DANDRIDGE PUBLIC LIBRARY

DAND 00038 125-

D1376969

DANDRIDGE MEMORIAL LIBRARY
DANDRIDGE, TENNESSEE 37725

"GOOD PEOPLE
BEGET
GOOD PEOPLE"

DANDRIDGE MEMORIAL LIBRARY
DANDRIDGE, TENNESSEE 37725

"GOOD PEOPLE BEGET GOOD PEOPLE"

A Genealogy of the Frist Family

WILLIAM H. FRIST, M.D.

WITH SHIRLEY WILSON, CG^SM

ROWMAN & LITTLEFIELD PUBLISHERS, INC.

Lanham • Boulder • New York • Toronto • Oxford

ROWMAN & LITTLEFIELD PUBLISHERS, INC.

Published in the United States of America
by Rowman & Littlefield Publishers, Inc.
A wholly owned subsidiary of
The Rowman & Littlefield Publishing Group, Inc.
4501 Forbes Boulevard, Suite 200, Lanham, Maryland 20706
www.rowmanlittlefield.com

PO Box 317
Oxford
OX2 9RU, UK

Copyright © 2004 by William H. Frist

All rights reserved. No part of this publication may be reproduced,
stored in a retrieval system, or transmitted in any form or by any
means, electronic, mechanical, photocopying, recording, or otherwise,
without the prior permission of the publisher.

British Library Cataloguing in Publication Information Available

Library of Congress Cataloging-in-Publication Data
Frist, William H.
   "Good people beget good people" : a genealogy of the Frist family / William H. Frist
with Shirley Wilson.
       p. cm.
   Includes bibliographical references (p.) and index
   ISBN 0-7425-3336-0 (hardcover : alk. paper) — ISBN 0-7425-3453-7 (bonded leather: alk. paper)
I. Frist family. II. Title.

BL240.3.F46 2004
215—dc22   2003018547

Printed in the United States of America

∞™ The paper used in this publication meets the minimum requirements of American
National Standard for Information Sciences—Permanence of Paper for Printed Library
Materials, ANSI/NISO Z39.48-1992.

This book is dedicated to my parents,
Dorothy Cate and Thomas Fearn Frist,
whose legacy is one of family love,
humility, and service to others

CONTENTS

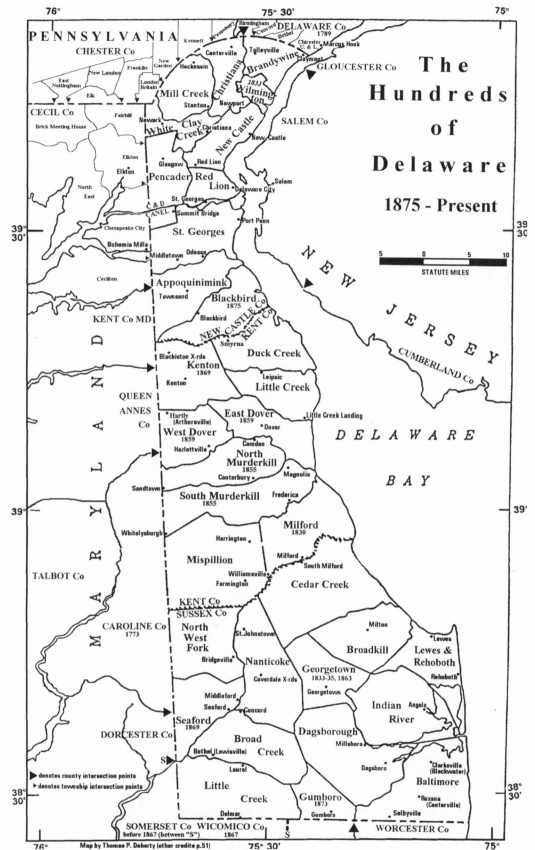

"The Hundreds of Delaware, 1875–Present," from Delaware Genealogical Society Research Guide, *3d ed.; used with permission of the Delaware Genealogical Society, the Delaware Public Archives, and Thomas P. Doherty.*

ILLUSTRATIONS

xi

- Elizabeth Helt Frist (1859–1935), wife of Jediah Frist
- Jediah and Elizabeth (Helt) Frist family, about 1891–1892, Vermillion County, Indiana
- Log home of Jediah and Elizabeth (Helt) Frist, Vermillion County, Indiana
- Farm home of Jediah and Elizabeth (Helt) Frist, built 1896, Vermillion County, Indiana
- Ren Leslie Frist (1881–1955), Vermillion County, Indiana
- Myrtle Maria Frist (1882–1974), Vermillion County, Indiana
- Mable Audrey Frist (1891–1946), wife of Harry Homer Frist
- Harry Homer Frist (1889–1983), Vermillion County, Indiana
- Harlow Peirce Frist (1891–1975), Vermillion County, Indiana
- Robert Jediah Frist, son of Harlow Peirce Frist, about 1944
- Russell E. and Mary Edith (Frist) Banes, about 1944
- Patricia Jo Frist and Herman Mayes, March 2001
- Mary Hazel Frist Harlan (1894–1984), Vermillion County, Indiana
- Marshall Alban Frist (1897–1966), Vermillion County, Indiana
- Webb Frist (1900–1957), Vermillion County, Indiana
- Jasper Nebeker Frist (1863–1934), founder of J. N. Frist Funeral Home, Clinton, Indiana
- Etta Lee Lambert Frist (1870–1955), wife of Jasper Nebeker Frist
- Children of Jasper Nebeker and Etta Lee (Lambert) Frist, about 1897
- White horse-drawn hearse, Frist Funeral Home, Clinton, Indiana, early 1900s
- The Frist Funeral Home's first ambulance, Clinton, Indiana
- Frist Funeral Home, Clinton, Indiana, about 1923
- Joseph Henry Frist (1866–1921), son of Jediah Rudolph Frist
- Mary Esther Frist Peters (1871–1952), daughter of Jediah Rudolph Frist
- Alban Frist (1873–1961) with wife Viola Adaline Jackson Frist, about 1905
- Franklin Peirce Frist (1869–1949), son of Jediah Rudolph Frist
- Tombstone of James and Henrietta (Little) Frist, Cecil County, Maryland, 2002
- Sidney Marietta "Etta" Frist Tyson (1868–1938)
- Joel Frist (1812–1891) of Wilmington, Delaware
- Tombstone of Annie James Frist, Cecil County, Maryland
- Dr. Henry M. "Harry" Frist of Wilmington, Delaware, the first in the family to become a doctor
- Jacob Frist (1817–1879) tombstone, Chattanooga, Tennessee

PREFACE

I love family. I love history. This genealogy is a product of my love for both.

This affection, I'm convinced, comes from my being the last of five children in a warm and loving family nurtured by two remarkable parents, Dorothy Cate and Thomas Fearn Frist. Their legacy is one that all of the five children are committed to carrying forth and passing to future generations.

Where did our ancestors come from? When did our family come to the United States? Where did the name Frist originate? These are just a few of the questions I set out to answer almost twenty years ago when I first began the journey that has led to this publication.

As a very young boy, I was fascinated by the stories my Aunt Bonnie (Margaret Randolph Cate) would tell us, as we gathered on her big porch, about all of our ancestors on the maternal Cate side of the family. My imagination would ignite as she vividly recounted the various lineages, occupations, and anecdotes. Her conversations would turn back the clocks of time.

She compiled her recollections and genealogical research in a family treasure, *The Armistead Family and Collaterals*. It provided countless hours of pleasure to me as a young boy, and indeed it was what led me to discover and record this genealogy of my father's side of the family—the Frists.

Indeed, the Frist who most affected my life was my dad. Thus, I have chosen his favorite saying, good people beget good people, to be the title of this work. These five words reflect his simplicity and purity in thinking, his humility, his appreciation of the strengths of others, his optimism, and his overall belief in the goodness of mankind.

My goal has been to create a recorded family history that will preserve past generations and bring a sense of time and place to present and future generations. Several members of the family, some of whom I have never met, have shared their collections and information about the Frist ancestry with me. I have had the opportunity to visit cemeteries, churches, and libraries. Stories and myths have been shared among relatives near and far. I have captured most of them in this book, immeasurably assisted by the professional guidance and research expertise of genealogist Shirley Wilson, who patiently, diligently, and successfully pursued the roads that too often brought me to a standstill.

This volume is my humble attempt to record permanently what we have collectively uncovered to date. A genealogy is truly never finished. I know this one is not. There is an endless trail back into time, and indeed as you will see there is an untold story before the late 1600s. I do hope this volume will spark some interest in others to delve further into our family history. It is almost certain to do so, and that is why publication at this juncture is appropriate. Maybe this work will lead to the discovery of some forgotten family Bible or faded family photographs. Indeed my own journey will continue, and thus I would appreciate any information on the family that others are willing to share (703 Bowling Avenue, Nashville, TN 37215).

I do thank all of the many people who assisted in this project, most of whom I recognize in the acknowledgments and reference in the footnotes. I personally thank all of the many Frist family members who have contributed generously to this project in so many ways. And, of course, I again express my love and appreciation to the loves of my life, the ones who bring me the ultimate joy, Karyn and the boys, who have encouraged me along the way as I have taken this journey.

William H. Frist, M.D.

ACKNOWLEDGMENTS

A work of this magnitude could not be completed without the assistance of the many individuals who willingly shared the results of their research on the Frist family or contributed in other ways. All of this information is truly appreciated, and the list below acknowledges those who made major contributions. Many more who contributed to the history of the family are footnoted within the text.

The work of Herman Mayes of Clinton, Indiana, has been invaluable in compiling this genealogy. Over a period of several years, Mayes collected the names and vital record dates of many of the descendants in this book through library visits and personal interviews. Gary Jones of Montezuma, Indiana, undertook the task of preserving Mayes's collection by entering the data in a computer genealogy program. The Tennessee Frists shared their family data with the Indiana Frists. When the Indiana project was completed in September 1991, they in turn shared it with the Tennessee Frists.

In March 2001, Patricia Frist of Clinton, Indiana, provided an abundance of scrapbook items and anecdotal material on the Indiana Frists from her private collection. This has added immeasurably to the overall content of this history. Regrettably, Pat did not live to see the book published; she died in April 2001.

Last, but far from least, Jane Frist of Montreat, North Carolina, collected materials over many years on the Frist family and shared that information for this publication, providing many helpful insights.

The list below acknowledges those who deserve special thanks.

Mary Edith Banes, Lafayette, Indiana

Mary Frist Barfield, Nashville, Tennessee

Ruth Connolly, Indianapolis, Indiana

Thomas P. Doherty, Wilmington, Delaware

Margaret Ann Foard Fowser, Medford Lakes, New Jersey

Clarence Harold Frist, Gadsden, Alabama

Donald Frist, Rising Sun, Maryland

Jane Frist, Montreat, North Carolina

Patricia Frist, Clinton, Indiana (died 2001)

Ronnie and Michelle Frist, Chattanooga, Tennessee

Margaret and Dan Hepner, Joppa, Maryland

Patricia Huguenin, Chattanooga, Tennessee

Gary and Judy Jones, Montezuma, Indiana

Herman Mayes, Clinton, Indiana

Geraldine Rosetta Frist Miller, Clarinda, Iowa (died 2002)

Ray Nichols, Wilmington, Delaware

J. Stanley Vetter, Rockingham, North Carolina

Cecil County Historical Society Library, Elkton, Maryland

Delaware Historical Society Library, Wilmington

Family History Library, Salt Lake City, Utah

Holy Trinity (Old Swedes) Church Foundation, Inc., Wilmington

Indiana State Library, Indianapolis

Maryland Public Archives, Annapolis

National Archives, Washington, D.C.

Tennessee State Library and Archives, Nashville,
*   especially Carol Roberts and Karina McDaniel*

A special thanks to the Delaware Public Archives in Dover, whose staff and facility are truly exceptional.

NUMBERING SYSTEM EXPLANATION

The numbering system selected for this book is a slightly modified version of the National Genealogical Society Quarterly System. For those unfamiliar with genealogical numbering systems, it is briefly explained here.

The small superscript numbers next to the names in the first and last sentence of each biographical sketch denote the generation, with the earliest proven ancestor Rudolph Frist being the first generation. This superscript generational number is also used for the first child in each set of children.

The actual numbering system begins with the earliest proven ancestor Rudolph Frist, who was assigned the number one. His two children are numbered two and three in the list of children following the biographical information on Rudolph. This assigned number remains the same for each person, whether listed as a parent or a child. When a child's number has a + sign at the left of it, additional information on that individual will be found later in the text. Follow the numbering in bold type at the left side of the page to locate the individual.

This numbering system continues throughout the book. It can be used to move forward through the text (by locating the child's number as an adult in subsequent text) or backward (by locating the adult's number as a child in previous text).

The index will enable readers to locate entries of interest. Married women were indexed under both their maiden name, if known, and their married name.

For the more recent generations where information was provided by a living person or when all biographical information came from one source, the text was footnoted only twice, once at the beginning and once at the end of each biographical sketch.

COMMENTS FROM THE COMPILER

*R*esearching and compiling this information for the Frist family has been an interesting and enjoyable experience for me. Despite the never ending questions that I was required to ask of them, members of the Frist family were all extremely courteous and friendly to me. I hope I have been able to convey in this genealogy what interesting and truly remarkable people they are.

While every effort has been made to avoid errors, in a compilation of this size some are almost inevitable. I take responsibility for them and apologize for any that may still exist.

This project is a culmination of my career of twenty-five years as a professional genealogist. I would like to thank my husband, Richard, for his patience and his invaluable computer expertise and my daughter, Carla, for her editorial assistance. My plans now call for at least semiretirement and time to enjoy my two granddaughters, Sarah and Rebecca.

Shirley Wilson, Certified Genealogist[SM]
106 Leeward Point
Hendersonville, Tennessee 37075
April 1, 2003

CHART OF FRIST DESCENDANTS

This chart is a brief outline of Frist descendants. It includes legally adopted children, but not foster or step children who are included within the text. Many of the birth and death dates listed here are approximated or are qualified in some manner within the text. Please refer to the text for more detailed information and documentation.

1 Rudolph Frist by 1740—1781–92
   2 Henry Frist about 1758–1821
    +possibly Galbraith—1789
     3 John Frist 1789–1847
      +Susannah Paulson Stidham 1792–after 1855
       4 Rebecca Ann Frist 1816–1854
        +Joseph Hahn 1812–1889
         5 John A. Hahn 1850–by 1871
         5 Samuel S. Hahn 1852–1918
          +Sophronia A. Mogle 1857–
           6 Infant (male) Hahn 1883–1883
       4 David H. Frist 1818–1865
        +Lydia E. Holliday 1823–1856
         5 Rachel Frist 1843–1850
         5 Joseph Andrew Frist 1845–1932
          +Rosetta Josephine Mitchell 1855–1925
           6 John Hulsey Frist 1875–1891
           6 Louisa Jane Frist 1881–1965
            +Lewis Patton 1878–1961

7 Clara Etta Patton 1901–1992
+Roy Manford Findley 1899–1963
8 Manferd Harold Findley 1920–
+Margeret L. Fessler 1919–2000
9 Marvin Lee Findley 1941–
+Frances Powers
9 Ronald Jack Findley 1943–
+Carolyn Cheatham
10 Jeffery Michael Findley
+Cindy Jean Kline
11 Ashley Marie Findley
11 Adam Kline Findley
11 Aubrey Nicole Findley
10 Kristin M. Findley
+Timothy Long
11 Haley Marie Long
11 Hanna Virginia Long
9 Kirk Allen Findley 1953–
+Catherine Forbes
*2nd Wife of Manferd Harold Findley:
+Thelma J. Fisher 1939–1992
8 Stanley Wayne Findley 1922–1992
+Leona Streigl 1924–
9 Connie Sue Findley 1943–
+John Stillions 1943–1973
10 Jody Kay Stillions
+Kevin Hahn
11 Noelle E. Hahn
11 Danielle Stillions Hahn
10 John M. Stillions 1964–1980s
9 Peggy Findley 1951–
+James M. Bixby
10 James Lee Bixby
*2nd Husband of Peggy Findley:
+Philip Neyens
10 Brad M. Neyens
7 Rosa Hannah Patton 1904–
+Harry Thompson
8 Paul Eugene Thompson 1935–1935
8 Harry Thompson–1936
8 Alice Thompson 193?–
8 Alvin Thompson 193?–
8 Robert Thompson
7 Donald Keith Patton 1922–1994
+Donna Pauline Hilleary 1922–
8 Douglas Patton
8 Debora Patton
6 Willibur Stiles Frist 1885–1930
+Orpha Lucille Geesaman 1898–1988
7 Geraldine Rosetta Frist 1924–2002

+Edward Dale Miller 1925–

   8 Judith Kay Miller 1948–

   +Richard Shoffit 1949–

   8 Linda Rae Miller 1951–

   +David Vader 1952–

      9 Aaron Kipp Vader 1978–

      9 Casey Ryan Vader 1983–

   8 Barbara Dale Miller 1954–

   +Terry Douglas Thompson 1952–

      9 Shawn Edward Thompson 1976–

      9 Heather Rose Thompson 1977–

      +Patrick Allen Rehder

         10 Chase Allen Rehder 2001–

   *2nd Husband of Barbara Dale Miller:

      +Francis Wayne Akers 1951–

      9 Cody Wayne Akers 1987–

   8 Shirley Jo Miller 1956–

   +Timothy Dean Roehl 1958–

      9 Aubrey Joy Roehl 1983–

      9 Elise Faith Roehl 1987–

7 Helen Marie Frist 1929–1972

+Glendon Amos Smith 1930–

   8 Vicky Jean Smith 1949–

   +Paul Anthony Pavlas

      9 Shelley Marie Pavlas 1972–

      +Robert Romauld Vouk 1966–

         10 Jacob Vouk 2001–

      9 Jenny Jean Pavlas 1975–

      9 Paul Anthony Pavlas, Jr. 1979–

      9 Lucas Glen Pavlas 1980–

   8 David Glendon Smith 1954–

   +Gwyn Eastman 1953–

      9 Derek Glendon Smith 1977–

      9 Brook Marie Smith 1980–

7 Raymond A. Frist 1930–

+Beverly Jean Brown 1934–

   8 Linda Lee Frist 1952–

   +Rick Thompson

      9 Lewis Harvey Thompson 1976–

      9 Eric Matthew Thompson 1979–

   8 Raymond Andrew Frist 1954–

   8 Cynthia Lucille Frist 1955–

   +David Carl Short 1952–

      9 David Andrew Short 1985–

      9 Carl Edward Short 1987–

   8 Julie Ann Frist 1957–

      9 Asha Rae Frist 1986–

   8 LeRae Opal Frist 1963–

   +Kurtiss Isles Humphrey 1957–

      9 Katelyn Janel Humphrey 1992–

9 Sean Kurtiss Humphrey 1995–
6 William Hawkins Frist 1885–1952
6 Nannie Elizabeth Frist 1890–1970
  +Fred Bridgman 1898–1971
    7 Thelma F. Bridgman 1916–
      +Paul Iocker
6 Samuel Victor Frist 1894–1918
5 John S. Frist 1848–after 1920
  +Elizabeth A. Bivans? 1838–by 1900
    6 Joseph E. Frist 1877–after 1920
      +Blanche R. Coloway 1887–1977
        7 Russell Edward Frist 1907–1963
          +Mary Ann 1912–
            8 Jimmy Dale Frist 1938–
              +Marva Olson 1939–1997
                9 Terry Michael Frist 1957–1973
                9 Steven Todd Frist 1960–
                  +Audrey Loftis 1968–
                    10 Sarah Elizabeth Frist 1997–1997
                    10 Jacob Michael Frist 1999–
                9 Julie Ann Frist 1962–
                  +Don Seiwert 1961–
                    10 Allison Seiwert 1985–
                    10 Phillip Seiwert 1989–
                9 Diane Sue Frist 1964–
                  +Jeff Hemann 1961–
                    10 Collin Hemann 1995–
                    10 Alec Hemann 1998–
5 Elizabeth A. Frist 1849–1849
5 Rebecca J. Frist 1850–1910
  +Henry Thomas 1842–by 1910
    6 Elmer E. Thomas 1868–
      +Della Jane Wilson 1872–
        7 Bertie Thomas 1894–
        7 Perry Thomas 1896–
        7 Hazel Thomas 1899–
    6 Lydia Ann Thomas 1870–
      +Samuel Albert Parker 1867–
    6 Cora Thomas 1872–
    6 Henry Thomas 1874–
    6 Viola May Thomas 1876–
      +Arthur W. Allen 1869–
        7 Ethel M. Allen 1894–
        7 Goldie Allen 1897–
        7 Ruth Allen 1900–
    6 Hendley Thomas 1880–
    6 Mary E. Thomas 1881–
    6 Amelia A. Thomas 1884–
    6 Roy C. Thomas 1890–
    6 Ira Thomas 1894–

*2nd Wife of David H. Frist:
  +Ruth J. Cate
4 William H. Frist 1823–1887
  +Catherine Reid 1827–1899
    5 James Jasper Frist 1850–1922
    5 Sarah J. Frist 1852–after 1910
      +Henry C. Rupe 1853–after 1910
        6 Ida M. Rupe 1874–1955
          +Jerome Jordan 1863–1933
        6 Susan Rupe 1877–
        6 William Rupe 1879–
        6 Charles H. Rupe 1882–1954
          +Flora E. Bullerdick 1883–after 1954
            7 Alice M. Rupe 1910–
            7 Clarence Rupe 1911–
        6 Anna L. Rupe 1884–1909
          +Smith M. Parry 1876–after 1909
        6 Jesse Rupe 1886–
        6 Roy Rupe 1889–
        6 Celia Florence Rupe 1891–
        6 Pearl Rupe 1893–
        6 Viola Ethel Rupe 1896–
    5 Catherine Letitia Frist 1854–1894
    5 Alphoretta Frist 1857–after 1922
    5 Pulaski Frist 1859–by 1870?
    5 Susan P. Frist 1861–
      +John N. Cook
        6 Ernie Cook
        6 Minnie Cook
        6 Keel Cook
    5 Samuel C. Frist 1862–
    5 Margaret A. Frist 1864–
      +Ruhle
    5 William O. Frist 1867–1929
      +Reba F. Juqua 1876–1944
        6 Garnet L. Frist 1894–
          +Willam H. Mungavin 1891–
        6 Paul H. Frist 1896–1959
          +Anabel
            7 Barbara Jane Frist 1918–
        *2nd Wife of Paul H. Frist:
          +Violet Genevieve Jelly 1901–1987
            7 Paul Jacque Frist 1922–
              +Helen Louise Hockett 1925–1993
                8 Paul Richard Frist 1944–
                  +Dorothy Mae Kelley 1949–
                    9 Gregory Paul Frist 1968–
                    9 Kellie Ann Frist 1971–
                8 Jack Edward Frist 1947–
                  +Pon Phanphon 1948–

9 Jinifer Phanphon Frist 1973–
9 Jeremiah Phanphon Frist 1984–
8 Dennis Michael Frist 1948–
+Joan Ellen Summers 1946–
9 David Michael Frist 1970–
9 Matthew James Frist 1973–
9 Mary Elizabeth Frist 1976–
8 Robert William Frist 1949–
+Louise Elaine Steele 1951–1994
9 Jeffery Robert Frist 1969–
+Deanna Baratta
10 Dakota Robert Frist 1990–
9 Tracy May Frist 1970–
8 Judith Ann Frist 1952–
8 Thomas Allen Frist 1953–
+Brenda Isaacs
9 Brad Alan Frist 1976–
9 Amy Jo Frist 1979–
*2nd Wife of Thomas Allen Frist:
+Teresa Lenigar
9 Krystal Frist 1985–
6 Helen Catherine Frist 1904–
+ Trafford B. Boyd
5 Russell Frist 1871–1930
+Sarah Viola Hunt 1874–1950
6 Marley Otto Frist 1893–1957
+Hester Vurnie Swinford 1893–1992
7 Russell Marrell Frist 1915–1989
+Vivian Maxine Lawson 1916–
8 Robert Russell Frist 1940–
+Beverley Griffith 1938–
9 Jeffery Allen Frist 1961–
*2nd Wife of Robert Russell Frist:
+Bonnie Johnson 1943–
9 Kimberly Renee Frist 1964–
9 Robert Douglas Frist 1969–
*3rd Wife of Robert Russell Frist:
+Dollie Bade 1945–
8 Phillip Stanley Frist 1945–
+Vickie Carol Haston 1947–
9 Phillip Steven Frist 1969–
+Rose Marie Gulli
10 Tyler Scott Gulli Frist 1990–
10 Steven Travis Frist 1995–
9 Patricia Ann Frist 1971–
+Harold Ceslo Avila
10 Wilson Ray Avila 2000–
10 Victoria Mackinzie Avila 2002–
4 John S. Frist 1826–1847
+Elizabeth Moon

5 Sarah Adaline Frist 1847–1849
4 Robert M. Frist 1828–1884
  +Ruth C. Meredith 1834–1887
    5 Hannah Etta Frist 1858–1936
      +John J. Stevens 1851–1934
        6 Roxie Elma Stevens 1886–by 1936
        6 John Roy Everett Stevens 1889–
        6 Jesse O. Laffe Stevens 1891–1955
          +Ella May Baxter 1894–1982
            7 Mildred Irene Stevens 1920–
              +Paul Vincent McBride
                8 Larry Paul McBride Parmer 1943–
                8 Garry Alan McBride Parmer 1943–1997
                  +Bettieanne Teresa Berdine
                    9 Laura Lee Parmer
                    9 Wesley Alan Parmer
              *2nd Husband of Mildred Irene Stevens:
                +Richard Parmer, Jr.
                8 Sherry Lee Parmer 1954–
                  +Donnie Ray Bryant
                8 Terry Lynn Parmer 1964–
                  +Robert Lyle Deadmon
                    9 Jeremiah Hunter Deadmon 1991–
                    9 Zachary Taylor Deadmon 1992–
    5 Martin Luther Frist 1868–after 1920
      +Samantha Jane Hewett
        6 Roscoe E. Frist 1897–1983
          +Ida Olson 1892–
        6 Olive Marie Frist 1902–
          +Walter L. Hanley 1896–
        6 Ruth C. Frist 1903–
          +Philip Helling 1897–
        6 Edna M. Frist 1906–
          +Nathan C. Sayre 1905–
4 Eliza Jane Frist 1830–
  +Joseph Moon
4 Mary Jane Frist 1831–1890
  +Charles F. Powell
    5 Mary E. Powell 1858–
    5 Joseph E. Powell 1860–
    5 Marion F. Powell 1868–
4 Jonas Lyman Paulson Frist 1834–1908
  +Amy E. Powell 1837–1920
    5 Cora Frist 1861–1941
      +James Putnam Goodrich 1864–1940
        6 Jean Goodrich 1893–1893
        6 Pierre Frist Goodrich 1894–1973
          +Dorothy Dugan–1987
            7 Frances Dorwin Goodrich 1921–
              +Edmond Poniatowski

*2nd Wife of Pierre Frist Goodrich:
+Enid Smith 1903–1996
5 Toda Juanita Frist 1865–1923
+Daniel Hecker
6 Sheldon Jonas Hecker 1912–1923
*2nd Wife of Henry Frist:
+Elizabeth Garretson 1774–1831
3 Susanna Frist 1793–1859
+Jeremiah Ford 1795–
3 Jediah Frist 1795–1826
+Mary Meredith 1798–1889
4 Elizabeth Frist 1820–by 1907
+Franklin Lloyd 1818–by 1864
5 Mary Esther Lloyd 1842–by 1900
5 Emily E. Lloyd 1845–by 1900
5 Ella F. Lloyd 1853–1932
+William C. Tindall 1853–1926
6 Franklin Lloyd Tindall 1880–
+Charlotte Maltman 1893–
7 William Cook Tindall 1917–1986
8 Terrance C. Tindall
+Paula L.
6 Roscoe Cook Tindall 1887–1957
+Lillian
7 Marcia Tindall 1919–
+Benbow
5 Elizabeth Jane Lloyd 1857–1939
+Joseph A. Randall –1908
6 John W. Randall 1890–95—by 1934
+Margaret
7 Elizabeth B. Randall 1912–
4 Henry Frist 1821–1864
+Catherine Campbell Stewart 1827–1893
5 William Stewart Frist 1846–1871
5 Horace V. Frist 1848–after 1900
5 Elizabeth Frist 1851–1853
5 Henry Campbell Frist 1853–1920
5 Robert Porter Frist 1856–
+Helen Bleyer
6 Helen C. Frist 1884–1884
6 Beatrice Campbell Frist 1885–
6 Robert Porter Frist, Jr. 1889–1943
6 Archie Campbell Frist 1893–1961
+Charlotte Geraldine Ayers 1899–1961
5 Herman Eschenberg Frist 1859–1933
+Margaret A. Hume 1868–1950
4 Esther Ann Frist 1823–1909
+Levi H. Springer 1824–by 1894
5 Sarah E. Springer 1846–by 1924
+Morris D. Crossan –1924

5 John E. Springer 1850—1877–87
  +Clara 1853–
    6 Elsie R. Springer 1877–
5 Levi Rudolph Springer 1854–by 1876
5 Marietta F. Springer 1856–1942
  +Willard Springer 1851–1936
    6 Harold L. Springer 1881–1969
      +Carolyn L. 1883–1968
        7 Harold L. Springer, Jr. 1907–
          +Susan Fitzgerald Halcomb 1914–
            8 Harold L. Springer III 1937–
            8 Charles Halcomb Springer 1940–
            8 William Lobdell Springer 1942–
            8 Steven Ellis Springer 1945–
        7 William L. Springer 1909–1987
          +Fredrika Nesbitt
            8 Margaret Springer
              +Marvel
                9 James McFaddin Marvel
            *2nd Husband of Margaret Springer:
              +Denham
                9 Margaret Stewart Denham
        7 John Willard Springer 1912–1938
        7 Sarah Louise Springer 1923–1989
          +Ralph Romano
            8 John Springer Romano Springer –1984
              +Barbara
                9 Jesse Romano Springer?
                9 Seth Romano Springer?
            8 Carolyn Margaret Romano Springer
          *2nd Husband of Sarah Louise Springer:
            +Lawrence O. Neal
    6 Helen S. Springer 1884–1948
      +Herbert C. Stout 1885–by 1934
        7 Marjorie S. Stout 1913–1993
          +Paul L. White 1913–1982
            8 Paul L. White, Jr. 1945–
              +Brenda Maddox 1950–
                9 Paul L. White III 1977–
                9 Rebecca L. White 1983–
                9 Christina L. White 1990–
    6 Willard Springer 1886–1956
      +Edna L. Martenis 1890–
        7 Elizabeth Springer 1918–1956
          +William Thomas Mahood
            8 William Thomas Mahood, Jr.
            8 Willard Springer Mahood
            8 Rebecca Elizabeth Mahood
        7 Marietta Springer 1923–
          +Patterson

7 Edna Nancy Springer 1924–
+Jacques du Pont
6 Sarah Edith Springer 1890–1975
+Howard L. Baumgartner
5 Edgar E. Springer 1858–
5 Kallena R. Springer 1869–1950
+Edwin J. Sheppard 1864–
6 Morris W. Sheppard 1891–1961
+Bessie F. 1875–
*2nd Wife of Morris W. Sheppard:
+Cora W.
6 Edwin Ross Sheppard 1895–1956
+Mildred Booker 1897–
6 Natalie Sheppard 1896–1928
+Joseph W. Dare
7 Marjorie Jane Dare 1924–
+Poor
6 Esther Sheppard 1899–1975
+Edward J. Graves –1953
7 Nancy A. Graves
7 Carolyn Julia Graves
+Allen
7 Eileen Graves? –1952
6 Margaret Sheppard 1903–
+Charles Logan
6 Helen Sheppard 1906–
+Joseph W. Dare
4 Mary Frist 1824–after 1891
+James Robinson –by 1864
5 Anna Robinson 1849–
+Richard Alexander
5 Samuel Robinson 1853–
*2nd Husband of Mary Frist:
+Elon J. Way 1810–
4 Jediah Rudolph Frist 1826–1907
+Marietta Groom 1829–1853
5 Ella Frist 1851–1853
*2nd Wife of Jediah Rudolph Frist:
+Mary Johnson Peirce 1834–1891
5 Samuel Meredith Frist 1856–1941
+Dora Hoagland 1868–1941
5 Jediah Frist 1859–1948
+Elizabeth Helt 1859–1935
6 Ren Leslie Frist 1881–1955
6 Myrtle Maria Frist 1882–1974
6 Esther Pearl Frist 1885–1887
6 Harry Homer Frist 1889–1983
+Mable Audrey Boyd 1891–1946
7 Emily Elizabeth Frist 1911–
+Samuel Pyle Saxton 1903–1980

7 Esther Louise Frist 1917–
+Paul Kenneth Foltz 1913–
  8 Carolyn Jeanette Foltz 1937–
  +Montelle H. Lowry 1934–
    9 Kenneth Russell Lowry 1958–
    +Marianne Shelton 1956–
      10 Joseph Blake Lowry 1986–
    9 Karen Janette Lowry 1960–
    +James Edward Yeatman 1960–
    *2nd Husband of Karen Janette Lowry:
    +Charles Farmer III
    *3rd Husband of Karen Janette Lowry:
    +Paul Beaugh 1960–
    9 Kelley Joan Lowry 1963–
    +John Royston Easby-Smith 1957–
      10 John Easby-Smith 1994–
      10 Nicholas Kelley Easby-Smith 1996–
  8 Margaret Ann Foltz 1939–
  +Frank Warren Hughes 1933–
    9 Jeen Anne Hughes 1961–
    +Timothy Mark Doty 1956–
      10 Sutton Myles Doty 1986–
    9 Robert Alan Hughes 1962–1994
  8 Ronald Glen Foltz 1942–1972
  8 Emily Sue Foltz 1944–1998
  +Jeffery Wayne Skjordahl 1942–
    9 Heidi Wane Skjordahl 1966–
    +Kenneth Alan Sorenson 1966–
      10 Erik Christian Sorenson 1989–
      10 Haley Wayne Sorenson 1991–
      10 Lars Haldan Sorenson 1993–
      10 Arne Jacob Sorenson 1994–
    9 Martin Scott Skjordahl 1968–
7 Shirley Mae Frist 1922–
+Melvin Maurice Jones 1915–1998
  8 Gary Lynn Jones 1946–
  +Judith Ann Rennick 1953–
    9 Eric Lynn Jones 1974–
    +Heather Anne Hodges 1979–
    9 Bradley Joe Jones 1977–
    +Melissa Ann Taylor 1977–
  8 Linda Darline Jones 1947–
  +Danny Dean Reed 1951–
    9 Christopher Alan Reed 1974–
    +Mary Jo Bartlett 1975–
      10 Brandi Nicole Reed 2000–
    9 Sherrie Ann Reed 1976–
  *2nd Husband of Linda Darline Jones:
  +Robert Arden Gosnell 1946–
  8 Glen Alan Jones 1950–

+Brenda Pritchard 1956–
9 Scott Alan Jones 1977–
9 Kelly Marie Jones 1979–1980
7 Myrtle Lee Frist 1927–1976
+Milton Royce King 1922–
8 Michael Edwin King 1949–
+Patricia Lynn Butz 1950–
8 Martin F. King 1950–
+Lettie Barbara Jones 1950–
9 Julie Rae King 1973–
+Samonn Chhim 1967–
10 Cameron Martin Chhim 1998–
10 Sarah Rae Chhim 1999–
9 Jennifer Jo King 1974–
8 Melvin H. King 1950–
+Sheila Ann Davidson 1955–
9 Lori Ann King 1970–1970
9 Heather Lee King 1971–
9 Jason Andrew King 1975–
9 Angela Dawn King 1978–
9 Carrie King 1980–
*2nd Wife of Melvin H. King:
+Deirdre Cannon 1951–
7 Patricia Jo Frist 1932–2001
6 Harlow Peirce Frist 1891–1975
+Helen Eliza Miller 1898–1993
7 Mary Edith Frist 1920–
+Russell E. Banes 1915–1971
8 Mary Lynn Banes 1950–
+Richard Harold Skeel 1949–
9 Eric Brian Skeel 1969–
+Theresa Naomi Dees 1970–
10 Alexis Lauren Skeel 1996–
9 Brittney Lynn Skeel 1974–
+Jeremy Varao 1974–
10 Genna Skye Varao 2000–
*2nd Husband of Mary Lynn Banes:
+Frederick William Lowell
7 Robert Jediah Frist 1925–1998
+Frances Lillian Vrabic 1929–
8 Robert Harlow Frist 1951–
+Ellen Louise Edwards 1955–
9 Andrew Robert Charles Frist 1982–
9 Alexander Edward George Frist 1987–
8 Dennis Franklin Frist 1954–
+Patti Ann Acheson 1956–
9 Johanna Denise Frist 1979–
9 Erin Elizabeth Frist 1981–
9 Lucas Peirce Frist 1983–
8 Karl David Frist 1959–

+Shirley Jeanne Shultz 1961–
    9 Katelyn Jeanne Frist 1988–
    9 Alisha Christine Frist 1988–
    9 Claire Elizabeth Frist 1994–
8 Douglas Mark Frist 1960–
+Mary Hope Roberts 1963–
    9 Samuel Taylor Frist 1986–
    9 Clayton Robert Frist 1989–
7 Betty Lou Frist 1930–1990
+Herman Francis Mayes 1926–
6 Mary Hazel Frist 1894–1984
+Hubert Harlan 1902–1981
6 Marshall Alban Frist 1897–1966
+Marjorie Blakesley 1901–1982
7 Harold B. Frist 1920–
+Beulah Thomas 1920–
8 Lisa Ann Frist 1955–
+Hendrik Harm Drenth 1969–
    9 Melissa Anne Drenth 1992–
    9 Jonathan Hendrick H. Drenth 1995–
7 Wayne Edward Frist 1925–1963
+Ruth Eddy 1924–
8 Michael Thomas Frist 1950–
+Judy Michel 1950–
9 Angela Ann Frist 1970–
+Murphy
    10 Christopher Lewis Murphy 1993–
    10 Dalton Jon Murphy 1997–
9 Nicole Marie Frist 1972–
    10 Blain Michael Frist 1991–
    10 Dustin Donavin Musser 1995–
    10 Trevor Jon Musser 1995–
    10 Bailee Marie Musser 1996–1996
8 Mershell Suzanne Frist 1951–
+Richard Putman 1948–
    9 Theresa J'Nae Putman 1979–
    9 Charisse Janelle Putman 1981–
8 Joan Marie Frist 1954–
+Jack Erwin 1956–
9 Chantelle Marie Erwin 1973–
+Joseph Steven Pliler
9 Christopher Erwin 1975–
+Carly Rachelle Quandt 1976–
    10 Tyson Bradley Erwin 1999–
6 Webb Frist 1900–1957
+Jessie
*2nd Wife of Webb Frist:
+Clara Jane
5 Jasper Nebeker Frist 1863–1934
+Etta Lee Lambert 1870–1955

6 Enid Lambretta Frist 1892–1973
  +Louis Jacob Lemstra 1897–1965
6 Donald Carrol Frist 1895–1959
5 Joseph Henry Frist 1866–1921
5 Franklin Peirce Frist 1869–1949
+Elizabeth Arletta Walker 1873–1947
5 Mary Esther Frist 1871–1952
+Charles Harvey Peters 1869–1948
5 Alban Frist 1873–1961
+Viola Adaline Jackson 1879–1961
*3rd Wife of Jediah Rudolph Frist:
+Mary Helen Nelson 1847–1934
3 James Frist 1797–1873
+Henrietta Little 1798–1847
4 Marietta Frist 1823–1909
4 Hannah Frist 1825–1909
4 John Frist 1828–1909
+Annie James 1831–1859
5 Ida May Frist 1852–1859
5 John Edgar Frist 1854–1912
+Margaret Ann Arthur 1859–1930
6 John Arthur Frist 1877–1936
+Sarah Smith 1859–1930
6 Anna Louise Frist 1878–1939
+John Oliver Jamison—1973
7 Violet Marie Jamison 1896–1992
+Edgar Heath Coney –1973
8 Jean Coney
+Robert Taylor
6 Bessie Frist 1884–
+Gutman
*2nd Wife of John Edgar Frist:
+Emma D. Cooper 1863–after 1920
6 Naomi Frist 1890–
+William P. Zink
7 William P. Zink, Jr. 1912–
7 Emma V. Zink 1916–
5 Eva James Frist 1856–1930
+George W. Stocksdale
6 Ida M. Stocksdale –1976
5 Harry Davis Frist 1858–1859
*2nd Wife of John Frist:
+Emily M. Holt—1894
5 Hattie M. Frist 1869–1939
+William Wirt Emmart 1869–1949
6 Dorothy Holt Emmart 1896–
+Ryland Newman Depster
7 Dorothy E. Depster
7 Ryland E. Depster

  6 Emily Walcott Emmart 1898–

   +Charles Kingsley Trueblood –1974

 5 Alpheus W. Frist 1876–1902

4 Abraham B. Frist 1825–30—by 1885

 +Elizabeth C. Patterson

  5 Martha Jane Frist 1848–1857

  5 Elizabeth Frist 1850–

  5 Harlin L. Frist 1851–1855

*2nd Wife of Abraham B. Frist:

 +Julia A. Myers 1836–1902

  5 Edmund M. Frist 1860–by 1870?

  5 Abram Bernard Frist 1861–1923

   +Georgianna L. Zimmer –by 1900

   6 Emma May Frist 1882–1964

    +Henry Heer 1882–

   6 Estella Elizabeth Frist 1884–1974

    +Harry H. Lyons 1887–1954

     7 Dorothy Alifair Lyons 1916–1929

     7 Howard Ross Lyons 1917–1984

      +Margaret V. Quinn –1976

       8 Howard Lawrence Lyons 1952–

        +Brenda Pavon 1961–

         9 Rebecca Anne Lyons 1987–

         9 Christopher Ross Lyons 1990–

     7 Martin Burnett Lyons 1920–

     7 Harry Raymond Lyons 1922–1998

   6 Julia O. Frist 1887–

    +John J. Cox 1892–

     7 Estella Elizabeth Cox 1915–

  *2nd Wife of Abram Bernard Frist:

   +Genevieve T. Quinn 1880–1934

    6 Melvin Bernard Frist 1902–1974

     +Margaret W. –1993

    6 Margaret Theresa Frist 1904–

     +William Behnken 1901–

    6 Donnelly Frist 1907–1972

    6 Genevieve Frist 1908–

     +Gilbert Reed 1894–1968

    6 Dolores Mary Frist 1910–1996

     +Joseph Klima –1984

      7 Dolores Lorraine Klima 1930–1996

       +Eugene Alfred Fischer, Jr. 1929–1989

        8 Eugene Alfred Fischer III 1951–

         +Deborah Ann Baum 1955–

         9 Marcia Lynn Fischer 1974–

          +Scott Christopher Ritchie Sheppard 1967–

           10 Tyler Christopher Sheppard 1999–

           10 Brianna Marie Sheppard 2000–

           10 Andrew Lee Sheppard 2002–

9 Dwayne Lee Fischer 1976–
8 Brian Joseph Fischer 1960–
+Deborah Ann Pivec 1961–
9 Michael Joseph Fischer 1991–
9 Nichole Michelle Fischer 1993–
8 Dawn Lee Fischer 1965–
+Christopher Casey 1967–
9 Scott Christopher Casey 1993–
9 Logan Patrick Casey 1995–
9 Brennan David Casey 1998–
7 Joseph Klima
+Jane
8 Sharon Klima
8 Keith Klima
6 Casper Bernard Frist 1914–1953
+Elenora Helen Pronek 1918–
7 Margaret Genevieve Frist 1937–
+Daniel Robert Hepner 1934–
8 Daniel Robert Hepner, Jr. 1956–
8 Donnelly Bernard Hepner 1958–
+Margie Ann Sadler
9 Amanda Joyce Hepner 1987–
8 David Joseph Hepner 1961–
+Dorthea Jean Hawes
9 Deanna Janielle Hepner 1986–
9 Dylan Joseph Hepner 1991–
8 Douglas William Hepner 1963–
+Julie Frankovich
9 Jonathan Douglas Hepner 1995–
9 Katilyn Christine Hepner 1996–
8 Danielle Margaret Hepner 1965–
+William J. Tallett
8 Donna Terese Hepner 1966–
7 Bernard George Frist 1944–
+Elizabeth Ann Adamski 1945–
8 Bernard George Frist, Jr. 1965–
+Victoria Lynn Pike
9 Parker D. Frist 1999–
8 Robert William Frist 1967–
+Jennifer Therris
9 Brandon William Frist 1991–
8 Bryan Joseph Frist 1970–
+Krisan Pfiefer
5 William Henry Frist 1863–1885
5 Hattie Mary Frist 1870–1930
+George F. Mohrlein 1864–
6 Vema L. Mohrlein 1891–
6 Casper G. Mohrlein 1895–
6 Julia Mohrlein 1904–
4 Thomas Lyttle Frist 1830–1873

+Sarah Elizabeth 1831–1900
 5 James Henry Frist 1852–1918
 5 Burton Kyle Frist 1856–1923
  +Virginia Wilson 1851–1916
   6 Ida D. Frist 1878–
   6 Walter B. Frist 1879–1881
   6 Edward Frist 1887–1923
   6 Fred Wilbur Frist 1888–1923
   6 Howard Frist 1889–
   6 Gertrude Rebecca Frist 1890–1956
 5 Selena Jane Frist 1857–1932
 5 Mary Emma Frist 1858–1938
 5 Jennie Louise Frist 1860–1926
 5 Alva Julia Frist 1866–1948
 5 Thomas Jackson Frist 1869–1925
  +Laura Jane Chapman
   6 Roy Thomas Frist 1907–
   6 Lucille C. Frist 1908–
   6 Neva M. Frist 1911–
 5 William Webster Frist 1874–1900
4 Henry Frist 1832–1846
4 William Frist 1835–1873
4 James Frist 1836–1908
 +Annie A. (Hartzell) Beam 1848–1883
 5 Lillian E. Frist 1875–
  +J. Ezra Stem
 5 Blanche H. Frist 1879–
  +Browning
4 Edmund Physick Frist 1838–1911
 +Mary Jane Haines 1834–1915
 5 George Edmund Frist 1863–
  +Henrietta McCullough 1868–
   6 Estella M. Frist 1887–
    +William Feathers
   6 Ethel B. Frist 1891–
    +William Knox
   6 Clara J. Frist 1894–
    +Alfred Miller
     7 Earl B. Miller 1914–
     7 Estella E. Miller 1916–
     7 Ernest L. Miller 1917–
   6 Robert F. Lewis Frist 1897–1967
    +Mary 1895–
     7 Dorothy J. Frist 1918–
   6 Sidney B. Frist 1900–
    +Earl Waddell
     7 Leona Waddell
     7 Gladys Waddell
     7 Robert Waddell
   6 Oliver Elwood Frist 1902–

      6 Raymond Presley Frist 1903–1983

       +Florence Mae Smith

        7 Raymond Frist, Jr.

        7 Wallace Philip Frist 1929–1999

    5 Garrison James Frist 1865–by 1920?

     +Pearl C. Updegrove 1873–

      6 Phillip E. Frist 1908–

       +Lorette Bourgious

        7 Norbert Leo Frist 1936–

          8 Lynn Frist 1972–

        7 Roger B. Frist

        7 Pearl Frist

         +Erickson

        7 Mary Frist

         +Ward

        7 Elizabeth Frist

         +Pasapia

    5 Sidney Marietta Frist 1868–1938

     +George Elim Tyson 1862–1942

      6 Lula May Tyson 1887–1975

       +Samuel James Churchman 1883–1947

        7 Sherwood James Churchman 1908–1969

         +Anna Carrie Reneer

       *2nd Wife of Sherwood James Churchman:

        +Gladys Shank

        7 Stillborn Infant Churchman 1909–1909

      6 John Earl Tyson 1888–1960

       +Ella Elizabeth Tosh 1889–1966

        7 Mary Grove Tyson 1909–1969

         +John Floyd Absher 1903–1957

          8 Martha Vianne Absher 1934–

           +Paul Albert Taylor 1935–

            9 Vianne Paula Taylor Gillespie 1956–

             +Douglas Willard Bolton

              10 Lee Edward Bolton 1975–

               +Shelley Kay Holland

                11 Emily Kay Bolton 1994–

              10 Gary Vernon Bolton 1979–

              10 Mark Albert Bolton 1980–

            9 Mary Margaret Taylor Gillespie 1957–

             +Richard Austin Roberts 1957–

              10 Leya Ann Roberts 1977–

              10 Christina Lynn Roberts 1980–

               +Shane Handel

            9 Edward Albert Taylor Gillespie 1959–1973

          *2nd Husband of Martha Vianne Absher:

           +Edward Charles Gillespie 1927–

        *2nd Husband of Mary Grove Tyson:

         +Oliver Graeser

        7 John Earl Tyson, Jr. 1911–1911

7 John Edwin Tyson 1916–2002
  +Claire McWilliams 1927–
7 Margaret Elizabeth Tyson 1921–1981
  +Vernon McMullen 1924–
    8 Tyrone Eric McMullen 1947–
    8 Dawne Doretta McMullen 1951–
    +James Paul Yale 1949–
      9 Michael Shawn Yale 1968–
6 Roy Leslie Tyson 1890–1891
6 Mary Eva Tyson 1892–
 +John Clarence Bell 1887–1970
  7 John Cyril Bell 1913–1935
6 Lilah Isabelle Tyson 1895–1897
6 Sara Elizabeth Tyson 1896–1991
6 Pearl Catharine Tyson 1899–1981
 +Charles Ellis Astle 1891–1967
  7 Dorothy Ellen Astle 1919–1919
  7 George Nelson Astle 1920–1945
  7 Evelyn Elizabeth Astle 1922–
   +S. Clyde Crowl, Jr. 1921–1961
    8 Linda Ann Crowl 1947–
    +Dirk Howard Harrington 1948–
      9 Beth Ann Harrington 1971–
      9 Dirk Howard Harrington, Jr. 1973–
    8 Patricia Jane Crowl 1949–
    +Robert V. Sigler 1949–
    8 Barbara June Crowl 1951–
    +Barry Wayne Thomas 1947–
      9 Paul William Thomas 1971–
      9 John Richard Thomas 1972–
  *2nd Husband of Evelyn Elizabeth Astle:
   +Peter Kowal 1919–
  7 Charles Ellis Astle, Jr. 1924–1924
6 Roland Cresswell Tyson 1901–1923
6 Harold Edward Tyson 1903–1969
 +Esther Ann Astle 1897–1989
  7 Naomi Astle Tyson 1924–
   +George Oliver Gross 1919–1973
    8 Emily Lois Gross 1950–
    +Charles Elward Turner 1949–
      9 Jeffery Edward Turner 1968–
      9 Tricia Marie Turner 1972–
    8 Ellen Elizabeth Gross 1951–
    +Geoffrey Lance Travers 1948–
      9 Leigh Ann Elizabeth Travers 1979–
    8 Carolyn Jeanne Gross 1956–
    8 Roger Alan Gross 1961–
  7 George Edward Tyson 1939–
   +Charlotte May Wood 1940–
    8 Daryl Leigh Tyson 1961–

8 Dean Allyn Tyson 1963–
8 Laura Lynn Tyson 1970–
6 Martin Moore Tyson 1905–1987
+Frances Evelyn Jackson 1907–
7 George Robert Tyson 1937–
+Helen May Hull 1939–
8 Mark Robert Tyson 1959–1976
5 Oscar Haines Frist 1870–1936
+Ella McDowell 1880–1937
6 Joseph Osmond Frist 1903–1979
+Blanche Lucille Ramsey 1903–1981
7 Ramsey Hudson Frist 1936–
+Judith Ann Nadolny
8 Heidi Margaret Frist 1964–
+Anthony Patrick Derry 1958–
9 Patrick James Derry 1991–
9 Allison Marie Derry 1994–1994
9 William Ramsey Derry 1995–
9 Thomas Hudson Derry 2000–
8 Jonathan Ramsey Frist 1967–
+Margaret Jane Shaw 1960–
9 Ian Shaw Frist 1989–
9 Jillian Claire Frist 1999–
8 Erica Ann Frist 1969–
+James Andrew Canfield 1971–
9 James Alexander Canfield 2000–
9 Ava Marie Canfield 2002–
7 Sidney Marie Frist 1938–1938
7 Michael Maria Frist 1944–
+Elwood G. Schell, Jr. 1953–
6 Charles E. Frist 1905–1926
6 James R. Frist 1907–1907
6 Ernest H. Frist 1909–1913
6 Mary Jane Frist 1911–1983
+William C. Lauver
6 Letitia Frist 1915–1978
+Clyde Farmer 1913–
7 William Farmer
7 Betty Farmer
5 John Cresswell Frist 1872–1945
+Olive A. Campbell 1896–1982
6 Delbert Sterling Frist 1912–1984
+Florence Worth 1918–
7 Delbert Lee Frist 1946–
+Louise Benjamin 1947–
8 Duane Cresswell Frist 1972–
8 Cynthia Louise Frist 1975–
+David Russell Dittmar 1974–
7 Debora Louise Frist 1950–
+William H. Ewing 1946–

8 Shannon Lee Ewing 1976–
+Clinton Miller
9 Curtis Wayne Miller 1995–
9 Clinton William Miller 1997–
9 Craig Walter Miller 1999–
8 Hope Noel Ewing 1979–
6 John Willard Frist 1914–1965
+Willa Alverta Tarbert 1916–2000
7 Charlotte Alma Frist 1939–
+Bruce Turner 1935–
8 Susan Renee Turner 1963–
+David Paul Polk 1962–
9 Breck Emmerson Polk 1992–
9 Madison Renee Polk 1995–
8 William Gregory Turner 1966–
+Kathryn Donna Nelson 1966–
9 Jordan Kaitlyn Turner 2000–2000
6 Donald Russell Frist 1922–
+Doris V. Tome 1920–1987
*2nd Wife of Donald Russell Frist:
+Elizabeth Ann Slauch 1932–
5 Oliver T. Frist 1875–1935
+Florence Gertrude Harrison 1879–1957
6 Garrison Kenneth Frist 1901–1928
+Mary Susan Kirk 1904–1979
7 Helen Kirk Frist 1923–
+Harry Walter Cooper 1924–
8 Harry Sherwood Cooper 1953–
+Nancy Nepa 1957–
9 Stephen Michael Cooper 1987–
8 Gail Beverly Cooper 1954–
+Thomas Brabson
9 Kurt Thomas Brabson 1979–
9 Kristine Marie Brabson 1982–
7 Dorothy Jean Frist 1924–1982
+Frank Benjamin Ordog 1916–1991
8 Garrison Kenneth Ordog 1946–
8 Mary Margaret Ordog 1947–
+Robert Parker
8 Thomas Frank Ordog 1958–
7 Florence Gertrude Frist 1926–
+David Carlton Morris 1925–1993
8 David William Morris 1950–
+Debra Reynolds
9 William Christopher Morris 1971–
9 Michael David Morris 1972–
*2nd Wife of David William Morris:
+Catherine Watson Roper
8 Kenneth Everett Morris 1954–
+Kristine Connelly

3 Mary Frist 1800–1801
3 Joseph L. Frist 1803–1840
3 Garretson Frist 1807–1831
3 William Frist 1809–1891
3 Joel Frist 1812–1891
  +Adrianna Morrison 1816–1876
    4 Joseph Adriana Frist 1838–1842
    4 George Frist 1840–1928
      +Catherine A. Simmons 1850–1936
        5 Homer Frist 1878–1930–34
          +Mary Harkins 1884–after 1934
            6 Margaret Helena Frist 1902–1973
              +Joseph Hendel Wallis
                7 Joan Helene Wallis 1929–
                  +Carroll Draper Hauptle 1923–
                    8 Mary Elizabeth Hauptle 1953–
                    8 Carroll Draper Hauptle, Jr. 1954–
                    8 Richard Simon Hauptle 1960–
                    8 Nancy Katherine Hauptle 1962–
                7 Joseph Hendel Wallis, Jr. 1932–
    4 Rachel Frist 1846–after 1900
    +Henry Waddington
    4 Henry M. Frist 1854–after 1920
    +Anna 1872–
3 Jacob Chester Frist 1817–1879
  +Ann Eliza Harris–1847
    4 Robert Harris Frist 1847–1903
      +Elizabeth Rachel Nebeker 1844–1924
        5 Anna Elizabeth Frist 1878–1964
          +John Hilton Foard 1869–1943
            6 Elizabeth May Foard 1902–1918
            6 Hilda Louise Foard 1905–1924
            6 Anna Roberta Foard 1907–1998
              +James Henry Smith 1910–1990
                7 Warren Foard Smith 1932–1983
                  +Helen Ballard 1934–
                    8 Terri Ann Smith 1969–
                7 Wendell Murray Smith 1935–
                  +Margaret McGregor 1935–
                    8 Karen Murray Smith 1958–
                      +Jared Wilson 1959–
                        9 Courtney Murray Wilson 1984–
                    8 Wendy Margaret Smith 1959–
                    +James Berge 1958–
                        9 Alison Margaret Berge 1983–
                        9 James Alexander Berge 1985–
                        9 Anna Elizabeth Berge 1989–
                    8 Kimberly Foard Smith 1960–
                    +Kent Quirk 1960–
                        9 Lincoln Joseph Quirk 1986–

9 Morgan Tilghman Quirk 1989–
8 Katherine McGregor Smith 1962–
+William Oakford 1962–
9 Alexander McGregor Oakford 1988–
9 Abigail Margaret Oakford 1991–
8 Jennifer Keith Smith 1967–
+Richard Piselli 1966–
9 Eric James Piselli 1993–
9 Kevin James Piselli 1996–
7 Janet Frances Smith 1941–
+Herbert Dann
8 Teresa Lynn Dann 1964–
8 Leslie Ann Dann 1966–
+Guido Jimenez-Cruz 1968–
8 Herbert Irving Dann III 1968–
+Kay Cockerill 1964–
7 Robert Henry Smith 1946–
+Elizabeth Brereton 1947–
8 Matthew Brereton Smith 1972–
8 Molly Elizabeth Brereton Smith 1975–
8 Thomas Lumley Smith 1978–
6 John Hilton Foard 1910–1944
6 Franklin Peach Foard 1912–
+Margaret Jane Hubert 1917–
7 Margaret Ann Foard 1938–
+Neil Wyatt Fowser 1937–
8 Mark Andrew Fowser 1960–
8 Scott Wyatt Fowser 1963–
8 Lori Jean Fowser 1971–
7 Franklin Peach Foard 1940–1945
7 Susan Jean Foard 1948–
+Bill Sizemore
8 Lisa Ann Sizemore
9 Lucas Sizemore 1998–
8 Brian Michael Sizemore
5 John Nebeker Frist 1881–1947
+Carrie Currender 1883–1946
6 Robert Currender Frist 1904–1969
+Helen Kathryn Casey 1901–
6 Margaret W. Frist 1909–
*2nd Wife of Jacob Chester Frist:
+Mary Ann Elizabeth Baldwin 1833–1920
4 James Ball Frist 1853–1925
+Harriet R. 1855–1883
5 Mary Frist 1879–1887
5 Sue Frist 1882–1883
5 Jake Frist 1882–1883
*2nd Wife of James Ball Frist:
+Permelia Corbin 1866–1935
5 Bertie L. Frist 1889–1959

+William Calvin Hartman 1870–1917
  6 John Hartman 1912–by 1917?
  6 Roy Frist Hartman 1915–
    +Miriam Houts 1913–
      7 William Roy Hartman 1935–
        +Clarice Levan 1935–
          8 Cynthia Yvonne Hartman 1957–
      7 Robert Jacob Hartman 1937–
        +Mary Green 1937–
          8 Robert Jason Hartman 1960–
          8 Todd Eugene Hartman 1962–
        *2nd Wife of Robert Jacob Hartman:
          +Virginia Craft
            8 Valerie Michele Hartman 1971–
  5 Joseph Byron Frist 1892–1958
4 Samuel Henry Frist 1855–1939
  +Mary Florence Curry 1863–1913
  5 Mabel Frist 1881–85––by 1900
  5 Estelle Frist 1885–1958
    +Sprague S. Rockwood 1877–1943
  5 Hillis D. Frist 1893–after 1914
4 Ann Elizabeth Frist 1859–1922
  +William M. Vetter 1855–1900
  5 Robert J. Vetter 1882–1929
  5 Willmary Vetter 1886–
    +Samuel W. Perry
  5 John Stanley Vetter 1890–1929
    +Effie Roselle Bird 1896–1965
      6 John Stanley Vetter, Jr. 1928–
        +Sallie Louisa Middlebrooks 1934–
          7 Sara Roselle Vetter 1956–
            +Michael Joseph Mayhew 1955–
              8 Sara O'Kelly Mayhew 1982–
              8 John Michael Mayhew 1985–
              8 Mary Katherine Mayhew 1992–
          7 Martha Elizabeth Vetter 1958–
4 Jacob Chester Frist 1862–1919
  +Jane Jones 1869–1953
  5 Mary Louise Frist 1898–1980
    +Mahlon Floyd Parker 1877–
  *2nd Husband of Mary Louise Frist:
    +Bob Tomlinson
  5 Helen Jones Frist 1901–1956
    +Argie Garner Cameron 1885–1943
      6 Alan Garner Cameron 1924–1974
        +Doloris Aucella
  5 John Chester Frist 1906–1959
    +Lois Elizabeth Ferran 1909–1998
      6 Jane Elizabeth Frist 1935–
        +Arnold Cornelius Harms 1929–

      7 Jane Alden Harms 1959–

      7 John David Frist Harms 1960–

      7 Robert Dale Harms 1962–

  6 Charlotte June Frist 1938–

    +James Robert Faucette 1933–1987

      7 Robert Chester Faucette 1963–

        +Mary Elizabeth Tota 1962–

          8 Avery Nicole Faucette 1996–

          8 Ryan James Faucette 2000–

      7 Jane Elizabeth Faucette 1965–

        +Douglas Randolph Moore 1958–

      7 Thomas James Faucette 1968–

        +Lynda Chang 1971–

  *2nd Husband of Charlotte June Frist:

    +John Calvin Chesnutt 1927–

  6 John Chester Frist, Jr. 1941–

    +Mary Corinne Brothers 1941–2000

      7 Corinne Ansley Frist 1968–

        + Timothy Scott Glover 1968–

          8 Nathaniel Scott Glover 2001–

      7 John Chester Frist III 1971–

        +Mary Virginia West 1973–

  6 Thomas Ferran Frist 1945–

    +Clare Elizabeth Strachan 1947–

      7 Lisa Kristin Frist 1984–

      7 John Daniel Frist 1988–

5 Thomas Fearn Frist 1910–1998

+Dorothy Harrison Cate 1910–1998

  6 Thomas Fearn Frist, Jr. 1938–

    +Patricia Gail Champion 1939–

      7 Patricia Champion Frist 1965–

        +Charles Anthony Elcan 1963–

          8 Lauren Champion Elcan 1994–

          8 Patricia Cate Elcan 1997–

          8 Carrington Frist Elcan 2001–

      7 Thomas Fearn Frist III 1968–

        +Julie Mead Damgard 1971–

          8 Caroline Mead Frist 2000–

          8 Annabel Damgard Frist 2002–

      7 William Robert Frist 1969–

        +Jennifer Catherine Rose 1971–

          8 Walker Ryan Frist 2000–

          8 Jacqueline Collins Frist 2002–

  6 Dorothy Cate Frist 1941–

    +Charles Ray Eller 1938–

      7 Deborah Frist Eller 1964–

        +Raymond Keach

          8 Ashley Nichole Frist Eller 1991–

  *2nd Husband of Dorothy Cate Frist:

    +Richard Boensch 1941–

6 Robert Armistead Frist 1942–
+Carol Len Knox 1944–
7 Robert Armistead Frist, Jr. 1967–
+Melissa Merriman 1967–
8 Eleanor Knox Frist 2001–
7 Carol Len Frist 1970–
+Scott McClain Portis 1966–
8 Leah Cannon Portis 1996–
8 Scott McClain Portis, Jr. 1999–
7 James Knox Frist 1972–
6 Mary Louise Frist 1946–
+Henry Lee Barfield II 1946–
7 Mary Lauren Barfield 1970–
+Lawson Coffee Allen 1970–
8 Harrison Cole Allen 1996–
8 Thomas Frist Allen 1998–
8 Lawson Cole Allen 2002–
7 Dorothy Frist Barfield 1971–
+John Claiborne Sifford 1971–
8 John Claiborne Sifford, Jr. 2003–
7 Corinne Cole Barfield 1973–
7 Lee Cole Barfield 1980–
6 William Harrison Frist 1952–
+Karyn Jean McLaughlin 1954–
7 William Harrison Frist, Jr. 1983–
7 Jonathan McLaughlin Frist 1985–
7 Bryan Edward Frist 1987–
4 Joseph Elmer Frist 1867–1940
+Alice Keefe 1877–1911
5 Paul Franklin Frist 1898–1961
+Kate Irene Groves 1908–
6 Robert Joe Frist 1923–1945
6 Sidney Donald Frist 1930–1973
+Norma Drucilla Roberts
7 Larry D. Frist 1950–1950
7 Pamela Susanne Frist 1953–
+Curtis L. Brown
8 Christopher Lee Brown 1976–
8 Eric Scott Brown 1980–
7 Ronald Gary Frist 1956–
+Carla M.
8 Alisha Dawn Frist 1980–
8 Amber Rachelle Frist 1984–
*2nd Wife of Ronald Gary Frist:
+Michelle Helene Major 1956–
5 James Charles Frist 1900–1944
+Sadie Estell Briggs 1899–1997
6 James Calvin Frist 1923–1952
6 Alley Evelyn Frist 1924–1983
+Erskine Gallant

6 Frank Emmett Frist 1925–
  +Avene Phillips 1931–1962
    7 Frankie Susan Frist 1952–
      +Robert Taylor Dixon 1959–
        8 Zachary Taylor Dixon 1988–
        8 Victoria Elizabeth Dixon 1991–
    7 Mona Frist 1959–
      +Darryl Willett
        8 Stephanie F. Willett 1981–
    *2nd Husband of Mona Frist:
      +Steve Byer 1960–
    7 James Leland Frist 1960–
      +Lisa Osburn 1961–
        8 Haley Nichole Frist 1995–
  *2nd Wife of Frank Emmett Frist:
  +Margaret (Contillo) Kensinger
6 Naomi Willmary Frist 1932–
  +William Rollins 1924–1958
    7 William Erik Rollins 1953–1977
6 Patricia Estelle Frist 1937–
  +Edward Leon Garrett
    7 Kymberly Briggitte Garrett Huguenin 1958–
      +Charles Thomas McKeehan 1957–
    7 Sharon Michelle Garrett Huguenin 1961–
      +Steven Ellis Lynn 1953–
    7 Mark Edward Garrett Huguenin 1969–
      +Kelly Key
  *2nd Husband of Patricia Estelle Frist:
  +Mark Tell Huguenin 1923–
5 Ernest Arnold Frist 1903–1968
4 Emmett Franklin Frist 1877–1933
+Annie C. Stroud 1879–1963
  5 Mary Emma Frist 1904–1960
  +Curtis Duke –1952
    6 Fred Duke 1925–
    +Julia Maxine Cothran 1926–
      7 Jennifer Lynn Duke 1951–
      +Mike Gunnells 1950–
        8 Emily Gunnells 1977–
        8 Laurie Gunnells 1979–
        8 Cristin Gunnells 1982–
      7 Julie Beth Duke 1953–
      +David Galloway 1952–
        8 Jennifer Kaye Galloway 1975–
        8 Julliana Galloway 1977–
        8 Jill Galloway 1981–
    6 Harry Duke 1927–
    6 Anne Elizabeth Duke 1929–1999
    +Jerry Jasper Thompson, Jr. 1928–2000
      7 Jerry Stephen Thompson 1955–

+Joye Lynne Beaube 1960–
    8 Kristin Lynne Thompson 1981–
    8 Mathew Steven Thompson 1988–
    8 Emily Ann Thompson 1988–
7 Charles David Thompson 1957–
+Kimberly Faye Mays 1961–
    8 Tyler Mark Thompson 1985–
    8 Derek Scott Thompson 1987–
    8 Cody Brent Thompson 1993–1994
    8 Summer Faith Thompson 1996–
5 Edward Franklin Frist 1908–1978
+Lee Burns Lancaster 1904–
5 Clarence Harold Frist 1913–
+Ida Lizzie Davis 1910–1997
2 Elizabeth Frist 1760–75–1802
+John Vining–by 1798
    3 Henry Vining
    3 James Vining
*2nd Husband of Elizabeth Frist:
+Hugh Mercer –by 1809

Part I
ORIGINS AND EARLY YEARS

The American origins of the Frist family can be found in Delaware. Rudolph Frist of Kent County, Delaware,[1] was the father of Henry Frist, who was born about 1758 in Delaware.[2] Henry is the progenitor of the Frist family of Christiana Hundred, New Castle County, Delaware. Many, but not all, American Frist families are descended from him. As to the country of origin and the time of arrival in America, research, family traditions, and some descendants have provided some hints but no conclusive proof.

A grandson of Henry through his son Joel (and Joel's wife Adrianna Morrison) was Henry M. "Harry" Frist, a prominent doctor in Wilmington, Delaware. In a biographical sketch published in 1894, Dr. Henry Frist was identified as "springing from Scotch and German ancestry that settled in this country over two centuries ago."[3] Morrison is an English or Scottish name,[4] and thus the German ancestry presumably came from the Frists. If accurate, this would place the arrival of the Frists in America in the late 1600s.

Jasper Nebeker Frist [1863–1934] wrote a letter in which he stated that his father, Jediah Rudolph "Dolph" Frist [1826–1907], a great-grandson of Rudolph Frist, told him that he [Jediah] was the fifth generation who settled at Wilmington, Delaware, in 1638.[5] Jasper's father said, "the first was Henry." He also mentioned Rudolph, identifying him as the father of another Henry. This particular Henry, born about 1758 in Delaware, is the man identified in this publication as the progenitor of the New Castle County Frist family. It seems logical that Jasper might know when the family arrived in America and it is remarkable that he was able to correctly identify his great-grandfather Henry Frist and his second great-grandfather Rudolph Frist. Whether Jasper was correct about a generation beyond Rudolph remains undetermined, but nothing has been located to document it.

An examination of the allied families initially failed to establish any link to the country of origin of the Frists, although eventually a pattern began to emerge. Henry himself reportedly married first to a Galbraith and then to Elizabeth Garretson.[6] Galbraith is usually a Scottish surname,[7] but it should be noted that this was not the wife from whom Joel's son Henry descended. He descended from Henry's second wife, Elizabeth, the daughter of James and Mary (Abraham) Garretson.[8]

The Garretsons were very early settlers in New Castle County who arrived in the 1600s. Garretsons of both Swedish and Dutch descent can be found in New Castle County, but the ones of interest to this project were Dutch.[9]

The Abraham family, whose members married into the Garretsons, has not been fully explored, but is believed to be Welsh.[10] Henry's eldest son, John, married a Stidham, descended from one of the very early Swedish settlers in the county.[11] The Nebekers married into the Frist family and were reportedly from Germany,[12] although they arrived during the time of the Swedish immigration and associated with both Swedish and Dutch immigrants. The Merediths, another family with a Welsh name,[13] also married into the Frist family. The Constantines were another allied family who were Swedish.[14]

Henry's name in the early court records was never spelled Heinrich or Hendrik, as might be expected of a recent immigrant. However, the name of his father, Rudolph Frist, was found in a 1760 deed as Rundolf and later in tax lists as Rudolf, the Modern German form of the Old German Hrodulf.[15]

Based on this information, it can be surmised that the ethnic background of the Frists must be Dutch or German, but conclusive proof as to the area from which they migrated and the time period in which they arrived is lacking.

THE ORIGIN OF THE FRIST SURNAME

The origin of the Frist surname has been obscured in the mists of time. Frist is a legitimate surname and is infrequently found in the telephone directories of German cities.[16] Regrettably, there is no concentration of Frists in any particular area of Germany. It was found as a surname in only one dictionary of surnames.[17] The meaning of the name was listed as "period, time limit."

It seems unusual that there is no tradition among the Frist descendants regarding the ethnic background of the family. Family members assume Dutch or German origin, perhaps from the sound of the name. This lack of tradition is a further indication that the family has been in America for many generations, giving the origin of the surname ample time to become obscured.

There is a strong family tradition that the Frist surname was changed, but there are differing versions as to what the original name was. While family tradition can often aid in determining the nationality of a family, it cannot be considered 100 percent accurate. Stories are often enhanced or altered over the years, until the original meaning is no longer clear.

Jediah Rudolph Frist, a grandson of old Henry Frist, migrated to Indiana, taking with him a trunk made of logs that he inherited from his uncle Garretson Frist.[18] The initials G. D. V. are carved into the trunk, and from this came the theory that the Frist name was originally DeVries.

Descendants of another branch of the Indiana Frist family theorized in the early 1900s that the Frist surname was originally spelled Fries. Cora Frist Goodrich, wife of Governor James P. Goodrich of Indiana, worked diligently but without success in the 1920s to establish Henry Frist as a Revolutionary soldier for the National Society, Daughters of the American Revolution. In order to do this, she had to prove that the name was Fries, because no Revolutionary War service could be found under the name Henry Frist. In pursuit of this, Cora obtained the following deposition from her cousin, which she shared with other family members.[19]

County of Ocean, State of New Jersey

I, Anna Robinson Alexander, being first duly sworn on my oath, depose and say that my grandmother, Mary Meredith Frist, who was born in 1797 [*sic*] and died in 1890 [*sic*], and who was the daughter-in-law of Henry Frist, born in 1758 and died in 1821, spent the last two years of her life in my home. The said Mary Meredith Frist's memory remained clear until the last.

The said Mary Meredith Frist frequently made the statement in my presence that the name "Frist" was variously spelled, some members of the family spelling it, "Fries."

And further affiant says not.   [signed] *H. Anna Alexander*

Sworn to before me this
8th day of September, 1927
J. A. Thompson Notary Public.

Henry Frist was identified using the surname Fries only once, in the 1800 census of New Castle County.[20]

There is evidence that the name was Freese or Freeze before it became Frist. Freeze was used when Henry was taxed in Christiana Hundred in New Castle County beginning in 1788 and ending in 1796.[21] There was no tax list in 1797, and in 1798 Henry was taxed as Frist for the first time and the Freese surname was not used again.[22] Similar spellings of Freese were used when Henry's father Rudolph was taxed in Dover Hundred in Kent County, Delaware, in the time period 1760 to 1781.[23]

EARLY IMMIGRANTS AND RESIDENTS

One branch of the family has passed down the legend that two Frist brothers jumped ship at a port in Chesapeake Bay.[24] If so, then records showing them as passengers arriving in America would be lacking. Many passenger lists from arriving ships did not survive. Several entries of interest were found among the surviving passenger lists and other types of immigrant records, but none could be conclusively tied to Rudolph or Henry Frist.

On 5 May 1631 David Peterson DeVries established the first colony in what is now known as Delaware. This small group fought constantly with the Indians and abandoned their colony in the summer of 1633.[25] Nothing was found to indicate that descendants settled in the area.

JACOB AND PHILIP FRIST OR FRIES

On 24 September 1737 two men who reportedly carried the surname Frist arrived in America. They were Jacob and Philip Frist, whose names were on a list of foreigners imported in the ship *St. Andrew Galley* with John Stedman as master from Rotterdam.[26]

There is good reason to question whether these two men were actually Frists. A second list of the same men on the same date showed them as Jacob Fries (who made his mark) and Philipp Fritsch.[27] In both cases they were listed side by side, lending credence to the theory that they were brothers.

Jacob Fries, born about 1716 or 1717, emigrated from the province of Friesland, Netherlands, to America and was the founder of Friesburg, Salem County, New Jersey.[28] The author of the book on this family believes that the two men on the *St. Andrew Galley* were brothers named Fries. He stated that Jacob's future wife, Anna Margaretha Herkin, whom Jacob married in America, was also on board the *St. Andrew Galley*. Jacob had a son named Henry, but he is not the Henry Frist of New Castle County. Jacob Fries's children are known and identified through church records in Salem County, New Jersey.[29]

Nothing is known of Jacob's brother Philip (if in fact he was a brother). Early records in Salem County, New Jersey, are insufficient to prove whether Philip Fries settled there, but he was not found in the church records where Jacob Fries and his family were so thoroughly recorded.

That there was a Philip Fries with ties to the Salem County, New Jersey, Fries family who was alive in 1772 is evidenced by the fact that Philip Fries, *Jr.* served as sponsor when a child was baptized on 15 November 1772 at Friesburg.[30] At that time, the term Jr. did not indicate that he was the son of Sr. The terms were used to differentiate between two men of the same name. Sr. was the older or better established man. This Philip Fries, Jr. might have been Jacob Fries's son who was born in 1757 and would have been fifteen years old in 1772. Whether or not he was the Philip Fries who married on 19 October 1777 to Catherine Bop at Old Swedes Church in Philadelphia remains uncertain.[31]

One deed was found that tends to support the possibility of a link between Salem County, New Jersey, and New Castle County, Delaware. On 26 December 1780 Elizabeth Lauderback of Gilesgrove in Salem County, New Jersey, widow of Peter Lauderback of Salem County, deceased, executed a deed to Charles Yoast and his wife Christine of Philadelphia for land in New Castle County.[32] Also named in the deed were Henry Lauderback of Salem County and Patience his wife; John Lauderback of Newbern Liberties of the City of Philadelphia and Anny his wife; George Lauderback of Gilesgrove; Catharine Till of New Jersey, widow; Jacob Fries of New Jersey, yeoman, and Elizabeth his wife; John Curry[?] of New Jersey and Julianna his wife; and James Gainer and his wife Sarah. Elizabeth Fries was a daughter of Peter and Elizabeth Lauderback and the others were her siblings. Jacob was identified in another part of the deed as Jacob Fries, Jr.

It is not certain who this particular Jacob Fries was, but he was not the immigrant listed above, whose first wife was Anna and whose second wife was Dorcas.[33] That Jacob Fries was of Upper Allways Creek in Salem County, New Jersey, on 21 October 1795, when he conveyed along with Dorcas, his wife, a small tract of land to Alexander Martin, merchant, of Oxford Township in Philadelphia County, Pennsylvania. The deed is four pages long, but conveyed just a small amount of land. The deed was recorded 26 January 1796.[34]

On 19 September 1738 Michel Fris and Simon Fries were among Palatines imported on the ship *The Thistle*, John Wilson, commander, from Rotterdam, but last from Plymouth in old England.[35]

THE PROBLEMS WITH IMMIGRANT NAMES

On 9 September 1738 a list of foreigners, including Jacob Fries, took the oath of allegiance after arriving in Pennsylvania on the ship *Glasgow*, Walter Sterling, master, from Rotterdam.[36] The foreigners were listed twice. One list gave only their names, and another gave their names and ages. The problems inherent in the spelling of names can be examined in these two different lists of the same people. This provides insight into the confusion about names on the early passenger lists and oaths of allegiance.

FIRST LIST	SECOND LIST
Valentine Krantz	*Valentine Grance age 32*
Jacob Triess	*Jacob Fries age 25*
Gottfried Zerfass	*Godfriet Serwaes age 40*
Melchior Clos	*Melcher Klass age 32*
Johan Peter	*Oberkehr Hans Peter Oberkeer age 33*
Deobalt Weber	*Deobald Weaver age 37*

RELIGION

Religion is normally a major factor in determining the ethnic origin of a family. Both Henry Frist and his wife Elizabeth (Garretson) Frist are buried in St. James Methodist Episcopal Church Cemetery in Newport, Delaware. Since it does not appear that the very early records of this church survived, it is not certain whether the Frists worshipped there. The fact that they were buried in the church cemetery suggests that they were members and also that they were not recent immigrants, who would be more likely to attend a Lutheran Church.

There were very few early records for the Frists recorded at Holy Trinity (Old Swedes) Church in Wilmington, Delaware, and none prior to 1800. The original church burying ground was established in 1638 and Holy Trinity (Old Swedes) Church was established in 1698 as a Swedish Lutheran church.[37] If the Frists were recent immigrants from Germany or Sweden, one might expect to find records of them, but the records are extant and the Frists were not there. This could be due to the fact that they were living in the Newport area, rather than in Wilmington, although the distance is only a few miles. In 1791 Holy Trinity (Old Swedes) Church became a Protestant Episcopal church.[38] It wasn't until Joel Frist and his family and Jediah Frist's widow and her family moved to Wilmington that records were found on the Frists at Holy Trinity (Old Swedes) Church.

A STUDY OF THE 1880 AND 1900 U.S. CENSUS

A study of the 1880 and 1900 U.S. census returns for men named Frist produced some interesting results. Contrary to family tradition, not all Frists were descended from Henry Frist of New Castle County, Delaware.

In 1880, examining just the male heads of Frist households, most were found to have birthplaces in Delaware, Maryland, Tennessee, Pennsylvania, Ohio, Iowa, and Indiana. Many of the Frists found in these seven states were descended from Henry Frist of New Castle County, Delaware. However, Frists were also found in New York, Illinois, Wisconsin, and Kentucky. If they were foreign born, most gave Germany as their place of birth, although two were found who listed England as a birthplace.

In the 1900 census there were many recent Frist immigrants with birthplaces primarily in Germany and Austria, although a few were found in Ireland, England, and Canada. There was one from Brussels and one from France, several of African American descent, and even one Native American.

The 1900 census provided one interesting entry. It was for Joseph Frist, who was the head of the household in New Castle County, Delaware.[39] He was thirty-five years of age and indicated that he had emigrated from Germany in 1895. Joseph was listed as born in Germany of parents born in Germany. His wife was Christina, who was born in July of 1879 in Germany of parents born in Germany. They had one son, William, born in December 1897 in Philadelphia of parents born in Germany. They could not yet read or write English and they rented a home. Joseph gave his occupation as laborer.

In 1900 and 1901 Joseph Frist was listed in the Wilmington, Delaware, city directories with wife Christina. He was employed at the H. & F. B. Company and resided at 1810 Wawaset Avenue in Wilmington.[40] No further records were found for this man, but his presence causes one to consider the possibility that he might have come to Wilmington because of some distant family tradition of kinfolk who migrated to that area.

REVOLUTIONARY WAR RECORDS

A descendant, Anna Alexander, located a Revolutionary War service record in Northampton County, Pennsylvania, for a man named Henry Fries who served as a sergeant in Capt. John Lyle's Company in the second battalion guarding British prisoners in 1780.[41] He was discharged on 12 May 1781. She made reference to another one by that name in New York.

Another Henry Fries served in the Second Battalion, first establishment in Capt. Shute's Fourth Company in New Jersey as a first lieutenant enlisting on 28 November 1775. He was shown as missing in action at Three Rivers on 8 June 1776.[42]

Henry Fries was on a list of unknown officers in the First and Second New Jersey Regiment on 2 April 1776 and a similar list for the New Jersey line dated 16 August 1776.[43]

While Henry Frist may well have served in the American Revolution, he was not found serving under the surname Frist. There are many possibilities for his service when the search is extended to spelling variants.

Part II
THE DESCENDANTS OF RUDOLPH FRIST

$\mathcal{T}$he Frists who descended from Rudolph and his son, Henry Frist, were not as dependent on farming for an occupation as most families in this era. However, no evidence was found to indicate an occupation for either Rudolph or Henry other than farming. Although Rudolph owned land in Kent County, Delaware, Henry was not a land owner in adjacent New Castle County.

Many descendants gravitated to industrialized occupations, becoming pattern makers, carpenters, coopers, coach and carriage makers, wheelwrights, railroad engineers, and one railroad station master. They also aspired to professions that required higher education and became doctors, dentists, nurses, educators, engineers, and lawyers. Today, some still till the soil in the occupation of their distant ancestors.

The Frists were not prolific. Rudolph Frist had only two children. Most of his descendants in the early generations had families of six to eight children when families of fourteen and sixteen children were not unusual. The child mortality rate was high in the nineteenth and early twentieth centuries, and some of the Frist children died young, although not significantly more than in other families. Many of those who survived to adulthood remained unmarried. A surprising number of those who married did not reproduce, which was somewhat unusual in a time frame when sophisticated methods of birth control were as yet unknown.

Henry had ten children by two wives, a larger family than any of his children had. One child died as an infant and another died single at age twenty-four. Two of the remaining eight children who grew to adulthood remained single and a third, although married, had no children. Although Henry had thirty-three grandchildren, the average family was less than seven children, not large in that era. Only twenty-four of Henry's grandchildren reproduced, and their average was just over four children per family. Because this pattern repeated itself in subsequent generations, the Frist surname continues to be an extremely uncommon one.

While all of Henry's eight sons survived to adulthood, only five of them married and procreated. His eldest son John migrated to Indiana, his son James moved to Maryland, and his youngest son Jacob went south to Tennessee. Descendants of his son Jediah, who died in New Castle County, also went to Indiana. Only one of Henry's two daughters lived to adulthood. She also died in New Castle County.

Research on an uncommon name is frequently complicated by numerous spelling variations, and many were found, including Friest, Fries, Fritz, Frieze, Freese, and Freeze. In written material, the name was occasionally transcribed as Frisk. In typed material, letters were reversed so that the name was occasionally found as First.

DELAWARE

After having been granted Delaware, on 25 October 1682, William Penn determined that the land should be divided into townships that were to be occupied by one hundred families. Each family, including servants, was presumed to have an average of ten people. The areas were referred to as hundreds. Originally, there were five in New Castle County, but more were added as the population increased.[1]

There have been only three counties in the state of Delaware, but the names have changed over the years. They are currently Kent, Sussex, and New Castle. The county of Kent was created in 1682, formerly known as St. Jones, with a county seat at Dover. It is located south of New Castle County. The county of New Castle, whose county seat today is Wilmington, was an original county created in 1673.

It was in Dover Hundred in Kent County that Henry Frist was raised, and it was in the rural area of Christiana Hundred in New Castle County where he spent his adult life, beginning as early as 1788.

RUDOLPH FRIES, FRIETS, FRIESS

On 27 September 1749 Rudolf Fries was among those foreigners from the Palatinate who arrived in Philadelphia on the ship *Isaac* with Robert Mitchell as captain and took the oath of allegiance.[2] They came from Rotterdam, but their last port in England was Cowes.

This may or may not be the same person as Rudolph Friets who on 12 November 1758 was a sponsor at Holy Trinity (Old Swedes) Church in Wilmington, Delaware, when Nicklas and Catharina Puschy's son Rudolph Puschy was baptized.[3] Also serving as a sponsor was Susanna Bauman.[4]

Some researchers believe that these two people who witnessed the baptism were the same two people, identified as Rudolph Friess and Susanna Baumaenn, who married on 25 February 1760 in the German Reformed Church in Philadelphia.[5] This seems unlikely, however, since Susanna Bauman was identified in Holy Trinity (Old Swedes) Church records as the wife of John Bauman and mother of five children born from 1750 through 1757 who were christened at Holy Trinity (Old Swedes) Church.[6] If John Bauman died while a member of Old Swedes Church, his death was not recorded there. It is possible that John and Susanna Bauman had an older daughter Susanna, born prior to their appearance in the records of Old Swedes Church, who was the bride in the 1760 marriage.

It is likely that the Rudolph Fries who arrived in Philadelphia in 1749 was the Rudolph Friess who married Susanna Baumaenn in Philadelphia in 1760, but even that remains unproven. An immigrant who arrived in America in 1749 with limited funds would probably require several years of work before he could afford to marry.

No information has been located thus far to prove that these records are for the Rudolph Frist, more often spelled Freese or other variations of the surname, who lived in Kent County, Delaware, in the 1760s.[7] One George Frees/Freese was taxed in Dover Hundred of Kent County from 1788 to 1791,[8] but may have no connection to the family.

FIRST GENERATION

1. Rudolph Frist[1] is the progenitor of the Frist family of Delaware, but very little is known about him. His place and date of birth are unknown, but the latter could be no later than 1740 and was probably considerably earlier. He died in Kent County, Delaware, between 1781 and 1792.[9]

On 26 February 1760 Rudolph Frist, husbandman (or farmer), bought fifty acres of land in Dover Hundred in Kent County, Delaware, from Abraham Galindo and his wife Elizabeth.[10] The land was described as being on the south side of the main branch of Dover River. David Caldwell and Will. Kellen were witnesses.

From 1760 and continuing through 1781 Rudolph Freeze or Freese was taxed in Dover Hundred in Kent County, Delaware.[11] He was not found after that year and died intestate in Kent County between 1781 and 1792.[12]

On 10 January 1792 Rudolph's daughter, Elizabeth Vining, and her husband, John, sold their undivided one-third share of her father's estate to her brother,

Henry.[13] On 8 November 1796 Rudolph's son, Henry Frist, and his daughter, Elizabeth Vining, executed a deed selling the land of their father Rudolph Frist to Alexander McCoy.[14] Both deeds were registered at the same time. The deed stated that there were only two children, so Rudolph's widow is presumed to have been alive in 1792 to receive the other one-third share.

Children of Rudolph Frist,[1] both probably born in Kent County, Delaware:

+ 2   i. Henry[2] Frist, born circa 1758; died 10 July 1821 New Castle County, Delaware;[15] married (1) about 1789; possibly to a Galbraith;[16] and (2) 3 January 1792 New Castle County Delaware, Elizabeth Garretson.[17]

3   ii. Elizabeth Frist, probably born 1760 to 1775;[18] died by 2 January 1802 New Castle County, Delaware;[19] married (1) by 1792 John Vining,[20] a blacksmith who died by 29 October 1798 New Castle, New Castle County, Delaware.[21] Elizabeth married (2) 25 October 1800 New Castle County, Delaware, Hugh Mercer.[22] Children, (a) Henry Vining and (b) James Vining, both not of legal age in 1803.[23] Hugh Mercer left a widow when he died intestate in New Castle County by 23 January 1809[24] and a minor daughter, Elizabeth Mercer born between 1797 and 1810.[25]

SECOND GENERATION

2. Henry[2] Frist (Rudolph[1]) was born circa 1758,[26] probably in Kent County, Delaware, the son of Rudolph Frist.[27] He died 10 July 1821 in New Castle County, Delaware.[28] He married about 1789, possibly to a **Galbraith**, whose given name is not known and who died that same year a few weeks after delivering their only child, John.[29] Henry married second on 3 January 1792 in New Castle County to **Elizabeth Garretson**.[30] Elizabeth was born 22 January 1774 in New Castle County,[31] the daughter of James and Mary (Abraham) Garretson.[32] She died 19 September 1831 in Newport, New Castle County, Delaware.[33]

In 1788 Henry was listed as Henry Freeze when taxed in Christiana Hundred in New Castle County.[34] He was alternately listed as Freese, Freeze, Frieze, or Fruze, and was taxed from 1789 through 1796.

On 10 January 1792 Henry Frist was of New Castle County, Delaware, when he purchased a tract of fifty acres of land in Kent County, Delaware, for thirteen pounds from his sister, Elizabeth Vining, and her husband, John.[35] The deed indicated that the land in question had been sold by Abraham Galindo of Kent County to Rudolph Frist on 26 February 1760. It further stated that Rudolph had died intestate in Kent County leaving two children Henry Frist and Elizabeth Frist, wife of John Vining. John and Elizabeth Vining conveyed their one-third undivided interest in the land. Joseph Boughman witnessed the deed.

On 8 November 1796 Henry Frist of Christiana Hundred in New Castle County and his wife Elizabeth sold this fifty-acre tract for thirty-four pounds, seventeen shillings, and three pence to Alexander McCoy of Dover Hundred in Kent County, Delaware.[36] Witnesses were G. Read, Jr. and J. Monro. John Vining witnessed the fact that Henry Frist received payment in full from Alexander McCoy.

Beginning in 1798 Henry was taxed as Henry Frist in Christiana Hundred, New Castle County.[37] He owned no land, but paid tax on personal property valued at $185.

In 1800 Henry was listed as Henry Fries, the head of the household in the census of New Castle County, Delaware.[38] He was listed as twenty-six to forty-five years of age. A total of five females lived in the household. His wife was twenty-six in 1800 and was probably the female listed as sixteen to twenty-six. Another female aged twenty-six to forty-five in the household may have been his widowed sister, Elizabeth Vining. There was also a female over forty-five years of age. This older woman could not have been his current mother-in-law, Mary Garretson, who was known to be deceased.[39] There were three other males in the household, but their ages were not compatible with the known dates of birth of his sons. Their nearest neighbors were Hance Nebucar, William Armon, and two Armstrong families.

In 1804 Henry, listed as Henry Fritz, paid tax on stock valued at $128.75 plus a personal tax on $200 in Christiana Hundred, New Castle County.[40] His total tax was a higher amount than many of his neighbors.

In 1810 Henry and Elizabeth lived in Christiana Hundred, New Castle County, Delaware, but not within the town of Newport.[41] Henry was over forty-five years of age, and Elizabeth was twenty-six to forty-five. The information on the children and their ages and sex is consistent with what is known about the family. They lived next door to Jacob Rothwell and John Whiteman. In 1816 Henry was taxed in Christiana Hundred on livestock valued at $64.

In 1820 Henry lived in Mill Creek Hundred in New Castle County.[43] He was over forty-five years of age. Two women lived with him, one over forty-five years (surely his wife Elizabeth) and another twenty-six to forty-five (probably his unmarried daughter Susannah who would have been twenty-seven). Five sons also lived with him, probably the five youngest. Living nearby were his two oldest sons, John and Jediah.[44]

When Henry died in New Castle County,[45] Jacob Rothwell and Jacob Ball were appointed on 1 August 1821 to appraise his estate.[46] The inventory of his estate was taken on 11 August 1821 and recorded on 24 February 1823. It totaled $347.25, and items included a horse cart, four horses, nine sheep, four lambs, four milk cows, four heifers, and four spring calves.

While Henry's occupation isn't known, sufficient farm animals and equipment were included in the inventory to conclude that he made his living primarily by farming. Elizabeth administered the estate and submitted an account on 24 February 1823, which listed notes on Michael Kinch, James Armon, and John Erwin totaling $140. Payments were made to John Frist for $10.96; to James Frist for $38.50; to Israel Garretson for $6.98; and to John Erwin, executor of Peter Garretson, for $225.07.

Henry owned no land in New Castle County, but instead rented land. The administrator's account in the estate of Peter Garretson indicated that on 25 March 1822 a sum of $225 was due from H. Frist for rent.[47]

Henry is buried in St. James Methodist Episcopal Church Cemetery in Newport, Christiana Hundred, New Castle County, Delaware. It isn't certain just how long the family had worshipped at this church or if they worshipped there at all. St. James Church was started in the 1760s, but the original church building was never finished and gradually fell into ruin.[48] In 1809 a fire completed the destruction and the families in Newport were said to have used the other St. James Church in nearby Stanton from time to time. There were numerous attempts to revive the church at Newport, but it wasn't until 1875 that anyone was completely successful. Henry's grandson Robert Harris Frist was the first to be married in the newly rebuilt church on 25 December 1875 when he wed Elizabeth R. Nebeker.[49]

Almost two years after Henry's death, his widow Elizabeth purchased a house and lot on the north side of Ayre Street in Newport on 15 March 1823 from John and Mary Boys and John H. and Lydia Stidham.[50] Witnesses to the deed were Clarissa Davis and Isaac Hendrickson.

In 1830 Elizabeth was the head of the household in Christiana Hundred, New Castle County.[51] She was fifty to sixty years of age, which is consistent with her known birth date. Two sons lived with her, one aged twenty to thirty and another aged ten to fifteen. The latter was surely their youngest son, Jacob Chester Frist, age thirteen. A female aged twenty to thirty also lived with Elizabeth. Her daughter Susanna would have been thirty-seven, but was still single and believed to be living with her mother.

Elizabeth wrote her will on 18 September 1831, and it was probated on 18 December 1832.[52] She left her house and lot in Newport to her daughter Susanna for her lifetime, to be divided among all of Elizabeth's children at Susanna's death. She left bequests to her sons James, Joseph, and Jacob and named her son Garretson as executor. On 18 December 1832 administration was granted to Joseph Derrickson, Garretson Frist having since died. On 25 December 1832 the estate was appraised.[53] Several items of significant value indicating a certain amount of

Trustee's Sale

OF

REAL ESTATE.

By virtue of an order of the Orphans' Court of the State of Delaware, in and for
New Castle County, made February Term, 1868, will be exposed to sale at

PUBLIC VENDUE,

ON

SATURDAY,

The 21st day of March, at 3 o'clock, P. M.

At the Hotel of Alex. Laws, in the village of Newport,
of said County,

ALL THAT CERTAIN LOT OR PIECE OF LAND WITH A

BRICK HOUSE

Thereon erected, situated in the village of Newport, in the County of New Castle
aforesaid, bounded and described as follows, to wit: Beginning at the North side
of Ayre street, thence by said street North 86 degrees Easterly four perches by said
street, thence North 4 degrees Westerly 8 perches and three feet, thence South 86
degrees Westerly 4 perches, and thence South 4 degrees Easterly 8 perches and
three feet to the place of beginning, containing 82½ perches of land more or less,
being the Real Estate of which ELIZABETH FRIST, deceased, died seized and
intestate.

And it is ordered that the purchaser or purchasers thereof be and appear at the next Orphans' Court for
New Castle County, that the Court may assign to him, her or them, the premises sold pursuant to said
order, he, she or they paying to the parties entitled, their just and proportionate shares of the purchase
money, respectively, or with sufficient surety or sureties to be approved by the Court entering into recogni-
zance to the State, to be taken and acknowledged in said Court in a penal sum, to be determined by the
said Court, with condition to pay to the parties entitled severally, their executors, administrators or assigns
respectively, their just and proportionate shares of the said purchase money, with interest from such time
as the Court may determine, in manner and form as may by the direction of the said Court be prescribed
and appointed in said condition.

Attendance will be given and terms of sale made known at the time and place
aforesaid by JOSHUA MARIS, Esquire, a Trustee, appointed by the Court to effect
said sale or by his Attorney.

BY ORDER OF THE COURT,

Attest, SAM'L. GUTHRIE, *Clerk, &c., &c.*

New Castle, February 24th, 1868.

Henry Eckel, Printer, Southeast corner of Fifth and Market Streets, Wilmington, Del.

*1868 Trustee's Sale of Real Estate, New Castle County, Delaware. Orphans' Court case file, Elizabeth
Frist, 1867, widow of Henry Frist. Reproduction courtesy of Delaware State Archives.*

wealth and comfort were included in the inventory—a silver watch valued at
$3.50, an eight-day clock worth $17, a small stove worth $3.50, and some old books.
The house contained two levels, according to the inventory. The items amounted
to $94.61, and all were purchased by James Frist at the valued amount. The estate
paid William G. Jones $5 for making the coffin and William Wasson $2 for digging

the grave. Dr. John Quimby was paid $52. Ultimately, $1.44 was distributed to each of the heirs—Susanna, Jediah (who was listed as deceased), James, Joseph, William, Jacob, and Joel. Actually, both Jediah and Garretson were deceased at that time, but Garretson died without issue whereas Jediah left heirs. Henry's eldest son John was not mentioned in this estate. John was Henry's child by his first marriage and Elizabeth was not his mother.

Elizabeth's daughter Susanna, who was willed the house in Newport, died 22 May 1859.[54] On 11 December 1867 Susanna's brother Joel Frist petitioned in Orphans' Court in New Castle County stating that Susanna had owned a brick house and lot on the north side of Ayre Street in Newport when she died.[55] Documents in this court case identified the five surviving children of Elizabeth Frist. It also named her deceased son Jediah's five children, with all but Henry surviving. Henry's children were also named. Joseph Fitzsimmons of Wilmington purchased the house for $670.80.

Elizabeth is buried beside Henry in St. James Cemetery in Newport, Delaware.[56] The monument includes both of their names as well as those of their sons Jediah, Joseph, and Garretson Frist, and their grandson Joseph Adriana "Joel" Frist, who died in 1842 at the age of two years.

Child of Henry[2] Frist by his first wife, born in New Castle County, Delaware:

+   4   i. JOHN[3] FRIST, born 1789;[57] died 2 October 1847 Preble County, Ohio;[58] married 21 February 1815 New Castle County, Delaware, Susannah Paulson Stidham.[59]

Children of Henry[2] and Elizabeth (Garretson) Frist, all born in New Castle County, Delaware:

     5   ii. SUSANNA FRIST, born 6 March 1793;[60] died 22 May 1859 New Castle County, Delaware;[61] married 11 February 1834 New Castle County, Delaware, Jeremiah Ford.[62] Jeremiah's occupation was lime dealer in 1850.[63] On 5 April 1855 Jeremiah Ford, age sixty of New Castle County, Delaware, deposed as to the accuracy of the 1815 marriage of his wife's half brother John Frist to Susannah Stidham;[64] no issue.

+   6   iii. JEDIAH FRIST, born 25 July 1795;[65] died 23 October 1826 New Castle County, Delaware;[66] married 4 March 1819 New Castle County, Delaware, Mary Meredith.[67]

+   7   iv. JAMES FRIST, born 19 September 1797;[68] died 11 December 1873 Cecil County, Maryland.[69] He married about the year 1821, Henrietta Little.[70]

     8   v. MARY FRIST, born 27 May 1800; died 18 May 1801 New Castle County, Delaware.[71]

9   vi. JOSEPH L. FRIST born 5 September 1803;[72] died 13 August 1840; buried St. James Cemetery, Newport, New Castle County, Delaware;[73] no issue.

10   vii. GARRETSON FRIST, born 16 February 1807;[74] died 1 October 1831; buried St. James Cemetery, Newport, New Castle County, Delaware; no issue.[75]

11   viii. WILLIAM FRIST, born 27 August 1809;[76] died 3 December 1891 New Castle County, Delaware, of debility;[77] buried Wilmington and Brandywine Cemetery, Wilmington, Delaware. He was sixty years old and his occupation was cooper in the 1870 census;[78] bought and sold several lots of land in Wilmington;[79] single at his death, no issue.

+   12   ix. JOEL FRIST, born 9 February 1812;[80] died 29 October 1891 Wilmington, New Castle County, Delaware;[81] married 28 September 1837 in Holy Trinity (Old Swedes) Church in Wilmington, New Castle County, Delaware, Adrianna Morrison.[82]

+   13   x. JACOB CHESTER FRIST born 27 January 1817;[83] died 18 March 1879 Chattanooga, Hamilton County, Tennessee;[84] married (1) 13 February 1845 Wilmington, New Castle County, Delaware, Ann Eliza Harris;[85] married (2) 1852 Chattanooga, Hamilton County, Tennessee, Mary Ann Elizabeth Baldwin.[86]

THIRD GENERATION

4. John[3] **Frist** (Henry[2], Rudolph[1]) was born in 1789 in New Castle County, Delaware, the son of Henry and his first wife, whose surname was perhaps Galbraith.[87] He died 2 October 1847 in Preble County, Ohio.[88] He married on 21 February 1815 in New Castle County to **Susannah Paulson Stidham**.[89] Susannah was born 23 November 1792 in Delaware,[90] the daughter of David and Rebecca (Paulson) Stidham of Christiana Hundred in New Castle County.[91] She died after 1855,[92] presumably in Preble County, Ohio.

John Frist was drafted on 25 May 1813 at New Castle, Delaware, during the War of 1812 and served as a private in a company of the Delaware Militia commanded by Colonel Caleb P. Bennett.[93] He was discharged on 30 July 1813.[94]

In 1820 John and Susannah lived in New Castle County.[95] Both were twenty-six to forty-five years of age. Three children lived with them, two boys and one girl, all under the age of ten.[96]

On 22 August 1821 John Frist and his wife, Susannah P. Frist, along with John Stidham and his wife, Sarah, and David Stidham, all of Christiana Hundred, sold Lot 8 in Mill Creek Hundred, consisting of three acres, to Samuel Meredith of Mill Creek Hundred.[97] The deed identified the lot as having been a part of the estate of the mother of Rebecca Paulson Stidham. Rebecca was identified as the mother of John Stidham and Susannah P. Frist. The deed was sworn in court on 21 August 1821 (the day before it was executed), but it wasn't recorded until 7 November 1837.[98]

In 1821 a tax list in Christiana Hundred in New Castle County showed John, using the surname Freist, as "gone."[99] John and Susannah migrated to Wayne County, Indiana, in time to appear in the 1830 census.[100] Four sons and a daughter lived with them.

They did not remain in Indiana long. On 8 July 1831 John purchased forty-two acres just across the Indiana state line in Preble County, Ohio, from William and Cynthia Tramel for $250.[101] The land was identified as the west half of Section 18, Township 9 Range 1 and witnesses were William and Richard B. Paine. In 1832 they can be found on the tax lists in Jefferson Township of Preble County, Ohio.[102]

Back in Delaware, Susannah's father David Stidham wrote his will on 24 August 1836, and it was probated on 9 April 1838 in New Castle County, leaving a $100 bequest to his daughter Susannah Frist.[103]

John Frist wrote his will on 30 September 1847, and it was probated on 18 March 1848 in Preble County, Ohio.[104] He left his estate to his wife, Susannah, for her natural life. He named all of his children except his son John S., who had predeceased him. He named his granddaughter Sarah, who was a baby when he wrote his will, but who died not long after the will was probated. John is buried in Pleasant Hill Cemetery in Preble County, Ohio.[105]

In 1850 his widow Susannah, age fifty-seven, and her daughter Eliza Jane, age twenty, lived with Susannah's son William Frist in Jefferson Township in Preble County, Ohio.[106] On 21 May 1855 Susannah applied from Preble County for bounty land based on John's service in the War of 1812.[107]

Children of John[3] and Susannah Paulson (Stidham) Frist:

+   14   i.   REBECCA ANN[4] FRIST, born about 1816 New Castle County, Delaware;[108] died 1854, presumably Preble County, Ohio;[109] married 23 March 1848 Preble County, Ohio, Joseph Hahn.[110]

+   15   ii. DAVID H. FRIST, born 12 April 1818 New Castle County, Delaware;[111] died 13 March 1865, presumably Villisca, Montgomery County, Iowa.[112] He married (1) 29 December 1842 Lydia E. Holliday[113] and (2) 25 March 1858 Ruth J. Cate.[114]

+   16   iii. WILLIAM H. FRIST, born about 1823 probably Wayne County, Indiana;[115] died 22 September 1887 Preble County, Ohio;[116] married Catherine Reid.[117]

     17   iv. JOHN S. FRIST, born 6 November 1826 probably in Wayne County, Indiana; died 14 August 1847 Wayne County, Indiana;[118] married

27 August 1846 Wayne County, Indiana, Elizabeth Moon.[119] Elizabeth Frist lived with Joseph and Elizabeth Moon in 1850 in Wayne County, Indiana.[120] John owned land in Wayne County, Indiana, at his death,[121] creating an estate that was probated.[122] One child, Sarah Adaline Frist born 21 June 1847 and died 22 July 1849.[123]

+ 18   v. ROBERT M. FRIST, born about 1828, probably in Wayne County, Indiana;[124] died 7 October 1884 Preble County, Ohio;[125] married (1) name unknown and (2) 20 August 1857 Fountain City, Wayne County, Indiana, Ruth C. Meredith.[126]

   19   vi. ELIZA JANE FRIST, born about 1830 in Wayne County, Indiana;[127] married 7 November 1850 Preble County, Ohio, Joseph Moon.[128]

+ 20   vii. MARY JANE FRIST, born about 1831[129] probably in Preble County, Ohio; died 6 August 1890 Warren, Huntington County, Indiana;[130] married 22 November 1849 Preble County, Ohio, Charles F. Powell.[131]

+ 21   viii. JONAS LYMAN PAULSON FRIST, born 20 June 1834 Preble County, Ohio; died 10 October 1908;[132] married 18 November 1853 Wayne County, Indiana, Amy E. Powell.[133]

6. Jediah³ Frist (Henry², Rudolph¹) was born on 25 July 1795 in Wilmington, New Castle County, Delaware, the son of Henry and Elizabeth (Garretson) Frist.[134] He died on 23 October 1826 in Christiana Hundred, New Castle County, Delaware.[135] He married on 4 March 1819 in New Castle County to **Mary Meredith**.[136] Mary was born on 10 August 1798, in Wilmington, the daughter of Samuel and Mary (Bowman) Meredith.[137] She died on 29 October 1889 in Wilmington, Delaware.[138]

In 1820 Jediah and Mary lived in New Castle County.[139] They were both listed as sixteen to twenty-six years of age, and one child had already been born to their union. Living with them was a male over forty-five years of age whose identity is unknown.

When Jediah died in 1826, he was only thirty-one years of age. The inventory of his estate, which amounted to almost $700, was dated 15 November 1827.[140] Payments were made to Elizabeth Frist, to Israel Garretson for rent, to Samuel Meredith, and to Charles Shoemaker, among others. On 12 February 1833 Mary Frist petitioned the court in New Castle County to be appointed guardian of the minor children of Jediah Frist.[141]

On 25 May 1839 Mary Frist purchased a lot on Orange Street in Wilmington, Delaware, with a two-story frame house and brick kitchen, from William Solomon and his wife Eliza for $500.[142]

In 1840 Mary was the head of the household, living in Wilmington in New Castle County.[143] She gave her age as thirty to forty, although she would actually have been forty-two. There was another female of the same age living with her as well as two females aged fifteen to twenty (daughters Esther, seventeen, and Mary, sixteen), two males, one aged twenty to thirty (son Henry, nineteen), and another male aged fifteen to twenty (son Jediah, fourteen).

In 1850 Mary headed a large family in New Castle County, living in Wilmington.[144] She was fifty-two years of age, born in Delaware, and she owned real estate valued at $600.

By 1870 Mary lived with her daughter Elizabeth Lloyd in Wilmington.[145] She was seventy-one years of age and owned real estate valued at $1000. In 1880 Mary lived with another daughter, Esther Springer, and Esther's husband, Levi, in Wilmington, Delaware.[146] She was eighty-two years old.

When Mary died in 1889, it was of general debility at the age of ninety-two. She is buried in Wilmington and Brandywine Cemetery in Wilmington, Delaware.[147] Her will was dated 5 March 1864, just two months after the death of her oldest son Henry. It was probated in New Castle County on 12 November 1889.[148] It named her son Jediah, her daughter and son-in-law Levi H. and Esther Ann Springer, her daughter Elizabeth widow of Franklin Lloyd, and her daughter Mary F. Robinson widow of James Robinson. Neither her son Henry nor his children were mentioned in her will.

On 30 January 1891 the inventory and appraisement of Mary's estate was recorded in New Castle County with Morris D. Crossan and George H. Tindall as appraisers. Elizabeth Lloyd signed this document, stating that she was certain that the inventory was inclusive.[149] It contained $700.35 cash on deposit with the Wilmington Savings Fund Society.

Children of Jediah[3] and Mary (Meredith) Frist, all born in Wilmington, New Castle County, Delaware:

+   22   i. ELIZABETH[4] FRIST, born 5 April 1820;[150] died by 1907 New Castle
            County, Delaware;[151] married 28 March 1841 New Castle County,
            Delaware, Franklin Lloyd.[152]

+   23   ii. HENRY FRIST, born 19 November 1821;[153] died 13 January 1864 New
            Castle County, Delaware;[154] married 13 May 1845 Wilmington, New
            Castle County, Delaware, Catherine Campbell Stewart.[155]

+   24   iii. ESTHER ANN "HESTER" FRIST, born 27 April 1823;[156] died
            16 October 1909 Wilmington, New Castle County, Delaware;[147]
            married 17 April 1845 Philadelphia, Pennsylvania, Levi H. Springer.[148]

+   25   iv. MARY FRIST, born 26 November 1824;[159] died after 1891;[160] married
            (1) 31 May 1846 New Castle County, Delaware, James Robinson of
            Delaware City, Delaware[161] and (2) between 1864 and 1867, Elon J.
            Way.[162]

+   26   v. JEDIAH RUDOLPH "DOLPH" FRIST, born 22 December 1826;[163]
died 13 November 1907 Vermillion County, Indiana;[164] married
(1) 2 January 1851 New Castle County, Delaware, Marietta Groom;[165]
(2) 15 August 1855 Chester County, Pennsylvania, Mary Johnson
Peirce;[166] and (3) 22 November 1892 Vermillion County, Indiana, Mary
Helen Nelson.[167]

7. James³ Frist (Henry², Rudolph¹) was born on 19 September 1797[168] in New
Castle County, Delaware, the son of Henry and Elizabeth (Garretson) Frist.[169] He
died 11 December 1873 in Cecil County, Maryland.[170] He married about the year
1821 to **Henrietta Little**, who was born in 1798[171] and died on 27 May 1847 in Cecil County, Maryland.[172]

Based on the places of their children's births, the family probably lived in Pennsylvania from about 1825 through at least 1830. In 1830 they were enumerated in
the census of Chester County, Pennsylvania.[173] Three sons (John, Abraham B., and
Thomas) and two daughters (Marietta and Hannah) had been born to their union.

James and Henrietta migrated from Chester County, Pennsylvania, to Cecil
County, Maryland. Children born between 1835 and 1840 list Maryland as their
place of birth. Although tax lists exist for Cecil County, Maryland, for the years between 1830 and 1840, James Frist is not listed on them.

By 1840 James and Henrietta Frist lived in Cecil County, Maryland, with a large
family of seven sons and two daughters.[174] The age and sex of the children fit precisely with the family found in Chester County, Pennsylvania, in 1830. In 1841 and
1842 James Frist was taxed in the seventh district of Cecil County, Maryland, on
$329 worth of livestock and $75 worth of household furniture.[175] He continued to
be taxed in a similar manner in the years from 1842 to 1847.

James never married again after Henrietta's death in 1847.[176] In 1848 their son
Abraham Frist appeared for the first time on the tax lists of Cecil County, Maryland.[177] Abraham paid tax on personal property valued at $200 and other property
worth $200. Abraham was the only son of James Frist found on the tax lists prior
to the Civil War.

In 1850 James lived in Cecil County, Maryland, the widowed head of the household, listed as William Frist.[178] Even though he was listed as William, he was in
fact James, and five of the proven children of James Frist lived with him—Marietta, Hannah, William, James, and Edmund. James Frist, not William, was taxed
in the seventh district of Cecil County in 1850 and throughout this period of
time.[179]

In 1860 James, his son Edmund, and his two oldest daughters, both of whom
never married, lived in the seventh district of Cecil County, Maryland.[180] James
owned personal property worth $1600, but was not a land owner.

In 1870 James and his two unmarried daughters remained living in Cecil County.[181] He was seventy-three years of age and owned personal property valued at $1000. His son Edmund lived nearby, listed in the census as Edward Frist.[182]

James wrote his will on 7 December 1873 and it was probated in Cecil County, Maryland.[183] He left his estate to his two unmarried daughters Marietta and Hannah. His estate packet revealed that a debt of $100 was due from the estate of Theodore Physick and listed personal property appraised at $345.30.[184] He and his wife are both buried in Hopewell United Methodist Church Cemetery in Cecil County, Maryland.[185] Their tombstone includes the name of their son Henry, who died at age fourteen.[186]

Children of James[3] and Henrietta (Little) Frist:

+ 27 i. MARIETTA[4] FRIST, born 8 October 1823[187] Delaware; died 10 June 1909 Baltimore City, Maryland;[188] did not marry, no issue.

+ 28 ii. HANNAH FRIST, born 14 December 1825[189] Pennsylvania; died 20 June 1909 Baltimore City, Maryland;[190] did not marry, no issue.

+ 29 iii. JOHN FRIST, born 1 January 1828 Pennsylvania;[191] died 8 November 1909 Baltimore City, Maryland;[192] married (1) about 1851, Annie James.[193] He married (2) on 14 May 1867 in Baltimore City, Maryland, Emily M. Holt.[194]

+ 30 iv. ABRAHAM B. a.k.a. ABRAM FRIST, born about 1825 to 1830, probably Chester County, Pennsylvania;[195] died by 12 February 1885;[196] married (1) 11 June 1845 Cecil County, Maryland, Elizabeth C. Patterson.[197] He married (2) 5 March 1859 Baltimore City, Maryland, Julia A. Myers.[198]

+ 31 v. THOMAS LYTTLE FRIST, born about 1830,[199] probably Chester County, Pennsylvania; died 21 January 1873 Charleston, Kanawha County, West Virginia;[200] married about 1851, Sarah Elizabeth.[201]

32 vi. HENRY FRIST, born 6 January 1832; died 30 July 1846 Cecil County, Maryland;[202] no issue.

33 vii. WILLIAM FRIST, born 1835 Maryland;[203] died 24 March 1873 Monroe, Ouachita County, Louisiana.[204] After the Civil War William started a carriage business in Port Deposit known as "W. Frist and Brother."[205] William was thirty-six years of age, unmarried, and working as a wheelwright in Ouachita County, Louisiana, in 1870.[206]

+ 34 viii. JAMES FRIST, born 11 April 1836 Maryland; died 3 April 1908 Baltimore City, Maryland;[207] married 26 November 1873 Baltimore City, Maryland, Annie A. (Hartzell) Beam.[208]

+ 35 ix. EDMUND PHYSICK a.k.a. EDWARD FRIST, born 15 May 1838, probably Cecil County, Maryland; died 15 September 1911 Cecil

County, Maryland;[209] married 9 February 1863 in Cecil County, Maryland, Mary Jane Haines.[210]

12. Joel[3] **Frist** (Henry[2], Rudolph[1]) was born on 9 February 1812 in Newport, New Castle County, Delaware, the son of Henry and Elizabeth (Garretson) Frist.[211] He died on 29 October 1891 in Wilmington, New Castle County, Delaware.[212] He married on 28 September 1837 to **Adrianna Morrison** in Wilmington, New Castle County, Delaware.[213] Adrianna was born on 21 September 1816 and died 31 January 1876 in Wilmington, New Castle County, Delaware.[214]

After his father died, Joel went to Wilmington in 1825, working for a time for Joseph A. Hunter and later for John Merrick.[215]

In 1840 Joel lived in New Castle County, Delaware.[216] He and Adrianna were twenty to thirty years of age. A son Joseph had been born to their union in 1838. Also living with them was a girl aged ten to fifteen whose identity is unknown.

On 17 March 1857 Joel Frist purchased a lot with a dwelling house in Wilmington, Delaware, from George David and his wife Jane of Wilmington for $1200.[217] The lot was located on the northwestern side of Shipley Street.

Carriage and wagon building was a prominent industry in Wilmington. In 1856 Joel combined his business ability with that of George Allmon and formed Frist and Allmon, a carriage factory located at the corner of Shipley and Seventh Streets in Wilmington.[218] The company was originally established in 1846 as Flagler & Company. Frist and Allmon were described as "practical men" who "commanded the confidence of the trade and are recognized as respectable dealers."[219]

On 20 January 1858 Joel Frist and his partner George Allmon advanced their business when they successfully bid on the property located at Shipley and Seventh Avenue, which they purchased for $2500 at a sheriff's sale.[220] The property had been owned by Joseph A. Hunter (for whom Joel had worked in years past) and was described as having "a frame coach maker's shop, brick blacksmith shop, and other buildings" on it.

The company employed from twelve to twenty workmen in a factory that was 64 × 58 feet in dimensions, five stories high with 17,000 square feet of floor space.[221] Another source described the company as four stories high with a basement that was used for a smith shop.[222] The offices and showrooms were on the first floor, wood and finishing shops were on the second floor, trimming and varnishing were done on the third floor, and the fourth floor was the paint shop. They were described as producing a variety of styles such as carriages, pony phaetons, buggies, and wagons and as having a large and imminently desirable class of customers for carriages built to order. These customers included the wealthy Lamot du Pont, with whom they did considerable business over the years. On 4 May 1882 du Pont was advised that they had sold his old carriage for

Map showing Frist and Allmon Carriage Shop, corner of West Seventh and Shipley Streets, Wilmington, Delaware. 1867 Atlas, G. M. Hopkins & Company. Reproduction courtesy of Delaware State Archives.

$40 and that while the "price seems low but it was the best I could do with it as it was old and out of stile [sic]."[223]

In 1860 Joel and Adrianna lived in Wilmington, New Castle County.[224] Joel owned real estate valued at $5200 and personal property worth $5000. Their three surviving children lived with them.

The Civil War brought strife and disruption to the North as well as to the South. In Wilmington, Delaware, the news in 1861 of the firing on Fort Sumter caused great excitement, and the streets were thronged with people. On 16 April 1861 Joel Frist was one of those in attendance when a Union demonstration was held at city hall in Wilmington.[225]

On 16 October 1866 Joel Frist and his wife, Adrianna, and George Allmon and his wife, Jane, all of Wilmington, sold a lot with three dwellings on it to Samuel W. McCauley of Wilmington for $2500.[226] This was not the Frist and Allmon facility, but property that the two had purchased in 1860.[227]

In 1876 when Adrianna died, the family lived at 709 Shipley Drive.[228] In 1880 Joel was the widowed head of the household in Wilmington.[229] His work as a coach maker continued, and he reported to the census taker that his parents were both born in Delaware. His daughter, Rachel, son George, daughter-in-law Catherine, and grandson, Homer, all lived with him.

Joel wrote his will on 6 August 1888 and died in 1891 at the age of eighty of cystitis while living at 709 Shipley Street, Wilmington, Delaware.[230] In his will, probated in New Castle County, he directed his executors to sell his real estate, including that which was jointly owned with his partner, George Allmon, and all of his personal property.[231] He left one-third of his estate to his son George, another one-third to his son Henry M., and the final one-third in trust to his sons George and Henry for the use of his daughter, Rachel Waddington, wife of Henry Waddington.

The inventory and appraisement of his estate was dated 1 December 1891 with George Frist and Dr. Henry M. Frist making oath that it was accurate. Joel's estate had no debts and no credits due.[232] The house was sold for $2000 and the carriage factory brought $5900. The estate totaled $8887.37.[233]

Joel and Adrianna are both buried in Wilmington and Brandywine Cemetery in Wilmington, Delaware.[234]

Children of Joel[3] and Adrianna (Morrison) Frist, all born in Wilmington, New Castle County, Delaware:

36　　i. JOSEPH ADRIANA[4] "JOEL" FRIST, born 24 March 1838; died 24 March 1842[235] Newport, New Castle County, Delaware; buried St. James Cemetery, Newport, New Castle County, Delaware.

+　37　　ii. GEORGE FRIST, born about February 1840;[236] died 14 September 1928 Wilmington, New Castle County, Delaware;[237] married about 1876, Catherine A. Simmons.[328]

38　　iii. RACHEL FRIST, born about 1846;[329] married 4 November 1886 Wilmington, New Castle County, Delaware, at Holy Trinity (Old Swedes) Church, Henry "Harry" Waddington.[240] In 1900 the Waddingtons lived in New Castle County.[241] Rachel stated that she was forty-seven, had been married twelve years [both inaccurate], and had no children. They owned their own home, and Henry was a railroad conductor born in Maryland of parents born in England; no issue.

+   39   iv. HENRY M. "HARRY" FRIST, born about December 1854 Wilmington, New Castle County, Delaware;[242] died after 1920;[243] married about 1897, Anna.[244]

13. Jacob Chester[3] **Frist** (Henry[2], Rudolph[1]) was born 27 January 1817 in New Castle County, Delaware,[245] the son of Henry and Elizabeth (Garretson) Frist.[246] He died 18 March 1879 in Chattanooga, Hamilton County, Tennessee.[247] He married on 13 February 1845 in Wilmington, New Castle County, Delaware, to **Ann Eliza Harris**,[248] who is believed to have died shortly after the birth of their first child in 1847. He married second in Chattanooga, Hamilton County, Tennessee, in 1852 to **Mary Ann Elizabeth Baldwin**.[249] She was born 7 September 1833 in Jefferson County, Tennessee,[250] the daughter of Isaac and Crissa (Cape) Baldwin.[251] Mary Ann died 20 February 1920 in Chattanooga, Hamilton County, Tennessee.[252]

In 1820 Jacob lived with his parents in New Castle County[253] and was probably the son aged ten to fifteen in the household of his widowed mother in 1830 in New Castle County.[254] Following the death of his first wife in 1847, Jacob moved to Richmond County, Georgia, where he was found living alone in 1850.[255] He was thirty-three years of age and his birthplace was Delaware. In 1850 and 1851 he was on the tax rolls of Richmond County paying a poll tax as "Jacob Frist R. R."[256]

By 1852 Jacob had moved to Chattanooga, Hamilton County, Tennessee, where he married for the second time to Mary Ann Elizabeth Baldwin, the ceremony performed by Reverend James Hickey of the Methodist Church.[257] The story of how he killed thirty-two snakes, mostly water moccasins, on the flats south of East Eleventh Street the day before their wedding has been published many times.[258] Many years later Mary Ann Frist was interviewed and an account of this was published in the Chattanooga newspaper.[259]

The Baldwins were among the fifty-three pioneer settlers of Chattanooga. There is a historical marker in Chattanooga honoring the family, and a downtown street bears their name.[260] They arrived in 1836, coming down the Tennessee River on a flatboat to Ross's Landing.[261] Mrs. Crissa Baldwin was one of ten founders of the Methodist Church there, now known as the Centenary Methodist Episcopal Church South.[262]

On 21 September 1852 Jacob Frist bought Lot 29 on Carter Street in Chattanooga from the East Tennessee Iron Manufacturing Company for $200.[263]

In 1860 Jacob and Mary lived at 315 Carter Street in Chattanooga, Hamilton County, Tennessee.[264] Jacob was forty-three and listed his occupation as carpenter. Mary was only twenty-six. Jacob's son Robert from his first marriage, thirteen years of age, and James, Samuel, and Elizabeth from his marriage to Mary

Ann, lived with them. They owned real estate valued at $800 and personal property worth $300.

On 22 September 1860 Jacob purchased eighty acres of land in the Fourth District of Hamilton County from Greenberry Hughes for $300,[265] a tract that he was to own for the remainder of his life.

The War between the States, as it was known in the South, surely had an impact on the Frist family of Chattanooga. Jacob's son Robert Harris Frist, by his first wife, served in that war, enlisting in 1862 at the age of fifteen in Company F of the Fourth Confederate Cavalry (McLemore's).[266] Although his muster rolls cited his enlistment age as seventeen, his actual birth year of 1847 is recorded in the family Bible and confirmed by census records. He served through 31 December 1864. Jacob's other sons were too young to serve.

Back in Delaware, Jacob's relatives were fighting for the United States in the Fifth Delaware Infantry. The Fifth Delaware was established for service in Delaware, and it is unlikely that those serving ever did battle against their Southern kinfolk.[267]

On 29 August 1868, when his mother's Delaware estate was being settled, Jacob executed a power of attorney to his brother Joel of Wilmington, Delaware, appointing him to accept his share of Elizabeth Frist's real estate.[268]

In 1870 Jacob and Mary still lived in Chattanooga.[269] They owned real estate valued at $700 and personal property worth $200. Jacob listed his occupation as pattern maker. Jacob's son Robert Harris Frist, by his first wife, was now twenty-three years old and living at home with the family along with six other children.

Jacob wrote his will in Chattanooga, Hamilton County, Tennessee, on 14 March 1879.[270] He left his house and lot on Carter Street in Chattanooga and eighty acres of land in the Fourth Civil District to his wife Mary for her life and to be disposed of by her will. He died of heart disease[271] at 11:00 p.m. on 18 March 1879 at the age of sixty-two in Chattanooga, Hamilton County, Tennessee.[272] His obituary stated that he had been a "skillful artisan," working as a pattern maker at Webster's Foundry and had commanded the respect and esteem of those who knew him in all walks of life.[273] He was buried in the old Citizens Cemetery.[274]

In 1880 Mary Frist was the head of the household in Chattanooga, living on Carter Street.[275] She was forty-seven years of age, born in Tennessee of parents born in South Carolina. Her daughter, Lizzie, and her three youngest sons lived with her. Her deceased husband's name was written in the census and then crossed off. Jacob was listed as a sixty-two-year-old pattern maker.

Signature of Jacob Chester Frist of Chattanooga, Tennessee, from an 1868 power of attorney to his brother Joel Frist of Wilmington, Delaware. Reproduction courtesy of Delaware State Archives.

In 1900 Mary Frist lived at 315 Carter Street in Chattanooga and Emmett, her youngest child, twenty years of age, lived with her.[276] She was sixty-six years of age and owned her home.

On 10 June 1903 Mary conveyed the south half of Lot No. 29 on Carter Street in Chattanooga "unto my son J. C. Frist."[277] This was the lot that her deceased husband Jacob had purchased in 1852.[278] In 1910 Mary lived alone at 315 Carter Street.[279] She was seventy-six years of age with her "own income."

In 1917 at the age of eighty-three Mary Frist was interviewed by the *Chattanooga Times* and revealed many details about her life.[280] At that time she lived in the same house at 315 Carter Street that Jacob had purchased in 1852. She was described as still retaining her dark brown/black hair "without one hair of gray." She stated that she was the mother of six children, twenty-one grandchildren, and seven great-grandchildren, six of whom lived in Delaware.[281] The seventh great-grandchild was described as a one year old who lived in Lookout Valley and was the "apple of her eye."

Mary died 20 February 1920 in Chattanooga of "softening of the brain" at the age of eighty-seven.[282] Her obituary indicated she had been a resident since 1836 and was a "woman of strong personality and vigorous mind." She was labeled as a person who "held pronounced views and could express them with exceptional ability when the occasion arose."[283] Jacob and Mary are both buried in Citizens Cemetery in Chattanooga, Hamilton County, Tennessee.[284]

Child of Jacob Chester[3] and Ann Eliza (Harris) Frist:

+   40   i. ROBERT HARRIS[4] FRIST, born 24 March 1847 Wilmington, New
Castle County, Delaware;[285] died 30 June 1903 Newport, New Castle
County, Delaware;[286] married on 25 December 1875, New Castle
County, Delaware, Elizabeth Rachel Nebeker.[287]

Children of Jacob Chester[3] and Mary Ann Elizabeth (Baldwin) Frist, all born in Chattanooga, Hamilton County, Tennessee:

+   41   ii. JAMES BALL FRIST, born 25 March 1853;[288] died 9 July 1925
Wauhatchie, Hamilton County, Tennessee;[289] married (1) about 1878,
Harriet R.;[290] married (2) 2 February 1887 Hamilton County,
Tennessee, Permelia "Melia" Corbin.[291]

+   42   iii. SAMUEL HENRY FRIST, born 19 September 1855;[292] died 23 October
1939 Chattanooga, Hamilton County, Tennessee;[293] married about 1881,
Mary Florence Curry,[294] who died 7 January 1913 in Chattanooga,
Hamilton County, Tennessee.[295]

+   43   iv. ANN ELIZABETH "LIZZIE" FRIST, born 7 October 1859;[296] died 15 January 1922 Chickamauga, Walker County, Georgia;[297] married 21 December 1880 Chattanooga, Hamilton County, Tennessee, William M. Vetter.[298]

+   44   v. JACOB CHESTER "JAKE" FRIST, born 2 April 1862;[299] died 2 January 1919 Meridian, Lauderdale County, Mississippi;[300] married 10 August 1897 Jackson County, Ohio, Jane "Jennie" Jones.[301]

+   45   vi. JOSEPH ELMER FRIST, born 29 November 1867;[302] died 11 September 1940 Hamilton County, Tennessee;[303] married about 1898, Chattanooga, Hamilton County, Tennessee, Alice "Allie" Keefe.[304]

+   46   vii. EMMETT FRANKLIN FRIST, born 9 April 1877;[305] died 5 August 1933 Gadsden, Etowah County, Alabama;[306] married 1903 Gadsden, Etowah County, Alabama, Annie C. Stroud.[307]

FOURTH GENERATION

14. Rebecca Ann⁴ Frist (John³, Henry², Rudolph¹) was born about 1816 in New Castle County, Delaware,[308] the daughter of John and Susannah Paulson (Stidham) Frist.[309] She died in 1854, presumably in Preble County, Ohio.[310] She married on 23 March 1848 in Preble County, Ohio, to **Joseph Hahn**.[311] Joseph was born 30 October 1812 in Butler County, Ohio,[312] the son of Michael and Rebecca (Jordan) Hahn.[313] He died 30 October 1889 in Preble County, Ohio.[314]

In 1850 Joseph and Rebecca lived in Jefferson Township, Preble County, Ohio.[315] They owned real estate valued at $1600, and Joseph's occupation was farmer. Four children lived with them, but three of these were children by Joseph's previous marriage to Sarah Garretson. Joseph had married on 15 December 1835 in Preble County, Ohio, to Sarah.[316] Sarah was the daughter of Gideon and Margaret (Moore) Garretson.[317]

After Rebecca's death in 1854,[318] Joseph married for a third time on 18 September 1856 to Mary (Gray) Porterfield, who was the widow of Samuel H. Porterfield.[319] In 1860 Joseph and his new wife Mary lived in Preble County.[320] They owned real estate valued at $5500 and personal property worth $1100.

By 1870 Joseph and Mary's land holdings in Preble County had increased to the amount of $10,000, with personal property worth $1700.[321] Joseph was fifty-eight and Mary was forty-five. Joseph and Mary were still living in Preble County at the time of the 1880 census with their youngest child, a daughter Sarah E.[322]

When Joseph died in 1889 in Preble County, Ohio,[323] he left a will dated 20 October 1886 that named his wife Mary and many of his children.[324] He divided his estate among his children including Samuel S., his only surviving son from his marriage to Rebecca Frist. His widow Mary died 6 June 1894 of cancer at New Paris, Preble County, Ohio.[325]

Children of Joseph and Rebecca Ann[4] (Frist) Hahn:

47   i.   JOHN A.[5] HAHN, born about 1850;[326] died by 4 January 1871;[327] no issue.

48   ii. SAMUEL S. HAHN, born about 1852;[328] died 26 October 1918 Mercer County, Ohio;[329] married 15 September 1881 Darke County, Ohio, Sophronia A. Mogle, born May 1857 Ohio, daughter of Sarah.[330] One son (unnamed), born 14 September 1883 and died 17 September 1883 Dublin Township, Mercer County, Ohio.[331]

15. David H.[4] Frist (John[3], Henry[2], Rudolph[1]) was born 12 April 1818 in New Castle County, Delaware,[332] the son of John and Susannah Paulson (Stidham) Frist.[333] He died 13 March 1865,[334] presumably in Villisca, Montgomery County, Iowa. He married first on 29 December 1842 to **Lydia E. Holliday**, who was born 19 February 1823 in Indiana and died on 5 September 1856 in Wayne County, Indiana.[335] He married for the second time on 25 March 1858 to **Ruth J. Cate**.[336]

On 12 May 1847 David H. Frist bought Lot #10 in the town of Middleborough in Wayne County, Indiana, for $25 from Jonas S. Stidham and Elizabeth his wife.[337] On 6 March 1849 David H. Frist sold the lot in Middleborough to Bently Mendenhall for $85.[338]

In 1850 David and Lydia lived in Wayne County, Indiana, with their first two children.[339] In this census David was listed as born in Pennsylvania and his occupation was farmer.

When Lydia died in 1856 at the age of thirty-three,[340] David was left with several young children to raise. It is thus not surprising that in 1858 David married again, to Ruth J. Cate.[341] David and Ruth migrated to Villisca, Montgomery County, Iowa, with his children in the fall of 1860, behind a team of oxen.[342]

Children of David H.[4] and Lydia E. (Holliday) Frist:

49   i.   RACHEL[5] FRIST, born 18 November 1843; died 11 January 1850 Wayne County, Indiana.[343]

+ 50   ii. JOSEPH ANDREW FRIST, born 16 July 1845 most likely in Wayne County, Indiana;[344] died 11 April 1932 Page County, Iowa;[345] married 28 February 1875 Page County, Iowa, Rosetta Josephine "Rosa" Mitchell.[346]

+ 51   iii. JOHN S. FRIST, born 22 March 1848 Wayne County, Indiana;[347] married about 1875 Elizabeth A., probably Bivans.[348]

52   iv. ELIZABETH A. FRIST, born 21 July 1849 Wayne County, Indiana; died 27 November 1849 Wayne County, Indiana.[349]

+   53   v. REBECCA J. FRIST, born 15 October 1850 Wayne County, Indiana; died 8 December 1910;[350] married about 1867, Henry Thomas.[351]

16. William H.[4] **Frist** (John[3], Henry[2], Rudolph[1]) was born about 1823, probably in Wayne County, Indiana,[352] the son of John and Susannah Paulson (Stidham) Frist.[353] He died 22 September 1887 in Preble County, Ohio.[354] He married **Catherine Reid**, who was born in 1827, the daughter of James and Peggy Reid.[355] She died on 9 September 1899 in Preble County, Ohio.[356]

William and Catherine lived all of their lives in Jefferson Township, Preble County, Ohio, where William farmed. In 1850 William, Catherine, and their infant son were in the Preble County census.[357]

By 1860 their family had grown to include five children.[358] William was thirty-seven years of age, a farmer who owned real estate valued at $1600 and personal property worth $300. By 1870 they had eight children.[359] William was forty-seven with real estate valued at $4100 and personal property worth $1410. His wife Catherine was forty-three. In 1880 five of their children lived with them, the oldest thirty years and the youngest age nine.[369]

On 15 October 1884 William H. Frist filed a lunacy inquest on his daughter Catherine Letilia [*sic*] Frist and on 23 October 1884 she was taken to the asylum at Dayton, Ohio.[361]

William wrote his will on 17 September 1887[362] and died in 1887 of malaria.[363] He left his estate, both real and personal, to his wife, Catherine, during her natural life and named his three surviving sons—James J., William O., and Russell. Catherine died in 1899 at the age of seventy-two.[364] Both are buried in New Paris, Preble County, Ohio.

Children of William H.[4] and Catherine (Reid) Frist, all born in Preble County, Ohio:

       54   i. JAMES JASPER[5] FRIST, born February 1850[365]; died 28 January 1922 Preble County, Ohio.[366] James was a farmer, remained single, and lived with his brother William; no issue.

+   55   ii. SARAH J. FRIST, born about 1852;[367] married 29 December 1872 Preble County, Ohio, Henry C. Rupe.[368]

       56   iii. CATHERINE LETITIA FRIST, born about 1854;[369] died 2 February 1894 Dayton, Ohio;[370] no issue.

       57   iv. ALPHORETTA "ELLA" FRIST, born about 1857;[371] listed as Evaretta Day of Oldtown, Ohio, in father's 1887 estate papers;[372] shown as Ella Day of Xenia in obituary of brother James Jasper Frist in 1922.[373]

       58   v. PULASKI FRIST, born about 1859;[374] probably died young. He was not with the family in 1870 census and was not named in his father's estate papers.

59   vi. SUSAN P. FRIST, born about 1861;[375] married 17 April 1880 Preble County, Ohio, John N. Cook.[376] She lived in Camden, Indiana, when her father died in 1887. Children as named in her father's estate papers (a) Ernie Cook, (b) Minnie Cook, and (c) Keel Cook.[377]

60   vii. SAMUEL C. FRIST, born about 1862.[378]

61   viii. MARGARET A. FRIST, born about 1864.[379] She married a man named Ruhle and lived in Vincennes, Knox County, Indiana, in 1887 when her father died.[380]

+   62   ix. WILLIAM O. FRIST, born June 1867;[381] died 22 May 1929 Preble County, Ohio;[382] married 25 November 1893 Preble County, Ohio, Reba F. Juqua.[383]

+   63   x. RUSSELL "POP" FRIST, born about 1871;[384] died 1930;[385] married about 1892, Sarah Viola Hunt.[386]

18. Robert M.[4] **Frist** (John[3], Henry[2], Rudolph[1]) was born about 1828,[387] probably in Wayne County, Indiana, the son of John and Susannah Paulson (Stidham) Frist.[388] He died 7 October 1884 in Preble County, Ohio.[389] His first wife, whose name is unknown, died on 8 March 1855, but they had no children.[390] He married for the second time on 20 August 1857 in Fountain City, Wayne County, Indiana, to **Ruth C. Meredith**, who was born in North Carolina in 1834.[391] She died on 22 April 1887 in Preble County, Ohio.[392]

On 12 August 1862 Robert enlisted in the Union Army at Hartford, Warren County, Iowa, and served as a private in Company B of the Thirty-Fourth Regiment of Iowa Volunteers.[393] At the time of his discharge, the examining surgeon noted that he was "in feeble health, very much emaciated and failing daily." His military discharge described him as 5' 8" weighing 114 pounds with blue eyes and dark hair, a farmer by occupation.[394]

On 3 September 1863 while living in Polk County, Iowa, Robert applied for an invalid pension based on his service in the Union Army. Robert signed a rambling statement that provided the following information:

> About November or December of 1862 my company was ordered from St. Louis, Missouri, down the Mississippi and that while on board the transport boat on the river I was placed on guard duty on a stormy night. I took a severe cold, but continued on guard duty though suffering with cold and hoarseness until the boat reached Helena, Arkansas, where I went into the hospital. Although I continued to serve until given a medical discharge on 21 April 1863, I was never well again.[395]

In 1870 Robert and Ruth lived in Warren County, Iowa.[396] Robert's occupation was carpenter, and he owned personal property worth $100. Robert was of Warren County, Iowa, on 7 January 1875 when he applied for an increase in his pension.[397]

By 1880 Robert, Ruth, and their two children Hanna and Martin had moved to Jefferson Township in Preble County, Ohio.[398] Robert was fifty-two and Ruth was forty-five years of age. She was born in North Carolina.

Robert was a resident of New Paris in Preble County, Ohio, on 20 January 1881 when an application was filed in Wayne County, Indiana, to increase his pension because of chronic diarrhea and disease of the lungs.[399]

Robert died in 1884 at the age of fifty-five and is buried in New Paris, Preble County, Ohio.[400] When Ruth died a few years later in 1887, she was buried in Springlawn Cemetery in Preble County, Ohio.[401]

Children of Robert M.[4] and Ruth C. (Meredith) Frist:

+   64   i. HANNAH ETTA[5] FRIST, born 30 May 1858 Indiana;[402] died 10 September 1936 Liberty, Union County, Indiana;[403] married about 1886, John J. Stevens.[404]

+   65   ii. MARTIN LUTHER FRIST, born 10 April 1868 Iowa;[405] died after 1920;[406] married 17 September 1896 Lee County, Iowa, Samantha Jane "Mattie" Hewett.[407]

20. Mary Jane[4] Frist (John[3], Henry[2], Rudolph[1]) was born about 1831, probably in Preble County, Ohio, the daughter of John and Susannah Paulson (Stidham) Frist.[408] She died 6 August 1890 in Warren, Huntington County, Indiana.[409] She married on 22 November 1849 in Preble County, Ohio, to **Charles F. Powell**.[410]

In 1860 the couple lived across the Ohio border in Wayne County, Indiana, with their daughter, Mary, and infant son Joseph.[411] Charles was listed as a carpenter with real estate valued at $1200 and personal property worth $250. Living with them was Michael Powell, age seventy-four, identified as a laborer.

By 1880 the family had moved to Jay County, Indiana.[412] Charles was a farmer. Two sons lived with them, Joseph E., age twenty, and Marion F., age twelve. Also living with them was Laura V. Stratton, age four. Nothing more is known about the family after Mary Jane's death in 1890 in Warren, Huntington County, Indiana.[413]

Children of Charles F. and Mary Jane[4] (Frist) Powell:

66   i. MARY E.[5] POWELL, born about 1858 Wayne County, Indiana.[414]

67   ii. JOSEPH E. POWELL, born about 1860 Wayne County, Indiana.[415]

68   iii. MARION F. (m) POWELL, born about 1868 in Indiana.[416]

21. Jonas Lyman Paulson[4] Frist (John[3], Henry[2], Rudolph[1]) was born on 20 June 1834 in Preble County, Ohio,[417] the son of John and Susannah Paulson (Stidham) Frist.[418] He died on 10 October 1908, presumably in Randolph County, Indiana.[419]

He married on 18 November 1853 in Wayne County, Indiana, to **Amy E. Powell**.[420] Amy was born in 1837 in Philadelphia, Pennsylvania, the daughter of Stephen Stackhouse Powell.[421] She died on 18 November 1920 in Indianapolis, Indiana.[422]

In 1860 they lived in Wayne County, Indiana.[423] Amy was listed in the census as "Amarinda" age twenty-two and Jonas was twenty-six. His occupation was carpenter, and they owned real estate valued at $2000 and personal property worth $100.

By 1880 Jonas and Amy had relocated to Randolph County, Indiana.[424] Jonas was forty-five years of age, and his occupation was tile maker. Amy was forty-two. Their two daughters lived with them. Jonas later operated a tile company in Lynn, Randolph County, Indiana, moving shortly after 1880 to Winchester, which is also in Randolph County.[425]

After Jonas died in 1908,[426] Amy lived with her daughter Mrs. Daniel Hecker in Indianapolis where she died in 1920.[427] She is buried in Fountain Park Cemetery in Randolph County, Indiana. Her funeral was held at the home of her daughter Cora Frist Goodrich, wife of Governor Goodrich, in Winchester, Randolph County, Indiana.[428]

Children of Jonas Lyman Paulson[4] and Amy E. (Powell) Frist:

+   69   i. CORA[5] FRIST, born 26 June 1861[429] probably Wayne County, Indiana;[430] died 31 October 1941 Winchester, Randolph County, Indiana;[431] married 15 March 1888 Lynn, Randolph County, Indiana, James Putnam Goodrich.[432]

        70   ii. TODA JUANITA FRIST, born 24 December 1865 near Richmond, Wayne County, Indiana;[433] died 20 February 1923;[434] married 17 October 1900, Daniel Hecker.[435] One son, Sheldon Jonas Hecker, born 1912, died March 1923 following a mastoid operation.[436]

22. Elizabeth[4] Frist (Jediah[3], Henry[2], Rudolph[1]) was born on 5 April 1820[437] in Wilmington, New Castle County, Delaware, the daughter of Jediah and Mary (Meredith) Frist.[438] She died in New Castle County, Delaware, by 1907.[439] She married on 28 March 1841 in New Castle County to **Franklin Lloyd**,[440] who was born about 1818 in Pennsylvania.[441] Franklin died by 5 March 1864.[442]

In 1850 the Lloyds lived in New Castle County, and Franklin was employed as a miller.[443] They owned real estate valued at $600.

When Elizabeth's mother Mary Frist wrote her will in New Castle County on 5 March 1864, it was clear that Elizabeth was already a widow.[444] In 1870 the widow Elizabeth was the head of the household, living in Wilmington, Delaware.[445] She owned real estate valued at $1500 and personal property worth $300. Her daughters Elizabeth and Ella lived with her as did her seventy-one-year-old mother Mary.

In 1880 Elizabeth was sixty years old and lived with her daughter Ella Tindall in Wilmington.[446] Her occupation was seamstress. In 1900 Elizabeth was eighty years old, still living with her daughter Ella Tindall.[447] She said she had borne four children but that only two were still living.

Elizabeth wrote her will on 3 July 1899 and died by 1907 when her estate was probated in New Castle County.[448] She left $100 to each of three grandchildren, John W. Randle, Frank L. Tindall, and Roscoe C. Tindall. She also named her two surviving daughters and their husbands.

Children of Franklin and Elizabeth[4] (Frist) Lloyd, all probably born in New Castle County, Delaware:

> 71   i. MARY ESTHER[5] LLOYD, born about 1842[449] and died by 1900;[450] no issue.
>
> 72   ii. EMILY E. LLOYD, born about 1845[451] and died by 1900;[452] no issue.
>
> +   73   iii. ELLA F. LLOYD, born about 1853;[453] died 16 July 1932 in New Castle County, Delaware;[454] married about 1879, William C. Tindall.[455]
>
> +   74   iv. ELIZABETH JANE LLOYD, born about 1857;[456] died 3 July 1939 Rehoboth Beach, Sussex County, Delaware;[457] married about 1890, Joseph A. Randle.[458]

23. Henry[4] Frist (Jediah[3], Henry[2], Rudolph[1]) was born on 19 November 1821 in Wilmington, New Castle County, Delaware,[459] the son of Jediah and Mary (Meredith) Frist.[460] He died 13 January 1864 in Wilmington, New Castle County, Delaware.[461] He married on 13 May 1845 at the Hanover Street Presbyterian Church in Wilmington, Delaware, to **Catherine Campbell Stewart**.[462] Catherine was born in 1827, the daughter of William and Elizabeth Stewart, and died 2 September 1893 in Wilmington, New Castle County, Delaware.[463]

On 8 June 1847 Henry Frist of Wilmington, carpenter, purchased land in Wilmington, New Castle County, Delaware, from Aquilla Thomas and his wife Phoebe Ann for $700.[464] In 1850 Henry and Catherine lived in New Castle County, Delaware, with their first two children.[465] This census indicated that Henry's occupation was pattern maker and he owned real estate valued at $700.

On 26 December 1855 Henry Frist was of Wilmington when he purchased a lot in Newport, New Castle County, Delaware, for $300 from William Meredith, formerly of New Castle County but now of Cecil County, Maryland.[466]

On 20 March 1858 Henry was of New Castle County when he purchased fifty-seven acres of land in Chester County, Pennsylvania, from Jesse McFaien and his wife Jane of Elk Township in Chester County.[467] Witnesses were William Foy and John Brown. The land was described as being in Elk Township in Chester County beginning at a stone in the public road leading from New London to Elkton.

If Henry ever lived on the land in Pennsylvania, it was not for any great length of time. In 1860 Henry and Catherine lived in New Castle County, Delaware.[468] Henry owned real estate valued at $4000 and personal property worth $300. Their five surviving children lived with them.

Henry was forty-one years of age on 17 November 1862 when he enlisted as a private in Company G of the Fifth Delaware Infantry of the Union Army at Wilmington, Delaware.[469] His enlistment was for a period of nine months, and he was mustered out on 10 August 1863. He was described as 5'7" with a light complexion and gray eyes when he enlisted and his occupation was pattern maker.[470]

Their son Horace V. Frist enlisted in that same unit on 27 November 1862, giving his age as sixteen, and served as a musician through 10 August 1863.[471] Horace was actually barely fourteen at his enlistment. His older brother, Henry's eldest son William S. Frist, waited until he was eighteen and enlisted on 13 July 1864 at Wilmington, Delaware, in Company F of the Seventh Delaware Infantry.[472]

William H. Richter stated some years later on Henry's behalf that he had been a strong, hardy man with no bodily ailment, but that while stationed with the Fifth Delaware near Perryville, Maryland, he caught a severe cold with chronic diarrhea from which he never recovered and from which he subsequently died.[473]

When Henry Frist died in 1864 at the age of forty-two years,[474] he still owned the land that he had purchased in 1858 in Chester County, Pennsylvania. This created an estate that was probated there with Joseph Richardson as administrator.[475] Richardson's petition indicated that the estate in Delaware was insufficient to pay the debts and requested that the court order the land in Chester County sold. The widow Catherine and minor children were also named.

On 30 March 1865 Joseph Richardson, acting as the administrator of Henry Frist deceased late of the City of Wilmington, sold the fifty-seven-acre tract to Joseph Taylor for $2901.[476] Witnesses were Joseph McCrea and John Kerr.

In 1870 Catherine was the head of the household in Wilmington and all five of her surviving children lived at home.[477] Henry's estate in New Castle County had never been settled. In February of 1871 Catherine filed a petition in Orphans' Court in New Castle County, along with her two eldest sons, William Stewart and Horace V. Frist.[478] She stated that Henry owned two tracts of land in the county at the time of his death. One was a lot with a two-story dwelling and a brick front on the north side of Kent Street (now Eighth Street) near Shipley in Wilmington. A second tract was in Newport on Christian Street with a two-story frame dwelling house on it. She requested the court to sell the land so that the estate could be divided among the heirs.

In 1880 Catherine, listed in the census as fifty years of age, lived in Wilmington with four of her children—Horace V., Henry "Harry" C., Robert P., and Herman E.[479] Catherine died in 1893 of Bright's disease and is buried in Holy Trinity (Old Swedes) Church Cemetery in Wilmington, New Castle, County, Delaware.[480]

Children of Henry[4] and Catherine Campbell (Stewart) Frist, all born in Wilmington, New Castle County, Delaware:

75   i. WILLIAM STEWART[5] FRIST, born 1846; died 8 November 1871 Wilmington, New Castle County, Delaware, of suicide at age twenty-five and buried Holy Trinity (Old Swedes) Cemetery in Wilmington;[481] served in Company F of the Seventh Delaware Infantry during the Civil War;[482] admitted to practice as an attorney 21 November 1870;[483] no issue.

76   ii. HORACE V. FRIST, born 14 October 1848.[484] Horace enlisted in the United States Army on 27 November 1862 and served as a private in Company G, Fifth Delaware Volunteers until he was discharged on 10 August 1863 at Wilmington, Delaware.[485] He lived in Wilmington and worked as a watchmaker in 1900.[486]

77   iii. ELIZABETH FRIST, born 13 November 1851; died 24 January 1853 Wilmington, New Castle County, Delaware.[487]

78   iv. HENRY CAMPBELL FRIST, born 13 September 1853;[488] died 15 August 1920 Wilmington, New Castle County, Delaware, of apoplexy and is buried in Holy Trinity (Old Swedes) Church Cemetery in his maternal grandmother Elizabeth Stewart's plot;[489] in 1900 census he lived as a boarder, still single;[490] no apparent issue.

+ 79   v. ROBERT PORTER FRIST, born 22 July 1856;[491] married 17 March 1883 New Castle County, Delaware, Helen M. "Nellie" Bleyer.[492]

+ 80   vi. HERMAN ESCHENBERG FRIST, born 13 January 1859;[493] died 21 February 1933 Wilmington, New Castle County, Delaware;[494] married 12 July 1917 New Castle County, Delaware, Margaret A. Hume.[495]

24. Esther Ann[4] "Hester" Frist (Jediah[3], Henry[2], Rudolph[1]) was born on 27 April 1823[496] in Wilmington, New Castle County, Delaware, the daughter of Jediah and Mary (Meredith) Frist.[497] She died 16 October 1909 in Wilmington, New Castle County, Delaware.[498] She married on 17 April 1845 to **Levi H. Springer** in Philadelphia, Pennsylvania.[499] Levi was born about 1824 in Delaware[500] and died in New Castle County, Delaware, by 14 April 1894.[501]

In 1850 Levi and Hester lived with Hester's mother Mary Frist in Wilmington, New Castle County.[502] Levi's occupation was carpenter.

By 1880 Levi and Esther had their own home on Orange Street in Wilmington.[503] Levi's occupation was listed as "keeps a shade and blind store." Three of their children lived with them. Their daughter Marietta was a school teacher and their son Edgar worked in a paper mill. Their youngest daughter, Kallena, was still in school. Also living with them was Esther's mother, Mary Frist.

On 7 February 1887 Levi served as one of the appraisers for the estate of his son John E. Springer. John's widow Clara E. Springer affirmed that the inventory contained all of the goods, chattels, and money of John E. Springer.[504] Levi wrote his will in Wilmington, Delaware, on 10 March 1876, and it was probated in New Castle County on 14 April 1894.[505] He named his wife, Esther Ann, and his surviving children.

In 1900 his widow Esther, age seventy-seven, lived with her daughter and son-in-law, Kallena and Edwin J. Sheppard, in New Castle County.[506]

Esther Ann Springer wrote her will in Wilmington, Delaware, on 20 August 1894, and it was probated on 3 November 1909 in New Castle County.[507] She owned property at four different locations in Wilmington. Her son-in-law Dr. Willard Springer was her executor. She named two grandchildren, Elsie R. Springer (daughter of her son John E. and Clara Springer) and Willard Springer, Jr. (son of Willard and Etta Springer). She left the bulk of her estate to be divided among her three daughters, who were named as Sally Crossan, Etta F. Springer, and Kallena R. Sheppard. There was no mention in her will of her son Edgar.

Children of Levi H. and Esther Ann[4] (Frist) Springer, all born in New Castle County, Delaware:

> 81   i. SARAH E.[5] "SALLY" SPRINGER, born about 1846;[508] died by 14 December 1924; married to Morris D. Crossan, who died 14 December 1924 in Wilmington, New Castle County, Delaware. His will left bequests to relatives of his deceased wife;[509] no issue.
>
> 82   ii. JOHN E. SPRINGER, born about 1850;[510] died between 1880 and 7 February 1887;[511] married Clara, who was born 1853 Delaware. One daughter, Elsie R. Springer, was born 1877 in Delaware. She was single when her grandmother Esther Ann Springer's estate was settled in 1909.[512]
>
> 83   iii. LEVI RUDOLPH SPRINGER, born about 1854;[513] died by 10 March 1876;[514] no issue.
>
> + 84   iv. MARIETTA F. "ETTA" SPRINGER, born 8 April 1856;[515] died 2 July 1942 New Castle County, Delaware;[516] married about 1881, Willard Springer.[517]
>
> 85   v. EDGAR E. SPRINGER, born about 1858;[518] probably died between 10 March 1876 and 14 April 1894. He was named in his father's 1876 will, but was not listed as a "party of interest" in the 1894 probate papers;[519] no issue.

+   86   vi. KALLENA R. SPRINGER, born January 1869;[520] died 22 November
              1950 New Castle County, Delaware;[521] married about 1891, Edwin J.
              Sheppard.[522]

25. Mary[4] **Frist** (Jediah[3], Henry[2], Rudolph[1]) was born 26 November 1824 in
Wilmington, New Castle County, Delaware,[523] the daughter of Jediah and Mary
(Meredith) Frist.[524] She died after 1891.[525] She married for the first time on 31
May 1846 in New Castle County, Delaware, to **James Robinson** of Delaware
City.[526] James died by 5 March 1864.[527] Mary married second between 1864 and
1867 to **Elon J. Way**.[528] Elon was born about 1810 in Pennsylvania.[529]

When Mary's mother wrote her will in New Castle County on 5 March 1864, she
named her daughter as Mary F. Robinson, widow of James.[530] By 1868 when the
estate of Mary's grandmother Elizabeth Frist was settled in New Castle County,
Mary had married Elon J. Way and was listed in the estate as Mary Y. Way.[531]

In 1870 Elon and Mary Way lived in Baltimore City, Maryland.[532] Elon was
sixty-one, and his occupation was Methodist Episcopal minister. He owned real estate valued at $8000 and personal property worth $21,000. Mary was forty-five
with real estate of her own valued at $2000. Five children lived with them, all
listed with the surname Way and all twelve years or older. Also living in the household was Mary's son by her first marriage Samuel, who was listed as a Robertson.[533] He was seventeen years of age and worked as an apprentice druggist.

In 1880 Elon and Mary lived in Baltimore City, Maryland.[534] Elon was a doctor,
age sixty-six, who was born in Pennsylvania. Mary was fifty-two.[535] Although
there were two adult Way daughters living with them, they must have been children of Elon since they were in their twenties and thirties. Mary and Elon could
have been married no more than sixteen years.

In 1891 Mary received a legacy of $100 from the estate of her mother, Mary.
Her mother had written her will in 1864, but it wasn't probated until 1891.[536]

Children of James and Mary[4] (Frist) Robinson:

    87   i. ANNA[5] ROBINSON, born about 1849; married by 1870, Richard
            Alexander.[537]
    88   ii. SAMUEL ROBINSON, born 1853 Delaware.[538]

26. Jediah Rudolph[4] **"Dolph" Frist** (Jediah[3], Henry[2], Rudolph[1]) was born on 22
December 1826 in Wilmington, New Castle County, Delaware,[539] the son of Jediah
and Mary (Meredith) Frist.[540] He died on 13 November 1907 in Vermillion
County, Indiana.[541] He married first on 2 January 1851 in New Castle County,
Delaware, to **Marietta Groom**.[542] Marietta was born on 3 November 1829 and died
on 21 September 1853 in New Castle County, Delaware.[543] He married second on

15 August 1855 in Chester, Pennsylvania, to **Mary Johnson Peirce** of Wilmington, Delaware.[544] Mary was born on 7 September 1834 in Cecil County, Maryland,[545] the daughter of Samuel and Mary (Ferree) Peirce.[546] She died 27 January 1891 in Vermillion County, Indiana.[547] Jediah married third on 22 November 1892 in Vermillion County, Indiana, to **Mary Helen Nelson,**[548] who was born on 2 February 1847 and died 18 May 1934.[549]

Jediah was raised in New Castle County and probably lived there until 1853, when his first wife, Marietta, died. After his second marriage in 1855 to Mary Johnson Peirce, the couple probably lived in Pennsylvania for a few years but eventually decided to migrate westward.

On 10 August 1861 Jediah R. Frist purchased two tracts of land in Helt Township in Vermillion County, Indiana, for $1500.[550] One tract of eighty acres was in Section 20, and the other tract of twenty-three acres was in Section 29, both in Township 15 North, Range 9 West. Although he bought and sold other tracts of land, this was the home place that he retained until his death many years later.

There is a family tradition that Jediah was not welcomed in Indiana when he first arrived, because of the loyalty of his Indiana neighbors to the Union. He reportedly returned to Delaware because of this. The fact that he returned to Delaware can now be confirmed. On 6 March 1868 Jediah Rudolph Frist was of Brandywine Hundred in New Castle County, Delaware, when he signed a power of attorney appointing his mother, Mary, to receive his share of the estate of his grandmother, Elizabeth Frist.[551]

Just how long Jediah remained in Delaware is unknown, but by 1870 he and his family had returned to Vermillion County, Indiana.[552] Jediah's occupation was farmer, and he owned real estate valued at $2600 and personal property worth $1000. In 1880 Jediah R. and Mary lived in Helt Township in Vermillion County, Indiana, with their five children.[553]

When Mary died on 28 January 1891 of consumption,[554] her funeral was delayed so that their two sons, Samuel of Oklahoma City and Joseph of El Paso, Texas, could participate. Two of Mary's sisters from Chester County, Pennsylvania, also attended. Her obituary described her as "a woman of such blameless life that she left not an enemy in the world." Mary is buried in Helt's Prairie Cemetery in Vermillion County, Indiana.[555]

Jediah remained a widower almost two years, marrying on 22 November 1892 to Mary Helen Nelson.[556] Mary was born on 2 February 1847,[557] twenty years younger than Jediah.

In 1900 Jediah and his new wife Mary lived in Helt Township in Vermillion County.[558] They indicated they had been married for seven years. Mary had borne no children. Jediah's youngest child Alban, who was twenty-six years of age, lived with them.

Jediah wrote his will in Vermillion County on 25 June 1904.[559] He left the rents and profits of all of his real estate and the right to live in the family home to his third wife Mary for as long as she remained a widow. The estate was to be divided among all of Jediah's children at her death or when she ceased to be a widow. He named his son Jasper N. Frist as executor.

Jediah died in 1907 in Vermillion County of apoplexy[560] and is buried in Helt's Prairie Cemetery. Most of Jediah's wealth was in his land. His estate was taxed on 143 acres in Helt Township, including the original 103 acres purchased in 1861. An inventory of his estate indicated that he had $325 in cash in the bank and it included a number of farm animals.[561] Mary remained a widow for the rest of life, dying on 18 May 1934 of "tuberculosis of the right knee."[562] She is buried in Thomas Cemetery in Newport, Vermillion County, Indiana.

Child of Jediah Rudolph[4] and Marietta (Groom) Frist:

89   i. ELLA[5] FRIST, born 8 October 1851; died 22 January 1853.[563]

Children of Jediah Rudolph[4] and Mary Johnson (Peirce) Frist, as named in his will:

90   ii. SAMUEL MEREDITH FRIST, born 15 November 1856 Delaware;[564] died 10 May 1941 Alhambra, Los Angeles County, California;[565] married 8 April 1894, Dora Hoagland,[566] born 26 May 1868 Vermillion County, Indiana, died 7 December 1941 Alhambra, Los Angeles County, California; both buried in Helt's Prairie Cemetery, Vermillion County, Indiana.[567] On 2 October 1938 he wrote his brother Jediah from Yuma, Arizona.[568] When Sam died, his wife Dora planned to come back from California to Vermillion County with his body, but she became ill herself. Sam's body was held in "cold storage" until her death seven months later when both of them were shipped back for a joint funeral.[569] Both the 1900 and 1920 census indicated that they had no children.[570]

+   91   iii. JEDIAH FRIST, born 28 February 1859[571] Chester County, Pennsylvania;[572] died 30 April 1948 Dana, Vermillion County, Indiana;[573] married 22 August 1880 Vermillion County, Indiana, Elizabeth Helt.[574]

+   92   iv. JASPER NEBEKER FRIST, born 26 December 1863 Vermillion County, Indiana;[575] died 5 February 1934 Vermillion County, Indiana;[576] married 7 December 1890 Vermillion County, Indiana, Etta Lee Lambert.[577]

93   v. JOSEPH HENRY FRIST, born 9 May 1866 Vermillion County, Indiana;[578] died 28 December 1921 and buried in Helt's Prairie

Cemetery, Vermillion County, Indiana.[579] He owned a clothing store in Montezuma, Indiana, and later "Joe Henry" and his brother Samuel went to El Paso, Texas, where Sam was manager of a lumberyard for O. T. Bassett, formerly of Indiana;[580] no issue.

94 vi. FRANKLIN PEIRCE FRIST, born 15 July 1869 Vermillion County, Indiana;[581] died 5 October 1949 El Paso, El Paso County, Texas; married 8 November 1907 El Paso, Texas, Elizabeth Arletta Walker, who was born 28 December 1873 Indiana.[582] She died 17 November 1947 El Paso, Texas.[583] Franklin owned a feed and seed store. Both are buried in Restlawn Cemetery in El Paso, Texas;[584] no issue.

95 vii. MARY ESTHER "MANIE" FRIST, born 12 September 1871 Vermillion County, Indiana;[585] died 25 May 1952 Vermillion County, Indiana;[586] married 24 March 1906 Vermillion County, Indiana, Charles Harvey Peters born 25 September 1869 and died 13 September 1948 Vermillion County, Indiana.[587] Both are buried in Helt's Prairie Cemetery, Vermillion County, Indiana. Charles was a railroad station agent and Marie operated a greenhouse where she grew flowers; no issue.[588]

96 viii. ALBAN "ABBIE" FRIST, born 31 December 1873 Vermillion County, Indiana;[589] died 17 May 1961 of arteriosclerotic heart disease in Vermillion County, Indiana;[590] married 10 September 1903, Viola Adaline Jackson.[591] She was born 22 June 1879 Hillsdale, Vermillion County, Indiana, the daughter of Josiah Cooper and Priscilla (Shane) Jackson, and died 3 September 1961 Vermillion County, Indiana.[592] Both are buried in Helt's Prairie Cemetery, Vermillion County, Indiana. Abbie was the sexton at Helt's Prairie Cemetery for many years; he was the last surviving sibling; no issue.[593]

27. Marietta⁴ Frist (James³, Henry², Rudolph¹) was born 8 October 1823 in Delaware, the daughter of James and Henrietta (Little) Frist.[594] She died on 10 June 1909 in Baltimore City, Maryland.[595]

In 1850 Marietta lived with her widowed father in Cecil County, Maryland,[596] and she was also lived with him in 1860.[597] She never married and lived most of her life with her sister Hannah, who also remained single.

On 17 March 1874 Marietta and her sister, Hannah Frist, purchased sixty and a half acres of land in Cecil County, Maryland, from the heirs of James Barnes for $1874.[598] The land was identified as the eastern portion of the farm called "Steelman's Delight."

In 1880 Marietta age fifty-six, her sister, Hannah, age fifty-four, and their seventeen-year-old nephew lived together in Rising Sun, Cecil County, Maryland.[599]

Their purchase of land in 1874 was a good investment for on 24 March 1888 the two sisters sold the sixty and a half acres known as "Steelman's Delight" to Joseph D. Summers for $3500.[600]

By 1900 the sisters had moved to Baltimore City, Maryland, where they rented a home.[601] As befitting the status of the older sister, Marietta was listed in the census as the head of the household. She was seventy-six years of age, and her parents were shown as born in Delaware.

Marietta died on 10 June 1909 in Baltimore City, Maryland,[602] just ten days before her sister, Hannah, died. She was buried in Hopewell United Methodist Church Cemetery in Cecil County, Maryland.[603]

28. Hannah[4] Frist (James[3], Henry[2], Rudolph[1]) was born 14 December 1825 in Pennsylvania, the daughter of James and Henrietta (Little) Frist.[604] She died 20 June 1909, in Baltimore City, Maryland.[605]

In 1850 Hannah lived with her widowed father in Cecil County, Maryland,[606] and she also lived with him in 1860.[607] She never married and lived most of her life with her sister, Marietta, who also remained single.

In 1880 Hannah, age fifty-four, lived with her sister, Marietta, age fifty-six, and their seventeen-year-old nephew in Rising Sun, Cecil County, Maryland.[608] By 1900 the two sisters had moved to Baltimore City, Maryland, where they rented a home.[609] It is interesting to note that in every census record, Hannah entered her birthplace as Pennsylvania, while her sister, Marietta, born just two years earlier, consistently stated her birthplace as Delaware. In 1900 Hannah also indicated that her parents were born in Pennsylvania, whereas Marietta gave their birthplace correctly as Delaware.

Hannah died 20 June 1909, in Baltimore City, Maryland,[610] just ten days after her sister, Marietta. She was buried in Hopewell United Methodist Church Cemetery in Cecil County, Maryland.[611]

29. John[4] Frist (James[3], Henry[2], Rudolph[1]) was born on 1 January of 1828 in Pennsylvania,[612] the son of James and Henrietta (Little) Frist.[613] John died 8 November 1909 in Baltimore City, Maryland.[614] He married about the year 1851 to **Annie James**, who was born 14 October 1831.[615] She died 4 July 1859 in Cecil County, Maryland.[616] He married second on 14 May 1867 in Baltimore City, Maryland, to **Emily M. Holt**.[617] She died in November 1894 in Baltimore City, Maryland.[618]

John's first wife Annie had borne him four children, Ida May, John E., Eva J., and Harry Davis Frist, when tragedy struck on 4 July 1859.[619] A group of citizens held a holiday picnic on an island in the Susquehanna River directly across from Port Deposit. Returning home near sundown, a party of fourteen were in a boat that struck a rock and overturned. Ten persons survived, including John and two of his children. His wife Annie and their other two children, the oldest daughter Ida May and the baby Harry, drowned.[620] Also in the boat were John's brother James and his sister Marietta Frist, who were able to save themselves. Annie and her two drowned children share a tombstone in Hopewell United Methodist Church Cemetery in Cecil County, Maryland.[621]

When the census was taken in 1860 John, thirty-five years of age, and his younger brother James, twenty-three years of age, lived in Ward Eighteen of Baltimore City, Maryland, and lived with Greg Howser and several other individuals.[622] John and James were employed as coach makers. The two children who survived the boating accident were not living with him.

When John married for the second time to Emily M. Holt in 1867, he was listed as a widower, and Emily was single.[623] In 1870 John was forty-two years of age and living in Ward Nineteen in Baltimore.[624] His two children from his first marriage, John E. and Eva J., lived with them. Emily had borne John one child, Hattie M., and John's coach making business was apparently thriving. He owned real estate valued at $2500 and personal property worth $4400. Emily owned real estate valued at $700 in her own right.

On 11 March 1874 John Frist purchased three lots of land in the village of Hampden in Baltimore County, Maryland, and on 14 August 1883 John and Emily M. Frist sold the three lots of land in the village of Hampden in Baltimore County, Maryland, to Annie W. Brewer.[625]

When Emily died in 1894 in Baltimore City, Maryland, she was buried in Loudon Park Cemetery.[626] In 1900 John was again widowed, the head of the household in Baltimore City, Maryland.[627] He was seventy-seven years of age and his occupation was carriage maker. He owned his home. His son Alpheus, still single at twenty-four, lived with him as did a married daughter and her family.

When John died in 1909, he too was buried in Loudon Park Cemetery in Baltimore City, Maryland.[628] On 15 November 1909 his children by his first marriage, John E. Frist and Eva J. Stocksdale, renounced their right to administer the estate, and his surviving child from his second marriage, Hattie Emmart, was appointed by the Orphans' Court of Baltimore City, Maryland.[629] Hattie sold two leasehold properties to settle the estate, one located at 825 N. Mount Street and another at 334 W. Preston Street.[630] On 20 December 1910 Hattie filed an account for the estate with one-third going to each of the three surviving children, John E. Frist, Eva J. Stocksdale, and Hattie M. Emmart.[631]

Children of John[4] and Annie (James) Frist:

  97   i. IDA MAY[5] FRIST, born 27 April 1852; died 4 July 1859 Cecil County, Maryland.[632]

+   98   ii. JOHN EDGAR FRIST, born 22 March 1854 Baltimore City, Maryland; died 25 July 1912 Baltimore County, Maryland;[633] married (1) 4 April 1876 Baltimore City, Maryland, Margaret Ann Arthur[634] and perhaps (2) Emma D. Cooper.[635]

     99   iii. EVA JAMES FRIST, born about 1856; died 12 November 1930 Baltimore City, Maryland;[636] married George W. Stocksdale.[637] One child, Ida M. Stocksdale, died 7 February 1976 without issue.[638]

     100   iv. HARRY DAVIS FRIST, born 15 January 1858; died 4 July 1859 Cecil County, Maryland.[639]

Children of John[4] and Emily M. (Holt) Frist:

+   101   v. HATTIE M. FRIST, born 10 July 1869 Baltimore City, Maryland; died 9 December 1939 Baltimore City, Maryland; married about 1893, William Wirt Emmart.[640]

     102   vi. ALPHEUS W. FRIST, born May 1876 Maryland.[641] He died May 1902 and is buried in Loudon Park Cemetery, Baltimore City, Maryland;[642] no issue.

30. Abraham B.[4] a.k.a. Abram Frist (James[3], Henry[2], Rudolph[1]) was probably born between 1825 and 1830, in Chester County, Pennsylvania, the son of James and Henrietta (Little) Frist.[643] He died by 12 February 1885.[644] He married on 11 June 1845 in Cecil County, Maryland, to **Elizabeth C. Patterson**,[645] the daughter of William and Martha (Moulton) Patterson.[646] Abraham married second on 5 March 1859 in Baltimore City, Maryland, to **Julia A. Myers**,[647] who was born in Maryland in 1836.[648] She died 4 February 1902.[649]

In 1830 Abraham's parents, James and Henrietta (Little) Frist, lived in Chester County, Pennsylvania, and it is believed that this is where he was born and raised.[650] He moved with his parents to Cecil County, Maryland, by 1840.

In 1848, 1849, and 1850 Abraham Frist was taxed in District Seven of Cecil County, Maryland, in the same district as his father, James.[651] Elizabeth bore three children to Abraham before their marriage began to disintegrate. On 5 March 1857 Abraham filed suit in Cecil County, Maryland, chancery court for a divorce from Elizabeth.[652] Abraham's bill of complaint stated that they had married in Cecil County in 1845 and lived together until 1856 when Elizabeth committed adultery with Washington Taylor of Cecil County. He further stated that Elizabeth left him in May of 1856 and "has lived with Washington Taylor ever since." In her answer to the bill of complaint, Elizabeth admitted that they were married in 1845 and lived together until some time in 1856. She denied that she committed adultery, stating that she was "acting in the capacity of housekeeper for

Washington Taylor." George McVey testified in the case, stating that Elizabeth's "reputation is not good. She has the reputation in the neighborhood of being an unchaste woman." John Burrows, Jr. testified that "Washington Taylor used to visit at the Frist home and that he generally came at night when her husband was away." Burrows stated that the two were in the house alone except for the Frist's two children, the oldest of whom was about seven years old. Mrs. Jane E. Burrows testified that she had talked to her [Elizabeth] about her conduct and "she admitted to me that she did wrong in keeping Taylor's company but she said there was nothing between them but friendship." She further testified that she heard Elizabeth tell Frist that "she would suffer death before she would live with him again." No one came forward to testify in Elizabeth's behalf, and the divorce decree was issued on 19 January 1858. Elizabeth is buried in the Patterson Cemetery near Perryville in Cecil County, Maryland, without a tombstone and thus her date of death is unknown.[653]

By 1860 Abraham and his second wife, Julia, had left the area and lived in Union Town, Monroe County, Virginia.[654] Abraham was listed as thirty-eight years of age, born in Delaware, a carpenter who owned personal property valued at $100. His wife Julia A. was twenty-four and born in Maryland. Two children lived with them. Elizabeth was ten years old and born in Maryland, the only surviving child from his first marriage. Edmund M., from his second marriage, was just four months old and born in Virginia.

Abraham's brother Thomas Frist, a carriage maker, and his wife Sarah lived two households from him.[655] Abraham and Thomas both fought for the Confederacy during the Civil War in the Monroe Guards.[656] The Monroe Guards were organized in the winter of 1859 and 1860, becoming part of the Twenty-Seventh Virginia Infantry in 1861. This regiment served in Stonewall Jackson's famous foot cavalry and helped to break the Federal center at the second battle of Manassas.[657]

By 1870 Abraham and Julia had moved back to Port Deposit, Cecil County, Maryland.[658] Abraham was listed in the census as Abram, born in Maryland and thirty-four years of age.[659] His occupation was wheelwright and he owned personal property valued at $600. His wife Julia was listed as thirty-two and born in Maryland. Three children lived with them, but neither of the two children who lived with them in 1860 was present.

On 4 November 1870 Abraham and Julia Frist were in Cecil County, Maryland, when they sold a tract of land in the Sixth Election District in Cecil County to David Craig for $350.[660] The land was described as three-fourths of an acre on Rosen run purchased from William H. Rowland and his wife on 9 June 1870. Shelden Beach was the witness.

On 18 May 1875 Abraham and Julia's three surviving children were baptized at the Presbyterian Church in Port Deposit, Cecil County, Maryland.[661]

In 1880 Abraham, listed as Abram in the census, and his wife Julia remained in Port Deposit, Cecil County, Maryland.[662] He was sixty-two years of age with an occupation of fisherman. Julia was forty-two. Their three youngest children lived with them.

Abraham was deceased when their son William Henry Frist died on 12 February 1885 just before his twenty-second birthday.[663] This death coming after her husband's must have been particularly difficult for Julia and her daughter, Hattie Mary, for the obituary included two poems. This was from his mother.

> His merry shout no more we hear,
>   no laughing child we see;
> No arms around my neck,
>   No loving words I hear.
> No kisses drop upon my cheek;
>   Those lips are sealed from me;
> Oh Lord! how can we give our Willie up
>   To anyone but thee.

And from his sister Hattie Mary came this poem.

> We had a little Willie once,
>   He was our joy and pride;
> We loved him – oh! perhaps too well,
>   For soon he slept and died.

On 9 May 1885 Abraham's widow Mrs. Julia Frist of Baltimore City married Harmon Harris of Port Deposit, Cecil County, Maryland, at the residence of Reverend W. W. Kyle of Chester County, Pennsylvania.[664] Julia would have been about fifty years of age in 1885. In 1860 one Harmon Harris was enumerated in the 1860 census of Cecil County, Maryland, living in the seventh district.[665] He was thirty-eight, a tanner with a wife and daughter Rebecca. In 1885 he would have been about sixty-three years of age.

In 1900 Harmon and Julia lived in Cecil County, Maryland, next door to Julia's daughter Hattie Mohrlein.[666] They owned their home, and Harmon listed his occupation as gardener. They both indicated that they had been married sixteen years, and Julia stated she had borne no children, an apparent reference to her most recent marriage.

Julia died 4 February 1902 in Port Deposit, Cecil County, Maryland, leaving Harmon Harris and two children surviving her.[667]

Children of Abraham B.[4] and Elizabeth C. (Patterson) Frist:

103 i. MARTHA JANE[5] FRIST, born 24 October 1848 Maryland; died 5 April 1857 Cecil County, Maryland.[668]

104 ii. ELIZABETH FRIST, born about 1850 Maryland.[669] She lived with her father in 1860,[670] but was not present in his 1870 household.[671]

105 iii. HARLIN L. FRIST, born 7 November 1851 Maryland; died 21 October 1855 Cecil County, Maryland.[672]

Children of Abraham B.[4] and Julia (Myers) Frist:

106 iv EDMUND M. FRIST, born about 1860 Monroe County, Virginia;[673] was not with his parents in 1870 and must have died young.[674]

+ 107 v. ABRAM BERNARD FRIST, born 22 October 1861 West Virginia; died 11 March 1923 Baltimore City, Maryland;[675] married (1) 8 May 1882 Cecil County, Maryland, Georgianna L. Zimmer.[676] He married (2) 17 June 1901 Baltimore City, Maryland, Genevieve T. "Jennie" Quinn.[677]

108 vi. WILLIAM HENRY FRIST, born 30 March 1863;[678] died 12 February 1885.[679]

+ 109 vii. HATTIE MARY FRIST, born 10 May 1870 Port Deposit, Cecil County, Maryland; died 30 July 1930 Baltimore City, Maryland; married about 1886, George F. Mohrlein.[680]

31. Thomas Lyttle[4] Frist (James[3], Henry[2], Rudolph[1]) was born in Chester County, Pennsylvania,[681] about 1830,[682] the son of James and Henrietta (Little) Frist. He died in Charleston, Kanawha County, West Virginia, on 21 January 1873.[683] He married about the year 1851 to **Sarah Elizabeth**, who was born 1831[684] in New York.[685] She died in October of 1900 in Kanawha County, West Virginia.[686]

Based on the birth dates and places of their children, the family lived in Maryland from 1852 until 1858 and moved to Virginia by 1860. In 1860 Thomas and his wife, Sarah E., lived in Monroe County, Virginia.[687] Thomas was thirty years of age and born in Pennsylvania, a carriage maker with real estate valued at $1100 and personal property worth $1000. Five children lived with them as well as Richard McCanis, a nineteen-year-old carriage maker agent.

Thomas died in Charleston, West Virginia, in 1873[688] and is buried in Spring Hill Cemetery.[689] On 21 August 1876 his widow Sarah E. Frist was deeded twelve acres of land in Kanawha County, West Virginia, by Helen L. Burton as executor of Edward C. Burton, deceased.[690]

In 1880 Sarah lived in Kanawha County, West Virginia, with eight children, ranging in age from ten to twenty-six years.[691] She was forty-eight years of age, born in New York of parents born in New York.

On 11 March 1892, Sarah sold the twelve acres of land that she bought in 1876 to the Charleston Water Works Company for $1500.[692]

In 1900 Sarah was sixty-eight years of age, had been married for fifty years, and was the mother of eight children who were all living.[693] All remained single and lived at home, except for Burton, who lived next door with his wife and family.[694] The youngest of the children was twenty-six years of age.

Sarah Elizabeth died in Kanawha County and was buried in Spring Hill Cemetery on 31 October 1900.[695] The family remained in Kanawha County, West Virginia, after Sarah's death. In 1920 her oldest daughter, Lena J., sixty years of age, was the head of the household.[696] All three of her sisters lived with her, all still single.

Children of Thomas Lyttle[4] and Sarah Elizabeth Frist:

110   i. JAMES HENRY[5] FRIST, born May 1852 Maryland; died 1918 Kanawha County, West Virginia, and buried Spring Hill Cemetery on 3 February 1918;[697] single in 1900.

\+ 111   ii. BURTON KYLE FRIST, born 17 April 1856 Maryland; died 27 November 1923 Kanawha County, West Virginia,[698] and buried Spring Hill Cemetery;[699] married about 1877,[700] Virginia Wilson.[701]

112   iii. SELENA JANE FRIST, born March 1857 Maryland;[702] died 30 September 1932 Kanawha County, West Virginia,[703] and buried Spring Hill Cemetery 2 October 1932;[704] no issue.

113   iv. MARY EMMA FRIST, born 18 October 1858 Maryland; died 16 April 1938 Kanawha County, West Virginia, and buried Spring Hill Cemetery;[705] no issue.

114   v. JENNIE LOUISE FRIST, born October 1860 Virginia;[706] died 30 October 1926 Kanawha County, West Virginia,[707] and buried Spring Hill Cemetery 2 November 1926;[708] no issue.

115   vi. ALVA JULIA FRIST, born November 1866 West Virginia;[709] died 31 October 1948 Kanawha County, West Virginia;[710] no issue.

\+ 116   vii. THOMAS JACKSON FRIST, born September 1869 West Virginia;[711] died 14 April 1925 Kanawha County, West Virginia;[712] married about 1906,[713] Laura Jane Chapman.[714]

117   viii. WILLIAM WEBSTER FRIST, born October 1874 West Virginia;[715] died 1900 Kanawha County, West Virginia, and buried Spring Hill Cemetery 20 June 1900.[716]

34. James[4] Frist (James[3], Henry[2], Rudolph[1]) was born 11 April 1836 in Maryland,[717] the son of James and Henrietta (Little) Frist of Cecil County, Maryland.[718] He died 3 April 1908 in Baltimore City, Maryland.[719] He married on 26 November

1873 in Baltimore City, Maryland, to **Annie A. (Hartzell) Beam**, a widow.[720] Annie Hartzell was born in 1848 in Maryland,[721] the daughter of Mary Ann (Shipley) Hartzell and the granddaughter of Peregrine Shipley.[722] She died 23 September 1883 in Baltimore County, Maryland.[723]

On 4 July 1859, James joined other family members for a holiday picnic on the Susquehanna River and narrowly avoided drowning.[724] Returning home near sundown, a party of fourteen were in a boat that struck a rock and overturned. Ten persons survived including James, his sister Marietta, and his older brother John, but John's wife Annie and two of their four children drowned.[725]

In 1860 James lived as a boarder, along with his older brother John, in the Greg Howser household in Baltimore County, Maryland.[726] Both men were coach makers.

When James and Annie Beam married in 1873, she was a widow of Baltimore County who worked as a tailoress. James was single and a carriage maker from Cecil County, Maryland.[727]

On 6 July 1877 James Frist purchased a tract of land in Baltimore County, Maryland, known as the addition to Peggy's Delight from Nancy Wisner and Mathias Wisner her husband for $70.65.[728] On 13 September 1879 James Frist and his wife Annie A. Frist sold this same tract of land to William Richards for $70.[729]

On 1 July 1879 James and Annie were among the heirs of Peregrine Shipley who sold a tract of land in Baltimore County, Maryland, to Barney Owings for $1175.[730] This deed identified Annie A. Frist as the daughter of Mary Ann Hartzell, who in turn was the daughter of Peregrine Shipley. The land in question was located on the south side of the Reisterstown Turnpike, beginning at the corner of a tract known as James Peacock's lot.

In 1880 James and Annie lived in Baltimore County, Maryland, where James operated a retail grocery store.[731]

Their 1873 marriage was not destined to be a long one. Annie died 23 September 1883[732] and on 12 October 1883 James Frist was appointed guardian of her orphan children, who were named as Allen W. Beam, Lilly Frist, and Blanche Frist.[733]

James died in 1908 in Baltimore City, Maryland, and is buried in Stone Chapel Cemetery in Baltimore County, Maryland.[734] He wrote his will on 14 February 1908 and it was probated in Baltimore City, Maryland, on 9 April 1908.[735] He left bequests to his sisters Marietta and Hannah Frist. The remainder of his estate went to his daughters Blanche H. Browning and Lillian E. Stern.

Children of James[4] and Annie A. (Hartzell) Frist, both probably born in Baltimore County, Maryland:

118   i. LILLIAN E.[5] FRIST, born about 1875;[736] married by 1908, J. Ezra Stern.[737]

119   ii. BLANCHE H. FRIST, born about 1879;[738] married by 1908, Browning.[739]

35. Edmund Physick[4] **a.k.a. Edward Frist** (James[3], Henry[2], Rudolph[1]) was born on 15 May 1838 probably in Cecil County, Maryland,[740] the son of James and Henrietta (Little) Frist.[741] He died on 15 September 1911 in Cecil County, Maryland.[742] He married on 9 February 1863[743] to **Mary Jane Haines**, the daughter of George Haines.[744] Mary was born on 14 June 1834 and died 14 March 1915 in Cecil County, Maryland.[745]

Edmund lived throughout his life in Cecil County, Maryland. In 1860 he lived with his widowed father in Cecil County, Maryland.[746] On 7 November 1866 Edmund and his brothers James and William purchased a patented improvement in force pumps from William S. Judd of Clanhassen, Carver County, Minnesota.[747] Whether this device was to be used in the business the brothers intended to establish remains uncertain.

On 25 June 1868 Edmund and William Frist of Port Deposit, Cecil County, Maryland, leased a lot in Port Deposit for ninety-nine years from John P. and Harriet Venneman.[748] On 2 July 1868 Edmund and William mortgaged this property to secure their debt to Jacob Tome for $2000.[749] A note at the bottom of this document indicated that Jacob Tome released the mortgage on 25 January 1870. On 21 May 1869 Edmund and William Frist, trading under the firm of William Frist and Brother, executed a document to Theodore J. Vanneman with the intention of closing their company and dispersing the assets to their creditors.[750]

By 1870 Edmund, his wife, Mary, and their three children had established their own home in Port Deposit, Cecil County, Maryland.[751] Edmund was listed as Edward in this census.[752]

In 1877 when Mary's father George Haines died, he left his daughter a bequest of $1000 with strings attached to it.[753] The money was reserved for Mary Frist and was not to be paid to Edmund P. Frist. It could be used to purchase a house and lot if Mary desired to do so. On 28 May 1878 a house and lot 34 in the town of Port Deposit in Cecil County were purchased for Mary Frist on a lease assignment from William W. Moore and Hannah his wife for $800.[754] The $200 remaining from the $1000 gift was given to Mary and the house was to descend to her children at her death.

In 1880 Edmund lived in Cecil County, and the census recorded him as a farmer who was forty-four years of age and whose wife Mary was forty-five.[755] Their four youngest children lived with them and their oldest son, George Edmund, lived with his aunts, Marietta and Hannah Frist.[756]

Twenty years later in 1900 Edmund and Mary remained residents of Port Deposit in Cecil County.[757] Edmund was sixty-two and Mary was sixty-five. Both were born in Maryland of parents born in Maryland. Mary indicated that she had borne six children and that all six were still living. Their three youngest sons lived with them, and their son George lived next door. [758]

Edmund died in 1911 and Mary died in 1915, both presumably in Cecil County, Maryland.[759] They are buried in Hopewell United Methodist Church Cemetery in Cecil County, Maryland.[760]

Children of Edmund Physick[4] and Mary Jane (Haines) Frist, all born in Cecil County, Maryland:

+ 120   i. GEORGE EDMUND[5] FRIST, born 22 December 1863;[761] married about 1885, Henrietta McCullough.[762]

+ 121   ii. GARRISON JAMES FRIST, born 1 September 1865;[763] probably died by 1920;[764] married about 1898, Pearl C. Updegrove.[765]

+ 122   iii. SIDNEY MARIETTA "ETTA" FRIST, born 26 March 1868;[766] died 5 October 1938 Cecil County, Maryland;[767] married 25 July 1886 in Cecil County, Maryland, George Elim Tyson.[768]

+ 123   iv. OSCAR HAINES FRIST, born 11 September 1870;[769] died 20 July 1936 Cecil County, Maryland;[770] married 27 November 1901 Cecil County, Maryland, Ella McDowell.[771]

+ 124   v. JOHN CRESSWELL FRIST, born 17 August 1872;[772] died July 1945 Cecil County, Maryland;[773] married 31 January 1914 Cecil County, Maryland, Olive A. Campbell.[774]

+ 125   vi. OLIVER T. FRIST, born 9 July 1875;[775] died December 1935 Cecil County, Maryland;[776] married 20 January 1901 Baltimore City, Maryland, Florence Gertrude Harrison.[777]

37. George[4] Frist (Joel[3], Henry[2], Rudolph[1]) was born about February of 1840 in New Castle County, Delaware,[778] the son of Joel and Adrianna (Morrison) Frist.[779] He died on 14 September 1928 in Wilmington, New Castle County, Delaware.[780] He married about 1876 in New Castle County[781] to **Catherine A. Simmons**.[782] She was born 25 December 1850 in Wilmington, Delaware, the daughter of Mr. Simmons and his wife Margaret (Ennis) Simmons.[783] She died 12 February 1936 in Wilmington, New Castle County, Delaware.[784]

In 1880 George, his wife, Catherine, and their son, Homer, lived with George's father, Joel, who was a coach maker.[785] George's occupation was body maker. By 1900 George and Catherine owned a mortgaged home in Wilmington, New Castle County, Delaware, and George continued to work as a coach maker.[786] Their only child, Homer, who was twenty-one years of age, lived with them.

George was retired by 1910, living in Wilmington, Delaware.[787] They had been married thirty years, and Catherine had borne one child who was still living. George wrote his will on 29 January 1924 and died in 1928 in Wilmington, New Castle County, Delaware.[788] His will left his entire estate to his wife, Catherine, and the petition indicated that both Catherine and a son, Homer, survived him. Catherine lived at 3003 Lancaster Avenue in Wilmington.

In 1930 George's widow Catherine and their son, Homer, lived together in Homer's home in Wilmington.[789] Catherine wrote her will on 8 May 1934 and died in 1936 in Wilmington, New Castle County, Delaware, of myocardial failure.[790] She left a bequest to her daughter-in-law, Mary Frist, and another to her niece Lillian Schofield of Wilmington. The bulk of her estate went to her only descendant, her granddaughter, Margaret Wallis of Wilmington. Catherine is buried in Delaware and Brandywine Cemetery in Wilmington, Delaware.[791]

Child of George[4] and Catherine A. (Simmons) Frist:

+ 126 i. HOMER[5] FRIST, born 9 June 1878 Wilmington, New Castle County, Delaware;[792] died after 1930[793] and probably by 8 May 1934 when his mother wrote her will;[794] married 24 June 1901, Mary Harkins.[795]

39. Henry M.[4] "Harry" Frist (Joel[3], Henry[2], Rudolph[1]) was born about December 1854 in Wilmington, Delaware, the son of Joel and Adrianna (Morrison) Frist.[796] He died after 1920.[797] He married about 1897 to **Anna**, who was born in April of 1872.[798]

At the age of fourteen Harry entered Taylor's Select Scientific and Commercial Academy where he later graduated.[799] In 1880 he lived in New Castle County and worked as a carriage trimmer.[800] Although he worked in the carriage industry with his father for a time, he later decided to study medicine. He graduated with honors from the Jefferson Medical College in 1888 and also graduated from the Philadelphia Charity Hospital and Professor Shoemaker's Hospital of Dermatology.[801] After completing his studies he returned to Wilmington, purchasing the practice of Dr. George H. Cantwell at Eighth and Spruce Streets where he pursued the medical profession.[802]

In 1900 Harry and his wife Anna lived in New Castle County, but remained childless.[803] His occupation was physician. In 1910 Harry owned his home in Wilmington, was divorced, and had three boarders living with him.[804] In 1920 he lived alone in the Gardner Hitchens household in New Castle County.[805] He was the first of a long line of medical professionals to descend from Henry and Elizabeth (Garretson) Frist. Nothing was found to indicate that he and his wife had children.

40. Robert Harris[4] Frist (Jacob Chester[3], Henry[2], Rudolph[1]) was born on 24 March 1847 in Wilmington, New Castle County, Delaware, the son of Jacob Chester and his first wife Ann Eliza (Harris) Frist.[806] He died 30 June 1903 in Newport, New Castle County, Delaware.[807] He married on 25 December 1875 in New Castle County, Delaware, to **Elizabeth Rachel Nebeker**.[808] She was born on 21 October 1844[809] in Wilmington, Delaware, the daughter of John M. and Mary

Ann Nebeker.[810] She died 2 October 1924 in Newport, Mill Creek Hundred, New Castle County, Delaware.[811]

Robert's mother died when he was a baby, and it isn't certain who cared for him in his early years. By the age of thirteen in 1860, he had arrived in Tennessee to live with his father and stepmother in Chattanooga.[812]

Two years later, and just a few days after his fifteenth birthday, Robert enlisted at Chattanooga on 1 April 1862 as a private in Company F of the Fourth Confederate Cavalry (McLemore's).[813] The military roster listed his age as seventeen at enlistment. He served part of the time as a scout and was on the muster rolls through December 31, 1864, but there was no record of his discharge. Surprisingly, Robert wasn't the youngest descendant of old Henry Frist who fought at such a young age. Back in Delaware, Horace V. Frist, Robert's cousin, fought for the Union, enlisting just after he turned fourteen.[814]

In 1870 twenty-three-year-old Robert lived at home in Chattanooga with his father, Jacob, and his stepmother.[815] Shortly afterward, Robert returned to his place of birth in Newport, New Castle County, Delaware, where he remained for the rest of his life and where in 1875 he married Elizabeth R. Nebeker.[816] They were the first couple to be married in the newly rebuilt St. James Methodist Episcopal Church.[817]

In 1880 they lived at 421 Ninth Street in Wilmington, Delaware.[818] Robert was thirty-two and his occupation was pattern maker. His wife Lizzie was thirty, and their first child Ann Eliza lived with them.

They were members of the St. James Methodist Episcopal Church in Newport in 1891, along with their two children, Ann Eliza, age thirteen, and John Nebeker Frist, age ten.[819] In 1900 Robert and Elizabeth lived in Christiana Hundred, New Castle County, Delaware, with their two children.[820]

Robert died in 1903 of pneumonia in Newport, New Castle County, Delaware, at the age of fifty-five.[821] In 1910 his widow Elizabeth was the head of household in Newport, New Castle County.[822] She was sixty-four years of age, had borne two children, and both were living. Her brother Hance Nebeker, age fifty-four, lived with her.

At the time of the 1920 census Elizabeth and her brother Hance Nebeker remained living in Newport, New Castle County, Delaware.[823] She was listed as seventy-five years of age, and Hance W. was listed as sixty years of age.

When Elizabeth died in 1924 in Newport, Mill Creek Hundred, New Castle County, Delaware, it was of acute indigestion and acute dilation of heart with gastric disturbance.[824] Their son, John N. Frist, relinquished administration of the estate to his sister, Anna E. Foard.[825] Elizabeth owned a three-story dwelling in Newport as well as a lot on Justice Street between Walnut and Augustine valued at $3500, an undivided half interest in a dwelling on the north side of Market Street worth $1000, and several other lots.

Elizabeth and Robert share a tombstone in St. James Cemetery in Newport, New Castle County, Delaware.[826] The reverse side of the tombstone contains an inscription for Elizabeth's brother Hance Watts Nebeker who was born 21 June 1849 and died 9 December 1925.[827]

Children of Robert Harris[4] and Elizabeth Rachel (Nebeker) Frist, both born in Newport, New Castle County, Delaware:[828]

+   127   i. ANNA ELIZABETH[5] A.K.A. ANN ELIZA FRIST, born 3 January
                1878;[829] died 29 July 1964 New Castle County, Delaware;[830] married
                28 November 1900 New Castle County, Delaware, John Hilton Foard.[831]

+   128   ii. JOHN NEBEKER FRIST, born 30 March 1881;[832] died 9 April 1947 New
                Castle County, Delaware;[833] married 27 January 1904 New Castle
                County, Delaware, Carrie Currender.[834]

41. James Ball[4] Frist (Jacob Chester[3], Henry[2], Rudolph[1]) was born on 25 March 1853 in Chattanooga, Hamilton County, Tennessee, the son of Jacob Chester and Mary Ann Elizabeth (Baldwin) Frist.[835] He died on 9 July 1925 at Wauhatchie, Hamilton County, Tennessee.[836] James married about 1878 to **Harriet R.**[837] She was born 17 July 1855 in Georgia and died 5 January 1883 in Chattanooga, Hamilton County, Tennessee.[838] James married second on 2 February 1887 in Hamilton County, Tennessee, to **Permelia "Melia" Corbin.**[839] She was born on 27 October 1866[840] and died 10 April 1935 in Hamilton County, Tennessee.[841]

James and his first wife left Tennessee shortly after their marriage for Texas where they were enumerated in the 1880 census living in Denton County.[842] James was twenty-seven, born in Tennessee of a father born in Delaware. Harriet was twenty-four and born in Georgia. Their one-year-old daughter, Mary, lived with them. James listed his occupation as farmer.

For reasons unknown, the family returned to Tennessee where disaster struck. In January of 1883 smallpox hit the city of Chattanooga and several members of the Frist family died. James's wife Harriet died 5 January 1883,[843] just days before their daughter Sue, a twin.[844] On 12 January 1883 their son, Jacob, was identified in the newspaper as the second twin of the Frist family who died.[845] Harriet and her children are buried in Citizens Cemetery.[846]

On 12 February 1887 James B. Frist and his new bride Permelia executed a deed of trust mortgaging a lot on Peeples Street in Chattanooga.[847]

In 1900 James and Permelia lived in Civil District Four of Hamilton County.[848] James was forty-seven and a farmer. His wife was thirty-three. They had been married thirteen years, and two children had been born to their union. In 1910 they owned a farm in Civil District Four of Hamilton County.[849] Both of their children lived at home with them. Polly Smith, identified as an aunt, and Adaline Corbin, identified as mother-in-law, also lived with them.

On 15 June 1925 James B. and Permelia Frist sold eighty acres of land to their two children, Joseph Byron Frist and Bertie Frist Hartman for $800.[850] The land had been purchased from James's mother Mary Ann Frist on 25 May 1886.

James was a farmer, and they resided on the family farm in Lookout Valley until his death in 1925 at Wauhatchie, Hamilton County, Tennessee.[851] In 1930 the widow Permelia was the head of the household in Hamilton County.[852] Living with her were her son Roy, her daughter Bertie, and Bertie's son Roy. Their farm home was valued at $3000. Permelia died in 1935 at the age of sixty-eight at her home in Lookout Valley.[853] James and his second wife are buried in Parker Cemetery in Hamilton County, Tennessee.[854]

Children of James Ball[4] and Harriet R. Frist, who all died young, and are buried in Citizens Cemetery:

129 i. MARY[5] FRIST, born 3 January 1879 Denton County, Texas;[855] died 12 November 1887 Chattanooga, Hamilton County, Tennessee.[856]

130 ii. SUE FRIST, born 14 June 1882; died 8 January 1883 Chattanooga, Hamilton County, Tennessee.[857]

131 iii. JACOB "JAKE" FRIST, born 14 June 1882; died 14 January 1883 Chattanooga, Hamilton County, Tennessee.[858]

Children of James Ball[4] and Permelia (Corbin) Frist, both born in Hamilton County, Tennessee:

+ 132 iv. BERTIE L. FRIST, born June 1889;[859] died 16 May 1959 St. Elmo, Hamilton County, Tennessee;[860] married 20 September 1911, William Calvin Hartman.[861]

133 v. JOSEPH BYRON FRIST, born August 1892;[862] died 24 August 1958 Chattanooga, Hamilton County, Tennessee;[863] no issue.

42. Samuel Henry[4] Frist (Jacob Chester[3], Henry[2], Rudolph[1]) was born on 19 September 1855 in Chattanooga, Hamilton County, Tennessee, the son of Jacob Chester and Mary Ann Elizabeth (Baldwin) Frist.[864] He died on 23 October 1939 in Chattanooga, Hamilton County, Tennessee.[865] He married about the year 1881 to **Mary Florence Curry**, who was born about 1863 in Tennessee.[866] She died on 7 January 1913 in Chattanooga, Hamilton County, Tennessee.[867]

On 4 March 1893 Samuel conveyed his interest in almost two acres of land in Hamilton County on the southeast side of Lookout Mountain to his wife, Mary Florence Frist.[868] Samuel and Mary Florence had purchased their interest in the land from James P. McMillin and his wife.

In 1900 the family lived in Civil District Seventeen of Hamilton County.[869] They owned their home and carried no mortgage on it. Their two surviving children, Estelle and Hillis, lived with them.

Samuel was a talented carpenter and pattern maker. He lived on the side of Lookout Mountain with a commanding view of downtown Chattanooga. In 1910 Samuel and Mary Florence lived in Civil District Four of Hamilton County.[870]

Mary Florence died in 1913 in Chattanooga of pneumonia at the age of fifty-two and is buried in Mt. Olivet Cemetery.[871]

On 31 December 1914 Samuel and his son, Hillis D. Frist, executed a deed in Hamilton County conveying Lot #1 in the McMillan Subdivision to Mrs. Sarah Estelle Crimm.[872]

In 1930 Samuel was retired and lived with his daughter Estelle Rockwood in Hamilton County.[873] Samuel died in 1939 at the age of eighty-four of arteriosclerosis and is buried in Parker Cemetery in Chattanooga.[874]

Children of Samuel Henry[4] and Mary Florence (Curry) Frist, all born in Chattanooga, Hamilton County, Tennessee:

134   i. MABEL[5] FRIST, born about 1881 to 1885; died by 1900; no issue.

135   ii. ESTELLE FRIST, born about 1885;[875] died December 1958 Chattanooga, Tennessee;[876] married about 1920, Sprague S. "Clarence" Rockwood born about 1877 Illinois;[877] died February 1943.[878] Both buried Greenwood Cemetery, Chattanooga, Tennessee; no issue.

136   iii. HILLIS D. FRIST, born about 1893;[879] died young, but after 1914;[880] no issue.

43. Ann Elizabeth[4] "Lizzie" Frist (Jacob Chester[3], Henry[2], Rudolph[1]) was born on 7 October 1859 in Chattanooga, Hamilton County, Tennessee, the daughter of Jacob Chester and Mary Ann Elizabeth (Baldwin) Frist.[881] She died on 15 January 1922 in Chickamauga, Walker County, Georgia.[882] She married on 21 December 1880 to **William M. Vetter** in Chattanooga, Hamilton County, Tennessee.[883] He was born about September 1855 in Indiana[884] and died in Chattanooga on 13 October 1900.[885]

Lizzie grew up in Chattanooga, the only girl in a family of seven children. On 15 August 1878 the following invitation was extended to Miss Lizzie Frist.[886]

> Can I have the pleasure of your company to attend the Lawn Party to be given tonight at Mr. McDevitts. Please answer by bearer and pardon the lateness of this message. Trusting to have your consent,
>
> I am yours
> *William M. Vetter*

Apparently Lizzie accepted, and the event prompted a courtship that ended in marriage two years later.[887] The newspaper reported on the "Happy Nuptials" stating that the wedding was held at the home of the bride's mother on Carter Street in Chattanooga. William was described as one of the city's "cleverest and most energetic young business men" and Lizzie was described as "an amiable and accomplished young lady—accomplished not only in the ornamental, but in those more substantial things that make the true wife." The couple departed for "Kentucky and Indiana, to spend a few weeks among relatives and friends."[888]

On 1 June 1900 the family lived in Civil District Fourteen in Chattanooga where Lizzie was born.[889] Both William and Elizabeth were in their mid-forties and they had been married twenty years. William's occupation was listed as foreman, and the couple owned a mortgaged home. Their three teenage children lived with them as did a brother-in-law John W. Vetter, age fifty-six, who was born in Indiana.[890]

William Vetter died in 1900 shortly after the census was taken. He had been employed by the Ross-Meehan Foundry Company and was a member of the Royal Arcanum and the Red Cross at the time of his death.[891]

In 1910 his widow Elizabeth was the head of the household in Walker County, Georgia, just across the Tennessee state line.[892] She was fifty years of age and had three children, who were all living. Her son Robert and daughter, Willmary, lived with her, and she owned a farm free of mortgage. In 1920 Elizabeth and all three of her adult children lived together in Walker County, Georgia.[893]

When Elizabeth died in 1922 at her home in Chickamauga, Walker County, Georgia, she was buried in Forest Hills Cemetery.[894] She was survived by her three children, her mother, Mary Frist, and four brothers.

Children of William and Ann Elizabeth[4] (Frist) Vetter:

137   i. ROBERT J.[5] VETTER, born 7 November 1882; died 16 June 1929 Chattanooga, Hamilton County, Tennessee, of pneumonia and is buried in Forest Hills Cemetery;[895] operated a store at Worley, Tennessee, and was a member of the M. E. Church South at the time of his death;[896] no issue.

138   ii. WILLMARY VETTER, born 1886; married, Samuel W. Perry. She resided in Birmingham, Alabama, in 1929, the year her brothers died.[897]

+   139   iii. JOHN STANLEY VETTER, born 1890; died 16 June 1929 Chattanooga, Hamilton County, Tennessee;[898] married about 1926, Effie Roselle Bird.[899]

44. Jacob Chester[4] "Jake" Frist (Jacob Chester[3], Henry[2], Rudolph[1]) was born 2 April 1862 in Chattanooga, Hamilton County, Tennessee, the son of Jacob

Chester and Mary Ann Elizabeth (Baldwin) Frist.[900] He died 2 January 1919 in Meridian, Lauderdale County, Mississippi.[901] He married on 10 August 1897 in Jackson County, Ohio, to **Jane "Jennie" Jones**.[902] Jennie was born 4 December 1869 in Ohio,[903] the daughter of John F. and Mary (Parry) Jones.[904] Jennie died 18 April 1953 in Fort Lauderdale, Broward County, Florida.[905]

In 1870 Jake was an eight-year-old boy, living in the household of his parents in Chattanooga, Hamilton County, Tennessee,[906] where he was raised and educated. In May of 1874 his monthly report from his teacher at a school in Chattanooga survived to provide an insight into his character. Jake did well in reading, writing, spelling, geography, and rhetoric with scores all 90 or above, but a 28 in music and bad scores in math pulled his overall average down. On the bright side, he received 100 percent in both attendance and deportment from his teacher Hattie Ackerman.[907]

In 1880 Jake lived at home with his widowed mother.[908] He was eighteen years of age and his occupation was baggage master. Three years later in January of 1883 when smallpox struck Chattanooga, Jacob's name was listed in Ward Three as a resident who was afflicted.[909] In 1884 Jake lived at home and had undertaken his first business venture by starting a grocery, known as Frist & Company, enlisting the aid of his older brother James.[910] This enterprise was short-lived, and Jake decided that the railroad seemed a sensible way out of the hometown and up fortune's ladder. He advanced from baggage master to conductor, gradually moving up the scale.

While living in Chattanooga, he met Jennie Jones, a popular girl with many a beau, who also had a head for business. She worked as a saleswoman with the D. B. Loveman Company in St. Elmo, Tennessee.[911] They were married on 10 August 1897 in Jackson County, Ohio.[912]

After their marriage they moved with the railroad, first to New Orleans and then to Hattiesburg, Mississippi, where their first child, Mary Louise, was born in 1898. In 1900 they lived in Hattiesburg, Perry County, Mississippi.[913] They had been married for three years. Jacob was thirty-five years of age and Jennie was twenty-nine. Their baby daughter Mary Louise lived with them as did Jennie's parents, John F. and Mary Jones.

While living in Perry County, Jennie's parents, John F. and Mary Jones, executed a trust deed for the south half of Lot 18 in St. Elmo in Hamilton County, Tennessee, in an undated deed that was registered in Perry County, Mississippi, on 29 January 1900.[914] Jennie had lent her parents the sum of $1000 and the deed of trust was executed to secure that debt. They remained in Perry County as least through 1901 when their second child, Helen Jones Frist, was born.

By 1903 the Frists had returned to New Orleans where they established a home at 2026 Camp Street and Jake worked as a conductor for the railroad.[915] Jake's father-in-law, John F. Jones, lived at the same address.

On 25 June 1903 Mrs. Jake Frist was listed in the newspaper in Perry County, Mississippi, as having visited for a few days and then returned home to New Orleans.[916] Both the Frist and Jones families can be found in the New Orleans city directories through 1905 at the address on Camp Street.

On 18 February 1905 Jake bought a large home in Meridian, Lauderdale County, Mississippi, at 1503 Twenty-Fourth Avenue from Charles P. and Mattie Wetherbee for $4000.[917] Meridian could not then be described as the "Old South," which was much to the advantage of the newcomers. The destruction wrought by the Civil War and the subsequent rebuilding made the place seem decidedly up to date and progressive. The trolley line ran in front of the house and cows grazed in back. It was one of the largest homes in town, covered with cupolas, balconies, bays, porches, and gingerbread typical of the Victorian era.[918]

Jake also purchased two lots in the Palace Avenue Survey located in the southwest quarter of the northwest quarter of Section Seven in Township Six, Range Sixteen East in Lauderdale County from K. Threefoot who was acting as trustee.[919]

They joined the First Presbyterian Church, sent the children to public school, and diligently set about the job of being good citizens, good neighbors, and good parents.[920] Their first son, John Chester Frist, was born in 1906 in Lauderdale County.

Jake was in sufficient financial condition that he could lend $1200.07 to J. E. Watts, necessitating the execution of a deed of trust, which was satisfied in full and canceled on 18 May 1909.[921]

With his move to Meridian, Jake had reached the level of stationmaster with the railroad. In 1910 Jake and Jennie lived in Meridian with three of the four children that were eventually born to them.[922] Several lodgers also lived with them. Dr. Sam Hairston, who was later to play such a pivotal role in the life of Jake and Jennie's son Thomas Fearn Frist, and Hairston's wife Nell lived with them along with another lodger, Roy Crompton. Jake and Jennie's son Thomas Fearn Frist was born in December of 1910.

On 22 December 1910 Jake bought an adjacent tract of land from F. L. and Willie L. Walton for $4000.[923] On 31 December 1910 Jake purchased yet another tract of land from R. C. and Mary E. Dunbar for $1000.[924]

Precisely when Jennie's parents, John F. and Mary Jones, died is uncertain, but they were deceased by 1 April 1912 when J. C. and Jennie Jones Frist, as heir of John F. Jones, sold the south half of Lot 18 of D. P. Shauf's Addition to St. Elmo in Civil District Four of Hamilton County, Tennessee, to T. Newell Fry and his wife Minnie.[925] This deed was sworn in court and Jennie's consent taken in Meridian, Lauderdale County, Mississippi.

Life seemed good and there was nothing to suggest anything but the continuation of the family's pleasurable climb toward solid middle class security.[926] Unfortunately, a job-related event was soon to alter the family's lifestyle.

In Meridian there were six terminal tracks running north and south and numbered from 1 to 6 at the station. Several pedestrian passageways crossed the tracks in this station. One of them led from the main waiting room across all the station tracks and was known as the main concourse. Incoming trains from both directions pulled entirely across the main concourse before coming to a stop.[927]

On 3 February 1914, the Alabama Great Southern passenger train No. 3 came into the Meridian Terminal Station on track No. 4 traveling southbound and stopped south of the main concourse. Jacob was standing on the platform between tracks 3 and 4, about 150 feet south of the main concourse. He noticed Mobile & Ohio passenger train No. 4, which was northbound, pulling in on track No. 3 at a rather high rate of speed. Passengers were crossing the tracks in front of the stopped Alabama Great Southern train, and he realized that other cars standing on track No. 2 would obscure the view of people approaching from the station. He broke into a run toward the main concourse, signaling with his hands and shouting a warning. Most people stopped clear of the track. One lady, Mrs. Emma P. Wood, age fifty-eight of Electric Mills, Mississippi, was walking along holding her three-year-old grandchild A. Harlan Scogin. She stopped directly in front of the fast approaching train on track No. 3. It looked as if they would be crushed by the train until Jake Frist sprang forward and pushed them out of the way. Jake was struck by the train, sustaining head injuries and a broken leg.[928]

The local *Meridian Star* stated that he was knocked about thirty feet by the train, breaking his leg below the knee and sustaining other injuries about the head and body.[929] The article further stated that he did not lose consciousness and had the presence of mind to ask that his wife be telephoned and that Dr. Samuel Hairston be summoned.

The doctor who attended him described the injuries that he sustained somewhat differently. Dr. H. S. Gully executed a deposition on 6 February 1915, failing to mention a head injury. He stated that Jake's left leg was fractured between the knee and ankle and that there was a contusion of the left hip and side. Dr. Gully reported that this disabled him for about a year and "he now walks with the aid of a stick and limps slightly."[930]

Friends and acquaintances from all over the United States wrote to Jake upon hearing of his injuries to express their concern and to wish him a rapid recovery. W. N. Jones of Chattanooga wrote on February 5, just a few days after the accident, that he had heard "about your wonderful sacrifice to save the life of a lady and little girl [*sic*]; and how close you came to losing your own." John Prince of Marks Rothenberg Company of New York wrote on 5 February 1914 that he would be coming to see him as soon as he could have visitors. James Hand of Purvis, Mississippi, wrote that "your brave act was such as our Savior would have us do, and

He will remember you in this." One writer used all capital letters to emphasize his point, "YOU MUST HAVE HERO BLOOD IN YOU."[931]

There was an almost immediate response from the community and among Jake's friends to reward him for his bravery, and an application was made on his behalf to the Interstate Commerce Commission for the Medal of Honor.[932] These medals were awarded to persons who endangered their own lives in saving others and were limited to railroad-related incidents.

A. Y. Harvey had been at the station in Meridian the day of the accident to meet some arriving guests. On 26 January 1915 he executed a deposition in Lauderdale County, Mississippi, that became a part of the official record of the event. He stated that if stationmaster Frist had not hurled himself against the woman and child, both would have been killed or seriously injured. He deposed that it was an "act of extreme daring on Mr. Frist's part and greatly endangered his life in my judgment."[933]

In a letter dated 25 February 1915, the chief of the Division of Safety for the Interstate Commerce Commission wrote to investigator H. C. McAdams that "On account of the prominence of the people who have interested themselves in securing this medal for Mr. Frist, it is deemed advisable to give this matter preferred attention." He then directed McAdams to go directly to Meridian to make the investigation.[934]

In March of 1915 Jake was awarded a Medal of Honor from President Woodrow Wilson through the Interstate Commerce Commission for his lifesaving action.[935] On 26 March 1915 he wrote the following letter to Mr. G. B. McGinty, secretary of the Interstate Commerce Commission, thanking them for the award:

> I beg to acknowledge receipt of the Bronze Medal, Button and letters from the
> President and yourself. I appreciate them more than I can describe, I shall
> hand them down to my children and hope my boys may do the same thing
> when they grow to be men should they ever have occasion to be placed in a
> like position. I think it the duty of every man, when women and children are
> in danger of being killed to try and save them.
>   Thanking you and all the commission for the beautiful medal, I am,
>   Yours sincerely,
>   *J. C. Frist*

In October of 1915 Jake was also awarded the Carnegie Medal and Award.[936] This award consisted of a bronze medal and $1000 to be used for the education of his children, as needed. This award was established on 15 April 1904 by Andrew Carnegie and rewards volunteer heroism performed at the risk of life by United States civilians.

#1077   Jacob C. Frist, aged fifty-two, station-master, saved Emma P. Wood and
A. Harlan Scogin, aged fifty-eight and three, respectively, from being run over
by a train, Meridian, Miss., February 3, 1914. Mrs. Wood, carrying Harlan in her
arms, was nearing a track on which a passenger-train was approaching at a speed
of ten or twelve miles an hour. When she was about two feet from the track, Frist
ran across the track and shoved her and the child backward. As he shoved them,
the bumper-timber struck him and knocked him fifteen feet. He received injuries that totally disabled him for nine months, one of his hips being permanently injured. Mrs. Wood was slightly injured.

On 19 February 1916 Jake wrote his will in Meridian, Lauderdale County, Mississippi, with E. R. McArthur and E. Woods as witnesses.[937] It was a very simple
will, leaving everything to his wife, Jennie Jones Frist, and naming her as ex-
ecutrix. It was probated in Lauderdale County on 26 March 1919.

Jacob Chester Frist died 2 January 1919 in Meridian, Lauderdale County, Mississippi, from a cerebral hemorrhage and was buried in Magnolia Cemetery.[938] The
family has always believed that Jake died as a result of the injuries he received in
the train accident. His obituary, while referring to the train wreck, stated that he
died of a "stroke of paralysis."[939] Jake was described as "one of the best known
men in Meridian" and "widely known in railroad circles in this section of the
south." The funeral was held at the Frist home on 4 January 1919 with burial at
Magnolia Cemetery in Meridian.[940]

The task of settling Jake's estate was no small one in that he owned real estate
both in Lauderdale County, Mississippi, and in Hamilton County, Tennessee. On
5 April 1919, in order to expedite the sale of his property, Jennie filed a lengthy
document in Hamilton County so that Jake's will could be probated in Hamilton
County, Tennessee, as well as in Lauderdale County, Mississippi.[941]

In 1920 the widow Jennie was the head of the Frist household in Meridian, Mississippi.[942] Her four children lived with her. Jennie had no occupation, and their
oldest daughter, Mary Louise, was teaching school.

In November of 1923 Jennie filed the final account on Jake's estate in Lauderdale County, listing only one claim against the estate for $33 by Dr. Ruth K. Ha-
ley and paying a total of $93.27 in taxes on the estate.[943]

With Jake's passing, some of the outward conditions of life changed for the
Frists, but little of its inner texture did. There was no pension, no insurance, no
Social Security, and no more income from his position as stationmaster. A certain
style of living was important to the Frists, for to them it reflected a certain way of
life that transcended material things. Although growing up in a proper house in a
good neighborhood among cultured people were not determinants, they helped
immeasurably in the years-long job of building character in children.[944]

Jennie Frist was thrown back on her own considerable inner resources to sustain the fundamental substance of their way of life on a much diminished income. She continued to live in Meridian, turning a portion of the house on Twenty-Fourth Street into a boardinghouse while she raised their children in other portions of the home.[945] Over the years Jennie sold some of the land that Jake had purchased earlier, usually making a tidy profit.[946]

Jennie's make-more-than-the-best-of-it attitude filled the house with interesting, cultured people who were well remembered by their children. Their boarders included a scholarly Episcopal minister named Reverend Penneyman, a young banker named Mose Gaston (who eventually rose to the office of bank president), a successful lumberman named Mahlon Parker (who later married their daughter Mary Louise), retired minor league baseball player Jerry Hairston, and at least two medical men. One was a pediatrician, Dr. Gail Reilly, and the other was Dr. Samuel H. Hairston, a brother to the retired baseball player. These were the people with whom the Frist children associated. They also learned from them on a daily basis and at communal dinners. Jennie instilled a strong sense of family among her children, enabling them to affectionately relate to each other with humor and respect.[947]

In 1930 Jennie was the head of a large household in Meridian, Lauderdale County, Mississippi, consisting mostly of boarders.[948] She owned a home valued at $10,000 and identified herself as "proprietress" of an "apartment house." Jennie listed both of her sons in the census, but indicated they were absent from the family home.

The years following the Great Depression were difficult for most everyone and must have been doubly so for a widow. On 18 September 1935 the family home at 1503 Twenty-Fourth Avenue was sold to the state of Mississippi for taxes.[949] With the sale of her home, Jennie moved to Fort Lauderdale, Florida. There, on 31 August 1936, she sold the last of her landholdings in Lauderdale County, Mississippi, to Ben F. and Polly Paine Cameron.[950]

The tradition of taking boarders into the home continued even after her move to Fort Lauderdale, Florida, and many of the boarders lived with her for years. Her Florida home was almost like a small nursing home as the residents lived out their lives while she cared for them.[951]

Jennie died 18 April 1953 in Fort Lauderdale, Broward County, Florida, and was buried next to her husband Jake in Magnolia Cemetery in Meridian, Lauderdale County, Mississippi.[952]

Children of Jacob Chester[4] and Jane (Jones) Frist:

+   140   i. MARY LOUISE[5] FRIST, born June 1898 New Orleans, Louisiana; died January 1980 Fort Lauderdale, Broward County, Florida;[953] married (1) 6 September 1925 Lauderdale County, Mississippi, Mahlon Floyd Parker;[954] married (2) Bob Tomlinson.

+   141   ii.   HELEN JONES FRIST, born 9 May 1901 Hattiesburg, Perry County,
Mississippi; died 21 August 1956 Fort Lauderdale, Broward County,
Florida;[955] married about 1923 New York, Argie Garner Cameron.

+   142   iii.   JOHN CHESTER "CHET" FRIST, born 29 October 1906 Lauderdale
County, Mississippi; died December 1959 Mobile, Alabama; married
17 May 1932 Farmville, Virginia, Lois Elizabeth "Betty" Ferran.[956]

+   143   iv.   THOMAS FEARN FRIST, born 15 December 1910 Lauderdale County,
Mississippi; died 4 January 1998 Nashville, Davidson County,
Tennessee; married 11 June 1935 Nashville, Davidson County,
Tennessee, Dorothy Harrison Cate.[957]

45. Joseph Elmer[4] **Frist** (Jacob Chester[3], Henry[2], Rudolph[1]) was born on 29 November 1867 in Chattanooga, Hamilton County, Tennessee, the son of Jacob Chester and Mary Ann Elizabeth (Baldwin) Frist.[958] He died on 11 September 1940 in Chattanooga, Hamilton County, Tennessee.[959] He married about the year 1898 to **Alice "Allie" Keefe**, who was born in May 1877 in Wauhatchie, Hamilton County, Tennessee, the daughter of J. A. Keefe.[960] She died on 16 January 1911 in Mission Ridge, Georgia.[961]

In 1900 when the census was taken Joseph and Allie lived in Civil District Fourteen of Chattanooga.[962] Joseph was thirty-two and his occupation was railroad engineer. Allie was twenty-three. One son Paul F. lived with them.

When Allie died on 16 January 1911 in Mission Ridge, Georgia, she was buried in the family burying ground in Wauhatchie, Hamilton County, Tennessee.[963] In 1920 Joe Elmer Frist lived as a lodger in the home of William Henry Griswell in Chattanooga.[964] Joe was fifty-one years, a widower who worked as a flagman for the railroad. His two youngest sons, "Jake" and Ernest, lived as boarders in Chattanooga in the home of Richard Forrester.[965]

On 10 January 1924 Joseph Elmer Frist, widower, conveyed forty acres of land to his son Paul Franklin Frist.[966] The land was described as being in the old Fourth District, but now in the new Second District of Hamilton County, having been conveyed to Joseph E. Frist by Sarah Young on 13 January 1921.

In 1930 Joseph lived next door to his son Paul in Hamilton County.[967] He owned a home valued at $500 and worked as a laborer.

Joseph died in 1940 in Chattanooga, Hamilton County, Tennessee, at the age of seventy-two from apoplexy and is buried in McGill Cemetery.[968] Some of his descendants still live in Chattanooga.

Children of Joseph Elmer[4] and Alice (Keefe) Frist, all born in Chattanooga, Hamilton County, Tennessee:

+   144   i.   PAUL FRANKLIN[5] FRIST, born 5 October 1898;[969] died 12 March 1961
Chattanooga, Hamilton County, Tennessee;[970] married January 1923
Chattanooga, Tennessee, Kate Irene Groves.[971]

+ 145 ii. JAMES CHARLES "JAKE" FRIST, born 11 November 1900;[972] died
8 March 1944 Chattanooga, Hamilton County, Tennessee;[973] married
1 January 1923 Chattanooga, Tennessee, Sadie Estell Briggs.[974]

146 iii. ERNEST ARNOLD FRIST, born 20 September 1903;[975] died
6 November 1968 Chattanooga, Tennessee;[976] employed by Hotel
Northern, 201 West Eighth Street, Chattanooga, Tennessee, in 1936[977]
and was a veteran of World War II;[978] no issue.

46. Emmett Franklin[4] Frist (Jacob Chester[3], Henry[2], Rudolph[1]) was born on
9 April 1877 in Chattanooga, Hamilton County, Tennessee, the son of Jacob
Chester and Mary Ann Elizabeth (Baldwin) Frist.[979] He died on 5 August 1933 in
Gadsden, Etowah County, Alabama.[980] He married in 1903 to **Annie C. Stroud**
in Gadsden, Etowah County, Alabama.[981] Annie was born on 5 March 1879, the
daughter of John William and Emma V. (Phillips) Stroud.[982] She died in February
1963 in Gadsden, Etowah County, Alabama.[983]

In 1900 Emmett lived at home in Chattanooga with his widowed mother
Mary.[984] His occupation was railroad conductor on the Southern Railway. After his
marriage to Annie Stroud in 1903, the family settled in Gadsden, Etowah County,
Alabama. In 1920 Emmett was a railroad conductor, and the two owned a mortgaged home in Gadsden.[985] Their three children lived with them. Although they
owned a home in Gadsden, Emmett was also listed in the census as a lodger living
in Birmingham, Jefferson County, Alabama, with James R. Hawkins and his wife
Stella.[986]

In 1930 Emmett, Annie and their youngest son, Harold, lived in Gadsden, Alabama and owned a home valued at $6000.[987] Emmett was still employed as a rail-
road conductor.

Emmett died in 1933 in Gadsden, Etowah County, Alabama,[988] and Annie died
in 1963 in Gadsden.[989] They are both buried in Forrest Cemetery in Gadsden.[990]

Children of Emmett Franklin[4] and Annie C. (Stroud) Frist, all born in Gadsden,
Etowah County, Alabama:

+ 147 i. MARY EMMA[5] FRIST, born August 1904; died 5 June 1960 Gadsden,
Alabama; married 5 May 1925 Gadsden, Alabama, Curtis Duke.[991]

148 ii. EDWARD FRANKLIN FRIST, born 30 August 1908; died 5 March 1978
Gadsden, Alabama;[992] married after 30 November 1936, Lee Burns
Lancaster, who was born 18 August 1904 in Eatonton, Georgia,
daughter of Clayton and Lena Jane (Burns) Lancaster.[993]

149 iii. CLARENCE HAROLD FRIST; born 5 June 1913; married 14 August
1965 Gadsden, Alabama,[994] Ida Lizzie Davis, who was born 5 June 1910
Cedartown, Georgia, the daughter of Robert David and Annie

(Randall) Davis.[995] Ida died 14 June 1997 at Gadsden, Alabama.[996] Harold's occupation was accountant. He was cashier and paymaster at Goodyear Tire and Rubber Company in Gadsden. He taught Sunday school at First Baptist Church for fifty-seven years and was a member of the Civitan Club for over thirty years. In 2003 Harold lives in Gadsden, Etowah County, Alabama.[997]

FIFTH GENERATION

50. Joseph Andrew[5] **Frist** (David H.[4], John[3], Henry[2], Rudolph[1]) was born 16 July 1845 most likely in Wayne County, Indiana, the son of David H. and Lydia E. (Holliday) Frist. He died 11 April 1932 in Page County, Iowa.[998] Joseph married on 28 February 1875 in Page County, Iowa, to **Rosetta Josephine "Rosa" Mitchell**.[999] Rosa was born 31 July 1855 in Iowa, the daughter of John B. and Lydia Mitchell.[1000] She died on 17 June 1925 in Iowa.[1001]

In the fall of 1860, Joseph migrated with his family from Indiana to Villisca in Montgomery County, Iowa,[1002] where he was to meet his wife and marry in 1875. In 1885 Joseph and Rosa were in Lincoln Township, Page County, Iowa.[1003] Joseph was thirty-nine and listed his occupation as farmer. Rosetta was twenty-nine and their first two children, John and Louise, lived with them. By 1891 the family lived in Montgomery County, Iowa.[1004]

In 1900 they remained living in Montgomery County.[1005] Rosa had borne six children and five were living. The four youngest children lived with them. Rosa's mother Lydia Mitchell, who was seventy-eight years of age, also lived with them. Lydia was born in March of 1822 in Pennsylvania. She had borne nine children but only five survived.

In 1920 Joseph, age seventy-four, and Rosa, age sixty-four, lived with their son William H. Frist in Page County, Iowa.[1006] Five years later in 1925 Joseph and Rosa remained in Page County, living with their son William who was to remain a bachelor all of his life.[1007]

In February 1925 they celebrated their golden wedding anniversary at their home southeast of Villisca, Iowa, with thirty of their relatives and friends.[1008] The Frists limited their celebration to just a few "owing to the illness of Mrs. Frist" and stated that it was the intention of their children to hold another celebration for them at a later date when Mrs. Frist regained her health.

Hopefully Rosa enjoyed the celebration, for she did not regain her health and instead died at her home a few months later.[1009] She was a member of the Advent Christian Church in Villisca.[1010] Joseph survived a few years longer, dying in 1932 in Page County, Iowa, of cardiac "decompension."[1011] They are both buried in Villisca Cemetery, Rose Hill Section.[1012]

Children of Joseph Andrew[5] and Rosetta Josephine (Mitchell) Frist:

150   i. JOHN HULSEY[6] FRIST, born 28 June 1875 Page County, Iowa;[1013] died
        15 March 1891 Montgomery County, Iowa, and buried Villisca
        Cemetery, Montgomery County, Iowa;[1014] no issue.

+ 151   ii. LOUISA JANE FRIST, born 29 July 1881 Page County, Iowa;[1015] died
        28 May 1965 Villisca, Iowa;[1016] married 28 March 1900 Montgomery
        County, Iowa, Lewis Patton.[1017]

+ 152 iii. WILLIBUR STILES FRIST,[1018] born 6 October 1885 in Coin, Page
        County, Iowa;[1019] died 7 July 1930 Iowa;[1020] married 18 March 1917,[1021]
        Orpha Lucille Geesaman.[1022]

153   iv. WILLIAM HAWKINS FRIST, born 6 October 1885 in Coin, Page
        County, Iowa;[1023] died 16 September 1952 at Clarinda, Iowa, buried
        Villisca Cemetery next to his parents;[1024] no issue.

154   v. NANNIE ELIZABETH FRIST, born 23 September 1890 Montgomery
        County, Iowa;[1025] died November 1970 Plymouth County Iowa;[1026]
        married 21 December 1910 Montgomery County, Iowa, Fred Bridgman
        born 16 September 1898 Montgomery County, Iowa, son of John and
        Kate (McEntire) Bridgman.[1027] Fred died October 1971 Plymouth
        County, Iowa.[1028] One daughter, Thelma F. Bridgman, was born about
        1916.[1029] She married Paul Iocker[1030] and was last known to be living
        near Sioux City or a town called Hawarden in Sioux County, Iowa.[1031]

155   vi. SAMUEL VICTOR FRIST, born 25 February 1894;[1032] served in World
        War I and was severely wounded in the face at Chateau Thierry near
        the Croix Rouge farm in France on 26 July 1918. He died 27 July 1918
        and was buried in France; no issue.[1033]

51. John S.[5] Frist (David H.[4], John[3], Henry[2], Rudolph[1]) was born 22 March 1848
in Wayne County, Indiana, the son of David H. and Lydia E. (Holliday) Frist.[1034]
John married, about 1875 to **Elizabeth A.**, probably Bivans, who was born in Ohio
in 1838.[1035]

John migrated with his parents to Villisca in Montgomery County, Iowa, in the
fall of 1860,[1036] where he met and married his wife. In 1880 John, Elizabeth, and
their two-year-old son lived in Marion County, Iowa.[1037] John was a farmer. Josiah
Bivans lived with them in 1880, a single man named as brother-in-law. Three
Childress children also lived with them, listed as stepchildren—Margaret E., age
sixteen; Mary E., age fourteen; and Rhoda A., age eleven. They were apparently
Elizabeth's children from an earlier marriage.

By 1900 Elizabeth had died and John was a widower living in Polk County,
Iowa.[1038] He was fifty-two years of age and his occupation was day laborer. In 1915

he was sixty-six years of age when he was enumerated in the Polk County, Iowa, state census.[1039] In 1920 John lived with his son Joseph in Polk County, Iowa.[1040] He was seventy-one years of age.

Child of John S.[5] and Elizabeth A. (Bivans?) Frist:

+   156   i. JOSEPH E.[6] FRIST, born September 1877; died after 1920;[1041] married on 29 November 1905 Polk County, Iowa, Blanche R. Coloway.[1042]

53. Rebecca J.[5] Frist (David H.[4], John[3], Henry[2], Rudolph[1]) was born 15 October 1850 in Wayne County, Indiana, the daughter of David H. and Lydia E. (Holliday) Frist.[1043] Rebecca died 8 December 1910.[1044] She married about 1867 to **Henry Thomas** who was born in Iowa in 1842.[1045] He died by 1910 in Dallas County, Iowa.[1046]

Rebecca was just shy of six years when her mother, Lydia, died. Her father remarried to Ruth Cate and in the fall of 1860 the family migrated to Villisca, Montgomery County, Iowa.[1047]

Rebecca married about 1867 to Henry Thomas, and in 1880 the family lived in Booneville, Dallas County, Iowa.[1048] Twenty years later in 1900, the family remained in Dallas County.[1049] Henry was fifty-eight and Rebecca was listed as fifty-one. They owned a mortgaged farm and had been married thirty-three years. Rebecca had borne ten children and eight were living.

Henry died by 1910 when the widow Rebecca was listed as the head of household in Dallas County, Iowa.[1050] She was sixty-one years of age and indicated that eight of the ten children she had borne were still living. Four children lived with her, and her son Elmer lived next door. She died shortly after the census was taken in December of 1910.[1051]

Children of Henry and Rebecca J.[5] (Frist) Thomas, all born in Iowa:

+   157   i. ELMER E.[6] THOMAS, born about 1868 Booneville, Dallas County, Iowa; married 19 September 1892 Dallas County, Iowa, Della Jane Wilson.[1052]

    158   ii. LYDIA ANN THOMAS, born about 1870 Warren County, Iowa; married 21 August 1889 Dallas County, Iowa, Samuel Albert Parker born 1867 Dallas County, Iowa, son of Simron and Anna (Rathburn) Parker.[1053]

    159   iii. CORA THOMAS, born about 1872.[1054]

    160   iv. HENRY THOMAS, born about 1874.[1055]

+   161   v. VIOLA MAY THOMAS, born about 1876 Polk County, Iowa;[1056] married 17 September 1893 Dallas County, Iowa, Arthur W. Allen.[1057]

    162   vi. HENDLEY THOMAS, born about 1880.[1058]

    163   vii. MARY E. "MANDE" THOMAS, born about July 1881.[1059]

    164   viii. AMELIA A. THOMAS, born about June 1884.[1060]

165   ix. ROY C. THOMAS, born about July 1890.[1061]

166   x. IRA THOMAS, born about April 1894.[1062]

55. Sarah J.[5] Frist (William H.[4], John[3], Henry[2], Rudolph[1]) was born about 1852 in Preble County, Ohio, the daughter of William H. and Catherine (Reid) Frist.[1063] She married 29 December 1872 in Preble County to **Henry C. Rupe**.[1064] Henry was born in September 1853 in Ohio.[1065]

In 1880 Henry and Sarah lived in Wayne County, Indiana.[1066] Henry was a farmer, aged twenty-seven, and Sarah was twenty-eight. Three children lived with them. They lived in Cox Mills, Indiana, in 1887 when her father died.[1067]

In 1900 Henry and Sarah remained in Wayne County.[1068] Both were forty-eight years of age. Henry was a farmer who rented his land. Sarah said she had borne ten children and that nine were living. In 1910 Henry and Sarah and their four youngest children lived together in Wayne County on their rented farm.[1069]

Children of Henry C. and Sarah J.[5] (Frist) Rupe:

167   i. IDA M.[6] RUPE, born 1874 Ohio; died 1955; married 4 December 1889, Jerome Jordan born 1863 and died 1933.[1070]

168   ii. SUSAN RUPE, born about 1877 Indiana.[1071]

169   iii. WILLIAM RUPE, born about 1879 Ohio. [1072]

170   iv. CHARLES H. RUPE, born 20 September 1882 Wayne County, Indiana; died 13 May 1954; married 2 April 1908, Flora E. Bullerdick born 28 December 1883 died after 1954.[1073] Two children, both born in Indiana, *(a)* Alice M. Rupe born about 1910 and *(b)* Clarence Rupe born about 1911.[1074]

171   v. ANNA L. RUPE, born 1 November 1884 Wayne County, Indiana; died 1909;[1075] married Smith M. Parry born 6 February 1876 died after 1909.[1076]

172   vi. JESSE RUPE, born about February 1886 Wayne County, Indiana.[1077]

173   vii. ROY RUPE, born about January 1889 Wayne County, Indiana.[1078]

174   viii. CELIA FLORENCE RUPE, born about November 1891 Wayne County Indiana.[1079]

175   ix. PEARL RUPE, born about August 1893 Wayne County, Indiana.[1080]

176   x. VIOLA ETHEL RUPE, born about November 1896 Wayne County, Indiana.[1081]

62. William O.[5] Frist (William H.[4], John[3], Henry[2], Rudolph[1]) was born June 1867[1082] in Preble County, Ohio, the son of William H. and Catherine (Reid) Frist.[1083] He died 22 May 1929 in Preble County, Ohio.[1084] He married on 25 November 1893 in Preble County, Ohio, to **Reba F. Juqua**.[1085] Reba was born in September of 1876, the daughter of Hiram Juqua.[1086] She died in 1944.[1087]

In 1900 William and Reba lived in Jefferson Township in Preble County, Ohio, with two of their children and William's brother James Frist, fifty years of age.[1088] By 1910 another child had been born to William and Reba.[1089] William's brother James remained living with them, sixty-one years of age.

In 1920 William and Reba lived in New Paris in Preble County.[1090] Only their daughter, Helen, and William's brother James, listed as sixty-nine years of age, still lived with them. James was listed by his middle name of Jasper.

William's will was written on 5 April 1917 and when he died in 1929 in Preble County, Ohio, he left his estate to his wife, Reba.[1091] He also mentioned minor children Garnet L. Mungavin of Richmond, Indiana, Paul H. Frist, and Helen C. Boyd. Reba died several years later in 1944.[1092] Both have tombstones at the cemetery in New Paris, Preble County, Ohio.

Children of William O.[5] and Reba F. (Juqua) Frist, all born in Preble County, Ohio:

> 177   i. GARNET L.[6] FRIST, born 7 June 1894; married 6 November 1913 Preble County, Ohio, William H. Mungavin[1093] born 1891 Preble County, Ohio, son of Thomas H. and Mary (Flattley) Mungavin.[1094] William was a telegraph operator.[1095] They lived in Wayne County, Indiana, without children in 1920 and William was listed in the census as born in Ireland of parents born in Ireland.[1096]
>
> + 178   ii. PAUL H. FRIST, born April 1896;[1097] died 1959;[1098] married (1) about 1917 Anabel,[1099] and (2) about 1921 to Violet Genevieve Jelly.[1100]
>
> 179   iii. HELEN CATHERINE FRIST, born 17 August 1904; married 5 April 1924 Preble County, Ohio, Trafford B. Boyd,[1101] born New Paris, Ohio, son of T. A. and Alice (Brown) Boyd;[1102] Trafford was a bookkeeper.[1103]

63. Russell[5] "Pop" Frist (William H.[4], John[3], Henry[2], Rudolph[1]) was born about 1871 in Preble County, Ohio, the son of William H. and Catherine (Reid) Frist.[1104] Russell died in 1930 in Pendleton, Madison County, Indiana.[1105] He married about 1892 to **Sarah Viola Hunt**, who was born about 1874.[1106] She died 27 September 1950 in Pendleton, Madison County, Indiana.[1107]

In 1900 Russell and Sarah lived in Madison County, Indiana.[1108] They had been married eight years, Sarah had borne one child, and that child lived with them. Russell's occupation was glass packer, and their family home was rented.

In 1920 they were in their late forties and owned their home in Madison County.[1109] Their only son, Marley, his wife, Hester, and their infant son Russell, who was named after his grandfather, lived with them.

Russell and Sarah both died in Pendleton, Madison County, Indiana.[1110] They are buried in Grove Lawn Cemetery, Pendleton, Indiana.

Child of Russell[5] and Sarah Viola (Hunt) Frist, probably born in Madison County, Indiana:

+   180   i. MARLEY OTTO[6] FRIST, born 12 January 1893; died 6 December 1957
                 Anderson, Madison County, Indiana;[1111] married 12 August 1911,[1112]
                 Hester Vurnie Swinford.[1113]

64. Hannah Etta[5] Frist (Robert M.[4], John[3], Henry[2], Rudolph[1]) was born on 30 May 1858 in Indiana, the daughter of Robert M. and Ruth C. (Meredith) Frist.[1114] She died on 10 September 1936 at Liberty, Union County, Indiana.[1115] She married about 1886 to **John J. Stevens**, who was born in August of 1851.[1116] He died in 1934.[1117]

In 1870 Hannah Etta lived at home with her parents in Warren County, Iowa.[1118] In 1880 she was in her early twenties but remained at home with her parents, who had moved to Preble County, Ohio.[1119]

After her marriage in 1886 to John J. Stevens, the couple moved to Union County, Indiana, where they lived in 1900.[1120] They had been married twelve years, Hannah had borne three children, and all three lived with them. John was a farm laborer, and they rented their home.

In 1920 they were in their sixties and still renting their home in Union County.[1121] One son, twenty-nine-year-old John E. Stevens, lived with them.

John died in 1934, and when Hannah died two years later in 1936 at Liberty, Union County, Indiana, she left two sons, John E. and Jesse O., and three unnamed grandchildren surviving her.[1122] The funeral was held at Edwards Memorial Church, and she is buried in West Point Cemetery.

Children of John J. and Hannah Etta[5] (Frist) Stevens, probably all born in Union County, Indiana:

      181   i. ROXIE ELMA[6] STEVENS, born about February 1886;[1123] died before her
                 mother.
      182   ii. JOHN ROY EVERETT STEVENS, born about November 1889;[1124] living
                 at home in 1920.[1125]
+   183   iii. JESSE O. LAFFE STEVENS, born 14 August 1891;[1126] died 29 March
                 1955 Alexandria, Virginia;[1127] married 27 November 1918 Fort
                 Madison, Lee County Iowa, Ella May Baxter.[1128]

65. Martin Luther[5] Frist (Robert M.[4], John[3], Henry[2], Rudolph[1]) was born 10 April 1868 in Iowa, the son of Robert M. and Ruth C. (Meredith) Frist.[1129] He married 17 September 1896 at Fort Madison in Lee County, Iowa, to **Samantha Jane "Mattie" Hewett.**[1130]

In 1880 Martin lived with his parents, who had moved to Preble County, Ohio.[1131] By 1920 Martin and his wife, Mattie, lived in Lee County, Iowa.[1132] They were both listed in the census as fifty years of age. Martin's occupation was general laborer, and their four children lived with them.

Children of Martin Luther[5] and Samantha Jane (Hewett) Frist, all born in Fort Madison, Lee County, Iowa:

184   i. ROSCOE E.[6] FRIST, born 21 August 1897;[1133] died July 1983 Michigan;[1134] married 8 June 1920 Lee County, Iowa, Ida Olson born 1892 Fort Madison, Iowa, daughter of August and Almeda (Richardson) Olson.[1135]

185   ii. OLIVE MARIE FRIST, born about 1902;[1136] married 5 March 1925 Lee County, Iowa, Walter L. Hanley born 1896 Chicago, Illinois.[1137]

186   iii. RUTH C. FRIST, born about 1903;[1138] married 14 June 1922 Fort Madison, Lee County, Iowa, Philip Helling born 1897 Fort Madison, Iowa, son of Joseph and Catherine (Rosen?) Helling.[1139]

187   iv. EDNA M. FRIST, born about 1906;[1140] married 7 July 1926 Lee County, Iowa, Nathan C. Sayre born about 1905 Washington, Iowa, son of David and Ester (Beembloom) Sayre.[1141]

69. Cora[5] Frist (Jonas Lyman Paulson[4], John[3], Henry[2], Rudolph[1]) was born on 26 June 1861[1142] probably in Wayne County, Indiana,[1143] the daughter of Jonas Lyman Paulson and Amy E. (Powell) Frist. Cora died 31 October 1941 in Winchester, Randolph County, Indiana.[1144] Cora married on 15 March 1888 in Lynn, Randolph County, Indiana, to **James Putnam Goodrich**.[1145] James was born 18 February 1864 in Winchester, Randolph County, Indiana, the son of John Baldwin and Elizabeth Putnam (Edger) Goodrich.[1146] He died 15 August 1940 in Winchester, Randolph County, Indiana.[1147]

In 1880 Cora lived with her parents in Randolph County, Indiana.[1148] She was eighteen and listed her occupation as school teacher. Both Cora and her future husband James Putnam Goodrich took and passed the Indiana state teacher's licensing examination, which at that time required no college degree, and began teaching in Randolph County.[1149] Although Cora continued to teach, James pursued other careers. He proposed after a whirlwind courtship, although it would be three years later in 1888 before they were married at Cora's hometown of Lynn.[1150]

James Putnam Goodrich taught school briefly after high school graduation, attended DePauw University for two years, and then studied law at the office of Watson and Engle. He was admitted to the bar in 1886 and went into partnership with his uncle Ches Macy.[1151]

In 1900 the family lived in White River Township in Randolph County in a rented home, and their only child, Pierre, lived with them.[1152] James was a lawyer in his home town for many years and served as state chairman of the Republican Party from 1901 to 1910. He became a highly successful businessman, and shortly after 1910 they moved to Indianapolis where they owned farm land, banks, and coal mines.[1153]

James served as the governor of Indiana from 8 January 1917 until 10 January 1921. An Indianapolis newspaper called him the "real father of the magnificent park system in Indiana."[1154] In 1920 they lived in Indianapolis, Indiana.[1155] James was fifty-five and Cora was fifty-eight. Even though he was the elected governor of Indiana at the time, his occupation was listed as attorney. Their son, Pierre, was twenty-five and no longer lived with them.

In 1920 James was a favorite son candidate for the presidential nomination, which he lost to Warren G. Harding, although he remained an important political figure in Indiana politics for many years.[1156]

On 25 February 1939 Cora wrote to her cousin that "Jim seems a little better, his heart stands more." Typical of a mother, she also commented that "Pierre has too much to do" and, typical of a grandmother, she mentioned that her granddaughter Nancy "is beautiful and a good student."[1157]

Cora was involved in many philanthropic organizations. She was a charter member of the Women's Club and a member of the Magazine Club. She was also in the Daughters of the American Revolution, serving as president in 1925 and 1926. She used her mother's line to prove descent from a Revolutionary ancestor. Her mother was Amy Powell, daughter of Stephen Stackhouse Powell and granddaughter of William Powell.[1158] Cora was an avid genealogist, and many of her letters to family members have been preserved and helped to establish certain branches of the family.

In 1939 Cora and James Goodrich donated $11,000 for the construction of a library in Lynn, Indiana, in memory of her parents, and it was named the Frist Memorial Library.[1159] A portrait of Mrs. Goodrich in a dark red dress hangs in the library.[1160]

James P. Goodrich died in 1940 of paralysis and heart ailment at the Randolph County Hospital in Winchester, Indiana. He was survived by his widow Cora; his son, Pierre; a granddaughter, Nancy; and three brothers, Edward S. Goodrich, Perry E. Goodrich, and William W. Goodrich.[1161]

Cora founded the Madonna class of the Winchester Presbyterian Church in 1914 and continued to teach and guide almost to the day she died.[1162] She died in 1941 at her home in Winchester, Randolph County, Indiana, at the age of eighty after a year-long illness.[1163] She and her husband are buried in Fountain Park Cemetery in Winchester.

Children of James Putnam and Cora[5] (Frist) Goodrich:

188   i. JEAN[6] GOODRICH, born and died 16 May 1893 Winchester, Indiana.[1164]

+   189   ii. PIERRE FRIST GOODRICH, born 10 September 1894 Winchester, Randolph County, Indiana;[1165] died 25 October 1973 Indianapolis, Indiana;[1166] married (1) 17 July 1920, Dorothy Dugan;[1167] married (2) 3 February 1941 Chicago, Illinois, Enid Smith.[1168]

73. Ella F.[5] Lloyd (Elizabeth Frist[4], Jediah[3], Henry[2], Rudolph[1]) was born about 1853, probably in New Castle County, Delaware, the daughter of Franklin and Elizabeth (Frist) Lloyd.[1169] She died 16 July 1932 in New Castle County, Delaware.[1170] She married **William C. Tindall** about 1879.[1171] He was born in August 1853 in New Jersey.[1172] He died on 7 March 1926 in New Castle County, Delaware.[1173]

In 1870 Ella lived at home in Wilmington, New Castle County, Delaware, with her widowed mother.[1174] By 1880 Ella had married to William C. Tindall and the two continued to live in Wilmington.[1175] They were both twenty-seven years of age, and their son Franklin and Ella's mother Elizabeth lived with them.

Twenty years later in 1900, they were both forty-six years of age, had been married for twenty-one years, and remained living in Wilmington, Delaware.[1176] Ella had borne two children and both lived with them. Also living with them at the age of eighty was Ella's mother, Elizabeth Lloyd.

William and Ella were residents of Wilmington in 1920,[1177] both listed as sixty-six years of age. William was a carpenter and home builder. Their son Franklin and daughter-in-law Charlotte lived with them as did their two-year-old grandson William C. Tindall.

William wrote his will on 8 May 1924 and died in 1926 in New Castle County, Delaware.[1178] His will named his wife, Ella, and his two sons. Ella and their son Frank lived in Wilmington, while their son Roscoe lived in Toughkenamon, Chester County, Pennsylvania. William's estate was valued at $82,334.29.

Ella wrote her will on 14 April 1927 and died in 1932 in New Castle County, Delaware.[1179] She named her sons Frank and Roscoe as well as a granddaughter Marcia, daughter of her son Roscoe. Frank still resided in Wilmington, and Roscoe lived in New Garden, Pennsylvania.

Children of William C. and Ella F.[5] (Lloyd) Tindall, probably born in Wilmington, New Castle County, Delaware:

+   190   i. FRANKLIN LLOYD[6] TINDALL, born April 1880; married about 1916,[1180] Charlotte Maltman.[1181]

191   ii. ROSCOE COOK TINDALL, born April 1887;[1182] died 7 October 1957
New Castle County, Delaware;[1183] married after 1900 to Lillian; Roscoe
worked as an architect and bequeathed his architectural library to
Annette Yates Maier for fifteen years of faithful service. One child,
Marcia Tindall, born 1919 in Delaware married by 1954 to Mr.
Benbow and lived in Arlington, Virginia, in 1957.[1184]

74. Elizabeth Jane[5] **Lloyd** (Elizabeth Frist[4], Jediah[3], Henry[2], Rudolph[1]) was
born about 1857 in Delaware, the daughter of Franklin and Elizabeth (Frist)
Lloyd.[1185] She died 3 July 1939 in Rehoboth Beach, Sussex County, Delaware.[1186]
She married about 1890 to **Joseph A. Randle**.[1187] Joseph died 8 January 1908 in
New Castle County, Delaware, and his brother-in-law William Tindall served as
the administrator of his estate.[1188]

Elizabeth J. Randle wrote her will in Wilmington on 13 November 1934. When
she died in 1939 in Rehoboth Beach, Sussex County, Delaware, her will was probated in New Castle County, Delaware.[1189] She left numerous bequests to various
nieces and nephews and mentioned her daughter-in-law Margaret Randle. Her
son was not named in the will and is believed to have predeceased her. He was not
included in the list of her next of kin. She left the bulk of her estate to her only
descendant, a granddaughter, Elizabeth B. Randle, who lived in Rehoboth Beach,
Delaware.

Child of Joseph A. and Elizabeth Jane[5] (Lloyd) Randle:

192   i. JOHN W.[6] RANDLE, born about 1890–1895; deceased by 1934 when his
mother wrote her will; married Margaret born 11 September 1837
[sic].[1190] One child, Elizabeth B. Randle, born 24 August 1912.[1191]

79. Robert Porter[5] **Frist** (Henry[4], Jediah[3], Henry[2], Rudolph[1]) was born on
22 July 1856 in Wilmington, New Castle County, Delaware, the son of Henry and
Catherine Campbell (Stewart) Frist.[1192] He married on 17 March 1883 in New
Castle County to **Helen M. "Nellie" Bleyer**.[1193]

In 1870 he was thirteen years old and lived with his widowed mother in Wilmington.[1194] In 1880 he was twenty-three years of age and remained at home with
his mother and siblings in Wilmington.[1195]

By 1920 Robert and Helen B. Frist had migrated westward to Los Angeles
County, California, where they rented a home.[1196] Robert's age was incorrectly
listed as fifty-two and he worked in commercial travel in the ship-building industry. Helen was fifty and a pianist in an orchestra. Three adult children lived with
them, Robert, Beatrice, and Archie.

Children of Robert Porter[5] and Helen (Bleyer) Frist, all born in Wilmington, New Castle County, Delaware:

193   i. HELEN C.[6] FRIST, born January 1884; died 16 July 1884 of cholera infantum.[1197]

194   ii. BEATRICE CAMPBELL "DIXIE" FRIST, born 8 November 1885 Wilmington, Delaware.[1198]

195   iii. ROBERT PORTER FRIST, JR., born 8 June 1889 Wilmington, Delaware; died 15 September 1943 Sacramento, California, of cancer and was buried in Long Beach, California.[1199] He lived in Amador County, California, was a transportation officer at Preston School, and was single at the time of his death; no issue.

196   iv. ARCHIE CAMPBELL FRIST, born 17 October 1893;[1200] died 14 August 1961 Los Angeles, California;[1201] married Charlotte Geraldine Ayers who was born 3 April 1899 in Miltonville, Cloud County, Kansas, the daughter of James W. and Carrie (Ferguson) Ayers and died 8 June 1961 of a heart attack in Long Beach, California, and was buried in Westminster Memorial Park, Westminster, California.[1202] He had served in World War I, worked as a projectionist at United Artist Theater, and was widowed at the time of his death.[1203] Archie and his wife were Mormons;[1204] no issue.

80. Herman Eschenberg[5] Frist (Henry[4], Jediah[3], Henry[2], Rudolph[1]) was born 13 January 1859 in Wilmington, New Castle County, Delaware, the son of Henry and Catherine Campbell (Stewart) Frist.[1205] Herman died 21 February 1933 in Wilmington, New Castle County, Delaware.[1206] He married on 12 July 1917 in New Castle County, Delaware, to **Margaret A. Hume**.[1207] Margaret was born 23 November 1868 in Delaware, the daughter of George W. and Elizabeth R. (Ralston) Hume.[1208] Margaret died 22 October 1950 in Wilmington, Delaware.[1209]

In 1920 Herman and Margaret lived in Wilmington.[1210] After Herman's death in 1933 due to acute dilation of the heart,[1211] Margaret continued to live in Wilmington. She wrote her will on 13 December 1942,[1212] and died eight years later in 1950 of osteoarthritis.[1213] Her will mentioned her deceased husband, Herman, and directed that his remains be removed from the vault where they were deposited and moved to her vault in Holy Trinity (Old Swedes) Church Cemetery in Wilmington. She bequeathed her estate to various friends and a cousin. Herman and Margaret A. (Hume) Frist had no children.

84. Marietta F.[5] "Etta" Springer (Esther Ann[4] Frist, Jediah[3], Henry[2], Rudolph[1]) was born 8 April 1856 in New Castle County, Delaware, the daughter of Levi H. and Esther Ann (Frist) Springer.[1214] Etta died 2 July 1942 in New Castle County, Delaware.[1215] She married about 1881 to **Willard Springer**, who was born in August 1851 in Delaware.[1216] He died 26 June 1936 in New Castle County, Delaware.[1217]

In 1880 Etta lived at home in New Castle County with her parents.[1218] In 1900 Etta and her husband, Willard, lived in Wilmington, New Castle County, Delaware.[1219] Willard was a physician, forty-eight years of age, and Etta was forty-four. She had borne four children, and all four lived with them, along with two servants. They had been married for nineteen years and owned their own home.

Willard was of Wilmington when he wrote his will on 6 January 1934, and it was probated in 1936 in New Castle County.[1220] He named his wife, Etta, and their four children. Both married daughters were listed as living in Wilmington with their mother. He left a sizable estate for this post-Depression era of $113,500, including a home at 1101 Madison Street in Wilmington.

Etta wrote her will on 24 September 1940, and it was probated in 1942 in New Castle County.[1221] She named her four children and mentioned a granddaughter Marjorie Stout White.

Their youngest child Sarah Edith died without issue on 15 April 1975 in New Castle County, Delaware.[1222] She was the last of her siblings to die and left a will and estate papers that established the names and locations of many of her nieces and nephews.

Children of Willard and Marietta F.[5] (Springer) Springer, all born in New Castle County, Delaware:

+   197   i. HAROLD L.[6] SPRINGER, born about October 1881;[1223] died 11 November 1969 Wilmington, New Castle County, Delaware;[1224] married about 1907 Carolyn L.[1225]

+   198   ii. HELEN S. SPRINGER, born about January 1884;[1226] died 30 August 1948 New Castle County, Delaware;[1227] married about 1912 Herbert C. Stout.[1228]

+   199   iii. WILLARD SPRINGER, born 8 April 1886; died 26 February 1956 New Castle County, Delaware;[1229] married about 1915 Edna L. Martenis.[1230]

    200   iv. SARAH EDITH SPRINGER, born about March 1890;[1231] died 15 April 1975; married by 1936 Howard L. Baumgartner; no issue.[1232]

86. Kallena R.[5] Springer (Esther Ann[4] Frist, Jediah[3], Henry[2], Rudolph[1]) was born in January of 1869 in New Castle County, Delaware, the daughter of Levi H. and Esther Ann (Frist) Springer.[1233] She died 22 November 1950 in Wilmington, New Castle County, Delaware.[1234] She married about 1891 to **Edwin J. Sheppard**, who was born in August 1864 in Delaware.[1235]

In 1880 Kallena lived at home in New Castle County with her parents.[1236] By 1900 Kallena had married to Edwin J. Sheppard, and the Sheppards lived in Wilmington, New Castle County, Delaware.[1237] They had been married nine years. Edwin was thirty-five and his profession was clerk. Kallena was thirty-one, had borne four children, and all four lived with them.

Kallena wrote her will on 28 December 1933 and it was probated seventeen years later in 1950 in Wilmington, New Castle County, Delaware.[1238] No husband was mentioned in her will, and he is presumed to have predeceased her. She left the residue of her estate to her children in equal shares and named her sons Morris and Edwin as executors. The probate record named her three surviving daughters, all of whom lived in Delaware, except for Esther Graves, who lived in Louisville, Kentucky.

When their son Edwin Ross Sheppard died in 1956 without issue, his probate record indicated that all siblings still lived in Delaware except for his brother Morris, who resided in Southern Pines, South Carolina.[1239]

Children of Edwin J. and Kallena R.⁵ (Springer) Sheppard, all born in New Castle County, Delaware:

> 201   i. MORRIS W.⁶ SHEPPARD, born November 1891;[1240] died 2 February 1961 New Castle County, Delaware;[1241] married (1) Bessie F. born 1875 Delaware and (2) Cora W. In 1956 he lived in Southern Pines, South Carolina; no issue.
>
> 202   ii. EDWIN ROSS SHEPPARD, born March 1895;[1242] died 13 January 1956 New Castle County, Delaware;[1243] married Mildred Booker born 1897 Delaware; probate lists his widow and siblings as next of kin; no issue.
>
> 203   iii. NATALIE SHEPPARD, born June 1896;[1244] died 25 March 1928 New Castle County, Delaware;[1245] married by 1924 Joseph W. Dare. Joseph and their daughter lived in Kingston, Pennsylvania, at the time of Natalie's death. One child, Marjorie Jane Dare, born about 1924[1246] married by 1956 Mr. Poor.[1247] After Natalie's death, Joseph W. Dare married her younger sister Helen.[1248]
>
> +   204   iv. ESTHER SHEPPARD, born September 1899;[1249] died 17 August 1975 New Castle County, Delaware;[1250] married Edward J. Graves.[1251]
>
> 205   v. MARGARET SHEPPARD, born 1903; married by 1950 Charles Logan.[1252]
>
> 206   vi. HELEN SHEPPARD, born 1906; married by 1930 Joseph W. Dare;[1253] living in Milford, Sussex County, Delaware, in 1961.[1254]

91. Jediah⁵ Frist (Jediah Rudolph⁴ Jediah³, Henry², Rudolph¹) was born on 28 February 1859 in Brandywine Township, Chester County, Pennsylvania,[1255] the son of Jediah Rudolph and Mary Johnson (Peirce) Frist.[1256] Jediah died on 30 April 1948 in Dana, Vermillion County, Indiana.[1257] He married in Vermillion County on 22 August 1880 to **Elizabeth Helt**.[1258] Elizabeth was born on 21 May 1859 in Helt Township in Vermillion County, Indiana, the daughter of Charles and Sarah (Taylor) Helt.[1259] She died on 12 August 1935 in Dana, Vermillion County, Indiana.[1260]

Jediah migrated westward with his family and in 1870 lived with his parents in Vermillion County, Indiana.[1261] In 1880 Jediah and his brother Samuel lived in the household of John F. Moore in Vermillion County, working as farm hands.[1262]

When Jediah married in Vermillion County in 1880 to Elizabeth Helt,[1263] he married into a well-established pioneer family. Elizabeth's father Charles Helt was from the early pioneer family that settled Helt Township. "Lizzie" was a first cousin to the mother of World War II correspondent Ernie Pyle.[1264] They lived in a log cabin that originally stood at the northeast corner of a large and more comfortable home that was built in 1896.[1265]

By 1900 Jediah and Elizabeth had six children living with them in Helt Township, Vermillion County.[1266] Elizabeth had borne seven children, but one had died. The census was taken on 1 June 1900, and Elizabeth had their eighth and last child Webb on 18 August 1900.[1267] In 1910 Jediah and Elizabeth lived with their seven surviving children on their farm in Helt Township, Vermillion County.[1268]

On 16 December 1930 there was a bank robbery in the city of Clinton, Indiana. The robbers headed north out of town turning west on what was known as the Summit Grove Road with the authorities in hot pursuit. They stopped in the road at the north side of Jediah's farm. Jediah was headed down the road, unaware of the excitement, when the robbers stopped him and took his vehicle. Unbeknownst to both Jediah and the robbers, a "governor" had been put on the car to keep it from "going too fast." The robbers were eventually caught on U.S. Highway 36, west of Dana, Indiana. Jediah's son Harlow, who had watched the event from a distance and hollered out to them about what was going on, later reported finding a bullet hole in his jacket.[1269]

Jediah was a grain and stock farmer as well as an auctioneer in Clinton. He had his own steam engineer and did custom threshing of grain for his friends, family, and neighbors. A "threshing dinner" after a hard day's work was good eating for everyone who participated.[1270]

Jediah also had a maple syrup camp on his farm. Older family members recall that he put an egg in the syrup while it was cooking, which was supposed to collect the debris from the syrup. Some remembered the eggs as being good while others thought they were too sweet.[1271]

Jediah was among those who helped establish the Methodist Hospital in Indianapolis and was on the board of trustees at Helt's Prairie Cemetery for many years. He and Elizabeth were members of Salem Methodist Episcopal Church, which later became the Salem United Methodist Church.[1272]

Elizabeth died in 1935 at their home in Dana of chronic myocarditis after a three-year illness.[1273] On 2 October 1938 Jediah's brother Samuel wrote to him from Yuma, Arizona, in response to several letters that Jediah had written.[1274] He spoke of several Frist family members including their "grandfather Jediah" and their "great grandparents Henry and Elizabeth Frist."

Jediah died in 1948 in Dana.[1275] He and his wife are buried in Helt's Prairie Cemetery in Vermillion County. Jediah and Elizabeth had eight children, all carefully entered in the Jediah Frist Family Bible with birth, death, and some marriage dates.[1276]

Children of Jediah[5] and Elizabeth (Helt) Frist, all born in Vermillion County, Indiana:

207   i. REN LESLIE[6] FRIST, born 16 June 1881; died 11 August 1955 Vermillion County Hospital, Clinton, Indiana; cement finisher and contractor in Dana, Indiana; buried Helt's Prairie, Vermillion County, Indiana; member Salem Methodist Church and the K. P. Lodge in Dana, Indiana;[1277] no issue.

208   ii. MYRTLE MARIA FRIST, born 20 October 1882; died 12 January 1974 El Paso, Texas, of cardiac arrest due to bilateral pneumonia and a ruptured duodenal ulcer;[1278] buried Restlawn Memorial Park, El Paso, Texas; graduated from Indiana Normal (now Indiana State University) and Arizona College. She was a school teacher;[1279] no issue.

209   iii. ESTHER PEARL FRIST, born 20 August 1885; died 17 August 1887 Vermillion County, Indiana; buried Helt's Prairie, Vermillion County, Indiana.[1280]

+ 210   iv. HARRY HOMER FRIST, born 30 November 1889; died 11 January 1983 Vermillion County, Indiana; married 19 February 1911 Coatesville, Hendricks County, Indiana, Mable Audrey Boyd.[1281]

+ 211   v. HARLOW PEIRCE FRIST, born 12 May 1891; died 12 March 1975 Vermillion County, Indiana;[1282] married 26 October 1919, Clinton, Vermillion County, Indiana, Helen Eliza Miller.[1283]

212   vi. MARY HAZEL FRIST, born 2 October 1894; died 23 July 1984 Carlsbad, New Mexico, of natural causes; buried Helt's Prairie, Vermillion County, Indiana; married 27 December 1952 Roswell, Chaves County, New Mexico, Hubert Harlan born 27 November 1902 Coatesville, Indiana, died 20 March 1981 Carlsbad, Eddy County, New Mexico, buried Carlsbad Cemetery, Carlsbad, New Mexico. Hazel was a school

teacher, and Hubert worked as a potash mine warehouseman. Hazel was the last survivor in her generation;[1284] no issue.

+   213   vii. MARSHALL ALBAN FRIST, born 1 March 1897; died 20 June 1966 Clinton, Vermillion County, Indiana;[1285] married 14 December 1919 Vermillion County, Indiana, Marjorie Blakesley.[1286]

     214   viii. WEBB FRIST, born 18 August 1900; died 27 October 1957 Indianapolis, Indiana, and buried Crown Hill Cemetery, Indianapolis, Indiana; married (1) Jessie and (2) Clara Jane. Webb was a construction contractor in Indianapolis and was survived by his wife Jane and two stepsons, *(a)* Clayton Stingley and *(b)* Ernest Brock, both of Indianapolis;[1287] no issue.

92. Jasper Nebeker[5] Frist (Jediah Rudolph[4], Jediah[3], Henry[2], Rudolph[1]) was born on 26 December 1863 in Vermillion County, Indiana, the son of Jediah Rudolph and Mary Johnson (Peirce) Frist.[1288] Jasper died 5 February 1934 in Vermillion County, Indiana.[1289] He married on 7 December 1890 in Vermillion County to **Etta Lee Lambert**, daughter of George M. and Melissa (Shapard) Lambert.[1290] Etta was born on 13 September 1870 in Vermillion County.[1291] She died on 6 January 1955 in Vermillion County, Indiana.[1292]

Jasper was a farmer and school teacher in his early years and later worked for N. C. Anderson in the grocery business. Still later he attended embalming school in Indianapolis. In 1887, still in his twenties, he founded the J. N. Frist Funeral Home in Clinton, Indiana, where he worked as a mortician.[1293] Like many other funeral homes then, the Frist Funeral Home doubled as a furniture store, a common occurrence in America before the turn of the century.[1294]

In 1900 Jasper and Etta lived in Clinton Township, Vermillion County.[1295] Their two children, Enid, age seven, and Don, age four, lived with them. Also living with them were Etta's widowed mother, Melissa, age fifty-nine, her two sisters Verda and Nellie, and Jasper's brother Frank. Frank was thirty years of age and working as a salesman in a dry goods store.

In the early 1900s, the Frist Funeral Home kept a white hearse that was drawn by white horses and reserved for women and children. Men had a black hearse that was pulled by black horses. The horses were also used for ambulance runs. The horses could tell when Jasper approached them whether it was an ambulance run or a funeral. If he was not hurried when harnessing them, the horses remained docile. If he approached hurriedly, the horses would prance with excitement in anticipation of the ambulance run.[1296]

Jasper was active in the community. He was a member of the Indiana State Board of Embalmers, serving in various capacities including that of president. He served as postmaster for the city of Clinton, Indiana, for nine years, as a member of the city council, and also as the Worshipful Master of his local Masonic lodge.[1297] In 1920 they lived in Clinton Township, Vermillion County, and Verda Lambert, identified as a sister-in-law, lived with them.[1298]

When Jasper died in 1934 after a relapse following an operation,[1299] his wife, Etta, and their daughter and son-in-law, Louis and Enid Lemstra, continued operating the Frist Funeral Home. Etta died in 1955 in Vermillion County.[1300] Both are buried in Roselawn Cemetery in Vigo County, Indiana. The Lemstras then operated the funeral home until their deaths.[1301]

Children of Jasper Nebeker[5] and Etta Lee (Lambert) Frist, both born in Vermillion County, Indiana:

215   i. ENID LAMBRETTA[6] FRIST, born 1 December 1892; died 7 October 1973, Vermillion County, Indiana; married 8 January 1921 Louis Jacob Lemstra born 13 June 1897 Grand Rapids, Michigan, died 6 November 1965; both buried Roselawn Cemetery, Vigo County, Indiana; part owners and active in the Frist Funeral Home.[1302] Enid was interested in genealogy and collected a lot of material about the Frist family. She was the national president of the Auxiliary of the American Legion; no issue.

216   ii. DONALD CARROL FRIST, born 15 May 1895; died 6 November 1959 Miguel de Allende, Mexico and is buried in Roselawn Cemetery, Vigo County, Indiana.[1303] He was a mortician who worked with the family at the Frist Funeral Home and also designed ladies apparel. He never married.

98. John Edgar[5] Frist (John[4], James[3], Henry[2], Rudolph[1]) was born 22 March 1854 in Baltimore City, Maryland, the son of John and Annie (James) Frist.[1304] John died 25 July 1912 in Baltimore County, Maryland.[1305] He married first on 4 April 1876 in Baltimore City, Maryland, to **Margaret Ann Arthur**.[1306] Margaret was born 9 July 1859 in Maryland, the daughter of John P. and Maria (Maroney) Arthur.[1307] Margaret died 19 February 1930 in Baltimore City, Maryland.[1308] John may have married second to **Emma D. Cooper**, who was born in December of 1863 in England.[1309]

On 4 July 1959, John was with the rest of his family when they went on a holiday picnic on the Susquehanna River in Cecil County, Maryland. When tragedy struck in the form of a boating accident, young John survived the accident that drowned his mother, brother, and sister.[1310] In 1870 he and his sister Eva lived with his father and stepmother in Baltimore City, Maryland.[1311] John's father was a coach maker, and young John Edgar at sixteen was following in his father's footsteps, working as a coach maker's apprentice.

John was working as a blacksmith in April of 1876 in Baltimore City, Maryland, when he married Margaret Ann Arthur, who was a shoe fitter of Baltimore City.[1312] In 1880 the two lived in their own home in Baltimore City, Maryland.[1313] John was a coach blacksmith and Margaret kept house and took care of their two children.

Their marriage was not a happy one and the first legal sign of trouble was on 24 December 1889, when they appeared in Baltimore City court on a bill of divorce, which was dismissed four days later.[1314]

From divorce papers filed much later, it was determined that John and Margaret went their separate ways about 1890.[1315] The date of their separation was their only area of agreement and exactly who abandoned whom remains uncertain.

In 1900 Margaret Frist was the head of her own household in Baltimore City, Maryland.[1316] She accurately listed herself as married and her occupation was nurse. Living with her were two of their three children, John A. Frist, age twenty-three, and Bessie Frist, age sixteen.

Her husband, John E. Frist, lived nearby with Emma D. Frist, who was thirty-six.[1317] John was a blacksmith, and the pair indicated they had been married for eleven years. This was wishful thinking on John's part, for he and Margaret were not yet divorced. One child had been born to John and Emma. Although no record of their marriage was found in Baltimore City or County, they could have easily married in a neighboring county or state.

Emma was born Emma Cooper, and she was from South Kensington, England, before her marriage.[1318] She came to America as a young girl and met John Edgar Frist in Baltimore.

On 30 November 1901 John sued Margaret Ann Frist for divorce, alleging that they were married on 4 April 1876 in Baltimore City and lived together until December 1889 when she abandoned him.[1319] He further indicated that they "have three children who are all of age." Margaret responded by denying that she deserted him, but stated instead that he had deserted her and "has been living in adultery with another woman" but has been contributing to her support and paying her house rent for eleven years until a month ago.

This petition was denied. A divorce decree was not granted until 7 April 1911 when Margaret filed against John on the grounds of abandonment in yet another lawsuit for divorce.[1320] Their daughter Annie L. Jamison testified in court regarding the divorce, stating that her parents separated in January of 1890. Annie said that her father "just went away and forgot to come back." At the time of the divorce in 1911, John lived on Homeland Avenue, Govans, Baltimore County, Maryland.

Less than two weeks after their divorce was final, John wrote his will on 19 April 1911 while living in "Govanstown," and it was probated just over a year later on 31 July 1912 in Baltimore County, Maryland.[1321] He left $100 to each of his children by his first wife Margaret—John Arthur Frist, "Anna May [*sic*] Jamison," and Bessie Gutman. He left the remainder of his estate to "my wife Emma" and appointed her executrix. He is buried in Mount Carmel Cemetery.[1322] His obituary described him as one of the best-known men in this locality and a wheelwright for fifteen years who died from paralysis due to Bright's disease.[1323] The information was obviously supplied by Emma, as only one surviving daughter (Emma's) was listed. She was Mrs. William P. Zink.

In 1920 Emma lived with her married daughter, Naomi Zink, in Baltimore County, Maryland.[1324] Emma was a fifty-six-year-old dressmaker who was born in England.

When John's first wife Margaret died in 1930 in Baltimore City, Maryland, her death certificate inaccurately listed her as the widow of John E. Frist.[1325] They had been divorced for almost twenty years. Margaret is buried in Loudon Park Cemetery in Baltimore City, Maryland, near her son, John Arthur Frist.[1326]

Children of John Edgar[5] and Margaret Ann (Arthur) Frist:

217   i. JOHN ARTHUR[6] FRIST, born about 1877;[1327] died 24 February 1936 Baltimore City, Maryland;[1328] married Sarah Smith born 15 August 1859[1329] daughter of Moses and Louisa (Bowen) Smith.[1330] She died 25 September 1930 Baltimore City, Maryland.[1331]

218   ii. ANNA LOUISE "ANNIE" FRIST, born about 1878;[1332] died 13 March 1939 Baltimore City, Maryland;[1333] married John Oliver Jamison,[1334] who died 22 November 1973 Baltimore, Maryland.[1335] One child, Violet Marie Jamison, born 8 September 1896 Baltimore, Maryland, died 15 November 1992 Baltimore City, Maryland. Violet married Edgar Heath Coney, who died 22 November 1973 in Baltimore City, Maryland (they had one child, Mrs. Robert [Jean] Taylor).[1336]

219   iii. BESSIE FRIST, born about 1884;[1337] married by April 1911 to Mr. Gutman.[1338]

Child of John Edgar[5] and Emma D. (Cooper) Frist:

220   iv. NAOMI FRIST, born September 1890; married about 1910 William P. Zink.[1339] Children, *(a)* William P. Zink, Jr. born 1912 and *(b)* Emma V. Zink born 1916, both in Baltimore City, Maryland.[1340]

101. Hattie M.[5] **Frist** (John[4], James[3], Henry[2], Rudolph[1]) was born 10 July 1869 in Baltimore City, Maryland, the daughter of John and Emily M. (Holt) Frist.[1341] Hattie died 9 December 1939 in Baltimore City, Maryland.[1342] She married about 1893 to **William Wirt Emmart**.[1343] William was born 7 May 1869, the son of Vernon S. and Eliza Jane (Hindes) Emmart.[1344] He died 31 December 1949 in Baltimore City, Maryland.[1345]

In 1870 Hattie lived with her parents in Ward 19 in Baltimore.[1346] Hattie was educated at Woman's Medical College of Baltimore and practiced medicine for several years prior to her marriage in a time frame when few women entered the profession.[1347] By 1900 Hattie had married, and the young couple with their two children lived with Hattie's parents in Baltimore City, Maryland.[1348]

William Wirt Emmart's father was in the mercantile business, but his grandfather had been an architect. William attended Baltimore public schools, was a student at Baltimore City College, and completed his professional training in architecture at the Maryland Institute.[1349] He began his career in 1900 with the firm of Ellicott and Emmart, branching out on his own in 1919. He was described as an architect "devoted to the improvement and ornamentation of Baltimore" and one who "is deeply interested in everything that tends to make Baltimore a more beautiful and desirable place of residence."[1350] Hattie's father John was described as "a representative of a pioneer family of Delaware."[1351]

Hattie died in 1939,[1352] and William followed her to the grave in 1949.[1353] Both are buried in Loudon Park Cemetery in Baltimore City, Maryland.

Children of William Wirt and Hattie M.⁵ (Frist) Emmart:

> 221   i. DOROTHY HOLT⁶ EMMART, born April 1896; married Ryland Newman Dempster. Two children, *(a)* Dorothy E. Dempster and *(b)* Ryland E. Dempster.[1354]
>
> 222   ii. EMILY WALCOTT EMMART, born August 1898; married by 1950 Charles Kingsley Trueblood, who died 1 November 1974 Baltimore, Maryland.[1355] Emily also became a doctor.[1356]

107. Abram Bernard⁵ Frist (Abraham B.⁴, James³, Henry², Rudolph¹) was born in 22 October 1861 in Monroe County, Virginia (now West Virginia), the son of Abraham B. and Julia (Myers) Frist.[1357] He died 11 March 1923 in Baltimore City, Maryland.[1358] He married first on 8 May 1882 in Cecil County, Maryland, to **Georgianna L. Zimmer**,[1359] who died by 1900.[1360] He married second on 17 June 1901 in Baltimore City, Maryland, to **Genevieve T. "Jennie" Quinn**.[1361] Jennie was born 17 July 1880 in Baltimore City, Maryland, the daughter of John and Mary (Cunningham) Quinn.[1362] Jennie died 1 July 1934 in Baltimore City, Maryland.[1363]

By 1870 Abram's family had moved from Virginia to Port Deposit, Cecil County, Maryland,[1364] and he remained living with them in 1880 in Port Deposit.[1365] Abram's marriage to Georgianna L. Zimmer in 1882 produced three children,[1366] but by 1900 Georgianna had died and Abram was the widowed head of the household in Baltimore City, Maryland.[1367] He was thirty-eight years of age and born in

West Virginia, an iron molder by profession. Three children by his deceased wife Georgiana lived with him.

In 1901 when he married in Baltimore City, Maryland, at Immaculate Conception Church to Genevieve "Jennie" T. Quinn, he was listed as born in Charleston, West Virginia.[1368] Another copy of the marriage record indicated that Abram was thirty-nine and a widower and Jennie was twenty-eight and single.[1369]

In 1920 Abram and Jennie lived in the City of Baltimore.[1370] Abram was listed as Bernard Frist, a carpenter, sixty years of age and born in Virginia. Jennie was fifty years of age.

Abram Bernard Frist died in 1923 in Baltimore City, Maryland, of a cerebral hemorrhage and was buried in Cedar Hill Cemetery.[1371] He was sixty-one years of age, formerly of Port Deposit, Maryland, and survived by his wife "Jennie T. Frist (nee Quinn)."[1372] His obituary requested that Charleston, West Virginia, newspapers should "please copy." Jennie died in 1934 in Baltimore City, Maryland.[1373] Her funeral was held at the home of her daughter Margaret Behnken and burial was at Cathedral Cemetery.[1374]

Children of Abram Bernard[5] and Georgianna L. (Zimmer) Frist:

> 223   i. EMMA MAY[6] FRIST, born 14 May 1882 Baltimore City, Maryland;[1375] died 16 September 1964 Baltimore City, Maryland, and buried Loudon Park Cemetery, Baltimore City, Maryland; married Henry Heer born 28 February 1882 Maryland son of Charles and Caroline (Glaeser) Heer. One child who died in infancy.[1376]

> +   224   ii. ESTELLA ELIZABETH "STELLA" FRIST, born about November 1884 Maryland;[1377] died 10 April 1974 Talbot County, Maryland, and buried Easton, Maryland; married Harry H. Lyons.[1378]

> 225   iii. JULIA O. FRIST, born about December 1887 Maryland;[1379] married John J. Cox born about 1892 in Maryland. One child, Estella Elizabeth "Little Stell" Cox, born about 1915 Maryland.[1380]

Children of Abram Bernard[5] and Genevieve T. (Quinn) Frist:

> 226   iv. MELVIN BERNARD FRIST, born 26 June 1902 Baltimore, Maryland; died 31 December 1974 Baltimore, Maryland, buried New Cathedral Cemetery;[1381] married Margaret W. died 15 May 1993 also buried New Cathedral Cemetery; lived at 2826 Roselawn Avenue in Baltimore and worked for Montgomery Ward on 25 November 1936 when he applied for a Social Security number.[1382]

> 227   v. MARGARET THERESA FRIST, born 22 February 1904 Baltimore, Maryland; married by 6 July 1934 William Behnken[1383] born 1901 died 198?; no issue.[1384]

228   vi. DONNELLY FRIST, born 12 April 1907 Baltimore, Maryland; died 26 January 1972 Baltimore City, Maryland, and buried New Cathedral Cemetery.[1385] Donnelly was a physical education teacher who taught boxing. He served in the United States Army Air Corps during World War II and was a "S. Sgt retired" at the time of his death.[1386]

229   vii. GENEVIEVE FRIST, born 28 December 1908 Baltimore, Maryland; married (1) to a man named Tom and (2) to Gilbert Reed born 1894 died 16 April 1968; no issue.[1387]

+   230   viii. DOLORES MARY FRIST, born 10 June 1910 Baltimore, Maryland; died 19 February 1996 Edgewood, Harford County, Maryland; married 12 June about the year 1929, Joseph Klima.[1388]

+   231   ix. CASPER BERNARD FRIST, born 1 December 1914 Baltimore City, Maryland; died 28 May 1953 Baltimore County, Maryland; married 18 September 1936 Baltimore City, Maryland, Elenora Helen Pronek.[1389]

109. Hattie Mary[5] Frist (Abraham B.[4], James[3], Henry[2], Rudolph[1]) was born 10 May 1870 in Port Deposit, Cecil County, Maryland, the youngest child of Abraham B. and Julia (Myers) Frist.[1390] Hattie died on 30 July 1930 Baltimore City, Maryland, and is buried in Loudon Park Cemetery in Baltimore City, Maryland.[1391] She married about the year 1886 to **George F. Mohrlein**, who was born in Maryland about February of 1864.[1392]

In 1880 Hattie lived with her parents in Port Deposit, Cecil County, Maryland.[1393] By 1900 she had married George Mohrlein, and the two lived in Cecil County, Maryland, next door to her stepfather and mother, Harmon and Julia Harris.[1394] By 1920 Hattie, her husband George, and their three children had moved to Baltimore City, Maryland.[1395]

Children of George F. and Hattie Mary[5] (Frist) Mohrlein, probably all born in Cecil County, Maryland:

232   i. VERNA L.[6] MOHRLEIN, born about April 1891.[1396]

233   ii. CASPER G. MOHRLEIN, born about May 1895.[1397]

234   iii. JULIA MOHRLEIN, born about 1904.[1398]

111. Burton Kyle[5] Frist (Thomas Lyttle[4], James[3], Henry[2], Rudolph[1]) was born 17 April 1856[1399] in Maryland, the son of Thomas Lyttle and Sarah Elizabeth Frist.[1400] He died 27 November 1923 in Kanawha County, West Virginia.[1401] Burton married about 1877,[142] to **Virginia Wilson**.[1403] Virginia was born 4 October 1851,[1404] the daughter of Andrew A. and Rebecca (Frame) Wilson.[1405] She died 16 January 1916 in Kanawha County, West Virginia.[1406]

In 1860 Burton lived with his parents in Monroe County, Virginia, now a part of West Virginia.[1407] In 1880 Burton was enumerated twice in the census. He was listed in the household of his widowed mother Sarah in Kanawha County, West Virginia, as a twenty-four-year-old son born in Maryland.[1408]

In the second enumeration, Burton was the head of his own household in Kanawha County, living just a few households from his mother and his siblings.[1409] Living with him was his wife, Virginia, and their two children, Ida D. and Walter B. Oddly, Burton was listed as born in Germany, and the two children were listed with a father born in Germany. Virginia's father was the sexton at Spring Hill Cemetery in Charleston, a job that was inherited by her brother Thomas after the death of their father.[1410]

In 1900 Burton and Virginia lived in Kanawha County, West Virginia, next door to his mother, Sarah Frist.[1411] Burton was forty-five years of age and correctly shown as born in Maryland. Virginia was forty-eight and they had been married twenty-two years. Virginia had borne seven children, and six were still living. Six of the seven children have been identified.

When Virginia died in 1916, she was buried in Spring Hill Cemetery in Charleston, Kanawha County, West Virginia.[1412] In 1920 Burton owned a mortgaged home in Charleston, Kanawha County, West Virginia.[1413] His occupation was cemetery sexton. Living with him were two adult children, Fred W., age thirty-six, and Gertrude, age twenty-three.

Burton died in 1923 and was buried next to his wife in Spring Hill Cemetery in Charleston.[1414]

Children of Burton Kyle[5] and Virginia (Wilson) Frist, all born in West Virginia:

235   i.   IDA D.[6] FRIST, born about November 1878.[1415]

236   ii. WALTER B. FRIST, born about 1879; died 1881 Kanawha County, West Virginia, buried Spring Hill Cemetery 7 September 1881.[1416]

237   iii. EDWARD FRIST, born about December 1887; died 1923 Kanawha County, West Virginia, and buried Spring Hill Cemetery.[1417]

238   iv. FRED WILBUR FRIST, born 3 October 1888;[1418] died 16 January 1923 and buried Kanawha County, West Virginia.[1419]

239   v. HOWARD FRIST, born about October 1889.[1420]

240   vi. GERTRUDE REBECCA FRIST, born 2 November 1890;[1421] died 28 January 1956 and buried Kanawha County, West Virginia.[1422]

116. Thomas Jackson[5] Frist (Thomas Lyttle[4], James[3], Henry[2], Rudolph[1]) was born in September of 1869 in West Virginia, the son of Thomas Lyttle and Sarah Elizabeth Frist.[1423] He died 14 April 1925 in Kanawha County, West Virginia.[1424] He married about the year 1906 to **Laura Jane Chapman**.[1425]

In 1880 Thomas lived with his widowed mother Sarah in Kanawha County, West Virginia,[1426] and twenty years later in 1900 he remained at home in Kanawha County with his mother.[1427]

By 1920 he had married to Laura, and they lived in Charleston, Kanawha County, West Virginia.[1428] Thomas owned a home free of mortgage and his occupation was proprietor of a grocery store.

Children of Thomas Jackson[5] and Laura Jane (Chapman) Frist:

> 241   i. ROY THOMAS[6] FRIST, born 27 April 1907 Charleston, Kanawha County, West Virginia.[1429]
>
> 242   ii. LUCILLE C. FRIST, born 27 September 1908 Charleston, Kanawha County, West Virginia.[1430]
>
> 243   iii. NEVA M. FRIST, born about 1911.[1431]

120. George Edmund[5] Frist (Edmund Physick[4], James[3], Henry[2], Rudolph[1]) was born on 22 December 1863 in Port Deposit, Cecil County, Maryland, the son of Edmund Physick and Mary Jane (Haines) Frist.[1432] He married about the year 1885 to **Henrietta McCullough**, who was born in 1868, also in Maryland.[1433]

In 1870 George lived with his parents in Cecil County, Maryland.[1434] By 1900 he had married Henrietta, and they lived in Cecil County, Maryland, next door to his parents.[1435] He was thirty-five years of age and a machinist. Henrietta was thirty-three, had borne seven children, and five were still living. All five surviving children lived with them.

By 1920 George and Henrietta had moved to Delaware County, Pennsylvania, to live with their son-in-law Alfred M. Miller and their daughter Clara.[1436] They were both listed in the census as aged fifty-two, although George was actually fifty-seven. They were born in Maryland of parents born in Maryland. George was a millwright in a sawmill. Their three youngest children lived with them.

Children of George Edmund[5] and Henrietta (McCullough) Frist:

> 244   i. ESTELLA M.[6] FRIST, born about March 1887;[1437] married William Feathers.[1438]
>
> 245   ii. ETHEL B. FRIST, born about January 1891;[1439] married William Knox; no issue.[1440]
>
> 246   iii. CLARA J. FRIST, born about January 1894;[1441] married Cecil County, Maryland, Alfred Miller. Children, *(a)* Earl B. Miller born 1914, *(b)* Estella E. Miller born 1916, and *(c)* Ernest L. Miller born 1917.[1442]
>
> 247   iv. ROBERT F. LEWIS FRIST, born 7 September 1897 Philadelphia, Pennsylvania; died January 1967 probably in Darby, Delaware County, Pennsylvania.[1443] On 30 November 1936 he applied for a Social

Security number while living in Darby, Delaware County, Pennsylvania;[1444] married about 1917 Mary born 1895 Pennsylvania. One child, Dorothy J. Frist, born 1918.[1445]

248   v. SIDNEY B. FRIST, born about April 1900;[1446] married after 1920 Earl Waddell. Children, *(a)* Leona Waddell, *(b)* Gladys Waddell, *(c)* Robert Waddell. In 1920 Sidney was glassblower at Drug Manufacturing Company.

249   vi. OLIVER ELWOOD FRIST, born about 1902.[1447] In 1920 Oliver was a millwright in sawmill.

250   vii. RAYMOND PRESLEY FRIST, born 18 December 1903 Port Deposit, Cecil County, Maryland; died 23 November 1983 probably in Darby, Delaware County, Pennsylvania;[1448] married Florence Mae Smith.[1449] In 1936 he worked for the Supplee-Willis-Jones Milk Company in Darby, Pennsylvania, and lived at 11120 Walnut Street in Collingdale, Pennsylvania, when he applied for a Social Security number.[1450] Two children, *(a)* Raymond Frist, Jr. and *(b)* Wallace Philip Frist born 17 September 1929 Ridley Park, Delaware County, Pennsylvania,[1451] and died 30 July 1999 Folsom, Delaware County, Pennsylvania.[1452]

121. Garrison James[5] Frist (Edmund Physick[4], James[3], Henry[2], Rudolph[1]) was born on 1 September 1865 in Cecil County, Maryland, the son of Edmund Physick and Mary Jane (Haines) Frist.[1453] He died by 1920, presumably in Cleveland, Ohio.[1454] He married about the year 1898 to **Pearl C. Updegrove**, who was born in Ohio in April 1873.[1455]

In 1870 Garrison lived with his parents in Cecil County, Maryland.[1456] By 1900 Garrison had met and married his wife Pearl, and they lived with her parents, Edmund B. and Jennie E. Updegrove, in Cuyahoga County, Ohio.[1457] They had only been married two years and had no children. Garrison and his wife's brother-in-law Ernest Ely, who also lived with the Updegroves, were listed as the owners of a bakery and their father-in-law Edmund Updegrove worked as a clerk in the bakery.

Garrison died by 1920, and the widow Pearl lived with her father, Edmund Updegrove, in Cleveland, Ohio.[1458] The bakery was apparently a thing of the past since her father Edmund listed no occupation and Pearl worked as a bookkeeper. Two grandchildren lived with Edmund, Mildred Updegrove, age twenty, who was a school teacher, and Pearl's son, Phillip Frist, age ten.

Child of Garrison James[5] and Pearl C. (Updegrove) Frist:

251   i. PHILLIP E.[6] FRIST, born 7 September 1908 Cleveland, Ohio; married Lorette Bourgious.[1459] Children, *(a)* Norbert Leo Frist born 19 January 1936 Putnam, Connecticut[1460] (who had a daughter Lynn Frist born in

1972),[1461] *(b)* Roger B. Frist,[1462] *(c)* Pearl Frist, who married an Erickson,[1463] *(d)* Mary Frist, who married a Ward,[1464] and *(e)* Elizabeth Frist, who married a Pasapia.[1465]

122. Sidney Marietta[5] "Etta" Frist (Edmund Physick[4], James[3], Henry[2], Rudolph[1]) was born on 26 March 1868[1466] in Cecil County, Maryland, the daughter of Edmund Physick and Mary Jane (Haines) Frist. Sidney died 5 October 1938 in Cecil County, Maryland.[1467] She married 25 July 1886 in Cecil County, Maryland, to **George Elim Tyson**.[1468] George was born 14 December 1862,[1469] the son of John Benjamin and Sarah Elizabeth (Gillespie) Tyson.[1470] He died 19 February 1942 at Port Deposit, Cecil County, Maryland.[1471]

In 1900 George and Sidney lived in Cecil County, Maryland.[1472] They had been married fourteen years, and Sidney had borne seven children, five of whom were still living. All five of those children lived with them. George's occupation was farmer, and he owned a mortgaged farm.

On 23 March 1901, George Tyson and his brother-in-law John Cresswell Frist purchased 134¼ acres of land in Cecil County, Maryland, from Sarah E. Fisher for $2600.[1473] On 20 October 1903, George E. and Sidney E. Tyson sold their interest in the land to John C. Frist for $300.[1474]

By 1920 George and Sidney had paid off the mortgage on their farm in Cecil County.[1475] Four of their children lived with them, Elizabeth, Rowland C., Harold E., and Martin M.

Sidney died in 1938 in Cecil County, Maryland.[1476] She was an active member of the Ladies Aid and for over fifty years a faithful member of the Hopewell Methodist Church. George died a few years later in 1942 at Port Deposit, Cecil County, Maryland.[1477] Both are buried in Hopewell United Methodist Church Cemetery in Cecil County, Maryland.

Children of George Elim and Sidney Marietta[5] (Frist) Tyson, all born in Cecil County, Maryland:

+   252   i. LULA MAY[6] TYSON, born 1 May 1887; died 2 June 1975 Cecil County, Maryland;[1478] married 14 January 1908 Samuel James Churchman.[1479]

+   253   ii. JOHN EARL TYSON, born 28 August 1888; died 26 March 1960 Cecil County, Maryland;[1480] married 7 October 1908 in Cecil County, Maryland, Ella Elizabeth Tosh.[1481]

      254   iii. ROY LESLIE TYSON, born 3 May 1890; died 9 April 1891; buried Hopewell United Methodist Church Cemetery, Port Deposit, Cecil County, Maryland.[1482]

      255   iv. MARY EVA TYSON, born 5 March 1892;[1483] married John Clarence Bell born 25 April 1887 died 6 September 1970 Cecil County, Maryland.[1484]

One son John Cyril Bell born 2 October 1913 and died 28 November 1935 Cecil County, Maryland.[1485] They lived in Glenolden, Pennsylvania, in 1938.[1486]

256 v. LILAH ISABELLE TYSON, born 24 February 1895; died 19 March 1897 Cecil County, Maryland.[1487]

257 vi. SARA ELIZABETH TYSON, born 1 December 1896; died January 1991 Cecil County, Maryland; never married.[1488]

+ 258 vii. PEARL CATHARINE TYSON, born 9 March 1899; died 26 February 1981 Cecil County, Maryland;[1489] married 23 February 1918 Cecil County, Maryland, Charles Ellis Astle.[1490]

259 viii. ROLAND CRESSWELL TYSON, born 26 April 1901; died 2 November 1923 Cecil County, Maryland, in hunting accident.[1491]

+ 260 ix. HAROLD EDWARD TYSON, born 10 February 1903;[1492] died 3 December 1969 Cecil County, Maryland;[1493] married about 1923 Esther Ann Astle.[1494]

+ 261 x. MARTIN MOORE TYSON, born 30 March 1905; died 9 November 1987 Cecil County, Maryland;[1494] married 7 July 1928 Cecil County, Maryland, Frances Evelyn Jackson.[1496]

123. Oscar Haines[5] Frist (Edmund Physick[4], James[3], Henry[2], Rudolph[1]) was born on 11 September 1870, in Cecil County, Maryland, the son of Edmund Physick and Mary Jane (Haines) Frist.[1497] He died on 20 July 1936 in Cecil County, Maryland.[1498] He married 27 November 1901 in Cecil County, Maryland, to **Ella McDowell**.[1499] Ella was born in 1880 and died on 8 May 1937 in Cecil County, Maryland.[1500]

In 1900 Oscar lived at home with his parents in Cecil County, Maryland.[1501] He married in 1901, and by 1920 Oscar and his wife, Ella, lived in Cecil County, Maryland, with their four surviving children.[1502] He was a blacksmith.

Oscar died in 1936 and was buried in Hopewell United Methodist Church Cemetery in Cecil County, Maryland.[1503] His widow Ella wrote her will in November of 1936, and it was probated in Cecil County, Maryland, on 25 August 1937.[1504] Ella named her son Joseph and daughters Mary F. Lauver and Letitia Farmer, who were her only surviving children.

Children of Oscar Haines[5] and Ella (McDowell) Frist, all born in Cecil County, Maryland:

+ 262 i. JOSEPH OSMOND[6] FRIST, born 11 March 1903; died 6 November 1979 Meadville, Crawford County, Pennsylvania;[1505] married 1929 Blanche Lucille Ramsey.[1506]

263 ii. CHARLES E. FRIST, born 2 August 1905; died 17 September 1926 Cecil County, Maryland; no issue.[1507]

264 iii. JAMES R. FRIST, born 16 April 1907; died 28 October 1907.[1508]

265 iv. ERNEST H. FRIST, born 4 March 1909; died 5 July 1913.[1509] He died at age four after setting his clothes on fire while playing with matches.[1510]

266 v. MARY JANE FRIST, born 1911, died 1983; married William C. Lauver.[1511]

267 vi. LETITIA FRIST, born 1915; died 1978 Cecil County, Maryland; married Clyde Farmer born 1913.[1512] Children, (a) William Farmer and (b) Betty Farmer.[1513]

124. John Cresswell[5] Frist (Edmund Physick[4], James[3], Henry[2], Rudolph[1]) was born on 17 August 1872 in Cecil County, Maryland, the son of Edmund Physick and Mary Jane (Haines) Frist.[1514] John died in July 1945 in Cecil County, Maryland.[1515] He married 31 January 1914 in Cecil County, Maryland, to **Olive A. Campbell**.[1516] Olive was born on 1 January 1896 in Port Deposit, Maryland, the daughter of Oliver and Sarah (Fisher) Campbell.[1517] She died in November 1982 in Cecil County, Maryland.[1518]

In 1900 John lived at home with his parents in Cecil County, Maryland.[1519] On 23 March 1901 John Cresswell Frist and his brother-in-law George E. Tyson purchased 134 1/4 acres of land in Cecil County, Maryland, from Sarah E. Fisher for $2600.[1520] On 20 October 1903 John bought George E. and Sidney E. Tyson's interest in the land for $300.[1521]

By 1920 John had married Olive, and they lived in Cecil County, Maryland.[1522] John was a farmer, forty-six years of age, and Olive was twenty-four years old. They owned their farm, and their first two children, Sterling and Willard, lived with them.

John wrote his will on 17 September 1932 and it was probated on 10 August 1945 in Cecil County, Maryland.[1523] He left his entire estate to his wife during her widowhood and named their three sons. John died in 1945, and Olive lived another thirty-seven years, dying in 1982. They are buried in Hopewell United Methodist Church Cemetery in Port Deposit, Cecil County, Maryland.[1524]

Children of John Cresswell[5] and Olive A. (Campbell) Frist, all born in Cecil County, Maryland:

+ 268 i. DELBERT STERLING[6] FRIST, born 28 January 1912; died 24 May 1984 Cecil County Maryland; married 21 June 1943 Cecil County, Maryland, Florence "Floss" Worth.[1525]

+ 269 ii. JOHN WILLARD "BUSS" FRIST, born 14 November 1914; died June 1965 in Oklahoma City, Oklahoma;[1526] married 3 July 1937 Cecil County, Maryland, Willa Alverta Tarbert.[1527]

+ 270 iii. DONALD RUSSELL FRIST, born 7 February 1922;[1528] married

(1) 6 October 1945 Cecil County, Maryland, Doris V. Tome and

(2) 6 January 1989 Cecil County, Maryland, Elizabeth Ann Slauch.

125. Oliver T.[5] Frist (Edmund Physick[4], James[3], Henry[2], Rudolph[1]) was born on 9 July 1875 in Cecil County, Maryland, the son of Edmund Physick[3] and Mary Jane (Haines) Frist.[1529] He died in December of 1935 in Cecil County, Maryland.[1530] He married on 20 January 1901 to **Florence Gertrude Harrison** in Baltimore City, Maryland.[1531] Florence was born in 1879,[1532] the daughter of John T. and Phoebe Rebecca (Plummer) Harrison and the granddaughter of James H. and Sarah Ann Plummer of Baltimore City, Maryland.[1533] She died 26 May 1957 in Oxford, Chester County, Pennsylvania.[1534]

In 1900 Oliver lived at home with his parents in Cecil County, Maryland.[1535] He married in 1901 to Florence Gertrude Harrison in Baltimore City, Maryland.[1536] When Florence's mother Sarah Ann Plummer died intestate on 28 March 1907 in Baltimore City, Maryland, her husband, James H. Plummer, survived her, and a lawsuit filed in Baltimore County identified all of Florence's aunts, uncles, and siblings.[1537]

In 1920 Oliver and Florence lived in Baltimore City, Maryland.[1538] Oliver was forty-four and worked as a machinist in a machine shop. Florence was forty. They rented their home, which was half of a double. Their son, Garrison, who was nineteen years of age, did not live with them.

Oliver wrote his will on 24 December 1934, and it was probated 3 January 1936 in Cecil County, Maryland.[1539] He left everything to his wife, Florence Gertrude Frist, without mentioning their son.

Oliver and Florence are both buried in Hopewell United Methodist Cemetery in Port Deposit, Cecil County, Maryland.[1540] They share a tombstone in the cemetery where their son and daughter-in-law are also buried.[1541]

Child of Oliver T.[5] and Florence Gertrude (Harrison) Frist:

+ 271 i. GARRISON KENNETH[6] FRIST, born 15 September 1901 Maryland;

died 24 May 1928 Port Deposit, Cecil County, Maryland;[1542] married

2 September 1922 Harford County, Maryland, Mary Susan Kirk.[1543]

126. Homer[5] Frist (George[4], Joel[3], Henry[2], Rudolph[1]) was born in 9 June 1878, in Wilmington, New Castle County, Delaware,[1544] the only child of George and Catherine A. (Simmons) Frist.[1545] Homer probably died by 8 May 1934.[1546] He married on 24 June 1901 to **Mary Harkins**,[1547] who was born in 1884 in Delaware[1548] and died after 8 May 1934.[1549]

In 1880 Homer was two years old and lived with his parents in the household of his paternal grandparents in Wilmington Hundred, New Castle County, Delaware.[1550] In 1900 Homer remained single and lived at home with his parents in Wilmington, Delaware.[1551]

In September of 1918, Homer and his wife, Mary, lived at 1815 Delaware Avenue in Wilmington, and he was employed as a street railway conductor. He was described as of medium height and build with blue eyes and sandy hair.[1552]

In 1920 Homer and Mary rented a home at 1815 Delaware Avenue in Wilmington.[1553] Their seventeen-year-old daughter, Margaret, lived with them. Living nearby was the Wallis family, whose son Joseph was to marry Margaret in 1926.[1554]

In 1930 Homer and his eighty-year-old mother Catherine lived together in Homer's house on Lancaster Avenue in Wilmington, Delaware.[1555] Both were listed as married, rather than widowed or divorced. Catherine was a widow and Homer had a wife, but she was not living in their household.

Homer probably died by 8 May 1934, when his mother wrote her will in New Castle County, Delaware, making a bequest to her daughter-in-law Mary Harkins Frist.[1556]

Child of Homer[5] and Mary (Harkins) Frist:

272   i. MARGARET HELENA[6] FRIST, born 17 June 1902 Wilmington, New Castle County, Delaware;[1557] died May 1973 Concordville, Delaware County, Pennsylvania;[1558] married 16 June 1926 New Castle County, Delaware, Joseph Hendel Wallis, son of Francis A. and Catherine (Hendel) Wallis, who was manager of an ice company.[1559] Children, both born in Wilmington, New Castle County, Delaware, *(a)* Joan Helene Wallis born 8 August 1929 married 14 June 1952 Carroll Draper Hauptle born 31 July 1923 Landsdowne, Pennsylvania (they had Mary Elizabeth Hauptle born 9 March 1953; Carroll Draper Hauptle, Jr. born 18 August 1954; Richard Simon Hauptle born 29 December 1960; and Nancy Katherine Hauptle born 1 November 1962, all born in Wilmington, Delaware)[1560] and *(b)* Joseph Hendel Wallis, Jr. born 27 September 1932.[1561] Joan (Wallis) Hauptle, her husband, Carroll, and her brother, Joseph, were all graduates of the University of Delaware.

127. Anna Elizabeth[5] a.k.a. Ann Eliza Frist (Robert Harris[4], Jacob Chester[3], Henry[2], Rudolph[1]) was born 3 January 1878 in Newport, New Castle County, Delaware, the daughter of Robert Harris and Elizabeth Rachel (Nebeker) Frist.[1562] She died in New Castle County, Delaware, on 29 July 1964.[1563] She married on 28 November 1900 in New Castle County to **John Hilton Foard**.[1564] John was born

9 May 1869, the seventh of nine children born to Eli and Mary E. (Billingsly) Foard.[1565] He died 8 September 1943 in New Castle County.[1566]

Anna met John Hilton Foard at the grocery store where he worked in Newport, Delaware. He lived in a room above the store. One night when the store caught on fire, John had to jump from his room window wearing his "long johns."[1567] After their marriage in 1900 in New Castle County, they lived with Anna's parents for several years.[1568]

John bought the store in Marshallton from Mrs. George Spicer[1569] and commuted from Newport by horse and wagon. It was located at the southwest corner of Newport Road and Washington Avenue opposite the Marshallton elementary school. It was a two-story building of brick and frame construction with a brick-floored porch across the front. There were hitching posts in front and two signs, one proclaiming "JH FOARD" and the other "POST OFFICE."

On the wall to the right of the front door was a slate that served as a call board for the local doctor. When there was sickness in the family, the name was listed on the slate. After checking the slate, the doctor would call upon the sick person. Patrons could find everything necessary for a rural country store including food, candy, hardware, seeds for planting, feed for stock, clothing, fabric, medicine, and veterinary supplies.[1570]

In 1920 they lived in New Castle County.[1571] John and his son John worked in the family store. Customers charged their groceries and during the Depression, accounts were carried for some time when customers couldn't pay.[1572]

John Hilton Foard wrote his will on 17 November 1938 and died in 1943 in New Castle County.[1573] He left land in Marshallton to his son Franklin and the land with his store and other buildings in Marshallton to his son John Hilton. He left a house to his daughter, Anna Roberta Foard Smith, and divided another bequest among the three of them. He left the residue of his estate to his widow Anna E. Foard.

Shortly after John Hilton Foard, Sr.'s death, their son John Hilton died on 17 June 1944 while serving in Italy in the United States Army.[1574] John had entered the service in May of 1942, serving in a commando division of the 141st Infantry of the Fifth Army. He survived the battles of Tunisia, Salerno, and Anzio, but was killed during the march to Northern Italy.[1575] His sister Anna Smith lived in Maplewood, New Jersey, at the time of his death, and his brother lived in Charleston, West Virginia. His estate amounted to $8,400, which included the combination store and dwelling house inherited from his father.

The family store was sold after the death of their son and the building was taken down.[1576] Anna did a lot of charity work and also served as president of the local PTA organization. She rented her home in Newport and used the money to purchase books that she lent to neighbors and friends in Marshalltown.[1577]

Anna resided at the Chariot Nursing Home in Wilmington until her death in New Castle County, Delaware, in 1964.[1578] She had written her will on 17 September 1956. Her heirs were listed as Franklin P. Foard of 700 Zee Street, Martinsville, Virginia, and Anna Roberta Smith of 36 N. Crescent, Maplewood, New Jersey.

Children of John Hilton and Anna Elizabeth[5] (Frist) Foard, all born in New Castle County, Delaware:

273 i. ELIZABETH MAY[6] FOARD, born 4 June 1902;[1579] died 26 October 1918 of flu;[1580] won the state spelling bee and received a silver trophy cup; no issue.

274 ii. HILDA LOUISE FOARD, born 26 March 1905;[1581] died 12 August 1924 from flu complications;[1582] she was an organist at the Episcopal Church; no issue.

+ 275 iii. ANNA ROBERTA FOARD, born 13 September 1907;[1583] died 5 January 1998 in Hightstown, Mercer County, New Jersey; married 4 July 1931 James Henry Smith.[1584]

276 iv. JOHN HILTON FOARD, born 3 February 1910;[1585] died 17 June 1944 in Italy during WWII;[1586] no issue.

+ 277 v. FRANKLIN PEACH FOARD, born 3 June 1912; married 21 August 1937 New Castle County, Delaware, Margaret Jane "Peg" Hubert.[1587]

128. John Nebeker[5] Frist (Robert Harris[4], Jacob Chester[3], Henry[2], Rudolph[1]) was born 30 March 1881 in New Castle County, Delaware, the son of Robert Harris and Elizabeth Rachel (Nebeker) Frist.[1588] He died 9 April 1947 in Newport, New Castle County, Delaware.[1589] John married on 27 January 1904 in New Castle County to **Carrie Currender**.[1590] Carrie was born near Newport, New Castle County, Delaware, on 15 January 1883, the daughter of Charles W. and Laura (Smith) Currender, both of New Castle County, Delaware.[1591] She died 3 October 1946 in New Castle County, Delaware.[1592]

In 1900 John lived with his parents in Christiana Hundred, New Castle County, Delaware.[1593] He was seventeen years of age and an apprentice pattern maker.

By 1910 John had married to Carrie, and they lived next door to John's widowed mother in Newport.[1594] They were both twenty-six years of age, had been married for six years, and were the parents of two children. John's occupation was pattern maker at a shipyard.

In September of 1918 when John registered for the draft, he gave his occupation as carpenter and his employer as Hance Nebeker, his uncle.[1595] John was described as of medium height and build with blue eyes and black hair.

In 1920 John and Carrie lived in New Castle County with their son Robert, age fifteen, and a niece, Bessie Grose.[1596]

Carrie died in 1946 of chronic glomerulus and nephritis and was buried at St. James Methodist Episcopal Church Cemetery in Newport, Delaware.[1597] They were living at 2 East Justis Street in Newport at that time, which is located right behind the cemetery.

John died in 1947 in Newport, New Castle County, Delaware, of pulmonary embolism and phlebitis of the left leg.[1598] His occupation was caretaker of St. James Newport Cemetery. His probate record in New Castle County indicated that he owned a residence valued at $3000 at 211 E. Market Street in Newport, Delaware, where his son Robert C. Frist lived.[1599] He was buried in St. James Newport Cemetery in Newport, Delaware, beside his wife.

Children of John Nebeker[5] and Carrie (Currender) Frist:

278   i. ROBERT CURRENDER[6] FRIST, born 2 July 1904 Newport, New Castle County, Delaware;[1600] died 31 December 1969 Wilmington, New Castle County, Delaware;[1601] married by 1936 to Helen Kathryn Casey, who was born 9 July 1901 in Philadelphia, Pennsylvania, the daughter of William Anthony and Mame (O'Conner) Casey.[1602] In 1936 Robert lived at 2 Justice Street in Newport and worked at Newport Fencing Company located nearby at 3 Justice Street.[1603] He later worked for the Pullman Company. From 1958 until his death he was chauffeur for Irene du Pont. Robert was buried in Lawncroft Cemetery in Linwood, Pennsylvania.[1604]

279   ii. MARGARET W. FRIST, born about 1909;[1605] probably died young, not with family in the 1920 census.

132. Bertie L.[5] Frist (James Ball[4], Jacob Chester[3], Henry[2], Rudolph[1]) was born in June 1889 in Chattanooga, Hamilton County, Tennessee, the daughter of James Ball and Permelia (Corbin) Frist.[1606] Bertie died on 16 May 1959 in St. Elmo near Chattanooga.[1607] She married on 20 September 1911 to **William Calvin Hartman**, who was born on 18 October 1870, the son of John Hartman.[1608] William died on 12 July 1917.[1609]

In 1900 Bertie lived with her parents in Civil District 4 of Hamilton County, Tennessee.[1610] Her husband, William Hartman, died in 1917 only six years after their marriage in 1911. By 1930 Bertie and her son Roy lived on the family farm with her widowed mother and her brother in Hamilton County, Tennessee.[1611] Bertie died in 1959 at the residence of her son Roy Hartman in St. Elmo, Tennessee, near Chattanooga.[1612]

Children of William Calvin and Bertie L.[5] (Frist) Hartman:

280   i. JOHN[6] HARTMAN, born 15 August 1912;[1613] died young, probably by 1917.[1614]

+   281   ii. ROY FRIST HARTMAN, born 2 May 1915[1615] Chattanooga, Hamilton
                  County, Tennessee; married 8 May 1934, Miriam Houts.[1616]

139. John Stanley[5] **Vetter** (Ann Elizabeth[4] Frist, Jacob Chester[3], Henry[2], Rudolph[1]) was born in 1890, the son of William and Ann Elizabeth (Frist) Vetter.[1617] He died 16 June 1929 in Chattanooga, Hamilton County, Tennessee.[1618] He married about 1926[1619] to **Effie Roselle Bird**, who was born 26 April 1896 in Lenoir County, North Carolina, the daughter of Louis Abner and Minnie Madora (Nunn) Bird.[1620] She died on 26 January 1965 at Mount Olive, Wayne County, North Carolina.[1621]

In 1920 John was thirty years of age and lived at home with his widowed mother, along with his brother and sister, in Walker County, Georgia.[1622]

On 15 June 1929 John sat up all night with his brother Robert, who was hospitalized in Chattanooga with pneumonia. When John came home on 16 June 1929, he went into their guest room to rest from the experience. Later that day his wife, Roselle, found him dead. Both brothers died in Chattanooga, Hamilton County, Tennessee, on the same day.[1623] John was a tinner by occupation and lived at 505 Baldwin Street in Chattanooga at the time of his death.[1624]

Their sister Willmary and John's widow Roselle arranged for a double funeral. John was buried in Mount Olive, Wayne County, North Carolina, and Robert was buried in Chattanooga.

After John's death, his widow moved back to her home in eastern North Carolina where she raised their only child. She died in 1965 at Mount Olive, Wayne County, North Carolina.[1625]

Child of John Stanley[5] and Effie Roselle (Bird) Vetter:

+   282   i. JOHN STANLEY[6] VETTER, JR., born 26 May 1928 Chattanooga,
                  Tennessee; married 23 January 1955 in Haddock, Jones County,
                  Georgia, Sallie Louisa Middlebrooks.[1626]

140. Mary Louise[5] **Frist** (Jacob Chester[4], Jacob Chester[3], Henry[2], Rudolph[1]) was born in June 1898 in New Orleans, Louisiana, the daughter of Jacob Chester and Jane (Jones) Frist.[1627] She died in Fort Lauderdale, Florida, January of 1980.[1628] She married first on 6 September 1925 in Lauderdale County, Mississippi, to **Mahlon Floyd Parker**.[1629] Mahlon was a widower who was born in 1877 in Iowa.[1630] Mary Louise married second in Nashville, Tennessee, in the late 1960s to **Bob Tomlinson**.[1631]

In 1900 Mary Louise lived with her parents in Perry County, Mississippi.[1632] In 1906 her parents moved to Meridian, Mississippi, in Lauderdale County where they lived in 1910.[1633] She attended Ward-Belmont Finishing School in Nashville, Tennessee, and then returned home to teach elementary school in Meridian.

Mary Louise met her husband to be, Mahlon Floyd Parker, when he boarded at her mother's home in Meridian. Friends and neighbors thought Mahlon might marry the widow Jane "Jennie" Frist, but instead he married her daughter.[1634] Mahlon was a prominent lumber dealer in Meridian for many years whose business, at the time of their marriage, was in Fort Lauderdale, Florida.[1635] The bride was described as being a young girl "of unusual graciousness" who possessed "exceptional charm."[1636] Following their marriage, the couple resided in Florida.

After Mahlon's death, Mary Louise married again in Nashville, Tennessee, in the late 1960s, to Bob Tomlinson. She was a family-oriented person and enjoyed the family gatherings in their home in Fort Lauderdale, Florida, as well as those in Nashville.[1617]

Mary Louise lived in Fort Lauderdale at the time of her death in 1980.[1638] She was buried 11 January 1980 next to her parents in Magnolia Cemetery in Meridian, Lauderdale County, Mississippi.[1639] She had no children.

141. Helen Jones[5] **Frist** (Jacob Chester[4], Jacob Chester[3], Henry[2], Rudolph[1]) was born 9 May 1901 in Hattiesburg, Perry County, Mississippi, the daughter of Jacob Chester and Jane (Jones) Frist.[1640] Helen died 21 August 1956 in Fort Lauderdale, Broward County, Florida.[1641] Helen married in New York about the year 1923 to **Argie Garner Cameron**.[1642] Argie was born in 1885 in Mississippi, the son of Benjamin Franklin and Sarah Elizabeth (Garner) Cameron of Meridian.[1643] He died 24 March 1943 in Meridian, Lauderdale County, Mississippi.[1644]

In 1906 Helen's family moved to Meridian, Mississippi, in Lauderdale County where they lived in 1910.[1645] She had just left for school in Bristol, Virginia, when she heard the news of her father's death on 2 January 1919.[1646]

In 1920 Helen was eighteen years of age and lived with her widowed mother in Meridian, Lauderdale County, Mississippi.[1647] Later she went to New York City to further her education, where she met her future husband, Argie Garner Cameron. Argie was also from Meridian, Mississippi.

Helen and Argie eloped and were married in New York about the year 1923. It was a private ceremony with no family present, much to the distress of Helen's family back home in Mississippi.[1648] They had one son, known as "Cam," who was born in 1924.

When Argie died in 1943, he was buried in Rose Hill Cemetery in Meridian, Lauderdale County, Mississippi.[1649] He died in Richmond, Virginia, where he was engaged in auditing the books of the Chesapeake and Ohio Railroad.[1650]

Helen and her son, Cam, often visited her family at their home in Florida. Helen died in 1956 and was buried next to her husband and his family in Rose Hill Cemetery in Meridian, Lauderdale County, Mississippi.[1651]

Child of Argie Garner and Helen Jones[5] (Frist) Cameron:

283   i. ALAN GARNER[6] "CAM" CAMERON, born 25 February 1924 New York City;[1652] died 22 August 1974 in Broward County, Florida, buried Lauderdale Memorial Park, Fort Lauderdale, Florida;[1653] married about 1970, Doloris Aucella. He lived in New York and in Sunrise, Broward County, Florida. He was a teacher at Fort Lauderdale University;[1654] no issue.

142. John Chester[5] "Chet" Frist (Jacob Chester[4], Jacob Chester[3], Henry[2], Rudolph[1]) was born 29 October 1906 in Meridian, Lauderdale County, Mississippi, the son of Jacob Chester and Jane (Jones) Frist.[1655] Chet died in December 1959 in Mobile, Alabama. He married on 17 May 1932 in Farmville, Virginia, to **Lois Elizabeth "Betty" Ferran**. Betty was born 6 September 1909 in Toccoa, Stephens County, Georgia, the daughter of Dr. Clarence and Hannah Elizabeth (Moore) Ferran. Betty died 26 August 1998 in Asheville, Buncombe County, North Carolina.

Chet was raised in Meridian, and he was only twelve when his father died. He attended high school in Meridian, where he was captain of the football team and "All Southern Guard" as well as Mississippi's best high school debater.

Following graduation from high school in Meridian, Chet received an appointment to West Point but decided instead to enroll at Southwestern University (now Rhodes College) in Memphis, Tennessee. He was a popular student, captain of the football team, president of the debating team and also of his fraternity Sigma Alpha Epsilon. He was a charter member of Omicron Delta Kappa, a national leadership fraternity that recognizes outstanding junior and senior men. He was also president of the student body and of the honor council. He worked as a head waiter in the school dining room to earn money to pay his way through college.

His younger brother Tommy, who considered him a sometimes father figure, followed him to Southwestern in 1927. The two brothers wrote their widowed mother frequently and supported her as best they could. They were a very close-knit family. Chet had thought of becoming a lawyer because he was skillful at debating, but while at Southwestern College he decided to become a minister.

In 1927, while considering the call to the ministry, he served the little church of Eastland Presbyterian in Memphis, Tennessee. He continued to serve the church during his summers at college and in his senior year.

Chet received a B.A. degree from Southwestern University at Memphis in 1928. He earned his B.D. degree in 1931 and a Th.M. degree in 1937, both from Union Theological Seminary in Richmond, Virginia. He was licensed as a minister by Winchester Presbytery at its meeting in Hancock, Maryland, in 1931. In 1944 he was given the honorary degree of doctor of divinity from Southwestern University.

While studying at Union Seminary in Richmond, he met his wife to be, Lois Elizabeth "Betty" Ferran. Betty had gone to Flora MacDonald College in North Carolina and was studying to be a Christian educator at the Presbyterian School of Education, which was then called ATS, Assembly's Training School. They met when Chet gallantly arose to give her his bus seat (on an empty bus). He had been noticing her at the school, which was across the road from his own school.

They were married in 1932 in Farmville, Virginia. Betty was the daughter of Dr. Clarence and Hannah Elizabeth (Moore) Ferran. Clarence was a Presbyterian minister in Orlando, Florida, and the son of Edgar and Lucy Mariah (Avery) Ferran.

Their first child Jane Elizabeth was born 26 January 1935 in Richmond, Virginia, while Chet was completing his master's degree.[1656] The family then lived in Moorefield, West Virginia, where Chet served his first pastorate at the Moorefield Presbyterian Church.

The family moved to Starkville, Mississippi, in 1937, where Chet served the First Presbyterian Church in Starkville and where their second child Charlotte June was born on 4 March 1938.[1657] Their third child John Chester was also born while they lived in Starkville on 22 July 1941, and Betty traveled to Memphis, Tennessee, for the birth.[1658]

Chet was pastor of the First Presbyterian Church in Tampa, Florida, where they lived from 1942 to 1947. Their last child Thomas Ferran was born 2 July 1945 in Tampa.[1659] Chet then became pastor of the Government Street Presbyterian Church in Mobile, Alabama. Chet was the moderator of the Synod of Alabama and also on the board of directors of Agnes Scott College in Decatur, Georgia.

Montreat, North Carolina, became a childhood retreat for Betty when her father, Clarence Ferran, began bringing the family there. The Frists followed suit, establishing a summer home in Montreat. In 1951 Betty began buying and remodeling homes in Montreat.

The story is told that the youngest child in the family, seven-year-old Tom, wandered around in Montreat to neighbors' homes for breakfast, because he "didn't like the dog food Mom cooked" for the family.[1660] One of the homes where he had been stopping was that of the evangelist Billy Graham. Billy's wife, Ruth, asked him to have his mom come over for tea, because she wanted to hear more about the dog food story. Betty went for a visit and explained that her son Tom must have been talking about the corned beef hash served from a can at the same time she was feeding the dog from another can. Betty was ten years older than Ruth, but the two women became best friends and enjoyed hunting for antiques and log cabins together. The friendship extended to their daughters. Betty's daughter Jane was ten years older than Gigi, the daughter of Billy and Ruth Graham. Despite the age difference, they too became great friends over the years.

Betty authored the books *No Wings in the Manse*, a true story of life at the busiest of homes, the pastor's. She also wrote *My Neighbors the Billy Grahams*, a memoir based on her friendship with the Grahams. She had no previous training in writing, but was great at telling stories that were interesting. She was an opposite to her husband. She was effervescent and excitable, talented in painting, writing, piano playing, gathering antiques, and designing and constructing houses. She knew the Bible by heart and could quote hundreds of verses. She was considered a theological conservative, although her lively personality was in conflict with her conservative background. She was a strict disciplinarian, but is remembered as being lots of fun, making monkey faces for the children, dancing the Charleston, telling stories, and playing hymns to a ragtime beat.

On Sunday nights in the summer, after supper at the Grahams' house, the two families would gather in the living room in front of the fireplace where Betty would joyfully belt out their favorite songs on the baby grand piano, leading them all in a fun-filled sing-along. She was a lively and beautiful brown-eyed brunette.

Chet is remembered by his children as gentle, kind, loving, thoughtful, patient, more liberal than his conservative wife, and understanding with a great sense of humor. He always had a twinkle in his eye, and his sense of humor was such that his friends enjoyed playing practical jokes on him.

He was also a man of principle. In the early days of desegregation in the 1950s, he took a stand with a few of his pastor friends in Mobile, Alabama, in support of Martin Luther King's efforts to desegregate buses in Montgomery. He was severely criticized by some parishioners and a cross was burned as a warning in the yard of one of the pastors where a strategy meeting was taking place.[1661] Chet stuck to what he considered to be right and retained his sense of perspective and humor. He was a great preacher and a great pastor. He served in some of the most prestigious and well-known churches of that time.

Chet died in December 1959 in Mobile, Alabama, of colon cancer. He is buried in Pine Crest Cemetery in Mobile, Alabama. His early death at the age of fifty-three brought many messages of sympathy. His brother Tommy said that he was the greatest man he ever knew and the day Chet died was the saddest day of his life.[1662] Donald G. Miller, professor at Union Theological Seminary in Richmond, Virginia, wrote on 8 January 1960 to Chet's daughter Charlotte Chesnutt:

> You, in your sorrow and loss, have much for which to be grateful. It is not given to us to choose our parents; but if you had been making a choice, you could not have chosen anyone finer than your Daddy. He had a personal warmth, and a capacity for friendship which few people have, and he had more warm friends than anyone I know.[1663]

After his death, Betty returned to Montreat, North Carolina. She served as an organist in a small chapel in Mexico for a period of time and then went to Fort Lauderdale. She eventually moved to Penny Farms Retirement Community near Jacksonville, Florida, where she met and married Clarence Myers, her second husband. They were married for nineteen years.

Betty died in 1998 in Asheville, Buncombe County, North Carolina, and is buried in Swannanoa, about five miles from Montreat, which is also in Buncombe County, North Carolina.[1664]

Children of John Chester[5] and Lois Elizabeth (Ferran) Frist:

+ 284   i. JANE ELIZABETH[6] FRIST, born 26 January 1935 Richmond, Virginia; married 14 June 1957 Mobile, Mobile County, Alabama, Arnold Cornelius "Arnie" Harms.[1665]

+ 285   ii. CHARLOTTE JUNE FRIST, born 4 March 1938 Starkville, Oktibbeha County, Mississippi; married (1) 25 August 1961 Montreat, Buncombe County, North Carolina, James Robert Faucette and (2) 25 November 1989 Montgomery, Montgomery County, Alabama, John Calvin Chesnutt.[1666]

+ 286   iii. JOHN CHESTER FRIST, JR., born 22 July 1941 Memphis, Shelby County, Tennessee; married 15 June 1963 Nashville, Davidson County, Tennessee, Mary Corinne Brothers.[1667]

+ 287   iv. THOMAS FERRAN FRIST, born 2 July 1945 Tampa, Hillsborough County, Florida; married 26 August 1972 San Jose, Costa Rica, Clare Elizabeth Strachan.[1668]

143. Thomas Fearn[5] Frist (Jacob Chester[4], Jacob Chester[3], Henry[2], Rudolph[1]) was born 15 December 1910 in Meridian, Lauderdale County, Mississippi, the son of Jacob Chester and Jane (Jones) Frist.[1669] He died on 4 January 1998 in Nashville, Davidson County, Tennessee. He married on 11 June 1935 in Nashville, Davidson County, Tennessee, to **Dorothy Harrison Cate**. Dorothy was born on 6 September 1910 in Hopkinsville, Christian County, Kentucky, the daughter of James Harrison and Mary Lucenia (Armistead) Cate. She died 6 January 1998 in Nashville, Davidson County, Tennessee.

"Tommy" Frist was eight years old when his father, the station master in Meridian, Mississippi, died, and he felt his loss keenly. Tommy grew up in Meridian with his older brother, "Chet," as a sometimes father substitute.

In 1927, Tommy followed Chet to Southwestern University (now Rhodes College) in Memphis, Tennessee. Tommy entered his freshman year at the age of sixteen, and his brother Chet was a senior.[1670] Chet excelled at most everything he did and felt called to a career in the Presbyterian ministry. Tommy gravitated to a vocation that was not of interest to Chet and selected medicine.[1671]

Dr. Samuel H. Hairston played a pivotal role in Tommy's decision to go into medicine. Dr. Hairston had been a boarder at the Frist home for a period of time and offered Tommy summer work in his hospital—sweeping wards, making beds, giving enemas, and emptying bedpans. Tommy worked for him all through his high school years, long before rigid rules about who did what in a hospital prevented a novice from helping. Tommy even tried his hand at sewing up wounds and helping in the operating room. Hairston also showed him the business end of medicine, putting him to work collecting accounts, "door to door, face to face."[1672]

In 1928 he transferred from Southwestern to the University of Mississippi, where he completed his undergraduate studies, graduating in 1931. He entered Vanderbilt Medical School in Nashville, Tennessee, that same year and graduated with an M.D. degree in 1933.

Always industrious, in part out of necessity and in part because of a lifelong entrepreneurial spirit, he worked his way through college and medical school. He arranged the transport of trunks for arriving students at Ole Miss, announced in the local gym the "away" athletic events via telephone, kept the campus vending machines stocked, and sold advertisements for desk blotters that he distributed to all students. At Vanderbilt he took great pride in continuing the boardinghouse tradition of his family by setting up the popular living arrangement that affectionately became known as "Pauper's Paradise."

In 1933 he met Dorothy Harrison Cate, the woman he was to marry, who was then an elementary school teacher in Nashville. After graduating from Vanderbilt, he left the area to serve a medical internship at the University of Iowa. While in Iowa, he suffered a collapsed lung. He recuperated in Meridian, Mississippi, and also in Florida, later returning to Iowa. Upon completion of his Iowa medical training, Dr. Frist returned to Nashville where he and Dr. William Cate (his future brother-in-law) began a medical practice in the Doctors Building in downtown Nashville.

Years later, former Tennessee governor Winfield Dunn described Frist's early years of medical practice as consisting "mainly of physical examinations at a dollar per person for the Interstate Insurance Company, work at the state penitentiary where he established a hospital for the tubercular inmates, and an occasional private patient."[1673]

On 11 June 1935 Thomas Fearn Frist married Dorothy Harrison Cate in Wightman Chapel at Scarritt College in Nashville, Tennessee. The ceremony was performed by the groom's brother, Reverend John Chester Frist.

Dorothy Harrison Cate was one of fourteen children born to James Harrison Cate. Dorothy was the middle of nine children born to his second wife Mary Lucenia Cate, who was a sister of his first wife. She was raised at Cate's mill in Hopkinsville, Kentucky. Most of the siblings eventually settled in Nashville. Dorothy graduated from George Peabody School for Teachers in Nashville in 1932 and also attended Ward-Belmont Finishing School for Girls.

Their first two children were born in Nashville, a son Thomas Fearn Frist, Jr. on 12 August 1938 and a daughter Dorothy Cate Frist on 4 June 1941. During World War II Dr. Frist served in the United States Air Force for four years from 1942 to 1946. He was a major in the Medical Corps, rising to the position of medical chief of staff at Maxwell Field in Alabama. Their third child, Robert Armistead Frist, was born in Montgomery, Alabama, on 27 October 1942.

After the war the Frists returned to the Nashville area, where a second daughter and their fourth child, Mary Louise Frist, was born on 10 October 1946. They lived on Sterling Road, then on Fairfax, and in 1951 bought a home at 703 Bowling Avenue in Nashville where they lived for the remainder of their lives. This home is currently owned by their youngest son, William H. Frist, and his family.

Dr. Frist was a man devoted to his family. Although he made medical rounds at the hospital every night, he was always home for the family dinner. He told his children about his day at the hospital, and they were encouraged to share how they had spent their day. One day in 1951 at the family dinner, his wife Dorothy announced that she had news for him. She told the whole family that she was expecting another child. This must have been a surprise, for Dr. Frist's knife came down on the butter dish, flipping it to the ceiling where it left a grease smear to the utter delight of the children.[1674] Their last child, William Harrison Frist, was born 22 February 1952 in Nashville.

Dr. Frist developed a huge, highly regarded medical practice, serving people throughout the middle Tennessee region. He traveled to many smaller communities in the early years of his career. He recognized the need of both citizens and doctors in these rural areas for access to better medical facilities. His commitment to the quality of and access to health care in these communities ultimately led to the development of Hospital Corporation of America (HCA).

In 1960 Dr. Frist founded Parkview Hospital and Park Vista Nursing Home in Nashville. He served as the chief executive of Parkview Hospital until it became Hospital Corporation of America. In 1968 Dr. Frist, at the instigation of his oldest son, joined son Tommy and Nashville businessman Jack Massey to found the Nashville, Tennessee-based Hospital Corporation of America. Parkview Hospital was its initial facility. The father focused his attention on clinical care and quality assurance while his son concentrated on marketing, finance, and business development.

The for-profit, investor-owned multi-hospital concept was new. It was untried and untested. Son Tommy Frist had witnessed the phenomenal success of the motel chain started by the father of one of his friends at Vanderbilt, Holiday Inns of America. Tommy reasoned the same concepts of standardizations and shared services of facilities linked together as a "chain" could realize economies of a similar scale in the health care field. He convinced his dad and Jack Massey to support his vision and thereby invented what became a new industry. Hospital Corporation of America pioneered the way to bring business-style management and market-based principles to the cottage industry of hospitals. By leveraging the economies of scale inherent in a multifacility chain and using the equity markets, it could afford to build hospitals in small towns and rural areas with poor access to health care. By managing its hospitals as a "tight ship," it also could afford better equipment, supplies, and personnel.

Dr. Frist served as president of HCA from its founding until 1970 when he was named its chief medical officer and chairman of the board of governors. He continued his active medical practice throughout this period. In 1982 HCA owned 376 hospitals with 51,059 beds, including an overseas operation that was started in 1973 with a hospital in Saudi Arabia.[1675] At its peak in 1987, the company owned or managed 500 hospitals. In 1990 it owned or managed 133 hospitals with assets of $4.5 billion.[1676]

Dr. Thomas Fearn Frist, Sr. became a nationally known cardiologist and internist with extensive background in hospital management. Building on his interest and commitment to senior citizens and his experience in starting Park Manor, a senior living retirement home affiliated with the Westminster Presbyterian Church, he and Jack C. Massey, along with some local businessmen, founded the American Retirement Corporation (ARC) with headquarters in the Nashville suburb of Brentwood.[1677] ARC's mission is to provide professional services of the highest quality in order to enhance the quality of life for older Americans and their families. It currently owns or provides services for more than fifty communities in sixteen states. In 1997 it became a publicly traded company on the New York Stock Exchange.[1678]

In 1990 Thomas Fearn Frist, Sr. was inducted into the Health Care Hall of Fame at its third event, held at Pennsylvania Hospital in Philadelphia.[1679] He was described as a "staunch advocate of the investor-owned hospital sector." The seventy-nine-year-old Frist, who survived a heart attack, two heart bypass operations, a broken neck from an auto accident, colon cancer, and a stroke, commented, "I've been a patient so often that I know what's important in a hospital."

> It's not mortar and brick that make a hospital. It is the warmth, compassion and attitude of good employees that leads to quality care.
>
> Thomas F. Frist, Sr., M.D., in a speech in 1970

During his career, Dr. Frist was associate professor emeritus of clinical medicine at Vanderbilt University Medical School and a fellow of the American College of Physicians. He was president of the Nashville Society of Internal Medicine, Southeastern Clinical Club, and Tennessee Heart Association as well as president of staff for both Nashville General and St. Thomas Hospitals. He was certified by the American Board of Internal Medicine. He was a founder and member of the board of directors of the Medical Benevolence Foundation for Presbyterian Medical Missionaries.

His civic and community contributions were not limited to the medical field. For years he served on the board of trust for Montgomery Bell Academy. He was co-founder of Knowles Senior Citizen Center on Broadway. He founded and was chairman of the board for Park Manor Presbyterian Apartments for the elderly. He was a member of the board of directors at the Nashville City Bank and vice chairman of the board at American Retirement Corporation. He served on the Health, Education, and Welfare Advisory Committee on Older Americans in Washington, D.C.

Dr. Frist's avocation was dabbling in real estate. Over a twenty-year period, he purchased a series of ten old houses on West End Avenue adjacent to his medical office building across from Vanderbilt. He loved fixing them up and then renting out the ground floors to other doctors, reserving the upper two floors for Vanderbilt nurses and students who appreciated the affordable housing. It was this land that he ultimately contributed to the construction of the new Vanderbilt Plaza Hotel developed with his good friend Jack Massey and others.

Dr. Frist also loved the beauty of Middle Tennessee's countryside. Each Sunday he and Dorothy would take long drives with friends and family looking at the land. They purchased two farms. One was a working farm, and the other was purchased for the family to enjoy the creeks and woodlands.[1680]

On 15 December 1997 in the twilight of his life, Dr. Frist prepared a letter "For my family and for future generations with great love" and it is included here in full. It captures simply and beautifully much of the philosophy of this revered man.

> Dear great-grandchild,
>
> My children have asked me to write down what I believe. They want their children and their children's children to know about some of the things that are important in life. That is why I have written you this letter. I am writing it to you, even though I cannot know you. I hope, as you read it, you will know me, and know your parents and grandparents, a little better.
>
> I am now 87 years old and so happy to be alive. I have had so many blessings and such a full life. Every day of my life has been happy. I hope what I have to tell you will help you know the happiness in life I have known.
>
> I believe in a few simple things. I learned about them a long time ago from my mother and my father, my sisters and my brother, my teachers and

my friends. I learned a lot in life, but I never changed these beliefs all the way through. This is what I believe.

I believe that religion is so very important. I was raised in the Presbyterian church in Meridian, Mississippi, and I never missed a Sunday from when I was three to when I was eighteen. I believe there is a God and in Jesus Christ. The only prayer I ever pray is thanking God for all the blessings I have.

I never pray when I'm in a tight spot because I think God, in his wisdom, knows what you need. I believe in the morality of religion—the Golden rule. I say something nice to people when they deserve it. When they don't deserve it, I say something nice about other people, so they know how to act and they always smile.

I believe that culture is so important. My mother was so kind, so giving, so unselfish. My wife, Dorothy, is the same. When you marry, marry someone who believes in the same things you do.

Be happy in your family life. Your family is the most important thing you can ever have. Love your wife or your husband. Tell your children how great they are. Encourage them in everything they do. I never punished my children, never raised my voice with them. If they know you expect them to do right, they will do right. If you praise them for the good things they do, the bad things will disappear.

Be happy in your career. I was a doctor. I loved being a doctor because it meant helping people, being with patients every minute. All my sons were doctors. It's a great thing to be a doctor. Whatever work you do, do it well. Remember any job worth doing is worth doing well. Always do a quality job.

Be happy in your community. Charity is so important. Be active. Don't be self satisfied. There's so much good to do in the world and so many different ways to do it.

In politics, I believe in voting for the man, not the party. I voted for President Reagan and President Bush because they were good leaders, not because they were Republicans. I am conservative. I believe the free enterprise system can do a better job at most things than the government can. People should learn to be self-reliant; when they are self-reliant, they will have self-respect.

I believe good people beget good people. If you marry the right person, then you will have good children. But everywhere else in life, too, good people beget good people. In your work, when you hire good people, they, in turn, will hire good people and right on down the line. That's how we built Hospital Corporation of America. From the board members right on down to the man in the boiler room and the woman who makes the beds, we wanted good people with integrity and high moral standards. We made such a difference in the world with HCA, and we did it because good people beget good people.

I believe life is made up of peaks and valleys. But the thing to remember is that the curve is always going up. The next peak is a little higher than the previous peak, the next valley isn't quite so low. The work gets better all the time. Think about wars and peacetime—that's the challenge for great leaders. Think about business—there are always recessions and good times, but the good times always get better. Think about politics—we'll get a bad president and then a great president who corrects the things the other one did; that's a great thing about the party system. Or think about medicine, which is how I spent my life. Right now, medicine is really at a peak as far as technology and science are concerned, but we're way down in a valley with the cost. In time, we'll get this fixed, too. I'm sure we will.

Finally, I believe it is so terribly important in life to stay humble. Use your talents wisely and use other people's talents to help other people. Don't think about the reward; that will probably come along if you don't go looking for it. (I always said at HCA that if we just concentrated on doing the best job we could of giving quality care, then the bottom line would take care of itself. And it did.) Always be confident. But never be cocky. Always stay humble.

So, my great-grandchildren, I hope you will live happy and long lives like I have. I hope this letter will help you. Maybe you will give it to your children, and they will give it to their children right on down the line. The world is always changing, and that's a good thing. It's how you carry yourself in the world that doesn't change—morality, integrity, warmth, and kindness are the same things in 1910 when I was born or in 2010 or later when you will be reading this. And that's a good thing, too.

Love,

Granddaddy

His wife Dorothy was focused on her home and family. She was described as a truly remarkable person, ever sensitive to the needs of others and enthusiastic beyond measure. She was constantly looking for opportunities to share her natural optimism with others and was a person whose impact can never be forgotten.[1681] Their children described her similarly as "the glue that held the family together,"[1682] "the backbone of the family,"[1683] and "the anchor of the family,"[1684] while another commented, "to see their values carried through future generations would be God's greatest blessing."[1685] After her death F. Karl VanDevender, M.D., remarked on how her husband spoke of Dorothy during their life.

> She was a wonderful mother. Her family was the center of her world. She was exactly the kind of wife any doctor would want. She was interested in his patients, liked to ride along on house calls, and was known to prescribe her favorite antibiotic to people who called when he wasn't home. And when he wasn't home, she understood.[1686]

Throughout her life, Dorothy Frist never strayed from her unselfish devotion to her five children and husband. It was Dorothy, affectionately known as "Dodie" in her later years, who almost daily hosted the neighborhood kids for dinner, fed the horses in the back field, and cared for the constant stream of animals the Frist children seemed to have (dogs, cats, turkeys, and even the occasional alligator and billy goat). Their five children attribute most of what successes they achieved to her strength and her support.

Whereas the common sense and the "street smarts" of the family were frequently attributed to Dr. Frist, it was to Dorothy Frist that the intelligence and critical thinking was credited. An avid reader always having an opinion on the latest current events, she was known to hold her tongue respectfully when Dr. Frist expressed his more conservative views, though when out of earshot she made sure her more progressive views were understood by all.

Thomas Fearn Frist died on 4 January 1998, and his beloved wife Dorothy died just two days later on 6 January 1998, both in Nashville, Tennessee. A joint funeral was held for them at Westminster Presbyterian Church in Nashville on 7 January 1998. The eulogy was by F. Karl VanDevender, M.D., who spoke at length about the Frists. His comment "One death is the story of the end of a long and illustrious life. Two deaths is a love story" is one that speaks volumes about their relationship.

They were buried at Mount Olivet Cemetery in Nashville, Davidson County, Tennessee. A memorial service was held the next day on 8 January 1998 at Westminster Presbyterian Church. Surviving them in 1998 were five children, fourteen grandchildren, and five great-grandchildren.

Children of Thomas Fearn[5] and Dorothy Harrison (Cate) Frist:

+   288   i. THOMAS FEARN[6] FRIST, JR., born 12 August 1938 Nashville, Davidson County, Tennessee; married 22 December 1961 Nashville, Tennessee, Patricia Gail "Trish" Champion.[1687]

+   289   ii. DOROTHY CATE FRIST, born 4 June 1941 Nashville, Davidson County, Tennessee; married (1) 9 March 1963 Nashville, Tennessee, Charles Ray Eller and (2) 1976 Nashville, Tennessee, Richard Boensch.[1688]

+   290   iii. ROBERT ARMISTEAD FRIST, born 27 October 1942 Montgomery, Montgomery County, Alabama; married 6 June 1964 Nashville, Tennessee, Carol Len Knox.[1689]

+   291   iv. MARY LOUISE FRIST, born 10 October 1946 Nashville, Davidson County, Tennessee; married 31 January 1968 Nashville, Tennessee, Henry Lee Barfield II.[1690]

+   292   v. WILLIAM HARRISON FRIST, born 22 February 1952 Nashville, Davidson County, Tennessee; married 14 March 1981 Lubbock, Lubbock County, Texas, Karyn Jean McLaughlin.[1691]

144. Paul Franklin⁵ Frist (Joseph Elmer⁴, Jacob Chester³, Henry², Rudolph¹) was born on 5 October 1898 in Chattanooga, Hamilton County, Tennessee, the son of Joseph Elmer and Alice (Keefe) Frist.[1692] Paul died on 12 March 1961 in Chattanooga, Hamilton County, Tennessee.[1693] He married in January of 1923 to **Kate Irene Groves** in Chattanooga, Tennessee.[1694] Kate was born on 17 January 1908 in Athens, McMinn County, Tennessee, the daughter of Elmer Lewis and Litty (Smith) Groves.[1695] Litty died when Kate was born,[1696] and her father remarried on 6 November 1912 to Emma Rentfro.[1697]

In 1900 Paul lived with his parents in Civil District 14 of Chattanooga.[1698] On 10 January 1924 Paul's father, Joseph Elmer Frist, a widower, conveyed forty acres of land to his son Paul Franklin.[1699] The land was described as being in the old fourth district, but now in the new second district of Hamilton County, having been conveyed to Joseph E. Frist by Sarah Young on 13 January 1921.

In 1930 Paul and his wife Kate lived in Hamilton County, Tennessee, with their son Robert.[1700] They owned a home valued at $1000, and Paul worked at an iron foundry.

On 24 July 1939 Paul worked for Hembree Milling Company in Chattanooga[1701] and he later worked at the Chattanooga Box and Paper Company while living at 2 West End Avenue in Chattanooga.[1702]

World War II took a heavy toll on the Frists. Their oldest son Joe served in the Forty-Second Rainbow Division under Brigadier General Harry Collins in the European theater.[1703] Kate was very close to her firstborn son and the two maintained a lengthy correspondence during the war.[1704] On 17 November 1944 Joe wrote to his mother, asking if "Pap" was working now and commenting, "I intend to come out of this ok." The Forty-Second Rainbow Division landed in France in December 1944 as part of the Seventh Army and began the push through France toward Germany.[1705]

On January 9, 1945, Joe wrote again to his mother commenting, "I don't know just what it is, but there is something wrong with me. I don't eat. And I only smoke and drink coffee. But I will get by. Some way." He thanked her for sending candy and asked her to send air mail stamps, which were very hard for the soldiers to get. Although he wrote the letter on January 9, he didn't get around to mailing it until January 15. On that same day, his mother, Kate, living in Charleston, South Carolina, where Pap was working, sat down to write Joe a letter.[1706] She explained to her son why she had moved saying, "It wasn't no home with out your dadie." She cautioned Joe, "pleas look to God to take care of you for darling he is your maker and will watch over you and I feel that he will bring you throw if you all ways look to him."

On January 16, 1945 Private First Class Robert J. Frist made the ultimate sacrifice for his country, giving his life in combat in France. He never received his mother's letter urging him to "look to God." On January 30, 1945, Kate wrote again to her son Joe, still not having learned of his death. She expressed her desire to see him, "Boy how I would love to see you but that can wait," not realizing that it couldn't wait. She explained, "dadie is now working on a hospital ship and likes his job much better." She closed with the wish that the war would soon be over, enclosing the air mail stamps that Joe was always requesting. Both of these letters were eventually returned to the family marked "deceased," the air mail stamps still inside.[1707]

On 15 February 1945 Katie Frist received the telegram from Washington, D.C., that every soldier's mother dreaded, informing her that her son had been killed in action.[1708]

> MRS. KATIE I FRIST
>
> ROUTE FOUR ST. ALMO, CHATTANOOGA, TENN
>
> THE SECRETARY OF WAR DESIRES ME TO EXPRESS HIS DEEP REGRET THAT YOUR SON PRIVATE FIRST CLASS ROBERT J FRIST WAS KILLED IN ACTION ON SIXTEEN JANUARY IN FRANCE CONFIRMING LETTER FOLLOWS.
> *J A ULIO THE ADJUTANT GENERAL*

On 19 March 1945, the United States War Department advised the Frists that their son was posthumously awarded the Purple Heart for military merit and wounds received in action. He was buried in a military cemetery with a chaplain of the Baptist faith officiating at the burial. On 12 June 1947, the War Department sent the family a photograph of the United States Military Cemetery in Epinal, France, where their son was buried.[1709] Joe's death entitled family members to an honorary membership in the National Association Rainbow Division Veterans, and Kate retained her membership for many years.[1710]

Paul died in 1961 in Chattanooga, Hamilton County, Tennessee[1711] and is buried in the Boydston Cemetery. Kate was a seamstress and worked hard all of her life. Her quilts and spreads were highly prized and she earned a good income selling them.[1712] She was known in her lifetime as a generous person to her friends and family. She was also a person who said what she felt and said it with a certain amount of profanity.[1713] As of April 2003, Kate is living in a rest home in Chattanooga, Tennessee, at the age of ninety-five. She outlived both of her sons and age has not dulled her colorful speech.

Children of Paul Franklin[5] and Kate Irene (Groves) Frist:

> 293   i. ROBERT JOE[6] FRIST, born 31 December 1923; died 16 January 1945
> in France during WWII; no issue.

+   294   ii. SIDNEY DONALD FRIST, born 25 June 1930 Chattanooga, Hamilton,
County, Tennessee;[1714] died 1 January 1973 Chattanooga, Tennessee;[1715]
married Norma Drucilla Roberts.[1716]

145. James Charles[5] **"Jake" Frist** (Joseph Elmer[4], Jacob Chester[3], Henry[2],
Rudolph[1]) was born on 11 November 1900 in Chattanooga, Hamilton County, Ten-
nessee, the son of Joseph Elmer and Alice (Keefe) Frist.[1717] He died on 8 March
1944 in Chattanooga, Tennessee.[1718] He married on 1 January 1923 to **Sadie Estell
Briggs**. Sadie was born 9 December 1899, the daughter of William C. and Hattie
T. (Deaver) Briggs.[1719] She died 5 October 1997.[1720]

In 1920 Jake and his younger brother Ernest lived as boarders in Chattanooga in the
home of Richard Forrester.[1721] Jake was nineteen at the time and worked at the Chattanooga Medical Company, possibly supporting Ernest, who had no listed occupation.

Although Jake married in 1923 to Sadie Estell Briggs, the two were not living
together in 1930. Sadie lived in Chattanooga with her parents and her three young
children.[1722] Jake's whereabouts are unknown.

Jake died in 1944 in Chattanooga, Tennessee, at the age of forty-three from ure-
mia and acute heart "dilatation" due to accidentally drinking carbon tetra chlo-
ride and is buried in Forest Hills Cemetery in Chattanooga.[1723] He was an em-
ployee of the Ross Mehan Foundry at the time of his death.

Children of James Charles[5] and Sadie Estell (Briggs) Frist, all born in Chattanooga, Hamilton County, Tennessee:

295   i. JAMES CALVIN[6] FRIST, born 26 October 1923; died 23 October 1952
Chattanooga, Tennessee; buried National Cemetery, Chattanooga,
Tennessee; World War II veteran, serving in the Army Air Corps as a
sergeant.[1724] He contracted liver disease during the Berlin airlift and
was given two years to live after discharge. He committed suicide after
experiencing the disease in its later stages[1725] and possibly also from
despondency over his inability to obtain employment;[1726] no issue.

296   ii. ALLEY EVELYN FRIST, born 19 November 1924; died 13 December
1983 Chattanooga, Tennessee;[1727] married 1954 Atlanta, Georgia,
Erskine Gallant born Anderson, South Carolina; divorced 1956; Evelyn
worked as a corporate secretary for Kobax Corporation for seventeen
years and was a stewardess with Eastern Airlines and Northwest
Royalties.[1728] She operated her own swimming pool construction
company; no issue.[1729]

+   297   iii. FRANK EMMETT FRIST, born 1 December 1925; married (1) 1951
Rossville, Georgia, Avene Phillips and (2) about 1969, Margaret
(Contillo) Kensinger.[1730]

298   iv. NAOMI WILLMARY FRIST, born 1 March 1932; married 8 April 1952 Anderson County, Tennessee, William Rollins born 30 May 1924 Copperhill, Tennessee, died 21 October 1958 Houston, Texas, buried National Cemetery, Chattanooga, Tennessee. Willmary lives in Chattanooga. One child, William Erik "Rick" Rollins born 4 April 1953 Oak Ridge, Tennessee, died 10 July 1977 Lookout Mountain, Tennessee.[1731]

+   299   v. PATRICIA ESTELLE FRIST, born 28 September 1937; married (1) December 1955, Edward Leon Garrett and (2) 22 May 1971 Trenton, Dade County, Georgia, Mark Tell Huguenin.[1732]

147. Mary Emma⁵ Frist (Emmett Franklin⁴, Chester³, Henry², Rudolph¹) was born in August of 1904 in Gadsden, Etowah County, Alabama, the only daughter of Emmett Franklin and Annie C. (Stroud) Frist.[1733] She died 5 June 1960 at Gadsden, Etowah County, Alabama. She married on 5 May 1925 in Gadsden to **Curtis Duke**. Curtis was born in Alabama, the son of B. W. Duke. He owned a farm supply store. He died 4 July 1952 at Gadsden. Both are buried there in Forrest Cemetery.[1734]

Children of Curtis and Mary Emma⁵ (Frist) Duke, all born in Gadsden, Etowah County, Alabama:

+   300   i. FRED⁶ DUKE, born 11 December 1925; married 15 June 1947 Gadsden, Etowah County, Alabama, Julia Maxine Cothran.[1735]

301   ii. HARRY DUKE, born 13 April 1927; died Gadsden, Alabama; never married, no issue.[1736]

+   302   iii. ANNE ELIZABETH DUKE, born 20 December 1929; died 30 May 1999 Gadsden, Etowah County, Alabama; married 13 June 1954 Etowah County, Alabama, Jerry Jasper Thompson, Jr.[1737]

SIXTH GENERATION

151. Louisa Jane⁶ Frist (Joseph Andrew⁵, David H.⁴, John³, Henry², Rudolph¹) was born 29 July 1881 in Valley Township, Page County, Iowa, the daughter of Joseph Andrew and Rosetta Josephine (Mitchell) Frist.[1738] She died 28 May 1965 at Villisca, Montgomery County, Iowa.[1739] She married 28 March 1900 in Montgomery County, Iowa, to **Lewis Patton**, who was born 12 December 1878 in DeWitt County, Illinois, the son of George W. and Hannah (Gardner) Patton.[1740] He died in 1961 in Montgomery County, Iowa.[1741]

In 1900 Lewis and Louisa lived in Jackson Township, Montgomery County, Iowa.[1742] They had no children as yet, and Lewis was a farmer. In 1920 they remained living in Jackson Township, Montgomery County, Iowa,[1743] and Lewis listed his occupation as "section railroad." Their daughter Rosa lived with them as did their married daughter Clara and son-in-law Roy Findley. Louisa's mother-in-law Hannah Patton also lived with them.

Lewis died in 1961, Louisa died in 1965, and both are buried in Arlington Cemetery, Washington Township, Montgomery County, Iowa.[1744]

Children of Lewis and Louisa Jane[6] (Frist) Patton:

+   303   i. CLARA ETTA[7] PATTON, born 12 October 1901 Villisca, Montgomery County, Iowa; died April 1992 Cedar Rapids, Iowa;[1745] married 22 November 1919 Montgomery County, Iowa, Roy Manford Findley.[1746]

    304   ii. ROSA HANNAH PATTON, born 10 September 1904 Missouri; died and buried Sioux City, Iowa; married 16 March 1930 Harry Thompson. Children, *(a)* Paul Eugene Thompson born 5 January 1935 died 1935, *(b)* Harry Thompson died 1936, *(c)* Alice Thompson born 14 April 193?, *(d)* Alvin Thompson born 9 March 193?, and *(e)* Robert Thompson.[1747]

    305   iii. DONALD KEITH PATTON (adopted), born 8 May 1922 Villisca, Iowa; died 1994 Villisca, Iowa; married 20 March 1942 Donna Pauline Hilleary born 8 July 1922. Children, *(a)* Douglas Patton and *(b)* Debora Patton.[1748]

152. Willibur Stiles[6] Frist (Joseph Andrew[5], David H.[4], John[3], Henry[2], Rudolph[1]) was born 6 October 1885 in Coin, Page County, Iowa, the son of Joseph Andrew and Rosetta Josephine (Mitchell) Frist.[1749] He died 7 July 1930, probably in Plymouth County, Iowa.[1750] He married 18 March 1917[1751] to **Orpha Lucille Geesaman**.[1752] Orpha was born in Villisca, Montgomery County, Iowa, on 18 March 1898, the daughter of John Henry and Allie (Whitead) Geesaman.[1753] She died 27 May 1988 in Clarinda, Page County, Iowa.[1754]

In 1920 Willibur and Orpha lived in Plymouth County, Iowa, with his sister Nannie Elizabeth Bridgman.[1755] When Willibur died in 1930, he was buried in Villisca Cemetery, rose hill section in Montgomery County, Iowa.[1756]

Orpha worked at Powell School in Red Oak and lived in Villisca, Iowa, in October of 1952 when she applied for a Social Security number.[1757]

Children of Willibur Stiles[6] and Orpha Lucille (Geesaman) Frist:

+   306   i. GERALDINE ROSETTA[7] "GERRY" FRIST, born 12 July 1924 Jackson, Dakota County, Nebraska; died 6 June 2002 Clarinda, Page County, Iowa; married 5 June 1947 Villisca, Montgomery County, Iowa, Edward Dale Miller.[1758]

+   307   ii. HELEN MARIE FRIST, born 10 January 1929 Page County, Iowa; died 14 May 1972 Chetek, Baron County, Wisconsin; married 3 April 1949 Villisca, Montgomery County, Iowa, Glendon Amos Smith.[1759]

+   308   iii. RAYMOND A. FRIST, born 31 July 1930 Page County, Iowa; married 29 September 1953 Omaha, Douglas County, Nebraska, Beverly Jean Brown.[1760]

156. Joseph E.[6] Frist (John S.[5], David H.[4], John[3], Henry[2], Rudolph[1]) was born in September 1877[1761] in Polk County, Iowa, the only child of John S. and Elizabeth A. Frist.[1762] Joseph married in Polk County on 29 November 1905 to **Blanche R. Coloway**.[1763] Blanche was born 1 August 1887.[1764] She died in April of 1977, probably in Des Moines, Iowa.[1765]

In 1880 Joseph lived with his parents in Marion County, Iowa.[1766] In 1900 he was twenty-two years of age, still single, and living with Mead and Jennie Person in Camp Township, Polk County, Iowa, next door to his widowed father.[1767]

By 1910 Joseph had married to Blanche, and they lived in Des Moines in Polk County, Iowa, with their three-year-old son, Russell E.[1768] In 1920 they lived in Camp Township, Polk County, Iowa.[1769] Joseph was forty-one years of age and Blanche was thirty-two. His father, John, lived with them, as did their twelve-year-old son, Russell E. They owned their own home on McKinney Street.

Child of Joseph E.[6] and Blanche R. (Coloway) Frist:

+   309   i. RUSSELL EDWARD[7] FRIST, born 30 August 1907 Polk County, Iowa; died September 1963 Polk County, Iowa;[1770] married about 1937 Mary Ann.[1771]

157. Elmer E.[6] Thomas (Rebecca J.[5] Frist, David H.[4], John[3], Henry[2], Rudolph[1]) was born about 1868 in Booneville, Dallas County, Iowa, the son of Henry and Rebecca J. (Frist) Thomas.[1772] He married on 19 September 1892 in Dallas County, Iowa, to **Della Jane Wilson**, who was born in 1872 in Iowa, the daughter of Rufus Wilson and his wife, whose maiden name was Harkrader.[1773]

In 1910 Elmer and Della lived in Dallas County, next door to his widowed mother.[1774] Elmer was forty-two years of age and a house carpenter. Della was thirty-six and indicated she had borne three children, all of whom lived with them. They had been married seventeen years.

Children of Elmer E.[6] and Della Jane (Wilson) Thomas, all born in Dallas County, Iowa:

310   i. BERTIE[7] THOMAS, listed as a male, born about 1894.[1775]
311   ii. PERRY THOMAS, born about 1896.[1776]
312   iii. HAZEL THOMAS, born about 1899.[1777]

161. Viola May[6] Thomas (Rebecca J.[5] Frist, David H.[4], John[3], Henry[2], Rudolph[1]) was born about 1876 in Polk County, Iowa, the daughter of Henry and Rebecca J. (Frist) Thomas.[1778] In 1880 she lived with her parents in Dallas County, Iowa.[1779] She married on 17 September 1893 in Dallas County, Iowa, to **Arthur W. Allen**.[1780] Arthur was born in September of 1869 in Indiana,[1781] the son of W. H. and Martha (Ray) Allen.[1782]

In 1900 Arthur and Viola lived in Dallas County, Iowa.[1783] Arthur was thirty years of age, a farmer, who rented his farm. Viola was twenty-three and the mother of three children. They had been married seven years.

Children of Arthur W. and Viola May[6] (Thomas) Allen:

313   i. ETHEL M.[7] ALLEN, born about June 1894.[1784]

314   ii. GOLDIE ALLEN, born about June 1897.[1785]

315   iii. RUTH ALLEN, born about March 1900.[1786]

178. Paul H.[6] Frist (William O.[5], William H.[4], John[3], Henry[2], Rudolph[1]) was born in April 1896 in Preble County, Ohio, the son of William O. and Reba F. Frist.[1787] He died in 1959.[1788] Paul married first about 1917 to **Anabel**.[1789] He married second about 1921 to **Violet Genevieve Jelly**, who was born 28 November 1901 in Richmond, Wayne County, Indiana, the daughter of Casper and Sophia (Morel) Jelly.[1790] Violet died in February of 1987.[1791]

By 1920 Paul H. Frist had married to Anabel, and they lived in Wayne County, Indiana.[1792] Paul was twenty-three and his occupation was telegraph operator with the railroad. Anabel was twenty, and their baby daughter, Barbara Jane, was a year and eight months old.

Paul and his second wife Violet operated the Countryside Inn at 417 North Spring Street for a period of time.[1793] Both are buried at the cemetery in New Paris, Preble County, Ohio.

Child of Paul H.[6] and Anabel Frist:

316   i. BARBARA JANE[7] FRIST, born about 1918, probably Preble County, Ohio.[1794]

Child of Paul H.[6] and Violet Genevieve (Jelly) Frist:

+   317   ii. PAUL JACQUE "JACK" FRIST, born 6 December 1922, probably Preble County, Ohio; married, about 1943,[1795] Helen Louise Hockett.[1796]

180. Marley Otto[6] Frist (Russell[5], William H.[4], John[3], Henry[2], Rudolph[1]) was born on 12 January 1893, probably in Madison County, Indiana, the son of Russell and Sarah Viola (Hunt) Frist.[1797] He died 6 December 1957 in Anderson, Madison County, Indiana.[1798] He married on 12 August 1911[1799] to **Hester Vurnie Swinford** in Anderson, Madison County, Indiana.[1800] Hester was born 6 October 1893 in Anderson, Indiana, the daughter of John and Mary (Manis) Swinford.[1801] She died on 23 December 1992 in Anderson, Indiana.[1802]

In 1920 Marley, his wife, Hester, and their infant son, Russell, lived in Madison County, Indiana, with his parents.[1803] In 1936 his wife Hester worked for Delco Remy Division, GMC.[1804]

Marley worked at Delco Remy Division, GMC for twenty years, retiring in 1946. In recent years he owned a farm in Anderson, Indiana. The Frists attended the Ingalls Methodist Church. Marley and his wife, Hester, are buried in Grove Lawn Cemetery in Pendleton, Indiana.[1805]

Child of Marley Otto[6] and Hester Vurnie (Swinford) Frist:

+   318   i. RUSSELL MARRELL[7] FRIST, born 25 August 1915 Anderson, Madison County, Indiana; died 30 October 1989 Anderson, Madison County, Indiana;[1806] married 29 August 1936 Anderson, Madison County, Indiana, Vivian Maxine Lawson.[1807]

183. Jesse O. Laffe[6] Stevens (Hannah Etta[5] Frist, Robert M.[4], John[3], Henry[2], Rudolph[1]) was born on 14 August 1891, probably in Liberty, Union County, Indiana, the son of John J. and Hannah Etta (Frist) Stevens.[1808] He died on 29 March 1955 in Alexandria, Virginia.[1809] He married on 27 November 1918 to **Ella May Baxter** in Fort Madison, Lee County, Iowa.[1810] Ella was born on 22 December 1894, the daughter of Charles and Minnie (Newport) Baxter.[1811] She died on 4 August 1982.[1812]

Child of Jesse O. Laffe[6] and Ella May (Baxter) Stevens:

+   319   i. MILDRED IRENE[7] STEVENS, born 2 September 1920 Fort Madison, Lee County, Iowa; married (1) Paul Vincent McBride and (2) 17 June 1949 Great Lakes, Michigan, Richard Parmer, Jr.[1813]

189. Pierre Frist[6] Goodrich (Cora[5] Frist, Jonas Lyman Paulson[4], John[3], Henry[2], Rudolph[1]) was born 10 September 1894 in Winchester, Randolph County, Indiana, the son of James Putnam and Cora (Frist) Goodrich.[1814] He died 25 October 1973 in Indianapolis, Marion County, Indiana.[1815] He married first on 17 July 1920 in Decatur to **Dorothy Dugan**.[1816] Dorothy was the daughter of Charles A. and Fanny B. (Dorwin) Dugan.[1817] She died in 1987.[1818] Pierre married second on 3 February 1941 in Chicago, Illinois, to **Enid Smith**.[1819] Enid was born on 17 May 1903 in Enid, Oklahoma.[1820] She died 26 November 1996.[1821]

In 1900 Pierre lived with his parents in Winchester, Randolph County, Indiana.[1822] Raised in Winchester at the family home, Pierre studied first at Wabash

College in Indiana and then graduated from Harvard University Law School in September of 1916.[1823]

In the summer of 1919 Pierre was introduced to Dorothy Dugan by his cousin Florence Goodrich.[1824] They were married on 17 July 1920 in a private ceremony at the bride's parents' home in Decatur and left for a two-month honeymoon on the West Coast.[1825]

Pierre and Dorothy settled in Indianapolis in 1923, two years after his father left the governor's office, where Pierre launched an interesting and diverse career. He was a financier, scholar, and lawyer, a senior partner in the firm of Goodrich, Campbell and Warren. He was founder and president of the P. F. Goodrich Corporation, an investment firm that he organized in 1925. He served on the boards of many companies in Indiana and was an active supporter of Indianapolis Symphony Society Inc. and the Indianapolis Symphonic Choir Inc., serving as director of both organizations.[1826]

The couple divorced in August of 1928, when their daughter, Nancy, was a young child.[1827] Pierre remained single for several years, and Dorothy married in 1933 to Louis Haerle, although the two remained in contact in regard to the rearing of their daughter.

In 1928 Pierre became acquainted with Enid Smith when she served as his nurse after he had back surgery at St. Vincent Hospital. The two married on 3 February 1941 in Chicago, but never had children.[1828]

Pierre died in 1973 in Indianapolis, Marion County, Indiana, at their residence at 4220 Central Avenue and his widow Enid survived him.[1829] He had retained his membership in the Winchester Presbyterian Church all of his life and had never relinquished the Goodrich family home in Winchester, Randolph County, Indiana.[1830] His estate was estimated at $24.6 million and the majority of it endowed three separate private foundations.[1831]

Pierre wrote eleven different wills before his final one on 3 March 1969. As late as May of 1978 his estate remained unsettled. His last will left $150,000 to his daughter, Nancy Poniatowski, with the stipulation that she not contest the will.[1832] The Internal Revenue Service originally claimed that the estate owed almost $20,000,000 in taxes, and the widow Enid Goodrich challenged that claim. This amount was later adjusted to $3,886,567[1833] and the IRS finally settled for approximately one million dollars.[1834] His widow Enid (Smith) Goodrich died 26 November 1996.[1835]

Child of Pierre Frist[6] and Dorothy (Dugan) Goodrich:

320   i. FRANCES DORWIN[7] "NANCY" GOODRICH, born 10 October 1921[1836] Decatur, Adams County, Indiana; married May 1952 Verncliff

(the Vincent Astor estate), Rhinebeck, New York, Prince Edmond Poniatowski of Poland.[1837] Prince Poniatowski was the son of Stanislas Poniatowski of Paris and grandson of Prince Andre and Elizabeth (Sperry) Poniatowski and a direct descendant of Stanislas August Poniatowski, last king of Poland.[1838] Nancy graduated from Tudor Hall in 1939 in Indianapolis and made her debut in New York and Indianapolis in 1942.[1839] She attended Vassar College in New York, studied in Europe at Oxford and the Sorbonne.[1840] After her marriage, the couple lived in New York and Paris, and traveled extensively. They were married for over twenty years, but had no children.

190. Franklin Lloyd[6] Tindall (Ella F.[5] Lloyd, Elizabeth[4] Frist, Jediah[3], Henry[2], Rudolph[1]) was born April of 1880, probably in New Castle County, Delaware, the son of William C. and Ella F. (Lloyd) Tindall.[1841] In 1900 he lived with his parents in Wilmington, New Castle County, Delaware.[1842] Franklin married, probably about the year 1916,[1843] to **Charlotte Maltman**,[1844] who was born in 1893 in Delaware.[1845]

In 1920 they lived with Frank's parents in Wilmington, Delaware.[1846] Frank was thirty-nine years of age and a shoe merchant. Their two-year-old son lived with them.

Child of Franklin Lloyd[6] and Charlotte (Maltman) Tindall:

321   i.   WILLIAM COOK[7] TINDALL born 28 June 1917 Wilmington, Delaware;[1847] died 16 July 1986 New Castle County, Delaware.[1848] In 1938 he lived at 1701 Broome Street, Wilmington, Delaware, and was employed by T. B. O'Toole.[1849] He had one child, Terrance C. Tindall, who married Paula L.[1850]

197. Harold L.[6] Springer (Marietta F.[5] Springer, Esther Ann[4] Frist, Jediah[3], Henry[2], Rudolph[1]) was born about October of 1881 in New Castle County, Delaware, the son of Willard and Marietta F. (Springer) Springer.[1851] He died on 11 November 1969 in Wilmington, New Castle County.[1852] He married about 1907 to **Carolyn L.**, who was born in 1883 in Delaware.[1853] Carolyn died 24 August 1968 in New Castle County.[1854]

In 1900 Harold lived with his parents in Wilmington, New Castle County, Delaware.[1855] In 1930 Harold and his wife, Carolyn, lived in Christiana Hundred, New Castle County, Delaware, with three children.[1856]

Harold wrote his will on 15 February 1963 while living in Christiana Hundred in New Castle County, but when he died in 1969 his estate was listed as being in Brandywine Hundred in New Castle County.[1857] Harold was a doctor and his estate amounted to over a million dollars.

Children of Harold L.[6] and Carolyn L. Springer, probably all born in New Castle County, Delaware:

322   i. HAROLD L.[7] SPRINGER, JR., born 8 September 1907; married Susan Fitzgerald Halcomb born 18 August 1914. Harold graduated from Princeton in 1929 and then joined the Du Pont Company in Richmond, Virginia.[1858] In 1975 they lived in Wilmington, Delaware. Four children, *(a)* Harold L. Springer III born 1937, *(b)* Charles Halcomb Springer born 1940, *(c)* William Lobdell Springer born 1942, *(d)* Steven Ellis Springer born 1945.[1859]

323   ii. WILLIAM L. SPRINGER, born 1909; died 10 October 1987 New Castle County, Delaware; married Fredrika Nesbitt.[1860] One child, Margaret Springer, who married (1) by 1961 Marvel and (2) by 1983 to a Denham.[1861] (Margaret had James McFaddin "Dick" Marvel and Margaret Stewart Denham, born by 1983.[1862])

324   iii. JOHN WILLARD SPRINGER, born about 1912;[1863] died 1938, no issue.[1864]

325   iv. SARAH LOUISE SPRINGER, born about 1923 (listed as adopted in the 1930 census);[1865] died 1989;[1866] married (1) by 1961 to Ralph Romano and (2) by 1969 Lawrence O'Neal. In 1975 she was listed as Sarah Springer in her aunt Edith Baumgartner's estate and lived in Wilmington.[1867] Children, both minors in 1961, *(a)* John Springer Romano Springer (who died in 1984 leaving a wife Barbara and sons Jesse Romano? Springer and Seth Romano? Springer) and *(b)* Carolyn Margaret Romano Springer. Both John and Carolyn changed their surname to Springer.[1868]

198. Helen S.[6] Springer (Marietta F.[5] Springer, Esther Ann[4] Frist, Jediah[3], Henry[2], Rudolph[1]) was born about January of 1884 in New Castle County, Delaware, the daughter of Willard and Marietta F. (Springer) Springer.[1869] Helen died on 30 August 1948 in New Castle County, Delaware.[1870] Helen married about the year 1912 to **Herbert C. Stout**.[1871] Herbert C. Stout was born in July 1885 in Delaware, the son of Henry W. and Emma (Roeder) Stout.[1872] He probably died by 6 January 1934.[1873]

In 1900 Helen lived with her family in Wilmington, New Castle County, Delaware.[1874] Her father, Willard, was a physician and his wife, four children, and two servants comprised the family. In 1900 Helen's future husband, Herbert Stout, lived in Kent County, Delaware, with his mother, Emma, who had married Charles Masters in 1896.[1875]

Herbert was probably deceased by 6 January 1934 when Helen's father Willard Springer wrote his will, as it made no mention of his son-in-law Herbert.[1876] Helen and her daughter, Marjorie, were both named in Willard's will as living in Wilmington with Helen's mother.[1877]

Helen wrote her will on 8 January 1946 and died in 1948 in New Castle County, Delaware.[1878] She left her entire estate to her daughter, Marjorie S. White.

Child of Herbert C. and Helen S.[6] (Springer) Stout, probably born in New Castle County, Delaware:

+   326   i. MARJORIE S.[7] STOUT, born 7 April 1913; died 10 October 1993 New Castle County, Delaware;[1879] married Paul L. White about 1944.[1880]

199. Willard[6] Springer (Marietta F.[5] Springer, Esther Ann[4] Frist, Jediah[3], Henry[2], Rudolph[1]) was born 8 April 1886 in New Castle County, Delaware, the son of Willard and Marietta F. (Springer) Springer.[1881] He died on 26 February 1956 in New Castle County, Delaware.[1882] He married about the year 1915 to **Edna L. Martenis**.[1883] She was born 20 April 1890, in Rochester, Monroe County, New York, the daughter of Jacob Weller and Jesse Foster (Boorman) Martenis.[1884]

In 1900 Willard lived with his parents in Wilmington, New Castle County, Delaware.[1885] By 1930 Willard and his wife, Edna, lived in Brandywine Hundred in New Castle County, Delaware, with three children.[1886] They rented their home, which was valued at $100,000, and Willard's occupation was leather manufacturer.

Willard was of Brandywine Hundred in New Castle County when he wrote his will on 13 September 1955.[1887] He named his wife and three daughters, Elizabeth Mahood, Marietta Patterson, and Nancy du Pont. His will established a trust for his estate of $375,000 and indicated that he owned land in Sussex County. His widow and daughters Elizabeth and Marietta lived in Rockland, Delaware, while Nancy lived in West Chester, Pennsylvania. His was listed as a banker on his death certificate and was buried in Lower Brandywine Cemetery in Wilmington, Delaware.[1888]

Children of Willard[6] and Edna L. (Martenis) Springer, all born in New Castle County, Delaware:

    327   i. ELIZABETH[7] SPRINGER, born about 1918;[1889] died 8 May 1956 New Castle County, Delaware; married William Thomas Mahood.[1890] Children, *(a)* William Thomas Mahood of Vermillion, who lived in South Dakota in 1975,[1891] *(b)* Willard Springer Mahood, who lived in Tokyo, Japan, in 1975,[1892] and *(c)* Rebecca Elizabeth Mahood who lived in Durham, New Hampshire, in 1975.[1893]

328   ii. MARIETTA SPRINGER, born about 1923;[1894] married by 1955

        Patterson; of Wilmington in 1975.[1895]

329   iii. EDNA NANCY SPRINGER, born about 1924;[1896] married by 1955

        Jacques du Pont of West Chester, Pennsylvania, in 1975.[1897]

204. Esther[6] Sheppard (Kallena R.[5] Springer, Esther Ann[4] Frist, Jediah[3], Henry[2], Rudolph[1]) was born in September of 1899 in New Castle County, Delaware, the daughter of Edwin J. and Kallena R. (Springer) Sheppard.[1898] She died 17 August 1975 in New Castle County.[1899] She married **Edward J. Graves**.[1900] Edward wrote his will while living in Louisville, Jefferson County, Kentucky, on 7 February 1952 and died on 3 August 1953 in Wilmington, Delaware, where his will was probated.[1901] He mentioned his wife, Esther, and his daughters Nancy and Carolyn. He left his home in Louisville, Kentucky, to his wife.

Esther's estate in Brandywine Hundred, New Castle County, Delaware, amounted to $143,975.33 when she died in 1975.[1902] Her probate record indicated that she had two daughters, Nancy A. Graves of Wilmington and Carolyn Allen of Louisville.

Children of Edward J. and Esther[6] (Sheppard) Graves:

330   i. NANCY A.[7] GRAVES.[1903]

331   ii. CAROLYN JULIA GRAVES;[1904] married by 1953 Allen.[1905]

332   iii. EILEEN GRAVES [?], born by 1950;[1906] died by 1952.[1907]

210. Harry Homer[6] Frist (Jediah[5], Jediah Rudolph[4], Jediah[3], Henry[2], Rudolph[1]) was born 30 November 1889 in Vermillion County, Indiana, the son of Jediah and Elizabeth (Helt) Frist.[1908] He died 11 January 1983 Clinton, Vermillion County, Indiana[1909] He married on 19 February 1911 to **Mable Audrey Boyd** in Coatesville, Hendricks County, Indiana.[1910] Mable was born on 8 July 1891 in Vermillion County, Indiana, the daughter of Albert E. and Emily (Skidmore) Boyd.[1911] Mable died on 11 April 1946 in Clinton, Vermillion County, Indiana.[1912]

Mable "never met a stranger" and was beloved by all for her even personality and disposition. If a hobo or tramp came to their door, Mable would "find" a chore for him to do so that she could give him a meal without him feeling that he was begging. She taught the golden hour Sunday school class at Salem Methodist Church for many years, belonged to the Women's Society of Christian Service of that church and was a member of the Helt's Prairie Home Economics Club.[1913]

In 1920 the family lived in Helt Township in Vermillion County with their first two children, Emily and Esther.[1914] Harry was a farmer from a very early age and recalled to his daughter that he drove a team of horses when he was so small that he couldn't see over them.[1915] He was a grain farmer, but also kept several milk cows most of the time. He didn't sell the milk, but instead separated the cream and the milk, selling only the cream. The skimmed milk called "blue john" was fed to the hogs to fatten them. Although he earned a living as a farmer, he supplemented his income during the 1940s as a supervisor for the highway department in the south district of Vermillion County. He also had a grain "separator" for his own use and did some custom threshing for others.[1916]

Harry had an exceptional collection of American Indian artifacts that he had found while plowing the fields with horses. He watched for the artifacts in the turned soil and eventually mounted his collection.[1917]

Mable died in 1946 in Clinton, Vermillion County, Indiana,[1918] from complications following gall bladder surgery at the Vermillion County Hospital in Clinton. After that, Harry sold the farm and moved to a small house in Clinton. He, like his father before him, served as a trustee on the Helt's Prairie Cemetery board for several years, helping to dig graves, mow the cemetery, and even start a new book for the location of burials. He belonged to the Farm Bureau and Modern Woodsmen. He attended the Methodist Church and was very active in the Republican Party. He could never completely retire, so he mowed yards for friends and neighbors as he got older and worked as a custodian for a short while at Wilson Ford Sales.[1919]

Harry Homer died in 1983 at the age of ninety-three, also in Clinton,[1920] from complications after breaking a leg and contracting pneumonia. Harry and his wife, Mable, are both buried in Helt's Prairie Cemetery in Vermillion County, Indiana.

Children of Harry Homer[6] and Mable Audrey (Boyd) Frist, all born in Vermillion County, Indiana:

333   i. EMILY ELIZABETH[7] FRIST; born 27 November 1911; married 8 July 1936 Vermillion County, Indiana, Samuel Pyle Saxton.[1921] Samuel was born 18 September 1903 Vermillion County, Indiana, died 13 June 1980 Clinton, Indiana; buried Walnut Grove, Clinton, Indiana.[1922] Samuel was a farmer and Emily a homemaker. They owned a farm in rural Hilldale, Indiana, where they raised grain and chickens, selling both fryers and eggs. They sold the farm and retired to Clinton.[1923]

+   334   ii. ESTHER LOUISE FRIST, born 3 June 1917; married 6 October 1935 Vermillion County, Indiana, Paul Kenneth Foltz.[1924]

+   335   iii. SHIRLEY MAE FRIST, born 13 May 1922; married 11 March 1943 Vermillion County, Indiana, Melvin Maurice Jones.[1925]

+   336   iv. MYRTLE LEE FRIST, born 29 October 1927; died 26 October 1976 Greenfield, Hancock County, Indiana;[1926] married 6 April 1947, Milton Royce King.[1927]

+   337   v. PATRICIA JO FRIST, born 19 May 1932; died 29 April 2001 Vermillion
              County, Indiana.[1928]

211. Harlow Peirce⁶ Frist (Jediah⁵, Jediah Rudolph⁴, Jediah³, Henry², Rudolph¹) was born on 12 May 1891 in Vermillion County, Indiana, the son of Jediah and Elizabeth (Helt) Frist.[1929] Harlow died on 12 March 1975 in Vermillion County, Indiana.[1930] He married on 26 October 1919 in Vermillion County, Indiana, to **Helen Eliza Miller**.[1931] Eliza was born on 9 August 1898, also in Vermillion County, the daughter of David and Lavina (VanDuyn) Miller.[1932] Eliza died of pneumonia on 5 May 1993 in Home Hospital in Lafayette, Indiana.[1933]

Harlow enlisted in the United States Army on 29 August 1918 at Newport, Indiana, during World War I. He was twenty-seven years of age, had light brown eyes and dark brown hair and a dark complexion. He was 5'7½" and his occupation was farmer. He was stationed in Chillicothe, Ohio, in a hospital as an orderly during a severe flu epidemic. He was honorably discharged at Camp Sherman, Ohio, on 11 July 1919 and his character was listed as "excellent."[1934]

Harlow married that same year to Helen Eliza Miller. She was a typical farmer's wife who helped to prepare huge "threshing meals." She was active in the Salem Methodist Church and was an active member of the Helt's Prairie Home Economics Club.[1935]

In 1920 they lived in Helt Township in Vermillion County.[1936] They were newly married and as yet had no children. Harlow's youngest brother Webb Frist lived with them.

During World War II Harlow served in the Citizens Auxiliary Police (CAP), an organization for World War I veterans who were too old for service but assisted in disasters such as train wrecks.[1937] He also belonged to the American Legion. He earned a living as a farmer, living on the farm of his father Jediah most of his life.[1938]

Eliza died of pneumonia in Home Hospital in Lafayette, Indiana.[1939] Harlow died in 1975 in Vermillion County of myocardial infarction and arteriosclerosis.[1940] He and his wife are buried in Helt's Prairie Cemetery in Vermillion County.

Children of Harlow Peirce⁶ and Helen Eliza (Miller) Frist, all born in Vermillion County, Indiana:

+   338   i. MARY EDITH⁷ FRIST, born 3 November 1920; married 6 June 1942
              Tippecanoe County, Indiana, Russell E. Banes.[1941]
+   339   ii. ROBERT JEDIAH FRIST, born 16 April 1925; died 23 October 1998
              Lafayette, Tippecanoe County, Indiana; married 3 September 1950
              Vermillion County, Indiana, Frances Lillian Vrabic.[1942]

+   340   iii. BETTY LOU FRIST, born 24 November 1930; died 3 May 1990
             Columbia, Boone County, Missouri;[1943] married 19 December 1948
             Vermillion County, Indiana, Herman Francis Mayes.[1944]

213. Marshall Alban[6] Frist (Jediah[5], Jediah Rudolph[4], Jediah[3], Henry[2], Rudolph[1]) was born on 1 March 1897 in Helt Township, Vermillion County, Indiana, the son of Jediah and Elizabeth (Helt) Frist.[1945] He died on 20 June 1966 in Clinton, Vermillion County, Indiana.[1946] He married on 14 December 1919 in Vermillion County to **Marjorie Blakesley**, the daughter of Lawrence Bruce and Eva (James) Blakesley.[1947] Marjorie was born on 10 September 1901 in Helt Township, Vermillion County, Indiana.[1948] Marjorie died on 5 March 1982 in Clinton, Indiana.[1949]

Marshall graduated from Clinton High School and served in World War I. By 1920 he had married Marjorie, and they lived in Helt Township in Vermillion County.[1950] They were newly married and as yet had no children. Marjorie was a homemaker.

Marshall graduated from the Cincinnati College of Embalming in 1924. He went to work for his uncle Jasper N. Frist at the Frist Funeral home in Clinton and eventually became part owner of the company. After forty years he sold his interest in the home to Harold B. Mack. Marshall and Marjorie were both active members of the Clinton Methodist Church.[1951]

Marshall died in 1966 in Clinton from emphysema.[1952] Marjorie died in 1982[1953] while she was on her way to a World Day of Prayer meeting at the Clinton Christian Church. Both are buried in Helt's Prairie, Vermillion County, Indiana.[1954]

Children of Marshall Alban[6] and Marjorie (Blakesley) Frist, both born in Vermillion County, Indiana:

+   341   i. HAROLD B.[7] FRIST, born 28 October 1920;[1955] married 12 December
             1942 in Saint Louis, Missouri, Beulah Thomas.[1956]

+   342   ii. WAYNE EDWARD FRIST, born 19 August 1925; died 1 October 1963
             Boone County, Iowa;[1957] married 19 November 1949 Boone County,
             Iowa, Ruth Eddy.[1958]

224. Estella Elizabeth[6] "Stella" Frist (Abram Bernard[5], Abraham B.[4], James[3], Henry[2], Rudolph[1]) was born about November 1884 in Maryland, the daughter of Abram Bernard[4] and Georgianna L. (Zimmer) Frist.[1959] She died 10 April 1974 in Talbot County, Maryland, and is buried in Easton, Maryland. She married on 16 January 1913 in Baltimore, Maryland to **Harry H. Lyons**, who was born in 1887 in Trappe, Maryland, and died in Talbot County, Maryland, in 1954. Harry worked as a purser on a steamboat.[1960]

In 1920 Harry and Stella lived in Talbot County, Maryland, with their two oldest children.[1961] Harry was a farmer.

Children of Harry H. and Estella Elizabeth[6] (Frist) Lyons, all born in Trappe, Talbot County, Maryland:

343   i. DOROTHY ALIFAIR[7] LYONS, born 2 October 1916; died 8 August 1929 Easton, Talbot County, Maryland.[1962]

344   ii. HOWARD ROSS LYONS, born 13 October 1917; died 10 October 1984 Chestertown, Kent County, Maryland; married Margaret V. Quinn died 1976 Chestertown, Maryland. One child, Howard Lawrence Lyons, born 5 June 1952, married 1 October 1983 Chestertown, Kent County, Maryland, Brenda Pavon born 8 August 1961 in Westchester, Pennsylvania, daughter of Daniel and Kay Pavon (they had two children, *(a)* Rebecca Anne Lyons born 16 May 1987 and *(b)* Christopher Ross Lyons born 8 March 1990).[1963]

345   iii. MARTIN BURNETT LYONS, born 31 July 1920; never married.[1964]

346   iv. HARRY RAYMOND LYONS, born 22 August 1922; died 13 August 1998 and buried in Easton, Talbot County, Maryland; never married.[1965]

230. Dolores Mary[6] Frist (Abram Bernard[5], Abraham B.[4], James[3], Henry[2], Rudolph[1]) was born 10 June 1910 in Baltimore City, Maryland; the daughter of Abram Bernard and Genevieve T. (Quinn) Frist.[1966] She died 19 February 1996 in Edgewood, Harford County, Maryland. She married 12 June about the year 1929 to **Joseph Klima**. Joseph Klima was born in Czechoslovakia, the son of Joseph and Anna Klima. He died in May of 1984 in Baltimore City, Maryland.

Joseph owned a home on the Bush River and worked at Bethlehem Steel Corporation in Baltimore, retiring as a ship fitter. Dolores worked at Bendix in Baltimore and retired as an assembler. Both are buried in Holly Hill Memorial Park in Baltimore City, Maryland.[1967]

Children of Joseph and Dolores Mary[6] (Frist) Klima, both born in Baltimore City, Maryland:

+   347   i. DOLORES LORRAINE[7] KLIMA, born 1 August 1930; died 6 September 1996 Baltimore City, Maryland; married 10 June 1950 Baltimore City, Maryland, Eugene Alfred "Moe" Fischer, Jr.

348   ii. JOSEPH KLIMA; married Jane. Two children, *(a)* Sharon Klima and *(b)* Keith Klima.

231. Casper Bernard[6] Frist (Abram Bernard[5], Abraham B.[4], James[3], Henry[2], Rudolph[1]) was born 1 December 1914 in Baltimore City, Maryland, the son of Abram Bernard and Genevieve T. (Quinn) Frist.[1968] He died 28 May 1953 in

Baltimore County, Maryland. He married 18 September 1936 at Sacred Heart of Mary Church in Baltimore City, Maryland, to **Elenora Helen Pronek**. Elenora was born 30 June 1918 in Baltimore City, Maryland, the daughter of Jerry J. and Elenora (Kubin) Pronek.

In 1920 Casper lived with his parents in Baltimore City, Maryland.[1969] After his death in 1953, his widow Elenora married again on 28 June 1969 to Robert Gummer. Robert died 15 December 2002 in Baltimore City, Maryland.[1970] Elenora lives in Baltimore County, Maryland.[1971]

Children of Casper Bernard[6] and Elenora Helen (Pronek) Frist, both born in Baltimore City, Maryland:

+   349   i. MARGARET GENEVIEVE[7] FRIST, born 16 April 1937; married 21 November 1953 Baltimore City, Maryland, Daniel Robert Hepner.

+   350   ii. BERNARD GEORGE FRIST, born 12 April 1944; married 11 April 1964 Baltimore County, Maryland, Elizabeth Ann Adamski.

252. Lula May[6] Tyson (Sidney Marietta[5] Frist, Edmund Physick[4], James[3], Henry[2], Rudolph[1]) was born on 1 May 1887 in Port Deposit, Cecil County, Maryland, the daughter of George Elim and Sidney Marietta (Frist) Tyson.[1972] Lula died on 2 June 1975 in Cecil County, Maryland.[1973] She married on 14 January 1908 to **Samuel James Churchman**.[1974] He was born on 3 November 1883 in Calvert, Cecil County, Maryland, the son of Charles and Katie (Moore) Churchman.[1975] Samuel died on 10 July 1947 in Cecil County, Maryland.[1976]

In 1900 Lula lived with her parents in Cecil County, Maryland.[1977] By 1920 she had married to Samuel, and the Churchmans lived in Cecil County, Maryland, with their eleven-year-old son Sherwood.[1978] Samuel was a foreman on a dairy farm, and they rented their home.

In 1936 Samuel was employed by the Joseph Bancroft and Sons Company in Wilmington, Delaware, and lived in Wilmington, Delaware.[1979]

Lula remained in Cecil County, Maryland, after Samuel's death in 1947.[1980] On 6 May 1974 she lived at 48 North Main Street in Port Deposit, Cecil County, Maryland, when she applied for benefits under her husband's Social Security number.[1981] Lula wrote her will on 21 August 1958, but it wasn't probated in Cecil County until 19 June 1975.[1982] She left her entire estate to her brother Martin Moore Tyson and appointed him executor of her will. At the time she wrote her will in 1958, her son, Sherwood, was still living but was then about fifty years of age and without children. Her estate papers indicate that only her brother and three sisters had an interest in her estate.

Lula and Samuel are both buried in Hopewell United Methodist Church Cemetery in Port Deposit, Cecil County, Maryland.[1983]

Children of Samuel James and Lula May[6] (Tyson) Churchman:

351   i. SHERWOOD JAMES[7] CHURCHMAN, born 22 April 1908; died
31 October 1969;[1984] married (1) Anna Carrie Reneer and (2)
November 1965 Gladys Shank.[1985]

352   ii. Stillborn infant, born 28 August 1909.[1986]

253. John Earl[6] Tyson (Sidney Marietta[5] Frist, Edmund Physick[4], James[3], Henry[2], Rudolph[1]) was born on 28 August 1888, in Cecil County, Maryland, the son of George Elim and Sidney Marietta (Frist) Tyson.[1987] He died on 26 March 1960 in Colora, Cecil County, Maryland.[1988] He married on 7 October 1908 in Cecil County, Maryland, to **Ella Elizabeth Tosh**.[1989] Ella was born on 16 April 1889.[1990] She died on 17 September 1966 in Cecil County, Maryland.[1991]

In 1900 John lived with his parents in Cecil County, Maryland.[1992] By 1920 John had married Ella, and they lived in Cecil County, Maryland.[1993] John was an undertaker in Colora, Maryland, and they owned their own home. Their two surviving children, eleven-year-old Mary G. and three-year-old John E., lived with them. Also living with them was Ella's mother, Mary G. Tosh, a sixty-seven-year-old widow. Their last child, Margaret Elizabeth, would be born in 1921.

John wrote his will on 28 January 1959, and it was probated on 6 April 1960 in Cecil County, Maryland.[1994] He left everything to his wife, Ella. In the event she did not survive him, he also named his three surviving children—John E. Tyson, Mary G. Graeser, and Margaret T. McMullen. John died in 1960 and is buried in West Nottingham Cemetery in Colora, Cecil County, Maryland.[1995]

Ella left no will when she died in 1966 in Cecil County, Maryland, but her estate identified all of her heirs.[1996] At the time of her death she owned two lots in Rising Sun as co-tenant with her son John Edwin Tyson and his wife, Claire. Ella is buried beside her husband in West Nottingham Cemetery.

Children of John Earl[6] and Ella Elizabeth (Tosh) Tyson, all born in Cecil County, Maryland:

+   353   i. MARY GROVE[7] TYSON, born 3 March 1909; died 31 January 1969;
married (1) 14 November 1931 John Floyd Absher and (2) 2 October
1957 Oliver Graeser.[1997]

    354   ii. JOHN EARL TYSON, JR., born 11 June 1911; died 11 June 1911.[1998]

    355   iii. JOHN EDWIN TYSON, born 24 May 1916;[1999] died 7 January 2002 Cecil
County, Maryland, and buried at West Nottingham Presbyterian
Cemetery in Colora, Cecil County, Maryland;[2000] married 3 May 1952
Claire McWilliams born 30 November 1927.[2001]

+   356   iv. MARGARET ELIZABETH TYSON, born 4 September 1921; died
              2 March 1981 probably Cecil County, Maryland; married 26 June 1946
              Vernon McMullen.[2002]

258. Pearl Catharine[6] **Tyson** (Sidney Marietta[5] Frist, Edmund Physick[4], James[3], Henry[2], Rudolph[1]) was born on 9 March 1899 in Port Deposit, Cecil County, Maryland, the daughter of George Elim and Sidney Marietta (Frist) Tyson.[2003] She died on 26 February 1981 in Cecil County, Maryland.[2004] She married 23 February 1918 in Cecil County, Maryland, to **Charles Ellis Astle**,[2005] who was born 3 October 1891[2006] and died on 3 March 1967 in Cecil County, Maryland.[2007]

In 1900 Pearl lived with her parents in Cecil County, Maryland.[2008] She died fourteen years after her husband in 1981 in Cecil County,[2009] and they are both buried in Hopewell Cemetery in Port Deposit, Maryland.

Children of Charles Ellis and Pearl Catharine[6] (Tyson) Astle, all born in Cecil County, Maryland:

     357   i. DOROTHY ELLEN[7] ASTLE, born 12 March 1919; died 7 August 1919
              Cecil County, Maryland.[2010]

     358   ii. GEORGE NELSON ASTLE, born 2 September 1920; died 2 January
              1945, Cecil County, Maryland;[2011] never married.

+   359   iii. EVELYN ELIZABETH ASTLE, born 2 April 1922; married (1) 2 March
              1946 S. Clyde Crowl, Jr. and (2) 18 April 1970 Peter Kowal.[2012]

     360   iv. CHARLES ELLIS ASTLE, JR., born 3 February 1924; died September
              1924 Cecil County, Maryland.[2013]

260. Harold Edward[6] **Tyson** (Sidney Marietta[5] Frist, Edmund Physick[4], James[3], Henry[2], Rudolph[1]) was born on 10 February 1903 in Port Deposit, Cecil County, Maryland, the son of George Elim and Sidney Marietta (Frist) Tyson.[2014] Harold died on 3 December 1969 in Cecil County, Maryland.[2015] He married about 1923 to **Esther Ann Astle**, who was born on 15 October 1897 in Cecil County, Maryland, the daughter of John Westly and Annie (Chandlee) Astle.[2016] She died on 29 May 1989 also in Cecil County, Maryland.[2017]

In 1920 Harold was sixteen and lived with his parents in Cecil County, Maryland.[2018] On 19 April 1937 he was employed at the J. Earl Tyson Company in Rising Sun, Maryland, and lived in Port Deposit.[2019]

Harold died in 1969 in Cecil County, Maryland.[2020] When his wife, Esther, died in 1989 in Cecil County, Maryland, an estate was opened because of a cloud on the title to real estate held by their son, George Edward Tyson, and his wife, Charlotte.[2021] George and Esther are buried in Hopewell Cemetery in Port Deposit, Cecil County, Maryland.

Children of Harold Edward[6] and Esther Ann (Astle) Tyson, probably both born in Cecil County, Maryland:

+ 361 i. NAOMI ASTLE[7] TYSON, born 26 January 1924; married 27 November 1948 George Oliver Gross.[2022]

362 ii. GEORGE EDWARD TYSON, born 15 November 1939; married 18 June 1960 Charlotte May Wood born 25 July 1940. Children, *(a)* Daryl Leigh Tyson born 21 June 1961, *(b)* Dean Allyn Tyson born 22 May 1963, and *(c)* Laura Lynn Tyson born 23 March 1970.[2023]

261. Martin Moore[6] Tyson (Sidney Marietta[5] Frist, Edmund Physick[4], James[3], Henry[2], Rudolph[1]) was born on 30 March 1905, the son of George Elim and Sidney Marietta (Frist) Tyson.[2024] In 1920 Martin lived with his parents in Cecil County, Maryland.[2025]

He married on 7 July 1928 in Cecil County, Maryland, to **Frances Evelyn Jackson**,[2026] who was born on 2 November 1907.[2027] Martin died 9 November 1987 and is buried at Asbury Methodist Cemetery in Port Deposit, Cecil County, Maryland.[2028] In 2003 his widow Frances lives in Chestertown, Maryland, near her son.

Child of Martin Moore[6] and Frances Evelyn (Jackson) Tyson:

363 i. GEORGE ROBERT[7] TYSON, born 1 July 1937, probably in Cecil County, Maryland; married 23 August 1958 Helen May Hull born 15 November 1939. One child, Mark Robert Tyson, born 24 June 1959; died 1 February 1976.[2029]

262. Joseph Osmond[6] Frist (Oscar Haines[5], Edmund Physick[4], James[3], Henry[2], Rudolph[1]) was born 11 March 1903 at Port Deposit, Cecil County, Maryland, the son of Oscar Haines and Ella (McDowell) Frist.[2030] He died 6 November 1979 in Meadville, Crawford County, Pennsylvania.[2031] Joseph married in 1929 to **Blanche Lucille Ramsey** of Conneaut Lake, Pennsylvania.[2032] Blanche was born 12 February 1903 in Meadville, Crawford County, Pennsylvania, the daughter of Charles William and Grace Leora (Hudson) Ramsey.[3033] Blanche died in June of 1981.[2034]

In his early twenties Joseph was employed by an English textile company. In 1928 he spent a year in Coventry, England, learning the process of making cellulose acetate yarn. In 1929 he was sent to Meadville, Pennsylvania, to help set up a new cellulose acetate factory. The company became American Viscose Corporation, later a part of the FMC Corporation. He was promoted to superintendent of spinning, a position he held until his retirement in 1968.

Joseph married in 1929 to Blanche Lucille Ramsey of Conneaut Lake, Pennsylvania.[2035] Blanche had been previously married to an Anderson and had two daughters, Ida Grace Anderson and Lorraine DeEmma Anderson.

Joseph died in 1979 in Meadville, Crawford County, Pennsylvania, after a long illness.[2036] He was a member of Masonic Lodge 408; Northwestern Commandery 25 of Meadville, Pennsylvania; Zem Zem Shrine Temple of Erie, Pennsylvania; and Crawford County Shrine Club.[2037]

Blanche died in 1981,[2038] and both are buried at Roselawn Memorial Gardens in Meadville, Crawford County, Pennsylvania.

Children of Joseph Osmond[6] and Blanche Lucille (Ramsey) Frist, all born in Meadville, Crawford County, Pennsylvania:

+   364   i. RAMSEY HUDSON[7] FRIST, born 16 August 1936; married Judith Ann Nadolny.[2039]

      365   ii. SIDNEY MARIE FRIST, born 23 January 1938; died 15 June 1938 Pittsburgh, Pennsylvania, and buried Rocky Glen Cemetery in Adamsville, Pennsylvania.[2040]

+   366   iii. MICHAEL MARIA FRIST, born 19 May 1944; married 17 March 1983 Conneaut Lake, Crawford County, Pennsylvania, Elwood G. Schell, Jr.[2041]

268. Delbert Sterling[6] Frist (John Cresswell[5], Edmund Physick[4], James[3], Henry[2], Rudolph[1]) was born on 28 January 1912 in Cecil County, Maryland,[2042] the son of John Cresswell and Olive A. (Campbell) Frist.[2043] He died on 24 May 1984 in Port Deposit, Cecil County, Maryland.[2044] He married on 21 June 1943 in Cecil County, Maryland, to **Florence "Floss" Worth**. Florence was born on 18 February 1918,[2045] the daughter of Hubert and Effie (Scott) Worth.

In 1920 Sterling lived with his parents in Cecil County, Maryland.[2046] He was a United States Navy veteran of World War II and a member of the American Legion Post 194 of Rising Sun. He worked as a building and bridge inspector for the Penn Central Railroad, retiring in 1974.[2047] He is buried in Hopewell Cemetery in Port Deposit, Cecil County, Maryland.[2048] In 2003 his widow Floss lives in Cecil County, Maryland.

Children of Delbert Sterling[6] and Florence (Worth) Frist, both born in Cecil County, Maryland:

+   367   i. DELBERT LEE[7] FRIST, born 31 January 1946; married 23 August 1969 Cecil County, Maryland, Louise Benjamin.[2049]

+   368   ii. DEBORA LOUISE FRIST, born 29 January 1950; married 19 May 1973 Cecil County, Maryland, William H. Ewing.[2050]

269. John Willard[6] "Buss" Frist (John Cresswell[5], Edmund Physick[4], James[3], Henry[2], Rudolph[1]) was born on 14 November 1914 in Cecil County, Maryland,[2051] the son of John Cresswell and Olive A. (Campbell) Frist.[2052] He died in June 1965 in Oklahoma City, Oklahoma.[2053] He married 3 July 1937 at the Hopewell Methodist Church in Port Deposit, Cecil County, Maryland, to **Willa Alverta Tarbert**.[2054] Alverta was born on 5 June 1916 in Chester, Pennsylvania, the daughter of Jacob and Esther (Coulson) Tarbert. Alverta died 4 July 2000 at Gilbert, Maricopa County, Arizona.[2055]

Buss went to Jacob Tome Institute in Port Deposit, and his occupation was auto mechanic. After his marriage in 1937 to Alverta, the family moved from Maryland to Cheyenne, Wyoming, in 1952. In 1959 Buss and Alverta divorced in Cheyenne, and he later remarried. He is buried in Oklahoma City, Oklahoma.

Child of John Willard[6] and Willa Alverta (Tarbert) Frist:

+   369   i. CHARLOTTE ALMA[7] FRIST, born 13 January 1939 Port Deposit,
              Cecil County, Maryland; married 18 August 1962 Reno, Nevada,
              Bruce Turner.[2056]

270. Donald Russell[6] Frist (John Cresswell[5], Edmund Physick[4], James[3], Henry[2], Rudolph[1]) was born 7 February 1922 in Colora, Cecil County, Maryland, the son of John Cresswell and Olive A. (Campbell) Frist.[2057] He married first on 6 October 1945 at Hopewell Methodist Church, Port Deposit, Maryland, to **Doris V. Tome**. Doris was born 4 November 1920 in Cecil County, Maryland, the daughter of Peter E. and Ella O. Tome.[2058] She died 6 July 1987 and is buried at Hopewell Cemetery, Port Deposit, Maryland.[2059] Donald married second on 6 January 1989 at Hopewell Methodist Church in Cecil County, Maryland, to **Elizabeth Ann Slauch**. Elizabeth was born 6 February 1932 in Oxford, Pennsylvania, the daughter of Harry and Kathryn (Martin) Slauch.[2060]

Donald retired in 1977 from the United States Government at Aberdeen Proving Ground. His wife Doris also worked at the Aberdeen Proving Ground, retiring in 1964. She was a member of the Ladies Auxiliary of the American Legion Post 194 at Rising Sun.[2061]

Donald operates a small parts business for Jeep and Pontiac and owns, restores, and collects antique cars as a hobby. He is the proud possessor of a 1955 Kaiser Manhattan, one of only 239 four-door Manhattans that were made that year.[2062] In past years he frequented car flea markets in this pursuit, but now limits his excursions to the fall flea market at Hershey, Pennsylvania. He and his second wife Elizabeth enjoy traveling to car shows. In 2003 they live in Rising Sun, Cecil County, Maryland.[2063]

271. Garrison Kenneth[6] Frist (Oliver T.[5], Edmund Physick[4], James[3], Henry[2], Rudolph[1]) was born on 15 September 1901 in Maryland, the son of Oliver T. and Florence Gertrude (Harrison) Frist of Port Deposit, Cecil County, Maryland.[2064]

He died 24 May 1928 in Cecil County, Maryland.[2065] He married on 2 September 1922 in Harford County, Maryland, to **Mary Susan Kirk**.[2066] Mary was born on 1 November 1904, the daughter of Ernest and Mercy Moore (Townsend) Kirk.[2067] She died 8 May 1979 in Cecil County, Maryland.[2068]

In 1920 Garrison was a boarder with John Kraus in Cecil County, Maryland.[2069] His occupation was steamfitter. He married in 1922 to Mary Susan and died just six years later in 1928 at the age of twenty-seven. He is buried in Hopewell United Methodist Church Cemetery in Port Deposit, Maryland.[2070]

His widow Mary Susan was left with three small children to raise. She died fifty-two years later in 1979 and is buried beside her husband in Cecil County, Maryland.[2071]

Children of Garrison Kenneth[6] and Mary Susan (Kirk) Frist, all probably born in Cecil County, Maryland:

+   370   i. HELEN KIRK[7] FRIST, born 15 January 1923;[2072] married 24 March 1951 Cherry Hill, Maryland, Harry Walter Cooper.[2073]

+   371   ii. DOROTHY JEAN FRIST, born 16 September 1924;[2074] died 5 June 1982 Lakeland, Polk County, Florida; married 2 July 1945 in Bartow, Polk County, Florida, Frank Benjamin Ordog.[2075]

+   372   iii. FLORENCE GERTRUDE FRIST, born 22 August 1926;[2076] married 29 June 1946 Chester County, Pennsylvania, David Carlton Morris.[2077]

275. Anna Roberta[6] Foard (Anna Elizabeth[5] Frist, Robert Harris[4], Jacob Chester[3], Henry[2], Rudolph[1]) was born 13 September 1907 in New Castle County, Delaware, the daughter of John and Anna Elizabeth (Frist) Foard.[2078] She died 5 January 1998 in Hightstown, Mercer County, New Jersey. She married 4 July 1931 in Marshallton, New Castle County, Delaware, to **James Henry Smith**.[2079] James was born in 29 March 1910 in Hightstown, Mercer County, New Jersey, the son of Tilghman James and Clara (Murray) Smith. He died in 1990.

James was a 1930 graduate of the University of Delaware, the son of a Methodist minister, and he served as president of the Equitable Society.[2080] Roberta was a school teacher.

Children of James Henry and Anna Roberta[6] (Foard) Smith:

+   373   i. WARREN FOARD[7] SMITH, born 15 May 1932 Brooklyn, New York; died 1983 East Orange, Essex County, New Jersey; married 1968 East Orange, Essex County, New Jersey, Helen Ballard.[2081]

+   374   ii. WENDELL MURRAY SMITH, born 15 May 1935 Brooklyn, New York; married 1957 Brockton, Plymouth County, Massachusetts, Margaret McGregor.[2082]

+ 375 iii. JANET FRANCES SMITH, born 6 April 1941 Hartford, Hartford County, Connecticut; married 1962 Maplewood, Essex County, New Jersey, Herbert Dann.[2083]

+ 376 iv. ROBERT HENRY SMITH, born 13 October 1946 Maplewood, Essex County, New Jersey; married 1970 Norwich, Chenango County, New York, Elizabeth Brereton.[2084]

277. Franklin Peach[6] Foard (Anna Elizabeth[5] Frist, Robert Harris[4], Jacob Chester[3], Henry[2], Rudolph[1]) was born 3 June 1912 in New Castle County, Delaware, the son of John and Anna Elizabeth (Frist) Foard.[2085] Franklin graduated from the University of Delaware where he played baseball and the saxophone in the band. He taught school for awhile after graduation.[2086]

On 21 August 1937 he married **Margaret Jane "Peg" Hubert** at St. Barnabas Protestant Episcopal Church in Marshallton, New Castle County, Delaware. Peg was born 20 August 1917, the daughter of Walter and Anna Florence (Brown) Hubert. Florence Brown was the daughter of a blacksmith who was also mayor of Bridgeville, Delaware, at one time.

Franklin worked as safety supervisor for Du Pont for about thirty years. During this period of time, they moved many times and spent two years in the Netherlands.

Peg managed a beauty school, which she later owned, and also taught Sunday school at the Methodist Church. After retiring from Du Pont, Franklin taught school for a year in Martinsville, Virginia, and later managed MARC Workshop, a facility for mentally retarded/brain damaged adults, for about six years. He enjoys creating poems to commemorate occasions, and Peg immortalizes his poetry in cross-stitch embroidery. In 2003 they live in Martinsville, Virginia.[2087]

Children of Franklin Peach[6] and Margaret Jane (Hubert) Foard, all born in Wilmington, New Castle County, Delaware:

+ 377 i. MARGARET ANN[7] FOARD, born 31 October 1938; married 20 June 1959 in Woodstown, Salem County, New Jersey, to Neil Wyatt Fowser.[2088]

378 ii. FRANKLIN PEACH FOARD, born 5 October 1940; died 1945 of leukemia.[2089]

379 iii. SUSAN JEAN FOARD, born 11 September 1948; married and divorced Bill Sizemore. Children, *(a)* Lisa Ann Sizemore (who had a son Lucas, born 1998) and *(b)* Brian Michael Sizemore.[2090]

281. Roy Frist[6] Hartman (Bertie L.[5] Frist, James Ball[4], Jacob Chester[3], Henry[2], Rudolph[1]) was born on 2 May 1915 in Chattanooga, Hamilton County, Tennessee, the son of William Calvin and Bertie L. (Frist) Hartman.[2091]

In 1930 he was fifteen years of age and lived with his grandmother, mother, and uncle on the family farm in Hamilton County.[2092] One of their nearby neighbors was the family of Jacob and Nettie Houts, who had three daughters, including one named Miriam, who was sixteen years of age.[2093] He married on 8 May 1934 to **Miriam Houts**, who was born on 2 December 1913 in Sayre, Alabama,[2094] probably the daughter of Jacob C. and Nettie Houts.[2095]

In August of 1958 when his maternal uncle Joseph Byron Frist died in Chattanooga, Tennessee, Roy served as the executor of his estate and was listed in his will as his sole heir.[2096] He inherited his entire estate of $1949.46. Roy lived at St. Elmo, Tennessee, in May of 1959, when his mother died.[2097]

Children of Roy Frist[6] and Miriam (Houts) Hartman:

380   i. WILLIAM ROY[7] HARTMAN, born 13 March 1935; married Clarice Levan born 20 September 1935. Child, Cynthia Yvonne Hartman born 28 January 1957.[2098]

381   ii. ROBERT JACOB HARTMAN, born 17 January 1937; married (1) before 1960 Mary Green born 25 November 1937; divorced 21 September 1970. Children by Mary Green, *(a)* Robert Jason Hartman born 1 November 1960 and *(b)* Todd Eugene Hartman born 27 November 1962. Robert Jacob married (2) 22 February 1971 Virginia Craft. Child by Virginia Craft, *(c)* Valerie Michele Hartman born 3 November 1971.[2099]

282. John Stanley[6] Vetter, Jr. (John Stanley[5], Ann Elizabeth[4] Frist, Jacob Chester[3], Henry[2], Rudolph[1]) was born on 26 May 1928 in Chattanooga, Hamilton County, Tennessee, the only child of John Stanley and Effie Roselle (Bird) Vetter.[2100] His father died when he was just over a year old, and his mother returned to her family's home in eastern North Carolina where he was raised. John received a B.S. degree from Wake Forest in 1949 and an M.D. from Duke University in 1954.

He married on 23 January 1955 to **Sallie Louisa Middlebrooks** in Haddock, Jones County, Georgia. Sallie was born on 25 July 1934 in Macon, Georgia, the daughter of Willis Price and Sara Louisa (O'Kelly) Middlebrooks. John works as a family physician and lives in Rockingham, Richmond County, North Carolina.[2101]

Children of John Stanley[6] and Sallie Louisa (Middlebrooks) Vetter, Jr.:

382   i. SARA ROSELLE[7] VETTER, born 12 July 1956 Trumball County, Ohio; married 19 May 1979 Rockingham, Richmond County, North Carolina, Michael Joseph Mayhew born 5 October 1955 Lexington, Davidson County, North Carolina. Sara earned a B.S. degree in nursing from the University of North Carolina in 1978 and works as a registered nurse.

Michael earned his B.S. from Catawba College in 1975. He earned his D.D.S. from the University of North Carolina in 1979, an M.S. in pedodontics in 1981, and an M.S. in orthodontics in 1986. He works as a pediatric orthodontist and dentist. Children, *(a)* Sara O'Kelly Mayhew born 13 May 1982 Boone, Watauga County, North Carolina, is a freshman at Meredith College in 2001, *(b)* John Michael Mayhew born 22 May 1985 Chapel Hill, Orange County, North Carolina, and *(c)* Mary Katherine Mayhew born 7 April 1992 Boone, Watauga County, North Carolina.

383   ii. MARTHA ELIZABETH VETTER, born 3 December 1958; Martha received a B.S. in nursing from the University of North Carolina in 1982, an M.A. in religion in 1989 (with concentration in biblical studies) from the Trinity Episcopal School for Ministry in Pittsburgh, Pennsylvania, and an M.Ed. in 1994 from Marymount University in Arlington, Virginia. She works as a Christian education teacher in Little Rock, Arkansas.

284. Jane Elizabeth[6] **Frist** (John Chester[5], Jacob Chester[4], Jacob Chester[3], Henry[2], Rudolph[1]) was born 26 January 1935 in Richmond, Virginia, the daughter of John Chester and Lois Elizabeth (Ferran) Frist.[2102] She lived in many areas of the country as the family followed her father's ministerial profession. She graduated from Peace College Preparatory School in Raleigh, North Carolina, in 1952, serving as valedictorian of her class.

In 1955 Jane illustrated her mother's book *No Wings in the Manse*. In the summer of 1955, she worked in the National Parks Ministry Program in Yellowstone National Park as a hostess/cashier and in advertising. In 1956 Jane graduated from Agnes Scott College in Decatur, Georgia, earning a B.A. degree, majoring in English literature and minoring in art. She received a master's degree in education from her combined work at Princeton Seminary and the University of Denver.

Jane married on 14 June 1957 to **Arnold Cornelius "Arnie" Harms** in Mobile, Alabama. Arnie was born 3 March 1929 in Chicago, Illinois, the son of Arnold Cornelius and Irene (Crowley) Harms, Sr. He received a degree in electrical engineering from UCLA and a divinity degree from Fuller Seminary in California. He attended Princeton Seminary for his master's degree and received his Ph.D. from Drew University. He is a minister and a professor. Arnie won a scholarship at Bonn University in Germany, precipitating a move to Germany. While there, Jane taught English to the Korean ambassador to Germany, Won Yil Sohn.

They returned to the United States so that Arnie could accept the position of assistant dean of Princeton University Chapel in Princeton, New Jersey. Jane operated a small nursery school for three years while they lived there. Their next move took the family to Denver, Colorado, where Arnie was professor of religion and philosophy at the University of Denver while Jane taught third grade. She served as an elder in the Presbyterian Church in Denver and also in Orlando, Florida. During summers Jane and her children traveled from Colorado to Montreat, North Carolina, where her family had established a summer home.

Jane sold real estate for thirty years, establishing Frist Realty in 1994 in Montreat, North Carolina. Since that time, she has listed and sold more than 80 percent of the properties in Montreat. She not only put the right people with the right houses, she matched people with people and claims responsibility for six marriages!

In 1998, she wrote and illustrated the book *Montreat, How I Love You.* Jane's hobbies are watercolor painting, writing poetry and prose, photography, computer graphics, jazzercise, and pool aerobics. In the fall of 2001 she purchased a motor home and spent the winter traveling, writing her second book, and visiting friends and relatives throughout Florida. In 2003 Jane Frist lives in Montreat, North Carolina, with her two poodles Rascal and Buffy.[2103]

Children of Arnold Cornelius and Jane Elizabeth[6] (Frist) Harms:

+   384   i. JANE ALDEN[7] HARMS, born 23 January 1959 Princeton, Mercer County, New Jersey.[2104]

+   385   ii. JOHN DAVID FRIST HARMS, born 24 September 1960 New Brunswick, Middlesex County, New Jersey.[2105]

+   386   iii. ROBERT DALE HARMS, born 26 May 1962 New Brunswick, Middlesex County, New Jersey.[2106]

285. Charlotte June[6] Frist (John Chester[5], Jacob Chester[4], Jacob Chester[3], Henry[2], Rudolph[1]) was born on 4 March 1938 in Starkville, Oktibbeha County, Mississippi, the daughter of John Chester and Lois Elizabeth (Ferran) Frist.[2107] She lived in many areas of the country as the family followed her father's ministerial profession. She attended Peace Junior College in Raleigh, North Carolina, for her last two years of high school. She was president of her class in both years and voted "best all around student." She went to Southwestern University (now Rhodes College) in Memphis, Tennessee, and the University of Florida at Gainesville. She joined Tri Delta Sorority and was voted its "most outstanding freshman." She graduated from the Presbyterian School of Christian Education at Richmond, Virginia, with a B.C.E. in 1961.

She married on 25 August 1961 in Gaither Chapel, Montreat, Buncombe County, North Carolina, to **James Robert Faucette.** James was born 20 January 1933 in Bristol, Sullivan County, Tennessee. He attended Davidson College, served in the military, and then graduated from King College in Bristol, Tennessee. He received his theological degree from Union in Richmond, Virginia. He was a Presbyterian minister serving pastorates in Virginia and Texas. Jim was also a prison chaplain in Louisville, Kentucky, and a hospital chaplain in Houston, Texas. He died 1 May 1987 in Houston, Texas.

Charlotte married for the second time on 25 November 1989 at Westminster Presbyterian Church in Montgomery, Alabama, to **John Calvin Chesnutt**.

Calvin was born 11 December 1927 in Thomasville, Georgia, the son of Dr. Thomas Henry and Chrissie Wright (Boney) Chesnutt. He received B.D. and Th.M. degrees from Columbia Theological Seminary in Decatur, Georgia, and his doctor of ministry from McCormick Seminary. He was a Presbyterian minister, retiring after serving churches in Alabama and South Carolina. Calvin was previously married on 7 September 1955 to Carolyn Crawford, and they divorced in 1981. Calvin is involved in volunteering and enjoys reading, carpentry, hunting, and cooking.

Charlotte has been employed in various jobs over the years—teaching, social service, and real estate. In 2003 she is retired to full-time volunteering and is an elder in the Presbyterian Church USA. She enjoys watercolor painting and walking. She and Calvin both enjoy gardening and entertaining family and friends including her three children, their spouses, and two grandchildren and Calvin's four children, their spouses, and seven grandchildren.[2108] They live in Montreat, North Carolina.

Children of James Robert and Charlotte June[6] (Frist) Faucette:

+   387   i. ROBERT CHESTER[7] FAUCETTE, born 25 March 1963 Martinsville, Virginia; married 6 October 1990 in Greensboro, Guilford County, North Carolina, Mary Elizabeth Tota.[2109]

+   388   ii. JANE ELIZABETH FAUCETTE, born 27 September 1965 Richmond, Virginia; married 15 September 2001 Black Mountain, North Carolina, Douglas Randolph Moore.[2110]

+   389   iii. THOMAS JAMES FAUCETTE, born 8 September 1968 Louisville, Jefferson County, Kentucky; married 10 April 1999 La Jolla, San Diego County, California, Lynda Chang.[2111]

286. John Chester[6] Frist, Jr. (John Chester[5], Jacob Chester[4], Jacob Chester[3], Henry[2], Rudolph[1]) was born on 22 July 1941 in Memphis, Shelby County, Tennessee, the son of John Chester and Lois Elizabeth (Ferran) Frist.[2112] He lived in many areas as the family followed his father's ministerial profession, but most of his childhood years were spent in Mobile, Alabama. He attended McCallie Preparatory School in Chattanooga, Tennessee, and did his undergraduate work at Southwestern University (now Rhodes College) in Memphis and later Vanderbilt

University in Nashville. "Johnny" married on 15 June 1963 in Nashville, Tennessee, to **Mary Corinne Brothers**.

Mary Corinne was born 12 June 1941 in Nashville, Davidson County, Tennessee, the daughter of Russell White and Mary Kate (Troup) Brothers, Sr. She grew up in Nashville, attending Woodmont Grammar School and later Harpeth Hall for Girls, where she graduated in 1959. In 1962 she received her bachelor of arts degree from Baylor University after three years of study. In 1963 she was awarded a teaching certificate from Vanderbilt University in Nashville. After their marriage Mary Corinne faithfully followed her husband Johnny through his years of medical school, internship, residency, and missionary service overseas. She taught school in the various cities where they lived. While living in Soonchun, South Korea, Mary Corinne taught in a one-room school house where she had seven different grade level preparations.

Johnny served as a major in the United States Army during the Vietnam conflict, from September of 1968 to September of 1969. He was a commanding officer in Company B Eighty-Second Airborne. He received the Bronze Star and the Army Commendation Medal. He undertook his surgical internship and residency program at the University of Florida in Gainesville. He also did a plastic surgery fellowship at the University of Florida followed by one at the Aesthetic Surgery Center in Rio de Janeiro, Brazil, completing the work in July of 1974. The family then located to Soonchun, South Korea, where he served as plastic and reconstructive surgery consultant at the Wilson Leprosy Center. In 1982 he returned to Korea for a second term as consultant at Wilson Leprosy center. He later served as plastic surgery consultant to the task force in Zaire and Ghana under the auspices of the Presbyterian Church USA. He also served as consultant to the Crippled Children's Service for twenty years in Nashville.

Dr. Frist has been in active practice as a plastic and reconstructive surgeon in Nashville since 1975. He is a member of the American Medical Association, the American Society of Plastic and Reconstructive Surgeons, the Southeastern Society of Plastic and Reconstructive Surgeons, the JB Lynch Plastic Surgery Society, the Woodward Surgical Society, the Tennessee Medical Association, and the Nashville Academy of Medicine. He has served as trustee, vice president, and later president of the Medical Benevolence Foundation (the fund-raising arm of the Presbyterian Church). He was chief of surgery at Parkview Medical Center for three years and later served as chief of staff at Parkview Medical Center.

On a personal level, he served as deacon of the First Presbyterian Church in Nashville. Both he and Mary Corinne were active members of the First Presbyterian Church and later Westminster Presbyterian Church. He is also a 1984 graduate of Colorado Outward Bound Course.

Mary Corinne was a former president of the Nashville Medical Auxiliary, a tutor in the Salvation Army's reading program, and a student of the Bible. In her later years she became a formidable doubles tennis player. She played competitively at the Belle Meade Country Club and in NALTA. She loved God's Word, her Labrador retrievers Beowulf and Chaucer, fishing with her husband, the great outdoors, and every one of her family and friends. She died suddenly on 20 December 2000 and was at that time a member of the Covenant Presbyterian Church in Nashville.[2113]

Children of John Chester[6] and Mary Corinne (Brothers) Frist, Jr.:

+ 390   i. CORINNE ANSLEY[7] FRIST, born 9 July 1968 Nashville, Davidson County, Tennessee; married 20 June 1992 Nashville, Tennessee, Timothy Scott Glover.[2114]

+ 391   ii. JOHN CHESTER FRIST III, born 12 June 1971 Gainesville, Alachua County, Florida; married 24 August 2002 Davidson County, Tennessee, Mary Virginia West.[2115]

287. Thomas Ferran[6] Frist (John Chester[5], Jacob Chester[4], Jacob Chester[3], Henry[2], Rudolph[1]) was born on 2 July 1945 in Tampa, Hillsborough County, Florida, the son of John Chester and Lois Elizabeth (Ferran) Frist.[2116] He grew up in Mobile, Alabama, spending summers in Montreat, North Carolina. He was fourteen when his father died. He attended McCallie School in Chattanooga, Tennessee, where he lettered in three sports. He was president of the senate and of the YMCA. He was awarded many military, academic, religious, and leadership awards at McCallie, including the Grayson Medal, which was the school's highest award. He graduated from Davidson College where he lettered in soccer and was president of his class and of his fraternity. As a sophomore he was secretary-treasurer of the student council. He was later awarded the distinguished alumni award. While at Davidson, he won a Rockefeller theological grant and a Fulbright scholarship to France and India. He spent his junior year of college at the University of Montpellier in France; and among other adventures, he hitchhiked to Israel and back. In India he spent a year teaching English and American literature at a university in Indore as well as doing research in comparative religions. Leaving India, he hiked in Nepal and visited Thailand and Cambodia on his way to South Vietnam. There he worked for almost a year and a half as a UNICEF volunteer. He built hospital wards in Saigon and Danang and was responsible for UNICEF's refugee and emergency work in I Corps (Danang, Hue, Quang Ngai), feeding five thousand children a day.

On his return to the United States, he worked at the Yale Psychiatric Institute while studying at Yale University in New Haven, Connecticut, for his M.P.H. degree. After being tried and acquitted in Montgomery, Alabama, for his refusal to serve in the military, he spent six months in Tanzania on a Yale grant studying social problems related to leprosy. He enjoyed his time there, traveling around on a trail bike and climbing Kilimanjaro.

During his years in New Haven, he met his future wife, Clare, who was teaching Spanish in Boston at the time. It was actually Clare's sister Cathy who met Tom first at a Yale reception. Cathy wrote in her diary right afterward that she had just met her future brother-in-law, and she then introduced the two in Boston. On 26 August 1972 Tom married in San Jose, Costa Rica, to **Clare Elizabeth Strachan**.

Clare was born 29 January 1947 in Costa Rica, the daughter of Robert Kenneth and Elizabeth (Walker) Strachan. The Strachans were British and American missionaries. Clare's grandparents were British missionaries who founded the Latin America Mission based in Costa Rica, as well as a major hospital, seminary, school, and radio station. Clare received a B.A. degree from Wheaton College in Illinois, where she was also homecoming queen. She earned an M.A. degree in Spanish from Middlebury College and also studied in Costa Rica and California.

After their marriage, they lived in Madrid, Spain, where Clare obtained her master's degree in Spanish literature. After spending three months in Venezuela, the family moved to Brazil, where they lived for the next fifteen years. There Tom was the founder and director of SORRI, a network of eight rehabilitation centers for the disabled in Brazil. He was also a founder of MORHAN, a national movement of over eighty grassroots organizations promoting the social integration of people affected by Hansen's disease, as well as the cofounder of several other organizations. He was named an honorary citizen of Bauru, São Paulo, Brazil, given the "keys" to the cities of Bauru and São José dos Campos, and had a small park in Bauru named in his honor.

In 1984 they returned to the United States for the birth of their daughter, Lisa Kristin Frist. This also enabled Tom to attend management programs at Columbia University and the Harvard Business School.

Back in Brazil in 1988, they adopted their son, John Daniel Frist. In 1989 they returned home to the United States when Tom was named president of the American Leprosy Missions. In 1994 he became president of the International Federation of Anti-Leprosy Organizations based in London, whose twenty-two member organizations had work in over one hundred countries.

Upon completion of his duties in this office, the family moved to Montreat, North Carolina, where Tom fulfilled his dream to write a novel. It is entitled *The Descendant* and was published in the fall of 2002, the story of a young man's search for his father, which leads him into a Brazilian world of ex-Confederates, leprosy, hate, prejudice, and finally love and a purpose for living. He had already written numerous scientific articles and a book entitled *Don't Treat Me Like I Have Leprosy!*

Tom consults and continues his support of SORRI and his interests in international and social issues, leprosy, and language and is on a number of boards. He travels widely and recently toured China, El Salvador, and Guatemala on consulting trips and also visited Tibet. He is extremely grateful for all that God has given him and loves family, tennis, hiking, traveling, adventures, being useful, reading, and laughing.

His wife Clare enjoys music, tennis, volunteering for school, church, and civic activities, and playing the piano for the local church. She also has written an unpublished devotional book on the Beatitudes, as well as two histories of her family, the Walkers and Strachans.

Tom recently accepted the invitation of the president of Nicaragua and other Central American business leaders to go there to work with government, business leaders, and nongovernmental organizations in a fascinating project to promote economic development and reduce rural poverty. In September of 2002 the Frists left their home in Montreat, North Carolina, to spend at least two years in Managua, Nicaragua, where Tom serves as executive director of Fundación Adelante.[2117]

Children of Thomas Ferran[6] and Clare Elizabeth (Strachan) Frist:

+ 392   i. LISA KRISTIN[7] FRIST, born 2 April 1984 in Atlantic City, Atlantic County, New Jersey.

+ 393   ii. JOHN DANIEL FRIST, born 10 May 1988 in Ourinhos, SP Brazil.

288. Thomas Fearn[6] Frist, Jr. (Thomas Fearn[5], Jacob Chester[4], Jacob Chester[3], Henry[2], Rudolph[1]) was born 12 August 1938 in Nashville, Davidson County, Tennessee, the son of Thomas Fearn and Dorothy Harrison (Cate) Frist.[2118] He attended Eakin and Woodmont Grammar Schools in Nashville and then went to Montgomery Bell Academy, where he excelled in athletics, including playing quarterback on the state championship team, and graduated with scholastic honors. He received his bachelor's degree in 1961 from Vanderbilt University in Nashville and his M.D. degree in 1965 from Washington University School of Medicine in St. Louis, Missouri.

On 22 December 1961 Thomas Fearn Frist, Jr. married his childhood sweetheart, **Patricia Gail "Trish" Champion**, in Nashville, Davidson County, Tennessee. Trish was born on 28 September 1939 in Ripley, Lake County, Tennessee. She attended Hillsboro High School in Nashville, where she was a cheerleader and class president, and was selected Miss Nashville High School in her junior year. She received a bachelor's degree from Vanderbilt University and did postgraduate work at Peabody College in Nashville. While at Vanderbilt, she was elected cheerleader and was president of Pi Beta Phi Sorority. She was elected Miss Vanderbilt by the student body and was chosen National Football Queen at the National Collegiate Competition in California.

Trish taught junior and senior English at Kirkwood High School in St. Louis while "Tommy" pursued his M.D. degree. Their first child, Patricia Champion Frist, was born in St. Louis in 1965 during Tommy's last year of medical school.

After receiving his medical degree, he served a surgical internship at Vanderbilt University Medical Center in Nashville prior to his service as an Air Force flight surgeon during the Vietnam War. He was assigned to a Strategic Air Command Unit in Warner Robins, Georgia, and it was here that their second child, Thomas Fearn Frist III, was born in 1968. A third son, William Robert Frist, was born the following year in Nashville.

While serving in the United States Air Force, Tommy developed the concept of a multi-hospital company and shared his idea with his father, who had founded Parkview Hospital and Park Vista Nursing Home in the early 1960s. His father, along with other investors, was in the process of converting the facilities into a not-for-profit entity.

After completing his military commitment, he and his family returned to Nashville where he pursued his multi-hospital concept. This concept later developed into the nation's largest and leading provider of healthcare services.

In 1968, Tommy founded Hospital Corporation of America (HCA) in Nashville, with his father, Dr. Thomas F. Frist, Sr. and Jack C. Massey. In 1977, he became president and chief operating officer of HCA and subsequently became chairman, president, and CEO in 1987. In 1989, he initiated a management-led leveraged buyout of HCA, which by the time of its initial public offering in 1992 was recognized as the largest and most successful management-led buyout in the history of corporate America. When HCA and another hospital company, Columbia, merged in February 1994, he served in a nonmanagement role as chairman of the board and after the company's merger in April 1995 with HealthTrust, Inc., as vice chairman of the board.

In August of 1997, Tommy was asked by the board of directors of Columbia/HCA to again become the chairman and CEO. Over the next three and a half years and in response to government investigation into fraud and abuse allegations by the prior management, he completely rebuilt the management team. He recruited and established one of the top boards of directors in corporate America, restructured the assets, rebuilt a strong balance sheet, and put in place state-of-the-art management controls. Most importantly, he rebuilt a systemwide culture that reflected the beliefs and values established early in the history of Hospital Corporation of America by its founders. After he settled the majority of the issues with the government and reestablished the company's reputation with all publics, he returned to the name so admired in the past—Hospital Corporation of America. In January 2001 he relinquished the title CEO to Jack Bovender while retaining the chairmanship until his official retirement in January 2002.

Trish and Tommy are prominent community leaders and nationally recognized philanthropists, and their contributions are numerous and widespread throughout the Nashville community and the nation as well. They have assumed major leadership roles in numerous local and national capital fund initiatives. They funded the Frist Teen Center at the Green Hills YMCA, the Frist Learning Center at Cheekwood, the Patricia Champion Frist building on the Vanderbilt University Campus, and the Frist Campus Center at Princeton, University. In addition to funding Frist Hall at Ensworth School, Trish and Tommy provided the major lead donation for the founding of the new Ensworth High School, a private coeducational high school scheduled to open in 2004. They also support the Nashville Zoo.

Recognizing the need for a downtown art museum in Nashville, the Frists partnered with the Frist Foundation in the creation of the Frist Center for Visual Arts, which opened in April of 2001. The center, housed in Nashville's beautifully restored, historic downtown post office, hosts major United States and international exhibitions as well as those by local, state, and regional artists.

Trish serves on the boards of SunTrust Bank of Nashville, SunTrust Banks, Inc. in Atlanta, the Community Foundation of Middle Tennessee, the Tennessee Performing Arts Foundation, and the Ensworth School. She is a partner in Frist Capital Partners, a member of the board of directors of the Frist Foundation, and a member of the advisory board for the Frist Center for the Visual Arts, and was involved in the development of the Frist Learning Center at Cheekwood.

Over his thirty-year career, Dr. Frist was active in numerous civic, charitable, and philanthropic endeavors. Next to his family and the founding of HCA, he considers these activities the most enjoyable and rewarding. He was always mindful that it was HCA that provided the time and the resources, both personal and company, as well as the platform to use his entrepreneurial skills to pioneer transformational efforts in the nonprofit sector. Special mention should be made of the lasting impact on charitable contributions nationwide made through his founding of the Alexis de Tocqueville Society in United Way and the Frist Foundation.

Today in 2003 Tommy is chairman of the board of the Frist Center for the Visual Arts, the Frist Foundation, Nashville Healthcare Council, and Hospital Corporation of America Foundation. In addition, he serves on the boards of Montgomery Bell Academy, the Harvard Business School, American Society of Corporate Executives, the Business Council, and Hospital Corporation of America.

His awards and honors over the years are numerous. In 1982 and 1983 he received the Silver Award by *Financial World* magazine as CEO of the Year. In 1985 he was the first recipient of the Alexis de Tocqueville award, United Way of Middle

Tennessee. He has been listed in the Forbes 400 since 1992. More recently, in 2002 he received the Distinguished Alumnus Award from Vanderbilt University.

He is an avid pilot and enjoys flying as well as tennis, biking, skiing, and running. The Frists live in Nashville in 2003.[2119]

Children of Thomas Fearn[6] and Patricia Gail (Champion) Frist, Jr.:

+   394   i. PATRICIA CHAMPION[7] FRIST, born 17 January 1965 St. Louis, Missouri; married 29 June 1991 Nashville, Davidson County, Tennessee, Charles Anthony Elcan.[2120]

+   395   ii. THOMAS FEARN FRIST III, born 16 February 1968 Warner Robins Air Force Base, Georgia; married 26 September 1998 Southampton, Suffolk County, New York, Julie Mead Damgard.[2121]

+   396   iii. WILLIAM ROBERT FRIST, born 29 December 1969 Nashville, Davidson County, Tennessee; married 28 June 1997 Nashville, Davidson County, Tennessee, Jennifer Catherine Rose.[2122]

289. Dorothy Cate[6] Frist (Thomas Fearn[5], Jacob Chester[4], Jacob Chester[3], Henry[2], Rudolph[1]) was born on 4 June 1941 in Nashville, Davidson County, Tennessee, the daughter of Thomas Fearn and Dorothy Harrison (Cate) Frist.[2123] She was the second child and first daughter in a family of five. She grew up in Nashville and fondly recalls her dad building a lighted skating rink for the children in the basement of their Fairfax Avenue home. After the family moved to the Bowling Avenue home, she remembers that they had horses, cats, a dog named Pogo, turkeys, and once an alligator that her brother Tommy brought home from Florida. Her horse was Chico, a stubborn animal who preferred not to "go" when urged to do so.

While in high school, she also attended the Joe Susan Modeling School in Nashville. After graduating from Hillsboro High School in 1959, she attended Peabody College in a business administration program. In 1961, her older brother Tommy flew her to Fort Lauderdale, Florida, where she lived in her grandmother Jennie Frist's home for a year. Her grandmother, who died in 1953, had owned a boardinghouse in Florida that was still in the family, so there was plenty of room. Her aunt Helen Cameron and her cousin Cam also lived in the boardinghouse.

"Dottie" pursued a career as a professional model during this period. Returning to Nashville, she married **Charles Ray Eller** on 9 March 1963 at Westminster Presbyterian Church in Nashville.

Charles was born on 7 September 1938 in Nashville, Tennessee. He earned a B.A. degree in business from David Lipscomb College in Nashville. He served in the air force for four years after their marriage. He was stationed at Fort Wainwright Air Force Base in Fairbanks, Alaska. Their only child, a daughter, Deborah Frist Eller, was born there on 8 February 1964. The Ellers divorced in 1971.

Returning to the Nashville area, Dottie married **Richard Boensch** in 1976. Richard was born 22 October 1941 in Nashville, Tennessee. He earned a B.A. and an M.A. degree in business administration from Peabody College. They moved to a home Dottie owned on Center Hill Lake near Cookeville, Putnam County, Tennessee. Dottie also owned a business, Tire Engineers and Auto Parts, in Cookeville. Richard managed the business and Dottie worked in it for eight years until their divorce in 1984.

Dottie lives in Nashville in 2003. She likes to travel and sew. She enjoys music, art, writing, and the theater. Her favorite sport is tennis. She directs her generous charitable activities toward helping children become better educated. She does volunteer work, both in the hospital and at Westminster Presbyterian Church. She remembers her mother as a loving person with a great heart. She recalls that her father, as busy as he was, always found time to attend the events that are so important in the lives of young children.[2124]

Child of Charles Ray and Dorothy Cate[6] (Frist) Eller:

+   397   i. DEBORAH FRIST[7] ELLER, born 8 February 1964 Fairbanks, Alaska; married in 1990 Raymond Keach.[2125]

290. Robert Armistead[6] Frist (Thomas Fearn[5], Jacob Chester[4], Jacob Chester[3], Henry[2], Rudolph[1]) was born on 27 October 1942 in Montgomery, Alabama, the son of Thomas Fearn and Dorothy Harrison (Cate) Frist.[2126] He grew up in Nashville, Tennessee, where he attended Montgomery Bell Academy (MBA). He was in the National Honor Society and Totomoi, an honorary fraternity at MBA, founded in 1954. He was president of the honor council. He was captain of both the basketball and tennis teams, quarterback of the football team and voted "most athletic." On the tennis team, he was NIL champion and regional champion in singles and doubles.

Following graduation from MBA, he enrolled at Vanderbilt University, where he played freshman basketball, was on the tennis team, and joined Phi Delta Theta Fraternity. He graduated with a B.S. degree. He met his wife to be, **Carol Len Knox,** in Sunday school at Westminster Presbyterian Church.

They were married on 6 June 1964 in Nashville, Tennessee, at the Westminster Presbyterian Church. Carol Len Knox was born on 8 March 1944 in Nashville, Tennessee, the daughter of James Hugh and Lura Evelyn (Notgrass) Knox, Jr. Carol attended Hillsboro High school, where she was in the National Honor Society and was also a cheerleader, a class officer, and voted "friendliest." She attended Vanderbilt University for two years from 1962 to 1964, where she was a member of Delta Delta Delta sorority. She received her B.S. in secondary education from the University of Virginia. She was a member of Lychnos Society, the women's honor society, and received the Z Society Book Award (for graduating as the top-ranking student in the school of education).

"Bobby" earned his M.D. degree at the University of Virginia in 1968. He completed his internship and residency in general and thoracic surgery at the University of Kentucky Albert B. Chandler Medical Center. He is a board certified general surgeon and cardiothoracic surgeon. He is a member of the Nashville Surgical Society and a Fellow of the American College of Surgeons. Bobby practiced cardiothoracic surgery in Nashville until his retirement in 1995.

He was the founder and a former director of Eyecare Corporation and Endeavor Technology. He was a former member of the board of directors of American Retirement Corporation, Mid South Health Plan, and OPTS. In 1978 he founded the Tar Heel Capital Corporation and is now its co-owner and chairman. The company currently owns and operates sixty-eight Wendy's restaurants in North and South Carolina. Bobby is a board member of HealthLeaders, Inc. and is also on the advisory board of Delta Capital.

His community service activities include past service as a trustee for Harding Academy and work with the Charles Davis Foundation. He currently serves as a director of the Dorothy Cate and Thomas F. Frist Foundation and as trustee of Westminster School (now Curry-Ingram Academy), and is on the Cumberland Heights Advisory Committee.

Carol has served as president of Harding Academy Auxiliary, chairman of Brentwood Academy Board of Trustees, and on the Heart Gala Benefit Board and the Eve of Janus Benefit for Children's Hospital. She has served on the boards of Cumberland Museum and Science Center, Belle Meade Plantation, and American Heart Association Middle Tennessee Chapter.

Currently, she is on the board of Harding Academy, the Nashville Public Library Foundation, and the Louisville Presbyterian Theological Seminary in Louisville, Kentucky. She works with the International Storytelling Center in Jonesborough, Tennessee. She is an elder at Westminster Church, chair of the Hillsboro Advisory Council, and a sustaining member of the Junior League of Nashville.

In 2003 the Frists live in Nashville and are members of Westminster Presbyterian Church. They love to go to Center Hill lake and enjoy boating and water sports. Carol enjoys reading, the theater, and music. Bobby loves to golf and has made three "holes in one."[2127]

Children of Robert Armistead[6] and Carol Len (Knox) Frist:

+   398   i. ROBERT ARMISTEAD[7] FRIST, JR., born 7 April 1967 Charlottesville, Albemarle County, Virginia; married 11 September 1999 in Nashville, Davison County, Tennessee, Melissa Merriman.[2128]

+ 399 ii. CAROL LEN FRIST, born 11 January 1970 Lexington, Fayette County, Kentucky; married 28 December 1991 Nashville, Davidson, County, Tennessee, Scott McClain Portis.[2129]

+ 400 iii. JAMES KNOX FRIST, born 11 July 1972 Lexington, Fayette County, Kentucky.[2130]

291. Mary Louise[6] **Frist** (Thomas Fearn[5], Jacob Chester[4], Jacob Chester[3], Henry[2], Rudolph[1]) was born on 10 October 1946 in Nashville, Tennessee, the second daughter in a family of five, to Thomas Fearn and Dorothy Harrison (Cate) Frist.[2131] She grew up in Nashville and loved being in the midst of her brothers and sister. There were games of football and badminton in the side yard and competitive games of Ping-Pong in the game room and balloon basketball in the front hall of the Bowling home. Life to her was ideal. She had loving and caring parents and siblings who provided the fun and activity she so enjoyed. Many an afternoon, she could be found riding her Tennessee walking horse "Molly," stabled in the barn in the back field. Neighborhood and school friends were always welcome at the Frist home. Mary developed a love for sports and played varsity tennis and basketball for Hillsboro High School.

After graduating from Hillsboro High School, Mary enrolled at the University of Alabama. In her sophomore year, she transferred to George Peabody College of Vanderbilt University in Nashville majoring in elementary education. She met **Henry Lee Barfield II**, her husband to be, on a blind date at the first football game of the season. They had a fun-filled courtship throughout their Vanderbilt years. They were married in their senior year on 31 January 1968 at Westminster Presbyterian Church in Nashville, Tennessee.

Henry Lee Barfield II was born on 22 July 1946 in Macon, Bibb County, Georgia, the son of Lee Bayne and Corinne Powers (Cole) Barfield. While at Vanderbilt, he was president of the senior class. He was elected Bachelor of Ugliness, a student recognition of the outstanding senior male. He served as vice president of his fraternity, Sigma Alpha Epsilon.

Lee received his B.A. degree in philosophy from Vanderbilt University in 1968, and Mary received her degree in elementary education. After they graduated from Vanderbilt University in June of 1968, they left for Newport, Rhode Island, where he attended naval officer candidate school and was commissioned as an ensign. He served in the anti-submarine warfare section of the navy, and they were stationed in Antigua in the West Indies for a year. In 1969, they were transferred to Norfolk, Virginia, where their first child, Mary Lauren, was born.

In July of 1971, they returned to Nashville and Lee enrolled at Vanderbilt Law School. In 1974 he received his J.D. degree from Vanderbilt and obtained his license to practice law in Tennessee. He is a partner with the law firm of Bass, Berry

& Sims, PLC. Lee is engaged in the trial of complex business and health law cases, including the defense of class action litigation.

Lee has served in a variety of professional, educational, community service, and philanthropic organizations over the years. He was president of the Nashville Bar Association in 1985 and served as a member and chairman of the board of directors of the Vanderbilt Law School Alumni Association in 1994. He was a member of the board of directors of the American Society of Law, Medicine, and Ethics from 1995 to 1998 and served on the board of Law Examiners for the State of Tennessee from 1989 to 2000.

Beyond the legal community, he has served on the boards of the Ensworth School, Harpeth Hall, and Brentwood Academy. He was president of the Ensworth Board of Trustees and the Brentwood Academy Board of Trustees.

Currently, he serves on the board of Montgomery Bell Academy, the Nashville Public Radio, and the Frist Center for Visual Arts. He has been a member of the board of directors of the YMCA of Nashville and Middle Tennessee since 1974 and was chairman of the board in 1992.

Two more daughters, Dorothy and Corinne, and a son, Cole, were born to Lee and Mary in Nashville. Four young children kept Mary very busy for years. She appreciates education and was always heavily involved in her children's schools. She served on the boards of the Ensworth School, Westminster Kindergarten, and the auxiliary boards of Montgomery Bell Academy and the Harpeth Hall School. She was a Girl Scout leader or a room mother most years. She served as chair of annual giving at Ensworth and the Montgomery Bell Academy spaghetti supper. She was a Sunday school teacher at Westminster Presbyterian Church for many years.

Her community contributions are not limited to her children. She has served on the auxiliary board of the Salvation Army and the boards of Friends of Children's Hospital and Cumberland Heights Alcohol and Drug Treatment Center.[2132] She was an active member of the Junior League of Nashville and chaired the YWCA Academy for Women of Achievement.

Mary serves on the boards of the National Vanderbilt Alumni Association, the Nashville Vanderbilt Club, and the YWCA Advisory Board. Mary and Lee serve together as chairs for the Peabody Roundtable.

Mary finds her greatest joy in the love she has for her husband, Lee, their children, grandchildren, extended family, and friends. She enjoys their many family activities such as golf, tennis, skiing, hiking, dancing, and travel. She was devoted to her parents and values their greatest legacy of love and compassion for others and their sense of honor and loyalty. They live in Nashville, Tennessee, in 2003.[2133]

Children of Henry Lee and Mary Louise[6] (Frist) Barfield II:

+   401   i. MARY LAUREN[7] BARFIELD, born 2 January 1970 Portsmouth,
            Virginia; married 28 August 1993, Nashville, Davidson County,
            Tennessee, Lawson Coffee Allen.[2134]

+   402   ii. DOROTHY FRIST BARFIELD, born 25 August 1971 Nashville,
            Davidson County, Tennessee; married 30 September 2000 Nashville,
            Tennessee, John Claiborne "Clay" Sifford.[2135]

+   403   iii. CORINNE COLE BARFIELD, born 29 October 1973 Nashville,
            Davidson County, Tennessee.[2136]

+   404   iv. LEE COLE BARFIELD, born 31 October 1980 Nashville, Davidson
            County, Tennessee.[2137]

292. William Harrison[6] Frist (Thomas Fearn[5], Jacob Chester[4], Jacob Chester[3], Henry[2], Rudolph[1]) was born on 22 February 1952 in Nashville, Davidson County, Tennessee, the son of Thomas Fearn and Dorothy Harrison (Cate) Frist.[2138] His earliest memories are of his father, leaving after dinner with his worn black doctor's bag in the right seat of his old (never new) Chevrolet car, to make his nightly rounds at the hospital. Bill Frist was raised with a passion for helping people and this sense of service has been the driving force in his life.

He graduated from Woodmont Grammar School and then went to Montgomery Bell Academy in Nashville, graduating in 1970. He was president of the student body and editor of the yearbook. Encouraged by his brother Tommy, he learned to fly and soloed when he was sixteen.

Frist enrolled in Princeton University, where he pursued premedical studies and health care policy at the Woodrow Wilson School of Public and International Affairs. He was active in student government while at Princeton.

While in college, Frist spent a summer interning with veteran Tennessee congressman Joe Evins in Washington, D.C. The "dean" of the state's congressional delegation told the young intern that should he ever want to serve in Congress, he should first excel in some field other than politics.

Frist noted the advice and, after graduating from Princeton in 1974, pursued a medical degree at Harvard Medical School. He graduated from Harvard with honors in 1978 and spent the next six years in surgical training at Massachusetts General Hospital in Boston and Southampton General Hospital in England.

It was during his residency in Boston that Frist met his wife to be, **Karyn Jean McLaughlin**. While Bill was at Massachusetts General Hospital, Karyn was teaching part time in Boston and working as a flight attendant. They married on 14 March 1981 in Lubbock, Texas.

A West Texas native, Karyn was born on 31 May 1954 in Lubbock, the daughter of William Eddie and Kathryn Louise (Loving) McLaughlin II.[2139] She was raised to value personal responsibility, self-reliance, and hard work. She earned a bachelor's degree in elementary education and special education from Texas Christian University in Fort Worth, Texas. She was rush chairman of Kappa Kappa Gamma sorority and president of the Pan-Hellenic Council. She taught children with physical and mental disabilities in Dallas public schools.

Their first child, William Harrison Frist, Jr., was born in Southampton, England. They would have two more sons, Jonathan McLaughlin, born in California, and Bryan Edward, born in Tennessee.

In 1985, Frist accepted the position of senior fellow and chief resident at the Stanford University School of Medicine. There he studied the new field of heart transplantation with transplant pioneer Norman Shumway. Bill Frist had found his niche.

After completing his surgical fellowship, Frist took his expertise back to his hometown of Nashville. In 1986, he became director of the Vanderbilt University Medical Center's heart and lung transplantation program.

He immediately began building on his bold vision for an innovative facility that would bring together in an unprecedented way transplant specialists and scientists from a broad range of disciplines. In 1989, he founded and became surgical director of the multi-organ Vanderbilt Transplant Center, which he developed into one of the premier transplant facilities in the United States.

During his twenty years in medicine, Bill Frist performed over 150 heart and lung transplant procedures, including the first lung transplant and the first pediatric heart transplant in Tennessee and the first successful combined heart-lung transplant in the Southeast. He also wrote over one hundred articles, chapters, and abstracts on medical research and coauthored the book *Grand Rounds in Transplantation.*

In 1989, Frist wrote and published *Transplant: A Heart Surgeon's Account of the Life-and-Death Dramas of the New Medicine.* His goal was to dispel myths about transplantation and encourage people to become organ donors. He lectured nationally on the subject and led a successful campaign to return the organ donor card to the back of the Tennessee driver's license.

Bill Frist had risen to the top of the medical profession at a remarkably young age. And he was devoting his life to what he loved the most—helping people. But Frist believed he could do even more for medicine, for patients, and eventually, for the people of Tennessee and the United States of America.

Frist then began exploring the idea of seeking public office. In 1990, he met with Howard Baker and talked with the former Tennessee senator and Senate majority leader about the benefits and burdens of public service. Baker told Frist that the U.S. Senate would provide the best forum for his talents, expertise, and ambitions. Frist officially launched his campaign for the Senate in 1994.

After defeating five opponents in a hard-fought primary, he faced a popular three-term senator who was also in line to become the next Democrat majority leader. The campaign unfolded as a battle between a career politician and a populist outsider—the citizen legislator. Bill Frist won by a resounding thirteen percentage points and became the first practicing physician elected to the Senate since 1928.

Six years later Frist won reelection with 66 percent of the vote and the largest margin of victory in a statewide election in the history of Tennessee. During that time, he also wrote his third book, *Tennessee Senators 1911–2002: Portraits of Leadership in a Century of Change.*

As a United States senator, Bill Frist has emerged as one of the leading voices on health issues in America today. He has fought hard to strengthen Medicare, provide seniors with better access to prescription drugs, and make health care more affordable and available to every American. His service on the Health, Labor, Education, and Pension Committee and as chairman of the subcommittee on public health positioned him to address these issues.

Frist's expertise in infectious diseases enabled him to take on one of the greatest threats to the health and security of our nation—bioterrorism. During the October 2001 anthrax attacks, the national spotlight shined on Frist as the calming voice to a frightened country. He worked quickly to pass landmark legislation to bolster America's defenses against bioterrorism. He then wrote his fourth book, *When Every Moment Counts*, to help families prepare for a potential bioterror attack.

As a member of the Foreign Relations Committee and chairman of the African Affairs subcommittee, Bill Frist has been a strong advocate for increasing funding for global HIV/AIDS. He proposed legislation that would create the first federal framework for the care, treatment, and prevention of HIV/AIDS around the world. As he did with bioterrorism, Frist has taken the fight against global HIV/AIDS beyond the Senate chamber. At least once a year, he travels to Sub-Saharan Africa as part of a medical mission team.

America's children have been another top priority for Frist. He strongly supported President Bush's *No Child Left Behind Act*, which provided regular testing, local control, more federal funding, and greater accountability and flexibility to our education system. Reducing childhood obesity, halting childhood vaccine shortages, and fighting drug abuse have been the focus of Frist's efforts to improve the health of our children.

Frist rose through the ranks of leadership in the U.S. Senate with unprecedented speed. In 2000 he was elected unanimously by his colleagues as chairman of the National Republican Senatorial Committee. Under his leadership, for the first time in history, the party of the president regained majority control of the U.S. Senate in midterm elections. Frist was also one of two congressional representatives to the United Nations General Assembly.

In 2002 he was unanimously elected as the eighteenth majority leader of the United States Senate. He is the ninth Republican to hold that post. He was elected after only eight years in the Senate, having served fewer total years in Congress than any majority leader in history.

Anyone who knows Bill Frist knows nothing means more to him than his family. He calls Karyn and sons Harrison, Jonathan, and Bryan his "foundation in life."

Karyn's life centers around her three sons. She serves on the regional board of Focus (Fellowship of Christians in Universities and Schools). She actively serves her community, devoting much of her time to raising awareness of and supporting women's health issues, including breast cancer and heart disease. She is a member of the National Alliance for the Mentally Ill and is on the board of the Children's Inn at the National Institutes of Health.

She is a strong advocate for the arts, serving on the boards in Washington, D.C., of the National Museum of Women in the Arts, Ford's Theatre, and the Meridian International Center, and in Nashville of the Frist Center for the Visual Arts. Having studied ballet in high school and college, she is on the boards of both the Nashville and Washington, D.C., ballet companies. She has served as an officer of the Senate Spouses as well as president of International Club I.

An avid exercise enthusiast her entire life, Karyn enjoys running, aerobics, and playing tennis and golf. In what few spare hours she has, she can be found in her garden or at her piano. She is a private pilot. Bill also enjoys flying (commercial, instrument licenses), running (seven marathons), and writing.

The Frists are active members of the National Presbyterian Church in Washington, D.C., and Westminster Presbyterian Church in Nashville. They reside in the family home on Bowling Avenue in Nashville, Tennessee, where Bill was born and raised, and they also have a home in Washington, D.C.[2140]

Children of William Harrison[6] and Karyn Jean (McLaughlin) Frist:

+   405   i. WILLIAM HARRISON[7] FRIST, JR., born 6 May 1983 Southampton, England.

+   406   ii. JONATHAN MCLAUGHLIN FRIST, born 11 October 1985 Stanford, California.

+   407   iii. BRYAN EDWARD FRIST, born 29 April 1987 Nashville, Davidson County, Tennessee.

294. Sidney Donald⁶ Frist (Paul Franklin⁵, Joseph Elmer⁴, Jacob Chester³, Henry², Rudolph¹) was born 25 June 1930 in Chattanooga, Hamilton County, Tennessee, the son of Paul Franklin and Kate Irene (Groves) Frist.[2141] He attended John A. Patten public school in Hamilton County. His sixth grade report card survived to document a fairly mediocre student, although he did excel in reading.[2142]

Sidney was raised in the shadow of his older brother Robert Joe Frist, who was killed in action in France during World War II. On 23 April 1948, just two months shy of his eighteenth birthday, Sidney enlisted in the United States Marine Corps for a three-year term.[2143] He was described as single, 69" high with gray eyes, brown hair, and a ruddy complexion. He was honorably discharged with the rank of private first class on 21 February 1950. He qualified as a rifle sharpshooter and was a refrigeration specialist, leaving the service with a Good Conduct Medal.

Sidney Donald married **Norma Drucilla Roberts**, the daughter of Norman L. and Roxy Roberts.[2144] Sidney seemed unable to settle down and to adjust to married life after his service in the marines and he and Norma eventually divorced.[2145]

Sidney died 1 January 1973 in Chattanooga, Hamilton County, Tennessee.[2146] He worked for an equipment company as a maintenance man. Norma remarried and died 30 March 1999 at Fort Oglethorpe, Georgia. She is buried in Hamilton Memorial Gardens in Chattanooga, Hamilton County, Tennessee.[2147]

Children of Sidney Donald⁶ and Norma Drucilla (Roberts) Frist, all born in Chattanooga, Hamilton County, Tennessee:

> 408   i. LARRY D.⁷ FRIST, born 9 August 1950; died 12 September 1950 Chattanooga, Tennessee; buried Boydston Cemetery.[2148]
>
> 409   ii. PAMELA SUSANNE FRIST, born 15 July 1953; married Curtis L. Brown son of Joe D. and Sandy Brown. Children, both born in Chattanooga, Hamilton County, Tennessee, *(a)* Christopher Lee Brown born 4 November 1976 and *(b)* Eric Scott Brown born 2 September 1980.[2149]
>
> +   410   iii. RONALD GARY "RONNIE" FRIST, born 29 November 1956; married (1) 14 August 1978 Carla M. and (2) 19 September 1998 Hamilton County, Tennessee, Michelle Helene Major.[2150]

297. Frank Emmett⁶ Frist (James Charles⁵, Joseph Elmer⁴, Jacob Chester³, Henry², Rudolph¹) was born on 1 December 1925 in Chattanooga, Hamilton County, Tennessee, the son of James Charles and Sadie Estell (Briggs) Frist.[2151] He served in the United States Navy during World War II.[2152] He married in 1951 to **Avene Phillips** in Rossville, Georgia. Avene was born 9 September 1931 in Chattanooga, Tennessee,[2153] the daughter of Anderson Phillips.[2154] She died at the age of thirty-one on 26 September 1962 in Chattanooga and is buried in the Forest Hills Cemetery.[2155]

Frank married again, possibly about the year 1969, to **Margaret (Contillo) Kensinger**. They divorced in 1971.[2156] Margaret continued to use the Frist surname and died in Chattanooga in March of 1991.[2157] In 2002 Frank lives in Georgia near his son Jimmy.[2158]

Children of Frank Emmett[6] and Avene (Phillips) Frist, all born in Chattanooga, Hamilton County, Tennessee:

+ 411 i. FRANKIE SUSAN[7] FRIST, born 5 March 1952; married 25 April 1987 Chattanooga, Tennessee, Robert Taylor Dixon.[2159]

+ 412 ii. MONA FRIST, born 5 August 1959; married (1) and divorced Darryl Willett. Mona married (2) 22 May 1993 Steve Byer.[2160]

+ 413 iii. JAMES LELAND FRIST, born 7 July 1960; married 29 June 1985 Chickamauga, Walker County, Georgia, Lisa Osburn.[2161]

299. Patricia Estelle[6] Frist (James Charles[5], Joseph Elmer[4], Jacob Chester[3], Henry[2], Rudolph[1]) was born on 28 September 1937 in Chattanooga, Hamilton County, Tennessee, the daughter of James Charles and Sadie Estell (Briggs) Frist.[2162] Her first marriage was in December 1955 to **Edward Leon Garrett** and they later divorced. Her second marriage was on 22 May 1971 in Trenton, Dade County, Georgia, to **Mark Tell Huguenin**, who adopted her children and gave them his surname.

Mark was born 24 October 1923 in Chewelah, Stevens County, Washington, the son of Mark Arthur and Magdelina "Maggie" (Gardner) Huguenin. In 2003 they live in Chattanooga, Tennessee. Mark is retired, and Pat enjoys volunteering at Memorial Hospital.[2163]

Children of Edward Leon and Patricia Estelle[6] (Frist) Garrett, all born in Chattanooga, Hamilton County, Tennessee:

414 i. KYMBERLY BRIGGITTE[7] GARRETT HUGUENIN, born 18 February 1958 Memorial Hospital; married 4 April 1981 Chattanooga, Tennessee, Charles Thomas McKeehan born 6 May 1957 Madisonville, Monroe County, Tennessee, son of Paul Richard and Swandla "Sally" (Jones) McKeehan. Tom is manager of Chattanooga Branch of Motion Industries and Kymberly is an account executive with Cuna Mutual Insurance. They live in Chattanooga, Tennessee, in 2003.

415 ii. SHARON MICHELLE GARRETT HUGUENIN, born 12 October 1961

Memorial Hospital; married May 2000 Savannah, Georgia, Steven Ellis Lynn born 30 March 1953 Columbia, Maury County, Tennessee. She has twin stepchildren, *(a)* Whitney Ruth Lynn and *(b)* Victoria Elizabeth Lynn, born 30 October 1989. Steve is vice president of marketing with S. P. Richards Company in Atlanta, Georgia. Sharon was a print model in New York. They live in Marietta, Georgia, in 2003.

416   iii. MARK EDWARD GARRETT HUGUENIN, born 12 July 1969 Erlanger Hospital; married 27 November 1993 Kelly Key. Mark is employed at Brock Candy Company and Kelly works in Sun Trust Bank and Mortgage Company. They live in Chattanooga, Tennessee, in 2003.

300. Fred[6] **Duke** (Mary Emma[5] Frist, Emmett Franklin[4], Jacob Chester[3], Henry[2], Rudolph[1]) was born 11 December 1925 in Gadsden, Etowah County, Alabama, the son of Curtis and Mary Emma (Frist) Duke.[2164] Fred served in the United States Navy during World War II. He married 15 June 1947 in Gadsden to **Julia Maxine Cothran**, who was born 8 October 1926 in Gadsden. He was employed at Allis-Chalmers Corporation. The family lives in Gadsden, Alabama, in 2002.[2165]

Children of Fred[6] and Julia Maxine (Cothran) Duke, both born in Gadsden, Etowah County, Alabama:

417   i. JENNIFER LYNN[7] DUKE, born 22 June 1951; married 17 December 1972 Gadsden, Etowah County, Alabama, Mike Gunnells born 26 August 1950 in Gadsden. Mike graduated from Jacksonville State University and owns a computer company called MCBA. Children, *(a)* Emily Gunnells born 6 March 1977 Huntsville, Madison County, Alabama, *(b)* Laurie Gunnells born 19 June 1979 Atlanta, Georgia, and *(c)* Cristin Gunnells born 28 October 1982 Atlanta, Georgia.[2166]

418   ii. JULIE BETH DUKE, born 1 May 1953; married 16 June 1973 Gadsden, Etowah County, Alabama, David Galloway born 13 February 1952 Gadsden. David is plant manager at Goodyear Tire & Rubber in Asheboro, North Carolina. Children, *(a)* Jennifer Kaye Galloway born 13 February 1975, *(b)* Julliana Galloway born 10 January 1977, and *(c)* Jill Galloway born 26 February 1981.[2167]

302. Anne Elizabeth[6] **Duke** (Mary Emma[5] Frist, Emmett Franklin[4], Jacob Chester[3], Henry[2], Rudolph[1]) was born 20 December 1929 in Gadsden, Etowah County, Alabama, the daughter of Curtis and Mary Emma (Frist) Duke.[2168] She died 30 May 1999 at Gadsden, Etowah County, Alabama. She married 13 June 1954 in Gadsden, Alabama, to **Jerry Jasper Thompson, Jr**. Jerry was born

17 March 1928. He died 10 September 2000 at Gadsden.

Jerry served in the United States Army in Korea and was supervisor at Goodyear Tire & Rubber in Gadsden. Both are buried at Forrest Cemetery in Gadsden.[2169]

Children of Jerry Jasper and Anne Elizabeth[6] (Duke) Thompson, Jr., both born in Gadsden, Etowah County, Alabama:

> 419   i.   JERRY STEPHEN[7] THOMPSON, born 9 August 1955; married Gadsden, Etowah County, Alabama, Joye Lynne Beaube born 29 August 1960; Jerry is area manager for Goodyear Tire & Rubber in Gadsden. Children, all born in Gadsden, Etowah County, Alabama, *(a)* Kristin Lynne Thompson born 4 November 1981, *(b)* Mathew Steven Thompson born 29 March 1988, and *(c)* Emily Ann Thompson born 29 March 1988.[2170]

> 420   ii. CHARLES DAVID THOMPSON, born 28 March 1957; married Chattanooga, Hamilton County, Tennessee, Kimberly Faye Mays born 6 July 1961 in Chattanooga, Tennessee; Charles graduated from Auburn University in electrical engineering and is manager of a computer office in Chattanooga. Children, *(a)* Tyler Mark Thompson born 25 September 1985 Chattanooga, Tennessee, *(b)* Derek Scott Thompson born 11 March 1987 Phoenix, Maricopa County, Arizona, *(c)* Cody Brent Thompson born 1 March 1993 Chattanooga, Tennessee, and died 14 February 1994 Chattanooga, Tennessee, and *(d)* Summer Faith Thompson born 3 August 1996 Chattanooga, Tennessee.[2171]

SEVENTH GENERATION

303. Clara Etta[7] Patton (Louisa Jane[6] Frist, Joseph Andrew[5], David H.[4], John[3], Henry[2], Rudolph[1]) was born 12 October 1901 in Villisca, Montgomery County, Iowa, the daughter of Lewis and Louisa Jane (Frist) Patton.[2172] She died April 1992 in Cedar Rapids, Iowa.[2173] She married 22 November 1919 in Red Oak, Montgomery County, Iowa, to **Roy Manford Findley**.[2174] He was born 14 August 1899, the son of Winfield Scott and Nonna May (Osborne) Findley, and died 9 December 1963 in Cedar Rapids, Boone County, Iowa.[2175]

Roy was a truck driver in Villisca, Iowa, and later worked for Link Belt as a machinist, retiring from the maintenance department of the City of Cedar Rapids.

Children of Roy Manford and Clara Etta[7] (Patton) Findley, both born in Villisca, Montgomery County, Iowa:

> +   421   i.   MANFERD HAROLD[8] FINDLEY, born 24 February 1920; married (1) 1940 Margaret L. Fessler and (2) 1971 Thelma J. Fisher.[2176]

> +   422   ii. STANLEY WAYNE FINDLEY, born 30 May 1922; died 5 June 1992

Cedar Rapids, Linn County, Iowa; married Leona Streigl.[2177]

306. Geraldine Rosetta[7] "Gerry" Frist (Willibur Stiles[6], Joseph Andrew[5], David H.[4], John[3], Henry[2], Rudolph[1]) was born 12 July 1924 in Jackson, Dakota County, Nebraska, the daughter of Willibur Stiles and Orpha Lucille (Geesaman) Frist.[2178] Gerry grew up near Villisca, Indiana. In 1942 she began teaching at Fairview Country School and later taught at Sunny Slope School. She married on 5 June 1947 at the Advent Christian Church in Villisca, Montgomery County, Iowa, to **Edward Dale Miller**. Edward was born 19 January 1925 in Clarinda, Page County, Iowa, the son of Ross Edward and Cassie Felicia (Lawson) Miller.

Gerry retired in 1980 after serving as McKinley School secretary for eleven years. She and Dale spent winters in Arizona for many years. Gerry loved hobbies, crafts, and quilt making and lovingly completed a quilt for each grandchild when they graduated from high school.

Gerry died 6 June 2002 in Clarinda, Page County, Iowa, just a day after her fifty-fifth wedding anniversary. Her husband, Dale, lives in Clarinda, Iowa, in 2003.[2179] Children of Edward Dale and Geraldine Rosetta[7] (Frist) Miller, all born in Clarinda, Page County, Iowa:

423   i. JUDITH KAY[8] MILLER, born 9 April 1948; married 4 December 1971 in Denton, Denton County, Texas, Richard Shoffit born 14 July 1949; divorced; no issue.[2180]

424   ii. LINDA RAE MILLER, born 30 April 1951; married 17 August 1974 Trinity Presbyterian Church, Clarinda, Page County, Iowa, David Vader born 19 July 1952 Hoven, Potter County, South Dakota. Children, both born in Omaha, Douglas County, Nebraska, *(a)* Aaron Kipp Vader born 26 March 1978 and *(b)* Casey Ryan Vader born 24 October 1983.[2181]

425   iii. BARBARA DALE MILLER, born 2 January 1954; married (1) 5 July 1975 Trinity Presbyterian Church, Clarinda, Page County, Iowa, Terry Douglas Thompson born 22 December 1952 Maryville, Nodaway County, Missouri; divorced. Barbara married (2) 8 November 1985 Bedford, Taylor County, Iowa, Francis Wayne Akers born 23 September 1951 Maryville, Nodaway County, Missouri. Children, *(a)* Shawn Edward Thompson born 14 January 1976 Junction City, Geary County, Kansas, *(b)* Heather Rose Thompson born 1 December 1977 Honolulu, Hawaii, married 20 August 1999 Patrick Allen Rehder (they have a son, Chase Allen Rehder, born 7 December 2001 in Omaha, Douglas County, Nebraska), and *(c)* Cody Wayne Akers born 21 May 1987 Clarinda, Page County, Iowa.[2182]

426   iv. SHIRLEY JO MILLER, born 3 August 1956; married 21 June 1980 Trinity Presbyterian Church, Clarinda, Page County, Iowa, Timothy Dean Roehl born 6 March 1958 Marshall, Lyon County, Minnesota. Children, *(a)* Aubrey Joy Roehl born 5 December 1983 and *(b)* Elise Faith Roehl born 9 March 1987, both born Milwaukee, Wisconsin.[2183]

307. Helen Marie[7] **Frist** (Willibur Stiles[6], Joseph Andrew[5], David H.[4], John[3], Henry[2], Rudolph[1]) was born 10 January 1929 south of Villisca in Page County, Iowa, at the farm home of her parents, Willibur Stiles and Orpha Lucille (Geesaman) Frist.[2184] She married on 3 April 1949 in Villisca, Montgomery County, Iowa, to **Glendon Amos Smith**. Glendon was born 2 August 1930 in Corning, Adams County, Iowa, the son of Art and Nora Neal Smith.

Helen died 14 May 1972 in Chetek, Baron County, Wisconsin, and is buried in Villisca City Cemetery in Villisca, Montgomery County, Iowa.[2185]

Children of Glendon Amos and Helen Marie[7] (Frist) Smith:

+   427   i. VICKY JEAN[8] SMITH, born 4 December 1949 Villisca, Montgomery County, Iowa; married 12 June 1971 Chetek, Barron County, Wisconsin, Paul Anthony Pavlas.[2186]

+   428   ii. DAVID GLENDON SMITH, born 19 March 1954, Aurora, Kane County, Illinois; married 21 August 1978 Gwyn Eastman.[2187]

308. Raymond A.[7] **Frist** (Willibur Stiles[6], Joseph Andrew[5], David H.[4], John[3], Henry[2], Rudolph[1]) was born 31 July 1930 south of Villisca in Page County, Iowa, the son of Willibur Stiles and Orpha (Geesaman) Frist.[2188] He married on 29 September 1953 in Omaha Nebraska, to **Beverly Jean Brown**. Beverly was born 9 January 1934 in Adams County, Iowa, the son of Boyd Darwin and Pansy Opal (Higgins) Brown.[2189]

Children of Raymond A.[7] and Beverly Jean (Brown) Frist:

429   i. LINDA LEE[8] FRIST, born 30 May 1952 Clarinda, Page County, Iowa; married and divorced Rick Thompson. Children, *(a)* Lewis Harvey Thompson born 26 April 1976 Oklahoma and *(b)* Eric Matthew Thompson born 17 November 1979 Japan.[2190]

430   ii. RAYMOND ANDREW FRIST, born 22 April 1954 Nebraska City, Otoe County, Nebraska.[2191]

431   iii. CYNTHIA LUCILLE FRIST, born 18 March 1955, Omaha, Douglas County, Nebraska; married David Carl Short born 13 February 1952. Children, *(a)* David Andrew Short born 6 May 1985 and *(b)* Carl

Edward Short born 11 April 1987, both born Yuma, Yuma County, Arizona.[2192]

432   iv. JULIE ANN FRIST, born 3 June 1957 Corning, Adams County, Iowa. One child, Asha Rae Frist born 24 January 1986 Yuma, Arizona.[2193]

433   v. LERAE OPAL FRIST, born 31 July 1963 Yuma, Yuma County, Arizona; married Kurtiss Isles Humphrey born 29 March 1957. Children, *(a)* Katelyn Janel Humphrey born 6 November 1992 and *(b)* Sean Kurtiss Humphrey born 7 September 1995, both in Lancaster, Los Angeles County, California.[2194]

309. Russell Edward[7] Frist (Joseph E.[6], John S.[5], David H.[4], John[3], Henry[2], Rudolph[1]) was born 30 August 1907[2195] in Polk County, Iowa, the only child of Joseph E. and Blanche R. (Coloway) Frist.[2196] In 1910 he was three years old and lived with his parents in Des Moines, Polk County, Iowa, [2197] and he also lived with them in 1920 in Camp Township, Polk County, Iowa.[2198] He married about the year 1937, probably in Polk County, to **Mary Ann**.[2199] She was born 5 March 1912 and her death date is unknown.[2200] Russell died in September of 1963 in Runnells, Polk County, Iowa.[2201]

Child of Russell Edward[7] and Mary Ann Frist:

+   434   i. JIMMY DALE[8] FRIST, born 24 April 1938 Polk County, Iowa; married 20 July 1956? Des Moines, Polk County, Iowa, Marva Olson.[2202]

317. Paul Jacque[7] "Jack" Frist (Paul H.[6], William O.[5], William H.[4], John[3], Henry[2], Rudolph[1]) was born on 6 December 1922, probably in Preble County, Ohio, the son of Paul H. and Violet G. Frist.[2203] He married, probably about the year 1943,[2204] to **Helen Louise Hockett**, who was born 23 June 1925 in Winchester, Randolph County, Indiana, the daughter of Clyde James and Cleo Marie (Newman) Hockett.[2205] She died 12 October 1993.[2206] In 2002 Paul lives in New Paris, Preble County, Ohio.

Children of Paul Jacque[7] and Helen Louise (Hockett) Frist, all probably born in Preble County, Ohio:

435   i. PAUL RICHARD[8] "DICK" FRIST, born 9 March 1944; married Dorothy Mae Kelley born 28 December 1949. Children, *(a)* Gregory Paul Frist born 27 June 1968 and *(b)* Kellie Ann Frist born 27 February 1971.[2207]

436   ii. JACK EDWARD FRIST, born 20 April 1947; married Pon Phanphon born 11 June 1948. Children, *(a)* Jinifer Phanphon Frist born 26 February 1973 and *(b)* Jeremiah Phanphon Frist born 20 April 1984.[2208]

437   iii. DENNIS MICHAEL FRIST, born 8 July 1948; married Joan Ellen
            Summers born 8 June 1946; Dennis was a career soldier. Children,
            (a) David Michael Frist born 3 September 1970, *(b)* Matthew James
            Frist born 13 March 1973, and *(c)* Mary Elizabeth Frist born
            16 September 1976.[2209]

438   iv. ROBERT WILLIAM FRIST, born 16 October 1949; married Louise
            Elaine Steele born 28 March 1951 in Richmond, Wayne County,
            Indiana, daughter of Howard Grandvalle and Marjorie Leona (Taylor)
            Steele. She died 2 December 1994 in Clearwater, Florida.[2210] Children,
            (a) Jeffery Robert Frist born 10 March 1969 married Deanna Baratta
            (and had Dakota Robert Frist born 22 December 1990) and *(b)* Tracy
            May Frist born 20 May 1970.[2211]

439   v. JUDITH ANN FRIST, born 12 February 1952.[2212]

440   vi. THOMAS ALLEN FRIST, born 22 July 1953; married (1) Brenda Isaacs
            and they had *(a)* Brad Alan Frist born 20 June 1976 and *(b)* Amy Jo
            Frist born 28 June 1979. Thomas married (2) Teresa Lenigar and they
            had *(c)* Krystal Frist born 16 August 1985.[2213] Teresa's child Kimberly
            from an earlier union is also a family member.

318. Russell Marrell[7] Frist (Marley Otto[6], Russell[5], William H.[4], John[3], Henry[2],
Rudolph[1]) was born on 25 August 1915 in Anderson, Madison County, Indiana,[2214]
the son of Marley Otto and Hester Vurnie (Swinford) Frist.[2215] He married on
29 August 1936 in Anderson, Madison County, Indiana, to **Vivian Maxine Lawson**.
Vivian was born on 2 January 1916, the daughter of Bessie Lane Lawson.

Vivian was a beautician and co-owned the Frist Health Food Store with her husband. Russell was employed with the Central Indiana Gas Company, also in Anderson. He was co-owner of both the Frist Health Food Store in Anderson, Indiana, and the Frist Party House, retiring after forty-two years. He was a member of
the Seventh-Day Adventist Church.[2216]

Russell died on 30 October 1989 in Anderson, Madison County, Indiana, and is
buried in Anderson Memorial Park Cemetery.[2217]

Children of Russell Marrell[7] and Vivian Maxine (Lawson) Frist, both born in
Madison County, Indiana:

+   441   i. ROBERT RUSSELL[8] FRIST, born 11 July 1940; married (1) December
            1961 Pendleton, Madison County, Indiana, Beverley Griffith;
            (2) March 1964 Lapel, Madison County, Indiana, Bonnie Johnson;
            and (3) 3 November 1976 Greenfield, Hancock County, Indiana,
            Dollie Bade.[2218]

+ 442 ii. PHILLIP STANLEY FRIST, born 11 October 1945; married 30 November 1968 Anderson, Madison County, Indiana, Vickie Carol Haston.[2219]

319. Mildred Irene[7] **Stevens** (Jesse O. Laffe[6], Hannah Etta[5] Frist, Robert M.[4], John[3], Henry[2], Rudolph[1]) was born on 2 September 1920 in Fort Madison, Lee County, Iowa, the daughter of Jesse O. Laffe and Ella May (Baxter) Stevens.[2220] She married first to **Paul Vincent McBride**. She married second on 17 June 1949 to **Richard Parmer, Jr.** in Great Lakes, Michigan. Richard is the son of Richard and Mabel (Watts) Parmer. Richard adopted the two boys from Mildred's first marriage and their surname was changed to Parmer.[2221]

Children of Paul Vincent and Mildred Irene[7] (Stevens) McBride, both born in Farragut, Kootenai County, Idaho:

443 i. LARRY PAUL[8] MCBRIDE PARMER, born 18 November 1943.[2222]

+ 444 ii. GARRY ALAN MCBRIDE PARMER, born 18 November 1943; died 17 June 1997 Richmond, Virginia;[2223] married in Falls Church, Virginia, Bettieanne Teresa Berdine.[2224]

Children of Richard and Mildred Irene[7] (Stevens) Parmer, Jr.:

445 iii. SHERRY LEE PARMER, born 17 January 1954 Kenansville, Duplin County, North Carolina; adopted child; married 1 September 1979 Hopewell, Virginia, Donnie Ray Bryant.[2225]

446 iv. TERRY LYNN PARMER, born 23 November 1964 Fort Belvoir, Fairfax County, Virginia; married 7 April 1990 Petersburg, Virginia, Robert Lyle Deadmon son of Robert and Carroll (Scott) Deadmon. Children, *(a)* Jeremiah Hunter Deadmon born 6 March 1991 and *(b)* Zachary Taylor Deadmon born 21 December 1992, both in Petersburg, Virginia.[2226]

326. Marjorie S.[7] **Stout** (Helen S.[6] Springer, Marietta F.[5] Springer, Esther Ann[4] Frist, Jediah[3], Henry[2], Rudolph[1]) was born 7 April 1913, probably in New Castle County, Delaware,[2227] the daughter of Herbert C. and Helen S. (Springer) Stout. She died 10 October 1993 in New Castle County, Delaware.[2228] She married about 1944 to **Paul L. White**.[2229] Paul was born 1 May 1913 in Wilmington, Delaware, the son of Abraham Lincoln and Mary White.[2230] He died 4 May 1982 in Sussex County, Delaware, while living in Wilmington, Christiana Hundred, New Castle County, Delaware.[2231]

Paul's will, written on 15 January 1977,[2232] named his wife, Marjorie, and a son, Paul L. White, Jr. Marjorie died in 1993 in New Castle County, Delaware,[2233] and both are buried in Silverbrook Cemetery.[2234]

Child of Paul L. and Marjorie S.[7] (Stout) White:

447   i. PAUL L.[8] WHITE, JR. born 13 May 1945 Wilmington, Delaware; married 1974 Wilmington, Delaware, Brenda Maddox born 9 September 1950 Wilmington, Delaware, daughter of William and Evelyn Maddox. Children, all born Wilmington, Delaware, *(a)* Paul L. White III born 2 February 1977, *(b)* Rebecca L. White born 4 February 1983, and *(c)* Christina L. White born 1 April 1990.[2235]

334. Esther Louise[7] Frist (Harry Homer[6], Jediah[5], Jediah Rudolph[4], Jediah[3], Henry[2], Rudolph[1]) was born on 3 June 1917 in Vermillion County, Indiana, the daughter of Harry Homer and Mable Audrey (Boyd) Frist.[2236] She married on 6 October 1935 to **Paul Kenneth Foltz** in Vermillion County.[2237] Paul was born on 20 July 1913, also in Vermillion County, the son of Paul and Hazel (Walther) Foltz.

When newly married they helped Paul's father, who had a dairy farm, deliver milk to area residents. They were grain farmers, but also sold milk on a much larger scale, employing mechanical milking machines and a refrigeration system. They were active members of the Farm Bureau for many years and faithful church members, first at the old Fairview Methodist Church and later as charter members of the newly combined Wayside United Methodist Church.

Esther worked at the Clinton Public Library for several years as assistant librarian and was a member of the Clinton Township Home Economics Club for many years. They raised four children and helped to educate a young man from Brazil named Loureno Batzner, who was sent to them by their son when he was a member of the Peace Corps.[2238]

Children of Paul Kenneth and Esther Louise[7] (Frist) Foltz, all born in Vermillion County, Indiana:

+   448   i. CAROLYN JEANETTE[8] FOLTZ, born 12 August 1937; married 24 November 1957 Clinton, Vermillion County, Indiana, Montelle H. "Monty" Lowry.[2239]

+   449   ii. MARGARET ANNE "PEGGY" FOLTZ, born 21 March 1939; married 29 May 1960 Clinton, Vermillion County, Indiana, Frank Warren Hughes.[2240]

450   iii. RONALD GLEN FOLTZ, born 3 October 1942; died 20 June 1972 Vermillion County, Indiana; buried Roselawn, Vigo County, Indiana. Ron graduated from Indiana University at Bloomington and served

in the Peace Corps in Brazil where he met Loureno Batzner, whom he sent to his parents at age sixteen to educate. He never married, although he had just become engaged when he was killed in a semi truck accident on State Route 63.[2241]

+ 451 iv. EMILY SUE FOLTZ, born 20 March 1944; died 11 September 1998 in Gurnee, Lake County, Illinois; married 12 September 1964 Clinton, Vermillion County, Indiana, Jeffery Wayne Skjordahl.[224]

Foster child of Paul Kenneth and Esther Louise (Frist) Foltz:

+ 452 i. LOURENO[1] BATZNER, born 31 January 1950; married 14 November 1986 Brazil, South America, Jeanne Marie Novello.[2243]

335. Shirley Mae[7] Frist (Harry Homer[6], Jediah[5], Jediah Rudolph[4], Jediah[3], Henry[2], Rudolph[1]) was born on 13 May 1922 in Vermillion County, Indiana, the daughter of Harry Homer and Mable Audrey (Boyd) Frist.[2244] Shirley graduated from Brown's Business College (now Indiana Business College) and worked as a secretary at Oakley-Kroger. She married on 11 March 1943 to **Melvin Maurice Jones** in Vermillion County.[2245]

Melvin was born on 25 December 1915 in Vermillion County, Indiana, the son of William and Ollie (Pritchard) Jones. Melvin was in the Army Air Corps during World War II, training as a bombardier and pilot. He served as a gunner, flying sixty-six missions while in England. He was awarded the Distinguished Flying Cross and other awards. Melvin relayed to his family that during his time as a gunner in England, his plane carried a bomb that did not drop, and it was necessary for both him and the pilot to get down in the "hole" to get the bomb loose and push it out of the plane. Melvin worked as a farmer for different landowners and as a mechanic, eventually retiring from the army ammunition plant at Newport, Indiana. Melvin served on the Montezuma Fire Department and was fire chief for a time. He served a term as township trustee for the Republican Party.[2246]

Shirley worked at the old Vermillion County Hospital for a time. She and Melvin were Methodists and more recently members of the Christian Church at Montezuma, Indiana. Melvin received his fifty-year Masonic pin in May of 1998. He died on 26 October 1998 at his residence in Montezuma, Parke County, Indiana. He is buried in Oakland Cemetery at Montezuma.[2247]

Children of Melvin Maurice and Shirley Mae[7] (Frist) Jones, all born in Clinton, Vermillion County, Indiana:

+ 453 i. GARY LYNN[8] JONES, born 11 September 1946; married 4 February 1972 Montezuma, Parke County, Indiana, Judith Ann Rennick.[2248]

+ 454 ii. LINDA DARLINE JONES, born 17 September 1947; married (1) 18 December 1970 Clay City, Clay County, Indiana, Danny Dean Reed and (2) 26 June 1999 Vigo County, Indiana, Robert Arden Gosnell.[2249]

+ 455 iii. GLEN ALAN JONES, born 21 March 1950; married 7 February 1976 Coloma, Parke County, Indiana, Brenda Pritchard.[2250]

336. Myrtle Lee[7] Frist (Harry Homer[6], Jediah[5], Jediah Rudolph[4], Jediah[3], Henry[2], Rudolph[1]) was born on 29 October 1927 in Vermillion County, Indiana, the daughter of Harry Homer and Mable Audrey (Boyd) Frist.[2251] She died on 26 October 1976 in Greenfield, Hancock County, Indiana.[2252] She married on 6 April 1947 to **Milton Royce King** at the Salem Methodist Church in Vermillion County.[2253] Milton was born on 21 November 1922 in Vermillion County, Indiana, the son of Frank and Minnie (Bottoms) King.

Milton served in the United States Army during World War II in the engineers and also as a cook. They owned and managed a restaurant in Dana, Indiana, and he later worked at Cleveland's Hatchery in Dana. Still later he worked as a salesman, selling first hogs and later cars. Myrtle enjoyed working in the school kitchen, and she and Royce managed the town swimming pool for several summers, because they enjoyed being around young people.

Myrtle died in 1976 in Greenfield, Hancock County, Indiana, from complications from cancer and is buried in Park Cemetery in Greenfield.[2254]

Children of Milton Royce and Myrtle Lee[7] (Frist) King, all born in Edgar County, Illinois:

456 i. MICHAEL EDWIN[8] KING, born 14 August 1949; married 4 September 1976 Greenfield, Hancock County, Indiana, Patricia Lynn Butz born about 22 February 1950; divorced 1981; no issue. Mike graduated from Indiana State University, worked as a salesman after graduating and in 2001 is employed at Lowe's in Anderson, Indiana.[2255]

+ 457 ii. MARTIN F. "MART" KING, born 28 October 1950; married 18 July 1970 Greenfield, Hancock County, Indiana, Lettie Barbara "Barb" Jones.[2256]

+ 458 iii. MELVIN H. KING, born 28 October 1950; married (1) 4 November 1969 Hancock County, Indiana, Sheila Ann Davidson and (2) 15 September 1990, Deirdre "Dee" Cannon.[2257]

337. Patricia Jo[7] Frist (Harry Homer[6], Jediah[5], Jediah Rudolph[4], Jediah[3], Henry[2], Rudolph[1]) was born 19 May 1932 at Clinton, Vermillion County, Indiana, the daughter of Harry Homer and Mable Audrey (Boyd) Frist.[2258] She died 29 April 2001 from heart failure following surgery for cancer. The funeral service was 1 May 2001 at First Methodist Church in Clinton, Vermillion County, Indiana, with burial at Helt's Prairie Cemetery on Wednesday, 2 May 2001.[2259]

Pat worked in several professions, taking classes to further her education. While working at Motor Freight Corporation, Pat graduated from Mi-Lady Beauty Academy in Terre Haute as a licensed beautician. She was one of the original employees hired when the Clinton State Bank opened in December 1964. She became a licensed property and casualty insurance agent in 1968 while working for Lang Helt Agency in Clinton.

Pat worked on several different election boards in Clinton and Fairview Park and served a term as vice president of the Young Republican Party of Vermillion County. Pat was an active member of the Clinton First United Methodist Church. She was a member of the Daughters of the American Revolution and Beta Sigma Chapter of Delta Theta Tau Sorority. She had an extensive collection of angels in different forms (statues, pictures, books, and jewelry).

As a "collector," she was also designated as the family historian and kept a large collection of Frist family materials (records of births, deaths, marriages, funerals, obituaries, news clippings, and lots of interesting stories). She contributed most of the anecdotes used in this publication relating to the Indiana branch of the Frist family.[2260]

338. Mary Edith[7] **Frist** (Harlow Peirce[6], Jediah[5], Jediah Rudolph[4], Jediah[3], Henry[2], Rudolph[1]) was born on 3 November 1920 in Helt Township, Vermillion County, Indiana, the daughter of Harlow Peirce and Helen Eliza (Miller) Frist.[2261] She married on 6 June 1942 to **Russell E. Banes** in Chapel Central Presbyterian Church in Tippecanoe County, Indiana. Russ was born on 17 November 1915 in White County, Indiana, the son of Edward and Mary (Neilson) Banes. He died on 10 November 1971 in Tippecanoe County, Indiana.

Mary Edith graduated from Purdue University in 1942 to become a school teacher. Her husband, Russ, was employed at Ross Gear, making gears for tanks on Blanchard Grinder. Russ served in the United States Navy Seabees during World War II and was stationed at Pearl Harbor, Hawaii. He and his brother Ernest left on the same day in March of 1943 for the navy. Another brother, Harold Banes, was a cook on the ship *Tuscaloosa* when it stopped in Pearl Harbor. At the same time, another ship carrying Russ's brother-in-law Robert J. Frist arrived in Pearl Harbor for repairs from damage a Japanese bomber had inflicted. The three sailors met and had Christmas dinner together on the *Tuscaloosa*.[2262]

Mary Edith taught homemaking and science in Tippecanoe County for ten years. She obtained her master's degree in 1957 from Indiana State University and Purdue. She retired in April of 1985 from Lafayette School Corporation after completing a total of forty-three years of teaching. She also served for a time as assistant principal. A front page article in the newspaper honored her for three decades of teaching and announced a retirement party.[2263]

Following the war, Russ became a salesman. He died in 1971 and is buried in Tippecanoe Memory Gardens in West Lafayette, Indiana. In 2003 Mary Edith lives in Lafayette, Tippecanoe County, Indiana, and spends time with her daughter in Las Vegas, Nevada.[2264]

Child of Russell E. and Mary Edith[7] (Frist) Banes:

+   459   i. MARY LYNN[8] BANES, born 12 March 1950 Lafayette, Tippecanoe County, Indiana; married (1) 2 February 1969 Lafayette, Tippecanoe County, Indiana, Richard Harold "Rick" Skeel;[2265] married (2) 26 October 2001 Las Vegas, Nevada, Frederick William Lowell.[2266]

339. Robert Jediah[7] Frist (Harlow Peirce[6], Jediah[5], Jediah Rudolph[4], Jediah[3], Henry[2], Rudolph[1]) was born on 16 April 1925 in Vermillion County, Indiana, the son of Harlow Peirce and Helen Eliza (Miller) Frist.[2267] He died on 23 October 1998 in Lafayette, Tippecanoe County, Indiana.[2268] He married on 3 September 1950 in Vermillion County, Indiana, to **Frances Lillian Vrabic.**[2269] Frances was born on 20 July 1929 in Vermillion County, Indiana, the daughter of Frank and Arkie Lillian (Whitehead) Vrabic.[2270]

Robert served in the navy in the South Pacific during World War II. He received his B.S. in vocational agriculture education in 1951 and his M.S. in extension education in 1962 from Purdue University.[2271]

In 1965 Robert received a Ph.D. from the University of Wisconsin. Frist was a vocational agriculture teacher and 4-H club leader. He became the 4-H and youth department head at Purdue University, retiring on 30 April 1985. He was named professor emeritus. He was a member of the Central Presbyterian Church in Lafayette, Masonic Lodge 123, Scottish Rite and Wabash Township Farmers Club 2.[2272]

Robert was the owner of the Frist trunk, a log-shaped trunk that contains the initials G. D. V., which was given to Jediah R. Frist by his uncle Garretson Frist.[2273]

Robert died in 1998 in Home Hospital in Lafayette and was buried on 27 October 1998 in Tippecanoe Memory Garden in West Lafayette, Indiana.[2274] His widow Frances is retired from Purdue University English Research Center and in 2002 resides in Brookston, White County, Indiana.[2275]

Children of Robert Jediah[7] and Frances Lillian (Vrabic) Frist:

+   460   i. ROBERT HARLOW[8] FRIST, born 8 August 1951 Vermillion County, Indiana; married 2 September 1979 Indianapolis, Marion County, Indiana, Ellen Louise Edwards.[2276]

+   461   ii. DENNIS FRANKLIN FRIST, born 7 December 1954 Tippecanoe
County, Indiana; married 5 March 1977 Tippecanoe County, Indiana,
Patti Ann Acheson.[2277]

+   462   iii. KARL DAVID FRIST, born 22 July 1959 Tippecanoe County, Indiana;
married 8 August 1981 Tippecanoe County, Indiana, Shirley Jeanne
Shultz.[2278]

+   463   iv. DOUGLAS MARK FRIST, born 1 November 1960 Tippecanoe County,
Indiana; married 22 May 1983 Deerfield, Lake County, Illinois, Mary
Hope Roberts.[2279]

340. Betty Lou[7] Frist (Harlow Peirce[6], Jediah[5], Jediah Rudolph[4], Jediah[3], Henry[2], Rudolph[1]) was born 24 November 1930 in Vermillion County, Indiana, the daughter of Harlow Peirce and Helen Eliza (Miller) Frist.[2280] She died on 3 May 1990 in Columbia, Boone County, Missouri.[2281] She married on 19 December 1948 in Vermillion County, Indiana, to **Herman Francis Mayes**.[2282] Herman was born 18 February 1926 in Vermillion County, Indiana.

Herman served in the United States Army during World War II in the European theater and worked as a research engineer. Betty worked as a secretary and sold Avon products. She was a member of Beta Sigma Pi Sorority, Fort Knightly Club of Columbia, and the Resident Wives of the College of Agriculture at the University of Missouri.

Herman's brother-in-law Robert J. Frist had inherited some letters written by Enid Frist Lemstra. Herman compiled information from the letters and devoted many hours to researching his wife's Frist family. As he traveled, he visited libraries and interviewed descendants. This eventually led to the compilation of the first Frist genealogy in September of 1991.[2283]

Betty died in 1990 in Columbia, Missouri, from severe breathing problems and is buried in Helt's Prairie Cemetery in Vermillion County, Indiana.[2284]

Herman is active in the Salem United Methodist Church and in 2003 resides in the dwelling built by Jediah Frist in 1896. He alternates his time between Clinton, Vermillion County, Indiana, and Florida.

341. Harold B.[7] Frist (Marshall Alban[6], Jediah[5], Jediah Rudolph[4], Jediah[3], Henry[2], Rudolph[1]) was born on 28 October 1920 in Vermillion County, Indiana, the son of Marshall Alban and Marjorie (Blakesley) Frist.[2285] In 1942 he graduated from Rose Polytechnic Institute (now Rose-Hulman Institute of Technology) in Terre Haute where he was a member of Tau Beta Pi Honorary Fraternity.[2286]

Harold married on 12 December 1942 to **Beulah Thomas** in Saint Louis, Missouri.[2287] Beulah was born on 13 June 1920 in Vermillion County, the daughter of James and Goldie (Nolan) Thomas.[2288] After their marriage, they lived in

Indianapolis, where Beulah worked as a teacher until retiring in 1980. Harold worked for the Allison Division of General Motors for many years before retiring as superintendent of quality engineering in 1980. They are members of the Avon Methodist Church[2289] and live in Hendricks County, Indiana, in 2002.

Child of Harold B.[7] and Beulah (Thomas) Frist:

+   464   i. LISA ANN[8] FRIST, born 14 November 1955 Indianapolis, Marion County, Indiana; married 28 December 1989 Avon, Hendricks County, Indiana, Hendrik Harm "Henk" Drenth.[2290]

342. Wayne Edward[7] Frist (Marshall Alban[6], Jediah[5], Jediah Rudolph[4], Jediah[3], Henry[2], Rudolph[1]) was born on 19 August 1925 in Vermillion County, Indiana, the son of Marshall Alban and Marjorie (Blakesley) Frist.[2291] He died at the age of thirty-eight on 1 October 1963 in Boone, Boone County, Iowa, and is buried there.[2292] He married on 19 November 1949 in Boone County, Iowa, to **Ruth Eddy**, who was born 2 August 1924 in Iowa.[2293] Wayne and Ruth later divorced.

Wayne graduated from Clinton High School, the Indianapolis College of Mortuary Science, and then served in the United States Navy as a pharmacist's mate.[2294] After his military service, he moved to Boone, Iowa, where he worked for John Deere Manufacturing.[2295]

Children of Wayne Edward[7] and Ruth (Eddy) Frist, all born in Boone, Boone County, Iowa:

+   465   i. MICHAEL THOMAS[8] FRIST, born 5 December 1950; married on 22 December 1969 Omaha, Douglas County, Nebraska, Judy Michel.[2296]
+   466   ii. MERSHELL SUZANNE FRIST, born 5 December 1951; married 15 April 1972 Boone, Boone County, Iowa, Richard Putman.[2297]
+   467   iii. JOAN MARIE FRIST, born 7 May 1954; married 7 April 1973 Boone, Boone County, Iowa, Jack Erwin.[2298]

347. Dolores Lorraine[7] Klima (Dolores Mary[6] Frist, Abram Bernard[5], Abraham B.[4], James[3], Henry[2], Rudolph[1]) was born 1 August 1930 in Baltimore City, Maryland, the daughter of Joseph and Dolores Mary (Frist) Klima.[2299] She died 6 September 1996 in Baltimore City, Maryland. She married 10 June 1950 in Baltimore City, Maryland, to **Eugene Alfred "Moe" Fischer, Jr.** Moe was born 4 May 1929 in Baltimore City, Maryland, the son of Eugene Alfred and Sadie Lee (Williams) Fischer, Sr. He died 26 December 1989 in Edgewood, Harford County, Maryland.

Moe worked for the Coca Cola Bottling Company in Baltimore City, Maryland, as a route salesman and was medically retired after forty years of service. He was known for his dry sense of humor and his kindheartedness. He enjoyed boating, fishing, and the Baltimore Colts and the Orioles. He was a creative person who could build and remodel most anything.

Dolores retired from the cafeteria staff at the Harford County School System in Edgewood, Maryland. She had a good sense of humor and was known as a caregiver to elderly family members. Dolores and Moe are buried in Holly Hill Memorial Park in Baltimore City, Maryland.[2300]

Children of Eugene Alfred and Dolores Lorraine[7] (Klima) Fischer, Jr., all born in Baltimore City, Maryland:

+ 468   i. EUGENE ALFRED[8] "GENE" FISCHER III, born 18 April 1951; married 23 June 1973 Edgewood, Harford County, Maryland, Deborah Ann "Debbie" Baum.[2301]

469   ii. BRIAN JOSEPH FISCHER, born 24 October 1960 Baltimore City, Maryland, married 26 May 1985 Joppa, Harford County, Maryland, Deborah Ann "Debbie" Pivec, who was born 5 March 1961 in Baltimore City, Maryland. Children, both born in Baltimore City, Maryland, *(a)* Michael Joseph Fischer born 11 April 1991 and *(b)* Nichole Michelle Fischer born 18 May 1993. They live in Joppa, Maryland, in 2003.[2302]

470   iii. DAWN LEE FISCHER, born 22 April 1965; married 12 September 1992 in Bel Air, Maryland, Christopher "Chris" Casey born 11 July 1967 New Haven Connecticut, son of Sherman and Julie Casey. Children, all born in Towson, Baltimore County, Maryland, *(a)* Scott Christopher Casey born 25 August 1993, *(b)* Logan Patrick Casey born 3 October 1995, and *(c)* Brennan David Casey born 2 November 1998. They live in Bel Air, Maryland. Chris is a 1991 graduate of the University of Maryland with a bachelor's degree in criminal justice. He is a Baltimore County police officer. Dawn is a respiratory therapist and completed her hospital training at Sinai Hospital of Baltimore. They live in Bel Air, Maryland, in 2003.[2303]

349. Margaret Genevieve[7] Frist (Casper Bernard[6], Abram Bernard[5], Abraham B.[4], James[3], Henry[2], Rudolph[1]) was born 16 April 1937 in Baltimore City, Maryland, the daughter of Casper Bernard and Elenora Helen (Pronek) Frist.[2304] She married 21 November 1953 at Saint Elizabeth Church in Baltimore City, Maryland, to **Daniel Robert Hepner**. Daniel was born 16 March 1934 in Baltimore City, Maryland, the son of Joseph and Laura (Slowik) Hepner, Sr. He is a retired maintenance planner and machinist. Margaret is a genealogy buff who has devoted many hours to searching for her Frist ancestry. The Hepners live in Joppa, Harford County, Maryland.

Children of Daniel Robert and Margaret Genevieve[7] (Frist) Hepner, all born in Baltimore City, Maryland:

471   i. DANIEL ROBERT[8] HEPNER, JR., born 7 August 1956; works in electrical signal maintenance for the railroad; single in 2003.[2305]

472   ii. DONNELLY BERNARD HEPNER, born 8 October 1958; married Margie Ann Sadler (separated in 2002); Donnelly is a heating and air conditioning technician. They have one child, Amanda Joyce Hepner born 27 May 1987.[2306]

473   iii. DAVID JOSEPH HEPNER, born 29 March 1961; married Dorthea Jean Hawes; David is a mechanical engineer. Children, *(a)* Deanna Janielle Hepner born 28 September 1986 and *(b)* Dylan Joseph Hepner born 8 September 1991.[2307]

474   iv. DOUGLAS WILLIAM HEPNER, born 14 October 1963; married Julie Frankovich; Douglas is in retail food management. Children, *(a)* Jonathan Douglas Hepner born 9 January 1995 and *(b)* Katilyn Christine Hepner born 4 July 1996.[2308]

475   v. DANIELLE MARGARET HEPNER, born 30 January 1965; married 14 September 2001 William J. Tallett; Danielle is a medical technician. Children of William J. Tallett by a previous union, *(a)* William James Tallett, Jr. born 15 September 1973 died 16 May 1996, *(b)* Heather Ann Tallett born 31 October 1976, *(c)* Michael Tallett born 8 April 1986, and *(d)* Mary Elizabeth Tallett born 11 August 1987.[2309]

476   vi. DONNA TERESE HEPNER, born 10 May 1966; college art teacher; single in 2003.[2310]

350. Bernard George[7] Frist (Casper Bernard[6], Abram Bernard[5], Abraham B.[4], James[3], Henry[2], Rudolph[1]) was born 12 April 1944 in Baltimore City, Maryland, the son of Casper Bernard and Elenora Helen (Pronek) Frist.[2311] He married on 11 April 1964 at Our Lady of Hope Church in Baltimore City, Maryland, to **Elizabeth Ann Adamski**. Elizabeth was born 2 March 1945 in Baltimore City, Maryland, the daughter of Stanislaus W. and Bertha (Lackl) Adamski. In 2003 they live in Baltimore where Bernard owns a slate and roofing business.[2312]

Children of Bernard George[7] and Elizabeth Ann (Adamski) Frist all born in Baltimore City, Maryland:

477   i. BERNARD GEORGE[8] FRIST, JR., born 13 June 1965; married Victoria Lynn Pike. They have one child, Parker D. Frist born 1 January 1999 Baltimore County, Maryland. Bernard works in environmental protection.[2313]

Photographs of the Indiana descendants are courtesy of Patricia Frist, unless otherwise noted. Photographs of the Tennessee descendants are courtesy of Mary Barfield, unless otherwise noted.

Henry and Elizabeth Frist tombstone, Saint James Methodist Episcopal Church cemetery, Newport, Delaware; includes several other family members (photo by compiler).

Left to right: Jonas Lyman Paulson Frist, daughter Toda Juanita Frist, wife Amy E. (Powell) Frist, and daughter Cora Frist, about 1885 to 1890 (used by permission of Randolph County, Indiana, Historical Society).

James Putnam Goodrich, Republican governor of Indiana from 1917 to 1921, husband of Cora (Frist) Goodrich (courtesy Liberty Trust, Inc.).

Joseph Andrew Frist and his brother John S. Frist, Iowa (courtesy Geraldine Miller family).

Clara Etta Patton (1901–1992), about 1904 (courtesy Geraldine Miller family).

Left to right: Stanley Findley and wife Leona, Manferd Findley and wife Margaret, about 1942 (courtesy Manferd Findley).

Jediah Rudolph Frist
(1826–1907), Vermillion
County, Indiana.

Mary Peirce Frist
(1834–1891), second wife of
Jediah Rudolph Frist.

Samuel Meredith Frist (1856–1941),
son of Jediah Rudolph Frist.

Jediah Rudolph Frist's wife and siblings, about 1892, shortly after Jediah's third marriage to Mary Nelson. *Left to right in the front row*: Mary Nelson Frist, Jediah Rudolph Frist, Mary Frist Robinson Way. *Left to right in back row*: Elizabeth Frist Lloyd and Esther Ann Frist Springer (courtesy Mary Barfield).

Jediah Frist (1859–1948), son of Jediah Rudolph Frist.

Elizabeth Helt Frist (1859–1935), wife of Jediah Frist.

Jediah and Elizabeth (Helt) Frist family, about 1891–1892, Vermillion County, Indiana. *Left to right*: Jediah Frist, Harry Homer Frist, and Elizabeth (Helt) Frist holding Harlow Peirce Frist. *Standing in back*: Ren Leslie Frist and Myrtle Maria Frist.

Log home of Jediah and Elizabeth (Helt) Frist, Vermillion County, Indiana.

Farm home of Jediah and Elizabeth (Helt) Frist, built 1896, Vermillion County, Indiana.

Ren Leslie Frist (1881–1955),
Vermillion County, Indiana.

Myrtle Maria Frist (1882–1974),
Vermillion County, Indiana.

Mable Audrey Frist (1891–1946), wife of Harry Homer Frist.

Harry Homer Frist (1889–1983), Vermillion County, Indiana.

Harlow Peirce Frist (1891–1975), Vermillion County, Indiana.

Robert Jediah Frist, son of Harlow Peirce Frist, standing in front of the home his grandfather Jediah built, about 1944 during World War II (courtesy Mary Edith [Frist] Banes).

Russell E. Banes, with wife Mary Edith (Frist) Banes, daughter of Harlow Peirce Frist, home on leave during World War II, about 1944 (courtesy Mary Edith [Frist] Banes).

Patricia Jo Frist, who contributed Frist family anecdotes, and Herman Mayes, who prepared the 1992 Frist data, after a meeting with compiler Shirley Wilson, March 2001 (photo by compiler).

Mary Hazel Frist Harlan (1894–1984), Vermillion County, Indiana.

Marshall Alban Frist (1897–1966), Vermillion County, Indiana.

Webb Frist (1900–1957), Vermillion County, Indiana.

Jasper Nebeker Frist (1863–1934), son of Jediah Rudolph Frist, and founder of J. N. Frist Funeral Home, Clinton, Indiana.

Photo Children of Jasper Nebeker and Etta Lee (Lambert) Frist, photo taken about 1897. *Left to right*: Donald Carroll Frist and Enid Lambretta Frist (courtesy Mary Barfield).

Etta Lee Lambert (1870–1955), wife of Jasper Nebeker Frist.

White horse-drawn hearse, Frist Funeral Home, Clinton,
Indiana, early 1900s (courtesy Patricia Frist).

The Frist Funeral Home's first ambulance, Clinton, Indiana
(courtesy Patricia Frist).

Frist Funeral Home, Clinton, Indiana, about 1923 (courtesy
Patricia Frist).

Mary Esther Frist Peters (1871–1952), daughter of Jediah Rudolph Frist.

Joseph Henry Frist (1866–1921), son of Jediah Rudolph Frist.

Alban Frist (1873–1961), son of Jediah Rudolph Frist, with wife Viola Adaline Jackson Frist, about 1905.

Franklin Peirce Frist (1869–1949), son of Jediah Rudolph Frist.

Tombstone of James and Henrietta (Little) Frist, Hopewell United Methodist Church Cemetery, Cecil County, Maryland, 2002 (courtesy Margaret Hepner).

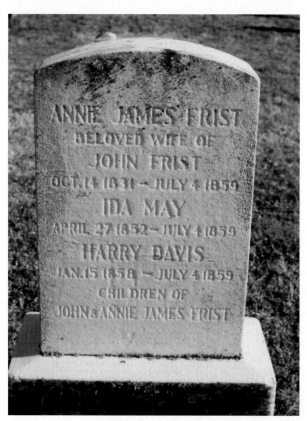

Tombstone of Annie James Frist, Hopewell United Methodist Church Cemetery in Cecil County, Maryland. Annie was the wife of John Frist and shares her tombstone with her two drowned children, Ida May Frist and Harry Davis Frist (photo by compiler).

Sidney Marietta "Etta" Frist Tyson (1868–1938) (courtesy Vianne Gillespie).

Joel Frist (1812–1891) of Wilmington, Delaware.

Dr. Henry M. "Harry" Frist of Wilmington, Delaware, the first in the family to become a doctor.

Jacob Frist (1817–1879) tombstone, Citizens Cemetery, Chattanooga, Tennessee (courtesy William H. Frist, M.D.).

Mary (Baldwin) Frist tombstone, Citizens Cemetery, Chattanooga, Tennessee (courtesy William H. Frist, M.D.).

Tombstone of Robert Harris Frist, son of Jacob Frist by his first wife, Saint James Church Cemetery, Newport, Delaware, 2001 (photo by compiler).

John Hilton and Ann Eliza (Frist) Foard (daughter of Robert Harris Frist) of Marshallton, Delaware, and their grandchildren, 1942. *Left to right*: Margaret Ann Foard, Anna Eliza (Frist) Foard holding Franklin Peach Foard, Jr., John Hilton Foard holding Janet Frances Smith, and Wendell Murray Smith. *In back*: Warren Foard Smith (courtesy Ann Fowser).

Mary Ann Elizabeth (Baldwin) Frist, from tintype about 1860–1865 (courtesy of Ronnie Frist, photograph duplication by Karina McDaniel, Tennessee State Library and Archives).

Ann Elizabeth "Lizzie" Frist Vetter (1859–1922), about 1885 (courtesy John Stanley Vetter, Jr.).

Mary Ann Elizabeth (Baldwin) Frist, 7 September 1915, on her 82nd birthday, Chattanooga, Tennessee.

Jane "Jennie" Jones (1869–1953), about 1890, age twenty-one.

Mary Ann (Baldwin) Frist and daughter Lizzie in front of log cabin, Chattanooga, Tennessee (courtesy of John Stanley Vetter, Jr.).

Jacob Chester "Jake" Frist (1861–1919), about 1895, age thirty-four.

Mary (Parry) Jones, mother of Jane "Jenny" (Jones) Frist, Chattanooga, Tennessee, about 1898.

Left to right: Jake Frist, mother-in-law Mary (Parry) Jones, wife Jennie, father-in-law John F. Jones, and children Mary Louise and Helen Jones Frist, about 1902–1903.

The Frist family home, Meridian, Mississippi, about 1908.

Jacob Chester "Jake" Frist wearing Medal for Lifesaving awarded in 1915.

The United States Medal for Lifesaving on Railroads (under Act of Congress 23 February 1903) (photo by Bill Lafevor).

Carnegie Medal (photo by Bill Lafevor).

Jacob Chester "Jake" Frist, about 1905, age forty-four.

Carnegie Medal, reverse side with Andrew Carnegie portrait, (J. E. Caldwell and Company, Philadelphia, patented 11 December 1906) (photo by Bill Lafevor).

John F. Jones and his granddaughter Helen Jones Frist,
about 1903.

Mary Louise Frist (1898–1980), about 1940.

Mary Louise, age six, and Helen Jones Frist, age three, about 1904.

Helen Jones Frist (1901–1956), about 1940.

Mary Louise, age ten, and Helen Jones Frist, age seven, about
1908, Meridian, Mississippi.

Jane "Jennie" (Jones) Frist, about 1940.

John Chester Frist age two, about 1908, Meridian, Mississippi
(courtesy John Chester Frist family).

John Chester Frist, about 1923
(courtesy John Chester Frist family).

Lois Elizabeth "Betty" Ferran (1909–1998) as a young woman
(courtesy John Chester Frist family).

John Chester Frist, as a young man
(courtesy John Chester Frist family).

John Chester Frist (1906–1959) in later years
(courtesy John Chester Frist family).

Betty (Ferran) Frist and her children. *Left to right*:
Charlotte, Betty, Jane, and Johnny with Tommy in front
(courtesy John Chester Frist family), about 1955 (courtesy
John Chester Frist family).

Reverend John Chester Frist and Dr. Billy Graham, at home in Mobile,
Alabama, 1950s (courtesy John Chester Frist family).

The Frist brothers. *Left to right*: Thomas
Fearn and John Chester.

Thomas Fearn
Frist, about 1912,
Meridian,
Mississippi.

Thomas Fearn
Frist, about 1916,
Meridian,
Mississippi.

Thomas Fearn
Frist, about 1920,
Meridian,
Mississippi.

Thomas Fearn
and Dorothy
Harrison (Cate)
Frist, 1935.

Dorothy Harrison Cate, as a young woman.

Thomas Fearn Frist, in uniform during World War II.

Dorothy Harrison (Cate) Frist, about 1943.

Dorothy Harrison (Cate) Frist and children. *Left to right back row*: Bobby, Dorothy, Tommy. *Left to right front row*: Mary, Billy, and Dottie.

Dr. Thomas Fearn and Dorothy Harrison (Cate) Frist and their children. *Left to right*: Bobby, Tommy, Dottie, and Mary.

Dr. Thomas Fearn Frist (1910–1998),
in later years.

Dorothy Harrison "Cate" Frist (1910–1998),
in later years.

The Frist family, December 1996, at the home of Thomas Fearn and Dorothy (Cate) Frist, 703 Bowling Avenue, Nashville.

The Frist family, December 2002, at the home of Robert Armistead and Carol (Knox) Frist, 1526 Page Road, Nashville.

478   ii. ROBERT WILLIAM FRIST, born 2 March 1967; married Jennifer Therris. They have one child, Brandon William Frist born 29 December 1991 Baltimore County, Maryland. Robert is in the carpentry and remodeling business.[2314]

479   iii. BRYAN JOSEPH FRIST, born 31 July 1970; married Krisan Pfiefer. Bryan is in transportation.[2315]

353. Mary Grove[7] **Tyson** (John Earl[6], Sidney Marietta[5] Frist, Edmund Physick[4], James[3], Henry[2], Rudolph[1]) was born on 3 March 1909, in Cecil County, Maryland, the daughter of John Earl and Ella Elizabeth (Tosh) Tyson.[2316] She died on 31 January 1969, Harford County, Maryland.[2317] She married first on 14 November 1931 to **John Floyd Absher**, the son of Joseph Preston and Martha Jane (Taliver) Absher,[2318] by whom she had one child. John was born on 3 February 1903 and died on 13 March 1957. She married second on 2 October 1957 to **Oliver Graeser**.[2319]

In 1966 when Mary's mother Ella Tyson died, Mary lived in Sanford, Florida.[2320]

Child of John Floyd and Mary Grove[7] (Tyson) Absher:

+   480   i. MARTHA VIANNE[8] ABSHER, born 9 December 1934; married (1) before 1956 to Paul Albert Taylor[2321] and (2) 15 November 1965 to Edward Charles Gillespie.

356. Margaret Elizabeth[7] **Tyson** (John Earl[6], Sidney Marietta[5] Frist, Edmund Physick[4], James[3], Henry[2], Rudolph[1]) was born on 4 September 1921 in Cecil County, Maryland, the daughter of John Earl and Ella Elizabeth (Tosh) Tyson.[2322] She died on 2 March 1981, probably in Cecil County, Maryland.[2323] She married on 26 June 1946 to **Vernon McMullen**, who was born on 14 April 1924.[2324]

In 1966 when Margaret's mother Ella Tyson died in Cecil County, Maryland, her estate identified her daughter Margaret and her grandchildren Tyrone and Dawne McMullen.[2325]

After Margaret died in 1981,[2326] Vernon wrote his will in July of 1982, and it was probated in Cecil County, Maryland, on 17 April 1990.[2327] He left a cash bequest to his grandson, Michael Shawn Yale. He left the remainder of his estate to his daughter, Dawne, some of which was in trust for the use of his son Tyrone.

Children of Vernon and Margaret Elizabeth[7] (Tyson) McMullen:

481   i. TYRONE ERIC[8] MCMULLEN, born 1 June 1947.[2328]

482   ii. DAWNE DORETTA MCMULLEN, born 2 January 1951; married 28 August 1968 James Paul Yale born July 1949; divorced. One child, Michael Shawn Yale, born 2 November 1968.[2329]

359. Evelyn Elizabeth[7] **Astle** (Pearl Catharine[6] Tyson, Sidney Marietta[5] Frist, Edmund Physick[4], James[3], Henry[2], Rudolph[1]) was born on 2 April 1922, in Cecil County, Maryland, the daughter of Charles Ellis and Pearl Catharine (Tyson) Astle.[2330] She married first on 2 March 1946 to **S. Clyde Crowl, Jr.**, who was born 16 May 1921 and died 18 December 1961 with burial in Hopewell United Methodist Church Cemetery in Cecil County, Maryland.[2331] Evelyn married second on 18 April 1970 to **Peter Kowal**, who was born on 11 July 1919.

Children of S. Clyde and Evelyn Elizabeth[7] (Astle) Crowl, Jr., all probably born in Cecil County, Maryland:

483 i. LINDA ANN[8] CROWL, born 28 June 1947; married 19 January 1970 Dirk Howard Harrington born 3 December 1948. Children, *(a)* Beth Ann Harrington born 22 June 1971 and *(b)* Dirk Howard Harrington, Jr. born 19 April 1973.[2332]

484 ii. PATRICIA JANE CROWL, born 26 September 1949; married 3 June 1972 Robert V. Sigler born 3 September 1949.[2333]

485 iii. BARBARA JUNE CROWL, born 2 June 1951; married 8 November 1969 Barry Wayne Thomas born 3 September 1947. Children, *(a)* Paul William Thomas born 25 March 1971 and *(b)* John Richard Thomas born 6 April 1972.[2334]

361. Naomi Astle[7] **Tyson** (Harold Edward[6], Sidney Marietta[5] Frist, Edmund Physick[4], James[3], Henry[2], Rudolph[1]) was born on 26 January 1924, probably in Cecil County, Maryland, the daughter of Harold Edward and Esther Ann (Astle) Tyson.[2335] She married on 27 November 1948 to **George Oliver Gross**, who was born on 18 August 1919 in York, Pennsylvania, the son of George Oliver and Ada May (Gross) Gross.[2336] On 17 July 1937 George lived in Bellemoore, Delaware, and was employed at the Elsworth L. Jones Company in Wilmington Delaware.[2337] He died on 3 September 1973 and is buried in Hopewell United Methodist Church Cemetery in Cecil County, Maryland.[2338] In 2003 his widow Naomi lives in Lewes, Delaware.

Children of George Oliver and Naomi Astle[7] (Tyson) Gross:

486 i. EMILY LOIS[8] GROSS, born 12 January 1950; married 7 October 1967 Charles Elward Turner born 13 November 1949. Children, *(a)* Jeffery Edward Turner born 14 January 1968 and *(b)* Tricia Marie Turner born 7 February 1972.[2339]

487 ii. ELLEN ELIZABETH GROSS, born 2 April 1951; married 20 December 1969 Geoffrey Lance Travers born 20 November 1948. They have one child, Leigh Ann Elizabeth Travers, born 11 August 1979.[2340]

488   iii. CAROLYN JEANNE GROSS, born 3 August 1956.[2341]

489   iv. ROGER ALAN GROSS, born 27 March 1961.[2342]

364. Ramsey Hudson[7] Frist (Joseph Osmond[6], Oscar Haines[5], Edmund Physick[4], James[3], Henry[2], Rudolph[1]) was born 16 August 1936 in Meadville, Crawford County, Pennsylvania, the son of Joseph Osmond and Blanche Lucille (Ramsey) Frist.[2343] He earned a B.S. degree in physics from Allegheny College in Meadville, Pennsylvania, in 1959. He received an M.S. degree and Ph.D. in biophysics from the University of Pittsburgh, completing the work in 1965. He was a United States Public Health Service postdoctoral fellow at the Virus Research Unit, Agricultural Research Council in Cambridge, England, from 1965 to 1967 and a postdoctoral fellow at the Biophysics Laboratory, University of Wisconsin in Madison from 1967 to 1969. Since 1969 he has been on the faculty of the biology department at West Virginia University at Morgantown, West Virginia, and serves as associate professor and associate chair.

Ramsey married **Judith Ann Nadolny**, the daughter of Edward Otto and Margaret Ruth (Gorman) Nadolny. They were divorced in 1979 and Judith remarried about 1983. In 2003 Ramsey lives in Morgantown, West Virginia.[2344]

Children of Ramsey Hudson[7] and Judith Ann (Nadolny) Frist:

+   490   i. HEIDI MARGARET[8] FRIST, born 4 February 1964 Pittsburgh, Pennsylvania; married 6 August 1988 Morgantown, Monongalia County, West Virginia, Anthony Patrick Derry.[2345]

+   491   ii. JONATHAN RAMSEY FRIST, born 3 June 1967 Cambridge, England; married Margaret Jane Shaw.[2346]

+   492   iii. ERICA ANN FRIST, born 26 July 1969 Madison, Dane County, Wisconsin; married 28 May 2000 Madison, Morgan County, Georgia, James Andrew Canfield.[2347]

366. Michael Maria[7] Frist (Joseph Osmond[6], Oscar Haines[5], Edmund Physick[4], James[3], Henry[2], Rudolph[1]) was born 19 May 1944 in Meadville, Crawford County, Pennsylvania, the daughter of Joseph Osmond and Blanche Lucille (Ramsey) Frist.[2348] She has sixteen years of education and a major in psychology. She worked as an employment specialist for Career Employment Choices, as a writer on horse shows for the Morgan Horse Association in Shelburne, Vermont, and as an employment interviewer and labor relations representative for Pennsylvania Labor and Industry in Harrisburg, Pennsylvania, for many years, retiring at age thirty-seven.

She married on 17 March 1983 at Conneaut Lake, Crawford County, Pennsylvania, to **Elwood G. Schell, Jr**. Elwood was born 14 February 1953 in Philadelphia, Pennsylvania, the son of Elwood G. and Mary Jane (McDonald) Schell. He devoted fourteen years to his education and worked twenty-five years for Chicago Bridge and Iron as a field supervisor, traveling in the United States and abroad, constructing water and oil storage tanks. Since 1996 he has worked at home as the administrator of building and maintenance for Conneaut School District. He is a member of Masonic Temple 234 and obtained his real estate license in 1999.

The Schells own a forty-acre farm called "Snail's Pace Acres" where they raise, breed, and sell Morgan show horses. Their horses are shown across the United States and at grand national and world competitions. They are members of the American Morgan Association and the Penn-Ohio Morgan Horse Association. They own twenty-two horses, three dogs, eight cats, a donkey, and a llama.[2349] In 2003 they live in Conneaut Lake, Pennsylvania.

367. Delbert Lee[7] **Frist** (Delbert Sterling[6], John Cresswell[5], Edmund Physick[4], James[3], Henry[2], Rudolph[1]) was born 31 January 1946 in Cecil County, Maryland, the son of Delbert Sterling and Florence (Worth) Frist.[2350] He married 23 August 1969, at Hopewell Methodist Church in Cecil County, Maryland, to **Louise Benjamin**. Louise was born 4 April 1947, the daughter of Rufus and Ruth (Williams) Benjamin. In 2003 they live in Port Deposit, Cecil County, Maryland.

Children of Delbert Lee[7] and Louise (Benjamin) Frist:

493   i. DUANE CRESSWELL[8] FRIST, born 14 January 1972.

494   ii. CYNTHIA LOUISE FRIST, born 22 April 1975; married 14 September 2002 Cecil County, Maryland, David Russell Dittmar born 26 May 1974 in New Jersey, son of Russell Dittmar.[2351]

368. Debora Louise[7] **Frist** (Delbert Sterling[6], John Cresswell[5], Edmund Physick[4], James[3], Henry[2], Rudolph[1]) was born 29 January 1950 in Cecil County, Maryland, the daughter of Delbert Sterling and Florence (Worth) Frist.[2352] She married 19 May 1973, at Hopewell Methodist Church in Cecil County, Maryland, to **William H. Ewing**. William was born 20 September 1946, the son of William and Martha (Love) Ewing. In 2003 they live in Rising Sun, Cecil County, Maryland.

Children of William H. and Debora Louise[7] (Frist) Ewing:

495   i. SHANNON LEE[8] EWING, born 14 October 1976; married 1994 Hopewell Methodist Church, Port Deposit, Cecil County, Maryland, Clinton Miller. Children, (a) Curtis Wayne Miller born 7 May 1995, (b) Clinton William Miller born 31 October 1997, and (c) Craig Walter Miller born 26 August 1999.

496   ii. HOPE NOEL EWING, born 18 July 1979.

369. Charlotte Alma[7] **Frist** (John Willard[6], John Cresswell[5], Edmund Physick[4], James[3], Henry[2], Rudolph[1]) was born 13 January 1939 in Port Deposit, Cecil

County, Maryland, the only child of John Willard and Willa Alverta (Tarbert) Frist.[2353] She went to Jacob Tome Institute in Port Deposit before moving with her parents in 1952 to Cheyenne, Wyoming, where she graduated from high school. She married on 18 August 1962 at Park Wedding Chapel in Reno, Nevada, to **Bruce Turner**. Bruce was born 25 August 1935 in Happy, Texas, the son of William Earl and Dovie Ethel (Myers) Turner.

Bruce was an assistant engineer at Motorola, Inc., retiring in 1998. His hobbies include woodworking, fishing, and drawing. Charlotte is a homemaker and worked as a warranty administrator. She too is retired and enjoys quilting and china painting. They live in Paradise, California.[2354]

Children of Bruce and Charlotte Alma[7] (Frist) Turner, both born in Upland, California:

> 497   i. SUSAN RENEE[8] TURNER, born 10 December 1963; married 2 April 1988 David Paul Polk born 12 May 1962 son of Bruce and Darlene Polk. Susan attended Mesa Community College and is a homemaker who enjoys sewing and crafts. Children, *(a)* Breck Emerson Polk born 10 February 1992 and *(b)* Madison Renee Polk born 16 August 1995, both in Mission Viejo, California.[2355]

> 498   ii. WILLIAM GREGORY TURNER, born 6 June 1966; married 8 May 1993 Kathryn Donna Nelson born 31 July 1966 daughter of Alan Curtis and Jo Ann (Wallen) Nelson. "Greg" graduated from the University of Arizona and McGeorge School of Law and is employed by the California Taxpayers Association as general counsel and legislative director. He enjoys golf and woodworking. One child, Jordan Kaitlyn Turner, born 11 January 2000 and died 29 November 2000.[2356]

370. Helen Kirk[7] Frist (Garrison Kenneth[6], Oliver T.[5], Edmund Physick[4], James[3], Henry[2], Rudolph[1]) was born on 15 January 1923, probably in Cecil County, Maryland, the daughter of Garrison Kenneth and Mary Susan (Kirk) Frist.[2357] She married on 24 March 1951 to **Harry Walter Cooper** in Methodist Parsonage, Cherry Hill, Maryland. Harry was born on 2 February 1924.

Children of Harry Walter and Helen Kirk[7] (Frist) Cooper:

> 499   i. HARRY SHERWOOD[8] COOPER, born 25 January 1953; married 3 February 1979 Catholic Church, Wilmington, New Castle County, Delaware, Nancy Nepa born 30 October 1957. One child, Stephen Michael Cooper, born 28 April 1987 Newark, New Castle County, Delaware.[2358]

> 500   ii. GAIL BEVERLY COOPER, born 16 May 1954; married 17 May 1976 Presbyterian Church, Nottingham, Chester County, Pennsylvania,

Thomas Brabson. Children, both born in Coatsville, Chester County, Pennsylvania, *(a)* Kurt Thomas Brabson born 3 June 1979 and *(b)* Kristine Marie Brabson born 18 September 1982.[2359]

371. Dorothy Jean[7] **Frist** (Garrison Kenneth[6], Oliver T.[5], Edmund Physick[4], James[3], Henry[2], Rudolph[1]) was born on 16 September 1924, probably in Cecil County, Maryland, the daughter of Garrison Kenneth and Mary Susan (Kirk) Frist.[2360] She died on 5 June 1982 and is buried in Lakeland, Polk County, Florida. She married on 2 July 1945 in Bartow, Polk County, Florida, to **Frank Benjamin Ordog**. He was born 21 March 1916 in Roebling, New Jersey, the son of Frank and Margaret Ordog.[2361] He died in August 1991.[2362]

Children of Frank Benjamin and Dorothy Jean[7] (Frist) Ordog:

> 501   i. GARRISON KENNETH[8] ORDOG, born 3 September 1946.
>
> 502   ii. MARY MARGARET ORDOG, born 12 September 1947 Lakeland, Polk County, Florida; married 23 June 1969 Bartow, Polk County, Florida, Robert Parker.
>
> 503   iii. THOMAS FRANK ORDOG, born 20 August 1958 Lorain, Lorain County, Ohio.

372. Florence Gertrude[7] **Frist** (Garrison Kenneth[6], Oliver T.[5], Edmund Physick[4], James[3], Henry[2], Rudolph[1]) was born on 22 August 1926, probably in Cecil County, Maryland, the daughter of Garrison Kenneth and Mary Susan (Kirk) Frist.[2363] She married on 29 June 1946 to **David Carlton Morris** in Presbyterian Church, Oxford, Chester County, Pennsylvania. David was born on 11 July 1925 in West Grove, Chester County, Pennsylvania, the son of Everett Vasher and Gertrude May (Fisher) Morris.[2364] David died 8 August 1993, probably in Oxford, Chester County, Pennsylvania.[2365]

Children of David Carlton and Florence Gertrude[7] (Frist) Morris, probably all born in Chester County, Pennsylvania:

> 504   i. DAVID WILLIAM[8] MORRIS, born 6 June 1950 West Grove, Chester County, Pennsylvania; married (1) 20 June 1970 Methodist Church, Landenburg, Chester County, Pennsylvania, Debra Reynolds. Children, *(a)* William Christopher Morris born 15 April 1971 Cheyenne, Wyoming, and *(b)* Michael David Morris born 29 December 1972 West Chester, Chester County, Pennsylvania. David married (2) 23 April 1977 Methodist Church, Claymont, New Castle County, Delaware, Catherine Watson Roper.[2366]

505   ii. KENNETH EVERETT MORRIS, born 12 March 1954; married
20 October 1984 Methodist Church, Oxford, Chester County,
Pennsylvania, Kristine Connelly.[2367]

373. Warren Foard[7] Smith (Anna Roberta[6] Foard, Anna Elizabeth[5] Frist, Robert Harris[4], Jacob Chester[3], Henry[2], Rudolph[1]) was born 15 May 1932 in Brooklyn, New York, the son of James Henry and Anna Roberta (Foard) Smith.[2368] He died in 1983 in East Orange, Essex County, New Jersey.[2369] He married in 1968 in East Orange, Essex County, New Jersey, to **Helen Ballard**, who was born 22 February 1934.

Warren attended Franklin and Marshall College and served in the United States Air Force, performing radio repair on airplanes. He was a medical technician and enjoyed photography.

Child of Warren Foard and Helen (Ballard) Smith:

506   i. TERRI ANN[8] SMITH, born 1969.[2370]

374. Wendell Murray[7] Smith (Anna Roberta[6] Foard, Anna Elizabeth[5] Frist, Robert Harris[4], Jacob Chester[3], Henry[2], Rudolph[1]) was born 15 May 1935 in Brooklyn, New York, the son of James Henry and Anna Roberta (Foard) Smith.[2371] Wendell was educated at Dartmouth College, receiving an A.B. degree in 1957 and an M.S. in mechanical engineering in 1958. He married in 1957 in Brockton, Plymouth County, Massachusetts, to **Margaret McGregor**, who was born 22 November 1935.

Wendell is a retired aeronautical engineer who enjoys sailing, traveling, tennis, golf, and sculpture. He is listed in *Who's Who in America*.[2372]

Children of Wendell Murray[7] and Margaret (McGregor) Smith:

507   i. KAREN MURRAY[8] SMITH, born 1958; married 1980 in Stamford,
Fairfield County, Connecticut, Jared Wilson born 1959. One child,
Courtney Murray Wilson born 1984.[2373]

508   ii. WENDY MARGARET SMITH, born 1959; married 1982 Stamford,
Fairfield County, Connecticut, James Berge born 1958. Children,
(a) Alison Margaret Berge born 1983, *(b)* James Alexander Berge born
1985, and *(c)* Anna Elizabeth Berge born 1989.[2374]

509   iii. KIMBERLY FOARD SMITH, born 1960; married 1983 Stamford,
Fairfield County, Connecticut, Kent Quirk born 1960. Children,
(a) Lincoln Joseph Quirk born 1986 and *(b)* Morgan Tilghman Quirk
born 1989.[2375]

510 iv. KATHERINE MCGREGOR SMITH, born 1962; married 1985 Stamford, Fairfield County, Connecticut, William Oakford born 1962. Children, *(a)* Alexander McGregor Oakford born 1988 and *(b)* Abigail Margaret Oakford born 1991.[2376]

511 v. JENNIFER KEITH SMITH, born 1967; married 1990 Stamford, Fairfield County, Connecticut, Richard Piselli born 1966. Children, *(a)* Eric James Piselli born 1993 and *(b)* Kevin James Piselli born 1996.[2377]

375. Janet Frances[7] **Smith** (Anna Roberta[6] Foard, Anna Elizabeth[5] Frist, Robert Harris[4], Jacob Chester[3], Henry[2], Rudolph[1]) was born 6 April 1941 in Hartford, Hartford County, Connecticut, the daughter of James Henry and Anna Roberta (Foard) Smith.[2378] She married in 1962 in Maplewood, Essex County, New Jersey, to **Herbert Dann**. Janet received her B.S. in nursing at Alfred University in 1963. She is a public health nurse and director of Home Health Agency. She enjoys traveling, reading, and hiking.[2379]

Children of Herbert and Janet Frances[7] (Smith) Dann:

512 i. TERESA LYNN[8] DANN, born 1964.[2380]

513 ii. LESLIE ANN DANN, born 1966; married 1994 Corning, Steuben County, New York, Guido Jimenez-Cruz born 18 April 1968.[2381]

514 iii. HERBERT IRVING DANN III, born 1968; married 1997 Lake Tahoe, California, Kay Cockerill born 16 October 1964.[2382]

376. Robert Henry[7] **Smith** (Anna Roberta[6] Foard, Anna Elizabeth[5] Frist, Robert Harris[4], Jacob Chester[3], Henry[2], Rudolph[1]) was born 13 October 1946 in Maplewood, Essex County, New Jersey, the son of James Henry and Anna Roberta (Foard) Smith.[2383] He received his A.B. degree at Wesleyan in 1968. He married in 1970 at Norwich, Chenango County, New York, to **Elizabeth Brereton**, who was born 24 February 1947. After his marriage, he enrolled at the University of Chicago and received his J.D. degree in 1972. He is a lawyer and educator. He received the Lifetime Achievement Award from Boston College Law School. He enjoys sports, hiking, and community service.[2384]

Children of Robert Henry[7] and Elizabeth (Brereton) Smith:

515 i. MATTHEW BRERETON[8] SMITH, born 1972.[2385]

516 ii. MOLLY ELIZABETH BRERETON SMITH, born 1975.[2386]

517 iii. THOMAS LUMLEY SMITH, born 1978.[2387]

377. Margaret Ann[7] **Foard** (Franklin Peach[6], Anna Elizabeth[5] Frist, Robert Harris[4], Jacob Chester[3], Henry[2], Rudolph[1]) was born 31 October 1938 in Wilmington, New Castle County, Delaware, the daughter of Franklin Peach and Margaret Jane (Hubert) Foard.[2388] She married 20 June 1959 in Woodstown, Salem County, New Jersey, to **Neil Wyatt Fowser**.

Neil was born 10 August 1937 in Salem, New Jersey, the son of Wyatt Earl and Naomi C. (Jones) Fowser. Neil and Ann are both graduates of the University of Delaware. Ann was a school occupational therapist from 1980 until her retirement in June 2001. She is a violist in the community orchestra and enjoys quilting. They live in Medford Lakes, New Jersey, in 2003.[2389]

Children of Neil Wyatt and Margaret Ann[7] (Foard) Fowser:

518   i. MARK ANDREW[8] FOWSER, born 21 August 1960, Fort Benjamin Harrison, Indianapolis, Marion County, Indiana. Mark is news director for WILM radio station in Wilmington, Delaware, and lives in Newark, Delaware.[2390]

519   ii. SCOTT WYATT FOWSER, born 18 February 1963, Wilmington, New Castle County, Delaware. Scott has a Ph.D. in engineering and is with Boeing in Los Angeles, California.[2391]

520   iii. LORI JEAN FOWSER, born 26 December 1971, Wilmington, New Castle County, Delaware. Lori was educated at the College of New Jersey and the University of Massachusetts at Lowell, and is a physicist. She is a clarinetist and is enrolled at the University of Maryland in September 2002 as a music major.[2392]

384. Jane Alden[7] Harms (Jane Elizabeth[6] Frist, John Chester[6], Jacob Chester[4], Jacob Chester[3], Henry[2], Rudolph[1]) was born 23 January 1959 in Princeton, Mercer County, New Jersey, the daughter of Arnold Cornelius and Jane Elizabeth (Frist) Harms.[2393] She graduated from Colorado State University in 1989 with a degree in communication. She won Best of Show in watercolor in Black Mountain, North Carolina; she is also talented in photography. She worked as a flight attendant with People Express Airlines and Continental Airlines for about seventeen years, traveling extensively around the world during work and vacations. She lived in Hawaii, Orlando, New Jersey, and New York. She recently worked at the George Vanderbilt Biltmore Estate and is now at the Asheville/Hendersonville Jet Port in North Carolina. Her hobbies include reading, skiing, and hiking.[2394]

385. John David Frist[7] Harms (Jane Elizabeth[6] Frist, John Chester[6], Jacob Chester[4], Jacob Chester[3], Henry[2], Rudolph[1]) was born 24 September 1960 in New Brunswick, Middlesex County, New Jersey, the son of Arnold Cornelius and Jane Elizabeth (Frist) Harms.[2395] He went to Fountain Valley prep school in Colorado Springs. After graduation, David worked in Heidelberg, Germany, for a year and then traveled in Europe with an extensive stay in Nepal and Dharmsala, India. After six years abroad, he returned to the United States where he worked as a photographer in New York City for about seven years. He photographed top models and helped to publish two books that included some of his photographs. He returned to Europe for another three years, working as a photojournalist in Madrid, Spain. He has licenses in insurance, mortgages, and real estate and worked for five years in stock brokerage companies in Orlando.

In 2003 he works as a certified financial planner in Orlando, Florida. His hobbies include hiking, skiing, and world travel. He enjoys riding daily on his horse Bo and canoeing on Lake Fairview in front of his Florida condo.[2396]

386. Robert Dale[7] Harms (Jane Elizabeth[6] Frist, John Chester[6], Jacob Chester[4], Jacob Chester[3], Henry[2], Rudolph[1]) was born 26 May 1962 in New Brunswick, Middlesex County, New Jersey, the son of Arnold Cornelius and Jane Elizabeth (Frist) Harms.[2397] He graduated from the University of Colorado in Boulder with a B.S. degree, majoring in biology. He sold time-shares in Breckenridge, Colorado, and in Orlando, Florida, for three years before starting his own insurance company in Winter Park, Florida. He bought a beautiful house with a pool and boathouse on Lake Maitland and enjoyed furnishing it with antiques. He lived there for several years, moving his insurance business into one wing of the house. In 1999 a devastating house fire destroyed all of the records of his insurance business and killed his beloved dogs. "Rob" was hospitalized with smoke inhalation but was otherwise unharmed. Since the house burned, Rob has worked in photography, is quite an accomplished poet and song writer, and also hopes to be a novelist.

Rob is a natural salesman with an easygoing personality and lots of enthusiasm. His hobbies include hiking, and he especially enjoyed climbing the 14,000-foot peaks in Colorado with a group that climbed for Save the Children. He also enjoys drawing and writing poetry. In 2003 Rob lives in Orlando, Florida, and is one of West Gate at Disney's top salesmen.[2398]

387. Robert Chester[7] Faucette (Charlotte June[6] Frist, John Chester[5], Jacob Chester[4], Jacob Chester[3], Henry[2], Rudolph[1]) was born 25 March 1963 in Martinsville, Virginia, the son of James Robert and Charlotte June (Frist) Faucette.[2399] He grew up in La Porte, Texas. He married on 6 October 1990 in Greensboro, Guilford County, North Carolina, at Our Lady of Grace Catholic Church to **Mary Elizabeth Tota**. Mary was born 24 March 1962 in Hoboken, Virginia, the daughter of Thomas and Nancy Tota. She grew up in Cliffside, New Jersey.

"Bobby" and Mary both obtained their Ph.D.s in clinical psychology from the University of North Carolina at Greensboro. Bobby works as a child psychologist at Child and Family Development, Inc. and Mary works as a psychologist specializing in pain management at Presbyterian Rehabilitation Center. They have two wonderful children who make their lives complete. Avery is in kindergarten and loves to learn, dance, and do arts and crafts. Ryan is fascinated by American flags and balloons. The Faucettes reside in Charlotte, North Carolina, in 2003.[2400]

Children of Robert Chester[7] and Mary Elizabeth (Tota) Faucette, both born in Charlotte, North Carolina:

521   i. AVERY NICOLE[8] FAUCETTE, born 14 October 1996.

522   ii. RYAN JAMES FAUCETTE, born 11 September 2000.

388. Jane Elizabeth[7] Faucette (Charlotte June[6] Frist, John Chester[5], Jacob Chester[4], Jacob Chester[3], Henry[2], Rudolph[1]) was born 27 September 1965 in Richmond, Virginia, the daughter of James Robert and Charlotte June (Frist) Faucette.[2401] "Janie" grew up in LaPorte, Texas, and received her B.A. degree from Trinity University in 1988. She taught school for eight years in Texas public schools and completed a "thru-hike" of the Appalachian Trail in the year 2000. It was during this hike that she became engaged to "Randy" Moore, at a stopover at Buzzard Rock in Virginia. Jane Elizabeth Faucette married on 15 September 2001 at Black Mountain, North Carolina, to **Douglas Randolph Moore**.

Randy was born 26 October 1958 in Georgetown, Georgetown County, South Carolina, the son of Paul Amos and Virginia (Graham) Moore. He grew up in Macon, Georgia, and has worked for both the Forest and Park Services. He also worked with juvenile delinquents in a therapeutic wilderness program. Randy, known on the trail as "Macon Tracks," has thru-hiked the Appalachian Trail three times (1987, 1993, 2000). He has also "end to end" hiked Vermont's Long Trail several times. He currently works for UMS, a utilities company.

Janie currently works with juvenile delinquents in a therapeutic wilderness program. Her trail name is "Not Yet." The Moores live at Black Mountain, North Carolina, in 2003.[2402]

389. Thomas James[7] Faucette (Charlotte June[6] Frist, John Chester[5], Jacob Chester[4], Jacob Chester[3], Henry[2], Rudolph[1]) was born 8 September 1968 in Louisville, Jefferson County, Kentucky, the son of James Robert and Charlotte June (Frist) Faucette.[2403] "Tom" attended the University of Texas at Austin where he met his wife to be, **Lynda Chang**.

On 10 April 1999 Thomas James Faucette married in La Jolla, San Diego County, California, to Lynda Chang. Lynda was born 28 December 1971 in Taipei, Taiwan, the daughter of Larry Chao-Der and Su (Yu-Yuen) Chang. She grew up in Houston, Texas, not far from where Tom lived. Tom was active in a pre-law fraternity, and Lynda was a cheerleader on the University of Texas cheerleading and dance team, Texas Pom. Both graduated from the University of Texas at Austin.

Tom has a career in quality assurance in the pharmaceutical industry. He enjoys tennis, basketball, golf, hiking, gardening, and home improvement projects. His hobbies include volunteering for KPBS (public television), reading, history, and current events. He plans to return to school for a graduate-level degree.

Lynda has a career in investor relations and business development in the biotechnology industry. She enjoys teaching aerobics classes, running, dancing, playing the piano, and pug dogs.

In June of 2001, Tom and Lynda purchased their first new home in San Diego and are enthused at being first-time home owners in California. In November of 2001 they adopted a feisty and friendly pug dog named "Butters" from Little Angels Pug Rescue (LAPR) in Pasadena, California. LAPR came to their April 1999 wedding with pugs in tow to serve as ring bearers.[2404]

390. Corinne Ansley[7] **Frist** (John Chester[6], John Chester[5], Jacob Chester[4], Jacob Chester[3], Henry[2], Rudolph[1]) was born 9 July 1968 in Nashville, Davidson County, Tennessee, the daughter of John Chester and Mary Corinne (Brothers) Frist.[2405] She graduated from Boston University in 1990. After graduation she joined Teach for America. She married 20 June 1992 in Nashville, Tennessee, to **Timothy Scott Glover**.

Tim was born 12 January 1968 in West Nyack, Rockland County, New York, the youngest of three children born to Robert Sheridan and Beryl (Scott) Glover. Tim's father earned a Ph.D. from Duke University and worked as a financial director for several universities. Tim moved with his family to Chapel Hill, North Carolina, then to West Hartford, Connecticut, and later to Tuscaloosa, Alabama. In 1990 Tim graduated from Bowdoin College in Brunswick, Maine. He joined Teach for America, teaching two years in urban New Orleans.

Tim taught high school science and math until 1996, when he joined Great Outdoor Provision Company. They provide and sell backpacks, fly rods, and camping gear, and Tim manages their Wilmington store and serves as a fly fishing expert. He is a dedicated father. Corinne helped build children's museums and science centers, was a freelance writer, and is currently a full-time mother. The Glovers live in Wilmington, New Hanover County, North Carolina, in 2003.[2406]

Child of Timothy Scott and Corinne Ansley[7] (Frist) Glover:

   523   i. NATHANIEL SCOTT[8] "NATHAN" GLOVER, born 25 May 2001 Wilmington, New Hanover County, North Carolina.

391. John Chester[7] **Frist III** (John Chester[6], John Chester[5], Jacob Chester[4], Jacob Chester[3], Henry[2], Rudolph[1]) was born 12 June 1971 in Gainesville, Alachua County, Florida, the son of John Chester and Mary Corinne (Brothers) Frist.[2407] He graduated in 1989 from Montgomery Bell Academy in Nashville, Tennessee. He attended Wake Forrest University in Winston-Salem, North Carolina, graduating in 1993 with a bachelor of arts degree in communications. After leaving college, "Chet" hiked the entire Appalachian Trail from Maine to Georgia, some 2,150 miles in all. Chet has also completed two marathons—the Rocket City Marathon in Huntsville, Alabama, and the original marathon, in Athens, Greece.

In January of 1994, he began working in the campaign of his father's cousin Bill Frist for the United States Senate. When Bill was elected senator in November of 1994, Chet moved to Washington, D.C., to join his staff as a legislative liaison. In the summer of 1995, he moved to Jackson Hole, Wyoming, where he worked for two years as a whitewater rafting guide on the Snake River. Returning to Nashville in 1997, Chet began working as a production coordinator for Scene Three, a Nashville-based production company. In October of 1999, he joined the Tennessee Film, Entertainment, and Music Commission as assistant director. He became acting director in August of 2000 and was appointed executive director in January 2001.

Chet's first date with his future wife, **Mary Virginia West**, was the grand opening of the Frist Center on 5 April 2001. Chet and Mary Virginia married on 24 August 2002 at The Hermitage, the home of Andrew Jackson in Davidson County, Tennessee. Mary Virginia was born 27 November 1973 in Nashville, Tennessee, the daughter of George Allen and Julie Ann (Simmons) West III. She was raised in Brentwood, Tennessee, and graduated from Brentwood Academy. She received her B.S. degree in early childhood development from the University of Tennessee in 1996. She is a paralegal for Kinnard, Clayton, and Beveridge in Nashville. She enjoys antique shopping, traveling, and cooking and is devoted to her family and friends. Chet and Mary Virginia live in Nashville, Tennessee.[2408]

392. Lisa Kristin[7] Frist (Thomas Ferran[6], John Chester[5], Jacob Chester[4], Jacob Chester[3], Henry[2], Rudolph[1]) was born 2 April 1984 in Atlantic City, Atlantic County, New Jersey, the daughter of Thomas Ferran and Clare (Strachan) Frist.[2409] She was first in her class all her years in high school, excelling in languages. She participates in a church youth group and Fellowship of Christian Athletes. She was named on her tennis team as "most valuable player" and as "player of the year" in her conference. She was chosen to be a page in the North Carolina legislature and to go to the North Carolina Governor's School. In 2002 after winning writing contests and scholarships from a number of local service clubs, she entered Princeton University as a freshman.[2410]

393. John Daniel[1] Frist (Thomas Ferran[6], John Chester[5], Jacob Chester[4], Jacob Chester[3], Henry[2], Rudolph[1]) was born 10 May 1988 in Ourinhos, SP Brazil, the adopted son of Thomas Ferran and Clare (Strachan) Frist.[2411] Daniel was adopted when he was two days old. He is in grade school, and participates in a church youth group and the tennis team. He is a fine artist and won third place in an art exhibition. He became a United States citizen in 1992. He enjoys video games, his many church and school friends, rap music, and basketball, and, beneath a quiet exterior, he is a real comedian.[2412]

394. Patricia Champion[7] Frist (Thomas Fearn[6], Thomas Fearn[5], Jacob Chester[4], Jacob Chester[3], Henry[2], Rudolph[1]) was born 17 January 1965 in St. Louis, Missouri, the daughter of Thomas Fearn and Patricia Gail (Champion) Frist.[2413] "Trisha" was raised in Nashville, Tennessee, and graduated from Harpeth Hall School in 1983. In 1987 she graduated from the University of Virginia with a B.A. in economics. She lived in Aspen, Colorado, Washington, D.C., and Boston, Massachusetts, before returning to Nashville where she met her husband to be, **Charles Anthony Elcan**. They were married on 29 June 1991 in Nashville, Tennessee.

"Chuck" was born 19 August 1963 in Nashville, the son of Paul Dillard and Jean (Page) Elcan. He was raised in Nashville and graduated from Father Ryan High School in 1982. In 1986, he graduated from Spring Hill College in Mobile, Alabama. Chuck founded and is CEO of MedCap Properties. He is on the board of the Land Trust for Tennessee and the YMCA Outdoor Center and Camp. He enjoys hunting, tennis, and flying. She enjoys flying and skiing and is on the board of the Women's Fund and the Ensworth School. They live in Nashville in 2003.[2414]

Children of Charles Anthony and Patricia Champion[7] (Frist) Elcan, all born in Davidson County, Tennessee:

> 524   i. LAUREN CHAMPION[8] ELCAN, born 22 September 1994.
> 525   ii. PATRICIA CATE ELCAN, born 10 November 1997.
> 526   iii. CARRINGTON FRIST ELCAN, born 12 July 2001.

395. Thomas Fearn[7] Frist III (Thomas Fearn[6], Thomas Fearn[5], Jacob Chester[4], Jacob Chester[3], Henry[2], Rudolph[1]) was born 16 February 1968 at Warner Robins Air Force Base, Georgia, the son of Thomas Fearn and Patricia Gail (Champion) Frist.[2415] "Tommy" graduated from Montgomery Bell Academy in Nashville, Tennessee. He went to Princeton University in New Jersey, where he graduated in 1991 with a B.A. degree in religion. He was a 1997 graduate of Harvard Business School, receiving an M.B.A. degree. This is where he met his wife to be, **Julie Mead Damgard**. They were married on 26 September 1998 at Southampton, Suffolk County, New York.

Julie Mead Damgard was born 14 January 1971 in Chicago, Cook County, Illinois, the daughter of John Michael and Darcy (Mead) Damgard II. Julie grew up in Washington, D.C., but also lived in New York City and Greenwich, Connecticut. She graduated from St. Paul's School, a boarding school in Concord, New Hampshire, and from Yale University, where she received a B.A. degree in history and was captain of the golf team. In 1997 she graduated from Harvard Business School with an M.B.A. degree.

Tommy has a career in investment management, enjoys tennis, and has a passion for flying. They live in Nashville in 2003.[2416]

Children of Thomas Fearn[7] and Julie Mead (Damgard) Frist III, both born in Nashville, Davidson County, Tennessee:

527   i.   CAROLINE MEAD[8] FRIST, born 24 October 2000.

528   ii. ANNABEL DAMGARD FRIST, born 4 April 2002.

396. William Robert[7] Frist (Thomas Fearn[6], Thomas Fearn[5], Jacob Chester[4], Jacob Chester[3], Henry[2], Rudolph[1]) was born 29 December 1969 in Nashville, Davidson County, Tennessee, the son of Thomas Fearn and Patricia Gail (Champion) Frist.[2417] He received his B.A. degree in art history from Princeton University in 1993. He married on 28 June 1997 in Nashville, Tennessee, to **Jennifer Catherine Rose**.

Jennifer was born 18 March 1971 in Maryville, Tennessee, the daughter of Ronald Gordon and Carole Josephine (Collins) Rusk. When her mother married her stepfather, Mike Rose, her surname was legally changed to Rose. Jennifer received a B.S. in computer science engineering from Vanderbilt University in 1993. "Billy" received his M.B.A. from Harvard University on 7 June 2001. He is associate administrator at Summit Medical Center in Nashville.

In 2003 Billy and Jennifer both have pilots' licenses and love to fly. They live in Nashville.[2418]

Children of William Robert[7] and Jennifer Catherine (Rose) Frist, both born in Nashville, Davidson County, Tennessee:

529   i.   WALKER RYAN[8] FRIST, born 19 June 2000.

530   ii. JACQUELINE COLLINS FRIST, born 12 June 2002.

397. Deborah Frist[7] Eller (Dorothy Cate[6] Frist, Thomas Fearn[5], Jacob Chester[4], Jacob Chester[3], Henry[2], Rudolph[1]) was born 8 February 1964 at Fort Wainwright Air Force Base in Fairbanks, Alaska, the daughter of Charles Ray and Dorothy Cate (Frist) Eller.[2419] Her younger years were spent in Nashville, but she moved in 1976 with her mother and stepfather to Cookeville, Tennessee. Early in life, she developed an interest in art. She won first place one year and second place another year in the art contest at the state fair in Cookeville. She graduated from Deberry Academy in Baxter, Tennessee, in 1982.

Deborah spent a year at David Lipscomb College in Nashville studying art design. In the summers she took lessons at the Watkins Institute College of Art and Design. She spent two years at Middle Tennessee State University in Murfreesboro, Tennessee, again in an art program.

In 1990 Deborah married **Raymond Keach** in Nashville, Tennessee, at Westminster Presbyterian Church. They moved to Michigan and Raymond attended Michigan State for two years. Their daughter, Ashley Nichole Frist, was born on 22 May 1991 in Lapeer, Michigan. They divorced in 1994 and Deborah returned to Nashville, Tennessee. Both Deborah and her daughter use the Eller surname.

Deborah is a freelance artist, working from her home in Nashville. She enjoys most sports, but especially tennis, snow skiing, and swimming. She does volunteer work and is active in the Westminster Presbyterian Church.[2420]

Child of Raymond and Deborah Frist[7] (Eller) Keach:

531   i. ASHLEY NICHOLE FRIST[8] ELLER, born 22 May 1991 Lapeer,
            Michigan. Ashley enjoys the sport of soccer.

398. Robert Armistead[7] Frist, Jr. (Robert Armistead[6], Thomas Fearn[5], Jacob Chester[4], Jacob Chester[3], Henry[2], Rudolph[1]) was born 7 April 1967 in Charlottesville, Albemarle County, Virginia, the son of Robert Armistead and Carol Len (Knox) Frist.[2421] "Bobby" attended Montgomery Bell Academy (MBA) in Nashville, Davidson County, Tennessee, graduating in 1985. During his junior year at MBA, Bobby founded Vintage Auto Detailing as an entrepreneurial enterprise limited to summers between his academic studies. Employing four of his high school friends, the business operated into Bobby's college years.

Upon graduation from MBA, Bobby went to Trinity University in San Antonio, Texas. There he majored in business with concentrations in marketing, economics, and finance. After his sophomore year at Trinity, Bobby chose to take a semester-long sabbatical to continue his academic studies and training in tae kwon do at California State, Fresno. Bobby attained a black belt (1st Dan) during his sabbatical in California.

After receiving a bachelor's degree in 1989 from Trinity University, he co-founded a multimedia development business named New Order Media with one of his classmates at Trinity University, Jeff McLaren. Joining this venture was Scott Portis, who had worked with Bobby back in high school in Vintage Auto Detailing. Throughout the early 1990s, New Order Media earned a strong reputation for developing innovative, computer-based healthcare education products for the world's largest medical publishers. Lippincott Williams & Wilkins was one of these publishers as well as other prestigious organizations like the American College of Physicians. A strategic decision was made in mid-1998 to focus exclusively on the healthcare industry. As a result, Bobby and Jeff's company changed its name to "HealthStream." What began as a two-person multimedia startup is now a leading provider of learning solutions for the healthcare industry with a staff of over 200 employees. There is an additional office in Denver as well as the corporate office in Nashville, Tennessee.

On 25 December 1998, Bobby became engaged to **Melissa Merriman**. Nine months later, they were married on 11 September 1999 at the Cathedral of the Incarnation in Nashville, Tennessee. Melissa was born 4 May 1967 in Erie, Pennsylvania, the daughter of Robert Frederick and Lois June (Schnelle) Merriman. She is the fifth child in a family of six. The family moved to Amarillo, Texas, when Melissa was three. She enjoyed basketball, track, and tennis while in junior high and high school in Texas, graduating from Tascosa High School in Amarillo in 1985. She attended Trinity University in San Antonio, where she was a member of Gamma Chi Delta sorority. She graduated magna cum laude from Trinity University with a B.A. in elementary education and a specialization in history. Her senior year at Trinity was devoted to travel in China with Trinity's education department, touring elementary and middle schools and meeting with educators at the university level.

After graduation Melissa taught second grade in San Antonio for two years. In 1993 she received an M.Ed. degree in human development counseling from Vanderbilt University. She taught second grade at the Ensworth School in Nashville for three years and coached track and cross-country teams. She worked for five years for the Dede Wallace Center in Nashville, a local not-for-profit community mental health center. She began as a community outreach coordinator and then became development manager.

Melissa enjoys running and has completed two marathons in under four hours, the Rock and Roll marathon in San Diego and the twenty-fifth anniversary of the Marine Corps marathon in Washington, D.C. In local 5k races, she took first overall in the One Race for Unity and second overall in the Susan G. Komen Race for the Cure. Melissa's greatest joys in life come from her family.

Under Bobby's leadership, HealthStream has flourished. The company raised $70 million within twelve months, including $45 million from an initial public offering in April of 2000. Since that time, the accounting firm of Deloitte & Touche awarded HealthStream a ranking on their prestigious "Technology Fast 500" list for two consecutive years, 2000 and 2001, as a top technology company in North America. Additionally, the Smithsonian Institution presented HealthStream with the Computerworld Smithsonian Commemorative Medallion in recognition of its achievement to innovatively use technology to contribute, empower, and advance society.

As the chief executive officer and chairman of the board of HealthStream, Bobby Frist's achievements have been widely recognized by his peers. He was awarded the 1999 Executive of the Year by the *Nashville Business Journal*. He was also named one of *Business Nashville*'s "High Tech 20" in April of 2001 and chosen by the same publication as a "40 under Forty" top local leader in June 2001. In October 2001, Bobby was featured for the third consecutive year in the Healthcare 100 most powerful and influential people in this industry in the Middle Tennessee region by the *Nashville Business Journal*. HealthStream's learning solutions are utilized in approximately 20 percent of the nation's hospitals, located in all fifty states.

Bobby Frist is a founding investor and board member for HealthLeaders, a healthcare industry publisher. He and Melissa are both actively involved in community service. Melissa currently serves on the boards of YMCA, Dede Wallace Center, and the Junior League of Nashville. Bobby is a board member of the Minnie Pearl Cancer Foundation and the Cumberland Science Museum. The Frists live in Nashville, Tennessee, in 2003.[2422]

Child of Robert Armistead[7] and Melissa (Merriman) Frist, Jr.:

532   i. ELEANOR KNOX[8] FRIST, born 1 September 2001 in Nashville, Davidson County, Tennessee.

399. Carol Len[7] Frist (Robert Armistead[6], Thomas Fearn[5], Jacob Chester[4], Jacob Chester[3], Henry[2], Rudolph[1]) was born 11 January 1970 in Lexington, Fayette County, Kentucky, the daughter of Robert Armistead and Carol Len (Knox) Frist.[2423] She grew up in Nashville, attending Harding Academy grade school. In 1984 she began high school at Brentwood Academy where she was active in varsity basketball and volleyball. A member of the Fellowship of Christian Athletes, she served as president in her junior and senior year and was also a homecoming attendant in both her sophomore and senior years. She was in the National Honor Society, serving as secretary of the club in her senior year. During her senior year at Brentwood Academy, she worked in Paris, France, at the ambassador's residence. Carol Len received two prestigious awards during her senior year of high school. She was awarded both the Bill Barron Award, given annually to an outstanding Brentwood Academy athlete, and the Andy Anderson Award, established to foster the attitudes and attributes displayed by Andy Anderson, who persevered through a brain tumor that eventually took his life.

Following graduation from Brentwood Academy in 1988, Carol Len enrolled at Furman University in Greenville, South Carolina, where she majored in health and exercise science. She was a member of Delta Delta Delta sorority and continued her membership in the Fellowship of Christian Athletes.

Carol Len met her husband to be, **Scott McClain Portis**, through her brother Bobby. Scott had trained in tae kwon do in 1985, becoming close friends with Bobby Frist. He later worked with Bobby at Vintage Auto Detailing. Carol Len and Scott were married on 28 December 1991 in Nashville, Tennessee, at Westminster Presbyterian Church.

Scott Portis was born 1 July 1966 in Indianapolis, Indiana, the son of Bill Scott and Dorothy (Conger) Portis (now Dorothy Durham). Scott's father is a prominent physician who was raised in Huntingdon, Tennessee. Scott moved with his mother in 1968 from Indiana to Tennessee and enrolled in 1980 at Montgomery Bell Academy. He played football at MBA. After graduation in 1984, he enrolled at Auburn University in Alabama where in 1989 he earned a B.S. degree in computer engineering. He was an active member of Beta Theta Pi fraternity and was the Auburn Freshman Orientation leader in 1987.

After their marriage, Scott worked for Electronic Data System in Detroit, Michigan, and Carol Len worked at a physical therapy sports medicine clinic. They moved to Atlanta, Georgia, with Electronic Data System, and Carol Len worked there as assistant director of a sports complex. In 1994 they returned to Nashville when Scott joined HealthStream (then New Order Media). He is currently vice president of technology. His civic activities include service on the board of the Boys and Girls Clubs of Middle Tennessee.

Carol Len enrolled at Belmont University in 1995 and obtained her master's degree in business administration in 1998. She has served on the advisory boards of the League for the Deaf and Hard of Hearing, the Center for Business Ethics at Belmont University, the Friends of Vanderbilt Children's Hospital, and the Eve of Janus. She raised $192,000 when she chaired the Eve of Janus 1999 benefit for the hematology/oncology program of Vanderbilt Children's Hospital. She is currently on the kindergarten committee at Westminster and the advisory board of Brentwood Academy.[2424]

Children of Scott McClain and Carol Len[7] (Frist) Portis, both born in Nashville, Davidson County, Tennessee:

> 533   i. LEAH CANNON[8] PORTIS, born 1 October 1996.
>
> 534   ii. SCOTT MCCLAIN PORTIS, JR., born 18 September 1999.

400. James Knox[7] Frist (Robert Armistead[6], Thomas Fearn[5], Jacob Chester[4], Jacob Chester[3], Henry[2], Rudolph[1]) was born 11 July 1972 in Lexington, Fayette County, Kentucky, the son of Robert Armistead and Carol Len (Knox) Frist.[2425] He grew up in Nashville, Tennessee, and attended Brentwood Academy. He enjoyed forensics and drama, performing in the high school play every year. He was in the National Honor Society and won awards for essay writing and English. He was voted "friendliest" and elected by the class to speak at graduation.

He graduated from Trinity University in San Antonio, Texas, with a B.A. degree in business administration and speech communications, studying for one semester at the American University in Paris. He is fluent in French and enjoyed traveling abroad. He was a member of Alpha Lambda Delta, a national academic honor society for freshmen.

Over the years, he has furthered his studies at the Watkins Film School in Nashville and the American Film Institute, Los Angeles Film School, UCLA, and the New York Film Academy, all in Los Angeles.

He is currently interested in the film industry and is studying directing, editing, and writing. He enjoys racquetball, tournament foosball, and golf. He lives in Los Angeles, California, in 2003.[2426]

401. Mary Lauren[7] Barfield (Mary Louise[6] Frist, Thomas Fearn[5], Jacob Chester[4], Jacob Chester[3], Henry[2], Rudolph[1]) was born 2 January 1970 at the Portsmouth Naval Hospital in Portsmouth, Virginia, the daughter of Henry Lee and Mary Louise (Frist) Barfield II.[2427] Her father was with the United States Navy, stationed in Portsmouth at the time. She grew up in Nashville and was a nationally ranked junior tennis player. In 1982 at the age of twelve, she was ranked ninth in the country. She graduated from the Ensworth School in 1984 and was honored as a Black Captain.[2428] She graduated from Harpeth Hall in 1988, where she was an All-American tennis player. She received a B.S. degree in human and organizational development from Vanderbilt University in 1992. There she met **Lawson Coffee Allen**, whom she married on 28 August 1993 in Nashville, Tennessee.

Lawson was born 6 March 1970 in Corpus Christi, Nueces County, Texas, the son of Sam Lawson and Phyllis (Coffee) Allen of Corpus Christi. He grew up in Corpus Christi, where he took an interest in sailing and drama. He played competitive tennis and soccer during his high school years. He graduated from Vanderbilt University in 1992 with a B.A. degree in public policy studies. He was an active member of the Sigma Chi Fraternity and later served as the chapter's alumni advisor. He was named the International Chapter Advisor of the Year in 2002.

Lawson is a principal in the Nashville investment management firm of Lee, Danner & Bass, Incorporated. He served as the president and as a director of the Nashville Society of Financial Analysts. He also served as a director of numerous nonprofit organizations including the YMCA, Friends of Warner Parks, and the Heart Gala.

After graduating from college, Mary Lauren became a certified tennis professional. She enjoyed coaching the Harpeth Hall school varsity tennis team in Nashville and was named Coach of the Year by *The Tennessean* in 1997. As a homemaker, Mary Lauren's main love is spending time with her husband, children, and extended family. The Allens live in Nashville in 2003.[2429]

Children of Lawson Coffee and Mary Lauren[7] (Barfield) Allen, all born at Centennial Medical Center in Nashville, Davidson County, Tennessee:

535   i. HARRISON COLE[8] ALLEN, born 26 September 1996.
536   ii. THOMAS FRIST ALLEN, born 23 November 1998.
537   iii. LAWSON COLE ALLEN, born 4 September 2002.

402. Dorothy Frist[7] Barfield (Mary Louise[6] Frist, Thomas Fearn[5], Jacob Chester[4], Jacob Chester[3], Henry[2], Rudolph[1]) was born 25 August 1971 in Nashville, Davidson County, Tennessee, the daughter of Henry Lee and Mary Louise (Frist) Barfield.[2430] Dorothy grew up in Nashville and attended the Ensworth School through eighth grade, where she was honored as a Black Captain.[2431] While at Brentwood Academy high school, she played varsity volleyball, tennis, and track. After graduating in 1990, she went to the University of Georgia where she was a member the water ski team and Kappa Alpha Theta sorority. She took a course from the National Outdoor Leadership School, spending the summer of 1992 rock climbing in the Wind River range in Wyoming. She graduated from the University of Georgia in 1994 with a B.S. degree from the college of family and consumer sciences.

After graduation Dorothy went to work for her "Uncle Billy" Frist in his campaign for the United States Senate. She traveled with Bill, his wife Karyn, and their sons around Tennessee and assisted in the Nashville campaign office as well. Afterwards, she moved to Jackson Hole, Wyoming, where she worked as a ski hostess in the winter and as a white-water raft guide on the Snake River in summer. In 1995 Dorothy trained and received her paragliding license. She returned to the National Outdoor Leadership School for a semester in Kenya, Africa. There, she climbed Mount Kenya, studied animal behavior, and lived with the Massai tribe. She then moved to Aspen, Colorado, where she worked as director of development for Challenge Aspen, a nonprofit organization that works with people who have mental and physical disabilities. This became her passion and she participated in many different Challenge Aspen camps and programs.

In 1999, Dorothy moved back to Nashville to be closer to her family. She learned to fly and soloed on 11 September 1999. Back at home, she met her husband to be. On 30 September 2000 in Nashville, Tennessee, at Westminster Presbyterian Church, she married **John Claiborne "Clay" Sifford**.

Clay was born 6 December 1971 in Charlotte, North Carolina, the son of David Falls and Mary (Donohue) Sifford. Clay lived in North Carolina until he was six years old and the family moved to Nashville. He attended Brentwood Middle School and High School where he lettered in baseball his sophomore year and in football all four years. He was elected captain of the football team his senior year and served in student government all four years. Clay went to Hampden Sydney College in Farmington, Virginia, where he was a member of Kappa Alpha Fraternity and played football and rugby. He graduated with a double major in political science and Spanish. He studied in San Jose, Costa Rica, for two summers where he learned to speak fluent Spanish. He is the owner of two companies in Nashville, Audio Visual Resources, Inc. and Sifford Media Services, Inc.

The Siffords live in Nashville in 2003. Dorothy is active in church and is on the boards of the YMCA bridge program and the YMCA restore ministries. She loves adventure and is an outdoor enthusiast. She loves running, biking, skiing, and snowboarding and is devoted to her family.[2432]

Child of John Claiborne and Dorothy Frist (Barfield) Sifford, born in Nashville, Davidson County, Tennessee:

538   i. JOHN CLAIBORNE SIFFORD, JR., born 2 May 2003.

403. Corinne Cole[7] Barfield (Mary Louise[6] Frist, Thomas Fearn[5], Jacob Chester[4], Jacob Chester[3], Henry[2], Rudolph[1]) was born 29 October 1973 in Nashville, Davidson County, Tennessee, the daughter of Henry Lee and Mary Louise (Frist) Barfield II.[2433] She grew up in Nashville and attended the Ensworth School through eighth grade. She received the faculty award and the sportsmanship award at graduation. She then attended Brentwood Academy, graduating in 1992. She was active on the student leadership team through school and in 1991 was the vice president for Fellowship of Christian Athletes. In 1992 she served as its president. She was voted "most athletic" in 1992. In 1996 she graduated cum laude from Vanderbilt University in Nashville with a B.S. degree, majoring in human and organizational development. She was a member of Tri Delta Sorority. She then entered Vanderbilt University School of Nursing and was a member of the Academic Society, Iota Chapter. She graduated in 1997 magna cum laude with a master's degree in nursing. Her specialty was acute critical care.

After graduation, Corinne worked at Baylor University Medical Center in Dallas, Texas, in their cardiac ICU section. She was named "Nurse of the Year 1999" at this facility. She currently works for Cardiology Consultants in Nashville and enjoys the reward of learning about the lives of her patients. She has been to Ghana, Peru, and Sudan on medical mission trips.

Corinne enjoys traveling, backpacking in Europe, inner-city involvement, Young Life, and Bible study. She likes to exercise and participated in the White Rock Marathon in Dallas, Texas. She appreciates music (country, Christian, and classical). She lives in Nashville in 2003.[2434]

404. Lee Cole[7] Barfield (Mary Louise[6] Frist, Thomas Fearn[5], Jacob Chester[4], Jacob Chester[3], Henry[2], Rudolph[1]) was born 31 October 1980 in Nashville, Davidson

County, Tennessee, the son of Henry Lee and Mary Louise (Frist) Barfield II.[2435] He grew up in Nashville and attended the Ensworth School through eighth grade, where he was honored as a Black Captain.[2436] He went to Montgomery Bell Academy where he received the P. M. Estes award for scholarship and leadership. He played varsity football and baseball. In his senior year the football team won the state championship. Cole received the game ball when he made a last-minute interception that kept Brentwood Academy from winning the game. He was voted "2nd team, All City linebacker" his junior year and "2nd team, All State offensive line" his senior year.

Cole enjoyed baseball year round. In the summer he received the "old timers" award, voted by the coaches, for being the best sixteen-year-old player in the city league. He was voted "All Region third baseman" his senior year at Montgomery Bell Academy, where he received the Coach's Award. Cole also had an interest in art at Montgomery Bell and received a silver award in a citywide art competition for one of his paintings. He was also an officer with Fellowship of Christian Athletes.

Cole's Uncle Tommy offered him the opportunity to take flying lessons, and he made his first solo flight at sixteen and received his license at age eighteen. He has greatly enjoyed flying and received his instrument license in 2002.

After graduation from Montgomery Bell Academy in 1999, Cole went to Princeton University in New Jersey where he majored in politics. He served on the executive committee of the USG (student government). He is president of AGAPE, a large Christian organization on campus. He is a member of the Cap and Gown Club and secretary of the Princeton Flying Club. He is also on a committee for minority issues, known as the Sustained Dialogue Committee.

In the summer of 2000, he worked at Centennial Hospital observing various doctors during surgery and rounds. In the summer of 2001 during the first year of the Bush administration, he worked as an intern at the White House in the Office of Legislative Affairs. In 2002 before his senior year at Princeton, Cole worked in Sudan doing medical missionary work with Samaritans Purse, an organization founded by Franklin Graham.

Cole has an adventuresome spirit and possesses a real sense of compassion, loyalty, and honor. In addition to his enthusiasm for flying, Cole enjoys skiing, golf, ice hockey, and tennis.[2437]

405. William Harrison[7] Frist, Jr. (William Harrison[6], Thomas Fearn[5], Jacob Chester[4], Jacob Chester[3], Henry[2], Rudolph[1]) was born 6 May 1983 in Southampton, England, the son of William Harrison and Karyn (McLaughlin) Frist.[2438] Harrison lived for a year in Boston, then a year in California. In 1986 the family moved to Nashville, where he spent his early years, attending the Ensworth School. In 1994 the family moved to Washington, D.C., where he graduated from St. Albans

School for Boys. He lettered in football, ice hockey, and baseball. He was elected captain of the football team and received the Coach's Award. He was All Interstate Athletic Conference (IAC) in baseball and football and was chosen Most Valuable Player in baseball in 2002. While at St. Albans, he received the Citizenship Award in 1996, the President's Student Service Award, the Bishop Walker Fellowship Award for summer study and medical mission work in Sudan, and the Headmaster's Spirit Award. He is a licensed pilot.

In 2002 he enrolled at Princeton University where he joined Sigma Alpha Epsilon Fraternity and was elected to the University Student Council.[2439]

406. Jonathan McLaughlin[7] **Frist** (William Harrison[6], Thomas Fearn[5], Jacob Chester[4], Jacob Chester[3], Henry[2], Rudolph[1]) was born 11 October 1985 in Stanford, California, the son of William Harrison and Karyn (McLaughlin) Frist.[2440] Jonathan moved with the family to Nashville in 1986, where he lived and attended the Ensworth School until 1994 when his father was elected to the U.S. Senate. In Washington, D.C., he attended St. Albans School for Boys. An avid rock climber, he was ranked seventh in the nation. At age sixteen, he climbed Mount Cotopaxi and Mount Chimborazo in Ecuador. He is active in the Government Club and earned varsity letters in wrestling and track (pole vaulting).[2441]

407. Bryan Edward[7] **Frist** (William Harrison[6], Thomas Fearn[5], Jacob Chester[4], Jacob Chester[3], Henry[2], Rudolph[1]) was born 29 April 1987 in Nashville, Davidson County, Tennessee, the son of William Harrison and Karyn (McLaughlin) Frist.[2442] Bryan was raised in Nashville and attended Ensworth School until 1994, when the family moved to Washington, D.C. He is a student at St. Albans School for Boys, where he was honored by being asked to give the Lower School Commencement Address in 2002. He received the Citizenship Award in 1999 and was elected to the Vestry in 2002 and 2003. As a freshman Bryan earned a varsity letter in wrestling. He enjoys all sports and is currently focusing on lacrosse.[2443]

410. Ronald Gary[7] **"Ronnie" Frist** (Sidney Donald[6], Paul Franklin[5], Joseph Elmer[4], Jacob Chester[3], Henry[2], Rudolph[1]) was born 29 November 1956 in Chattanooga, Hamilton County, Tennessee, the son of Sidney Donald and Norma Drucilla (Roberts) Frist.[2444] He grew up in Chattanooga where he married on 14 August 1978 to **Carla M**. They divorced in October of 1994.

On 19 September 1998 Ronnie married for the second time to **Michelle Helene Major**. Michelle was born 4 December 1956 at Lockbourne Air Force Base in Columbus, Franklin County, Ohio, the daughter of Eugene Andrew and Beverly Lee Major. Michelle is from an air force military background. Her mother, who is now deceased, was a veteran of the Korean conflict. Her father is retired from the air force and lives in Washington, D.C. It is thus not surprising to find that Michelle herself served in the United States Navy, a Vietnam veteran.

In 2003 the Frists live in Chattanooga where Ronnie owns Ronnie Frist Painting and Remodeling, a home repair business. Michelle is in retail merchandizing and works for an advertising company based in Atlanta, Georgia. They are the proud possessors of many antiques and family treasures from Ronnie's grandmother Kate Frist. The tintype photograph of Mary Baldwin Frist, a copy of which can be found in this publication, was among these treasures.[2445]

Children of Ronald Gary[7] and Carla M. Frist, both born in Chattanooga, Hamilton County, Tennessee:

> 539   i. ALISHA DAWN[8] FRIST, born 29 September 1980.
>
> 540   ii. AMBER RACHELLE FRIST, born 8 August 1984.

411. Frankie Susan[7] Frist (Frank Emmett[6], James Charles[5], Joseph Elmer[4], Jacob Chester[3], Henry[2], Rudolph[1]) was born 5 March 1952 in Memorial Hospital, Chattanooga, Hamilton County, Tennessee, the daughter of Frank Emmett and Avene (Phillips) Frist.[2446] She grew up in Chattanooga and married there on 25 April 1987 to **Robert Taylor Dixon**.

Robert was born 27 October 1959 in Chattanooga, Tennessee, the son of William Carl and Sybil Jane (Taylor) Dixon. Robert has a degree in art and is a fireman. He enjoys golf.

Susan has a B.A. in math and is a real estate agent. They both are involved with their children and in church activities.[2447]

Children of Robert Taylor and Frankie Susan[7] (Frist) Dixon:

> 541   i. ZACHARY TAYLOR[8] DIXON, born 13 June 1988.
>
> 542   ii. VICTORIA ELIZABETH DIXON, born 8 January 1991.

412. Mona[7] Frist (Frank Emmett[6], James Charles[5], Joseph Elmer[4], Jacob Chester[3], Henry[2], Rudolph[1]) was born 5 August 1959 in Chattanooga, Tennessee, the daughter of Frank Emmett and Avene (Phillips) Frist.[2448] She grew up in Chattanooga. She married first to **Darryl Willett** and they divorced. Mona married second on 22 May 1993 to **Steve Byer**. Steve was born 25 May 1960 in Chattanooga, Tennessee, the son of Frank and Anita (Batson) Byer.[2449]

Child of Darryl and Mona[7] (Frist) Willett:

> 543   i. STEPHANIE F.[8] WILLETT, born 12 July 1981.

413. James Leland[7] **Frist** (Frank Emmett[6], James Charles[5], Joseph Elmer[4], Jacob Chester[3], Henry[2], Rudolph[1]) was born 7 July 1960 in Chattanooga, Tennessee, the son of Frank Emmett and Avene (Phillips) Frist.[2450] He grew up in Chattanooga and married on 29 June 1985 in Chickamauga, Walker County, Georgia, to **Lisa Osburn**. Lisa was born 14 October 1961 in Chickamauga, Georgia, the daughter of Bobby and Jane (McDaniel) Osburn. The Frists live in Rossville, Georgia, in 2003.[2451]

Child of James Leland[7] and Lisa (Osburn) Frist:

> 544   i. HALEY NICHOLE[8] FRIST, born 15 September 1995.

EIGHTH GENERATION

421. Manferd Harold[8] **Findley** (Clara Etta[7] Patton, Louisa Jane[6] Frist, Joseph Andrew[5], David H.[4], John[3], Henry[2], Rudolph[1]) was born 24 February 1920 in Villisca, Montgomery County, Iowa, the son of Roy Manford and Clara Etta (Patton) Findley.[2452] He married first in 1940 to **Margaret L. Fessler**, who was born 3 September 1919 in Cedar Rapids, Linn County, Iowa, the daughter of Floyd Fessler. He served in the United States Navy during World War II. Manferd and Margaret were married until 1965, and Margaret died in the year 2000.

Manferd married second in 1971 to **Thelma J. Fisher**, who was born 30 May 1939 and died 7 November 1992 at Villisca, Montgomery County, Iowa. In 2003 he lives in Central City, Iowa, and still works almost daily in his shop.[2453]

Children of Manferd Harold[8] and Margaret L. (Fessler) Findley, all born in Cedar Rapids, Iowa:

> 545   i. MARVIN LEE[9] FINDLEY, born 12 October 1941; married Frances Powers.[2454]
>
> \+   546   ii. RONALD JACK FINDLEY, born 15 April 1943; married Carolyn Cheatham.[2455]
>
> 547   iii. KIRK ALLEN FINDLEY, born 29 December 1953; married Catherine Forbes.[2456]

422. Stanley Wayne[8] **Findley** (Clara Etta[7] Patton, Louisa Jane[6] Frist, Joseph Andrew[5], David H.[4], John[3], Henry[2], Rudolph[1]) was born 30 May 1922 in Villisca, Montgomery County, Iowa, the son of Roy Manford and Clara Etta (Patton) Findley.[2457] He married **Leona Streigl**, who was born 17 June 1924 in Cedar Rapids, Linn County, Iowa, the daughter of Wesley and Elizabeth (Barr) Streigl. He served in the United States Navy during World War II. He died 5 June 1992 in Cedar Rapids, Linn County, Iowa.[2458]

Children of Stanley Wayne[8] and Leona (Streigl) Findley:

548   i.   CONNIE SUE[9] FINDLEY, born 15 September 1943; married John Stillions born 16 July 1943 died 20 May 1973. Children, *(a)* Jody Kay Stillions married Kevin Hahn (they had Noelle E. Hahn and Danielle Stillions Hahn) and *(b)* John M. Stillions born 21 April 1964 and died 1980s.[2459]

549   ii. PEGGY FINDLEY, born 18 July 1951; married (1) James M. Bixby and (2) Philip Neyens. Children, *(a)* James Lee Bixby and *(b)* Brad M. Neyens.[2460]

427. Vicky Jean[8] Smith (Helen Marie[7] Frist, Willibur Stiles[6], Joseph Andrew[5], David H.[4], John[3], Henry[2], Rudolph[1]) was born 4 December 1949 in Villisca, Montgomery County, Iowa, the daughter of Glendon Amos and Helen Marie (Frist) Smith.[2461] She married 12 June 1971 at the Advent Christian Church in Chetek, Barron County, Wisconsin, to **Paul Anthony Pavlas**.[2462]

Children of Paul Anthony and Vicky Jean[8] (Smith) Pavlas:

550   i.   SHELLEY MARIE[9] PAVLAS, born 4 October 1972 Shell Lake, Washburn County, Wisconsin; married 9 September 2000 Robert Romauld Vouk, who was born 13 May 1966. One son, Jacob Vouk born 22 August 2001.[2463]

551   ii. JENNY JEAN PAVLAS, born 14 August 1975 Shell Lake, Washburn County, Wisconsin.[2464]

552   iii. PAUL ANTHONY PAVLAS, JR., born 16 January 1979 St. Paul, Ramsey County, Minnesota.[2465]

553   iv. LUCAS GLEN PAVLAS, born 6 March 1980 St. Paul, Ramsey County, Minnesota.[2466]

428. David Glendon[8] Smith (Helen Marie[7] Frist, Willibur Stiles[6], Joseph Andrew[5], David H.[4], John[3], Henry[2], Rudolph[1]) was born 19 March 1954 in Aurora, Kane County, Illinois, the son of Glendon Amos and Helen Marie (Frist) Smith.[2467] He married 21 August 1978 to **Gwyn Eastman**, born 17 August 1953.[2468]

Children of David Glendon[8] and Gwyn (Eastman) Smith, both born in Rice Lake, Barron County, Wisconsin:

554   i.   DEREK GLENDON[9] SMITH, born 6 May 1977.

555   ii. BROOK MARIE SMITH, born 5 June 1980.

434. Jimmy Dale[8] Frist (Russell Edward[7], Joseph E.[6], John S.[5], David H.[4], John[3], Henry[2], Rudolph[1]) was born 24 April 1938 in Polk County, Iowa, the only child of

Russell Edward and Mary Ann Frist.[2469] He married on 20 July 1956? in Des Moines, Iowa,[2470] to **Marva Olson** who was born 29 July 1939. Marva died 29 October 1997 in Indianola, Iowa, and is buried in Runnells, Polk County, Iowa. Jimmy Dale lives in Runnells, Iowa, in 2002.

Children of Jimmy Dale[8] and Marva (Olson) Frist, all born in Iowa:

556 i. TERRY MICHAEL[9] FRIST, born 30 January 1957; died June 1973 Indianola, Warren County, Iowa.[2471]

+ 557 ii. STEVEN TODD FRIST, born 1 August 1960; married 9 June 1996 Iowa City, Johnson County, Iowa, Audrey Loftis.[2472]

558 iii. JULIE ANN FRIST, born 25 November 1962; married 20 August 1983 Don Seiwert born 7 September 1961. Children, *(a)* Allison Seiwert born 29 December 1985 and *(b)* Phillip Seiwert born 5 October 1989; they live in Indianola, Iowa.[2473]

559 iv. DIANE SUE FRIST, born 18 January 1964; married 3 May 1986 Jeff Hemann born 2 October 1961. Children, *(a)* Collin Hemann born 26 April 1995 and *(b)* Alec Hemann born 16 June 1998; they live in Des Moines, Iowa.[2474]

441. Robert Russell[8] Frist (Russell Marrell[7], Marley Otto[6], Russell[5], William H.[4], John[3], Henry[2], Rudolph[1]) was born on 11 July 1940 in Anderson, Madison County, Indiana, the son of Russell Marrell and Vivian Maxine (Lawson) Frist.[2475] He married first in December 1961 in Pendleton, Madison County, Indiana, to **Beverley Griffith**. Beverley was born in 1938 in Marion, Madison County, Indiana. They divorced on 3 April 1963. Robert married second in March 1964 in Lapel, Madison County, Indiana, to **Bonnie Johnson**. Bonnie was born in 1943 in Lapel, Indiana, and was employed as a teacher. They divorced on 22 May 1974. Robert married third on 3 November 1976 in Greenfield, Hancock County, Indiana, to **Dollie Bade**. Dollie was born on 22 July 1945 in Homestead, Dade County, Florida, and was employed as a secretary. Robert lives in Chattanooga, Hamilton County, Tennessee, in 2002.[2476]

Child of Robert Russell[8] and Beverley (Griffith) Frist:

560 i. JEFFERY ALLEN[9] FRIST, born 1 November 1961 Lakeland, Polk County, Florida.

Children of Robert Russell[8] and Bonnie (Johnson) Frist, both born at Saint Johns Hospital in Anderson, Madison County, Indiana:

561 ii. KIMBERLY RENEE FRIST, born 29 October 1964.
562 iii. ROBERT DOUGLAS "ROBBIE" FRIST, born 18 December 1969.

442. Phillip Stanley[8] **Frist** (Russell Marrell[7], Marley Otto[6], Russell[5], William H.[4], John[3], Henry[2], Rudolph[1]) was born on 11 October 1945 in Anderson, Madison County, Indiana, the son of Russell Marrell and Vivian Maxine (Lawson) Frist.[2477] He attended Andrews University in Berrien Springs, Michigan, for a year and Indiana University at Bloomington, Indiana, for another year. He then served two years from 1966 to 1968 in the United States Army.

He married on 30 November 1968 in Anderson, Madison County, Indiana, to **Vickie Carol Haston**. Vickie was born on 16 November 1947 in Anderson, Madison County, Indiana, the daughter of Ray and Velma (Nevins) Haston. She is a homemaker and worked as a bookkeeper.

After their marriage, Phillip went to Ball State in Muncie, Indiana, where he obtained his B.S. degree in 1970. His dental training was acquired at Indiana University School of Dentistry where he graduated in 1975. He has since been employed as a dentist. The Frists live in Anderson, Madison County, Indiana, in 2003.[2478]

Children of Phillip Stanley[8] and Vickie Carol (Haston) Frist, both born at Saint Johns Hospital in Anderson, Madison County, Indiana:

> 563   i. PHILLIP STEVEN[9] FRIST, born 22 June 1969; married 5 November 1994 Rose Marie Gulli. Children, *(a)* Tyler Scott Gulli Frist born 1990 (adopted by Steven, child of Rose Marie Gulli) and *(b)* Steven Travis Frist born 6 October 1995.[2479]
>
> 564   ii. PATRICIA ANN FRIST, born 10 May 1971; married 4 August 1996 Harold Ceslo Avila. Children, *(a)* Wilson Ray Avila born 5 July 2000 Anderson, Madison County, Indiana, and *(b)* Victoria Mackinzie Avila born 2002.[2480]

444. Garry Alan[8] **McBride Parmer** (Mildred Irene[7] Stevens, Jesse O. Laffe[6], Hannah Etta[5] Frist, Robert M.[4], John[3], Henry[2], Rudolph[1]) was born on 18 November 1943 in Farragut, Kootenai County, Idaho, the son of Paul Vincent and Mildred Irene (Stevens) McBride.[2481] He was adopted by his mother Mildred's second husband, Richard Parmer, Jr., and assumed his surname. Garry Alan died on 17 June 1997 in Richmond, Virginia.[2482] He married to **Bettieanne Teresa Berdine** in Falls Church, Virginia. Bettieanne is the daughter of Stanley Berdine.

Children of Garry Alan[8] McBride and Bettieanne Teresa (Berdine) Parmer:

> 565   i. LAURA LEE[9] PARMER.
> 566   ii. WESLEY ALAN PARMER.

448. Carolyn Jeanette[8] **Foltz** (Esther Louise[7] Frist, Harry Homer[6], Jediah[5], Jediah Rudolph[4], Jediah[3], Henry[2], Rudolph[1]) was born on 12 August 1937 in

Vermillion County, Indiana, the daughter of Paul Kenneth and Esther Louise (Frist) Foltz.[2483] She married on 24 November 1957 in Clinton, Vermillion County, Indiana, to **Montelle H. "Monty" Lowry**. Monty was born on 23 October 1934, also in Vermillion County.

After serving in the United States Army, Monty worked as a painter and contractor. Both Monty and Carolyn sold for Metropolitan Life Insurance for a time while living in Clinton.

In the early 1970s they moved to Columbus, Mississippi, where Monty owned his own contracting business, working on old antebellum homes. Carolyn worked in car sales. They were active in the Methodist Church and lived in Columbus until the summer of 2000 when they moved back to the "home place" in Clinton, Vermillion County, Indiana.[2484]

Children of Montelle H. and Carolyn Jeanette[8] (Foltz) Lowry, all born in Vermillion, County, Indiana:

567   i. KENNETH RUSSELL[9] LOWRY, born 23 November 1958; married 3 October 1981 Columbus, Lowndes County, Mississippi, Marianne Shelton born 18 September 1956 Columbus, Mississippi. Marianne is a nursery school teacher. Kenneth works in the trucking business and started his own company in the year 2000. Adopted child, Joseph Blake Lowry born 29 June 1986 Alabama.[2485]

568   ii. KAREN JANETTE LOWRY, born 6 August 1960; married (1) 3 October 1981 Columbus, Mississippi, James Edward "Bud" Yeatman born 6 September 1960 Columbus, Lowndes County, Mississippi, and divorced 1987. Karen married (2) 1 June 1991 Columbus, Mississippi, Charles Farmer III born Cairo, Alexander County, Illinois; divorced in 1998, and (3) 25 March 2000 Paul Beaugh born 4 January 1960 Fort Riley, Kansas. Karen works for Tom Bigbee Dam and Locks and Paul manages a fish farm at Columbus, Mississippi. Charles Farmer had two children by a previous union, *(a)* Charles "Chase" Farmer IV born 1978 and *(b)* Wesley Farmer born 1982. Paul Beaugh had two children by a previous union, *(a)* Karen Nicole Beaugh and *(b)* Savannah Beaugh.[2486]

569   iii. KELLEY JOAN LOWRY, born 11 February 1963; married 18 May 1991 Columbus, Mississippi, John Royston Easby-Smith born 24 December 1957 West Germany. Kelley works for television stations in the Little Rock area and John, a graduate of the University of Arkansas, is a mechanical engineer. Children, both born in Little Rock, Arkansas, *(a)* John "Jack" Easby-Smith born 11 August 1994 and *(b)* Nicholas Kelley Easby-Smith born 30 December 1996.[2487]

449. Margaret Anne[8] **"Peggy" Foltz** (Esther Louise[7] Frist, Harry Homer[6], Jediah[5], Jediah Rudolph[4], Jediah[3], Henry[2], Rudolph[1]) was born on 21 March 1939 in Vermillion County, Indiana, the daughter of Paul Kenneth and Esther Louise (Frist) Foltz.[2488] She married on 29 May 1960 Clinton, Vermillion County, Indiana, to **Frank Warren Hughes**.

Frank was born on 15 March 1933 in Vigo County, Indiana, the son of Frank and Laverne (Anstead) Hughes. He served in the United States Army and was a high school science teacher, retiring from North Vigo High School at Terre Haute, Indiana.

Peggy has worked at several occupations including banking. She served on an election board for many years and volunteered for the Light House Mission in Terre Haute, serving on the board for a period of time. Both have been active in the United Methodist Church.[2489]

Children of Frank Warren and Margaret Anne[8] (Foltz) Hughes, both born in Vermillion County, Indiana:

> 570   i. JEEN ANNE[9] HUGHES, born 18 February 1961; married 11 June 1983 Parke County, Indiana, Timothy Mark Doty born 17 September 1956 Vigo County, Indiana, son of Robert and Betty (Sutton) Doty. Jeen worked as a police dispatcher and Tim is part owner of Commercial Radio Services in Terre Haute. Children of Timothy Doty by a previous union, born Vigo County, Indiana, are Timothy Mark "Timmy" Doty born 26 June 1975 and Samuel D. Doty born 14 February 1979. Timothy and Jeen Anne (Hughes) Doty had one child, Sutton Myles Doty born 26 December 1986.[2490]

> 571   ii. ROBERT ALAN HUGHES, born 11 March 1962; died 14 February 1994 Kissimmee, Florida;[2491] buried Roselawn Cemetery, Terre Haute, Indiana. "Rob" graduated from Purdue University at Lafayette, Indiana, in 1980 and was listed in *Outstanding Young Men of America in 1987*. He was manager of the telecommunications department of Watkins Motor Lines, Inc. in Florida when he died; no issue.[2492]

451. Emily Sue[8] **Foltz** (Esther Louise[7] Frist, Harry Homer[6], Jediah[5], Jediah Rudolph[4], Jediah[3], Henry[2], Rudolph[1]) was born on 20 March 1944 in Clinton, Vermillion County, Indiana, the daughter of Paul Kenneth and Esther Louise (Frist) Foltz.[2493] She died on 11 September 1998 in Gurnee, Lake County, Illinois, from a severe asthma attack and is buried in Roselawn Cemetery in Terre Haute, Indiana.[2494] She married on 12 September 1964 to **Jeffery Wayne Skjordahl** in Clinton, Vermillion County, Indiana. Jeffery was born on 13 February 1942 in Illinois, the son of Arthur and Amelia (Sienke) Skjordahl.

Jeffery worked for Underwriters Laboratories in the Chicago area. Sue studied nursing at old St. Anthony's Hospital in Terre Haute, but interrupted her studies to marry and have children. Later she went back to school to become a registered nurse and obtained her master's degree in St. Louis, Missouri. She helped to establish four different emergency medical establishments from the "ground up," assisting in locating the sites and overseeing the building.

Children of Jeffery Wayne and Emily Sue[8] (Foltz) Skjordahl:

572 i. HEIDI WANE[9] SKJORDAHL, born 21 November 1966 Savannah, Georgia; married 23 May 1987 Valparaiso, Porter County, Indiana, Kenneth Alan Sorenson born 3 October 1966 son of John and Norma (Acker) Sorenson. Children, *(a)* Erik Christian Sorenson born 7 October 1989 Westchester, Chester County, Pennsylvania, *(b)* Haley Wayne Sorenson born 30 April 1991 Valparaiso, Porter County, Indiana, *(c)* Lars Haldan Sorenson born 31 January 1993 Valparaiso, Porter County, Indiana, and *(d)* Arne Jacob Sorenson born 18 December 1994 Valparaiso, Porter County, Indiana.[2495]

573 ii. MARTIN SCOTT SKJORDAHL, born 5 July 1968 San Bernardino, California. He studied at Embry Aviation University at Prescott, Arizona, to become a commercial airline pilot. After graduation, he worked at Underwriters Laboratories and, with a partner, eventually started a computer "dot.com" company.[2496]

452. Loureno[1] Batzner (Esther Louise[7] Frist, Harry Homer[6], Jediah[5], Jediah Rudolph[4], Jediah[3], Henry[2], Rudolph[1]) was born on 31 January 1950 in Chapeco, S.C. Brazil, South America.[2497] Loureno became the foster child of Paul Kenneth and Esther Louise (Frist) Foltz when their son Ron met him during a period in Brazil with the Peace Corps and sent him at the age of sixteen to his parents to be educated. He graduated from Clinton High School and Indiana State University at Terre Haute.

Loureno eventually moved back to Brazil where he met **Jeanne Marie Novello**; they married on 14 November 1986 in Brazil. Jeanne was born on 18 June 1956 in Concordia, Brazil, and works as a pediatrician. Loureno worked in sales in the United States and as a county agent in South America. He built and owns a supermarket known as Global.[2498]

Children of Loureno[1] and Jeanne Marie (Novello) Batzner:

574 i. LOUISE NOVELLO[2] BATZNER, born 31 December 1987 Brazil, SA.

575 ii. CLARISSA NOVELLO BATZNER, born 8 November 1994 Chapeco, S.C., Brazil, SA.

453. Gary Lynn[8] **Jones** (Shirley Mae[7] Frist, Harry Homer[6], Jediah[5], Jediah Rudolph[4], Jediah[3], Henry[2], Rudolph[1]) was born on 11 September 1946 in Clinton, Vermillion County, Indiana, the son of Melvin Maurice and Shirley Mae (Frist) Jones.[2499] As a teen, Gary was in the J. N. Frist Chapter of the Order of De Molay, named for Gary's second great-uncle Jasper Nebeker Frist. After graduating from high school, Gary took computer training in Indianapolis and went to work for Eastern Panhandle near Montezuma. Gary served four years in the United States Air Force, spending three years at Ramstein Air Force Base in Kaiserslautern, Germany.

Gary married on 4 February 1972 to **Judith Ann Rennick** in Montezuma, Parke County, Indiana. Judith was born on 14 January 1953 in Danville, Vermillion County, Illinois, the daughter of Floyd and Helen (Keen) Rennick. Judy worked at the local newspaper *The Daily Clintonian* after they were married and was a "stay at home" mom until their boys were in school. She earns a living in marketing and accounting, working for Child Adult Resources Services in Rockville, Indiana.

Gary works as an equipment analyst for a gas pipeline company. He assisted Herman Mayes with the first Frist family genealogy compiled in 1991 by doing the data entry using the names, dates, and places provided to him by Herman Mayes. In 2003 Gary and Judy live in Montezuma, Indiana, and are members of the Christian Church.[2500]

Children of Gary Lynn[8] and Judith Ann (Rennick) Jones, both born in Clinton, Vermillion County, Indiana:

576   i. ERIC LYNN[9] JONES, born 12 March 1974; married 17 October 1998 United Methodist Church, Boonville, Warrick County, Indiana, Heather Anne Hodges born 16 June 1979 Evansville, Vanderburgh County, Indiana, daughter of Wesley G. and Sarah L. Hodges. Eric attended Indiana University and works at AET in Vigo County, Indiana. Heather attends Indiana University. They live in Montezuma, Indiana, and are active in the Christian Church.[2501]

577   ii. BRADLEY JOE JONES, born 23 May 1977; married 25 September 1999 Williamsport, Warren County, Indiana, Melissa Ann Taylor born 31 January 1977 Vermillion County, Indiana. Brad graduated from Rose-Hulman University in Terre Haute, Indiana, in May 1999 as a civil engineer and works for Hannum, Wagle, & Cline. They attend church in Terre Haute near where they live.[2502]

454. Linda Darline[8] **Jones** (Shirley Mae[7] Frist, Harry Homer[6], Jediah[5], Jediah Rudolph[4], Jediah[3], Henry[2], Rudolph[1]) was born on 17 September 1947 in Clinton, Vermillion County, Indiana, the only daughter of Melvin Maurice and Shirley

Mae (Frist) Jones.[2503] Linda attended nursing school and became a licensed practical nurse.

She married first on 18 December 1970 to **Danny Dean Reed** in Clay City, Clay County, Indiana. Danny was born on 25 July 1951 in Indiana, the son of Rex and Lillian (Scott) Reed.

Linda and Danny were divorced in 1984. Linda married second on 26 June 1999 in Vigo County, Indiana, to **Robert Arden Gosnell**. "Bob" was born 18 June 1946 at Danville, Hendricks County, Illinois. He was in the United States Army for seven years, three of them in Vietnam, where he was wounded twice. After leaving the army, he worked as a semi truck driver for thirty-five years.

Linda worked in various nursing homes and in 2001 is employed at the Women's Correction Facility in Rockville, Indiana, as an LPN.[2504]

Children of Danny Dean and Linda Darline[8] (Jones) Reed:

578   i. CHRISTOPHER ALAN[9] "CHRIS" REED, born 22 July 1974 Tampa, Hillsborough County, Florida; married 28 September 1996 Trinity Church, Shepardsville, Vigo County, Indiana, Mary Jo Bartlett born 27 December 1975. Chris works for the Wal-Mart at Greencastle, Indiana. Child, Brandi Nicole Reed born 3 December 2000 Terre Haute, Vigo County, Indiana.[2505]

579   ii. SHERRIE ANN REED, born 19 October 1976 Brazil, Clay County, Indiana. Sherrie attended Indiana Business College and is a certified nurse's aide working at Vermillion Convalescent Center.[2506]

455. Glen Alan[8] Jones (Shirley Mae[7] Frist, Harry Homer[6], Jediah[5], Jediah Rudolph[4], Jediah[3], Henry[2], Rudolph[1]) was born on 21 March 1950 in Clinton, Vermillion County, Indiana, the son of Melvin Maurice and Shirley Mae (Frist) Jones.[2507] He married on 7 February 1976 to **Brenda Pritchard** in Coloma, Parke County, Indiana. Brenda was born on 4 October 1956 in Indiana, the daughter of Ralph and Margaret (Firestone) Pritchard.

Glen attended Rose-Hulman University in Terre Haute, Indiana. He was a precinct committeeman for the Republican Party in Montezuma and an active member of the Montezuma Volunteer Fire Department, along with his father and brother. He was the co-owner of Central Hardwoods, Inc. and in 2001 owns a pallet business in Montezuma, Indiana.[2508]

Children of Glen Alan[8] and Brenda (Pritchard) Jones, both born in Clinton, Vermillion County, Indiana:

580   i. SCOTT ALAN[9] JONES, born 4 April 1977; attended Franklin College and graduated from Indiana State University. He coaches and umpires for basketball games.[2509]

581   ii. KELLY MARIE JONES, born 14 August 1979; died 2 January 1980 Montezuma, Indiana, a victim of sudden infant death syndrome; buried Coloma, Parke County, Indiana.[2510]

457. Martin F.[8] **"Mart" King** (Myrtle Lee[7] Frist, Harry Homer[6], Jediah[5], Jediah Rudolph[4], Jediah[3], Henry[2], Rudolph[1]) was born on 28 October 1950 in Edgar County, Illinois, the son of Milton Royce and Myrtle Lee (Frist) King.[2511] Mart graduated from Indiana State University, working during and afterward at WTHI-TV both on and off the screen. He married on 18 July 1970 to **Lettie Barbara "Barb" Jones** in Greenfield, Hancock County, Indiana. Barb was born on 4 January 1950, the daughter of Emil and Viola (Arther) Jones. Barb worked in the secretarial field.

Mart worked on the board of Home Missions for the Southern Baptist Convention and served for a year as vice president at a Christian college in Kansas City, Missouri.[2512]

Children of Martin F.[8] and Lettie Barbara (Jones) King, both born in Vigo County, Indiana:

582   i. JULIE RAE[9] KING, born 1 February 1973; married 14 January 1995 Jackson, Madison County, Tennessee, Samonn "Sam" Chhim born 5 June 1967 Cambodia, son of Khorn and Soth Chhim. Julie and Samonn both graduated from Union University in Jackson, Tennessee. Children, both born in Jackson, Madison County, Tennessee, *(a)* Cameron Martin Chhim born 16 July 1998 and *(b)* Sarah Rae Chhim, born 19 December 1999.[2513]

583   ii. JENNIFER JO KING, born 11 August 1974; graduated from Union University in Jackson, Tennessee, and teaches school in Jackson.[2514]

458. Melvin H.[8] **King** (Myrtle Lee[7] Frist, Harry Homer[6], Jediah[5], Jediah Rudolph[4], Jediah[3], Henry[2], Rudolph[1]) was born on 28 October 1950 in Edgar County, Illinois, the son of Milton Royce and Myrtle Lee (Frist) King.[2515] He married first on 4 November 1969 to **Sheila Ann Davidson** in Greenfield, Indiana. Sheila was born in 1955 and they divorced in 1983.

Melvin married second on 15 September 1990 to **Deirdre "Dee" Cannon**. Dee was born on 15 April 1951 in Indianapolis, Marion County, Indiana, the daughter of Paul and Elizabeth (Kelly) Cannon. Melvin worked for Dollar General Stores and also as a cook.[2516]

Children of Melvin H.[8] and Sheila Ann (Davidson) King:

584   i. LORI ANN[9] KING, born 18 April 1970 Hancock County, Indiana; died 19 April 1970 Greenfield, Hancock County, Indiana.

585   ii. HEATHER LEE KING, born 25 December 1971 Hancock County, Indiana.

586   iii. JASON ANDREW KING, born 25 September 1975.

587   iv. ANGELA DAWN KING, born 11 April 1978.

588   v. CARRIE KING, born 1980 Rochester, Fulton County, Indiana.

459. Mary Lynn[8] Banes (Mary Edith[7] Frist, Harlow Peirce[6], Jediah[5], Jediah Rudolph[4], Jediah[3], Henry[2], Rudolph[1]) was born on 12 March 1950 in Lafayette, Tippecanoe County, Indiana, the daughter of Russell E. and Mary Edith (Frist) Banes.[2517] She married first on 2 February 1969 to **Richard Harold "Rick" Skeel** in Trinity United Methodist Church in Lafayette, Tippecanoe County, Indiana.

Rick was born on 28 July 1949 in Pennsylvania, the son of Samuel and Alene (Coldiron) Skeel. He graduated from Purdue University in 1971. He taught and coached in Indiana, Ohio, New York, and Florida.

Mary Lynn graduated from Purdue in 1972, earning a master's degree in 1978. She was a speech pathologist in Ohio, New York, Indiana, Maryland, and Florida.

Rick and Mary Lynn were divorced in April 2000, and in 2001 Rick makes his home in Florida, where he coaches at the college level. Mary Lynn worked in Apple Valley School Corporation in California and recently moved to Las Vegas where she is a speech pathologist for Rose Warren School.[2518] On 26 October 2001 she married second in Las Vegas, Nevada, to **Frederick William Lowell**. In 2003 their home is in Las Vegas, Nevada, where "Fred" is a security guard and paralegal.[2519]

Children of Richard Harold and Mary Lynn[8] (Banes) Skeel:

589   i. ERIC BRIAN[9] SKEEL, born 19 August 1969 Tippecanoe County, Indiana; united with Theresa Naomi Dees born 19 January 1970 Orlando, Orange County, Florida, daughter of Stephen and Theresa (Krick) Dees. Eric graduated from the University of Ohio and is district manager in southern states for an ice-making machine company. Theresa Naomi Dees had a child Ashley Lauren Dees born 26 August 1989 Orlando, Florida. Child of Eric Brian Skeel and Theresa Naomi Dees is Alexis Lauren Skeel born 20 June 1996 Daytona Beach, Volusia County, Florida.[2520] They live in Port Orange, Florida.

590   ii. BRITTNEY LYNN SKEEL, born 20 June 1974 Cincinnati, Hamilton County, Ohio; married 28 November 1998 Florida to Jeremy Varao born 21 September 1974 son of Irene Varao. Brittney graduated from Central Florida University in 1998 and taught school in Florida and Nevada. Jeremy is a graphic artist and chef. One child, Genna Skye Varao, born 21 January 2000 Daytona Beach, Volusia County, Florida.[2521] They live in Las Vegas, Nevada.

460. Robert Harlow⁸ Frist (Robert Jediah⁷, Harlow Peirce⁶, Jediah⁵, Jediah Rudolph⁴, Jediah³, Henry², Rudolph¹) was born on 8 August 1951 in Vermillion County, Indiana, the son of Robert Jediah and Frances Lillian (Vrabic) Frist.[2522] Robert graduated from Purdue University in 1974 in landscape architecture and interior design. He married on 2 September 1979 in Indianapolis, Marion County, Indiana, to **Ellen Louise Edwards**.

Ellen was born on 29 July 1955 in Pennsylvania, the daughter of Andrew Wood and Evelyn (Conrad) Edwards. She graduated from Purdue in 1977 in consumer and family sciences. Robert is the executive vice president of design and marketing with Rowland Company and Ellen was also employed with Rowland as a retail buyer. In 2001 they live in Indianapolis, Indiana.[2523]

Children of Robert Harlow⁸ and Ellen Louise (Edwards) Frist, both born in Indianapolis, Marion County, Indiana:

> 591   i. ANDREW ROBERT CHARLES⁹ "DREW" FRIST, born 21 December 1982; plans to enter college in fall 2001 in computer graphics.
>
> 592   ii. ALEXANDER EDWARD GEORGE FRIST, born 20 January 1987.

461. Dennis Franklin⁸ Frist (Robert Jediah⁷, Harlow Peirce⁶, Jediah⁵, Jediah Rudolph⁴, Jediah³, Henry², Rudolph¹) was born on 7 December 1954 in Tippecanoe County, Indiana, the son of Robert Jediah and Frances Lillian (Vrabic) Frist.[2524] He married on 5 March 1977 in Tippecanoe County, Indiana, to **Patti Ann Acheson**.

Patti was born on 28 June 1956, also in Tippecanoe County, the daughter of Claude Densel and Elnora Letha (Klaiber) Acheson. Dennis graduated from Purdue University in 1976 and earns a living as a chemical operator and draftsman with Eli Lilly at Tippecanoe. Patti graduated from Purdue University in 1978 in consumer and family sciences. She works for the Tippecanoe School Corporation. In 2001 they live in West Lafayette, Indiana, and their three children are all college students.[2525]

Children of Dennis Franklin⁸ and Patti Ann (Acheson) Frist, all born in Lafayette, Tippecanoe County, Indiana:

> 593   i. JOHANNA DENISE⁹ FRIST, born 19 July 1979.
>
> 594   ii. ERIN ELIZABETH FRIST, born 27 August 1981.
>
> 595   iii. LUCAS PEIRCE "LUKE" FRIST, born 17 April 1983.

462. Karl David⁸ Frist (Robert Jediah⁷, Harlow Peirce⁶, Jediah⁵, Jediah Rudolph⁴, Jediah³, Henry², Rudolph¹) was born on 22 July 1959 in Tippecanoe County, Indiana, the son of Robert Jediah and Frances Lillian (Vrabic) Frist.[2526] David graduated from Purdue University in 1979 with an associate degree in agricultural management and works in project maintenance at Wabash National Corporation. He married on 8 August 1981 in Tippecanoe County to **Shirley Jeanne Shultz**.

Shirley was born on 12 December 1961, also in Tippecanoe County, the daughter of Virgil Lee and Doris Jeanne (Schrader) Shultz. Shirley attended Ball State in 1980 and 1981. She graduated from Purdue University in 1985 with a B.S. in elementary education and teaches third grade at Battle Ground Elementary School. They live in Battle Ground, Indiana, in 2002.[2527]

Children of Karl David[8] and Shirley Jeanne (Shultz) Frist, all born in Lafayette, Tippecanoe County, Indiana:

    596   i. KATELYN JEANNE[9] FRIST, born 27 May 1988.
    597   ii. ALISHA CHRISTINE FRIST, born 27 May 1988.
    598   iii. CLAIRE ELIZABETH FRIST, born 30 January 1994.

463. Douglas Mark[8] Frist (Robert Jediah[7], Harlow Peirce[6], Jediah[5], Jediah Rudolph[4], Jediah[3], Henry[2], Rudolph[1]) was born on 1 November 1960 in Tippecanoe County, Indiana, the son of Robert Jediah and Frances Lillian (Vrabic) Frist.[2528] He married on 22 May 1983 in Deerfield, Lake County, Illinois, to **Mary Hope Roberts**. Mary was born on 2 November 1963 in Deerfield, Illinois, the daughter of Donald George and Phyllis Sandra (Wexler) Roberts.

Doug graduated from Purdue University in 1984 with a B.S. in mechanical engineering technology and is employed by Coty USLLC as an equipment engineering manager. Mary received a B.S. degree in consumer and family sciences from Purdue University in 1984 and is a high school special education teacher. In 2001 they live in North Carolina.[2529]

Children of Douglas Mark[8] and Mary Hope (Roberts) Frist:

    599   i. SAMUEL TAYLOR[9] FRIST, born 16 October 1986 Indianapolis, Marion County, Indiana.
    600   ii. CLAYTON ROBERT FRIST, born 17 May 1989 Chicago, Cook County, Illinois.

464. Lisa Ann[8] Frist (Harold B.[7], Marshall Alban[6], Jediah[5], Jediah Rudolph[4], Jediah[3], Henry[2], Rudolph[1]) was born on 14 November 1955 in Indianapolis, Marion County, Indiana, the daughter of Harold B. and Beulah (Thomas) Frist.[2530] She graduated from Franklin College (cum laude) in 1978 and did graduate work at Ball State and the University of Indianapolis where she received her master's degree. She was an art teacher at Pendleton and Custer-Baker middle schools in Franklin, Indiana, and a member of the Avon Methodist Church.

She married on 28 December 1989 to **Hendrik Harm "Henk" Drenth** in Avon, Indiana. Hendrik was born on 6 March 1969 in Amsterdam, Holland, the son of Dethmer and Jetsy (Olijslager) Drenth. They lived in Europe for about a year after their marriage. In 2001, they live on a farm in rural Indiana and have several horses. Hendrik is a financial consultant and Lisa teaches art.[2531]

Children of Hendrik Harm and Lisa Ann[8] (Frist) Drenth:

> 601   i. MELISSA ANNE[9] DRENTH, born 24 February 1992.
>
> 602   ii. JONATHAN HENDRICK H. DRENTH, born 26 October 1995.

465. Michael Thomas[8] Frist (Wayne Edward[7], Marshall Alban[6], Jediah[5], Jediah Rudolph[4], Jediah[3], Henry[2], Rudolph[1]) was born on 5 December 1950 in Boone, Boone County, Iowa, the son of Wayne Edward and Ruth (Eddy) Frist.[2532] He married on 22 December 1969 in Omaha, Douglas County, Nebraska, to **Judy Michel**. Judy was born on 1 December 1950 in Boone County. Michael earns a living as a dry wall worker and Judy is a housekeeper and superintendent at a motel in Ames, Iowa.[2533]

Children of Michael Thomas[8] and Judy (Michel) Frist, both born in Boone County, Iowa:

> 603   i. ANGELA ANN[9] FRIST, born 30 May 1970; married a Murphy and divorced in 1999. Children, both born in Iowa, *(a)* Christopher Lewis Murphy born 10 January 1993 and *(b)* Dalton Jon Murphy born 3 January 1997.[2534]
>
> 604   ii. NICOLE MARIE FRIST, born 18 July 1972. Children, all born in Iowa, *(a)* Blain Michael Frist born 17 December 1991, *(b)* Dustin Donavin Musser born 3 April 1995, *(c)* Trevor Jon Musser born 3 April 1995, and *(d)* Bailee Marie Musser born and died 22 December 1996.[2535]

466. Mershell Suzanne[8] Frist (Wayne Edward[7], Marshall Alban[6], Jediah[5], Jediah Rudolph[4], Jediah[3], Henry[2], Rudolph[1]) was born on 5 December 1951 in Boone, Boone County, Iowa, the daughter of Wayne Edward and Ruth (Eddy) Frist.[2536] Mershell was named for her grandfather Marshall Frist. She married on 15 April 1972 in Boone, Boone County, Iowa, to **Richard Putman**. Richard was born on 16 January 1948 in Perry, Iowa. Richard earned his living as a diesel mechanic and was in the Iowa Air Guard. Richard and Mershell divorced in October of 1995. Mershell is a secretary and is also in the Iowa Air Guard.[2537]

Children of Richard and Mershell Suzanne[8] (Frist) Putman, both born in California:

> 605   i. THERESA J'NAE[9] PUTMAN, born 30 July 1979.
>
> 606   ii. CHARISSE JANELLE PUTMAN, born 25 April 1981.

467. Joan Marie[8] **Frist** (Wayne Edward[7], Marshall Alban[6], Jediah[5], Jediah Rudolph[4], Jediah[3], Henry[2], Rudolph[1]) was born 7 May 1954 in Boone, Boone County, Iowa, the daughter of Wayne Edward and Ruth (Eddy) Frist.[2538] She married on 7 April 1973 in Boone, Boone County, Iowa, to **Jack Erwin**. Jack was born on 16 January 1956 in Perry, Dallas County, Iowa, and works as a district manager for Hilano Potato Chip Company. Joan works at Principal Insurance.[2539]

Children of Jack and Joan Marie[8] (Frist) Erwin, both born in Iowa:

607   i. CHANTELLE MARIE[9] ERWIN, born 18 August 1973; married Joseph Steven Pliler.[2540]

608   ii. CHRISTOPHER ERWIN, born 27 May 1975; married 2 August 1997 Carly Rachelle Quandt born 7 September 1976. One child, Tyson Bradley Erwin born 14 January 1999.[2541]

468. Eugene Alfred[8] **"Gene" Fischer III** (Dolores Lorraine[7] Klima, Dolores Mary[6] Frist, Abram Bernard[5], Abraham B.[4], James[3], Henry[2], Rudolph[1]) was born on 18 April 1951 in Baltimore City, Maryland, the son of Eugene Alfred and Dolores Lorraine[6] (Klima) Fischer, Jr.[2542] He married on 23 June 1973 in Edgewood, Harford County, Maryland, at Trinity Lutheran Church to **Deborah Ann "Debbie" Baum**.

Debbie was born 22 October 1955 in Baltimore City, Maryland, the daughter of Henry Russell and Angeline Adeline (DiBlasio) Baum. She is a computer specialist and worked for twenty-four years in civil service. She is currently in the United States Marine Corps and is working toward an associate degree in applied science in information technology. She is known as a caregiver and enjoys crafts and crocheting.

Gene graduated from Edgewood High School in 1970. He attended a local community college for over a year and had a one-year degree in engineering drafting from Maryland Drafting Institute. He retired from the United States Marine Corps as a gunnery sergeant with twenty years of service in 1992. He was a military policeman and combat photographer. He works as a computer draftsman and designer. He is known for his great sense of humor and practical jokes. He enjoys sporting events, and he and Debbie both enjoy pleasure boating. In 2003 they live in Fredericksburg, Virginia.[2543]

Children of Eugene Alfred[8] and Deborah Ann (Baum) Fischer III:

+   609   i. MARCIA LYNN[9] FISCHER, born 30 January 1974 Portsmouth, Virginia; married 27 September 1997 Frederick, Maryland, Scott Christopher Ritchie Sheppard.[2544]

610   ii. DWAYNE LEE FISCHER, born 3 July 1976 Quantico, Virginia. Dwayne attended junior college and is working on an associate degree in

applied science in general studies. He is known as a hard worker with a good sense of humor. He enjoys baseball and was second team all county in high school, playing second base.[2545]

480. Martha Vianne[8] Absher (Mary Grove[7] Tyson, John Earl[6], Sidney Marietta[5] Frist, Edmund Physick[4], James[3], Henry[2], Rudolph[1]) was born on 9 December 1934 in Rising Sun, Cecil County, Maryland, the daughter of John Floyd and Mary Grove (Tyson) Absher.[2546] She married first before 1956 to **Paul Albert Taylor**, who was born on 21 August 1935. In 1966 when her grandmother Ella Tyson died in Cecil County, Maryland, Ella's estate identified Martha Vianne's three children and indicated that the family lived in De Bary, Florida.[2547]

Martha Vianne married second on 15 November 1965 to **Edward Charles Gillespie**, who was born on 5 May 1927 in St. Louis, Missouri, the son of Herman Behrman and Olive (Gepson) Gillespie.[2548] He adopted Martha Vianne's children and their names were changed to Gillespie. The Gillespies live in Peoria, Arizona, in 2003.

Children of Paul Albert and Martha Vianne[8] (Absher) Taylor.

611   i. VIANNE PAULA[9] TAYLOR GILLESPIE, born 15 September 1956 Aberdeen Proving Grounds, Maryland, married 14 February 1975 Douglas Willard Bolton. Children, *(a)* Lee Edward Bolton born 28 July 1975 married Shelley Kay Holland daughter of John and Freda Holland (Lee and Shelley had Emily Kay Bolton born 9 November 1994),[2549] *(b)* Gary Vernon Bolton born 13 July 1979, and *(c)* Mark Albert Bolton born 8 September 1980.[2550]

612   ii. MARY MARGARET TAYLOR GILLESPIE, born 17 September 1957 San Jose, California; married 4 December 1976 Richard Austin Roberts born 25 December 1957. Children, *(a)* Leya Ann Roberts born 15 September 1977 and *(b)* Christina Lynn Roberts born 20 January 1980[2551] married 14 February 2002 Shane Handel.[2552]

613   iii. EDWARD ALBERT TAYLOR GILLESPIE, born 10 November 1959 Fort Huachuca, Arizona; died 27 May 1973.[2553]

490. Heidi Margaret[8] Frist (Ramsey Hudson[7], Joseph Osmond[6], Oscar Haines[5], Edmund Physick[4], James[3], Henry[2], Rudolph[1]) was born 4 February 1964 in Shady Side Hospital in Pittsburgh, Allegheny County, Pennsylvania, the daughter of Ramsey Hudson and Judith Ann (Nadolny) Frist.[2554] Heidi grew up in Morgantown, West Virginia. She graduated from West Virginia University in August of 1987 with a bachelor of arts degree, majoring in sociology with a minor in fine arts.

In July of 1986 Heidi met **Anthony Patrick Derry**. Two years later on 6 August 1988 they were married at St. John's University Parish in Morgantown, Monongalia County, West Virginia.

Anthony was born 2 September 1958 in Braddock, Pennsylvania, the son of Regis Allen Angelo and Esther Marie (Jones) Derry. Anthony grew up in West Mifflin, Pennsylvania, and joined the navy in November of 1976 where he served as a hull technician fireman apprentice. After leaving the navy in July of 1978, Anthony attended Computer Systems Institute in Pittsburgh, where he received his associate degree in specialized business, systems analysis in 1983. In 1985 he moved to Morgantown, West Virginia, where he took a job with West Virginia Network for Educational Telecomputing (WVNET) as a systems programmer. Anthony was appointed by Governor Gaston Caperton in March of 1995 to serve on the West Virginia Board of Examiners of Psychologists. In 1998 he was elected to serve on the Monongalia County Board of Education and in the year 2000 he was elected to the position of vice president of that board.

Heidi is employed as a purchasing assistant at WVNET and was elected by her colleagues to represent classified staff at an institutional level and to serve as president of staff council at WVNET. Volunteer activities include being the last PTO president for Wiles Hill Elementary School before it was closed in the spring of 1999 and service with Pack 60 Cub Scouts. Heidi is a devoted wife and mother, participating in many of her children's activities and supporting her husband in his political career. In June of 2001, Anthony accepted a position as a UNIX coordinator at the University of Maryland at College Park and the Derrys plan to move to Maryland.[2555]

Children of Anthony Patrick and Heidi Margaret[8] (Frist) Derry, all born in Morgantown, Monongalia County, West Virginia:

614   i. PATRICK JAMES[9] DERRY, born 22 August 1991.
615   ii. ALLISON MARIE DERRY, born 6 May 1994; died 6 May 1994.
616   iii. WILLIAM RAMSEY DERRY, born 2 November 1995.
617   iv. THOMAS HUDSON DERRY, born 23 January 2000.

491. Jonathan Ramsey[8] Frist (Ramsey Hudson[7], Joseph Osmond[6], Oscar Haines[5], Edmund Physick[4], James[3], Henry[2], Rudolph[1]) was born 3 June 1967 in Cambridge, England, the son of Ramsey Hudson and Judith Ann (Nadolny) Frist.[2556] He married **Margaret Jane Shaw**. Margaret was born 11 November 1960 in Gallipolis, Gallia County, Ohio, the daughter of Kenneth Alden and Wilda Jane (Landrum) Shaw. In 2003 they live in Morgantown, West Virginia.[2557]

Children of Jonathan Ramsey[8] and Margaret Jane (Shaw) Frist, both born in Morgantown, Monongalia County, West Virginia:

618   i. IAN SHAW[9] FRIST, born 7 October 1989.

619   ii. JILLIAN CLAIRE FRIST, born 27 May 1999.

492. Erica Ann[8] Frist (Ramsey Hudson[7], Joseph Osmond[6], Oscar Haines[5], Edmund Physick[4], James[3], Henry[2], Rudolph[1]) was born 26 July 1969 in Madison, Dane County, Wisconsin, the daughter of Ramsey Hudson and Judith Ann (Nadolny) Frist.[2558] She grew up in West Virginia and graduated from West Virginia University with a B.A. in liberal arts with concentration on business administration. She moved to northern Virginia in 1992 and worked for a government contract as administrative assistant and later financial analyst. She resigned to return to school for her education degree, but took a temporary position with America Online, which turned into a six-year career.

Erica met her future husband at America Online. On 28 May 2000 Erica married in Madison, Morgan County, Georgia, to **James Andrew Canfield**.

James was born 25 April 1971 in Athens, Clarke County, Georgia, the son of Thomas Joseph and Mary Jane (Attaway) Canfield. James works for America Online as principal interface designer. In 2002 they live in Arlington, Virginia, and are working with an architect to add a new master bedroom and family room for their growing family.[2559]

Children of James Andrew and Erica Ann[8] (Frist) Canfield, both born in Arlington, Virginia:

620   i. JAMES ALEXANDER[9] CANFIELD, born 22 October 2000.

621   ii. AVA MARIE CANFIELD, born 10 June 2002.

NINTH GENERATION

546. Ronald Jack[9] Findley (Manferd Harold[8], Clara Etta[7] Patton, Louisa Jane[6] Frist, Joseph Andrew[5], David H.[4], John[3], Henry[2], Rudolph[1]) was born 15 April 1943 in Cedar Rapids, Linn County, Iowa, the son of Manferd Harold[7] and Margaret L. (Fessler) Findley. He married **Carolyn Cheatham**.[2560]

Children of Ronald Jack[9] and Carolyn (Cheatham) Findley:

622   i. JEFFERY MICHAEL[10] FINDLEY; married Cindy Jean Kline. Children, *(a)* Ashley Marie Findley, *(b)* Adam Kline Findley, and *(c)* Aubrey Nicole Findley.

623   ii. KRISTIN M. FINDLEY; married Timothy Long. Children, *(a)* Haley Marie Long and *(b)* Hanna Virginia Long.

557. Steven Todd⁹ Frist (Jimmy Dale⁸, Russell Edward⁷, Joseph E.⁶, John S.⁵, David H.⁴, John³, Henry², Rudolph¹) was born 1 August 1960 in Iowa, the son of Jimmy Dale and Marva (Olson) Frist.²⁵⁶¹ Steve received his B.S. degree in biology from Simpson College in August of 1990 and his master of art in teaching at the University of Iowa in August of 1997. Steve married on 9 June 1996 in Iowa City, Johnson County, Iowa, to **Audrey Loftis.**

Audrey was born 18 June 1968 in Nashville, Davidson County, Tennessee, the daughter of Keith and Janice (Lollar) Loftis. Audrey obtained a B.S. degree in microbiology from Mississippi State University in May 1990 and attended the University of Alabama at Birmingham for doctoral work in molecular and cellular biology. She does research in human gene therapy. She enjoys Japanese antiques, especially woodblock prints.

Steve enjoys woodworking and Japanese antiques, especially swords. He planned to complete his Ph.D. at Iowa State University in 2002. They live in Des Moines, Iowa.²⁵⁶²

Children of Steven Todd⁹ and Audrey (Loftis) Frist:

624   i. SARAH ELIZABETH¹⁰ FRIST, born 24 January 1997 Iowa City, Iowa; died 24 January 1997 Iowa City, Johnson County, Iowa.

625   ii. JACOB MICHAEL FRIST, born 17 October 1999 Des Moines, Iowa.

609. Marcia Lynn⁹ Fischer (Eugene Alfred⁸, Dolores Lorraine⁷ Klima, Dolores Mary⁶ Frist, Abram Bernard⁵, Abraham B.⁴, James³, Henry², Rudolph¹) was born 30 January 1974 in Portsmouth, Virginia, the daughter of Eugene Alfred⁷ and Deborah Ann (Baum) Fischer III.²⁵⁶³ She married 27 September 1997 at All Saints Episcopal Church in Frederick, Frederick County, Maryland, to **Scott Christopher Ritchie Sheppard.**

Scott was born 11 April 1967 in Baltimore City, Maryland, the son of Gene and Donna (Fulford) Sheppard. Scott was educated in Carroll County, Maryland. He is a district manager of Toy Works. He is known as a hard worker, enjoys sporting events, and is an Orioles fan.

Marcia graduated from Germanna Community College in 1996 with an associate degree in applied science in general studies. She worked for ten years at K-B Toys where she was a retail store manager and training manager. She is currently a homemaker and medical billing specialist. She is known as a dedicated hard worker and caregiver. She enjoys scrap booking, crafts, and softball. She was on the second team all county in high school as a right fielder.[2564] They live in Myersville, Maryland, in 2002.

Children of Scott Christopher Ritchie and Marcia Lynn[9] (Fischer) Sheppard:

626   i. TYLER CHRISTOPHER[10] SHEPPARD, born 15 April 1999 Olney, Montgomery County, Maryland.

627   ii. BRIANNA MARIE SHEPPARD, born 20 May 2000 Olney, Montgomery County, Maryland.

628   iii. ANDREW LEE SHEPPARD, born 24 March 2002 Frederick, Frederick County, Maryland.

Part III

THE GARRETSONS OF
NEW CASTLE COUNTY, DELAWARE

*T*he second wife of Henry Frist of New Castle County, Delaware, the progenitor of many of America's Frist families, was Elizabeth Garretson. This narrative establishes her Garretson ancestry.

There were many Garretsons in the early records of New Castle County, Delaware. Several different families arrived in the 1600s and remained for many generations, populating the area. All known families were at least partially investigated, and several separate and apparently unrelated lines emerged.

Hendrick Garretson, who died in New Castle County, Delaware, in 1721 had a brother Powell, also known as Paul,[1] and the two men left many descendants whose records can be found in Holy Trinity (Old Swedes Church) in Wilmington, Delaware. They owned land in several areas of the county. One tract, located near two tracts that were owned by Conrad Constantine, was on Herring Run, a stream that flows into Red Clay Creek.[2]

Jan Gerritsen van der Hof, also known as John Garretson, was the progenitor of the line of interest to Elizabeth Garretson, wife of Henry Frist of New Castle County, Delaware.[3]

Very few records were found at Holy Trinity (Old Swedes) Church on Jan Gerritsen van der Hof and his descendants, who were Dutch rather than Swedish, except when a descendant married into the Abraham family, who were known to be members of Holy Trinity (Old Swedes) Church.[4]

Although many Garretsons were investigated, due to time constraints and the complexity of the Garretson family, only the direct line of descent to Elizabeth (Garretson) Frist is included in this compilation.[5]

1. John[1] Garretson a.k.a. Jan Gerritsen van der Hof was probably born by about 1640.[6] He died by 5 March 1694/1695 in New Castle County, Delaware.[7] He married **Ann**, although it is uncertain whether she mothered his children.[8]

John was an early landowner and planter in New Castle County, Delaware. He reportedly came to Delaware between 1657 and 1664 from Gelderland in Holland.[9] He was in New Castle County by 1 April 1676 when a tract of 440 acres was surveyed for him and John Ogle on the west side of the Delaware River and on the south side of Christina Creek next to the upper side of Swartnutt Island.[10]

On 21 February 1682/1683, Jan Gerritsen Verhoof became a naturalized citizen in New Castle County, along with Hendrik Gerritzen and Paul Gerritzen.[11]

In 1684 a tract of 400 acres identified as "New Vien" was surveyed and divided.[12] It was located on Christina Creek at the mouth of the Dividing Branch adjacent to land patented by Robert Hutchinson. On the "fifth day of the sixth month" in 1684, William Penn granted this 400-acre tract called "New Vien" to John Garretson.[13]

John Garretson wrote his will on 28 November 1694 in New Castle County and it was probated on 5 March 1694/1695.[14] Although his land was patented in the name of John Garretson, his will was written "John Garretson Vanderhofe." He signed the will simply "John Garretson" and his descendants used the surname Garretson. His will divided his land equally among his sons. He left his plantation to his son Garret and requested that he help his brothers, Casparius and Cornelius, clear a portion of his land for them equal to the plantation tract.

John named his wife, Ann, as well as sons Garret, Casparius, and Cornelius. He mentioned "daughters," but did not name them and they remain unidentified. Robert Hutchinson, his 1684 neighbor, witnessed his will along with Robert Dyer. No source was located to document the birth years of his children, and the dates shown here are estimated. However, on 1 July 1695, the eldest son Garret was still a minor.[15]

Children of John[1] a.k.a. Jan Gerritsen van der Hof and possibly Ann Garretson, all probably born in New Castle County, Delaware:

+   2   i.   GARRET[2] GARRETSON, born about 1676 to 1680; died between 1754 and 1758 New Castle Hundred, New Castle County, Delaware;[16] married Charity Hussey.[17]

      3   ii.   CASPARIUS GARRETSON, born about 1678; died 1726 Christiana Hundred, New Castle County, Delaware; married Ann.[18]

      4   iii.   CORNELIUS GARRETSON, born about 1681; died between 21 January 1765 and March 1765 New Castle Hundred, New Castle County,

Delaware; no issue.[19] He made bequests to many of his relatives, referring to his nephews, nieces, and other relatives as "cousins." He left his real estate to his brother Casparius's sons John and William Garretson.

2. Garret[2] **Garretson** (John[1] a.k.a. Jan Gerritsen van der Hof) must have been born about 1676 to 1680,[20] probably in New Castle County, Delaware,[21] the son of John Garretson a.k.a. Jan Gerritsen van der Hof.[22] He died between 20 January 1754 and 6 January 1758 in New Castle Hundred, New Castle County, Delaware.[23] He married **Charity Hussey**.[24] Charity was born 4 October 1681, the daughter of John and Rebecca (Perkins) Hussey.[25]

The will of John Hussey dated 18 February 1707 named a daughter Charity, wife of Garret Garretson.[26] John Hussey was a Quaker and his son-in-law Garret was also a member of the Society of Friends, participating in the Kennett Monthly Meeting.[27] Garret did not appear frequently in the minutes of Kennett Monthly Meeting, which included the area of New Castle where he and Charity lived.[28]

On the "16th day of the 3rd month" in 1720, Garret and Charity Garretson witnessed the Quaker marriage of Ann Garretson, widow, to Nathan Hussey at the Kennett Monthly Meeting in New Castle County.[29] When Garret's brother Casparius wrote his will in 1726, Garret and his brother Cornelius were witnesses along with F. V. Land and Edward Blake.[30]

On the "11th day of the 10th month" in 1729 Garret and Charity witnessed the Quaker marriage of their son John Garretson to Margaret Colender.[31] Also present were their children Rebecca Garretson, Hulda Garretson, and Mary Garretson. In 1732 Garret was appointed, along with Abraham Marshall, William Lovis, and Thomas Collingsworth, to attend a quarterly Quaker meeting.[32]

Relatively few county records were found for Garret, and he apparently lived his entire life at "New Vien" on the land he inherited from his father. Garret wrote his will on 20 January 1754 in Hundred and County of New Castle in Delaware.[33] He died by 6 January 1758 when his will was probated in New Castle County.[34]

He made no provision for a wife and she is believed to have predeceased him. Minutes of the Kennett Monthly Quaker Meeting indicate that she was living in 1745,[35] but no records of the birth dates of their children were found.

Garret named ten children in his will. Birth dates are estimated and the children are listed below in the order that he named them in the will. This is probably the correct birth order for the daughters, but possibly not for the sons. He left five shillings to his son John and "cut him off" from any further part of his real and personal estate. He mentioned his grandsons James and John and identified them as minor sons of his son Cornelius Garretson deceased. His sons Eliakim and Jedediah were to receive his real and personal estate, to be divided equally between them.

Children of Garret[2] and Charity (Hussey) Garretson:

5   i. JOHN[3] GARRETSON, born about 1705–1709; married "11th day of 10th month" in 1729 Kennett Monthly Meeting, New Castle County, Delaware, Margaret Colender daughter of Nicholas Colender.[36]

6   ii. ANNA GARRETSON, born about 1709; "Cousin Ann Hussey" was named in the will of Cornelius Garretson in 1765.[37]

7   iii. REBECCA GARRETSON, born about 1710.

8   iv. HULDA GARRETSON, born about 1712; married 12 August 1750 William Goodwind at Holy Trinity (Old Swedes) Church in Wilmington, New Castle County, Delaware.[38] Her brother Jedidiah's 1766 will named a sister Hulda Gooding.[39]

9   v. MARY GARRETSON, born about 1714; married by 1765 Scot [sic].[40]

10   vi. SARAH GARRETSON, will written 1776 and probated in 1793, New Castle County, Delaware.[41] She named her brother Jediah, a nephew Eliakim Garretson, and her unmarried sister Elizabeth Garretson.

11   vii. ELIZABETH GARRETSON, born about 1723; died between 2 February 1802 and 26 June 1802 Newport, Christiana Hundred, New Castle County, Delaware.[42] Elizabeth never married. She left her real estate to "my well beloved relation" Jediah Garretson and also left a bequest to Elizabeth Frist and another to Ester Garretson. Elizabeth Garretson sold a lot in Newport, New Castle County, Delaware, to Jediah Garretson on 8 December 1800.[43]

+ 12   viii. CORNELIUS GARRETSON, born by about 1725;[44] died by 13 August 1750 New Castle County, Delaware;[45] married Rebecca.[46]

13   ix. ELIAKIM GARRETSON, born about 1718–1722;[47] died 1761 in New Castle Hundred, New Castle County, Delaware; married 25 September 1747 Lydia Walter, a Quaker of Chester County, Pennsylvania.[48]

14   x. JEDEDIAH GARRETSON, born about 1720–1725;[49] wrote his will and died 1766 New Castle County, Delaware.[50] He named a son Eliakim and sisters Huldah Gooding, Mary Scott, and both Sarah and Elizabeth Garretson.

12. Cornelius[3] Garretson (Garret[2], John[1] a.k.a. Jan Gerritsen van der Hof) was born about 1725 in New Castle County, Delaware,[51] the son of Garret and Charity (Hussey) Garretson.[52] He died by 13 August 1750 in New Castle County, Delaware.[53] He married in Pennsylvania in October of 1744 to **Rebecca**.[54]

On 1 March 1741 Cornelius Garretson, Jr., weaver, was of New Castle city and county when he purchased a lot and dwelling house in the city of New Castle from Sigfredus Alrich and his wife Elizabeth.[55] The land was described as having been deeded to Alrich in 1736 by John Gooding. It was described when sold to Alrich as a 200-foot square, bounded on the north by the road leading to Maryland, on the east and south by other lands of Alrich, and on the west by Beaver Street. When the land was sold to Cornelius, it was found to be 124 feet in length along Beaver Street and only 155.5 feet in length on the Maryland Road. Beaver Street was also identified as the road leading to the town marsh.

When Cornelius died in New Castle County in 1750, he still owned this tract of land, which descended to his two sons. On 17 April 1756 when Daniel McGinnis and his wife Mary sold lots along Beaver Street in New Castle Town to John Land, the lots were described as formerly in the possession of Gideon Griffith, and lately of Cornelius Garretson.[56]

Children of Cornelius[3] and Rebecca Garretson:

+   15   i. JAMES[4] GARRETSON, born 4 January 1745;[57] New Castle County,
                Delaware; died 5 March 1782 New Castle County, Delaware;[58] married
                10 April 1770 Wilmington, New Castle County, Delaware, Mary
                Abrams a.k.a. Abrahams.[59]

      16   ii. JOHN GARRETSON, born about 1749.[60]

15. James[4] Garretson (Cornelius[3], Garret[2], John[1] a.k.a. Jan Gerritsen van der Hof) was probably born on 4 January 1745,[61] in New Castle County, Delaware, the son of Cornelius Garretson.[62] He probably died 5 March 1782 in New Castle County, Delaware.[63] He married on 10 April 1770 at Old Swedes Church in Wilmington, New Castle County, Delaware, to **Mary Abrams**.[64] The surname Abrams was found in the church records sometimes as Abram and sometimes as Abraham or Abrahams, but Abraham is used hereinafter.

The birth year of Mary Abraham, daughter of Joseph and Margret (Farrys) Abraham, was recorded in Old Swedes Church as 16 November 1745.[65] This date is precisely one year different from the date of 16 November 1744 that a descendant of Mary's recorded in 1930.[66] Mary died between 23 and 29 August 1786 in New Castle County, Delaware.[67]

In 1765 when James's grand-uncle Cornelius Garretson died, he left ten pounds to him, but did not mention James's brother, John Garretson.[68]

In 1772 James Garretson was listed as the administrator when the intestate estate of his father-in-law, Joseph Abraham of Christiana Hundred in New Castle County, was probated in New Castle County.[69] He was not specifically named in this record as Joseph's son-in-law and no heirs were mentioned.

Although the Abraham family worshiped at Old Swedes Church in Wilmington, New Castle County, Delaware,[70] there is ample evidence that they lived in Newport, New Castle County, Delaware. On 7 January 1757 Joseph Abraham, farmer, and Margaret his wife of Newport, New Castle County, Delaware, sold five acres of land to Joseph Jones for twenty-one pounds.[71] On 22 August 1770 Joseph Abraham was of Newport, New Castle County, Delaware, when he sold a lot in Newport to Allen Cunningham.[72]

On 15 May 1775 James Garretson was living in Christiana Hundred in New Castle County, Delaware, when he and Mary sold the lot of land and the dwelling house that he had inherited from his father, Cornelius, in New Castle to Joseph Enos of New Castle Hundred for thirty-five pounds.[73] Witnesses were Jacob Morton and Mary Enos. The land was described as having been purchased on 1 March 1741 by James's father Cornelius Garretson from Sigfredus Alrich and located near Beaver Street. According to the deed, Cornelius died intestate leaving only two sons, James and John, to survive him. John sold his share to his brother James on 15 May 1770. Although the legal description had changed slightly over the ensuing years, it was identified as the same land.

A death date for James Garretson of 5 March 1783 was recorded by a descendant in 1930.[74] The inventory of his estate was dated 28 March 1782 and identified him as a weaver,[75] an occupation that his father had also followed. This inventory was dated *before* the family death date.[76] Thus, assuming the inventory date is correct, the correct date for James Garretson's death was 5 March 1782.

The inventory wasn't recorded in Christiana Hundred, New Castle County, Delaware, until 29 December 1787 after his wife, Mary, died. The administration was handled by Hance Stamcast. An amount paid to Isaac Abraham, Ann Lewis, Joseph Garretson and Sarah his wife, heirs of Joseph Abraham deceased was mentioned in the accounting.[77] This entry provides conclusive proof that this James Garretson was the same one who married Mary Abraham and served as administrator of her father's estate.

On 29 April 1786 the heirs of Joseph Abraham deeded four and a fourth acres to their brother Isaac Abraham.[78] The heirs, all siblings, were identified in the deed as Isaac Abraham; Mary Garretson, widow of James Garretson; Ann Lewis, widow of David Lewis; and Sarah Garretson, wife of Joseph Garretson. Mary was further identified in the deed as formerly Mary Abraham of Christiana Hundred, New Castle County, Delaware, a spinster by profession.

Mary Garretson's will was written on 23 August 1786 and it was probated 29 August 1786 in New Castle County, with Hance Stamcast as executor.[79] There can be no mistaking the fact that this was the correct Mary Garretson. Her probate file, containing the original will, included an inventory of her estate that identified her as Mary Garretson, widow of James Garretson of Christiana Hundred, New Castle County, Delaware, weaver.[80] An account dated May 1786 from her brother Isaac Abraham was mentioned.

Her will stated that "my daughter Elizabeth shall have my case of drawers and all my wearing apparel" and that certain items are to be kept by "my Aunt Elizabeth Garretson for the other two children until they come to the age of twenty-one years." Although Mary identified Elizabeth as her aunt, she was actually the aunt of her deceased husband James Garretson. "Aunt Elizabeth" was the unmarried sister of James's father Cornelius Garretson.

When the aunt, Elizabeth Garretson, died in 1802 in New Castle County, her will mentioned both Jediah Garretson and Elizabeth Frist,[81] but made no mention of Gideon Garretson.

Children of James[4] and Mary (Abraham) Garretson, all born in New Castle County, Delaware:

17   i. JOSIAH OR JEDIAH[5] GARRETSON, born 9 January 1772;[82] died by 10 October 1807 in Newport, New Castle County, Delaware.[83] Jediah's estate was administered by Susanna Garretson and included debts to both Gideon Garretson and Henry Frist.

18   ii. ELIZABETH GARRETSON, born 22 January 1774;[84] died 19 September 1831 Newport, New Castle County, Delaware;[85] married 3 January 1792, Henry Frist.[86] Please see the Frist section for further information on Henry and Elizabeth (Garretson) Frist.

19   iii. GIDEON GARRETSON, born 12 January 1778;[87] died by 9 December 1862 Preble County, Ohio;[88] married about 1805, Margaret Moore.[89]

Part IV

THE ABRAHAMS OF NEW CASTLE COUNTY, DELAWARE

*J*ames and Mary (Abraham) Garretson were the parents of Elizabeth Garretson, wife of Henry Frist of New Castle County, Delaware. This is the story of Mary Abraham's ancestry.

William Abraham was an early settler whose records can be found at Holy Trinity (Old Swedes) Church in Wilmington, New Castle County, Delaware. The surname Abraham was spelled many ways in the records of Old Swedes Church including Abrahams, Abrams, and Abram. Abraham will be used in this compilation to minimize confusion.

1. William Abraham[1] married at Old Swedes Church in Wilmington, New Castle County, Delaware, on 1 December 1715 to **Maria Constantine**.[1] Maria was the daughter of Conrad and Christina/Kerstin Constantine of New Castle County, Delaware.[2] Conrad's father was Constantinus Gronberg, a Swedish soldier from Mark Brandenburg, Germany, who migrated to America in the mid-1600s.[3] Conrad dropped his father's surname and adopted the patronymic surname of Constantine.[4] Conrad's wife, Christina, was the widow of Pelle Hendrickson a.k.a. Parker, who died by 1684.[5]

William and Maria had only one known child, a son Joseph.[6] It is uncertain whether or not they remained in New Castle County after their son, Joseph, grew to manhood but no records were found to prove that they did.

Only known child of William[1] and Maria (Constantine) Abraham, baptized at Old Swedes Church:

+   2   i. JOSEPH[2] ABRAHAM, born 18 February 1716 New Castle County, Delaware;[7] died by 1772;[8] married 1744 New Castle County, Delaware, Margret Farrys.[9]

2. Joseph[2] Abraham (William[1]) was born 18 February 1716 in New Castle County, Delaware, the son of William and Maria (Constantine) Abraham.[10] He died by 1772 in Christiana Hundred, New Castle County, Delaware.[11] He married in 1744 in New Castle County, Delaware, to **Margret Farrys**.[12]

On 16 May 1740 he purchased a lot containing thirty-two perches in Newport, Christiana Hundred, from his uncle Augustine Constantine and Augustine's wife Janet.[13]

On 18 August 1741 Joseph purchased a tract of land containing four and a quarter acres in Christiana Hundred in New Castle County from Augustine Constantine.[14] Joseph owned this land for the rest of his life and his four surviving heirs sold it after he died.[15]

Joseph married in 1744 in New Castle County, Delaware, to Margret Farrys.[16] Margret's name was listed variously in the church records as Margret, Margretha, and Margrete.

On 19 May 1748 Joseph Abraham and John Garretson were listed as the administrators of John Hyland, a weaver who owned land on Christina Creek.[17]

On 16 January 1749 Joseph Abraham served, along with Jonas Walderaver, as administrator of the estate of his uncle Augustine Constantine.[18]

On 7 January 1757 Joseph Abraham of Newport, farmer, and Margaret his wife, sold five acres of land to Joseph Jones for twenty-one pounds.[19] The land bounded that of Anthony Cadman, James McMullin, and Peter Garretson.

On 15 August 1757 Joseph Abraham of "Newport Ayer" in Christiana Hundred and Margaret his wife sold four acres of marsh land to John Conrad Gary, saddler, for forty pounds.[20] The land was identified as being in Newport and being part of the great marsh, having been purchased from Augustine Constantine in 1740.

On 20 November 1758 Joseph Abraham of Newport, farmer, executed a deed to Conrad Garretson for Conrad's Cripple, a five-acre tract of land in Newport.[21] This was done by Joseph in accordance with the will of Augustine Constantine, Conrad's uncle.

In 1764 Joseph and his family were listed on Borrell's list of church members at Old Swedes Church in Wilmington.[22] Joseph was shown as a fifty-year-old farmer. Margret was listed as his forty-year-old wife. Four children lived with them—

Maria, who was sixteen; Sarah, who was thirteen; and William and Anna, who were both under ten.

On 22 August 1770 Joseph Abraham was of Newport, Delaware, when he sold a lot in Newport to Allen Cunningham.[23] The land was identified as a tract of thirty-two perches sold to Joseph by Augustine Constantine and his wife Janet on 16 May 1740 and recorded in Deed Book M:463.

By 1772 Joseph Abraham had died, and James Garretson was listed as the administrator when the estate was probated in Christiana Hundred, New Castle County.[24] On 21 April 1779 amounts were paid to Soloman Springer and Nehemiah Delaplane and an amount was due from Joseph's son-in-law David Lewis.[25]

On 29 April 1786 three of the four surviving heirs of Joseph Abraham sold four and one-fourth acres of Joseph's land to their brother Isaac Abraham.[26] The four were identified as follows:

- Mary (Abraham) Garretson of New Castle County and Christiana Hundred, the daughter of Joseph Abraham and the widow of James Garretson of New Castle County, deceased.
- Ann Lewis, widow of David Lewis.
- Sarah Garretson, wife of Joseph Garretson.
- Isaac Abraham.

Children of Joseph[2] and Margret (Farrys) Abraham, as listed in the birth and baptismal records of Old Swedes Church, Wilmington, New Castle County, Delaware:

3   i. MARIA[3] a.k.a. MARY ABRAHAM, born 16 November 1745;[27] died between 23 and 29 August 1786 in New Castle County, Delaware;[28] married 10 April 1770 New Castle County, Delaware, James Garretson.[29] Please see the section on James and Mary (Abraham) Garretson for information on this family.

4   ii. AGNES ABRAHAM, born 12 October 1746; probably died by 1764.[30]

5   iii. SARAH ABRAHAM, born 12 October 1748; married 9 January 1770 New Castle County, Delaware, Joseph Garretson.[31]

6   iv. MARGRET ABRAHAM, born 14 December 1750; probably died by 1764.[32]

7   v. WILLIAM ABRAHAM, born 16 December 1752; probably died between 1764[33] and 1786.[34]

8   vi. ANNE ABRAHAM, born 19 March 1755; married David Lewis.[35]

9   vii. HANNAH ABRAHAM, born 23 May 1757; probably died by 1764.[36]

10   viii. JOSEPH ABRAHAM, born 20 July 1759, probably died by 1764.[37]

11   ix. ISAAC ABRAHAM, born 3 March 1763; died by 15 November 1790
           Christiana Hundred, New Castle County, Delaware;[38] married
           24 March 1785 Jennet "Jane" Smith.[39]

12   x. BENJAMIN ABRAHAM, born 3 May 1765; probably died by 1786.[40]

Part V

WILLIAM PARRY OF WALES
AND THE ALLIED JONES FAMILY

*J*ane "Jennie" Jones was the wife of Jacob Chester Frist of Chattanooga, Tennessee, who died in Meridian, Mississippi. Jennie's parents were John F. and Mary (Parry) Jones. This section outlines Mary's paternal Parry family of Wales and links it to her husband, John F. Jones.

William and Mary (Griffith) Parry lived in Llanfihangel tre'r-Beirdd Parish, Anglesey County, Wales. Anglesey is an island and also a county located off the northwest coast of Wales in the Irish Sea. It is separated from the coast by the Menai, a narrow strait. The entire island is approximately twenty-six by thirty miles with a port city of Amlwch in the north. Amlwch was a tiny fishing village until 1768 when copper was discovered on nearby Parys Mountain.[1]

Locating the immigrant ancestor is almost always a challenge. In the case of the Parrys, the search was somewhat easier because they migrated within a group that settled in Jackson County, Ohio. The immigrant ancestor Griffith Parry was identified in Jackson County as being from Gorslwyd, Rhosybol, Anglesey, Wales.[2] It was also fortunate that both Griffith and his older brother married in Wales before coming to America and Griffith had a child born in Wales.

Complicating the research is the limited number of surnames in use in Wales. Thus it cannot be assumed or even suggested that people living in the same area with the same surname are related. Parry, although not one of the most common surnames, is not an unusual one.

There were several factors that proved helpful in the identification of the two immigrant brothers, John and Griffith Parry. One was that both brothers married apparent sisters in the same location in Wales.[3] Another was that the birth record of the child born to Griffith and Jane (Evans) Parry identified Griffith as a miner whose abode was Caecwtta,[4] the same location mentioned in American records as the homeplace in Wales of Griffith's wife Jane (Evans) Parry.[5] Caecwtta is also located near Rhosybol, Anglesey, Wales.

Locating a nearby Parry family with two brothers the right age to be John and Griffith Parry was the final step in the process. Although specific birth dates are missing for the two men in Jackson County, Ohio, John Parry was consistent in listing 1815 as his birth year in the census, and Griffith Parry's birth year was listed in the census as either 1817 or 1818, except for one year when it was recorded as 1820.

When Griffith Parry died in Jackson County, Ohio, on 21 January 1884, one source stated that he died at sixty-six years and seven months[6] and another sixty-six years and six months.[7] This projects to a birth date of June or July of 1817. While this is not a perfect match with the birth records in Wales, in view of the proximity of Llanfihangel tre'r-Beirdd Parish, just a few miles from Gorslwyd, Rhosybol, Anglesey, Wales[8] where Griffith Parry lived with his wife, Jane (Evans) Parry, the descendency seems correct. There is also the fact that both brothers, John and Griffith Parry, named a son William and a daughter Mary.

1. William Parry[1] was born in Wales, probably by the year 1792, for he married about the year 1810 to **Mary Griffith**, spinster.[9] The exact date and place of their marriage is unknown.

William and Mary were living in Ty Mawr when their first child, Ann, was born and baptized on 22 May 1812 at the Ty Mawr chapel in Llanfihangel tre'r-Beirdd Parish, Anglesey County, Wales.[10] The birth record indicated that Llanfihangel tre'r-Beirdd was both William's parish and that of Mary's before their marriage.

By the time their second child, a son John, was born in 1814 their residence was listed as Beydy Coch.[11] The child was still baptized at Ty Mawr chapel in Llanfihangel tre'r-Beirdd Parish. Two more children were born to their marriage, Griffith in 1816 and Mary in 1819, both baptized at the same chapel while the couple lived in Beydy Coch.[12]

Children of William[1] and Mary (Griffith) Parry of Wales, all born in Llanfihangel Tre'r-beirdd Parish, Anglesey County, Wales:

2   i. ANN[2] PARRY, born 28 March 1812.[13]

3   ii. JOHN PARRY, born 31 January 1814;[14] married 1840 in Amlwch, Anglesey, Wales, Ann Evans born 1820 Wales daughter of William Evans.[15] Children, all born in Jackson or Gallia County, Ohio, *(a)* Mary

A. Parry born about 1844,[16] *(b)* Catherine Parry born about 1846,[17] *(c)* William Parry born about 1851,[18] *(d)* Jane Parry born about 1854,[19] and *(e)* Thomas Parry born about 1857.[20] John's occupation was lawyer with real estate valued at $300 in 1850 and farmer in 1860 with $1000 in real estate.

+   4   iii. GRIFFITH PARRY, born 21 August 1816;[21] died 21 January 1884 in Jackson County, Ohio;[22] married (1) 1840 Amlwch, Anglesey, Wales, Jane Evans daughter of William Evans[23] and (2) 15 April 1852 Jackson County, Ohio, Jane Jones.[24]

    5   iv. MARY PARRY, born 13 March 1819.[25]

4. Griffith[2] **Parry** (William[1]) was born 21 August 1816 and baptized at Ty Mawr Chapel, Llanfihangel Parish, Anglesey County, Wales, the apparent son of William and Mary (Griffith) Parry.[26] He died on 21 January 1884 in Jackson County, Ohio.[27] He married first in the year 1840 in Amlwch, Anglesey, Wales,[28] to **Jane Evans**, the daughter of William Evans, of Caecwtta, Rhosybol, Wales.[29] Jane was born in Wales in the year 1820[30] and died 12 February 1848 in Jackson County, Ohio.[31] Griffith married second on 15 April 1852 in Jackson County, Ohio, to **Jane Jones**.[32] His second wife, Jane, was born about 1823 and died 28 February 1901 in Jackson County, Ohio.[33]

Presumably, Griffith grew up in Llanfihangel tre'r-Beirdd Parish, Anglesey County, Wales, but headed north along with his older brother John, to work in the mines at or around Parys Mountain. According to information in America, he and Jane were from Gorslwyd, Rhosybol, Anglesey, Wales.[34]

Following his marriage in 1840 in Amlwch,[35] to Jane Evans,[36] their first child was baptized at Amlwch, Anglesey, Wales, on 28 February 1840.[37] At the christening, Griffith was listed as a miner whose abode was Caecwtta, pronounced Ki-coot-a and identified as a farm.[38] This may have been the farm of Jane's parents, since Caecwtta was specifically listed in American records as where she was from in Wales.[39] Although Caecwtta hasn't been placed on a map, it was used as an address for miners in the 1881 census of Amlwch.[40]

Griffith's brother John married Ann Evans, also identified as a daughter of William Evans. While it is likely that they were sisters, the surname Evans is so common in Wales that it is impossible to be certain without further research.

The two brothers migrated to America by 13 August 1841 when Griffith and John Parry purchased land in Jackson County, Ohio.[41] The land was identified as the southwest quarter of the southwest quarter and also the southeast quarter of the southwest quarter, both in Section 34 in Township 7, Range 17, containing slightly more than eighty-two acres of land. It was purchased from Thomas Murry of Gallia County, Ohio. Witnesses were James M. Cole and William Griffith.

In 1846 Griffith Parry was chosen as a deacon in Sardis Church, which had recently been established by Welsh immigrants.[42] He was described as a gifted speaker, a "good and unwordy explainer," and an excellent Sunday school teacher. He was "tender and meek in his temperament and careful not to hurt the feelings of others."

His first wife, Jane, died 12 February 1848 and is buried in Sardis Cemetery in Jackson County, Ohio.[43] The brothers also owned land in Gallia County. Shortly after Jane's death, Griffith Parry and his brother John Parry and John's wife Ann of Gallia County, Ohio, executed a document in Jackson County on 19 April 1849 that indicated they planned to separate a portion of their property in order to build a steam mill.[44] The lot was part of the east half of the northeast quarter of Section 4, Township 6, Range 17 in Gallia County, Ohio, and was conveyed to John Owens and William Lewis. John's wife Ann Parry relinquished her dower interest in this tract of land. Griffith was a widower at the time.

In 1850 Griffith was the widowed head of the household in Madison Township, Jackson County, Ohio, living next door to his brother John.[45] He was thirty years of age and born in Wales. His occupation was laborer, and he owned real estate valued at $300. His son, William, and daughter, Mary, lived with him.

On 5 January 1852 Griffith Parry of Jackson County initiated a land swap with his brother John by selling him the north quarter of the east half of the northeast quarter of Section 4, Township 6, Range 17 consisting of thirty-eight acres for $200.[46] On that same day John Parry and his wife, Ann, conveyed forty-one acres in the southwest quarter of the southwest quarter of Section 34, Township 7, Range 17 to Griffith Parry for $200.[47]

On 15 April 1852 Griffith married for the second time in Jackson County, Ohio, to Jane Jones.[48] Although Jane was not identified as Mrs. Jane Jones in the marriage records, it is likely, as will be seen, that she was previously married.

On 3 March 1854 John Parry and his wife Ann and Griffith Parry and his wife Jane sold part of the east half of the northeast quarter of Section 4, Township 6, Range 17 to Hugh Humphreys for $600.[49] This was the mill tract and the deed included the opening of a road by John Parry from the mill yard to the county road.

On 24 April 1857 Jane executed a quitclaim to Owen Evans and Nathaniel Davis relinquishing any claim she might have in the southeast quarter of the southwest quarter of Section 25, Township 6, range 18 and also the southwest quarter of the southeast quarter of Section 25, Township 6, range 18.[50] Witnesses were J. Edward Jones and John Lloyd. This land was not owned by either of the Parry brothers and apparently had nothing to do with their land holdings.

On 23 September 1857 John Parry and his wife, Ann, of Jackson County, Ohio, conveyed all of their claim to the northeast quarter of the northeast quarter of Section 4, Township 6, Range 17 containing thirty-eight acres of land to Griffith Parry with Ann Parry relinquishing her dower interest in the land.[51]

In 1860 Griffith and his second wife, Jane, lived in Madison Township, Jackson County, Ohio.[52] Griffith was forty-three years of age, a farmer from North Wales, who owned real estate valued at $1200 and personal property worth $400. Jane was thirty-seven, born in South Wales in 1823. Three Jones children lived with them— Thomas, age sixteen; John, age fourteen; and Ann, age twelve. These children have not been identified, but might belong to Jane Jones Parry from a previous union.

In 1870 Griffith Parry's stature and fortune had continued to climb.[53] He owned real estate valued at $1400 and personal property worth $1600. Their son Hugh worked on the farm and was the only child still living at home.

In 1880 Griffith and Jane headed a slightly larger household in Madison Township, Jackson County.[54] An eleven-year-old nephew named Charles Jones lived with them, as did their daughter Mary Jones, who was thirty-six, and her ten-year-old daughter Jane Jones. Oddly, Mary's daughter was listed as the niece of Griffith Parry and not his granddaughter. Their son Hugh Parry and his wife, Sarah, lived next door.

Griffith died of consumption on 21 January 1884 at the age of sixty-six years[55] and is buried in Sardis Cemetery in Jackson County.[56] Griffith had written his will on 22 October 1883 and added a codicil on 14 January 1884, and it was probated on 12 March 1884.[57] Witnesses were John E. Jones and Edward Jones.

He left his son Hugh the south half of the southeast quarter of Section 33, Range 17 in Madison Township. He left the "farm home that we now reside on" to his wife Jane for her natural life and described it as part of the southwest quarter of the southwest quarter in Section 34, along with some other land. The total was about seventy-two acres. The farm home was to go to his son Hugh when his wife died. This was the first tract of land the brothers purchased in 1841 when they arrived in America. He also mentioned his son William and his daughter, Mary Jones. He stipulated in his will that his daughter, Mary, was to be paid $500 after his wife Jane's death, if Mary was living at the time. If Mary had died, the $500 was to be given half to his son William and half to his granddaughter Jane, daughter of his daughter, Mary. Thus, his will conclusively identified Jane as his granddaughter and not a niece, as listed in the previously cited census.

His widow Jane Parry died 28 February 1901 at the age of seventy-eight and was buried in Sardis Cemetery.[58]

Children of Griffith[2] and Jane (Evans) Parry:

6   i.   WILLIAM[3] PARRY, born 21 February 1840 Amlwch, Anglesey, Wales;[59] died by 12 March 1884 Jackson County, Ohio.[60] Children, *(a)* Samuel Parry and *(b)* Jane Parry.[61]

+   7   ii.   MARY F. PARRY, born about July 1843 Jackson County, Ohio;[62] died by 1 April 1912, New Orleans, Louisiana;[63] married 1 April 1869 Jackson County, Ohio, John F. Jones.[64]

Children of Griffith[2] and his second wife, Jane Jones Parry:

8   iii. HUGH PARRY, born about 1853 Ohio;[65] married about 1879 Sarah Williams born 7 May 1861 Gallia County, Ohio, died 17 June 1888 Jackson County, Ohio.[66] She is buried in Sardis Cemetery.[67] Son Griffith Parry born and died 18 November 1883.[68]

9   iv. DANIEL PARRY, born about 1856 Ohio;[69] died 6 July 1865 Jackson County, Ohio, and buried Sardis Cemetery.[70]

10   v. DAVID PARRY, born about 1859 Ohio;[71] died 4 November 1860 and buried Sardis Cemetery, Jackson County, Ohio.[72]

7. Mary F.[3] Parry (Griffith[2], William[1]) was born about July of 1843 in Jackson County, Ohio, the daughter of Griffith and Jane (Evans) Parry.[73] She died by 1 April 1912 in New Orleans, Louisiana.[74] She married on 1 April 1869 in Jackson County, Ohio, to **John F. Jones**.[75] John was born in February of 1822 in Ohio.[76] He died by 1 April 1912 in New Orleans, Louisiana.[77]

In 1850 seven-year-old Mary lived in her widowed father's household in Madison Township, Jackson County, Ohio, with her older brother William.[78] In 1860 Mary, age seventeen, lived with her father and stepmother and three half siblings in Jackson County, Ohio.[79]

When Mary married John F. Jones, she was twenty-six years of age and John was twenty-one years her senior. Oddly, in 1870 just a year after their 1869 marriage, Mary was the head of the household in Madison Township, Jackson County, Ohio, and John F. Jones was not living with her.[80] She was twenty-seven years of age and listed herself as "keeping house." She owned real estate valued at $1600. Both of her parents were foreign born. Her newborn daughter "Jennie," age five months (born in December), lived with her as did Jane Parry, a domestic servant, who was sixteen years of age.

By 1880 Mary Jones had moved back home with her father, Griffith Parry, in Madison Township, Jackson County, taking along her ten-year-old daughter Jane.[81] Mary was thirty-six and listed as married, but once again her husband of eleven years, John F. Jones, was not living with her. There was also a Charles Jones, age eleven, in the household, identified as a nephew.

On 30 May 1888 John F. Jones resurfaced in Hamilton County, Tennessee, when he purchased Lot 134 in Civil District 3 from J. E. Bullington and his wife Rosa Lee Bullington for $200.[82] The land was located in the North Chattanooga Land Company Addition and was subject to all the conditions set out in the deed to Bullington with regard to the sale of intoxicating liquors.

On 26 June 1889 John F. Jones purchased the south half of Lot 18 and Lot 45 in Civil District 17 of Hamilton County from D. F. and Annie Shauf for $1550, giving notes for payment.[83] This particular purchase of land, which John F. and Mary Jones owned until they died, was to generate many records in two different states.

From the time of their marriage in 1869, it was twenty-three years before John F. Jones and his wife, Mary Jones, were found together in a public record. On 6 August 1892 they were of Hamilton County, Tennessee, when they executed a deed of trust to the Chattanooga National Building and Loan Association for the property John had purchased in 1889.[84] The property was identified as being in St. Elmo. A note in the margin indicated that the debt had been discharged on 16 December 1898.

John and Mary Jones, and presumably their daughter, Jennie, lived in Chattanooga, Hamilton County, Tennessee, on 10 August 1897 when Jennie married Jacob Chester "Jake" Frist of Hamilton County, Tennessee.[85] The marriage took place in Jackson County, Ohio.

On 10 December 1898 John F. Jones mortgaged the south half of Lot 18 in St. Elmo, Tennessee, to the South Chattanooga Savings Bank.[86] By 12 December 1898 John F. and Mary Jones were of Perry County, Mississippi, when they acknowledged this deed in court. The front of the deed contained a marginal note that the debt had been discharged.

On 10 November 1899 John F. and Mary Jones sold Lot 123 of the North Chattanooga Land Company to E. L. Simmons for $35.[87] On 13 November 1899 this deed was sworn in court in Hattiesburg, Perry County, Mississippi.

John F. and Mary Jones executed a trust deed for the south half of Lot 18 in St. Elmo in an undated deed that was registered in Perry County, Mississippi, on 29 January 1900.[88] The deed indicated that John F. Jones was indebted to Mrs. Jennie Frist in the sum of $1000 and the mortgage was executed to secure that debt.

In 1900 John F. and Mary Jones were living together in the household of their married daughter, Jennie Frist, in Hattiesburg, Perry County.[89] John was seventy-eight years of age and Mary was fifty-seven. They had been married for thirty-one years. Mary indicated she had borne only one child and stated that her parents were foreign born. John said that his father was born in Illinois and his mother in New York.

When their daughter, Jennie Frist, and her husband, Jake, moved to New Orleans with the railroad in 1903, John F. and Mary Jones went with them and lived at the same address, 2026 Camp Street.[90] Their exact death dates remain uncertain, but they were not with Jake and Jennie Frist when the 1910 census was taken.

John F. and Mary Jones both died in New Orleans, Louisiana, by 1 April 1912 according to an affidavit dated 10 November 1915, which was filed in Hamilton County, Tennessee, by J. C. Frist.[91] This document indicated that John F. Jones had died intestate leaving Jennie Jones Frist as his only child and heir at law. He still owned Lot 18 in Hamilton County, Tennessee.

On 1 April 1912 J. C. and Jennie Jones Frist, as heir of John F. Jones, sold the south half of Lot 18 of D. P. Shauf's Addition to St. Elmo in Civil District 4 to T. Newell Fry and his wife Minnie.[92] This deed was sworn in court and Jennie's consent taken in Meridian, Lauderdale County, Mississippi, where the Frists had moved in 1906.

Only child of John F. and Mary F.[3] (Parry) Jones, born in Madison Township, Jackson County, Ohio:

11   i. JANE[4] "JENNIE" JONES, born 4 December 1869 Jackson County, Ohio; died 18 April 1953 Fort Lauderdale, Broward County, Florida;[93] married 10 August 1897 in Jackson County, Ohio, Jacob Chester "Jake" Frist.[94] Please see the Frist section of this publication for additional information on Jacob Chester and Jane (Jones) Frist.

NOTES

Part I

1. Kent County, Delaware, Deed Book F2:148–149, microfilm 14, Delaware Public Archives, Dover, Delaware.

2. Henry Frist tombstone, St. James Methodist Episcopal Church Cemetery, Newport, Delaware, photo taken July 2001 by compiler Shirley Wilson (106 Leeward Point, Hendersonville, TN 37075). Also Joel Frist household, 1880 U.S. census, New Castle County, Delaware, population schedule, enumeration district 12, sheet 23, line 42, stamped p. 283, microfilm 1254119, Family History Library, Salt Lake City, Utah.

3. "Every Evening," *History of Wilmington* (Wilmington, Delaware: "Every Evening," 1894).

4. George J. Jones, *German-American Names*, 2d ed. (Baltimore: Genealogical Publishing Co., 1995), p. 360.

5. Letter from Jasper Nebeker Frist to Cora Goodrich, undated, from Patricia Frist Genealogical Collection. Patricia Frist of Clinton, Indiana, now deceased, devoted years to collecting family materials on the Indiana branch of the Frist family. Before her death, she shared her written, personal recollections, genealogical clippings, and photographs with the compiler. Newspaper clippings were often from unidentified newspapers and undated, but many were probably from *The Daily Clintonian*, Clinton, Indiana. Numbered items used in this publication in regard to her collection refer to her comments on numbered photographs. Most comments were included in this publication, but not all photographs. Copies held in 2002 by compiler. Materials from this collection are hereinafter cited as the Patricia Frist Genealogical Collection.

6. Letter from Mrs. James P. Goodrich (née Cora Frist of Winchester, Indiana) to relative "Mayne," surname not stated, 14 December 1926. Cora was a great-granddaughter of Henry Frist and the wife of Governor James Goodrich of Indiana. Copy of letter from genealogical collection of Senator William H. Frist, M.D. (703 Bowling Avenue, Nashville, TN 37215). Senator Frist is a second great-grandson of Henry Frist and has collected material on the Frists over a period of many years.

7. George J. Jones, *German-American Names*, 2d ed. (Baltimore: Genealogical Publishing Co., 1995), p. 170.

8. Refer to the Garretson section of this publication for the complex proof of Elizabeth's ancestry.

9. John Garretson van der Hof will, New Castle County, Delaware Will Book B:13–14, microfilm 6539, Family History Library, Salt Lake City, Utah.

10. Brian James Ensley and Corinne Winget submitters, Descendants of Morgan Abraham born 1660/1665 Caerwys, Clodock County and Hereford County, Wales (undocumented), *Ancestral File*, version 4.19, 8 January 2002, Family History Library, Salt Lake City, Utah. This lists a son, William Abraham, born about 1693 in Clodock County, Herefordshire, Wales, who married Maria Constantin, born 1693 New Castle County, Delaware.

11. Jack Stidham, *The Descendants of Timothy Stidham. Vol. 1* (Morristown, Tennessee: J. Stidham, 1978), p. 30b, microfilm 1697293 item 1, Family History Library, Salt Lake City, Utah. Also Alice Reinders, "Delaware Settlers, 1693," *National Genealogical Society Quarterly* 53 (September 1965): 205. Four of the immigrant's sons were on this 1693 list of Swedish immigrants. Author states that some may be Dutch.

12. William G. Nebeker, "Line of Descent of Nebekers," printed genealogical chart (Salt Lake City, Utah: privately printed, no date); copy held in 2002 by compiler.

13. Elsdon C. Smith, *New Dictionary of American Family Names* (New York: Gramercy Publishing Company, 1988), p. 349.

14. Peter Stebbins Craig, *The 1693 Census of the Swedes on the Delaware* (Winter Park, Florida: SAG Publications, 1993), pp. 101–2.

15. E. G. Withycombe, *The Oxford Dictionary of English Christian Names*, 3d ed., (Oxford: Oxford University Press, 1977), p. 259.

16. Das Telefonbuch, www.telefonbuch.de/NSAPI/anfrage, downloaded 17 January 2002 by compiler.

17. George J. Jones, *German-American Names*, 2d edition (Baltimore: Genealogical Publishing Co., 1995), p. 146.

18. *The Sunday Star*, 19 September 1943, city unknown, clipping from Patricia Frist Genealogical Collection, copy held in 2002 by compiler.

19. Herman Mayes (11207 South 200 East, Clinton, IN 47842), copy provided in May 2001 and held in 2002 by compiler. Every Frist genealogical collection included a copy of this letter. Both the birth and death dates for Mary Meredith Frist, who was born in 1798 and died in 1889, are wrong.

20. Henry Fries household, 1800 U.S. census, New Castle County, Delaware, p. 183, line 17; National Archives micropublication M32, roll 4.

21. Henry Freeze entry, New Castle County, Delaware Assessment Lists, 1788 Christiana Hundred, p. 16, record group 2535, microfilm roll 1 (41), Delaware Public Archives, Dover, Delaware.

22. New Castle County, Delaware Tax Lists RG 2535.000 roll 2, no pagination, Delaware Public Archives, Dover, Delaware.

23. Kent County, Delaware, levy assessments, record group 3535, microfilm rolls 2 and 3 for Dover and Jones Hundreds, Delaware Public Archives, Dover, Delaware. Name was also spelled Frees and Freese.

24. Letter from Ramsey Hudson Frist (633 Jones Avenue, Morgantown, WV 26505) 18 December 2000 to compiler. Frist stated that his father had been told this story.

25. Henry C. Peden, Jr., *Colonial Delaware Soldiers and Sailors 1638–1776* (Westminster, Maryland: Family Line Publications, 1995), p. 52.

26. Ralph Strassburger and William Hinke, *Pennsylvania German Pioneers, Volume I 1727–1755* (Norristown, Pennsylvania: Pennsylvania German Society, 1934), p. 178, list of 26 September 1737.

27. Ralph Strassburger and William Hinke, *Pennsylvania German Pioneers, Volume I 1727–1755* (Norristown, Pennsylvania: Pennsylvania German Society, 1934), p. 180, second list dated 26 September 1737.

28. Charles Starne Belsterling, *Paternal Ancestors of Florence Fries Belsterling* (New York: no publisher, 1938); Family History Library microfilm 17141 item 5, Salt Lake City, Utah.

29. Charlotte D. Meldrum, *Early Church Records of Salem County, New Jersey* (Westminster, Maryland: Family Line Publications, 1996), pp. 230, 233.

30. Charlotte D. Meldrum, *Early Church Records of Salem County, New Jersey* (Westminster, Maryland: Family Line Publications, 1996), pp. 195, 233.

31. *Record of Pennsylvania Marriages Prior to 1810. Vol. I* (Baltimore: Genealogical Publishing Co., 1987), p. 374.

32. Philadelphia County, Pennsylvania, Deed Book D:22:455, microfilm 21917, Family History Library, Salt Lake City, Utah.

33. Charles Starne Belsterling, *Paternal Ancestors of Florence Fries Belsterling* (New York: no publisher, 1938), Family History Library microfilm 17141 item 5, Salt Lake City, Utah.

34. Philadelphia County, Pennsylvania, Deed Book D:53:391, microfilm 21932, Family History Library, Salt Lake City, Utah.

35. Ralph Strassburger and William Hinke, *Pennsylvania German Pioneers, Volume I 1727–1755* (Norristown, Pennsylvania: Pennsylvania German Society, 1934), p. 223.

36. Ralph Strassburger and William Hinke, *Pennsylvania German Pioneers, Volume I 1727–1755* (Norristown, Pennsylvania: Pennsylvania German Society, 1934), p. 205.

37. Informational flyer, Holy Trinity (Old Swedes) Church Foundation, Inc., Holy Trinity (Old Swedes) Church, 606 Church Street, Wilmington, DE 19801.

38. Ibid.

39. 1900 U.S. census New Castle County, Delaware, population schedule, Wilmington Hundred, Wilmington City, enumeration district 31, sheet 15 line 100, dwelling and family 272; National Archives micropublication T623, roll 155.

40. *Wilmington City Directory and Business Gazetteer* (Wilmington, Delaware: Wilmington Advertising Agency, 1900 and 1902).

41. L. J. Lemstra (Clinton, Indiana) letter dated 26 August 1927 to "Cousin" Anna Alexander (1200 Gilpin Avenue, Wilmington, DE), Patricia Frist Genealogical Collection, copy held in 2002 by compiler.

42. The New Jersey Historical Records Survey Program, *Index of the Official Register of the Officers and Men of New Jersey in the Revolutionary War* (1941; reprint, Baltimore: Genealogical Publishing Co., 1965) p. 47.

43. Index to Papers of Continental Congress, p. 211, 1799, Delaware Public Archives, Dover, Delaware.

Part II

1. Thomas P. Doherty, ed., *Delaware Genealogical Research Guide*, 2d ed. (Wilmington, Delaware: Delaware Genealogical Society, 1997) p. 5.

2. Ralph Strassburger and William Hinke, *Pennsylvania German Pioneers, Volume I 1727–1755* (Norristown, Pennsylvania: Pennsylvania German Society, 1934), p. 415.

3. Records of Holy Trinity (Old Swedes) Church, baptisms, Wilmington, Delaware, p. 830, 1758.

4. Ibid.

5. *Record of Pennsylvania Marriages Prior to 1810* (Baltimore: Genealogical Publishing Co., 1987), 1:670.

6. Bauman entries, Index to Baptisms and Births in the 1700s in Old Swedes Church Records, citing Burr 552 original p. 809, Burr 563 original p. 815, Burr 570 original p. 819, Burr 578 original p. 823, and Burr 587 original p. 828, Holy Trinity (Old Swedes) Church, Wilmington, Delaware.

7. Kent County, Delaware, levy assessments, Record Group 3535, microfilm rolls 2 and 3 for Dover and Jones Hundreds, Delaware Public Archives, Dover, Delaware. Name was also spelled Frees and Freese.

8. Doherty, Thomas P. (3321 N. Rockfield Dr., Wilmington DE 19810-3238) genealogical report 2 February 2003 to compiler.

9. Kent County, Delaware, Deed Book F2:148–149, microfilm 14, Delaware Public Archives, Dover, Delaware.

10. Kent County, Delaware, Deed Book P:198, Delaware Public Archives, Dover, Delaware. Rudolph was listed as "Rundolf" in this deed.

11. Kent County, Delaware, levy assessments, Record Group 3535, microfilm rolls 2 and 3 for Dover and Jones Hundreds, Delaware Public Archives, Dover, Delaware. Name was also spelled Frees and Freese.

12. Kent County, Delaware, Deed Book F2:148–149, microfilm 14, Delaware Public Archives, Dover, Delaware.

13. Ibid.

14. Ibid.

15. Henry Frist tombstone, St. James Methodist Episcopal Church Cemetery, Newport, Delaware, photo taken July 2001 by compiler Shirley Wilson (106 Leeward Point, Hendersonville, TN 37075).

16. Letter from Mrs. James P. Goodrich (née Cora Frist of Winchester, Indiana) to relative "Mayne," surname not stated, 14 December 1926. Cora wrote that "I have the information you need from the old family Bible." Copy from genealogical collection of Senator William H. Frist, M.D. (703 Bowling Avenue, Nashville, TN 37215), previously discussed. Relationships were proved through other sources, but exact dates could not always be retrieved from another source.

17. Letter from Mrs. James P. Goodrich (née Cora Frist of Winchester, Indiana) to relative "Mayne," surname not stated, 14 December 1926. Also Frist tombstone, Newport Methodist Episcopal Church Cemetery, Newport, Delaware.

18. Kent County, Delaware, Deed Book F2:148–149, microfilm 14, Delaware Public Archives, Dover, Delaware. The dower release on this deed in 1796 indicates that Elizabeth was of legal age. The birth date is an estimate.

19. Elizabeth Mercer probate record, 1802, New Castle County, Delaware, Delaware Public Archives, Dover, Delaware.

20. Kent County, Delaware, Deed Book F2:148–149, microfilm 14, Delaware Public Archives, Dover, Delaware. The Vining connection was a late discovery and has not been fully researched.

21. John Vining probate record, 1802–1808, New Castle County, Delaware, Delaware Public Archives, Dover, Delaware.

22. Delaware Historical Society card file, Wilmington, Delaware, citing New Castle Presbyterian Church record located in vault of New Castle Wilmington Trust Bank.

23. John Vining probate record, 1802–1808, New Castle County, Delaware, Delaware Public Archives, Dover, Delaware. This information was located so late in the research process that it was not possible to initiate a careful search for descendants, but records in New Castle County, Delaware, indicate that there were descendants.

24. Hugh Mercer probate record, 1809–1815, New Castle County, Delaware, Delaware Public Archives, Dover, Delaware. Rachel Mercer was mentioned in the probate several times, but not named as widow.

25. Elizabeth Mercer guardianship, 1810–1828, New Castle County, Delaware Orphans' Court, Record Group 2840.039, Delaware Public Archives, Dover, Delaware. Whether Elizabeth was the daughter of Hugh and Elizabeth (Frist) Vining Mercer or that of Hugh's widow remains undetermined. Descendants of Elizabeth Frist Vining Mercer have not been fully researched, due to time restrictions.

26. Letter from Mrs. James P. Goodrich (née Cora Frist of Winchester, Indiana) to relative "Mayne," surname not stated, 14 December 1926. Also Frist tombstone, Newport Methodist Episcopal Church Cemetery, Newport, Delaware.

27. Kent County, Delaware, Deed Book F2:148–149, microfilm 14, Delaware Public Archives, Dover, Delaware.

28. Henry Frist tombstone, St. James Methodist Episcopal Church Cemetery, Newport, Delaware, photo taken July 2001 by compiler.

29. Letter from Mrs. James P. Goodrich (née Cora Frist of Winchester, Indiana) to relative "Mayne," surname not stated, 14 December 1926.

30. Ibid.

31. Ibid.

32. Refer to the Garretson section of this publication for the complex proof of Elizabeth's ancestry.

33. Henry Frist tombstone, St. James Methodist Episcopal Church Cemetery, Newport, Delaware, photo taken July 2001 by compiler.

34. Henry Freeze [*sic*] entry, New Castle County, Delaware, Assessment Lists, 1788 Christiana Hundred, p. 16, record group 2535, microfilm 1 (41), Delaware Public Archives, Dover, Delaware.

35. Kent County, Delaware, Deed Book F2:147, microfilm 14, Delaware Public Archives, Dover, Delaware.

36. Kent County, Delaware, Deed Book F2:148, microfilm 14, Delaware Public Archives, Dover, Delaware.

37. Henry Frist entry, New Castle County, Delaware, Tax Lists, 1798 Christiana Hundred, p. 10, line 3, microfilm 6532, Family History Library, Salt Lake City, Utah.

38. Henry Fries [*sic*] household, 1800 U.S. census, New Castle County, Delaware, p. 183, line 17; National Archives micropublication M32, roll 4.

39. Mary Garretson will, New Castle County, Delaware, Will Book M:217–218, microfilm 6540, Family History Library, Salt Lake City, Utah.

40. Henry Fritz [*sic*] entry, New Castle County, Delaware, Assessment Lists, 1804 Christiana Hundred, no pagination, p. 12, line 27, Record Group 2535, microfilm 1 (41), Delaware Public Archives, Dover, Delaware.

41. Henry Frist household, 1810 U.S. census, New Castle County, Delaware, p. 157, line 11, microfilm 224381, Family History Library, Salt Lake City, Utah.

42. Henry Friest [*sic*] entry, New Castle County, Delaware, Assessment Lists, 1816 Christiana Hundred, no pagination, p. 11, line 30, Record Group 2535, microfilm 1 (41), Delaware Public Archives, Dover, Delaware.

43. Henry Frist household, 1820 U.S. census, New Castle County, Delaware, p. 127, line 12; National Archives micropublication M33, roll 4.

44. John Frist household, 1820 U.S. census, New Castle County, Delaware, p. 113, line 18; National Archives micropublication M33, roll 4. Also Jediah Frist household, 1820 U.S. census, New Castle County, Delaware, p. 111, line 34; National Archives micropublication M33, roll 4.

45. Henry Frist tombstone, St. James Methodist Episcopal Church Cemetery, Newport, Delaware, photo taken July 2001 by compiler.

46. Henry Frist probate record, 1823, New Castle County, Delaware, Delaware Public Archives, Dover, Delaware. Name, date, and county are all that is necessary to locate a probate record in this facility.

47. Peter Garretson probate record, 1820–1827, New Castle County, Delaware, Delaware Public Archives, Dover, Delaware.

48. Charles A. Silliman, *The Episcopal Church in Delaware 1785–1954* (Wilmington, Delaware: The Protestant Episcopal Church in the Diocese of Delaware, 1982), pp. 93–94.

49. St. James Methodist Episcopal Church, Newport, Delaware, Register No. 1 1874–1935, p. 102. Also Mary Sam Ward, *Our Spiritual Heritage* (Newport, Delaware: The Women of St. James, no date),

p. 10, St. James Methodist Episcopal Church, Newport. Variant spellings of the name are Nebecker, Nebuker, and Nebaker, among others.

50. New Castle County, Delaware, Deed Book A4:141–143, microfilm 6585, Family History Library, Salt Lake City, Utah.

51. Elizabeth Frist household, 1830 U.S. census, New Castle County, Delaware, Christiana Hundred, p. 35, line 2; National Archives micropublication M19, roll 12.

52. Elizabeth Frist will, New Castle County, Delaware, Will Book S1:557–558, microfilm 6543, Family History Library, Salt Lake City, Utah.

53. Elizabeth Frist probate record, 1832–1833, New Castle County, Delaware, Delaware Public Archives, Dover, Delaware.

54. Letter from Enid Lemstra to her cousin Anna Alexander in Wilmington, Delaware, 26 August 1927. Lemstra was second great-granddaughter of Henry Frist, copy held in March 2001 by the compiler. The dates listed in this letter are consistent with those approximated by the census records cited in this compilation. The letter cites a "family Bible in Baltimore."

55. Elizabeth Frist Orphans' Court case file, 1867, record group 2840, New Castle County, Delaware, Delaware Public Archives, Dover, Delaware.

56. Frist tombstone, St. James Methodist Episcopal Church Cemetery, Newport, Delaware, photo taken July 2001 by compiler.

57. Letter, Enid Lemstra to Anna Alexander, Wilmington, Delaware, 26 August 1927.

58. John Frist 1812 file, Bounty Land Warrant Application Files, 1812–1855, Can No. 1014, Bundle No. 22, Unindexed bounty land files; Record Group 15, National Archives, Washington, D.C.

59. New Castle County, Delaware, Marriage Record Volume 6:2, Delaware Public Archives, Dover, Delaware.

60. Elizabeth Frist will, New Castle County, Delaware, Will Book S1:557–558, microfilm 6543, Family History Library, Salt Lake City, Utah. Exact date from Letter, Mrs. James P. Goodrich (née Cora Frist) to "Mayne," surname not stated, 14 December 1926.

61. Letter, Enid Lemstra to Anna Alexander, Wilmington, Delaware, 26 August 1927.

62. Mary Fallon Richards and John C. Richards, eds., *Delaware Marriages and Deaths from Newspapers 1729–1853* (Westminster, Maryland: Family Line Publications, 1997), p. 81.

63. Jeremiah Ford household, 1850 U.S. census, New Castle County, Delaware, population schedule, Christiana Hundred, District 13, p. 366, dwelling 701, family 731, microfilm 6437, Family History Library, Salt Lake City, Utah.

64. Jeremiah Ford deposition in John Frist 1812 file, Bounty Land Warrant Application Files, 1812–1855, Can No. 1014, Bundle No. 22, Unindexed bounty land files, Record Group 15, National Archives, Washington, D.C.

65. Elizabeth Frist Orphans' Court case file, 1867, record group 2840, New Castle County, Delaware, Delaware Public Archives, Dover, Delaware. Exact date from letter, Mrs. James P. Goodrich (née Cora Frist) to "Mayne," surname not stated, 14 December 1926.

66. Jedediah Frist probate record, 1827–1831, New Castle County, Delaware, Delaware Public Archives, Dover, Delaware.

67. Herman Mayes Genealogical Collection, copy held in 2003 by compiler. Mayes (11207 South 200 East, Clinton, IN 47842) collected many birth, marriage, and death dates for the Frist family through visits to libraries, state archives, and personal interviews with descendants. Gary Jones (P.O. Box 142, Montezuma, IN 47862) entered them in a computer program. Mayes did not retain notes, documents, or record sources. When his work could be documented, it was found to be accurate. Relationships were documented through other sources. Rather than omit undocumented dates that are probably accurate, I have chosen to cite his collection.

68. Elizabeth Frist will, New Castle County, Delaware, Will Book S1:557–558, microfilm 6543, Family History Library, Salt Lake City, Utah. Exact date from Donna J. Robertson, compiler, *Tombstone Inscriptions of Cecil County, Maryland* (Largo, Florida: privately printed, 1995), p. 180. Also

tombstone at Hopewell United Methodist Church Cemetery in Cecil County, Maryland, photographed July 2002 by compiler Shirley Wilson (106 Leeward Point, Hendersonville, TN 37075).

69. Donna J. Robertson, compiler, *Tombstone Inscriptions of Cecil County, Maryland* (Largo, Florida: privately printed, 1995), p. 180. Also tombstone at Hopewell United Methodist Church Cemetery in Cecil County, Maryland, photographed July 2002 by compiler Shirley Wilson (106 Leeward Point, Hendersonville, TN 37075).

70. Donna J. Robertson, compiler, *Tombstone Inscriptions of Cecil County, Maryland* (Largo, Florida: privately printed, 1995), p. 180. Also tombstone at Hopewell United Methodist Church Cemetery in Cecil County, Maryland, photographed July 2002 by compiler Shirley Wilson. Marriage date approximated from birth of first child.

71. Letter, Mrs. James P. Goodrich (née Cora Frist) to "Mayne," surname not stated, 14 December 1926.

72. Elizabeth Frist will, New Castle County, Delaware, Will Book S1:557–558, microfilm 6543, Family History Library, Salt Lake City, Utah. Exact date from letter, Mrs. James P. Goodrich (née Cora Frist) to "Mayne," surname not stated, 14 December 1926.

73. Jediah Frist tombstone, St. James Methodist Episcopal Church Cemetery, Newport, Delaware, photo taken July 2001 by compiler. This also lists Joseph L. Frist.

74. Elizabeth Frist will, New Castle County, Delaware, Will Book S1:557–558, microfilm 6543, Family History Library, Salt Lake City, Utah. Also Garretson Frist tombstone, St. James Church Cemetery, New Castle County, Delaware, photographed July 2001 by compiler.

75. Garretson Frist Probate, New Castle County, Delaware, Will Book S1:435–436, administration of estate granted to his sister Susan, microfilm 6543, Family History Library, Salt Lake City, Utah. Also Garretson Frist tombstone, St. James Methodist Episcopal Church Cemetery, Newport, Delaware, photo taken July 2001 by compiler.

76. Elizabeth Frist will, New Castle County, Delaware, Will Book S1:557–558, microfilm 6543, Family History Library, Salt Lake City, Utah. Exact date from Letter, Mrs. James P. Goodrich (née Cora Frist) to "Mayne," surname not stated, 14 December 1926.

77. Wilmington, Delaware, Death Register 1888–1895, p. 270, microfilm 2188030, Family History Library, Salt Lake City, Utah.

78. William Frist household, 1870 U.S. census, New Castle County, Delaware, population schedule, p. 210B, dwelling 329, family 334; National Archives micropublication M593, roll 121.

79. New Castle County, Delaware, Deed Book E9:488–490 and Deed Book P9:168–170, Delaware Public Archives, Dover, Delaware.

80. Letter, Mrs. James P. Goodrich (née Cora Frist) to "Mayne," surname not stated, 14 December 1926.

81. Joel Frist death record (1891), Wilmington, Delaware, Death Register, Record Group 1500 p. 79 #42288, Delaware Public Archives, Dover, Delaware.

82. Frist–Morrison marriage, marriage card file, Delaware Public Archives, Dover, Delaware. This record was not found at Holy Trinity (Old Swedes) Church, Wilmington, Delaware.

83. Jacob Frist Family Bible, Chattanooga, Tennessee, descended to Jacob's grandson Paul Franklin Frist and given by Paul's widow Kate to William H. Frist, M.D. (703 Bowling Avenue, Nashville, TN 37215). Jacob entered his own birth date and place as well as the fact that he was son of Henry and Elizabeth Frist.

84. Jacob Frist Family Bible, Chattanooga, Tennessee, descended to Jacob's grandson Paul Franklin Frist and given by Paul's widow Kate to William H. Frist, M.D. (703 Bowling Avenue, Nashville, TN 37215).

85. New Castle County, Delaware, Marriage Record Volume 44:27, Record Group 1325, Delaware Public Archives, Dover, Delaware.

86. Zella Armstrong, *Hamilton County and Chattanooga, Tennessee, Volume 1* (1931; reprint, Johnson City, Tennessee: Overmountain Press, 1993), p. 209.

87. Letter, Enid Lemstra to Anna Alexander, Wilmington, Delaware, 26 August 1927.

88. John Frist 1812 file, Bounty Land Warrant Application Files, 1812–1855, Can No. 1014, Bundle No. 22, Unindexed bounty land files; Record Group 15, National Archives, Washington, D.C.

89. New Castle County, Delaware, Marriage Record Volume 6:2, Delaware Public Archives, Dover, Delaware. Also John Frist 1812 file, Bounty Land Warrant Application Files, 1812–1855, Can No. 1014, Bundle No. 22, Unindexed bounty land files; Record Group 15, National Archives, Washington, D.C. This file gives the date as on or about 23 February 1815.

90. Jack Stidham, *The Descendants of Timothy Stidham Volume 1* (Morristown, Tennessee: J. Stidham, 1978), p. 82.

91. David Stidham will, New Castle County, Delaware, Will Book T1:373, microfilm 6543, Family History Library, Salt Lake City, Utah.

92. John Frist 1812 file, Bounty Land Warrant Application Files, 1812–1855, Can No. 1014, Bundle No. 22, Unindexed bounty land files; Record Group 15, National Archives, Washington, D.C. Susannah applied in 1855, but her death is not listed in this record.

93. John Frist 1812 file, Bounty Land Warrant Application Files, 1812–1855, Can No. 1014, Bundle No. 22, unindexed bounty land files; Records of the Veterans Administration, Record Group 15, National Archives, Washington, D.C.

94. Ibid.

95. John Frist household, 1820 U.S. census, New Castle County, Delaware, p. 113, line 18; National Archives micropublication M33, roll 4.

96. If John and Susannah had two sons born by 1820, only one, David H. born in 1818, has been identified. It may be that the approximated date for their second son of 1823 is wrong.

97. New Castle County, Delaware, Deed Book Y4:297–299, microfilm 6595, Family History Library, Salt Lake City.

98. This 1837 date was after their father David wrote his will (he had since married again), but before it was probated. A deed is sworn in court on or after the date it is executed. One date is probably an error, possibly due to the excessive length of time between the execution of the deed and the date it was recorded.

99. John Freist entry, New Castle County, Delaware, Assessment Lists, 1821 Christiana Hundred error list, p. 2, column 2, line 9, Record Group 1535, microfilm 10, Delaware Public Archives, Dover, Delaware.

100. John Frist household, 1830 U.S. census, Wayne County, Indiana, p. 55, line 5; National Archives micropublication M19, roll 29.

101. Audrey Gilbert, *Preble County, Ohio, Land Records Volume III 1828–1833 Books 9–13* (West Alexandria, Ohio: privately printed, 1992), p. 104.

102. Audrey Gilbert, *Preble County, Ohio, Personal Property Tax Lists 1827–1834* (West Alexandria, Ohio: privately printed, no date), p. 90.

103. David Stidham will, New Castle County, Delaware, Will Book T1:373, microfilm 6543, Family History Library, Salt Lake City, Utah.

104. John Frist will, Preble County, Ohio, Will Book C:178. Probate Court, Eaton, Ohio.

105. Audrey Gilbert, *Obituary Abstracts 1877–1895 from Preble County Newspapers in Preble County, Ohio, Volume II* (Utica, Kentucky: McDowell Publications, 1983), p. 18.

106. William Frist household, 1850 U.S. census, Preble County, Ohio, population schedule, Jefferson Township, p. 469, dwelling and family 1227; National Archives micropublication M432, roll 723.

107. John Frist 1812 file, Bounty Land Warrant Application Files, 1812–1855, Can No. 1014, Bundle No. 22, Unindexed bounty land files; Record Group 15, National Archives, Washington, D.C.

108. Joseph Hahn household, 1850 U.S. census, Preble County, Ohio, population schedule, Jefferson Township, p. 468, dwelling and family 1220; National Archives micropublication M432, roll 723.

109. Herman Mayes Genealogical Collection.

110. Rose Shilt, *Preble County, Ohio, Marriage Records 1841–1859 Volume III* (Union City, Indiana: Gateway to the West Publications, no date), p. 50.

111. David H. Frist Family Bible, inherited and owned by Geraldine Frist Miller, deceased (formerly of 415 South Eighteenth Street, Clarinda, IA 51632), copy held in 2003 by compiler. Mrs. Miller was the great-granddaughter of David H. and Lydia E. (Holliday) Frist.

112. Herman Mayes Genealogical Collection.

113. David H. Frist Family Bible.

114. Ibid.

115. William Frist household, 1850 U.S. census, Preble County, Ohio, population schedule, Jefferson Township, p. 469, dwelling and family 1227; National Archives micropublication M432, roll 723.

116. Audrey Gilbert, *Preble County, Ohio, Deaths 1867–1907* (Utica, Kentucky: McDowell Publications, no date), p. 57.

117. Audrey Gilbert, *Probate Abstracts Preble County, Ohio, Estates and Guardianships Cases 2000 through 2999* (West Alexandria, Ohio: privately printed, 1998), p. 24.

118. Beverly Yount, *Tombstone Inscriptions in Wayne County, Indiana, Volume IV* (Fort Wayne, Indiana: Fort Wayne Public Library, 1970), p. 51. This cites his exact birth and death dates. Also John Frist will, Preble County, Ohio, Will Book C:178. Probate Court, Eaton, Ohio. While John S. is not named in his father's will, his daughter, Sarah, is.

119. Beverly Yount, *Tombstone Inscriptions in Wayne County, Indiana, Volume IV* (Fort Wayne, Indiana: Fort Wayne Public Library, 1970), p. 51.

120. Joseph Moon household, 1850 U.S. census, Wayne County, Indiana, population schedule, p. 240, dwelling and family 334; National Archives micropublication M432, roll 180.

121. Wayne County, Indiana, Deed Book 9:467, microfilm 1753568, Family History Library, Salt Lake City, Utah.

122. Wayne County, Indiana, Court Order Probate Record Volume 3 1845–1848, p. 514, microfilm 1839242. Also final accounting when the heir Susan A. Frist died, Wayne County, Indiana, Volume E 1848–1851, pp. 9, 210, 513, microfilm 413530, both from Family History Library, Salt Lake City, Utah.

123. Beverly Yount, *Tombstone Inscriptions in Wayne County, Indiana, Volume IV* (Fort Wayne, Indiana: Fort Wayne Public Library, 1970), p. 51.

124. Robert M. Frist household, 1870 U.S. census Warren County, Iowa, population schedule, city of Hartford, p. 430, dwelling 53, family 55; National Archives micropublication M593, roll 423.

125. Audrey Gilbert, *Obituary Abstracts 1877–1895 from Preble County Newspapers in Preble County, Ohio, Volume II* (Utica, Kentucky: McDowell Publications, 1983), p. 14.

126. Robert M. Frist Civil War Soldiers Pension File #32387 and Widows Pension File #321253, National Archives, Washington, D.C. This source mentions but does not name the first wife.

127. William Frist household, 1850 U.S. census, Preble County, Ohio, population schedule, Jefferson Township, p. 469, dwelling and family 1227; National Archives micropublication M432, roll 723.

128. Rose Shilt, *Preble County, Ohio, Marriage Records 1841–1859 Volume III* (Union City, Indiana: Gateway to the West Publications, no date), p. 89.

129. Charles Powell household, 1860 U.S. census, Wayne County, Indiana, population schedule, Wayne Township, stamped p. 747, dwelling 1525, family 1542; National Archives micropublication M653, roll 308.

130. Audrey Gilbert, *Obituary Abstracts 1877–1895 from Preble County Newspapers in Preble County, Ohio, Volume II* (Utica, Kentucky: McDowell Publications, 1983), p. 53 citing *New Paris Mirror* August 14, 1890.

131. Rose Shilt, *Preble County, Ohio, Marriage Records 1841–1859 Volume III* (Union City, Indiana: Gateway to the West Publications, no date), p. 102.

132. Herman Mayes Genealogical Collection. Also death record, book of Lynn #L-1 p. 40, Randolph County Health Department, Winchester, Indiana.

133. Herman Mayes Genealogical Collection.

134. Elizabeth Frist Orphans' Court case file, 1867, Record Group 2840, New Castle County, Delaware, Delaware Public Archives, Dover, Delaware. Exact date from Letter, Mrs. James P. Goodrich (née Cora Frist) to "Mayne," surname not stated, 14 December 1926.

135. Jedediah Frist probate record, 1827–1831, New Castle County, Delaware, Delaware Public Archives, Dover, Delaware.

136. Herman Mayes Genealogical Collection.

137. Shirley Swenson, ed., *The Nebeker Family Book* (No place: Nebeker Family Association, 1979), p. 57, Family History Library, Salt Lake City, Utah.

138. Wilmington, Delaware, Death Register 1888–1895, p. 84, microfilm 2188030, Family History Library, Salt Lake City, Utah.

139. Jediah Frist household, 1820 U.S. census, New Castle County, Delaware, p. 111, line 18; National Archives micropublication M33, roll 4.

140. Jedediah Frist probate record, 1827–1831, New Castle County, Delaware, Delaware Public Archives, Dover, Delaware.

141. New Castle County, Delaware, Orphans' Court Records Book O:428–429, microfilm 0006549, Family History Library Salt Lake City, Utah.

142. New Castle County, Delaware, Deed Book C5:177–178, microfilm 6597, Family History Library, Salt Lake City, Utah.

143. Mary Frist household, 1840 U.S. census, New Castle County, Delaware, City of Wilmington, p. 165, line 26; National Archives micropublication M704, roll 33.

144. Mary Frist household, 1850 U.S. census, New Castle County, Delaware, population schedule, City of Wilmington, Ninth Ward, p. 024, dwelling 323, family 328, microfilm 6437, Family History Library, Salt Lake City, Utah.

145. Elizabeth Lloyd household, 1870 U.S. census, New Castle County, Delaware, population schedule, City of Wilmington, p. 383, dwelling 163, family 174; National Archives micropublication M593, roll 121.

146. Levi H. Springer household, 1880 U.S. census, New Castle County, Delaware, population schedule, City of Wilmington, enumeration district 5, p. 132B, dwelling 320, family 435, microfilm 1254118, Family History Library, Salt Lake City, Utah.

147. Wilmington, Delaware, Death Register 1888–1895, p. 84, microfilm 2188030, Family History Library, Salt Lake City, Utah.

148. Mary Frist probate record, 1889–1891, New Castle County, Delaware, Delaware Public Archives, Dover, Delaware.

149. Mary First [*sic*] probate record, 1891, New Castle County, Delaware, Delaware Public Archives, Dover, Delaware. This probate is filed incorrectly under the surname First.

150. Mary Frist probate record, 1889–1891, New Castle County, Delaware, Delaware Public Archives, Dover, Delaware. Exact birth date from Herman Mayes Genealogical Collection.

151. Elizabeth Lloyd probate record, 1907–1908, New Castle County, Delaware, Delaware Public Archives, Dover, Delaware.

152. Lloyd–Frist marriage, card file, Delaware Historical Society, Wilmington, Delaware, citing Asbury M. E. Church.

153. Elizabeth Frist Orphans' Court case file, 1867, Record Group 2840, New Castle County, Delaware, Delaware Public Archives, Dover, Delaware. This probate for Henry's grandmother named all of her children and grandchildren including Henry, who was specifically named as Jediah's son. Exact birth date is from Herman Mayes Genealogical Collection.

154. Mary Fallon Richards and John C. Richards, eds., *Delaware Marriages and Deaths from Newspapers 1729–1853* (Westminster, Maryland: Family Line Publications, 1997), p. 95.

155. Catherine Campbell Stewart Frist, Civil War Delaware Widow's Pension Application #193503, National Archives, Washington, D.C.

156. Mary Frist probate record, 1889–1891, New Castle County, Delaware, Delaware Public Archives, Dover, Delaware. Exact date from Herman Mayes Genealogical Collection.

157. Esther Ann Springer probate record, 1909–1910, New Castle County, Delaware, Delaware Public Archives, Dover, Delaware.

158. Herman Mayes Genealogical Collection.

159. Mary Frist probate record, 1889–1891, New Castle County, Delaware, Delaware Public Archives, Dover, Delaware. Exact date from Herman Mayes Genealogical Collection.

160. Mary Frist probate record, 1889–1891, New Castle County, Delaware, Delaware Public Archives, Dover, Delaware.

161. Mary Fallon Richards and John C. Richards, eds., *Delaware Marriages and Deaths from Newspapers 1729–1853* (Westminster, Maryland: Family Line Publications, 1997), p. 209.

162. Elizabeth Frist probate record, 1867, New Castle County, Delaware, and Elizabeth Frist, 1867, Orphans' Court Case Files New Castle County, Delaware, Record Group 2840, Delaware Public Archives, Dover, Delaware. Probate and Orphans' Court record of Mary's grandmother Elizabeth Frist both list her as Mary Y. Way.

163. Mary Frist probate record, 1889–1891, New Castle County, Delaware, Delaware Public Archives, Dover, Delaware. Frank Peirce Frist Family Bible; Frank was a son of Jediah Rudolph Frist. Frank and his wife, Arletta Walker, had no children, but recorded many dates on their Frist and Walker siblings. Copy of data pages held in 2003 by compiler, from Patricia Frist Genealogical Collection, previously discussed.

164. Jediah Frist obituary, *Clinton Plaindealer*, Clinton, Indiana, 15 November 1907.

165. Herman Mayes Genealogical Collection.

166. Mary Fallon Richards and John C. Richards eds., *Marriages from the Delaware Gazette 1854–1859, 1861–1864* (Camden, Maine: Picton Press, no date), p. 37.

167. Vermillion County, Indiana, Marriage Book 6:495, County Clerk, Newport, Indiana.

168. Donna J. Robertson, compiler, *Tombstone Inscriptions of Cecil County, Maryland* (Largo, Florida: privately printed, 1995), p. 180. Also tombstone at Hopewell United Methodist Church Cemetery in Cecil County, Maryland, photographed July 2002 by compiler Shirley Wilson (106 Leeward Point, Hendersonville, TN 37075).

169. Elizabeth Frist will, New Castle County, Delaware, Will Book S1:557–558, microfilm 6543, Family History Library, Salt Lake City, Utah.

170. Donna J. Robertson, compiler, *Tombstone Inscriptions of Cecil County, Maryland* (Largo, Florida: privately printed, 1995), p. 180. Also tombstone photographed in July 2002 by compiler Shirley Wilson (106 Leeward Point, Hendersonville, TN 37075).

171. Donna J. Robertson, compiler, *Tombstone Inscriptions of Cecil County, Maryland* (Largo, Florida: privately printed, 1995), p. 180. Also tombstone photographed July 2002 by compiler Shirley Wilson (106 Leeward Point, Hendersonville, TN 37075). Marriage date approximated from birth of first child.

172. Donna J. Robertson, compiler, *Tombstone Inscriptions of Cecil County, Maryland* (Largo, Florida: privately printed, 1995), p. 180. Also tombstone photographed July 2002 by compiler Shirley Wilson (106 Leeward Point, Hendersonville, TN 37075).

173. James Frist household, 1830 U.S. census, Chester County, Pennsylvania, New Garden Township, p. 303, line 22, National Archives micropublication M19, roll 148.

174. James Frist household, 1840 U.S. census Cecil County, Maryland, p. 254, line 13; National Archives micropublication M704, roll 164.

175. James Frist entries, Cecil County, Maryland, 1841–1842 Tax Assessments, District 7, alphabetical by district, no pagination, Cecil County Historical Society Library, Elkton, Maryland.

176. Donna J. Robertson, compiler, *Tombstone Inscriptions of Cecil County, Maryland* (Largo, Florida: privately printed, 1995), p. 180.

177. Abraham Frist entry, Cecil County, Maryland, 1848 Tax Assessments, District 7, alphabetical by district, no pagination, Cecil County Historical Society Library, Elkton, Maryland.

178. William Frist household, 1850 U.S. census, Cecil County, Maryland, population schedule, Port Deposit, p. 157, dwelling 1050, family 1066; National Archives micropublication M432, roll 290. This is the only record where he was found as William, and he was never found with the initial W.

179. James Frist entry, Cecil County, Maryland, 1850 Tax Assessments, District 7, alphabetical by district, no pagination, Cecil County Historical Society Library, Elkton, Maryland.

180. James Frist household, 1860 U.S. census, Cecil County, Maryland, population schedule, Seventh District, p. 590, dwelling 1938 and family 1896; National Archives micropublication M653, roll 472.

181. James Frist household, 1870 U.S. census, Cecil County, Maryland, population schedule, Seventh District, Port Deposit p. 257, dwelling and family 206; National Archives micropublication M593, roll 583.

182. Edward Frist household, 1870 U.S. census, Cecil County, Maryland, population schedule, Seventh District p. 271, dwelling and family 421; National Archives micropublication M593, roll 583.

183. James Frist will, Cecil County, Maryland, Will Book E12:296, Orphans' Court, Elkton, Maryland.

184. James Frist probate record, Cecil County, Maryland, 9 February 1874, Register of Wills, Elkton, Maryland.

185. Donna J. Robertson, compiler, *Tombstone Inscriptions of Cecil County, Maryland* (Largo, Florida: privately printed, 1995), p. 180.

186. James and Henrietta Little Frist tombstone, Hopewell United Methodist Church Cemetery, Cecil County, Maryland, photographed in July 2002 by compiler.

187. Marietta Frist death certificate #23025 (1909), Health Department, City of Baltimore, Maryland, microfilm CR 48,145, Maryland State Archives, Annapolis, Maryland.

188. Ibid.

189. Hannah Frist death certificate #C23208 (1909), Health Department, City of Baltimore, Maryland, microfilm CR 48,145, Maryland State Archives, Annapolis, Maryland.

190. Ibid.

191. John Frist death certificate #C27264 (1909), Health Department, City of Baltimore, Maryland, Maryland State Archives, Annapolis, Maryland.

192. John Frist burial card, Lot 81, Section J, permit A1525, Loudon Park Cemetery, Baltimore City, Maryland. Also John Frist death certificate #C27264 (1909), Health Department, City of Baltimore, Maryland.

193. Donna J. Robertson, compiler, *Tombstone Inscriptions of Cecil County, Maryland* (Largo, Florida: privately printed, 1995), p. 170.

194. Baltimore City, Maryland, Marriage Index 1851–1885 citing Book 1:140; microfilm CR 1669, Maryland State Archives, Annapolis, Maryland.

195. James Frist household, 1830 U.S. census, Chester County, Pennsylvania, New Garden Township, p. 303, line 22, National Archives micropublication M19, roll 148. Abraham listed a different state for his birth in every census, but this is where his parents were in 1830.

196. Obituary of son William H. Frist, *Cecil Democrat*, Elkton, Maryland, 21 February 1885, Margaret Hepner Genealogical Collection. Hepner is a great-granddaughter (600 Falcon Bridge Drive, Joppa, MD 21085). This obituary identifies William H. Frist's father as "the late Abraham Frist." Copy held in 2003 by compiler.

197. Frist–Patterson marriage record, Margaret Hepner Genealogical Collection (600 Falcon Bridge Drive, Joppa, Maryland 21085). Margaret is the granddaughter of Abram Bernard Frist and collected many documents on this branch of the family. Copy of original marriage held in 2003 by compiler.

198. Baltimore City, Maryland, Marriage Index 1851–1885, microfilm CR 1669, Maryland State Archives, Annapolis, Maryland.

199. Rose W. Peterson, compiler, *Spring Hill Cemetery, Charleston, West Virginia, Volume III, L–R* (Nitro, West Virginia: Peterson Quality Associates, 1995), p. 197.

200. Rose W. Peterson, compiler, *Spring Hill Cemetery, Charleston, West Virginia, Volume III, L–R* (Nitro, West Virginia: Peterson Quality Associates, 1995), p. 197. Also Sarah E. Frist household, 1880 U.S. census, Kanawha County, West Virginia, population schedule, Charleston, enumeration district 61, p. 454, dwelling and family 136; National Archives micropublication T9, roll 1405.

201. Thomas Frist household, 1860 U.S. census, Monroe County, Virginia, population schedule, Union Town, post office Peterstown, p. 947B, line 2; National Archives micropublication M653, roll 1363.

202. James and Henrietta Little Frist tombstone, Hopewell United Methodist Church Cemetery, Cecil County, Maryland; photographed in July 2002 by compiler. Tombstone also listed their son Henry.

203. William Frist household, 1850 U.S. census, Cecil County, Maryland, population schedule, p. 157, dwelling 1050, family 1066; National Archives micropublication M432, roll 290. This is the only record found where James Frist was listed as William.

204. Thomas and William Frist obituary, Index of Obits and Marriages in *Baltimore Sun* 1871–1875, Volume 1 A–J, Enoch Pratt Library, Baltimore City, Maryland.

205. 1867, 1868, 1869 Cecil County, Maryland, Tax Assessment Lists, Seventh District, Town of Port Deposit, W. Frist & Brother, carriages materials $800, Cecil County Historical Society Library, Elkton, Maryland.

206. 1870 U.S. census, Ouachita County, Louisiana, population schedule, Monroe, Ward Eight, stamped p. 85, dwelling and family 201, microfilm 552025, Family History Library, Salt Lake City, Utah.

207. James Frist death certificate #11012 (1908), Baltimore City, Maryland, microfilm CR48140, Maryland State Archives, Annapolis, Maryland.

208. Baltimore City, Maryland, Marriage Book 4:152, microfilm CR 10,279, Maryland State Archives, Annapolis, Maryland. Also Baltimore County, Maryland, Land Record 114:180–181, microfilm CR 1110, Maryland State Archives, Annapolis, Maryland. She was a widow when she married and this deed proves her maiden name.

209. Donna J. Robertson, compiler, *Tombstone Inscriptions of Cecil County, Maryland* (Largo, Florida: privately printed, 1995), p. 197.

210. Cecil County, Maryland, Marriages 1840–1863:82, Marriage Office, Elkton, Maryland.

211. Elizabeth Frist will, New Castle County, Delaware, Will Book S1:557–558, microfilm 6543, Family History Library, Salt Lake City, Utah. Exact date from Letter, Mrs. James P. Goodrich (née Cora Frist) to "Mayne," surname not stated, 14 December 1926.

212. Wilmington, Delaware, Death Register 1888–1895, p. 258, microfilm 2188030, Family History Library, Salt Lake City, Utah.

213. Frist–Morrison marriage, marriage card file, Delaware Public Archives, Dover, Delaware. This record was not found at Holy Trinity (Old Swedes) Church in Wilmington, Delaware.

214. Wilmington, Delaware, Death Register 1871–1879, p. 126, microfilm 2188029, Family History Library, Salt Lake City, Utah.

215. *Harkness' Magazine*, September 1872 to August 1874, p. 120, Wilmington, Delaware, Public Library.

216. Joel Frist household, 1840 U.S. census, New Castle County, Delaware, Wilmington, p. 178, line 4; National Archives micropublication M704, roll 33.

217. New Castle County, Delaware, Deed Book 26:279–281, Delaware Public Archives, Dover, Delaware.

218. *Delaware's Industries, An Historical and Industrial Review* (Philadelphia: Keighton Printing House, 1891), p. 196–197.

219. Ibid.

220. New Castle County, Delaware, Deed Book C7:511–513, Delaware Public Archives, Dover, Delaware.

221. J. Thomas Scharf, *History of Delaware 1609–1888, Volume II* (1888; reprint, Westminster, Maryland: Family Line Publications, 1990), 802.

222. *Harkness' Magazine* September 1872 to August 1874, p. 120, Wilmington, Delaware Public Library.

223. du Pont letters, Hagley Museum and Library, Wilmington, Delaware.

224. Joel Frist household, 1860 U.S. census, New Castle County, Delaware, population schedule, City of Wilmington, Ward Three, p. 837, dwelling and family 1235, microfilm 803098, Family History Library, Salt Lake City, Utah.

225. J. Thomas Scharf, *History of Delaware 1609–1888, Volume 1* (Philadelphia: L. J. Richards & Company, 1888), p. 332.

226. New Castle County, Delaware, Deed Book G8:463–464, Delaware Public Archives, Dover, Delaware.

227. New Castle County, Delaware, Deed Book M7:82, Delaware Public Archives, Dover, Delaware.

228. Wilmington, Delaware, Death Register 1871–1879, p. 126, microfilm 2188029, Family History Library, Salt Lake City, Utah.

229. Joel Frist household, 1880 U.S. census, New Castle County, Delaware, population schedule, enumeration district 12, page 23, line 42, stamped p. 283; microfilm 1254119, Family History Library, Salt Lake City, Utah.

230. Wilmington, Delaware, Death Register 1888–1895, p. 258, microfilm 2188030, Family History Library, Salt Lake City, Utah.

231. Joel Frist probate record, 1891–1892, New Castle County, Delaware, Delaware Public Archives, Dover, Delaware.

232. Joel First [*sic*] probate record, 1891, New Castle County, Delaware, Delaware Public Archives, Dover, Delaware. Part of this estate is incorrectly filed in a separate listing under the surname First.

233. Joel Frist probate record, 1891–1892, New Castle County, Delaware, Delaware Public Archives, Dover, Delaware.

234. Research report 15 September 1984 from Thomas Ferran Frist (current address P.O. Box 1204, 98 Frist Road, Montreat, NC 28757 but in 1984 living in Boston, Massachusetts), copy from William H. Frist, M.D. Genealogical Collection.

235. Frist combination tombstone, photograph from William H. Frist, M.D. Genealogical Collection.

236. George Frist household, 1900 U.S. census, New Castle County, Delaware, population schedule. City of Wilmington, Ward Seven, enumeration district 26, sheet 8, line 37, dwelling 137, household 147; National Archives micropublication T623, roll 155. Also Joel Frist household, 1860 U.S. census, New Castle County, Delaware, population schedule, City of Wilmington, Ward Three, p. 837, dwelling and family 1235, microfilm 803098, Family History Library, Salt Lake City, Utah.

237. George Frist probate record, 1928 #11913, New Castle County, Delaware, Delaware Public Archives, Dover, Delaware.

238. Mrs. Catherine Frist death certificate #307 (1936), State of Delaware, Division of Vital Records. Marriage date approximated from birth of first child.

239. Joel Frist household, 1860 U.S. census, New Castle County, Delaware, population schedule, City of Wilmington, Ward Three, p. 837, dwelling and family 1235, microfilm 803098, Family History Library, Salt Lake City, Utah.

240. Waddington–Frist marriage, Marriage Book E:102, Holy Trinity (Old Swedes) Church, Church Archives, Wilmington, Delaware.

241. Henry Waddington household, 1900 U.S. census, New Castle County, Delaware, Wilmington, enumeration district 20, sheet 3, line 51, p. 245a; National Archives micropublication T623, roll 154.

242. Joel Frist household, 1860 U.S. census, New Castle County, Delaware, population schedule, City of Wilmington, Ward Three, p. 837, dwelling and family 1235, microfilm 803098, Family History Library, Salt Lake City, Utah. Also Harry M. Frist household, 1900 U.S. census New Castle County, Delaware, population schedule, enumeration district 35, sheet 19B, line 96, dwelling 397, family 408; National Archives micropublication T623, roll 155.

243. Gardner Hitchens household, 1920 U.S. census, New Castle County, Delaware, population schedule, enumeration district 92, sheet 4A, line 17, dwelling 57, family 65; National Archives micropublication T625, roll 202. Harry lived with this man in 1920.

244. Harry M. Frist household, 1900 U.S. census New Castle County, Delaware, population schedule, enumeration district 35, sheet 19B, line 96, dwelling 397, family 408; National Archives micropublication T623, roll 155.

245. Jacob Frist tombstone, Citizens Cemetery, Chattanooga, Tennessee, photograph from William H. Frist, M.D. Genealogical Collection.

246. Jacob Frist Family Bible. Also Elizabeth Frist will, New Castle County, Delaware, Will Book S1:557–558, microfilm 6543, Family History Library, Salt Lake City, Utah.

247. Jacob Frist obituary, *Chattanooga Daily Times*, Chattanooga, Tennessee, 19 March 1879, from Senator William H. Frist, M.D. Genealogical Collection.

248. New Castle County, Delaware, Marriage Record, Volume 44:27, Record Group 1325, Delaware Public Archives, Dover, Delaware.

249. Zella Armstrong, *Hamilton County and Chattanooga, Tennessee, Volume 1* (1931; reprint, Johnson City, Tennessee: Overmountain Press, 1993), p. 209.

250. Jacob Frist Family Bible.

251. Jacob Frist Family Bible. The Bible does not prove Crissa's surname, but Mary Ann (Baldwin) Frist's death certificate does.

252. Mary Ann (Baldwin) Frist death certificate #43304 (1920), p. 153, Hamilton County, Tennessee, Tennessee State Library and Archives, Nashville, Tennessee.

253. Henry Frist household, 1820 U.S. census, New Castle County, Delaware, p. 127, line 12; National Archives micropublication M33, roll 4.

254. Elizabeth Frist household, 1830 U.S. census, New Castle County, Delaware, Christiana Hundred, p. 35, line 2; National Archives micropublication M19, roll 12.

255. Jacob Frist household, 1850 U.S. census, Richmond County, Georgia, population schedule, 73rd division, p. 483, household 660; National Archives micropublication M432, roll 81.

256. Tax lists, Richmond County, Georgia, Court of Ordinary, microfilm 234628, Family History Library, Salt Lake City, Utah.

257. Zella Armstrong, *Hamilton County and Chattanooga, Tennessee, Volume 1* (1931; reprint, Johnson City, Tennessee: Overmountain Press, 1993), p. 209.

258. *Art Work of Chattanooga, Tennessee* (Chicago: Gravure Illustration Company, 1917), p. 10.

259. Mary Ann Baldwin Frist interview, in unpublished manuscript of Wiltse, pp. 9–13, Chattanooga Public Library, Chattanooga, Tennessee. This was published in *Chattanooga News*, Chattanooga, Tennessee, 2 February 1917, copy from William H. Frist, M.D. Genealogical Collection.

260. "Williams Family Owns Early Land Purchases," *Chattanooga News Free Press*, Chattanooga, Tennessee, 17 July 1956, copy from William H. Frist, M.D. Genealogical Collection.

261. Centenary Methodist Church Historical Committee, *Centenary The Story of a Church* (Chattanooga: privately printed, 1962), pp. 17–18, copy from William H. Frist, M.D. Genealogical Collection.

262. Zella Armstrong, *Hamilton County and Chattanooga, Tennessee, Volume 1* (1931; reprint, Johnson City, Tennessee: Overmountain Press, 1993), p. 240.

263. Hamilton County, Tennessee, Deed Book 33:483, Register of Deeds, Chattanooga, Tennessee.

264. Jacob Frist household, 1860 U.S. census, Hamilton County, Tennessee, population schedule, Chattanooga, District 14, stamped p. 114B, dwelling 734, family 535; National Archives micropublication M653, roll 1253.

265. Hamilton County, Tennessee, Deed Book 14:305, Record N, Volume 1, Register of Deeds, Chattanooga, Tennessee.

266. Robert H. Frist service record, Compiled Service Records of Confederate Soldiers Who Served in Organizations from Tennessee, Company F, Fourth Confederate Cavalry (McLemore's), National Archives micropublication M268, roll 17, Tennessee State Library and Archives, Nashville, Tennessee.

267. Horace V. Frist Military Pension Application #909478, Fifth Delaware Infantry Regiment, National Archives, Washington, D.C.

268. Elizabeth Frist Orphans' Court case file, 1867, New Castle County, Delaware, Record Group 2840, Delaware Public Archives, Dover, Delaware.

269. Jacob Frist household, 1870 U.S. census, Hamilton County, Tennessee, population schedule, p. 698, dwelling 172, family 212; National Archives micropublication M593, roll 1532.

270. Hamilton County, Tennessee, Will Book 1:139, microfilm 83, Tennessee State Library and Archives, Nashville, Tennessee.

271. Jacob Frist death record (1879), Chattanooga, Tennessee, microfilm M-21, Tennessee State Library and Archives, Nashville, Tennessee.

272. Jacob Frist obituary, *Chattanooga Daily Times*, Chattanooga, Tennessee, 19 March 1879, clipping from William H. Frist, M.D. Genealogical Collection.

273. Ibid.

274. Mary Ann Frist interview, *Chattanooga News*, Chattanooga, Tennessee, 2 February 1917, clipping from William H. Frist, M.D. Genealogical Collection.

275. Mary Frist household, 1880 U.S. census, Hamilton County, Tennessee, population schedule, Chattanooga, p. 172, family 150; National Archives micropublication T9, roll 1259.

276. Mary E. Frist household, 1900 U.S. census, Hamilton County, Tennessee, population schedule, enumeration district 59, sheet 53, line 19; National Archives micropublication T623, roll 1574.

277. Hamilton County, Tennessee, Deed Book 169:460, Record M, Volume 7, Register of Deeds, Chattanooga, Tennessee.

278. Hamilton County, Tennessee, Deed Book 33:483, Register of Deeds, Chattanooga, Tennessee.

279. Mary E. Frist household, 1910 U.S. census, Hamilton County, Tennessee, population schedule, enumeration district 50, sheet 9, line 21; National Archives micropublication T624, roll 1502.

280. Mary Ann Frist interview, *Chattanooga News*, Chattanooga, Tennessee, 2 February 1917, clipping from William H. Frist, M.D. Genealogical Collection.

281. Her numbers don't match the records found. It is true that she had six children, but only nineteen living grandchildren were located (twenty-three if you include those who died in infancy), and the nineteen included the two belonging to her stepson Robert Harris Frist. She was accurate in stating that she had seven great-grandchildren (not including several who died as infants). She was also accurate in stating that six of them lived in Delaware, the children of her stepson Robert Harris Frist.

282. Mary Ann Frist death certificate #43304 (1920), p. 153, Hamilton County, Tennessee, Tennessee State Library and Archives, Nashville, Tennessee.

283. Mary Ann Frist obituary, *Chattanooga Daily Times*, Chattanooga, Tennessee, 22 February 1920, clipping from William H. Frist, M.D. Genealogical Collection.

284. The Historical Records Survey, *Hamilton County Tombstone Inscriptions, Volume II* (Nashville, Tennessee: Works Progress Administration, 1939), p. 6, Citizens Cemetery, Tennessee State Library and Archives, Nashville, Tennessee.

285. Jacob Frist Family Bible.

286. Robert Harris Frist, Death Register, Record Group 1500, p. 68 #65474, New Castle County, Delaware, Delaware Public Archives, Dover, Delaware.

287. St. James Methodist Episcopal Church, Newport, Delaware, Register No. 1 1874–1935, p. 102.

288. Jacob Frist Family Bible.

289. Jacob Frist Family Bible and James B. Frist obituary, *Chattanooga Daily News*, Chattanooga, Tennessee, 10 July 1925, p. 3, column 1.

290. James Frist household, 1880 U.S. census, Denton County, Texas, population schedule, precinct 3, enumeration district 105, p. 105B, dwelling and family 206; National Archives micropublication T9, roll 1300.

291. Hamilton County, Tennessee, Marriage Book 1884–1888, p. 266, County Clerk, Chattanooga, Tennessee.

292. Jacob Frist Family Bible.

293. Samuel Henry Frist death certificate #21603 (1939), Tennessee Bureau of Vital Records, Nashville, Tennessee.

294. Mrs. Estell Frist Rockwood obituary, *Chattanooga Times*, Chattanooga, Tennessee, 9 December 1958, p. 15, column 8, identifies her mother as Florence M. Curry Frist. Also Hamilton County, Tennessee, Deed Book 109:405 Record E:109, Hamilton County Register of Deeds, Chattanooga, Tennessee, identified her as Mary Florence.

295. Mrs. S. H. Frist death record (1913), Chattanooga Death Records, Volume 1911–1923, p. 24, microfilm M-21, Tennessee State Library and Archives, Nashville, Tennessee.

296. Jacob Frist Family Bible lists her as Susan Elizabeth both at birth and at her death, but descendants say she was Ann Elizabeth.

297. Mrs. Elizabeth Vetter obituary, undated clipping from unidentified newspaper, in family papers of William M. Vetter inherited and owned by his grandson John Stanley Vetter, M.D. (FristHealth Richmond Family Medicine, 921 Long Drive, Suite 101, Rockingham, NC 28379), copy held in 2003 by compiler.

298. "Happy Nuptials," undated clipping from unidentified newspaper, in family papers of William M. Vetter inherited and owned by his grandson John Stanley Vetter, M.D. (FristHealth Richmond Family Medicine, 921 Long Drive, Suite 101, Rockingham, NC 28379), copy held in 2003 by compiler.

299. Jacob Frist Family Bible.

300. Jacob Chester Frist death certificate #1519 (1919), Mississippi State Department of Health, Jackson, Mississippi.

301. Frist–Jones marriage, Jackson County, Ohio, Marriage Book J:399 #4247, Probate Court, Jackson, Ohio.

302. Jacob Frist Family Bible.

303. Joseph Elmer Frist death certificate #20872 (1940), Tennessee Bureau of Vital Records, Nashville, Tennessee.

304. Alice Frist obituary, 19 January 1911, *Chattanooga Daily Times*, Chattanooga, Tennessee, page 3, column 1.

305. Jacob Frist Family Bible.

306. Jacob Frist Family Bible.

307. Frist Family Group Sheets provided March 2001 by son Clarence Harold Frist (419 Turrentine Avenue, Gadsden, AL 35901) to compiler.

308. Joseph Hahn household, 1850 U.S. census, Preble County, Ohio, population schedule, Jefferson Township, p. 468, dwelling and family 1220; National Archives micropublication M432, roll 723.

309. John Frist will, Preble County, Ohio, Will Book C:178, Probate Court, Eaton, Ohio.

310. Herman Mayes Genealogical Collection.

311. Rose Shilt, *Preble County, Ohio, Marriage Records 1841–1859 Volume III* (Union City, Indiana: Gateway to the West Publications, no date), p. 50.

312. Audrey Gilbert, *Obituary Abstracts 1877–1895 from Preble County Newspapers in Preble County, Ohio, Volume II* (Utica, Kentucky: McDowell Publications, 1983), p. 150 citing *New Paris Mirror* 14 June 1894. Joseph's obituary listed all three of his marriages.

313. *History of Preble County, Ohio* (1881; reproduction, Evansville, Indiana: Unigraphic, Inc., 1972), p. 259.

314. Audrey Gilbert, *Obituary Abstracts 1877–1895 from Preble County Newspapers in Preble County, Ohio, Volume II* (Utica, Kentucky: McDowell Publications, 1983), p. 150 citing *New Paris Mirror* 14 June 1894.

315. Joseph Hahn household, 1850 U.S. census, Preble County, Ohio, population schedule, Jefferson Township, p. 468, dwelling and family 1220; National Archives micropublication M432, roll 723.

316. Mrs. Don Short and Mrs. Dale Bowers, *Preble County, Ohio, Marriage Records 1831–1840 From Marriage Book A Volume II* (No place, privately printed, no date), p. 23.

317. *History of Preble County, Ohio, with Illustrations and Biographical Sketches* (1881; reprint, Evansville, Indiana: Unigraphic Inc., 1972), p. 259.

318. Herman Mayes Genealogical Collection.

319. Rose Shilt, *Preble County, Ohio, Marriage Records 1841–1859 Volume III* (Union City, Indiana: Gateway to the West Publications, no date), p. 50.

320. Joseph Hahn household, 1860 U.S. census, Preble County, Ohio, population schedule, Jefferson Township, dwelling 1339, family 1288, p. 175, stamped p. 88; National Archives micropublication M653, roll 1026.

321. Joseph Hahn household, 1870 U.S. census, Preble County, Ohio, population schedule, Jefferson Township, stamped p. 137, dwelling 200, family 199; National Archives micropublication M593, roll 1259.

322. Joseph Hahn household, 1880 U.S. census, Preble County, Ohio, population schedule, enumeration district 199, sheet 20, line 40, dwelling and family 9, stamped p. 118, microfilm 1255060, Family History Library, Salt Lake City, Utah.

323. Audrey Gilbert, *Obituary Abstracts 1877–1895 from Preble County Newspapers in Preble County, Ohio, Volume II* (Utica, Kentucky: McDowell Publications, 1983), p. 150 citing *New Paris Mirror* 14 June 1894.

324. Audrey Gilbert, *Probate Abstracts Estates and Guardianships Preble County, Ohio, Cases 5000 to 5999 Book 5* (West Alexandria, Ohio: privately printed, 1999), p. 155 citing case #5814.

325. Audrey Gilbert, *Obituary Abstracts 1877–1895 from Preble County Newspapers in Preble County, Ohio, Volume II* (Utica, Kentucky: McDowell Publications, 1983), p. 150 citing *New Paris Mirror* 14 June 1894

326. Joseph Hahn household, 1860 U.S. census, Preble County, Ohio, population schedule, Jefferson Township, dwelling 1339, family 1288, p. 175, stamped p. 88; National Archives micropublication M653, roll 1026.

327. Audrey Gilbert, *Preble County, Ohio, Probate Abstracts Estates and Guardianships Cases 3000 through 3999* (West Alexandria, Ohio: privately printed, 1998), p. 125. In this court record, Samuel S. Hahn was named as son of the deceased Rebecca Hahn and heir of Susan Frist, thus John A. Hahn had died.

328. Joseph Hahn household, 1860 U.S. census, Preble County, Ohio, population schedule, Jefferson Township, dwelling 1339, family 1288, p. 175, stamped p. 88; National Archives micropublication M653, roll 1026.

329. Audrey Gilbert, *Abstracts from Preble County, Ohio, Newspaper Obituaries Book VII 1915–1918* (West Alexandria, Ohio: privately published, 1999), p. 167.

330. Darke County Genealogical Society, *Darke County, Ohio, Marriages 1851–1898* (No place: Darke County Genealogical Society, no date), p. 112.

331. The Mercer County Chapter of the Ohio Genealogical Society, *Probate Court Death Records Mercer County, Ohio, Book 1 1867–1888* (Celina, Ohio: no publisher, no date), p. 74.

332. John Frist will, Preble County, Ohio, Will Book C:178, Probate Court, Eaton, Ohio. Also David H. Frist Family Bible, previously discussed.

333. John Frist will, Preble County, Ohio, Will Book C:178, Probate Court, Eaton, Ohio.

334. David H. Frist Family Bible.

335. David H. Frist Family Bible.

336. David H. Frist Family Bible.

337. Wayne County, Indiana, Deed Book 9:438, microfilm 1753568, Family History Library, Salt Lake City, Utah.

338. Wayne County, Indiana, Deed Book 11:463, microfilm 1753569, Family History Library, Salt Lake City, Utah.

339. David Frist household, 1850 U.S. census, Wayne County, Indiana, population schedule, Wayne Township, p. 241, dwelling and family 254; National Archives micropublication M432, roll 180.

340. David H. Frist Family Bible.

341. David H. Frist Family Bible.

342. "Mr. and Mrs. Joseph A. Frist Celebrate Their 50th Anniversary," *Villisca Review and Letter*, Villisca, Iowa, newspaper clipping on fiftieth wedding anniversary of David and Lydia Frist's son Joseph, undated, possibly February 1925, typescript copy held in 2003 by compiler.

343. David H. Frist Family Bible.

344. Ibid.

345. Joseph Andrew Frist death record (1939), Page County, Iowa, Death Records Volume 2, p. 77, microfilm 1535553, Family History Library, Salt Lake City, Utah.

346. Page County, Iowa, Marriage Record Book 1:567, microfilm 1035209, Family History Library, Salt Lake City, Utah.

347. David H. Frist Family Bible.

348. John S. Frist household, 1880 U.S. census, Marion County, Iowa, population schedule, enumeration district 118, line 10, dwelling 91, family 93, stamped p. 482; National Archives micropublication T9, roll 354, Joseph Bivans identified as a brother-in-law lived with them, so Elizabeth A. may be née Bivans.

349. David H. Frist Family Bible.

350. Ibid.

351. David H. Frist Family Bible revealed that Rebecca married a man named Thomas. And Henry Thomas household, 1880 U.S. census, Dallas County, Iowa, population schedule, Boone Township, p. 275, dwelling and family 25; National Archives micropublication T9, roll 335. This census revealed the identity of her husband.

352. John Frist will, Preble County, Ohio, Will Book C:178, Probate Court, Eaton, Ohio. Also William Frist household, 1850 U.S. census, Preble County, Ohio, population schedule, Jefferson Township, p. 469, dwelling and family 1227; National Archives micropublication M432, roll 723.

353. John Frist will, Preble County, Ohio, Will Book C:178, Probate Court, Eaton, Ohio.

354. William H. Frist probate record, Preble County, Ohio, Will Book F:347, Probate Court, Eaton, Ohio.

355. Audrey Gilbert, *Probate Abstracts Preble County, Ohio, Estates and Guardianships Cases 2000 through 2999* (West Alexandria, Ohio: privately printed, 1998), p. 24.

356. Audrey Gilbert, *Obituary Abstracts 1896–1900 from Preble County Newspapers in Preble County, Ohio, Volume III* (No place, privately printed, 1985), p. 120.

357. William Frist household, 1850 U.S. census, Preble County, Indiana, population schedule, Jefferson Township, p. 469, dwelling and family 1227; National Archives micropublication M432, roll 723.

358. William H. Frist household, 1860 U.S. census, Preble County, Ohio, population schedule, Jefferson Township, p. 176, dwelling 1343, family 1292; National Archives micropublication M653, roll 1026.

359. William Frist household, 1870 U.S. census, Preble County, Ohio, population schedule, p. 138, dwelling and family 210; National Archives micropublication M593, roll 1259.

360. William H. Frist household, 1880 U.S. census, Preble County, Ohio, population schedule, Jefferson Township, enumeration district 199, sheet 21, line 42, dwelling and family 9, stamped p. 119; National Archives micropublication T9, roll 1060.

361. Audrey Gilbert, *Probate Abstracts Estates and Guardianships Preble County, Ohio, Book 4* (West Alexandria, Ohio: privately printed, 1999), p. 33 #5169.

362. William H. Frist probate record, Preble County, Ohio, Will Book F:347, Probate Court, Eaton, Ohio.

363. Audrey Gilbert, *Preble County, Ohio, Deaths 1867–1907* (Utica, Kentucky: McDowell Publications, no date), p. 57 and Audrey Gilbert, *Obituary Abstracts 1877–1895 from Preble County Newspapers in Preble County, Ohio, Volume II* (Utica, Kentucky: McDowell Publications, 1983), p. 34.

364. Audrey Gilbert, *Obituary Abstracts 1896–1900 from Preble County Newspapers in Preble County, Ohio, Volume III* (No place, privately printed, 1985), p. 120.

365. Audrey Gilbert, *Preble County, Ohio, the 1900 Federal Census* (Owensboro, Kentucky: Cook & McDowell Publications, 1980), p. 302.

366. Audrey Gilbert, *Abstracts from Preble County, Ohio, Newspaper Obituaries Book VIII 1919–1922* (West Carrollton, Ohio: Electronic Print Imagine Corporation, 2000), p. 144.

367. William H. Frist household, 1860 U.S. census, Preble County, Ohio, population schedule, Jefferson Township, p. 176, dwelling 1343, family 1292; National Archives micropublication M653, roll 1026.

368. Audrey Gilbert, *Preble County, Ohio, Marriages 1860–1898* (Owensboro, Kentucky: McDowell Publications, 1981), p. 93.

369. William H. Frist household, 1860 U.S. census, Preble County, Ohio, population schedule, Jefferson Township, p. 176, dwelling 1343, family 1292; National Archives micropublication M653, roll 1026.

370. Audrey Gilbert, *Obituary Abstracts 1877–1895 from Preble County Newspapers in Preble County, Ohio, Volume II* (Utica, Kentucky: McDowell Publications, 1983), p. 146. Catherine Letitia Frist died at the Dayton, Ohio, asylum.

371. William H. Frist household, 1860 U.S. census, Preble County, Ohio, population schedule, Jefferson Township, p. 176, dwelling 1343, family 1292; National Archives micropublication M653, roll 1026.

372. Audrey Gilbert, *Probate Abstracts Estates and Guardianships Preble County, Ohio, Cases 5000 to 5999 Book 5* (West Alexandria, Ohio: privately printed, 1999), p. 93 #5503.

373. Audrey Gilbert, *Abstracts from Preble County, Ohio, Newspaper Obituaries Book VIII 1919–1922* (West Carrollton, Ohio: Electronic Print Imagine Corporation, 2000), p. 144.

374. William H. Frist household, 1860 U.S. census, Preble County, Ohio, population schedule, Jefferson Township, p. 176, dwelling 1343, family 1292; National Archives micropublication M653, roll 1026.

375. William Frist household, 1870 U.S. census, Preble County, Ohio, population schedule, p. 138, dwelling and family 210; National Archives micropublication M593, roll 1259.

376. Audrey Gilbert, *Preble County, Ohio, Marriages 1860–1898* (Owensboro, Kentucky: McDowell Publications, 1981), p. 22.

377. Audrey Gilbert, *Probate Abstracts Estates and Guardianships Preble County, Ohio, Cases 5000 to 5999 Book 5* (West Alexandria, Ohio: privately printed, 1999), p. 93 citing file #5503.

378. William Frist household, 1870 U.S. census, Preble County, Ohio, population schedule, p. 138, dwelling and family 210; National Archives micropublication M593, roll 1259. Samuel C. was listed as eight years old in this census, but nothing further was found on him and he was not with the family in 1880.

379. William Frist household, 1870 U.S. census, Preble County, Ohio, population schedule, p. 138, dwelling and family 210; National Archives micropublication M593, roll 1259.

380. Audrey Gilbert, *Probate Abstracts Estates and Guardianships Preble County, Ohio, Cases 5000 to 5999 Book 5* (West Alexandria, Ohio: privately printed, 1999), p. 93 #5503 and copy of original provided by descendant to compiler, no source provided.

381. Audrey Gilbert, *Preble County, Ohio, the 1900 Federal Census* (Owensboro, Kentucky: Cook & McDowell Publications, 1980), p. 302.

382. Audrey Gilbert, *Probate Abstracts Estates and Guardianships Preble County, Ohio* (West Alexandria, Ohio: Privately printed, 2001), p. 62 citing file #12401.

383. Audrey Gilbert, *Preble County, Ohio, Marriages 1860–1898* (Owensboro, Kentucky: McDowell Publications, 1981), p. 38.

384. William H. Frist household, 1880 U.S. census, Preble County, Ohio, population schedule, Jefferson Township, , enumeration district 199, sheet 21, line 42, dwelling and family 9, stamped p. 119; National Archives micropublication T9, roll 1060.

385. Herman Mayes Genealogical Collection.

386. Russell Frist household, 1900 U.S. census, Madison County, Indiana, population schedule, Green Township, enumeration district 92, sheet 10, dwelling 179, family 184, stamped p. 323; National Archives micropublication T623, roll 386. This census proves the first name and the date of the marriage. Sarah Viola's surname came from Herman Mayes Genealogical Collection.

387. Robert M. Frist household, 1870 U.S. census, Warren County, Iowa, population schedule, city of Hartford, p. 430, dwelling 53, family 55; National Archives micropublication M593, roll 423.

388. John Frist will, Preble County, Ohio, Will Book C:178, Probate Court, Eaton, Ohio.

389. Audrey Gilbert, *Obituary Abstracts 1877–1895 from Preble County Newspapers in Preble County, Ohio, Volume II* (Utica, Kentucky: McDowell Publications, 1983), p. 14.

390. E. Coates deposition, Robert M. Frist's Civil War Soldiers Pension File #32387 and Widows Pension File #321253, National Archives, Washington, D.C.

391. Robert M. Frist, Civil War Soldiers Pension File #32387 and Widows Pension File #321253, National Archives, Washington, D.C.

392. Audrey Gilbert, *Obituary Abstracts 1877–1895 from Preble County Newspapers in Preble County, Ohio, Volume II* (Utica, Kentucky: McDowell Publications, 1983), p. 31.

393. Robert M. Frist, Civil War Soldiers Pension File #32387 and Widows Pension File #321253, National Archives, Washington, D.C.

394. Ibid.

395. Ibid.

396. Robert M. Frist household, 1870 U.S. census, Warren County, Iowa, population schedule, city of Hartford, p. 430, dwelling 53, family 55; National Archives micropublication M593, roll 423.

397. Robert M. Frist, Civil War Soldiers Pension File #32387 and Widows Pension File #321253, National Archives, Washington, D.C.

398. Audrey Gilbert, *Preble County, Ohio, 1880 Census* (Utica, Kentucky: McDowell Publications, 1983), p. 206.

399. Robert M. Frist, Civil War Soldiers Pension File #32387 and Widows Pension File #321253, National Archives, Washington, D.C.

400. Audrey Gilbert, *Obituary Abstracts 1877–1895 from Preble County Newspapers in Preble County, Ohio, Volume II* (Utica, Kentucky: McDowell Publications, 1983), p. 14.

401. Audrey Gilbert, *Obituary Abstracts 1877–1895 from Preble County Newspapers in Preble County, Ohio, Volume II* (Utica, Kentucky: McDowell Publications, 1983), p. 31.

402. Herman Mayes Genealogical Collection.

403. Hannah Etta Stevens obituary, *Liberty Herald*, Liberty, Indiana, 17 September 1936, p. 1.

404. John Stevens household, 1900 U.S. Census, Union County, Indiana, population schedule, Centre Township, enumeration district 130, sheet 5, dwelling and family 92, stamped p. 276; National Archives micropublication T623, roll 406.

405. Ruth C. Frist, Civil War Widows Pension File #321253, National Archives, Washington, D.C.

406. Martin L. Frist household, 1920 U.S. census, Lee County, Iowa, population schedule, Madison Township, enumeration district 85, sheet 21, line 59; National Archives micropublication T625, roll 499.

407. Roscoe E. Frist marriage application, Lee County, Iowa, Marriage Volume 14 1919–1922, p. 221, microfilm 1903295, Family History Library, Salt Lake City, Utah. Roscoe is Martin's son, and his own marriage record names his parents.

408. John Frist will, Preble County, Ohio, Will Book C:178, Probate Court, Eaton, Ohio.

409. Audrey Gilbert, *Obituary Abstracts 1877–1895 from Preble County Newspapers in Preble County, Ohio, Volume II* (Utica, Kentucky: McDowell Publications, 1983), p. 53 citing *New Paris Mirror* August 14, 1890.

410. Rose Shilt, *Preble County, Ohio, Marriage Records 1841–1859, Volume III* (Union City, Indiana: Gateway to the West Publications, no date), p. 102.

411. Charles Powell household, 1860 U.S. census, Wayne County, Indiana, population schedule, Wayne Township, stamped p. 747, dwelling 1525, family 1542; National Archives micropublication M653, roll 308.

412. Charles F. Powell household, 1880 U.S. census, Jay County, Indiana, population schedule, Bearcreek Township, enumeration district 152, sheet 11, stamped p. 385, dwelling 102, family 108, microfilm 1254287, Family History Library, Salt Lake City, Utah.

413. Audrey Gilbert, *Obituary Abstracts 1877–1895 from Preble County Newspapers in Preble County, Ohio, Volume II* (Utica, Kentucky: McDowell Publications, 1983), p. 53 citing *New Paris Mirror* August 14, 1890.

414. Charles Powell household, 1860 U.S. census, Wayne County, Indiana, population schedule, Wayne Township, stamped p. 747, dwelling 1525, family 1542; National Archives micropublication M653, roll 308.

415. Ibid.

416. Charles F. Powell household, 1880 U.S. census, Jay County, Indiana, population schedule, Bearcreek Township, enumeration district 152, sheet 11, stamped p. 385, dwelling 102, family 108, microfilm 1254287, Family History Library, Salt Lake City, Utah.

417. Herman Mayes Genealogical Collection and death record, book of Lynn #L-1 p. 40, Randolph County Health Department, Winchester, Indiana.

418. John Frist will, Preble County, Ohio, Will Book C:178, Probate Court, Eaton, Ohio.

419. Herman Mayes Genealogical Collection. Also death record, book of Lynn #L-1 p. 40, Randolph County Health Department, Winchester, Indiana.

420. Herman Mayes Genealogical Collection.

421. Ruby Haskins Ellis and Anna Petty Neal, *Lineage Book National Society of the Daughters of American Colonists, Volume 11, 1001–2000* (Washington, D.C: Judd & Detweiler, 1930), application of Mrs. James P. Goodrich, Winchester, Indiana, #1164.

422. Amy Frist obituary, *The Richmond Item*, Richmond, Indiana, 16 November 1920, p. 3.

423. Jonas Frist household, 1860 U.S. census, Wayne County, Indiana, population schedule, Wayne Township, p. 748, dwelling 1528, family 1545; National Archives micropublication M653, roll 308.

424. Jonas L. P. Frist household, 1880 U.S. census, Randolph County, Indiana, population schedule, City of Lynn, p. 271; National Archives micropublication T9, roll 307.

425. Dane Starbuck, *The Goodriches: An American Family* (Indianapolis, Indiana: Liberty Fund, Inc., 2001), p. 25.

426. Herman Mayes Genealogical Collection.

427. Amy Frist obituary, *The Richmond Item*, Richmond, Indiana, 16 November 1920, p. 3.

428. Ibid.

429. Dane Starbuck , *The Goodriches: An American Family* (Indianapolis, Indiana: Liberty Fund, Inc., 2001), p. 25.

430. Jonas Frist household, 1860 U.S. census, Wayne County, Indiana, population schedule, Wayne Township, p. 748, dwelling 1528, family 1545; National Archives micropublication M653, roll 308. Her birthplace is questionable, some say Randolph County, Indiana.

431. "Mrs. James P. Goodrich, Widow of State's World War Governor, Dies," *The Indianapolis Star*, Indianapolis, Indiana, 1 November 1941, p. 12.

432. Dane Starbuck, *The Goodriches: An American Family* (Indianapolis, Indiana: Liberty Fund, Inc., 2001), pp. 29–30.

433. Toda Juanita Frist Hecker obituary, undated from unknown newspaper, Patricia Frist Genealogical Collection, copy held in 2003 by compiler.

434. Toda Juanita Frist Hecker obituary and Sheldon Jonas Hecker obituary, both undated from unknown newspapers, Patricia Frist Genealogical Collection, copies held in 2003 by compiler.

435. Ibid.

436. Sheldon Jonas Hecker obituary, undated from unknown newspaper, Patricia Frist Genealogical Collection, copy held in 2003 by compiler.

437. Herman Mayes Genealogical Collection.

438. Mary Frist probate record, 1889–1881, New Castle County, Delaware, Delaware Public Archives, Dover, Delaware.

439. Elizabeth Lloyd probate record, 1907–1908, New Castle County, Delaware, Delaware Public Archives, Dover, Delaware.

440. Lloyd–Frist marriage, card file, Delaware Historical Society, Wilmington, Delaware, citing Asbury M. E. Church.

441. Franklin Lloyd household, 1850 U.S. census, New Castle County, Delaware, population schedule, p. 307B, dwelling 507, family 527, microfilm 6437, Family History Library, Salt Lake City, Utah.

442. Mary Frist probate record, 1889–1891, New Castle County, Delaware, Delaware Public Archives, Dover, Delaware.

443. Franklin Lloyd household, 1850 U.S. census, New Castle County, Delaware, population schedule, p. 307B, dwelling 507, family 527, microfilm 6437, Family History Library, Salt Lake City, Utah.

444. Mary Frist probate record, 1889–1891, New Castle County, Delaware, Delaware Public Archives, Dover, Delaware.

445. Elizabeth Lloyd household, 1870 U.S. census, New Castle County, Delaware, population schedule, p. 383, dwelling 163, family 174; National Archives micropublication M593, roll 121.

446. William C. Tindall household, 1880 U.S. census, New Castle County, Delaware, population schedule, Wilmington, enumeration district 14, sheet 64, line 41, dwelling 470, family 576, stamped p. 361, microfilm 1254119, Family History Library, Salt Lake City, Utah.

447. William Tindall household, 1900 U.S. census, New Castle County, Delaware, population schedule, Wilmington, enumeration district 28, sheet 23, line 7; National Archives micropublication T623, roll 155.

448. Elizabeth Lloyd probate record, 1907–1908, New Castle County, Delaware, Delaware Public Archives, Dover, Delaware.

449. Franklin Lloyd household, 1850 U.S. census, New Castle County, Delaware, population schedule, p. 307B, dwelling 507, family 527, microfilm 6437, Family History Library, Salt Lake City, Utah.

450. William Tindall household, 1900 U.S. census, New Castle County, Delaware, population schedule, Wilmington, enumeration district 28, sheet 23, line 7; National Archives micropublication T623, roll 155. Elizabeth Lloyd listed two children as deceased.

451. Franklin Lloyd household, 1850 U.S. census, New Castle County, Delaware, population schedule, p. 307B, dwelling 507, family 527, microfilm 6437, Family History Library, Salt Lake City, Utah.

452. William Tindall household 1900 U.S. census, New Castle County, Delaware, population schedule, Wilmington, enumeration district 28, sheet 23, line 7; National Archives micropublication T623, roll 155. Elizabeth Lloyd listed two children as deceased.

453. Elizabeth Lloyd household, 1870 U.S. census, New Castle County, Delaware, population schedule, p. 383, dwelling 163, family 174; National Archives micropublication M593, roll 121.

454. Ella Tindall probate record, 17579, 1932, New Castle County, Delaware, Delaware Public Archives, Dover, Delaware.

455. Elizabeth Lloyd probate record, 1907–1908, New Castle County, Delaware, Delaware Public Archives, Dover, Delaware.

456. Elizabeth Lloyd household, 1870 U.S. census, New Castle County, Delaware, population schedule, p. 383, dwelling 163, family 174; National Archives micropublication M593, roll 121.

457. Elizabeth J. Randle probate record, 20581, 1939, New Castle County, Delaware, Delaware Public Archives, Dover, Delaware.

458. Elizabeth Lloyd probate record, 1907–1908, New Castle County, Delaware, Delaware Public Archives, Dover, Delaware. Her mother's will written in 1899 proves that she was married to Joseph A. Randall by that year, but the marriage probably took place about 1890.

459. Herman Mayes Genealogical Collection.

460. Elizabeth Frist Orphans' Court case file, 1867, Record Group 2840, New Castle County, Delaware, Delaware Public Archives, Dover, Delaware. Although Henry was not named in his mother's will, all five of Jediah's children were named in the estate of Jediah's mother, Elizabeth Frist.

461. Mary Fallon Richards and John C. Richards, eds., *Delaware Marriages and Deaths from Newspapers 1729–1853* (Westminster, Maryland: Family Line Publications, 1997), p. 95.

462. Catherine C. Frist, Civil War Delaware Widow's Pension Application #193503, National Archives, Washington, D.C.

463. Catherine Frist, Church Yard Record #572, Holy Trinity (Old Swedes) Church, Church Archives, Wilmington, Delaware.

464. New Castle County, Delaware, Deed Book Y5:116, Delaware Public Archives, Dover, Delaware.

465. Henry Frist household, 1850 U.S. census, New Castle County, Delaware, population schedule, p. 49, dwelling 696, family 728, microfilm 6437, Family History Library, Salt Lake City, Utah.

466. New Castle County, Delaware, Deed Book U6:337–339, Delaware Public Archives, Dover, Delaware.

467. New Castle County, Delaware, Deed Book G6:298–299, Delaware Public Archives, Dover, Delaware.

468. Henry Frist household, 1860 U.S. census, New Castle County, Delaware, population schedule, City of Wilmington, Ward Three, p. 850, dwelling 1324, family 1428, microfilm 803098, Family History Library, Salt Lake City, Utah.

469. Henry Frist service record, U.S. War Department, Delaware Military Service Records Fifth Delaware Infantry, National Archives, Washington, D.C.

470. Henry and Catherine Frist, Civil War Delaware Widow's Pension Application #193503, National Archives, Washington, D.C.

471. Horace V. Frist service record, U.S. War Department, Delaware Military Service Records, Fifth Delaware Infantry, National Archives, Washington, D.C.

472. William S. Frist service record, U.S. War Department, Delaware Military Service Records, Seventh Delaware Infantry, National Archives, Washington, D.C.

473. Catherine C. Frist, Civil War Delaware Widow's Pension Application #193503, National Archives, Washington, D.C.

474. Mary Fallon Richards and John C. Richards, eds., *Delaware Marriages and Deaths from Newspapers 1729–1853* (Westminster, Maryland: Family Line Publications, 1997), p. 95.

475. Henry Frist loose estate, Chester County, Pennsylvania, Orphans Court Docket 24, p. 549, Chester County Archives, West Chester, Pennsylvania.

476. Chester County, Pennsylvania, Deed Book X6:604–606, Chester County Archives, West Chester, Pennsylvania.

477. Catherine Frist household, 1870 U.S. census, New Castle County, Delaware, population schedule, Wilmington, p. 210B, dwelling 323, family 328; National Archives micropublication M593, roll 121.

478. Henry Frist Orphans' Court case file, 1865–1877, New Castle County, Delaware, Record Group 2840, Delaware Public Archives, Dover, Delaware.

479. Catherine C. Frist household, 1880 U.S. census, New Castle County, Delaware, population schedule, Wilmington, enumeration district 16, sheet 47, line 14 [edge of page damaged, lines counted], dwelling 414, family 420, stamped p. 425; National Archives micropublication T9, roll 119.

480. Catherine Frist burial, Church Yard Record #572, Holy Trinity (Old Swedes) Church Archives, Wilmington, Delaware.

481. William Frist burial, Church Yard Record Book A:177 #983, Holy Trinity (Old Swedes) Church Archives, Wilmington, Delaware.

482. William S. Frist service record, U.S. War Department, Delaware Military Service Records, Seventh Delaware Infantry, National Archives, Washington, D.C.

483. J. Thomas Scharf, *History of Delaware 1609–1888, Volume 1* (1888; reprint, Westminster, Maryland: Family Line Publications, 1990), pp. 563–564.

484. Catherine C. Frist, Civil War Delaware Widow's Pension Application #193503, National Archives, Washington, D.C.

485. Horace V. Frist, U.S. Military Pension file #909478, #1008, Bundle 7, National Archives, Washington, D.C.

486. Horace V. Frist household, 1900 U.S. census, New Castle County, Delaware, population schedule, Wilmington, enumeration district 24, sheet 3, line 35 dwelling 80, family 86; National Archives micropublication T623, roll 155.

487. Catherine C. Frist, Civil War Delaware Widow's Pension Application #193503, National Archives, Washington, D.C.

488. Ibid.

489. Henry Campbell Frist burial, Church Yard Record #1227, Holy Trinity (Old Swedes) Church Archives, Wilmington, Delaware.

490. George W. Ortlin hotel, 1900 U.S. census, New Castle County, Delaware, population schedule, Wilmington, enumeration district 26, sheet 2, line 54 dwelling 23, family 27; National Archives micropublication T623, roll 155.

491. Catherine C. Frist, Civil War Delaware Widow's Pension Application #193503, National Archives, Washington, D.C.

492. New Castle County, Delaware, Volume 41:42, Delaware Public Archives, Dover, Delaware.

493. Catherine C. Frist, Civil War Delaware Widow's Pension Application #193503, National Archives, Washington, D.C.

494. Herman Frist burial, Church Yard Record #1379, Holy Trinity (Old Swedes) Church Archives, Wilmington, Delaware.

495. Frist–Hume marriage, Marriage Book M-2:75, Holy Trinity (Old Swedes) Church Archives, Wilmington, New Castle County, Delaware.

496. Herman Mayes Genealogical Collection.

497. Mary Frist probate record, 1889–1881, New Castle County, Delaware, Delaware Public Archives, Dover, Delaware.

498. Esther Ann Springer probate record, 1909–1910, New Castle County, Delaware, Delaware Public Archives, Dover, Delaware.

499. Herman Mayes Genealogical Collection.

500. Mary Frist household, 1850 U.S. census, New Castle County, Delaware, population schedule, p. 024, dwelling 322, family 338, microfilm 6437, Family History Library, Salt Lake City, Utah.

501. Levi H. Springer probate record, 1894, New Castle County, Delaware, Delaware Public Archives, Dover, Delaware.

502. Mary Frist household, 1850 U.S. census, New Castle County, Delaware, population schedule, p. 024, dwelling 322, family 338, microfilm 6437, Family History Library, Salt Lake City, Utah.

503. Levi H. Springer household, 1880 U.S. census, New Castle County, Delaware, population schedule, enumeration district 5, p. 132B, dwelling 320, family 435, microfilm 1254118, Family History Library, Salt Lake City, Utah.

504. John E. Springer probate record, 1887, New Castle County, Delaware, Delaware Public Archives, Dover, Delaware.

505. Levi H. Springer probate record, 1894, New Castle County, Delaware, Delaware Public Archives, Dover, Delaware.

506. Edwin J. Sheppard household, 1900 U.S. census, New Castle County, Delaware, population schedule, Wilmington, enumeration district 45, sheet 24, line 32; National Archives micropublication T623, roll 156.

507. Esther Ann Springer probate record, 1909–1910, New Castle County, Delaware, Delaware Public Archives, Dover, Delaware.

508. Mary Frist household, 1850 U.S. census, New Castle County, Delaware, population schedule, p. 024, dwelling 322, family 338, microfilm 6437, Family History Library, Salt Lake City, Utah.

509. Morris D. Crossan probate record, 8198, 1924, New Castle County, Delaware, Delaware Public Archives, Dover, Delaware.

510. Mary Frist household, 1850 U.S. census, New Castle County, Delaware, population schedule, p. 024, dwelling 322, family 338, microfilm 6437, Family History Library, Salt Lake City, Utah.

511. John E. Springer household, 1880 U.S. Census, New Castle County, Delaware, population schedule, Wilmington, Ward 8, enumeration district 17, sheet 1, line 1, dwelling and family 1, microfilm 1254119, Family History Library, Salt Lake City, Utah. Also John E. Springer probate record, 1887, New Castle County, Delaware, Delaware Public Archives, Dover, Delaware.

512. Esther Ann Springer probate record, 1909–1910, New Castle County, Delaware, Delaware Public Archives, Dover, Delaware.

513. Herman Mayes Genealogical Collection.

514. Levi H. Springer probate record, 1894, New Castle County, Delaware, Delaware Public Archives, Dover, Delaware. Levi Rudolph not named in the will or listed as an heir.

515. Willard Springer household, 1900 U.S. census, New Castle County, Delaware, population schedule, Wilmington Hundred, enumeration district 16, sheet 1, line 39, p. 201; National Archives micropublication, T623, roll 154.

516. Etta F. Springer probate record, 24822, 1942 New Castle County, Delaware, Delaware Public Archives, Dover, Delaware.

517. Willard Springer household, 1900 U. S. census, New Castle County, Delaware, population schedule, Wilmington Hundred, enumeration district 16, sheet 1, line 39, p. 201; National Archives micropublication T623, roll 154.

518. Levi H. Springer household, 1880 U.S. census, New Castle County, Delaware, population schedule, enumeration district 5, p. 132B, dwelling 320, family 435, microfilm 1254118, Family History Library, Salt Lake City, Utah.

519. Levi H. Springer probate record, 1894, New Castle County, Delaware, Delaware Public Archives, Dover, Delaware.

520. Edwin J. Sheppard household, 1900 U.S. census, New Castle County, Delaware, population schedule, Wilmington, enumeration district 45, sheet 24, line 32; National Archives micropublication T623, roll 156.

521. Kallena Sheppard probate record, 29157, 1950, New Castle County, Delaware, Delaware Public Archives, Dover, Delaware.

522. Edwin Sheppard household, 1900 U.S. census, New Castle County, Delaware, population schedule, Wilmington, enumeration district 45, sheet 24, line 32; National Archives micropublication T623, roll 156.

523. Herman Mayes Genealogical Collection.

524. Mary Frist probate record, 1889–1881, New Castle County, Delaware, Delaware Public Archives, Dover, Delaware.

525. Mary Frist probate record, 1889–1891, New Castle County, Delaware, Delaware Public Archives, Dover, Delaware. Mary Y. Way named in this estate for her mother.

526. Mary Fallon Richards and John C. Richards eds., *Delaware Marriages and Deaths from Newspapers 1729–1853* (Westminster, Maryland: Family Line Publications, 1997), p. 209.

527. Mary Frist probate record, 1889–1891, New Castle County, Delaware, Delaware Public Archives, Dover, Delaware.

528. Elizabeth Frist probate record, 1867, New Castle County, Delaware, and Elizabeth Frist, Orphans' Court case file, 1867, New Castle County, Delaware, Record Group 2840, both from Delaware Public Archives, Dover, Delaware. Both records for Mary's grandmother, Elizabeth Frist, name her as Mary Y. Way.

529. Elon Way household, 1870 U.S. census, Baltimore County, Maryland, population schedule, Baltimore, Ward 3, p. 507B, line 7; National Archives micropublication M593, roll 572.

530. Mary Frist probate record, 1889–1891, New Castle County, Delaware, Delaware Public Archives, Dover, Delaware.

531. Elizabeth Frist Orphans' Court case file, 1867, New Castle County, Delaware, Record Group 2840, Delaware Public Archives, Dover, Delaware.

532. Elon Way household, 1870 U.S. census, Baltimore County, Maryland, population schedule, Baltimore, Ward Three, p. 507B, line 7; National Archives micropublication M593, roll 572.

533. Robinson was the spelling in all other records found.

534. E. J. Way household, 1880 U.S. census, Baltimore County, Maryland, population schedule, City of Baltimore, enumeration district 31, sheet 18, line 19, dwelling 145, family 183, stamped p. 524; National Archives micropublication T9, roll 498.

535. A more accurate age would have been fifty-six.

536. Mary Frist probate record, 1889–1891, New Castle County, Delaware, Delaware Public Archives, Dover, Delaware.

537. Herman Mayes Genealogical Collection.

538. Elon Way household, 1870 U.S. census, Baltimore County, Maryland, population schedule, Baltimore, Ward Three, p. 507B, line 7; National Archives micropublication M593, roll 572.

539. Frank Peirce Frist Family Bible, from Patricia Frist Genealogical Collection.

540. Mary Frist probate record, 1889–1881, New Castle County, Delaware, Delaware Public Archives, Dover, Delaware.

541. Jediah Frist obituary, *Clinton Plaindealer*, Clinton, Indiana, 15 November 1907, clipping from Patricia Frist Genealogical Collection.

542. Herman Mayes Genealogical Collection.

543. Marietta Frist tombstone, Wilmington and Brandywine Cemetery, Wilmington, Delaware, photograph from William H. Frist, M.D. Genealogical Collection.

544. Mary Fallon Richards and John C. Richards, eds., *Marriages from the Delaware Gazette 1854–1859, 1861–1864* (Camden, Maine: Picton Press, no date), p. 37.

545. Alban Frist birth record, Vermillion County, Indiana, Birth Records, Volume 1, p. 100, County Clerk, Newport, Indiana. Alban was a son.

546. Herman Mayes Genealogical Collection.

547. Mary J. Frist obituary, handwritten, no date, from Patricia Frist Genealogical Collection.

548. Vermillion County, Indiana, Marriage Book 6:495, County Clerk, Newport, Indiana.

549. Herman Mayes Genealogical Collection.

550. Vermillion County, Indiana, Deed Book 17:354, Courthouse, Newport, Indiana.

551. Elizabeth Frist, Orphans' Court case file, 1867, New Castle County, Delaware, Record Group 2840, Delaware Public Archives, Dover, Delaware.

552. Jediah R. Frist household, 1870 U. S. census, Vermillion County, Indiana, population schedule, Subdivision #222 Helt Township, p. 34, dwelling 225, family 233; National Archives micropublication M593, roll 365.

553. Jediah R. Frist household, 1880 U.S. census, Vermillion County, Indiana, population schedule, Helt Township, enumeration district 192, p. 92B, dwelling 133, family 136; National Archives micropublication T9, roll 318.

554. Mary Frist obituary, no date from unidentified newspaper, copy from Patricia Frist Genealogical Collection.

555. Patricia Frist Genealogical Collection.

556. Vermillion County, Indiana, Marriage Book 6:495, County Clerk, Newport, Indiana.

557. Herman Mayes Genealogical Collection.

558. Jediah Frist household, 1900 U.S. census, Vermillion County, Indiana, population schedule, Helt Township, enumeration district 91, sheet 9, line 40, dwelling and family 173; National Archives micropublication T623, roll 408.

559. Jediah R. Frist will, Vermillion County, Indiana, Will Book 4:121-3, County Clerk, Newport, Indiana.

560. Jediah Frist obituary, *Clinton Plaindealer*, Clinton, Indiana, 15 November 1907, clipping from Patricia Frist Genealogical Collection.

561. Jediah Rudolph Frist, estate packet #483, Vermillion County, Indiana, Circuit Court, Newport, Indiana.

562. Herman Mayes Genealogical Collection.

563. Herman Mayes Genealogical Collection.

564. Frank Peirce Frist Family Bible.

565. Samuel Frist tombstone, Helt's Prairie Cemetery, Vermillion County, Indiana. Viewed in March 2001 by compiler.

566. Vermillion County, Indiana, Marriage Book 6:586, County Clerk, Newport Indiana.

567. Dora Frist tombstone, Helt's Prairie Cemetery, Vermillion County, Indiana. Viewed in March 2001 by compiler.

568. Patricia Frist Genealogical Collection.

569. Mr. and Mrs. Samuel Frist obituary, undated from unknown newspaper, Patricia Frist Genealogical Collection.

570. Samuel Frist household, 1900 U.S. census, Los Angeles County, California, population schedule, enumeration district 103, sheet 7, line 29; National Archives micropublication T623, roll 91. Also Samuel Frist household, 1920 U.S. census, Los Angeles County, California, population schedule, enumeration district 580, sheet 16A, line 47; National Archives micropublication T625, roll 118.

571. Frank Peirce Frist Family Bible.

572. "Jediah Frist, Pioneer County Resident Dead," undated obituary from unknown newspaper, Patricia Frist Genealogical Collection.

573. Ibid.

574. Vermillion County, Indiana, Marriage Book 5:354, County Clerk, Newport, Indiana.

575. Frank Peirce Frist Family Bible.

576. "Frist Celebrates 100 Years," *Daily Clintonian*, Clinton, Indiana, 26 December 1987. Clipping from Patricia Frist Genealogical Collection, background information on the Frist Funeral Home in Clinton, Indiana.

577. *History of Parke and Vermillion Counties Indiana* (Indianapolis, Indiana: B. F. Bowen & Company, 1913), p. 580.

578. Frank Peirce Frist Family Bible.

579. Joseph Henry Frist tombstone, Helt's Prairie Cemetery, Vermillion County, Indiana. Viewed in March 2001 by compiler.

580. Patricia Frist Genealogical Collection.

581. Frank Peirce Frist Family Bible.

582. Ibid.

583. Ibid.

584. Patricia Frist Genealogical Collection.

585. Frank Peirce Frist Family Bible.

586. Ibid.

587. Charles and Mary Peters tombstones, Helt's Prairie Cemetery, Vermillion County, Indiana. Viewed in March 2001 by compiler.

588. Patricia Frist Genealogical Collection.

589. Frank Peirce Frist Family Bible.

590. Frist Funeral Home Record, Clinton, Indiana, Patricia Frist Genealogical Collection.

591. Frank Peirce Frist Family Bible.

592. "Last Rites for Viola Frist, 82, to be Wednesday" undated clipping from unknown newspaper, Patricia Frist Genealogical Collection.

593. "Alban Frist, 87, Dies at Hospital," 17 May 1961, from unknown newspaper, Patricia Frist Genealogical Collection.

594. Marietta Frist death certificate #23025 (1909), Health Department, City of Baltimore, Maryland, microfilm CR 48,145, Maryland State Archives, Annapolis, Maryland.

595. Ibid.

596. William Frist household, 1850 U.S. census, Cecil County, Maryland, population schedule, Port Deposit, p. 157, dwelling 1050, family 1066; National Archives micropublication M432, roll 290. This is the only record found where James Frist was listed as William.

597. James Frist household, 1860 U.S. census, Cecil County, Maryland, population schedule, Seventh District, p. 590, dwelling 1938 and family 1896; National Archives micropublication M653, roll 472.

598. Cecil County, Maryland, Land Record AWM1:137–139, Land Office, Elkton, Maryland.

599. Marietta Frist household, 1880 U.S. census, Cecil County, Maryland, population schedule, Rising Sun, enumeration district 15, p. 208A, dwelling and family 6; National Archives micropublication T9, roll 507.

600. Cecil County, Maryland, Land Record JAD15:196–197, Land Office, Elkton, Maryland.

601. Marietta Frist household, 1900 U.S. census, Baltimore County, Maryland, population schedule, City of Baltimore, enumeration district 200, sheet 14, line 76, stamped p. 180; National Archives micropublication T623, roll 614.

602. Marietta Frist death certificate #23025 (1909), Health Department, City of Baltimore, Maryland, microfilm CR 48,145, Maryland State Archives, Annapolis, Maryland.

603. Donna J. Robertson, compiler, *Tombstone Inscriptions of Cecil County, Maryland* (Largo, Florida: privately printed, 1995), p. 180.

604. Hannah Frist death certificate #C23208 (1909), Health Department City of Baltimore, Maryland, microfilm CR 48,145, Maryland State Archives, Annapolis, Maryland.

605. Ibid.

606. William Frist household, 1850 U.S. census, Cecil County, Maryland, population schedule, Port Deposit, p. 157, dwelling 1050, family 1066; National Archives micropublication M432, roll 290. This is the only record found where James Frist was listed as William.

607. James Frist household, 1860 U.S. census, Cecil County, Maryland, population schedule, Seventh District, p. 590, dwelling 1938 and family 1896; National Archives micropublication M653, roll 472.

608. Marietta Frist household, 1880 U.S. census, Cecil County, Maryland, population schedule, Rising Sun, enumeration district 15, p. 208A, dwelling and family 6; National Archives micropublication T9, roll 507.

609. Marietta Frist household, 1900 U.S. census, Baltimore County, Maryland, population schedule, City of Baltimore, enumeration district 200, sheet 14, line 76, stamped p. 180; National Archives micropublication T623, roll 614.

610. Hannah Frist death certificate #C23208 (1909), Health Department City of Baltimore, Maryland, microfilm CR 48,145, Maryland State Archives, Annapolis, Maryland.

611. Donna J. Robertson, compiler, *Tombstone Inscriptions of Cecil County, Maryland* (Largo, Florida: privately printed, 1995), p. 180.

612. John Frist death certificate # C27264 (1909), Health Department, City of Baltimore, Maryland, Maryland State Archives, Annapolis, Maryland.

613. Ibid.

614. John Frist burial card, Lot 81, Section J, permit A1525, Loudon Park Cemetery, Baltimore City, Maryland.

615. Donna J. Robertson, compiler, *Tombstone Inscriptions of Cecil County, Maryland* (Largo, Florida: privately printed, 1995), p. 170. Also Annie James Frist tombstone, Hopewell United Methodist Church Cemetery in Cecil County, Maryland, photographed July 2002 by compiler Shirley Wilson (106 Leeward Point, Hendersonville, TN 37075).

616. "Accident and Loss of Life on the Susquehanna," *Cecil Democrat*, Elkton, Maryland, 9 July 1859, p. 2. Clipping from Margaret Hepner Genealogical Collection.

617. Baltimore City, Maryland, Marriage Index 1851–1885 citing Book 1:140; microfilm CR 1669, Maryland State Archives, Annapolis, Maryland.

618. Emily M. Frist burial card, Lot 81, Section J, permit 27152, Loudon Park Cemetery, Baltimore City, Maryland.

619. "Accident and Loss of Life on the Susquehanna," *Cecil Democrat*, Elkton, Maryland, 9 July 1859, p. 2. Clipping from Margaret Hepner Genealogical Collection.

620. Donna J. Robertson, compiler, *Tombstone Inscriptions of Cecil County, Maryland* (Largo, Florida: privately printed, 1995), p. 170.

621. Annie James Frist tombstone, Hopewell United Methodist Church Cemetery, Cecil County, Maryland, photographed in July 2002 by compiler.

622. Greg Howser household, 1860 U.S. census, Baltimore County, Maryland, population schedule, City of Baltimore, 18th Ward, p. 504, dwelling 2914, family 3170; National Archives micropublication M653, roll 465.

623. Baltimore City, Maryland, Marriage Index 1851–1885 citing Book 1:140; microfilm CR 1669, Maryland State Archives, Annapolis, Maryland.

624. John Frist household, 1870 U. S. census, Baltimore County, Maryland, population schedule, City of Baltimore, Ward 19, p. 284, line 24; National Archives micropublication M593, roll 580.

625. Baltimore County, Maryland, Deed Book 137:264, microfilm CR 1122, Maryland State Archives, Annapolis, Maryland.

626. Emily M. Frist burial card, Lot 81, Section J, permit 27152, Loudon Park Cemetery, Baltimore City, Maryland.

627. John Frist household, 1900 U.S. census, Baltimore County, Maryland, population schedule, City of Baltimore, enumeration district 199, sheet 7, line 78; National Archives micropublication T623, roll 614.

628. John Frist burial card, Lot 81, Section J, permit A1525, Loudon Park Cemetery, Baltimore City, Maryland.

629. Baltimore City, Maryland, Records of Orphans' Court, Book 105:548, microfilm CR 315, Maryland State Archives, Annapolis, Maryland.

630. Baltimore City, Maryland, Records of Orphans' Court, Book 105:469, microfilm CR 315, Maryland State Archives, Annapolis, Maryland.

631. John Frist final accounting, Orphans' Court, Baltimore City, Maryland, Book 204:446, microfilm CR 9616, Maryland State Archives, Annapolis, Maryland.

632. Donna J. Robertson, compiler, *Tombstone Inscriptions of Cecil County, Maryland* (Largo, Florida: privately printed, 1995), p. 170. Also Annie James Frist tombstone, Hopewell United Methodist Church Cemetery in Cecil County, Maryland, photographed July 2002 by compiler Shirley Wilson (106 Leeward Point, Hendersonville, TN 37075).

633. John Edgar Frist death certificate (1912), Baltimore County, Maryland, Board of Health, F1912, Series C322-19, Acc. No. 50,126-19, location 2/56/9/8, Maryland State Archives, Annapolis, Maryland.

634. Baltimore City, Maryland, Marriage Index 1851–1885, microfilm CR 1669, Maryland State Archives, Annapolis, Maryland.

635. John Frist obituary, *The Jeffersonian*, Baltimore County, Maryland, 22 July 1912, page 5, column 3, microfilm M2936 January 1912–December 1912, Maryland State Archives, Annapolis, Maryland.

636. Eva Frist Stocksdale burial card, Lot 81, Section J, #11761, Loudon Park Cemetery, Baltimore City, Maryland.

637. Ida M. Stocksdale burial card, lot 81, grave 12 with undated obituary notice, Loudon Park Cemetery, Baltimore Maryland. Obituary lists her father as George W. Stocksdale.

638. Ida M. Stocksdale burial card, lot 81, grave 12 with undated obituary notice, Loudon Park Cemetery, Baltimore Maryland.

639. Donna J. Robertson, compiler, *Tombstone Inscriptions of Cecil County, Maryland* (Largo, Florida: privately printed, 1995), p. 170. Also Annie James Frist tombstone, Hopewell United Methodist Church Cemetery in Cecil County, Maryland, photographed July 2002 by compiler Shirley Wilson (106 Leeward Point, Hendersonville, TN 37075).

640. Hattie M. Emmart death certificate 11768 (1939), Maryland State Department of Health, Baltimore City, Maryland.

641. John Frist household, 1900 U.S. census, Baltimore County, Maryland, population schedule, City of Baltimore, enumeration district 199, sheet 7, line 78; National Archives micropublication T623, roll 614.

642. Alpheus W. Frist burial card, Lot 81, Section J, permit 37657, Loudon Park Cemetery, Baltimore City, Maryland.

643. James Frist household, 1830 U.S. census, Chester County, Pennsylvania, New Garden Township, p. 303, line 22; National Archives micropublication M19, roll 148. Abraham's birth year was found in three census listings, all cited in this sketch, one indicating 1822, another 1836, and a third 1818. He was taxed in 1848 in Cecil County, so the birth year of 1836 is clearly wrong. It is possible that he was the firstborn son.

644. Obituary of son William H. Frist, *Cecil Democrat*, Elkton, Maryland, 21 February 1885, Margaret Hepner Genealogical Collection. Hepner is a great-granddaughter (600 Falcon Bridge Drive, Joppa, MD 21085). This obituary identifies William H. Frist's father as "the late Abraham Frist." Copy held in 2003 by compiler.

645. Cecil County, Maryland, Marriage Book 1840–1851:39, Maryland State Archives, Annapolis, Maryland.

646. Mrs. Arthur (Elsie) Patterson Beaven, *Records of Callender and Patterson Family Cemetery* (Perryville, Maryland: Captain Jeremiah Baker Chapter DAR, 1942), page entitled "History of Families in Cemetery."

647. Baltimore City Marriage Index 1851–1885, microfilm CR 1669, Maryland State Archives, Annapolis, Maryland.

648. Abraham Frist household, 1860 U.S. census, Monroe County, Virginia, population schedule, City of Union Town, Post Office Peterstown, p. 947B, line 12; National Archives micropublication M653, roll 1363.

649. Julia Harris death certificate (1902) Cecil County, Maryland, copy from Margaret Hepner Genealogical Collection, copy held in October 2002 by compiler. Margaret obtained the copy from the Maryland State Archives, Annapolis, Maryland.

650. James Frist household, 1830 U.S. census, Chester County, Pennsylvania, New Garden Township, p. 303, line 22; National Archives micropublication M19, roll 148.

651. Cecil County, Maryland, Tax Assessments Book 1847–1848, Book 1849, and Book 1850, District Seven, no pagination, alphabetical by district, Cecil County Historical Society Library, Elkton, Maryland.

652. *Abraham B. Frist vs. Elizabeth C. Frist*, divorce filed 24 March 1857, Cecil County, Maryland, Chancery Court metal boxes Ended A-G, loose packet #300, Land Office, Elkton, Maryland.

653. Mrs. Arthur (Elsie) Patterson Beaven, compiler, *Records of Callender and Patterson Family Cemetery* (Perryville, Maryland: Captain Jeremiah Baker Chapter NSDAR, 1942), copies from Margaret Hepner Genealogical Collection obtained from DAR Library, Washington, no pagination.

654. Abraham Frist household, 1860 U.S. census, Monroe County, Virginia, population schedule, City of Union Town, Post Office Peterstown, p. 947B, line 12; National Archives micropublication M653, roll 1363.

655. Thomas Frist household, 1860 U.S. census, Monroe County, Virginia, population schedule, Union Town, post office Peterstown, p. 947B, line 2; National Archives micropublication M653, roll 1363.

656. Oren F. Morton, *A History of Monroe County, West Virginia* (Staunton, Virginia: The McClure Company, 1916), pp. 429, 440.

657. Oren F. Morton, *A History of Monroe County, West Virginia* (Staunton, Virginia: The McClure Company, 1916), p. 433.

658. Abram Frist household, 1870 U.S. census, Cecil County, Maryland, population schedule, Port Deposit, p. 243, dwelling and family 2; National Archives micropublication M593, roll 583.

659. This was four years younger than he was in 1860, so there is an obvious error.

660. Cecil County, Maryland, Deed Book 4:276, Land Records Office, Elkton, Maryland.

661. Clifton Morse Brubaker, "Copy of the Records from the Church Register of the Port Deposit Presbyterian Church 1938–1943—Book 1 for the 150th Port Deposit Presbyterian Church Celebration 1838–1988," p. 30. This is an unpublished manuscript available at the Port Deposit Library, Port Deposit, Maryland.

662. Abram Frist household, 1880 U.S. census, Cecil County, Maryland, population schedule, Port Deposit, enumeration district 17, p. 258A, dwelling and family 65; National Archives micropublication T9, roll 507.

663. Obituary of son William H. Frist, *Cecil Democrat*, Elkton, Maryland, 21 February 1885, Margaret Hepner Genealogical Collection. Hepner is a great-granddaughter (600 Falcon Bridge Drive, Joppa, MD 21085). This obituary identifies William H. Frist's father as "the late Abraham Frist." Copy held in 2003 by compiler.

664. "Married," Harris–Frist marriage, *Cecil Whig*, Elkton, Maryland, 9 May 1885, p. 3, Cecil County Library, Elkton, Maryland.

665. Genealogical Society of Cecil County, *1860 U.S. Census for Cecil County, Maryland* (Charlestown, Maryland: Genealogical Society of Cecil County, 1989), p. 19.

666. Harman [*sic*] Harris household, 1900 U.S. census, Cecil County, Maryland, population schedule, Port Deposit, enumeration district 25, sheet 2, dwelling 38, family 38; National Archives micropublication T623, roll 620.

667. Julia Harris death certificate (1902) Port Deposit, Cecil County, Maryland, from Margaret Hepner Genealogical Collection, obtained from Maryland State Archives, Annapolis, Maryland. Copy held in October 2002 by compiler

668. *Cecil County, Maryland, Tombstone Inscriptions, Districts 7, 8, & 9* (No place: Genealogical Society of Cecil County, 1992), p. 51.

669. Abraham Frist household, 1860 U.S. census, Monroe County, Virginia, population schedule, City of Union Town, Post Office Peterstown, p. 947B, line 12; National Archives micropublication M653, roll 1363.

670. Ibid.

671. Abram Frist household, 1870 U.S. census, Cecil County, Maryland, population schedule, Port Deposit, p. 243, dwelling and family 2; National Archives micropublication M593, roll 583.

672. *Cecil County, Maryland, Tombstone Inscriptions, Districts 7, 8, & 9* (No place: Genealogical Society of Cecil County, 1992), p. 51.

673. Abraham Frist household, 1860 U.S. census, Monroe County, Virginia, population schedule, City of Union Town, Post Office Peterstown, p. 947B, line 12; National Archives micropublication M653, roll 1363.

674. Abram Frist household, 1870 U.S. census, Cecil County, Maryland, population schedule, Port Deposit, p. 243, dwelling and family 2; National Archives micropublication M593, roll 583.

675. Abram B. Frist death certificate #73652 (1923), Health Department, Baltimore City, Maryland. Copy of original provided by Margaret Hepner (600 Falcon Bridge Drive, Joppa, MD 21085) and held in 2003 by compiler. This man's middle name was found as Bernard, Burton, and Burnett in various documents cited elsewhere, but two sons were given the middle name Bernard.

676. Frist–Zimmer marriage, Cecil County, Maryland, copy of original held in 2003 by compiler, Margaret Hepner Genealogical Collection.

677. Baltimore City, Maryland, Marriage Index 1886–1914, original card index, Maryland State Archives, Annapolis, Maryland.

678. Miss Audrey Abraham (Port Deposit, MD 21904), telephone conversation 14 August 2002 with compiler.

679. Obituary of son William H. Frist, *Cecil Democrat*, Elkton, Maryland, 21 February 1885, Margaret Hepner Genealogical Collection. Hepner is a great-granddaughter (600 Falcon Bridge Drive, Joppa, MD 21085). This obituary identifies William H. Frist's father as "the late Abraham Frist." Copy held in 2003 by compiler.

680. Hattie Mary Mohrlein death certificate E59382 (1930), Health Department, Baltimore City, Maryland. Also George F. Morhline [*sic*] household, 1900 U.S. census, Cecil County, Maryland, population schedule, Port Deposit, enumeration district 25, sheet 2, dwelling 37, family 37; National Archives micropublication T623, roll 620.

681. Thomas Frist household, 1860 U.S. census, Monroe County, Virginia, population schedule, Union Town, post office Peterstown, p. 947B, line 2; National Archives micropublication M653, roll 1363.

682. Rose W. Peterson, compiler, *Spring Hill Cemetery, Charleston, West Virginia, Volume III, L–R* (Nitro, West Virginia: Peterson Quality Associates, 1995), p. 197.

683. Thomas and William Frist obituary, Index of Obits and Marriages in *Baltimore Sun* 1871–1875, Volume 1 A–J, Enoch Pratt Library, Baltimore City, Maryland.

684. Rose W. Peterson, compiler, *Spring Hill Cemetery, Charleston, West Virginia, Volume III, L–R* (Nitro, West Virginia: Peterson Quality Associates, 1995), p. 197.

685. Thomas Frist household, 1860 U.S. census, Monroe County, Virginia, population schedule, Union Town, Peterstown, p. 947B, line 2; National Archives micropublication M653, roll 1363.

686. Rose W. Peterson, compiler, *Spring Hill Cemetery, Charleston, West Virginia, Volume III, L–R* (Nitro, West Virginia: Peterson Quality Associates, 1995), p. 197.

687. Thomas Frist household, 1860 U.S. census, Monroe County, Virginia, population schedule, Union Town, Peterstown, p. 947B, line 2; National Archives micropublication M653, roll 1363.

688. Thomas and William Frist obituary, Index of Obits and Marriages in *Baltimore Sun* 1871–1875, Volume 1 A–J, Enoch Pratt Library, Baltimore City, Maryland.

689. Rose W. Peterson, compiler, *Spring Hill Cemetery, Charleston, West Virginia, Volume III, L–R* (Nitro, West Virginia: Peterson Quality Associates, 1995), p. 197.

690. Kanawha County, West Virginia, Deed Book 32:452, microfilm 460,432, Family History Library, Salt Lake City, Utah.

691. Sarah Frist household, 1880 U.S. census, Kanawha County, West Virginia, population schedule, Charleston, enumeration district 61, p. 454, dwelling and family 136; National Archives micropublication T9, roll 1405.

692. Kanawha County, West Virginia, Deed Book 58:581, microfilm 460,445, Family History Library, Salt Lake City, Utah.

693. Sarah E. Frist household, 1900 U.S. census, Kanawha County, West Virginia, population schedule, enumeration district 44, sheet 4, line 31, stamped p. 172, dwelling 79, family 82; National Archives micropublication T623, roll 1762.

694. Burton Frist household, 1900 U.S. census, Kanawha County, West Virginia, population schedule, p. 172, enumeration district 44, sheet 4, dwelling 80 family 83; National Archives micropublication T623, roll 1762.

695. Rose W. Peterson, compiler, *Spring Hill Cemetery, Charleston, West Virginia, Volume III, L–R* (Nitro, West Virginia: Peterson Quality Associates, 1995), p. 197.

696. Lena J. Frist household, 1920 U.S. census, Kanawha County, West Virginia, population schedule, Charleston, precinct 25, enumeration district 111, sheet 9, line 93; National Archives micropublication T625, roll 1958.

697. Rose W. Peterson, *Spring Hill Cemetery, Charleston, West Virginia, Volume III, L–R* (Nitro, West Virginia: Peterson Quality Associates, 1995), p. 197.

698. Burton Kyle Frist death record (1923), Kanawha County, West Virginia, Volume 2:187, microfilm 460367, Family History Library, Salt Lake City, Utah.

699. Rose W. Peterson, *Spring Hill Cemetery, Charleston, West Virginia, Volume III, L–R* (Nitro, West Virginia: Peterson Quality Associates, 1995), p. 197.

700. Burton Frist household, 1880 U.S. census, Kanawha County, West Virginia, population schedule, Charleston, sheet 18, stamped p. 454, line 28; National Archives micropublication T9, roll 1405.

701. W. S. Laidley, *History of Charles and Kanawha County, West Virginia, and Representative Citizen* (1911; reprint, Waynesville, North Carolina: Don Mills, 1993), p. 918.

702. Sarah E. Frist household, 1900 U.S. census, Kanawha County, West Virginia, population schedule, enumeration district 44, sheet 4, line 31, stamped p. 172, dwelling 79, family 82; National Archives micropublication T623, roll 1762. Although the census says 1856, the correct year must be 1857.

703. Selena Jane Frist death record, Kanawha County, West Virginia, Volume 3:195, microfilm 460367; Family History Library, Salt Lake City, Utah.

704. Rose W. Peterson, *Spring Hill Cemetery, Charleston, West Virginia, Volume III, L–R* (Nitro, West Virginia: Peterson Quality Associates, 1995), p. 197.

705. Ibid.

706. Sarah E. Frist household, 1900 U.S. census, Kanawha County, West Virginia, population schedule, enumeration district 44, sheet 4, line 31, stamped p. 172, dwelling 79, family 82; National Archives micropublication T623, roll 1762.

707. Jennie Louise Frist death record (1926), Kanawha County, West Virginia, Volume 2:278, microfilm 460367, Family History Library, Salt Lake City, Utah.

708. Rose W. Peterson, *Spring Hill Cemetery, Charleston, West Virginia, Volume III, L–R* (Nitro, West Virginia: Peterson Quality Associates, 1995), p. 197.

709. Rose W. Peterson, *Spring Hill Cemetery, Charleston, West Virginia, Volume III, L–R* (Nitro, West Virginia: Peterson Quality Associates, 1995), p. 197. Also Sarah E. Frist household, 1900 U.S. census, Kanawha County, West Virginia, population schedule, enumeration district 44, sheet 4, line 31, stamped p. 172, dwelling 79, family 82; National Archives micropublication T623, roll 1762. She was shown in cemetery book as born in November 1863 but was age thirty-three in 1900 census.

710. Rose W. Peterson, *Spring Hill Cemetery, Charleston, West Virginia, Volume III, L–R* (Nitro, West Virginia: Peterson Quality Associates, 1995), p. 197.

711. Sarah E. Frist household, 1900 U.S. census, Kanawha County, West Virginia, population schedule, enumeration district 44, sheet 4, line 31, stamped p. 172, dwelling 79, family 82; National Archives micropublication T623, roll 1762.

712. Rose W. Peterson, *Spring Hill Cemetery, Charleston, West Virginia, Volume III, L–R* (Nitro, West Virginia: Peterson Quality Associates, 1995), p. 197.

713. Marriage estimated from birth date of first child.

714. Roy Thomas Frist social security application 235-50-2020, U.S. Social Security Administration. Roy was a son, and his application listed his parents as Thomas Jackson Frist and Laura Jane Chapman.

715. Sarah E. Frist household, 1900 U.S. census, Kanawha County, West Virginia, population schedule, enumeration district 44, sheet 4, line 31, stamped p. 172, dwelling 79, family 82; National Archives micropublication T623, roll 1762.

716. Rose W. Peterson, *Spring Hill Cemetery, Charleston, West Virginia, Volume III, L–R* (Nitro, West Virginia: Peterson Quality Associates, Inc., 1995), p. 197.

717. James Frist death certificate #11012 (1908), Baltimore City, Maryland, microfilm CR48140, Maryland State Archives, Annapolis, Maryland.

718. William Frist household, 1850 U.S. census, Cecil County, Maryland, population schedule, Port Deposit, p. 157; National Archives micropublication M432, roll 290. This is the only record where the father James Frist was found listed as William, and he was never found with the initial W.

719. James Frist death certificate #11012 (1908), Baltimore City, Maryland, microfilm CR48140, Maryland State Archives, Annapolis, Maryland.

720. Baltimore City, Maryland, Marriage Book 4:152, microfilm CR 10,279, Maryland State Archives, Annapolis, Maryland.

721. James Frist household, 1880 U.S. census, Baltimore County, Maryland, population schedule, City of Baltimore, p. 248, sheet 12, line 1, microfilm 1254501, Family History Library, Salt Lake City, Utah.

722. Baltimore County, Maryland, Land Record 114:180-181, microfilm CR 1110, Maryland State Archives, Annapolis, Maryland.

723. Annie A. Frist obituary, *Baltimore Sun*, Baltimore City, Maryland, 26 September 1883, Margaret Hepner Genealogical Collection. Copy held in 2003 by compiler.

724. "Accident and Loss of Life on the Susquehanna," *Cecil Democrat*, Elkton, Maryland, 9 July 1859, p. 2, clipping from Margaret Hepner Genealogical Collection.

725. Donna J. Robertson, compiler, *Tombstone Inscriptions of Cecil County, Maryland* (Largo, Florida: privately printed, 1995), p. 170.

726. Greg Howser household, 1860 U.S. census, Baltimore County, Maryland, population schedule, City of Baltimore, Eighteenth Ward, p. 504, dwelling 2914, family 3170; National Archives micropublication M653, roll 465.

727. Baltimore City, Maryland, Marriage Book 4:152, microfilm CR 10,279, Maryland State Archives, Annapolis, Maryland.

728. Baltimore County, Maryland, Land Record 104:330–331, microfilm CR 1105, Maryland State Archives, Annapolis, Maryland.

729. Baltimore County, Maryland, Land Record 131:138–139, microfilm CR 1119, Maryland State Archives, Annapolis, Maryland.

730. Baltimore County, Maryland, Land Record 114:180–181, microfilm CR 1110, Maryland State Archives, Annapolis, Maryland.

731. James Frist household, 1880 U.S. census, Baltimore County, Maryland, population schedule, City of Baltimore, p. 248, sheet 12, line 1, microfilm 1254501, Family History Library, Salt Lake City, Utah.

732. Annie A. Frist obituary, *Baltimore Sun*, Baltimore City, Maryland, 26 September 1883, Margaret Hepner Genealogical Collection. Copy held in 2003 by compiler.

733. Baltimore City, Maryland, Orphans' Court Book RTB 55:461, Maryland State Archives, Annapolis, Maryland.

734. James Frist death certificate #11012 (1908), Baltimore City, Maryland, microfilm CR48140, Maryland State Archives, Annapolis, Maryland.

735. James Frist will, Baltimore City, Maryland, Will Book 102:334, microfilm CR 170, Maryland State Archives, Annapolis, Maryland.

736. James Frist household, 1880 U.S. census, Baltimore County, Maryland, population schedule, City of Baltimore, p. 248, sheet 12, line 1, microfilm 1254501, Family History Library, Salt Lake City, Utah.

737. James Frist will, Baltimore City, Maryland, Will Book 102:334, microfilm CR 170, Maryland State Archives, Annapolis, Maryland.

738. James Frist household, 1880 U.S. census, Baltimore County, Maryland, population schedule, City of Baltimore, p. 248, sheet 12, line 1, microfilm 1254501, Family History Library, Salt Lake City, Utah.

739. James Frist will, Baltimore City, Maryland, Will Book 102:334, microfilm CR 170, Maryland State Archives, Annapolis, Maryland.

740. Donna J. Robertson, compiler, *Tombstone Inscriptions of Cecil County, Maryland* (Largo, Florida: privately printed, 1995), p. 197.

741. James Frist household, 1860 U.S. census, Cecil County, Maryland, population schedule, Seventh District, p. 590, dwelling 1938 and family 1896; National Archives micropublication M653, roll 472.

742. Donna J. Robertson, compiler, *Tombstone Inscriptions of Cecil County, Maryland* (Largo, Florida: privately printed, 1995), p. 197.

743. Cecil County, Maryland, Marriages 1840–1863:82, Marriage Office, Elkton, Maryland.

744. George Haines probate packet, Cecil County, Maryland, 12 April 1877, Register of Wills, Elkton, Maryland.

745. Donna J. Robertson, compiler, *Tombstone Inscriptions of Cecil County, Maryland* (Largo, Florida: privately printed, 1995), p. 197.

746. James Frist household, 1860 U.S. census, Cecil County, Maryland, population schedule, Seventh District, p. 590, dwelling 1938 and family 1896; National Archives micropublication M653, roll 472.

747. Cecil County, Maryland, Land Record, Mortgages, CHH1:488, Land Office, Elkton, Maryland.

748. Cecil County, Maryland, Land Record, HRT3:420–421, Land Office, Elkton, Maryland.

749. Cecil County, Maryland, Land Record, Mortgages, HRT2:608-610, Land Office, Elkton, Maryland.

750. Cecil County, Maryland, Land Record, DS2:254–256, Land Office, Elkton, Maryland.

751. Edward Frist household, 1870 U.S. census, Cecil County, Maryland, population schedule, Port Deposit, seventh district, p. 271, dwelling and family 421; National Archives micropublication M593, roll 583.

752. The given names Edward and Edmund were both used, so much so that it is uncertain which is correct, but descendants believe and his tombstone reads Edmund.

753. George Haines probate packet, Cecil County, Maryland, 12 April 1877, Register of Wills, Elkton, Maryland.

754. Cecil County, Maryland, Land Record AWM10:73–74, Land Office, Elkton, Maryland.

755. Edward Frist household, 1880 U.S. census, Cecil County, Maryland, population schedule, Port Deposit, p. 271B, line 40, National Archives micropublication T9, roll 507.

756. Marietta Frist household, 1880 U.S. census, Cecil County, Maryland, population schedule, Rising Sun, enumeration district 15, p. 208A, dwelling and family 6; National Archives micropublication T9, roll 507.

757. Edward Frist household, 1900 U.S. census, Cecil County, Maryland, population schedule, Port Deposit, enumeration district 25, sheet 9, line 100; National Archives micropublication T623, roll 620.

758. George E. Frist household, 1900 U.S. census, Cecil County, Maryland, population schedule, enumeration district 25, sheet 9, line 93; National Archives micropublication T623, roll 620. Henrietta's surname from Herman Mayes Genealogical Collection.

759. Donna J. Robertson, compiler, *Tombstone Inscriptions of Cecil County, Maryland* (Largo, Florida: privately printed, 1995), p. 197. Exact dates from Herman Mayes Genealogical Collection.

760. Donna J. Robertson, compiler, *Tombstone Inscriptions of Cecil County, Maryland* (Largo, Florida: privately printed, 1995), p. 197.

761. Edward Frist household, 1870 U.S. census, Cecil County, Maryland, population schedule, Port Deposit, 7th district, p. 271, dwelling and family 421; National Archives micropublication M593, roll 583. Exact date from Herman Mayes Genealogical Collection.

762. George E. Frist household, 1900 U.S. census, Cecil County, Maryland, population schedule, enumeration district 25, sheet 9, line 93; National Archives micropublication T623, roll 620. Henrietta's surname from Herman Mayes Genealogical Collection.

763. Edward Frist household, 1870 U.S. census, Cecil County, Maryland, population schedule, Port Deposit, 7th district, p. 271, dwelling and family 421; National Archives micropublication M593, roll 583. Exact date from Herman Mayes Genealogical Collection.

764. Edmund Updegrove household, 1920 U.S. census, Cuyahoga County, Ohio, population schedule, Cleveland, enumeration district 527, sheet 18, line 97; National Archives micropublication T625, roll 1374. Pearl living with her father, listed as widowed.

765. Edmund B. Updegrove household, 1900 U.S. census, Cuyahoga County, Ohio, population schedule, Cleveland Township, enumeration district 102, sheet 11, line 93, stamped p. 29A; National Archives micropublication T623, roll 1255.

766. Donna J. Robertson, compiler, *Tombstone Inscriptions of Cecil County, Maryland* (Largo, Florida: privately printed, 1995), p. 194.

767. Ibid.

768. Cecil County, Maryland, Marriages 1886–1896:292, Marriage Office, Elkton, Maryland.

769. Edward Frist household, 1880 U.S. census, Cecil County, Maryland, population schedule, Port Deposit, p. 271B, line 40; National Archives micropublication T9, roll 507. Exact date from Herman Mayes Genealogical Collection.

770. Donna J. Robertson, compiler, *Tombstone Inscriptions of Cecil County, Maryland* (Largo, Florida: privately printed, 1995), p. 203.

771. Cecil County, Maryland, Marriages 1896–1911:96, Marriage Office, Elkton, Maryland.

772. Edward Frist household, 1880 U.S. census, Cecil County, Maryland, population schedule, Port Deposit, p. 271B, line 40; National Archives micropublication T9, roll 507. Exact date from Herman Mayes Genealogical Collection.

773. Donna J. Robertson, compiler, *Tombstone Inscriptions of Cecil County, Maryland* (Largo, Florida: privately printed, 1995), p. 197.

774. Cecil County, Maryland, Marriages 1910–1914:112, Marriage Office, Elkton, Maryland.

775. Edward Frist household, 1880 U.S. census, Cecil County, Maryland, population schedule, Port Deposit, p. 271B, line 40; National Archives micropublication T9, roll 507. Exact date from Herman Mayes Genealogical Collection.

776. Oliver Frist obituary, *Cecil County News*, Elkton, Maryland, 11 December 1935, column 3, Cecil County Historical Society Library, Elkton, Maryland. Also Donna J. Robertson, compiler, *Tombstone Inscriptions of Cecil County, Maryland* (Largo, Florida: privately printed, 1995), p. 215.

777. Baltimore City, Maryland, Marriage Index 1886–1914, original card index, Maryland State Archives, Annapolis, Maryland.

778. George Frist household, 1900 U.S. census, New Castle County, Delaware, population schedule. City of Wilmington, Ward 7, enumeration district 26, sheet 8, line 37, dwelling 137, household 147; National Archives micropublication T623, roll 155.

779. Joel Frist household, 1880 U.S. census, New Castle County, Delaware, population schedule, Wilmington Hundred, enumeration district 12, page 23, line 42, stamped p. 283, dwelling 225, family 228, microfilm roll 1254119, Family History Library, Salt Lake City, Utah.

780. George Frist probate record, 11913, 1928, New Castle County, Delaware, Delaware Public Archives, Dover, Delaware.

781. Joel Frist household, 1880 U.S. census, New Castle County, Delaware, population schedule, Wilmington Hundred, enumeration district 12, page 23, line 42, stamped p. 283, dwelling 225, family

228, microfilm 1254119, Family History Library, Salt Lake City, Utah. Marriage date approximated from birth of their first child Homer.

782. Mrs. Catherine Frist death certificate #307 (1936), Delaware Division of Vital Records, Dover, Delaware.

783. Ibid.

784. Catherine A. Frist probate record, 18905, 1936, New Castle County, Delaware, Delaware Public Archives, Dover, Delaware.

785. Joel Frist household, 1880 U.S. census, New Castle County, Delaware, population schedule, Wilmington Hundred, enumeration district 12, page 23, line 42, stamped p. 283, dwelling 225, family 228, microfilm 1254119, Family History Library, Salt Lake City, Utah.

786. George Frist household, 1900 U.S. census, New Castle County, Delaware, population schedule. City of Wilmington, Ward Seven, enumeration district 26, sheet 8, line 37, dwelling 137, household 147; National Archives micropublication T623, roll 155.

787. George Frist household, 1910 U.S. census, New Castle County, Delaware, population schedule, Wilmington City, enumeration district 40, sheet 2B, line 96, dwelling 39, family 52; National Archives micropublication T624, roll 147.

788. George Frist probate record, 11913, 1928, New Castle County, Delaware, Delaware Public Archives, Dover, Delaware.

789. Homer Frist household, 1930 U.S. census, New Castle County, Delaware, population schedule, Wilmington City, enumeration district 277, sheet 41A, line 13; National Archives micropublication T626, roll 290.

790. Catherine A. Frist probate record, 18905, 1936, New Castle County, Delaware, Delaware Public Archives, Dover, Delaware.

791. Catherine A. Frist death certificate #307 (1936), Delaware Department of Vital Records, Dover, Delaware.

792. Raymond H. Banks, compiler, *The Banks Compilation of Birth Data of Men with Links to New Castle County, Delaware, [including the city of Wilmington] Who Were Born 1873–1900* (No place: privately published, 1996).

793. Homer Frist household, 1930 U.S. census, New Castle County, Delaware, population schedule, Wilmington City, enumeration district 277, sheet 41A, line 13; National Archives micropublication T626, roll 290.

794. Catherine A. Frist probate record, 18905, 1936, New Castle County, Delaware, Delaware Public Archives, Dover, Delaware.

795. Herman Mayes Genealogical Collection.

796. Joel Frist household, 1860 U.S. census, New Castle County, Delaware, population schedule, City of Wilmington, Ward Three, p. 837, dwelling and family 1235, microfilm 803098, Family History Library, Salt Lake City, Utah. Also Harry M. Frist household, 1900 U.S. census New Castle County, Delaware, population schedule, enumeration district 35, sheet 19B, line 96, dwelling 397 family 408; National Archives micropublication T623, roll 155.

797. Gardner Hitchens household, 1920 U.S. census, New Castle County, Delaware, population schedule, enumeration district 92, sheet 4A, line 17, dwelling 57, family 65; National Archives micropublication T625, roll 202. Harry lived with this man in 1920.

798. Harry M. Frist household, 1900 U.S. census, New Castle County, Delaware, population schedule, enumeration district 35, sheet 19B, line 96, dwelling 397, family 408; National Archives micropublication T623, roll 155.

799. "Every Evening," *History of Wilmington, the Commercial, Social, and Religious Growth of the City during the Past Century* (Wilmington, Delaware: "Every Evening," 1894), 252.

800. Harry Frist household, 1880 U.S. census, New Castle County, Delaware, population schedule, E. Wilmington, enumeration district 12, p. 297, dwelling 281, family 290; National Archives micropublication T9, roll 119.

801. "Every Evening," *History of Wilmington, the Commercial, Social, and Religious Growth of the City during the Past Century* (Wilmington, Delaware: "Every Evening," 1894), 252.

802. Ibid.

803. Harry M. Frist household, 1900 U.S. census, New Castle County, Delaware, population schedule, enumeration district 35, sheet 19B, line 96, dwelling 397 family 408; National Archives micropublication T623, roll 155.

804. 1910 U.S. census, New Castle County, Delaware, population schedule, City of Wilmington, Ward Eight, enumeration district 50, sheet 18, line 11; National Archives micropublication T624, roll 147.

805. Gardner Hitchens household, 1920 U.S. census New Castle County, Delaware, population schedule, enumeration district 92, sheet 4A, line 17, dwelling 57, family 65; National Archives micropublication T625, roll 202.

806. Jacob Frist Family Bible.

807. Robert Harris Frist, Death Register, Record Group 1500, p. 68, #65474, New Castle County, Delaware, Delaware Public Archives, Dover, Delaware.

808. St. James Methodist Episcopal Church, Newport, Delaware, Register No. 1 1874–1935, p. 102.

809. Nebeker Family Record, copy provided in August 2002 by Ann Fowser (3742 Asbury Avenue, Ocean City, NJ 08226) to compiler.

810. Elizabeth Frist death certificate #2569 (1924), Delaware Department of Vital Records, Dover, Delaware.

811. Ibid.

812. Jacob Frist household, 1860 U.S. census, Hamilton County, Tennessee, population schedule, Chattanooga, district 14, stamped p. 114B, dwelling 734, family 535; National Archives micropublication M653, roll 1253.

813. Robert Frist service record, Compiled Service Records of Confederate Soldiers Who Served in Organizations from Tennessee, Fourth (McLemore's) Cavalry. National Archives Micropublication M231, reel 17, Tennessee State Library and Archives, Nashville, Tennessee.

814. Horace V. Frist service record, U.S. War Department, Delaware Military Service Records Fifth Delaware Infantry, National Archives, Washington, D.C.

815. Jacob Frist household, 1870 U.S. census, Hamilton County, Tennessee, population schedule, p. 698, dwelling 172, family 212; National Archives micropublication M593, roll 1532.

816. St. James Methodist Episcopal Church, Newport, Delaware, Register No. 1 1874–1935, p. 102.

817. Mary Sam Ward, *Our Spiritual Heritage* (Newport, Delaware: The Women of St. James, no date), p. 10, St. James Methodist Episcopal Church office, Newport.

818. Robert H. Frist household, 1880 U.S. census, New Castle County, Delaware, population schedule, enumeration district 18, sheet 43, line 45; National Archives micropublication T9, roll 119.

819. St. James Methodist Episcopal Church, Newport, Delaware, Register No. 1 1874–1935, p. 10, Families, St. James Methodist Episcopal Church office, Newport.

820. Robert Frist household, 1900 U.S. census, New Castle County, Delaware, population schedule, Christiana Hundred, Newport, enumeration district 51, sheet 3, line 82, dwelling 68, family 72; National Archives micropublication T623, roll 156.

821. Robert Harris Frist, Death Register, Record Group 1500, p. 68 #65474, New Castle County, Delaware, Delaware Public Archives, Dover, Delaware.

822. Elizabeth Frist household, 1910 U.S. census, New Castle County, Delaware, population schedule, enumeration district 74, sheet 3A, family and dwelling 49, p. 227[?]; National Archives micropublication T624, roll 146.

823. Elizabeth Frist household, 1920 U.S. census, New Castle County, Delaware, population schedule, enumeration district 148, sheet 5B, line 66, dwelling and family 54; National Archives micropublication T625, roll 204.

824. Elizabeth Nebeker Frist death certificate #2569 (1924), Delaware Department of Vital Records, Dover, Delaware.

825. Elizabeth R. Frist probate record, 1924, New Castle County, Delaware, Delaware Public Archives, Dover, Delaware.

826. Frist tombstone, St. James Methodist Episcopal Church Cemetery, Newport, Delaware, photographed July 2001 by compiler.

827. Nebeker Family Record, copy provided in August 2002 by Ann Fowser (3742 Asbury Avenue, Ocean City, NJ 08226) to compiler, lists these birth and death dates. The Frist tombstone, St. James Methodist Episcopal Church Cemetery, Newport, Delaware, photographed July 2001 by compiler, states he was born 21 January 1848.

828. St. James Methodist Episcopal Church, Newport, Delaware, Register No. 1 1874–1935, pp. 46 and 48, St. James Methodist Episcopal Church office, Newport.

829. St. James Methodist Episcopal Church, Newport, Delaware, Register No. 1 1874–1935, pp. 46 and 48, St. James Methodist Episcopal Church office, Newport. She was listed in these records and in census records as Ann Eliza Frist, but descendants state that her name was Anna Elizabeth Frist.

830. Anna E. Foard probate record, 48521, 1964, New Castle County, Delaware, Delaware Public Archives, Dover, Delaware.

831. Frist–Foard marriage, card file, Delaware Historical Society, Wilmington, Delaware.

832. St. James Methodist Episcopal Church, Newport, Delaware, Register No. 1 1874–1935, pp. 46 and 48, St. James Methodist Episcopal Church office, Newport. Also John Nebeker Frist, Delaware death certificate #1122 (1947), Delaware Department of Vital Records, Dover, Delaware. Death certificate gives year of birth as 1882.

833. John Nebeker Frist, Delaware death certificate #1122 (1947), Delaware Department of Vital Records, Dover, Delaware.

834. Frist–Currender marriage, card file, Delaware Public Archives, Dover, Delaware.

835. Jacob Frist Family Bible.

836. James B. Frist, obituary, *Chattanooga Daily News*, Chattanooga, Tennessee, 10 July 1925, p. 3, column 1.

837. James Frist household, 1880 U.S. census, Denton County, Texas, population schedule, precinct 3, enumeration district 105, p. 105B, dwelling and family 206; National Archives micropublication T9, roll 1300.

838. The Historical Records Survey, *Hamilton County Tombstone Inscriptions, Volume II* (Nashville, Tennessee: Works Progress Administration, 1939), p. 6, Citizens Cemetery, Tennessee State Library and Archives, Nashville, Tennessee.

839. Hamilton County, Tennessee, Marriage Book 1884–1888, p. 266, County Clerk, Chattanooga.

840. Letter from Steve Daugherty (P.O. Box 626, Hixson, TN 37343) 11 December 2000 to compiler citing Melia Frist tombstone, Parker Cemetery on Drew Road, Lookout Valley, Hamilton County, Tennessee. Property owned in 1995 by Miles C. Koger per Hamilton County, Tennessee, Deed Book 3020:196 recorded 27 August 1984.

841. Permelia Frist obituary, *Chattanooga Daily Times*, Chattanooga, Tennessee, 11 April 1935, page 3, column 1.

842. James Frist household, 1880 U.S. census, Denton County, Texas, population schedule, precinct 3, enumeration district 105, p. 105B, dwelling and family 206; National Archives micropublication T9, roll 1300.

843. "Death of Mrs. Frist," *Chattanooga Times*, Chattanooga, Tennessee, 6 January 1883, clipping from Jane Frist Genealogical Collection. Jane (P.O. Box 272, 102 Frist Road, Montreat, NC 28757) is a cousin of William H. Frist, M.D. and spent years researching the Frist family. Copy from William H. Frist, M.D. Genealogical Collection.

844. The Historical Records Survey, *Hamilton County Tombstone Inscriptions, Volume II* (Nashville, Tennessee: Works Progress Administration, 1939), p. 6, Citizens Cemetery, Tennessee State Library and Archives, Nashville, Tennessee. Also "Yesterday's Deaths," *Chattanooga Daily Times*, Chattanooga, Tennessee, 15 January 1883, clipping from Jane Frist Genealogical Collection.

845. "Yesterday's Deaths," *Chattanooga Daily Times*, Chattanooga, Tennessee, 15 January 1883, clipping from Jane Frist Genealogical Collection.

846. The Historical Records Survey, *Hamilton County Tombstone Inscriptions, Volume II* (Nashville, Tennessee: Works Progress Administration, 1939), p. 6, Citizens Cemetery, Tennessee State Library and Archives, Nashville, Tennessee.

847. Hamilton County, Tennessee, Deed Book 56:7, Record D, Volume 3, Register of Deeds, Chattanooga, Tennessee.

848. James Frist household, 1900 U.S. census, Hamilton County, Tennessee, population schedule, enumeration district 43, sheet 12, line 6; National Archives micropublication T623, roll 1574.

849. James Frist household, 1910 U.S. census, Hamilton County, Tennessee, population schedule, Civil District Four, enumeration district 84, sheet 54, line 46; National Archives micropublication T624, roll 1501.

850. Hamilton County, Tennessee, Deed Book 476:614, Record H, Volume 19, Register of Deeds, Chattanooga, Tennessee.

851. James B. Frist obituary, *Chattanooga Daily News*, Chattanooga, Tennessee, 10 July 1925, p. 3, column 1.

852. James B. Frist household, 1930 U.S. census, Hamilton County, Tennessee, population schedule, enumeration district 33-82, sheet 5B, dwelling 91, family 93, microfilm 21, Tennessee State Library and Archives, Nashville, Tennessee. This is an erroneous and confusing census entry. James B. First would have been seventy-seven, had he been living. James B. Frist is the listed head of household, but the mark for male has been changed to female and the age of sixty-three is correct for his wife Permelia. In addition, Joe B. Hartman, who is inaccurately listed as the fourteen-year-old grandson, is actually the thirty-seven-year-old son, Joe B. Frist. Roy F. Frist, who is inaccurately listed as the thirty-seven-year-old son is in fact the fourteen-year-old grandson, Roy F. Hartman.

853. Permelia Frist obituary, *Chattanooga Daily Times*, Chattanooga, Tennessee, 11 April 1935, page 3, column 1.

854. The Historical Records Survey, *Hamilton County Tombstone Inscriptions, Volume I* (Nashville, Tennessee: Works Progress Administration, 1939), p. 156, citing Parker Cemetery, Tennessee State Library and Archives, Nashville, Tennessee.

855. James Frist household, 1880 U.S. census, Denton County, Texas, population schedule, precinct 3, enumeration district 105, p. 105B, dwelling and family 206; National Archives micropublication T9, roll 1300

856. The Historical Records Survey, *Hamilton County Tombstone Inscriptions, Volume II* (Nashville, Tennessee: Works Progress Administration, 1939), p. 6, citing Citizens Cemetery, Tennessee State Library and Archives, Nashville, Tennessee.

857. Ibid.

858. Ibid.

859. James Frist household, 1900 U.S. census, Hamilton County, Tennessee, population schedule, enumeration district 43, sheet 12, line 6; National Archives micropublication T623, roll 1574.

860. Bertie Hartman obituary, *Chattanooga Daily Times*, Chattanooga, Tennessee, 17 May 1959, p. 29, column 7.

861. Bertie Hartman obituary, *Chattanooga Daily Times*, Chattanooga, Tennessee, 17 May 1959, p. 29, column 7. Date of marriage is from Herman Mayes Genealogical Collection.

862. Joseph Byron Frist obituary, *Chattanooga Daily Times*, Chattanooga, Tennessee, 26 August 1958, page 9, column 8.

863. Ibid.

864. Jacob Frist Family Bible.

865. Samuel Henry Frist death certificate #21603 (1939), Tennessee Bureau of Vital Records, Nashville, Tennessee.

866. Mrs. Estell [*sic*] Frist Rockwood obituary, *Chattanooga Times*, Chattanooga, Tennessee, 9 December 1958, p. 15, column 8. This identifies her mother as Florence M. Curry Frist. Also James Frist household, 1900 U.S. census, Hamilton County, Tennessee, population schedule, enumeration district 43, sheet 12, line 6; National Archives micropublication T623, roll 1574, provides year and place of birth.

867. Mrs. S. H. Frist death record (1913), Chattanooga Death Records, Volume 1911–1923, p. 24, microfilm M-21, Tennessee State Library and Archives, Nashville, Tennessee.

868. Hamilton County, Tennessee, Deed Book 109:405 Record E:109, Hamilton County, Chattanooga, Tennessee, Resister of Deeds, Chattanooga, Tennessee.

869. Samuel Frist household, 1900 U.S. census, Hamilton County, Tennessee, population schedule, enumeration district 72, sheet 27, line 30; National Archives micropublication T623, roll 1575.

870. Samuel Frist household, 1910 U.S. census, Hamilton County, Tennessee, population schedule, enumeration district 84, sheet 11A, line 7; National Archives micropublication T624, roll.1501.

871. Mrs. S. H. Frist death record (1913), Chattanooga Death Records, Volume 1911–1923, p. 24, microfilm M-21, Tennessee State Library and Archives, Nashville, Tennessee.

872. Hamilton County, Tennessee, Deed Book 317:387, Register of Deeds, Chattanooga, Tennessee.

873. Sprague S. Rockwood household, 1930 U.S. census, Hamilton County, Tennessee, population schedule, enumeration district 33-82, line 24, dwelling 173, family 177; microfilm 21, Tennessee State Library and Archives, Nashville, Tennessee.

874. Samuel Henry Frist death certificate #21603 (1939), Tennessee Bureau of Vital Records, Nashville, Tennessee.

875. Samuel Frist household, 1900 U.S. census, Hamilton County, Tennessee, population schedule, enumeration district 72, sheet 27, line 30; National Archives micropublication T623, roll 1575.

876. Mrs. Estell [*sic*] Frist Rockwood obituary, *Chattanooga Times*, Chattanooga, Tennessee, 9 December 1958, p. 15, column 8. This identifies her husband as Sprague S. Rockwood, not Clarence.

877. Sprague S. Rockwood household, 1930 U.S. census, Hamilton County, Tennessee, population schedule, enumeration district 33-82, line 24, dwelling 173, family 177; microfilm 21, Tennessee State Library and Archives, Nashville, Tennessee.

878. Herman Mayes Genealogical Collection.

879. Samuel Frist household, 1900 U.S. census, Hamilton County, Tennessee, population schedule, enumeration district 72, sheet 27, line 30; National Archives micropublication T623, roll 1575.

880. Hamilton County, Tennessee, Deed Book 317:387, Register of Deeds, Chattanooga, Tennessee.

881. Jacob Frist Family Bible records her name as Susan Elizabeth Frist, both at birth and death, but descendants state her name was Ann Elizabeth.

882. Mrs. Elizabeth Vetter obituary, undated clipping from unidentified newspaper, in family papers of William M. Vetter inherited and owned by their grandson John Stanley Vetter, M.D. (FristHealth Richmond Family Medicine, 921 Long Drive, Suite 101, Rockingham, NC 28379), copy held in 2003 by compiler.

883. "Happy Nuptials," undated clipping from unidentified newspaper, in family papers of William M. Vetter inherited and owned by his grandson John Stanley Vetter, M.D. (FristHealth Richmond Family Medicine, 921 Long Drive, Suite 101, Rockingham, NC 28379), copy held in 2003 by compiler.

884. William Vetter household, 1900 U.S. census, Hamilton County, Tennessee, population schedule, enumeration district 58, sheet 1, line 21; National Archives micropublication T623, roll 1574.

885. William Vetter, obituary, 14 October 1900, *Chattanooga Daily Times*, Chattanooga, Tennessee; clipping from unknown and undated newspaper, from John Stanley Vetter, M.D. (FristHealth Richmond Family Medicine, 921 Long Drive, Suite 101, Rockingham, NC 28379), copy held in 2003 by compiler.

886. Miss Lizzie Frist letter dated 15 August 1878 from William M. Vetter, owned by his grandson John Stanley Vetter, M.D. (FristHealth Richmond Family Medicine, 921 Long Drive, Suite 101, Rockingham, NC 28379), copy held in 2003 by compiler.

887. "Happy Nuptials," undated clipping from unidentified newspaper, in family papers of William M. Vetter inherited and owned by his grandson John Stanley Vetter, M.D. (FristHealth Richmond Family Medicine, 921 Long Drive, Suite 101, Rockingham, NC 28379).

888. This would indicate that the Tennessee Frists were in touch with their Indiana Frist relatives.

889. William Vetter household, 1900 U.S. census, Hamilton County, Tennessee, population schedule, enumeration district 58, sheet 1, line 21; National Archives micropublication T623, roll 1574.

890. The fact that he was listed as brother-in-law is an indication that it was Elizabeth who provided the information to the census taker.

891. William Vetter, obituary, *Chattanooga Daily Times*, Chattanooga, Tennessee, 14 October 1900; clipping from unknown and undated newspaper, from John Stanley Vetter, M.D. (FristHealth Richmond Family Medicine, 921 Long Drive, Suite 101, Rockingham, NC 28379), copy held in 2003 by compiler.

892. Elizabeth Vetter household, 1910 U.S. census, Walker County, Georgia, population schedule, Crawfish Springs Match District, enumeration district 139, sheet 11, line 61, dwelling 220, family 222; National Archives micropublication T624, roll 214.

893. Elizabeth Vetter household, 1920 U.S. Census, Walker County, Georgia, population schedule, enumeration district 173, sheet 14B and 15A, line 94, stamped p. 66 and 67, dwelling 295, family 294; National Archives micropublication T625, roll 281.

894. Mrs. Elizabeth Vetter obituary, undated clipping from unidentified newspaper, in family papers of William M. Vetter inherited and owned by their grandson John Stanley Vetter, M.D. (FristHealth Richmond Family Medicine, 921 Long Drive, Suite 101, Rockingham, NC 28379), copy held in 2003 by compiler.

895. Robert J. Vetter, Tennessee death certificate #15129 (1929), Tennessee Bureau of Vital Records, Nashville, 17 June 1929.

896. "Vetter Brothers Die Fourteen Hours Apart," *Chattanooga Daily News*, Chattanooga, Tennessee, 17 June 1929, page 3, column 2.

897. "Vetter Brothers Die Fourteen Hours Apart," *Chattanooga Daily News*, Chattanooga, Tennessee, 17 June 1929, page 3, column 2. Also biographical material provided December 2000 by John Stanley Vetter, M.D. (921 Long Drive, Suite 101, Rockingham, NC 28379) to compiler. Vetter is a son of John Stanley Vetter.

898. "Vetter Brothers Die Fourteen Hours Apart," *Chattanooga Daily News*, Chattanooga, Tennessee, 17 June 1929, page 3, column 2.

899. Biographical material provided by John Stanley Vetter, M.D. (921 Long Drive, Suite 101, Rockingham, NC 28379) to compiler December 2000. Vetter is a son of John Stanley Vetter.

900. Jacob Frist Family Bible.

901. Jacob Chester Frist, death certificate #1519 (1919), Mississippi State Department of Health, Jackson.

902. Jackson County, Ohio, Marriage Book J:399 #4247, Probate Court, Jackson, Ohio.

903. Magnolia Cemetery Records, Meridian, Mississippi, photograph taken April 2002 by compiler.

904. Jake C. Frist household, 1900 U.S. census, Perry County, Mississippi, population schedule, enumeration district 89, sheet 11, line 35; National Archives micropublication T623, roll 824.

905. Magnolia Cemetery, Meridian, Mississippi, photograph taken April 2002 by compiler.

906. Jacob Frist household, 1870 U.S. census, Hamilton County, Tennessee, population schedule, stamped p. 698, dwelling 172, family 212; National Archives micropublication M593, roll 1532.

907. Jacob Frist report card; original owned by granddaughter Mary Barfield (1026 Chancery Lane S., Nashville, TN 37215-4552).

908. Mary Frist household, 1880 U.S. census, Hamilton County, Tennessee, population schedule, Chattanooga, p. 172, family 150; National Archives micropublication T9, roll 1259.

909. "Small-Pox," *Chattanooga Daily Times*, Chattanooga, Tennessee, 12 January 1883, clipping from Jane Frist Genealogical collection.

910. *Norwood's Directory of Chattanooga 1884–1885* (Chattanooga, Tennessee: C. W. Norwood, 1884), microfilm 2, Chattanooga Public Library, Chattanooga, Tennessee.

911. Thomas Fearn Frist, M.D. "The Frist Story," no date, p. 14, from William H. Frist, M.D. Genealogical Collection (703 Bowling Avenue, Nashville, TN 37215). Several versions of this typescript exist, and they differ slightly in content.

912. Jackson County, Ohio, Marriage Book J:399 #4247, Probate Court, Jackson, Ohio.

913. Jacob Frist household, 1900 U.S. census Perry County, Mississippi, population schedule, enumeration district 89, sheet 11, line 35, dwelling 198, family 203; National Archives micropublication T623, roll 824.

914. Hamilton County, Tennessee, Deed Book 152:279–280, Register of Deeds, Chattanooga, Tennessee.

915. *Soard's New Orleans City Directory for 1903* (New Orleans: Soard's Directory County Ltd., 1903), p. 353.

916. Jean Strickland and Patricia N. Edwards compilers, *Perry County, Mississippi, W.P.A. Manuscripts Newspaper Items* (Moss Point, Mississippi: Ben Strickland, 1997), p. 143.

917. Lauderdale County, Mississippi, Deed Record 76:28, Chancery Court, Meridian, Mississippi.

918. Frist, "The Frist Story," no date, p. 15, from William H. Frist, M.D. Genealogical Collection (703 Bowling Avenue, Nashville, TN 37215).

919. Lauderdale County, Mississippi, Deed of Trust Book 74:525, Chancery Court, Meridian, Mississippi.

920. Frist, "The Frist Story," no date, p. 15, from William H. Frist, M.D. Genealogical Collection (703 Bowling Avenue, Nashville, TN 37215).

921. Lauderdale County, Mississippi, Deed of Trust Book 93:345, Chancery Court, Meridian, Mississippi.

922. Jacob C. Frist household, 1910 U.S. census, Lauderdale County, Mississippi, population schedule, enumeration district, 42, sheet 18B, dwelling 256, family 282; National Archives micropublication T624, roll 746.

923. Lauderdale County, Mississippi, Deed Record 106:244, Chancery Court, Meridian, Mississippi.

924. Lauderdale County, Mississippi, Deed Record 106:254, Chancery Court, Meridian, Mississippi.

925. Hamilton County, Tennessee, Deed 271:458–459, Record K, Volume 11, Register of Deeds, Chattanooga, Tennessee.

926. Frist, "The Frist Story," no date, p. 9, from William H. Frist, M.D. Genealogical Collection (703 Bowling Avenue, Nashville, TN 37215).

927. Jacob Chester Frist, Medal of Honor Case File #25, Record Group 134, Interstate Commerce Commission, Item 14, National Archives, Washington, D.C.

928. Jacob Chester Frist, Medal of Honor Case File #25, Record Group 134, Interstate Commerce Commission, Item 14, National Archives, Washington, D.C.

929. "Heroic Deed of Jake Frist Nearly Cost Him His Life," *The Meridian Star*, Meridian, Mississippi, 4 February 1914, p. 4.

930. Jacob Chester Frist, Medal of Honor Case File #25, Record Group 134, Interstate Commerce Commission, Item 35, National Archives, Washington, D.C.

931. Ibid.

932. Life-Savings Medals under Public Act 98, an Act to Promote the Security of Travel upon Railroads Engaged in Interstate Commerce, approved 23 February 1905.

933. Jacob Chester Frist, Medal of Honor Case File #25, Record Group 134, Interstate Commerce Commission, Item 27, National Archives, Washington, D.C.

934. Jacob Chester Frist, Medal of Honor Case File #25, Record Group 134, Interstate Commerce Commission, Item 20, National Archives, Washington, D.C.

935. Interstate Commerce Commission, Acts Annotated, Ch. 4, Section 44, p. 3315–3317, 1930.

936. Jacob Chester Frist, Award No. 1077, Carnegie Hero Fund Commission (2307 Oliver Building, 535 Smithfield St., Pittsburgh, PA 15222-2394).

937. Lauderdale County, Mississippi, Wills 1915–1931, p. 53, Probate Court, Meridian, Mississippi.

938. Jacob Chester Frist, death certificate #1519 (1919), Mississippi State Department of Health, Jackson.

939. "Death of J. C. Frist at Noon Today Follows Stroke of Paralysis," *The Meridian Star*, Meridian, Mississippi, 2 January 1919, p. 3.

940. "Funeral of Mr. Frist to be at 10:30 O'clock," *The Meridian Star*, Meridian, Mississippi, 3 January 1919, p. 2.

941. Hamilton County, Tennessee, Deed Book 452:17–23, Record J, Volume 18 Register of Deeds, Chattanooga, Tennessee.

942. Jennie Frist household, 1920 U.S. census, Lauderdale County, Mississippi, population schedule, enumeration district 45, sheet 7B, dwelling 147, family 155; National Archives micropublication T625, roll 882.

943. J. C. Frist estate #6869, Box 328, Chancery Court, Lauderdale County, Mississippi, Department for Archives and History, Meridian, Mississippi.

944. Frist, "The Frist Story," no date, p. 16, from William H. Frist, M.D. Genealogical Collection (703 Bowling Avenue, Nashville, TN 37215).

945. Ibid.

946. Lauderdale County, Mississippi, Deed Record 143:17, 143:64, 144:344, 144:345, Chancery Court, Meridian, Mississippi.

947. Thomas Fearn Frist narrative labeled Family History Jacobson Excerpts, owned by William H. Frist, M.D. (703 Bowling Avenue, Nashville, TN 37215), pp. 18 and 19.

948. Jennie Frist household, 1930 U.S. census, Lauderdale County, Mississippi, population schedule, Meridian, enumeration district 32-6, supervisor's district 9, sheet 5A, stamped p. 111, line 4; National Archives micropublication T626, roll 1153.

949. Lauderdale County, Mississippi, Record of Lands Sold to State Volume 2:51–52, Chancery Court, Meridian, Mississippi.

950. Lauderdale County, Mississippi, Deed Record 243:269, Chancery Court, Meridian, Mississippi.

951. Charlotte Chesnutt (P.O. Box 412, Montreat, NC 28757), grand-daughter of Jacob Chester Frist, communication to Shirley Wilson 6 July 2001.

952. Magnolia Cemetery, Meridian, Mississippi, photograph taken April 2002 by compiler.

953. Karen Dover, abstractor, *Lauderdale County Cemetery Records, Volume IV* (Meridian, Mississippi: Lauderdale County Department of Archives and History, 1992), p. 71.

954. Lauderdale County, Mississippi, Marriage Records, white, Book 27:547, Lauderdale County, Mississippi, Department of Archives and History, Meridian, Mississippi.

955. Helen Cameron, death certificate #23337 (1956), Volume 1814, Florida Department of Vital Records, Jacksonville.

956. Biographical material provided by daughters Jane Elizabeth Frist (P.O. Box 272, 102 Frist Road, Montreat, NC 28757) and Charlotte June Chesnutt (P.O. Box 412, Montreat, NC 28757) to compiler.

957. William H. Frist, M.D. Genealogical Collection. Frist is a son.

958. Jacob Frist Family Bible.

959. Joseph Elmer Frist death certificate #20872 (1940), Tennessee Bureau of Vital Records, Nashville, Tennessee.

960. Alice Frist obituary, 19 January 1911, *Chattanooga Daily Times*, Chattanooga, Tennessee, page 3, column 1.

961. Ibid.

962. Joseph Frist household, 1900 U.S. census, Hamilton County, Tennessee, population schedule, enumeration district 59, sheet 53, line 28; National Archives micropublication T623, roll 1574.

963. Alice Frist obituary, 19 January 1911, *Chattanooga Daily Times*, Chattanooga, Tennessee, page 3, column 1.

964. William Henry Griswell household, 1920 U.S. census, Hamilton County, Tennessee, population schedule, Tennessee, enumeration district 163, sheet 6, line 77; National Archives micropublication T625, roll 1742.

965. Richard Forrester household, 1920 U.S. census, Hamilton County, Tennessee, enumeration district 197, sheet 3, lines 14 and 15; National Archives micropublication T625, roll 1743.

966. Original deed, Ronnie Frist Genealogical Collection. Deed was registered in Hamilton County, Tennessee, Deed Book 5, Volume 15, p. 356. Copy held in 2003 by compiler. Ronnie (1718 Gray Road, Chattanooga, TN 37421) is Kate's grandson. When Kate moved to a nursing home in 2001, several large trunks of information came into his possession; hereinafter cited as Ronnie Frist Genealogical Collection.

967. Joe E. Frist household, 1930 U.S. census, Hamilton County, Tennessee, population schedule, enumeration district 33-82, sheet 5B, dwelling 88, family 90, microfilm 21, Tennessee State Library and Archives, Nashville, Tennessee.

968. Joseph Elmer Frist death certificate #20872 (1940), Tennessee Bureau of Vital Records, Nashville, Tennessee.

969. Jacob Frist Family Bible.

970. Paul F. Frist obituary, *Chattanooga Daily Times*, Chattanooga, Tennessee, 13 March 1961, p. 9, column 7.

971. Interview with Kate (Groves) Frist, 28 February 2002, in Chattanooga, Tennessee, by compiler. Kate lives in a rest home.

972. Jacob Frist Family Bible lists him as Jacob C. Frist, but descendants state that his name was James Charles Frist and he used the nickname "Jake."

973. James C. Frist death certificate #5468 (1944), Tennessee Division of Vital Statistics, Nashville, Tennessee.

974. Biographical material, from Naomi Willmary (Frist) Rollins (4911 Alabama Avenue, Chattanooga, TN 37409) dated 13 November 2001 provided to compiler. Mrs. Rollins is the daughter of Sadie Briggs.

975. Jacob Frist Family Bible.

976. Ernest Arnold Frist, 413-03-2340, Social Security Death Index, *Ancestry.com* (Provo, Utah: MyFamily.com, Inc., 1998–2003), drawn from *Social Security Death Benefits Index* of the U.S. Social Security Administration.

977. Ernest Arnold Frist, social security application 413-03-2340, U.S. Social Security Administration.

978. Ernest A. Frist obituary, *Chattanooga News–Free Press*, Chattanooga, Tennessee, 7 November 1968, p. 4.

979. Jacob Frist Family Bible.

980. Jacob Frist Family Bible.

981. Frist Family Group Sheets provided March 2001 by son Clarence Harold Frist (419 Turrentine Avenue, Gadsden, AL 35901) to compiler.

982. Ibid.

983. Ibid.

984. Mary E. Frist household, 1900 U.S. census, Hamilton County, Tennessee, population schedule, enumeration district 59, sheet 53, line 19; National Archives micropublication T623, roll 1574.

985. Emmett Frist household, 1920 U. S. census, Etowah County, Alabama, population schedule, Gadsden, enumeration district 92, sheet 6, line 99, dwelling 139, family 155; National Archives micropublication T625, roll 15.

986. James R. Hawkins household, 1920 U.S. census, Jefferson County, Alabama, population schedule, Birmingham, enumeration district 35, sheet 17, line 96, 4115 Avenue D; National Archives micropublication T625, roll 23.

987. Emmet [sic] F. Frist household, 1930 U.S. census, Etowah County, Alabama, population schedule, enumeration district 28-5, supervisor's district 3, sheet 14A, stamped p. 76?, dwelling 251, family 332; National Archives micropublication T626, roll 16.

988. Tombstone, Forrest Cemetery, Gadsden, Alabama.

989. Jacob Frist Family Bible.

990. Frist Family Group Sheets provided by son Clarence Harold Frist (419 Turrentine Avenue, Gadsden, AL 35901) to compiler.

991. Frist Family Group Sheet provided March 2001 by Clarence Harold Frist (419 Turrentine Avenue, Gadsden, AL 35901) to compiler. Clarence is a brother.

992. Ibid.

993. Lee Frist, social security application 422-01-1510, U.S. Social Security Administration. At the time of this application dated 30 November 1936 her surname was Outlaw.

994. Frist Family Group Sheets provided March 2001 by son Clarence Harold Frist (419 Turrentine Avenue, Gadsden, AL 35901) to compiler.

995. Ida Frist, social security application 420-52-1813, U.S. Social Security Administration.

996. Ida Frist, 420-52-1813, Social Security Death Index, *Ancestry.com*.

997. Frist Family Group Sheet and biographical material provided October 2001 by Clarence Harold Frist (419 Turrentine Avenue, Gadsden, AL 35901) to compiler.

998. Page County, Iowa, Death Records Volume 2, p. 77, microfilm 1535553, Family History Library, Salt Lake City, Utah.

999. Page County, Iowa, Marriage Record Book 1:567, microfilm 1035209, Family History Library, Salt Lake City, Utah.

1000. *History of Page County, Iowa* (Des Moines, Iowa: Iowa Historical Society, 1880), p. 776.

1001. Frist Family Group Sheets and family records provided April/May 2001 by Shirley Findley (119 East Twenty-Second Street, Loveland, CO 80538) to compiler.

1002. "Mr. and Mrs. Joseph A. Frist Celebrate Their 50th Anniversary" *Villisca Review and Letter*, Villisca, Iowa, newspaper clipping on fiftieth wedding anniversary of David and Lydia Frist's son Joseph, undated, possibly February 1925, typescript copy held in 2003 by compiler.

1003. 1885 Page County, Iowa, state census, population schedule, entry 114/120, microfilm 1020170, Family History Library, Salt Lake City. Utah.

1004. 1891 Montgomery County, Iowa, state census, population schedule, p. 20; microfilm 1022209, Family History Library, Salt Lake City, Utah.

1005. Joseph Frist household, 1900 U.S. census, Montgomery County, Iowa, population schedule, Jackson Township, enumeration district 108, sheet 11, line 4; National Archives micropublication T623, roll 450.

1006. William H. Frist household, 1920 U.S. census, Page County, Iowa, population schedule, enumeration district 118, p. 1A, dwelling and family 15; National Archives micropublication T625, roll 506.

1007. 1925 Page County, Iowa, state census, population schedule, microfilm 1429485, Family History Library, Salt Lake City, Utah.

1008. "Mr. and Mrs. Joseph A. Frist Celebrate Their 50th Anniversary," *Villisca Review and Letter*, Villisca, Iowa, newspaper clipping on fiftieth wedding anniversary of David and Lydia Frist's son Joseph, undated, possibly February 1925, typescript copy held in 2003 by compiler.

1009. Frist Family Group Sheets and family records provided April/May 2001 by Shirley Findley (119 East Twenty-Second Street, Loveland, CO 80538) to compiler.

1010. Rosetta Frist, obituary, Obituary *Villisca Review and Letter*, Villisca, Iowa, no date, copy held by compiler.

1011. Page County, Iowa, Death Records Volume 2, p. 77, microfilm 1535553, Family History Library, Salt Lake City, Utah.

1012. Montgomery County Genealogical Society and Bicentennial Committee, *Cemetery Records Montgomery County, Iowa, Townships of Douglass Washington East (Jackson)* (Des Moines, Iowa: Iowa Genealogical Society, 1984), p. 103.

1013. David H. Frist Family Bible, previously discussed.

1014. Montgomery County Genealogical Society and Bicentennial Committee, *Cemetery Records Montgomery County, Iowa, Townships of Douglass Washington East (Jackson)* (Des Moines, Iowa: Iowa Genealogical Society, 1984), p. 93.

1015. David H. Frist Family Bible.

1016. Montgomery County Genealogical Society and Bicentennial Committee, *Cemetery Records Montgomery County, Iowa, Townships of Douglass Washington East (Jackson)* (Des Moines, Iowa: Iowa Genealogical Society, 1984), p. 49, citing Section Four, Row 14.

1017. Montgomery County, Iowa, Marriage Record Book 6:93, microfilm 1,481,225, Family History Library, Salt Lake City, Utah.

1018. Willibur is pronounced Wilbur; the unusual spelling is confirmed by daughter Geraldine Miller (415 S. Eighteenth Street, Clarinda, IA 51632-2515) in telephone conversation 39 May 2001 with compiler.

1019. David H. Frist Family Bible.

1020. Montgomery County Genealogical Society and Bicentennial Committee, *Cemetery Records Montgomery County, Iowa, Townships of Douglass Washington East (Jackson)* (Des Moines, Iowa: Iowa Genealogical Society, 1984), p. 120.

1021. Herman Mayes Genealogical Collection.

1022. Orpha Frist, social security application 485-38-3895, U.S. Social Security Administration.

1023. David H. Frist Family Bible.

1024. Manferd Findley (4555 Jordan Grove Road, Central City, IA 52214), telephone conversation 23 March 2001 with compiler.

1025. David H. Frist Family Bible.

1026. Nannie Bridgeman, 478-80-5885, Social Security Death Index, *Ancestry.com.*

1027. Montgomery County, Iowa, Marriage Record Volume 9:200, microfilm 1,481,227, Family History Library, Salt Lake City, Utah.

1028. Fred Bridgeman, 480-44-6425, Social Security Death Index, *Ancestry.com.*

1029. Fred Bridgman household, 1920 U.S. census, Plymouth County, Iowa, population schedule, enumeration district 138, sheet 3B, dwelling and family 58; National Archives micropublication T625, roll 506.

1030. Spelling of this surname is uncertain, possibly Eyeocker or Ayeocker.

1031. Biographical material provided by Shirley Findley (119 East Twenty-Second Street, Loveland, CO 80538).

1032. David H. Frist Family Bible.

1033. Frist Family Group Sheet and obituary, no date, no newspaper, provided by Shirley Findley (119 East Twenty-Second Street, Loveland, CO 80538).

1034. David H. Frist Family Bible.

1035. John Frist household, 1880 U.S. census, Marion County, Iowa, population schedule, enumeration district 118, sheet 10, dwelling 91, family 93, stamped p. 482; National Archives micropublication T9, roll 354. Josiah Bivans lived with them, a single man listed as brother-in-law.

1036. "Mr. and Mrs. Joseph A. Frist Celebrate Their 50th Anniversary" *Villisca Review and Letter*, Villisca, Iowa, newspaper clipping on fiftieth wedding anniversary of David and Lydia Frist's son Joseph, undated, possibly February 1925, typescript copy held in 2003 by compiler.

1037. John Frist household, 1880 U.S. census, Marion County, Iowa, population schedule, enumeration district 118, sheet 10, dwelling 91, family 93, stamped p. 482; National Archives micropublication T9, roll 354.

1038. John Frist household, 1900 U.S. census, Polk County, Iowa, population schedule, Camp Township, enumeration district 62, sheet 11, stamped p. 47; National Archives micropublication T623, roll 453.

1039. John Frist household, 1915 Polk County, Iowa state census, population schedule, Camp township, #206, microfilm 1462725, Family History Library, Salt Lake City, Utah.

1040. Joseph Frist household, 1920 U.S. census, Polk County, Iowa, population schedule, Camp Township, Runnells enumeration district 69, sheet 1, line 7 stamped p 58; National Archives micropublication T625, roll 507.

1041. Ibid.

1042. Pioneer Sons and Daughters Genealogical Society, *Marriages Polk County, Iowa, Book 12 1905–1906* (Des Moines, Iowa: Iowa Genealogical Society, 1986), p. 17.

1043. David H. Frist Family Bible.

1044. David H. Frist Family Bible.

1045. Henry Thomas household, 1880 U.S. census, Dallas County, Iowa, population schedule, Boone Township, 275, dwelling and family 25; National Archives micropublication T9, roll 335.

1046. Rebecca Thomas household, 1910 U.S. census, Dallas County, Iowa, population schedule, enumeration district 19, sheet 8, dwelling 173, family 181; National Archives micropublication T624, roll 399.

1047. "Mr. and Mrs. Joseph A. Frist Celebrate Their 50th Anniversary" *Villisca Review and Letter*, Villisca, Iowa, newspaper clipping on fiftieth wedding anniversary of David and Lydia Frist's son Joseph, undated, possibly February 1925, typescript copy held in 2003 by compiler.

1048. Henry Thomas household, 1880 U.S. census, Dallas County, Iowa, population schedule, Boone Township, 275, dwelling and family 25; National Archives micropublication T9, roll 335.

1049. Henry Thomas household, 1900 U.S. census, Dallas County, Iowa, population schedule, Van Meter Township, enumeration district 18, page 14, line 13, stamped p. 224; National Archives micropublication T623, roll 427.

1050. Rebecca Thomas household, 1910 U.S. census, Dallas County, Iowa, population schedule, enumeration district 19, sheet 8, dwelling 173, family 181; National Archives micropublication T624, roll 399.

1051. David H. Frist Family Bible.

1052. Dallas County, Iowa, Marriage Record 1852–1902, p. 149, microfilm 1034112 Item 2, Family History Library, Salt Lake City, Utah.

1053. Dallas County, Iowa, Marriage Record 1852–1902, p. 110, microfilm 1034112 Item 2, Family History Library, Salt Lake City, Utah.

1054. Henry Thomas household, 1880 U.S. census, Dallas County, Iowa, population schedule, Boone Township, p. 275, dwelling and family 25; National Archives micropublication T9, roll 335.

1055. Ibid.

1056. Ibid.

1057. Dallas County, Iowa, Marriage Record 1852–1902, p. 162, microfilm 1034112 Item 2, Family History Library, Salt Lake City, Utah.

1058. Henry Thomas household, 1880 U.S. census, Dallas County, Iowa, population schedule, Boone Township, p. 275, dwelling and family 25; National Archives micropublication T9, roll 335.

1059. Henry Thomas household, 1900 U.S. census, Dallas County, Iowa, population schedule, Van Meter Township enumeration district 80, sheet 14, line 13, stamped p. 224; National Archives micropublication T623, roll 427.

1060. Ibid.

1061. Ibid.

1062. Ibid.

1063. William H. Frist household, 1860 U.S. census, Preble County, Ohio, population schedule, Jefferson Township, p. 176, dwelling 1343, family 1292; National Archives micropublication M653, roll 1026.

1064. Audrey Gilbert, *Preble County, Ohio, Marriages 1860–1898* (Owensboro, Kentucky: McDowell Publications, 1981), p. 93.

1065. Henry Rupe household, 1880 U.S. census, Wayne County, Indiana, population schedule, Wayne Township, enumeration district 68, sheet 331, line 9, dwelling 280, family 287, stamped p. 240; National Archives micropublication T9, roll 322.

1066. Ibid.

1067. William H. Frist, obituary, Audrey Gilbert, *Obituary Abstracts 1877–1895 from Preble County Newspapers in Preble County, Ohio, Volume II* (Utica, Kentucky: McDowell Publications, 1983), p. 34; and Henry Rupe household, 1880 U.S. census, Wayne County, Indiana, population schedule, Wayne Township, enumeration district 68, sheet 331, line 9 dwelling 280, family 287, stamped p. 240; National Archives micropublication T9, roll 322.

1068. Henry Rupe household, 1900 U.S. census, Wayne County, Indiana, population schedule, Wayne Township, enumeration district 156, sheet 6, dwelling 134, family 138; National Archives micropublication T623, roll 412.

1069. Henry C. Rupe household, 1910 U.S. census, Wayne County, Indiana, population schedule, Wayne Township, enumeration district 189, sheet 4B, stamped p. 250B, dwelling and family 70; National Archives Micropublication T624, roll 388.

1070. Beverly Yount, compiler, *Tombstone Inscriptions in Wayne County, Indiana, Volume IV* (Fort Wayne, Indiana: Fort Wayne Public Library, 1970), p. 79.

1071. Henry Rupe household, 1880 U.S. census, Wayne County, Indiana, population schedule, Wayne Township, enumeration district 68, sheet 331, line 9, dwelling 280, family 287, stamped p. 240; National Archives micropublication T9, roll 322.

1072. Ibid.

1073. Beverly Yount, compiler, *Tombstone Inscriptions in Wayne County, Indiana, Volume IV* (Fort Wayne, Indiana: Fort Wayne Public Library, 1970), p.89.

1074. Charles H. Rupe household, 1920 U.S. census, Wayne County, Indiana, soundex code R-100; National Archives micropublication M1560, roll 164. Enumeration district not legible on microfilm, could not locate.

1075. Beverly Yount, compiler, *Tombstone Inscriptions in Wayne County, Indiana, Volume IV* (Fort Wayne, Indiana: Fort Wayne Public Library, 1970), p. 87.

1076. Ibid.

1077. Henry Rupe household, 1900 U.S. census, Wayne County, Indiana, population schedule, Wayne Township, enumeration district 156, sheet 6, dwelling 134, family 138; National Archives micropublication T623, roll 412.

1078. Ibid.

1079. Ibid.

1080. Ibid.

1081. Ibid.

1082. Audrey Gilbert, *Preble County, Ohio, the 1900 Federal Census* (Owensboro, Kentucky: Cook & McDowell Publications, 1980), p. 302.

1083. William H. Frist probate record, Preble County, Ohio, Will Book F:347, Probate Court, Eaton, Ohio.

1084. Audrey Gilbert, *Probate Abstracts Estates & Guardianships Preble County, Ohio* (West Alexandria, Ohio: privately printed, 2001), p. 62 citing file #12401.

1085. Audrey Gilbert, *Preble County, Ohio, Marriages 1860–1898* (Owensboro, Kentucky: McDowell Publications, 1981), p. 38.

1086. Audrey Gilbert, *Abstracts from Preble County, Ohio, Newspaper Obituaries Book VII 1915–1918* (West Alexandria, Ohio: privately published, 1999), p. 172.

1087. Herman Mayes Genealogical Collection.

1088. Audrey Gilbert, *Preble County, Ohio, the 1900 Federal Census* (Owensboro, Kentucky: Cook & McDowell Publications, 1980), p. 302.

1089. Audrey Gilbert, *Preble County, Ohio, 1910 Census* (Utica, Kentucky: McDowell Publications, 1984), p. 106.

1090. Audrey Gilbert, *Preble County, Ohio, 1920 Census* (No place: no publisher, 1993), p. 93.

1091. Audrey Gilbert, *Probate Abstracts Estates and Guardianships Preble County, Ohio* (West Alexandria, Ohio: privately printed, 2001), p. 62 citing file #12401.

1092. Herman Mayes Genealogical Collection.

1093. Audrey Gilbert, *Preble County, Ohio, Marriages 1907–1915* (Utica, Kentucky: McDowell Publications, no date), p. 131.

1094. Ibid.

1095. Ibid.

1096. William Mungavin household, 1920 U.S. census, Wayne County, Indiana, population schedule, Wayne Township, City of Richmond, enumeration district 179, sheet 6, family 162, stamped p. 22; National Archives micropublication T625, roll 474.

1097. Audrey Gilbert, *Preble County, Ohio, the 1900 Federal Census* (Owensboro, Kentucky: Cook & McDowell Publications, 1980), p. 302.

1098. Herman Mayes Genealogical Collection.

1099. Paul H. Frist household, 1920 U.S. census, Wayne County, Indiana, population schedule, City of Richmond, enumeration district 179, sheet 7B, dwelling 174, family 177; National Archives micropublication T625, roll 474.

1100. Violet Genevieve Frist, 308-44-1056, Social Security Death Index, *Family Search* (Salt Lake City: Family History Library, 2001). The SSDI portion of *Family Search* is from the *Social Security Death Benefits Index* of the U.S. Social Security Administration.

1101. Audrey Gilbert, *Preble County, Ohio, Marriages 1916–1926* (West Alexandria, Ohio: privately printed, 1998), p. 145.

1102. Ibid.

1103. Ibid.

1104. William H. Frist household, 1880 U. S. census, Preble County, Ohio, population schedule, Jefferson Township, , enumeration district 199, sheet 21, line 42, dwelling and family 9, stamped p. 119; National Archives micropublication T9, roll 1060.

1105. Herman Mayes Genealogical Collection.

1106. Russell Frist household, 1900 U.S. census, Madison County, Indiana, population schedule, Green Township, enumeration district 92, sheet 10, dwelling 179, family 184, stamped p. 323; National Archives micropublication T623, roll 386.

1107. Herman Mayes Genealogical Collection.

1108. Russell Frist household, 1900 U.S. census, Madison County, Indiana, population schedule, Green Township, enumeration district 92, sheet 10, dwelling 179, family 184, stamped p. 323; National Archives micropublication T623, roll 386.

1109. Russell Frist household, 1920 U.S. census, Madison County, Indiana, population schedule, Anderson Township, enumeration district 101, sheet 9A, stamped p. 170, dwelling 191, family 205; National Archives micropublication T625, roll 448.

1110. Herman Mayes Genealogical Collection.

1111. Marley Otto Frist obituary, *Anderson Daily Bulletin*, Anderson, Indiana, undated clipping from Patricia Frist Genealogical Collection.

1112. Herman Mayes Genealogical Collection.

1113. Hester Frist, social security application 313-03-2844 dated 25 November 1936, U.S. Social Security Administration.

1114. Robert M. Frist household, 1870 U.S. census, Warren County, Iowa, population schedule, city of Hartford, p. 430, dwelling 53, family 55; National Archives micropublication M593, roll 423. Hannah Etta was listed as Henrietta in this census. Exact date of birth from Herman Mayes Genealogical Collection.

1115. Hannah Etta Stevens obituary, *Liberty Herald*, Liberty, Indiana, 17 September 1936, p. 1.

1116. John J. Stevens household, 1900 U.S. census, Union County, Indiana, population schedule, Centre Township, enumeration district 130, sheet 5, dwelling and family 92, stamped p. 276; National Archives micropublication T623, roll 406.

1117. Hannah Etta Stevens obituary, *Liberty Herald*, Liberty, Indiana, 17 September 1936, p. 1.

1118. Robert M. Frist household, 1870 U.S. census, Warren County, Iowa, population schedule, city of Hartford, p. 430, dwelling 53, family 55; National Archives micropublication M593, roll 423.

1119. Audrey Gilbert, *Preble County, Ohio, 1880 Census* (Utica, Kentucky: McDowell Publications, 1983), p. 206.

1120. John J. Stevens household, 1900 U.S. census, Union County, Indiana, population schedule, Centre Township, enumeration district 130, sheet 5, dwelling and family 92, stamped p. 276; National Archives micropublication T623, roll 406.

1121. John J. Stevens household, 1920 U.S. census, Union County, Indiana, population schedule, Centre Township enumeration district 131, sheet 19A, line 17, dwelling 410, family 425; National Archives micropublication T625, roll 460.

1122. Hannah Etta Stevens obituary, *Liberty Herald*, Liberty, Indiana, 17 September 1936, p. 1.

1123. John J. Stevens household, 1900 U.S. census, Union County, Indiana, population schedule, Centre Township, enumeration district 130, sheet 5, dwelling and family 92, stamped p. 276; National Archives micropublication T623, roll 406.

1124. Ibid.

1125. John J. Stevens household, 1920 U.S. census, Union County, Indiana, population schedule, Centre Township enumeration district 131, sheet 19A, line 17, dwelling 410, family 425; National Archives micropublication T625, roll 460.

1126. John J. Stevens household, 1900 U.S. census, Union County, Indiana, population schedule, Centre Township, enumeration district 130, sheet 5, dwelling and family 92, stamped p. 276; National Archives micropublication T623, roll 406. Exact date from Herman Mayes Genealogical Collection.

1127. Herman Mayes Genealogical Collection.

1128. Lee County, Iowa, Marriage Record 13:418, microfilm 1,903,294, Family History Library, Salt Lake City, Utah.

1129. Ruth C. Frist, Civil War Widows Pension File #321253, National Archives, Washington, D.C.

1130. Roscoe E. Frist marriage application, Lee County, Iowa, Marriage Volume 14 1919–1922, p. 221, microfilm 1903295, Family History Library, Salt Lake City, Utah. Roscoe was their son, and Roscoe's own marriage proves his parents.

1131. Audrey Gilbert, *Preble County, Ohio, 1880 Census* (Utica, Kentucky: McDowell Publications, 1983), p. 206.

1132. Martin L. Frist household, 1920 U.S. census, Lee County, Iowa, population schedule, Madison Township, enumeration district 85, sheet 21, line 59; National Archives micropublication T625, roll 499.

1133. Roscoe E. Frist, social security application 373-01-4147, U.S. Social Security Administration.

1134. Roscoe E. Frist, 373-01-4147, Social Security Death Index, *Family Search*.

1135. Lee County, Iowa, Marriage Volume 14 1919–1922, p. 221, microfilm 1903295, Family History Library, Salt Lake City, Utah.

1136. Martin L. Frist household, 1920 U.S. census, Lee County, Iowa, population schedule, Madison Township, enumeration district 85, sheet 21, line 59; National Archives micropublication T625, roll 499.

1137. Lee County, Iowa, Marriage Volume 16 1924–1927, p. 156, microfilm 1903296, Family History Library, Salt Lake City, Utah. Record indicates Walter's parents unknown as he was raised in Illinois Children's Home in Chicago, Illinois.

1138. Martin L. Frist household, 1920 U.S. census, Lee County, Iowa, population schedule, Madison Township, enumeration district 85, sheet 21, line 59; National Archives micropublication T625, roll 499.

1139. Lee County, Iowa, Marriage Volume 15 1922–1924, p. 20, microfilm 1903295, Family History Library, Salt Lake City, Utah.

1140. Martin L. Frist household, 1920 U.S. census, Lee County, Iowa, population schedule, Madison Township, enumeration district 85, sheet 21, line 59; National Archives micropublication T625, roll 499.

1141. Lee County, Iowa, Marriage Volume 16 1924–1927, p. 442, microfilm 1903296, Family History Library, Salt Lake City, Utah.

1142. Dane Starbuck, *The Goodriches: An American Family* (Indianapolis: Liberty Fund, Inc., 2001), p. 25.

1143. Jonas Frist household, 1860 U. S. census, Wayne County, Indiana, population schedule, Wayne Township, p. 748, dwelling 1528, family 1545; National Archives micropublication M653, roll 308. There is some question regarding where Cora was born, but her parents were living in Wayne County the year before her birth.

1144. Cora Frist obituary, *The Indianapolis Star*, Indianapolis, Indiana, 1 November 1952 p. 2.

1145. Dane Starbuck, *The Goodriches: An American Family* (Indianapolis: Liberty Fund, Inc., 2001), p. 30.

1146. Dane Starbuck, *The Goodriches: An American Family* (Indianapolis: Liberty Fund, Inc., 2001), pp. 13 and 493.

1147. James P. Goodrich, obituary, *The Indianapolis Star*, Indianapolis, Indiana, 16 August 1940, p. 1.

1148. Jonas L. P. Frist household, 1880 U.S. census, Randolph County, Indiana, population schedule, City of Lynn, p. 271; National Archives micropublication T9, roll 307.

1149. Dane Starbuck, *The Goodriches: An American Family* (Indianapolis: Liberty Fund, Inc., 2001), pp. 25–26.

1150. Dane Starbuck, *The Goodriches: An American Family* (Indianapolis: Liberty Fund, Inc., 2001), p. 30.

1151. Dane Starbuck, *The Goodriches: An American Family* (Indianapolis: Liberty Fund, Inc., 2001), pp. 27 and 28.

1152. James P. Goodrich household, 1900 U.S. census, Randolph County, Indiana, population schedule, White River Township, enumeration district 136, sheet 4, line 70, dwelling 87 family 88; National Archives micropublication T623, roll 399.

1153. "Only Son Fondly Remembers Baking in Home at Winchester," *The Indianapolis Star*, Indianapolis, Indiana, 27 September 1964, p. 4, Section 7.

1154. Ibid.

1155. J. P. Goodrich household, 1920 U.S. census, Marion County, Indiana, population schedule, Center Township, enumeration district 119, sheet 9, line 91, no dwelling number, family 181; National Archives micropublication T625, roll 452.

1156. Wilbur D. Peat, *Portraits and Painters of the Governors of Indiana 1800–1978*, revised and edited by Diane Gail Lazarus, sketches of governors by Lana Ruegamer (Indianapolis: Indiana Historical Society, 1978).

1157. Patricia Frist Genealogical Collection, copy of letter held in 2003 by compiler.

1158. Ruby Haskins Ellis and Anna Petty Neal, *Lineage Book of National Society of the Daughters of American Colonists Volume II 1001–2000* (Washington, D.C.: Judd & Detweiler, 1930), #1164.

1159. Dane Starbuck, *The Goodriches: An American Family* (Indianapolis: Liberty Fund, Inc., 2001), p. 283.

1160. Dane Starbuck, *The Goodriches: An American Family* (Indianapolis: Liberty Fund, Inc., 2001), p. 284.

1161. James P. Goodrich obituary, *The Indianapolis Star*, Indianapolis, Indiana, 16 August 1940, p. 1.

1162. "Mrs. James P. Goodrich, Widow of State's World War Governor, Dies," *The Indianapolis Star*, Indianapolis, Indiana, 1 November 1941, p. 12.

1163. Ibid.

1164. Dane Starbuck, *The Goodriches: An American Family* (Indianapolis: Liberty Fund, Inc., 2001), p. 38.

1165. Ibid.

1166. "Pierre F. Goodrich Dies; Business Executive Had Diversified Career," *The Indianapolis Star*, Indianapolis, Indiana, 26 October 1973, p. 1.

1167. Dane Starbuck, *The Goodriches: An American Family* (Indianapolis: Liberty Fund, Inc., 2001), p. 125.

1168. Dane Starbuck, *The Goodriches: An American Family* (Indianapolis: Liberty Fund, Inc., 2001), p. 285.

1169. Elizabeth Lloyd household, 1870 U.S. census, New Castle County, Delaware, p. 383, dwelling 163, family 174; National Archives micropublication M593, roll 121.

1170. Ella Tindall probate record, 17579, 1932, New Castle County, Delaware, Delaware Public Archives, Dover, Delaware.

1171. William Tindall household, 1900 U.S. census, New Castle County, Delaware, population schedule, Wilmington, enumeration district 28, sheet 23, line 7; National Archives micropublication T623, roll 155.

1172. Ibid.

1173. William C. Tindall probate record, 14047, 1926, New Castle County, Delaware, Delaware Public Archives, Dover, Delaware.

1174. Elizabeth Lloyd household, 1870 U.S. census, New Castle County, Delaware, population schedule, p. 383 dwelling 163 family 174; National Archives micropublication M593, roll 121.

1175. William C. Tindall household, 1880 U.S. census, New Castle County, Delaware, population schedule, Wilmington, enumeration district 14, sheet 64, line 41, dwelling 470, family 576, stamped p. 361; microfilm 1254119, Family History Library, Salt Lake City, Utah.

1176. William Tindall household, 1900 U.S. census, New Castle County, Delaware, population schedule, Wilmington, enumeration district 28, sheet 23, line 7; National Archives micropublication T623, roll 155.

1177. William Tindall household, 1920 U.S. census, New Castle County, Delaware, population schedule, Wilmington, enumeration district 73, sheet 3, line 75, dwelling 41, family 50; National Archives micropublication T625, roll 203.

1178. William C. Tindall probate record, 14047, 1926, New Castle County, Delaware, Delaware Public Archives, Dover, Delaware.

1179. Ella Tindall probate record, 17579, 1932, New Castle County, Delaware, Delaware Public Archives, Dover, Delaware.

1180. Marriage date approximated from birth date of first child.

1181. William Cook Tindall (son), social security application 222-07-0954, U.S. Social Security Administration.

1182. William Tindall household, 1900 U.S. census, New Castle County, Delaware, population schedule, Wilmington, enumeration district 28, sheet 23, line 7; National Archives micropublication T623, roll 155.

1183. Roscoe C. Tindall probate record, 37833, 1957, New Castle County, Delaware, Delaware Public Archives, Dover, Delaware.

1184. Ibid.

1185. Elizabeth Lloyd household, 1870 U.S. census, New Castle County, Delaware, population schedule, p. 383 dwelling 163 family 174; National Archives micropublication M593, roll 121.

1186. Elizabeth J. Randle probate record, 20581, 1939, New Castle County, Delaware, Delaware Public Archives, Dover, Delaware.

1187. Elizabeth Lloyd probate record, 1907–1908, New Castle County, Delaware, Delaware Public Archives, Dover, Delaware. This proves she married to Joseph Randle by 1899, but the marriage probably took place about 1890.

1188. Joseph A. Randle probate record, 1908, New Castle County, Delaware, Delaware Public Archives, Dover, Delaware.

1189. Elizabeth J. Randle probate record, 20581, 1939, New Castle County, Delaware, Delaware Public Archives, Dover, Delaware.

1190. Elizabeth J. Randle probate record, 20581, 1939, New Castle County, Delaware, Delaware Public Archives, Dover, Delaware. This birth date for her daughter-in-law Margaret was listed in the probate record but cannot possibly be correct. A more likely date would be 1897.

1191. Elizabeth J. Randle probate record, 20581, 1939, New Castle County, Delaware, Delaware Public Archives, Dover, Delaware.

1192. Catherine C. Frist, Civil War Delaware Widow's Pension Application #193503, National Archives, Washington, D.C.

1193. New Castle County, Delaware Volume 41:42, Delaware Public Archives, Dover, Delaware.

1194. Catherine Frist household, 1870 U.S. census, New Castle County, Delaware, population schedule, Wilmington, p. 210B, dwelling 323, family 328; National Archives micropublication M593, roll 121.

1195. Catherine C. Frist household, 1880 U.S. census, New Castle County, Delaware, population schedule, Wilmington, enumeration district 16, sheet 47, line 14 [edge of page damaged, lines counted], dwelling 414, family 420, stamped p. 425; National Archives micropublication T9, roll 119.

1196. Robert Frist household, 1920 U.S. census, Los Angeles County, California, enumeration district 100. sheet 7A; stamped p. 246, dwelling 142, family 180; National Archives micropublication T625, roll 104.

1197. Wilmington, Delaware Death Register 1881–1888, p. 122, Delaware Public Archives, Dover, Delaware.

1198. Archie C. Frist obituary, *Long Beach Press-Telegram*, Long Beach, California, 15 August 1961 B-2, named a nephew William W. Rollins of Los Alamos, New Mexico, so Beatrice may have married a Robbins.

1199. Robert Porter Frist, death certificate 43 064668, California Department of Health Services.

1200. Archie C. Frist death certificate 61-080746, Los Angeles County, California, California Department of Health Services.

1201. Archie C. Frist death certificate 61-080746, Los Angeles County, California, California Department of Health Services. Also Archie C. Frist obituary, *Long Beach Press–Telegram*, Long Beach, California, 15 August 1961 B-2.

1202. Family Archives Record Sheet, microfilm 1274101, Family History Library, Salt Lake City, Utah.

1203. Archie C. Frist obituary, *Long Beach Press–Telegram*, Long Beach, California, 15 August 1961 B-2.

1204. Family Archives Record Sheet, microfilm 1274101, Family History Library, Salt Lake City, Utah.

1205. Catherine C. Frist, Civil War Delaware Widow's Pension Application #193503; National Archives, Washington, D.C.

1206. Holy Trinity (Old Swedes) Church, Church Yard Record #1379, Wilmington, Delaware.

1207. Frist–Hume marriage, Marriage Record Book M-2:75, Holy Trinity (Old Swedes) Church Archives, Wilmington, Delaware.

1208. Margaret Hume Frist death certificate #2981 (1950), Delaware Bureau of Vital Statistics, Dover, Delaware.

1209. Margaret Hume Frist #1490, Church Yard Record, Holy Trinity (Old Swedes) Church, Wilmington, Delaware.

1210. Herman Frist household, 1920 U.S. census, New Castle County, Delaware, population schedule, Wilmington, enumeration district 112, sheet 6B, line 889, dwelling 126, family 136; National Archives micropublication T625, roll 202.

1211. Holy Trinity (Old Swedes) Church, Church Yard Record #1379, Wilmington, Delaware.

1212. Margaret Hume Frist #26762, New Castle County, Delaware, Register of Wills, microfilm 741, Delaware Public Archives, Dover, Delaware.

1213. Margaret Hume Frist #1490, Church Yard Record, Holy Trinity (Old Swedes) Church, Wilmington, Delaware.

1214. Etta F. Springer death certificate 1704 (1942), Delaware Division of Vital Statistics, Dover, Delaware.

1215. Etta F. Springer probate record, 24822, 1942, New Castle County, Delaware, Delaware Public Archives, Dover, Delaware.

1216. Willard Springer household, 1900 U.S. census, New Castle County, Delaware, population schedule, Wilmington Hundred, enumeration district 16, sheet 1, line 39, p. 201; National Archives micropublication, T623, roll 154.

1217. Willard Springer probate record, 20759, 1936, New Castle County, Delaware, Delaware Public Archives, Dover, Delaware.

1218. Levi H. Springer household, 1880 U.S. census, New Castle County, Delaware, population schedule, City of Wilmington, enumeration district 5, p. 132B, dwelling 320, family 435, microfilm 1254118, Family History Library, Salt Lake City, Utah.

1219. Ibid.

1220. Willard Springer probate record, 20759, 1936, New Castle County, Delaware, Delaware Public Archives, Dover, Delaware.

1221. Etta F. Springer probate record, 24822, 1942, New Castle County, Delaware, Delaware Public Archives, Dover, Delaware.

1222. Edith Sarah Baumgartner probate record, 65875, 1975, New Castle County, Delaware, Delaware Public Archives, Dover, Delaware.

1223. Willard Springer household, 1900 U.S. census, New Castle County, Delaware, population schedule, Wilmington Hundred, enumeration district 16, sheet 1, line 39, p. 201; National Archives micropublication, T623, roll 154.

1224. Harold L. Springer probate record, 56073, 1969, New Castle County, Delaware, Delaware Public Archives, Dover, Delaware.

1225. Carolyn L. Springer probate record, 53971, 1968, New Castle County, Delaware, Delaware Public Archives, Dover, Delaware. Date of marriage approximated from birth of first child.

1226. Willard Springer household, 1900 U.S. census, New Castle County, Delaware, population schedule, Wilmington Hundred, enumeration district 16, sheet 1, line 39, p. 201; National Archives micropublication, T623, roll 154.

1227. Helen S. Stout probate record, 29860, 1948, New Castle County, Delaware, Delaware Public Archives, Dover, Delaware.

1228. Frist Family Group Sheet provided by grandson Paul L. White (118 Montchan Drive, Wilmington, DE 19807), 9 November 2001, to compiler.

1229. Willard Springer, Jr. death certificate 518 (1956), State of Delaware, Bureau of Vital Statistics, Dover, Delaware.

1230. Edna L. Springer, social security application 221-30-7022, U.S. Social Security Administration. Date of marriage approximated from birth of first child.

1231. Willard Springer household, 1900 U.S. census, New Castle County, Delaware, population schedule, Wilmington Hundred, enumeration district 16, sheet 1, line 39, p. 201; National Archives micropublication, T623, roll 154.

1232. Edith Baumgartner probate record, 65875, 1975, New Castle County, Delaware, Delaware Public Archives, Dover, Delaware.

1233. Levi H. Springer household, 1880 U.S. census, New Castle County, Delaware, population schedule, City of Wilmington, enumeration district 5, p. 132B, dwelling 320, family 435, microfilm 1254118, Family History Library, Salt Lake City, Utah. Also Edwin J. Sheppard household, 1900 U.S. census, New Castle County, Delaware, population schedule, Wilmington, enumeration district 45, sheet 24, line 32; National Archives micropublication T623, roll 156.

1234. Kallena Sheppard probate record, 29157, 1950, New Castle County, Delaware, Delaware Public Archives, Dover, Delaware.

1235. Edwin J. Sheppard household, 1900 U.S. census, New Castle County, Delaware, population schedule, Wilmington, enumeration district 45, sheet 24, line 32; National Archives micropublication T623, roll 156.

1236. Levi H. Springer household, 1880 U.S. census, New Castle County, Delaware, population schedule, City of Wilmington, enumeration district 5, p. 132B, dwelling 320, family 435, microfilm 1254118, Family History Library, Salt Lake City, Utah.

1237. Edwin J. Sheppard household, 1900 U.S. census, New Castle County, Delaware, population schedule, Wilmington, enumeration district 45, sheet 24, line 32; National Archives micropublication T623, roll 156.

1238. Kallena Sheppard probate record, 29157, 1950, New Castle County, Delaware, Delaware Public Archives, Dover, Delaware.

1239. Edwin R. Sheppard probate record, 36506, 1956, New Castle County, Delaware, Delaware Public Archives, Dover, Delaware.

1240. Edwin J. Sheppard household, 1900 U.S. census, New Castle County, Delaware, population schedule, Wilmington, enumeration district 45, sheet 24, line 32; National Archives micropublication T623, roll 156.

1241. Morris W. Sheppard probate record, 42966, 1961 estate amounted to $1,006,207.25, New Castle County, Delaware, Delaware Public Archives, Dover, Delaware.

1242. Edwin J. Sheppard household, 1900 U.S. census, New Castle County, Delaware, population schedule, Wilmington, enumeration district 45, sheet 24, line 32; National Archives micropublication T623, roll 156.

1243. Edwin R. Sheppard probate record, 36506, 1956, New Castle County, Delaware, Delaware Public Archives, Dover, Delaware.

1244. Edwin J. Sheppard household, 1900 U.S. census, New Castle County, Delaware, population schedule, Wilmington, enumeration district 45, sheet 24, line 32; National Archives micropublication T623, roll 156.

1245. Natalie Dare probate record, 11605, 1928, New Castle County, Delaware, Delaware Public Archives, Dover, Delaware.

1246. Joseph W. Dare household, 1930 U.S. census, New Castle County, Delaware, population schedule, Wilmington, enumeration district 59, p. 213, dwelling 77, family 78; National Archives micropublication T626, roll 289.

1247. Natalie Dare probate record, 11605, 1928, New Castle County, Delaware, Delaware Public Archives, Dover, Delaware.

1248. Joseph W. Dare household, 1930 U.S. census, New Castle County, Delaware, population schedule, Wilmington, enumeration district 59, p. 213, dwelling 77, family 78; National Archives micropublication T626, roll 289.

1249. Edwin J. Sheppard household, 1900 U.S. census, New Castle County, Delaware, population schedule, Wilmington, enumeration district 45, sheet 24, line 32; National Archives micropublication T623, roll 156.

1250. Esther S. Graves probate record, 66410, 1975, New Castle County, Delaware, Delaware Public Archives, Dover, Delaware.

1251. Herman Mayes Genealogical Collection.

1252. Kallena Sheppard probate record, 29157, 1950, New Castle County, Delaware, Delaware Public Archives, Dover, Delaware.

1253. Edwin R. Sheppard probate record, 36506, 1956, New Castle County, Delaware, Delaware Public Archives, Dover, Delaware.

1254. Morris W. Sheppard probate record, 42966, 1961, estate amounted to $1,006,207.25, New Castle County, Delaware, Delaware Public Archives, Dover, Delaware.

1255. Birth record of son Ren Leslie Frist, Vermillion County, Indiana, Birth Records Volume 1, p. 284, Newport, Indiana.

1256. Frank Peirce Frist Family Bible.

1257. Helt's Prairie Cemetery, Vermillion County, Indiana.

1258. Vermillion County, Indiana, Marriage Book 5:354, County Clerk, Newport, Indiana.

1259. Mrs. Elizabeth Frist obituary, 13 August 1935 from unknown newspaper, clipping from Patricia Frist Genealogical Collection.

1260. Frist Funeral Home Record, Clinton, Indiana, Patricia Frist Genealogical Collection.

1261. Jediah R. Frist household, 1870 U.S. census, Vermillion County, Indiana, population schedule, Subdivision #222 Helt Township, p. 34, dwelling 225, family 233; National Archives micropublication M593, roll 365.

1262. John F. Moore household, 1880 U.S. census, Vermillion County, Indiana, population schedule, Helt Township, p. 94; National Archives micropublication T9, Roll 318.

1263. Vermillion County, Indiana, Marriage Book 5:354, County Clerk, Newport, Indiana.

1264. Patricia Frist Genealogical Collection Item 14.

1265. Patricia Frist Genealogical Collection Item 17.

1266. Jediah Frist household, 1900 U.S. census, Vermillion County, Indiana, population schedule, Helt Township enumeration district 91, sheet 1A, stamped p. 213, dwelling and family 1; National Archives micropublication T623, roll 408.

1267. "Webb Frist, 57 Dies at Capital," undated obituary from unknown newspaper, Patricia Frist Genealogical Collection. Also Patricia Frist Genealogical Collection Item 65.

1268. Jediah Frist household, 1910 U.S. census, Vermillion County, Indiana, population schedule, enumeration district 123, sheet 3A, stamped p. 124, family and dwelling 48; National Archives micropublication T624, roll 384.

1269. Patricia Frist Genealogical Collection Item 13.

1270. Ibid.

1271. Ibid.

1272. Ibid.

1273. Frist Funeral Home Record, Clinton, Indiana, Patricia Frist Genealogical Collection.

1274. Patricia Frist Genealogical Collection; letter from Samuel Frist to Jediah Frist 2 October 1938, copy held in 2003 by compiler.

1275. Helt's Prairie Cemetery, Vermillion County, Indiana.

1276. Jediah Frist Family Bible, from Patricia Frist Genealogical Collection, copy held in 2003 by compiler.

1277. "Ren L. Frist Dies Today Following Two-Day Illness," undated obituary from unknown newspaper, Patricia Frist Genealogical Collection. Also Patricia Frist Genealogical Collection Item 24.

1278. Myrtle Marie Frist death certificate 0-100 (1974), Texas Department of Health, Austin; copy from Patricia Frist Genealogical Collection.

1279. Miss Myrtle Frist obituary, 14 January 1974, unidentified newspaper, Patricia Frist Genealogical Collection. Also Patricia Frist Genealogical Collection Item 26.

1280. Jediah Frist Family Bible.

1281. Ibid.

1282. Harlow Peirce Frist death certificate (1975), Vermillion County, Indiana, Board of Health.

1283. Frist–Miller marriage, copy of original marriage license provided June 2001 by daughter Mary Edith Banes (2229 Rainbow Drive, Lafayette, IN 47904-2311) to compiler.

1284. Hazel Frist Harlan obituary, undated from unidentified newspaper, Patricia Frist Genealogical Collection. Also Patricia Frist Genealogical Collection Items 58 and 59.

1285. Marshall Frist, 303-01-5203, Social Security Death Index, *Family Search.*

1286. Vermillion County Historical Society, *Vermillion County Indiana, History & Families* (Paducah, Kentucky: Turner Publishing Company, 1990), p. 156.

1287. "Webb Frist, 57 Dies at Capital," undated obituary from unknown newspaper, Patricia Frist Genealogical Collection. Also Patricia Frist Genealogical Collection Item 65.

1288. Frank Peirce Frist Family Bible.

1289. "Frist Celebrates 100 Years," *The Daily Clintonian*, Clinton, Indiana, 26 December 1987, clipping from Patricia Frist Genealogical Collection. Also Frank Peirce Frist Family Bible.

1290. *History of Parke and Vermillion Counties Indiana* (Indianapolis, Indiana: B. F. Bowen & Company, 1913), p. 580. The spelling Shapard was used in this publication.

1291. Frank Peirce Frist Family Bible.

1292. Ibid.

1293. *History of Parke and Vermillion Counties Indiana* (Indianapolis, Indiana: B. F. Bowen & Company, 1913), pp. 580–581.

1294. Patricia Frist Genealogical Collection Item 67.

1295. Jasper Frist household, 1900 U.S. census, Vermillion County, Indiana, population schedule, Clinton Township, enumeration district 89, sheet 20, line 65; National Archives micropublication T623, roll 408.

1296. Patricia Frist Genealogical Collection Item 70.

1297. *History of Parke and Vermillion Counties Indiana* (Indianapolis, Indiana: B. F. Bowen & Company, 1913), pp. 580–581.

1298. Jasper Frist household, 1920 U.S. census, Vermillion County, Indiana, population schedule, Helt Township, enumeration district, p. 4A dwelling 72, family 73; National Archives micropublication T625, roll 472.

1299. "Frist Celebrates 100 Years," *The Daily Clintonian*, Clinton, Indiana, 26 December 1987, clipping from Patricia Frist Genealogical Collection. Also Frank Peirce Frist Family Bible.

1300. "Frist Celebrates 100 Years," *The Daily Clintonian*, Clinton, Indiana, 26 December 1987, clipping from Patricia Frist Genealogical Collection.

1301. Ibid.

1302. Patricia Frist Genealogical Collection Items 75 and 77.

1303. Patricia Frist Genealogical Collection Item 76.

1304. John Edgar Frist death certificate (1912), Baltimore County, Maryland, Board of Health, F1912, Series C322-19, Acc. No. 50,126-19, location 2/56/9/8, Maryland State Archives, Annapolis.

1305. Ibid.

1306. Baltimore City, Maryland, Marriage Index 1851–1885, microfilm CR 1669, Maryland State Archives, Annapolis, Maryland.

1307. Margaret Arthur Frist death certificate #E-54242 (1930), Health Department, City of Baltimore City, Maryland.

1308. Ibid.

1309. John E. Frist household, 1900 U.S. census, Baltimore County, Maryland, population schedule, Ninth District, enumeration district 40, sheet 16, line 42, stamped p. 133; National Archives micropublication T623, roll 607. It is uncertain when or if John E. Frist married Emma Cooper. What is certain is that in 1900 he was still married to Margaret Arthur.

1310. Letter, *Cecil Democrat*, Elkton, Maryland, 9 July 1859, p. 2.

1311. John Frist household, 1870 U.S. census, Baltimore County, Maryland, population schedule, City of Baltimore, Ward 19, p. 284, line 24; National Archives micropublication M593, roll 580.

1312. Baltimore City, Maryland, Marriage Index 1851–1885, microfilm CR 1669, Maryland State Archives, Annapolis, Maryland.

1313. John Frist household, 1880 U.S. census, Baltimore County, Maryland, population schedule, Eight Ward, enumeration district 78, sheet 33, line 1, stamped p. 46; National Archives micropublication T9, roll 500.

1314. Baltimore City Equity Index, Circuit Court #2, p. 121 citing file #290, Maryland State Archives, Annapolis, Maryland. This file could not be located and apparently does not exist.

1315. Bill of divorce, *John Edgar Frist vs. Margaret Ann Frist*, Baltimore County, Maryland, Circuit Court, Equity Docket packet #9127, Maryland State Archives, Annapolis, Maryland.

1316. Margaret Frist household, 1900 U.S. census, Baltimore County, Maryland, population schedule, Ninth District, enumeration district 40, sheet 14, line 65, stamped p. 131; National Archives micropublication T623, roll 607.

1317. John E. Frist household, 1900 U.S. census, Baltimore County, Maryland, population schedule, Ninth District, enumeration district 40, sheet 16, line 42, stamped p. 133; National Archives micropublication T623, roll 607.

1318. John Frist obituary, *The Jeffersonian*, Baltimore County, Maryland, 22 July 1912, page 5, column 3, microfilm M2936 January 1912–December 1912, Maryland State Archives, Annapolis, Maryland.

1319. Bill of divorce, *John Edgar Frist vs. Margaret Ann Frist*, Baltimore County, Maryland, Circuit Court, Equity Docket packet #9127, Maryland State Archives, Annapolis, Maryland.

1320. Bill of divorce, *Margaret Ann Frist vs. John Edgar Frist*, Baltimore City, Maryland, Circuit Court Equity case file #11793-B, Box 282, Maryland State Archives, Annapolis, Maryland.

1321. John Edgar Frist will, Baltimore County, Maryland, Book 16:467, microfilm CR 123, Maryland State Archives, Annapolis, Maryland.

1322. John Edgar Frist death certificate (1912), Baltimore County, Maryland, Board of Health, F1912, Series C322-19, Acc. No. 50,126-19, location 2/56/9/8, Maryland State Archives, Annapolis, Maryland.

1323. John Frist obituary, *The Jeffersonian*, Baltimore County, Maryland, 22 July 1912, page 5, column 3, microfilm M2936 January 1912–December 1912, Maryland State Archives, Annapolis, Maryland.

1324. William P. Jink [*sic*] household, 1920 U.S. census, Baltimore County, Maryland, population schedule, City of Baltimore, enumeration district 452, sheet 7A, line 44; National Archives micropublication T625, roll 667.

1325. Margaret Arthur Frist death certificate #E-54242 (1930), Health Department, City of Baltimore City, Maryland.

1326. Margaret Ann Arthur Frist burial card, Lot 203 E ½, Section Elder, permit 80171, Loudon Park Cemetery, Baltimore City, Maryland.

1327. John Frist household, 1880 U.S. census, Baltimore County, Maryland, population schedule, Eighth Ward, enumeration district 78, sheet 33, line 1, stamped p. 46; National Archives micropublication T9, roll 500.

1328. John A. Frist burial card, Lot 203 E ½, Section Elder, permit 89701, Loudon Park Cemetery, Baltimore City, Maryland.

1329. Sarah Frist death certificate E-60865 (1930), Health Department, City of Baltimore City, Maryland. This birth year from Sarah's death certificate appears accurate in that she was seventy-one at death in 1930. John's birth year, although estimated from census, is consistently given as 1877. Thus, he married a woman almost twenty years his senior.

1330. Sarah Frist death certificate E-60865 (1930), Health Department, City of Baltimore City, Maryland.

1331. Ibid.

1332. John Frist household, 1880 U.S. census, Baltimore County, Maryland, population schedule, Eighth Ward, enumeration district 78, sheet 33, line 1, stamped p. 46; National Archives micropublication T9, roll 500.

1333. Anna Louise Jamison burial card with undated and unidentified obituary clipping, Lot 203 E½, Section Elder, Loudon Park Cemetery, Baltimore City, Maryland.

1334. Margaret Arthur Frist death certificate #E-54242 (1930), Health Department, City of Baltimore City, Maryland. The informant was Mrs. Anna L. Jamison whose address on the death certificate was the same as Margaret Frist's.

1335. John Jamison burial card with undated and unidentified obituary clipping, Lot 203 E ½, Grave 1, Loudon Park Cemetery, Baltimore City, Maryland.

1336. Edgar H. Coney burial card with undated and unidentified obituary clipping, Lot 203 E ½, Section Elder, Grave 5, Loudon Park Cemetery, Baltimore City, Maryland.

1337. Margaret Frist household, 1900 U.S. census, Baltimore County, Maryland, population schedule, Ninth District, enumeration district 40, sheet 14, line 65, stamped p. 131; National Archives micropublication T623, roll 607.

1338. John Edgar Frist will, Baltimore County, Maryland, Book 16:467, microfilm CR 123, Maryland State Archives, Annapolis, Maryland. Bessie was named as Bessie Gutman in her father's will.

1339. William P. Jink [*sic*] household, 1920 U.S. census, Baltimore County, Maryland, population schedule, City of Baltimore, enumeration district 452, sheet 7A, line 44; National Archives micropublication T625, roll 667.

1340. Ibid.

1341. Hattie M. Emmart death certificate 11768 (1939), Maryland State Department of Health, Baltimore City, Maryland.

1342. Ibid.

1343. John Frist household, 1900 U.S. census, Baltimore County, Maryland, population schedule, City of Baltimore, enumeration district 199, sheet 7, line 78; National Archives micropublication T623, roll 614.

1344. Henry Fletcher Powell, *Tercentenary History of Maryland, Volume 3* (Chicago: S. J. Clark Publishing Company, 1925), p. 360.

1345. William W. Emmart burial transmit permit #81434 (1950), Baltimore City Health Department, Baltimore City, Maryland.

1346. John Frist household, 1870 U.S. census, Baltimore County, Maryland, population schedule, City of Baltimore, Ward Nineteen, p. 284, line 24; National Archives micropublication M593, roll 580.

1347. "Mrs. W. W. Emmart Dies at Glyndon," *The Sun*, Baltimore City, Maryland, 10 December 1939, p. 22, column 1.

1348. John Frist household, 1900 U.S. census, Baltimore County, Maryland, population schedule, City of Baltimore, enumeration district 199, sheet 7, line 78; National Archives micropublication T623, roll 614.

1349. Henry Fletcher Powell, *Tercentenary History of Maryland, Volume 3* (Chicago: S. J. Clark Publishing Company, 1925), pp. 360–361.

1350. Ibid.

1351. Ibid.

1352. Hattie M. Emmart death certificate 11768 (1939), Maryland State Department of Health, Baltimore City, Maryland.

1353. William W. Emmart burial transmit permit #81434 (1950), Baltimore City Health Department, Baltimore City, Maryland.

1354. Henry Fletcher Powell, *Tercentenary History of Maryland, Volume 3* (Chicago: S. J. Clark Publishing Company, 1925), p. 360.

1355. Charles K. Trueblood interment permit, Lot 81, Section J, Loudon Park Cemetery, Baltimore City, Maryland.

1356. "Mrs. W. W. Emmart Dies at Glyndon," *The Sun*, Baltimore City, Maryland, 10 December 1939, p. 22, column 1.

1357. Abram B. Frist death certificate #73652 (1923), Heath Department, City of Baltimore City, Maryland. This man's middle name was found as Bernard, Burton, and Burnett in various documents cited elsewhere, but two sons were given the middle name Bernard.

1358. Abram B. Frist death certificate #73652 (1923), Heath Department City of Baltimore City, Maryland. Copy of original provided by Margaret Hepner (600 Falcon Bridge Drive, Joppa, MD 21085) and held in 2003 by compiler.

1359. Frist–Zimmer marriage, Cecil County, Maryland, copy of original from Margaret Frist Hepner Genealogical Collection (600 Falcon Bridge Drive, Joppa, MD 21085) provided to compiler 1 April 2002. Margaret is the granddaughter of Abram Bernard Frist.

1360. Abram Frist household, 1900 U.S. census, Baltimore County, Maryland, population schedule, City of Baltimore, enumeration district 289, sheet 17, house number 1112, dwelling 319, family number illegible; National Archives micropublication T623, roll 618.

1361. Frist–Quinn marriage, Immaculate Conception Church, Baltimore City, Maryland, copy of original from descendant Margaret Frist Hepner Genealogical Collection.

1362. Jennie Frist death certificate #02807 (1934), Health Department, City of Baltimore City, Maryland.

1363. Ibid.

1364. Abram Frist household, 1870 U.S. census, Cecil County, Maryland, population schedule, Port Deposit, p. 243, dwelling and family 2; National Archives micropublication M593, roll 583.

1365. Abram Frist household, 1880 U.S. census, Cecil County, Maryland, population schedule, Port Deposit, enumeration district 17, p. 258A, dwelling and family 65; National Archives micropublication T9, roll 507.

1366. Abram Frist household, 1900 U.S. census, Baltimore County, Maryland, population schedule, City of Baltimore, enumeration district 289, sheet 17, house number 1112, dwelling 319, family number illegible; National Archives micropublication T623, roll 618.

1367. Ibid.

1368. Frist–Quinn marriage, Immaculate Conception Church, Baltimore City, Maryland, copy of original from descendant Margaret Frist Hepner Genealogical Collection (600 Falcon Bridge Drive, Joppa, MD 21085).

1369. Baltimore City, Maryland, Marriage Index 1886–1914, original card index, Maryland State Archives, Annapolis, Maryland.

1370. Bernard Frist household, 1920 U.S. census, Baltimore County, Maryland, population schedule, City of Baltimore, enumeration district 187, sheet 4, line 15, dwelling 69, family 89; National Archives micropublication T625, roll 658.

1371. Abram B. Frist death certificate #73652 (1923), Heath Department, City of Baltimore City, Maryland. Copy of original provided by Margaret Hepner (600 Falcon Bridge Drive, Joppa, MD 21085) and held in 2003 by compiler.

1372. Abraham Burnett Frist obituary, *Baltimore Sun*, Baltimore, Maryland, 12 March 1923, p. 10, column 1, microfilm roll 365, Maryland State Law Library, Annapolis, Maryland.

1373. Jennie Frist death certificate #02807 (1934), Health Department, City of Baltimore, Baltimore City, Maryland.

1374. "Funeral at the home of her daughter Margaret Behnken," Jennie T. Frist obituary, undated from unknown newspaper, copy from Margaret Hepner Genealogical Collection.

1375. Abram Frist household, 1900 U.S. census, Baltimore County, Maryland, population schedule, City of Baltimore, enumeration district 289, sheet 17, house number 1112, dwelling 319, family number illegible; National Archives micropublication T623, roll 618. Also Interview with Martin Burnett Lyons (30588 Kingston Road, Easton, MD 21601), son of Estella Elizabeth Frist Lyons, September 2002 by Margaret Hepner (600 Falcon Bridge Drive, Joppa, MD 21085). Information conveyed 26 September 2002 to compiler.

1376. Interview with Martin Burnett Lyons (30588 Kingston Road, Easton, MD 21601), son of Estella Elizabeth Frist Lyons, September 2002 by Margaret Hepner (600 Falcon Bridge Drive, Joppa, MD 21085). Information conveyed 26 September 2002 to compiler.

1377. Abram Frist household, 1900 U.S. census, Baltimore County, Maryland, population schedule, City of Baltimore, enumeration district 289, sheet 17, house number 1112, dwelling 319, family number illegible; National Archives micropublication T623, roll 618.

1378. Interview with Martin Burnett Lyons (30588 Kingston Road, Easton, MD 21601), son of Estella Elizabeth Frist Lyons, September 2002 by Margaret Hepner (600 Falcon Bridge Drive, Joppa, MD 21085). Information conveyed 26 September 2002 to compiler.

1379. Abram Frist household, 1900 U.S. census, Baltimore County, Maryland, population schedule, City of Baltimore, enumeration district 289, sheet 17, house number 1112, dwelling 319, family number illegible; National Archives micropublication T623, roll 618.

1380. Interview with Martin Burnett Lyons (30588 Kingston Road, Easton, MD 21601), son of Estella Elizabeth Frist Lyons, September 2002 by Margaret Hepner (600 Falcon Bridge Drive, Joppa, MD 21085). Information conveyed 26 September 2002 to compiler. Also John J. Cox household, 1920 U.S. census, Baltimore City, Maryland, population schedule, Ward 8, enumeration district 114, sheet 20, dwelling 438, family 452; National Archives micropublication T624, roll 657.

1381. New Cathedral Cemetery, 4300 Old Frederick Road, Baltimore City, Maryland.

1382. Melvin Bernard Frist, social security application 215-09-8288, U.S. Social Security Administration.

1383. "Funeral at the home of her daughter Margaret Behnken," Jennie T. Frist obituary, undated from unknown newspaper, copy from Margaret Hepner Genealogical Collection, held in 2003 by compiler.

1384. Frist Family Group Sheet provided 2 April 2002 by Margaret Frist Hepner (600 Falcon Bridge Drive, Joppa, MD 21085), daughter of Casper Bernard Frist to compiler.

1385. Donnelly F. Frist obituary, undated clipping from unknown newspaper, copy from Margaret Hepner Genealogical Collection and New Cathedral Cemetery, 4300 Old Frederick Road, Baltimore City, Maryland.

1386. Ibid.

1387. Frist Family Group Sheet provided 2 April 2002 by Margaret Frist Hepner (600 Falcon Bridge Drive, Joppa, MD 21085) to compiler.

1388. Frist Family Group Sheet provided June 2002 by Gene and Debbie Fischer III (11615 Joy Lane, Fredericksburg, VA 22407) to compiler. Gene is a grandson of Dolores Mary Frist Klima.

1389. Frist Family Group Sheet provided 2 April 2002 by Margaret Frist Hepner (600 Falcon Bridge Drive, Joppa, MD 21085) to compiler.

1390. Hattie Mary Mohrlein death certificate E59382 (1930), Health Department, City of Baltimore City, Maryland.

1391. Ibid.

1392. George F. Morhline [*sic*] household, 1900 U.S. census, Cecil County, Maryland, population schedule, Port Deposit, enumeration district 25, sheet 2, dwelling 37, family 37; National Archives micropublication T623, roll 620.

1393. Abram Frist household, 1880 U.S. census, Cecil County, Maryland, population schedule, Port Deposit, enumeration district 17, p. 258A, dwelling and family 65; National Archives micropublication T9, roll 507.

1394. George F. Morhline [*sic*] household, 1900 U.S. census, Cecil County, Maryland, population schedule, Port Deposit, enumeration district 25, sheet 2, dwelling 37, family 37; National Archives micropublication T623, roll 620.

1395. George F. Mohrlein household, 1920 U.S. census, Baltimore County, Maryland, population schedule, City of Baltimore, enumeration district 156, sheet 9, line 73; National Archives micropublication T625, roll 662.

1396. George F. Morhline [*sic*] household, 1900 U.S. census, Cecil County, Maryland, population schedule, Port Deposit, enumeration district 25, sheet 2, dwelling 37, family 37; National Archives micropublication T623, roll 620.

1397. Ibid.

1398. George F. Mohrlein household, 1920 U.S. census, Baltimore County, Maryland, population schedule, City of Baltimore, enumeration district 156, sheet 9, line 73; National Archives micropublication T625, roll 662.

1399. Rose W. Peterson, *Spring Hill Cemetery, Charleston, West Virginia, Volume III, L–R* (Nitro, West Virginia: Peterson Quality Associates, 1995), p. 197.

1400. Thomas Frist household, 1860 U.S. census, Monroe County, Virginia, population schedule, Union Town, post office Peterstown, p. 947B, line 2; National Archives micropublication M653, roll 1363.

1401. Rose W. Peterson, *Spring Hill Cemetery, Charleston, West Virginia, Volume III, L–R* (Nitro, West Virginia: Peterson Quality Associates, 1995), p. 197.

1402. Burton Frist household, 1880 U.S. census, Kanawha County, West Virginia, population schedule, Charleston, sheet 18, stamped p. 454, line 28; National Archives micropublication T9, roll 1405.

1403. W. S. Laidley, *History of Charles and Kanawha County, West Virginia, and Representative Citizen* (no date; reprint, Waynesville, North Carolina: Don Mills, 1993), p. 918.

1404. Rose W. Peterson, *Spring Hill Cemetery, Charleston, West Virginia, Volume III, L–R* (Nitro, West Virginia: Peterson Quality Associates, 1995), p. 197.

1405. W. S. Laidley, *History of Charles and Kanawha County, West Virginia, and Representative Citizen* (no date; reprint, Waynesville, North Carolina: Don Mills, 1993), p. 918.

1406. Rose W. Peterson, *Spring Hill Cemetery, Charleston, West Virginia, Volume III, L–R* (Nitro, West Virginia: Peterson Quality Associates, 1995), p. 197.

1407. Thomas Frist household, 1860 U.S. census, Monroe County, Virginia, population schedule, Union Town, post office Peterstown, p. 947B, line 2; National Archives micropublication M653, roll 1363.

1408. Sarah Frist household, 1880 U.S. census, Kanawha County, West Virginia, population schedule, Charleston, enumeration district 61, p. 454, dwelling and family 136; National Archives micropublication T9, roll 1405.

1409. Burton Frist household, 1880 U.S. census, Kanawha County, West Virginia, population schedule, Charleston, sheet 18, stamped p. 454, line 28; National Archives micropublication T9, roll 1405.

1410. W. S. Laidley, *History of Charles and Kanawha County, West Virginia, and Representative Citizen* (no date; reprint, Waynesville, North Carolina: Don Mills, 1993), p. 918.

1411. Burton Frist household, 1900 U.S. census, Kanawha County, West Virginia, population schedule, p. 172, enumeration district 44, sheet 4, dwelling 80 family 83; National Archives micropublication T623, roll 1762.

1412. Rose W. Peterson, *Spring Hill Cemetery, Charleston, West Virginia, Volume III, L–R* (Nitro, West Virginia: Peterson Quality Associates, 1995), p. 197.

1413. Burton Frist household, 1920 U.S. census, Kanawha County, West Virginia, population schedule, Charleston precinct 25, enumeration district 110, sheet 9, line 33; National Archives micropublication T625, roll 1958.

1414. Rose W. Peterson, *Spring Hill Cemetery, Charleston, West Virginia, Volume III, L–R* (Nitro, West Virginia: Peterson Quality Associates, 1995), p. 197.

1415. Burton Frist household, 1900 U.S. census, Kanawha County, West Virginia, population schedule, p. 172, enumeration district 44, sheet 4, dwelling 80 family 83; National Archives micropublication T623, roll 1762.

1416. Rose W. Peterson, *Spring Hill Cemetery, Charleston, West Virginia, Volume III, L–R* (Nitro, West Virginia: Peterson Quality Associates, 1995), p. 197.

1417. Ibid.

1418. Rose W. Peterson, *Spring Hill Cemetery, Charleston, West Virginia, Volume III, L–R* (Nitro, West Virginia: Peterson Quality Associates, 1995), p. 197. The birth date from the tombstone was interpreted as 1883, but 1888 was in the 1900 census and is a more likely date.

1419. Rose W. Peterson, *Spring Hill Cemetery, Charleston, West Virginia, Volume III, L–R* (Nitro, West Virginia: Peterson Quality Associates, 1995), p. 197.

1420. Burton Frist household, 1900 U.S. census, Kanawha County, West Virginia, population schedule, p. 172, enumeration district 44, sheet 4, dwelling 80 family 83; National Archives micropublication T623, roll 1762.

1421. Ibid.

1422. Ibid.

1423. Sarah E. Frist household, 1900 U.S. census, Kanawha County, West Virginia, population schedule, enumeration district 44, p. 4, stamped p. 172, dwelling 79, family 82; National Archives micropublication T623, roll 1762.

1424. Rose W. Peterson, *Spring Hill Cemetery, Charleston, West Virginia, Volume III, L–R* (Nitro, West Virginia: Peterson Quality Associates, 1995), p. 197.

1425. Roy Thomas Frist, social security application 235-50-2020, U.S. Social Security Administration; Roy was a son, and his application listed his parents as Thomas Jackson Frist and Laura Jane Chapman. Marriage date estimated from birth of first child.

1426. Sarah Frist household, 1880 U.S. census, Kanawha County, West Virginia, population schedule, Charleston, enumeration district 61, p. 454, dwelling and family 136; National Archives micropublication T9, roll 1405.

1427. Sarah E. Frist household, 1900 U.S. census, Kanawha County, West Virginia, population schedule, enumeration district 44, p. 4, stamped p. 172, dwelling 79, family 82; National Archives micropublication T623, roll 1762.

1428. Thomas J. Frist household, 1920 U.S. census, Kanawha County, West Virginia, population schedule, Charleston Ward 14, enumeration district 112, sheet 9, line 58, address 1699 Piedmont; National Archives micropublication T625, roll 1958.

1429. Roy Thomas Frist, social security application 235-50-2020, U.S. Social Security Administration.

1430. Lucille Chapman Frist, social security application 236-30-5073, U.S. Social Security Administration.

1431. Thomas J. Frist, household, 1920 U.S. census, Kanawha County, West Virginia, population schedule, Charleston Ward 14, enumeration district 112, sheet 9, line 58, address 1699 Piedmont; National Archives micropublication T625, roll 1958.

1432. Edward Frist household, 1870 U.S. census, Cecil County, Maryland, population schedule, seventh district p. 271, dwelling family 421; National Archives micropublication M593, roll 583. Exact date from Herman Mayes Genealogical Collection.

1433. George E. Frist household, 1900 U.S. census, Cecil County, Maryland, population schedule, enumeration district 25, sheet 9, line 93; National Archives micropublication T623, roll 620 and Herman Mayes Genealogical Collection.

1434. Edward Frist household, 1870 U.S. census, Cecil County, Maryland, population schedule, seventh district p. 271, dwelling family 421; National Archives micropublication M593, roll 583.

1435. George E. Frist household, 1900 U.S. census, Cecil County, Maryland, population schedule, enumeration district 25, sheet 9, line 93; National Archives micropublication T623, roll 620.

1436. Edward Frist family in Alfred Miller household, 1920 U.S. census, Delaware County, Pennsylvania, population schedule, enumeration district 217, sheet 5A, line 46, dwelling 87, family 109; National Archives micropublication T625, roll 1560.

1437. George E. Frist household, 1900 U.S. census, Cecil County, Maryland, population schedule, enumeration district 25, sheet 9, line 93; National Archives micropublication T623, roll 620.

1438. Herman Mayes Genealogical Collection.

1439. George E. Frist household, 1900 U.S. census, Cecil County, Maryland, population schedule, enumeration district 25, sheet 9, line 93; National Archives micropublication T623, roll 620.

1440. Herman Mayes Genealogical Collection.

1441. George E. Frist household, 1900 U.S. census, Cecil County, Maryland, population schedule, enumeration district 25, sheet 9, line 93; National Archives micropublication T623, roll 620.

1442. Alfred M. Miller household, 1920 U.S. census, Delaware County, Pennsylvania, population schedule, enumeration district 217, sheet 5A, line 41, dwelling 87, family 108 109; National Archives micropublication T625, roll 1560.

1443. Robert F. Lewis, 161-05-4728, Social Security Death Index, *Family Search*.

1444. Robert F. Lewis Frist, social security application 161-05-4728, U.S. Social Security Administration.

1445. Robert L. [*sic*] Frist household, 1920 U.S. census, Delaware County, Pennsylvania, enumeration district 158, sheet 17B, line 65, dwelling 357, family 369; National Archives micropublication T625, roll 1560.

1446. George E. Frist household, 1900 U.S. census, Cecil County, Maryland, population schedule, enumeration district 25, sheet 9, line 93; National Archives micropublication T623, roll 620.

1447. Ibid.

1448. Raymond Frist, 180-01-2646, Social Security Death Index, *Family Search*.

1449. Wallace Philip Frist, social security application 211-20-6533, U.S. Social Security Administration.

1450. Raymond Presley Frist, social security application 180-01-2646, U.S. Social Security Administration.

1451. Wallace Philip Frist, social security application 211-20-6533, U.S. Social Security Administration.

1452. Wallace Philip Frist, 211-20-6533, Social Security Death Index, *Family Search*.

1453. Edward Frist household, 1870 U.S. census, Cecil County, Maryland, population schedule, 7th District, Port Deposit, p. 271, dwelling and family 421; National Archives micropublication M593, roll 583. Exact date from Herman Mayes Genealogical Collection.

1454. Edmund Updegrove household, 1920 U.S. census, Cuyahoga County, Ohio, population schedule, Cleveland, enumeration district 527, sheet 18, line 97; National Archives micropublication T625, roll 1374.

1455. Edmund B. Updegrove household, 1900 U.S. census, Cuyahoga County, Ohio, population schedule, Cleveland Township, enumeration district 102, sheet 11, line 93, stamped p. 29A; National Archives micropublication T623, roll 1255.

1456. Edward Frist household, 1870 U.S. census, Cecil County, Maryland, population schedule, 7th District, Port Deposit, p. 271, dwelling and family 421; National Archives micropublication M593, roll 583.

1457. Edmund B. Updegrove household, 1900 U.S. census, Cuyahoga County, Ohio, population schedule, Cleveland Township, enumeration district 102, sheet 11, line 93, stamped p. 29A; National Archives micropublication T623, roll 1255.

1458. Edmund Updegrove household, 1920 U.S. census, Cuyahoga County, Ohio, population schedule, Cleveland, enumeration district 527, sheet 18, line 97; National Archives micropublication T625, roll 1374.

1459. Norbert Leo Frist, social security application 041-28-0103, U.S. Social Security Administration. Also Lynn Frist letter, 6 January 1991 (PO Box 143, East Lyme, CT 06333), Jane Frist Genealogical Collection, copy held in 2003 by William H. Frist, M.D.

1460. Norbert Leo Frist, social security application 041-28-0103, U.S. Social Security Administration.

1461. Lynn Frist letter, 6 January 1991 (PO Box 143, East Lyme, CT 06333), Jane Frist Genealogical Collection, copy held in 2003 by William H. Frist, M.D.

1462. Ibid.

1463. Ibid.

1464. Ibid.

1465. Ibid.

1466. Donna J. Robertson, compiler, *Tombstone Inscriptions of Cecil County, Maryland* (Largo, Florida: privately printed, 1995), p. 194.

1467. Mrs. George E. Tyson obituary, *Cecil Whig*, Elkton, Maryland, 14 October 1938, page 8, column 1, Cecil County Historical Society Library, Elkton, Maryland.

1468. Cecil County, Maryland, Marriages 1886–1896:292, Marriage Office, Elkton, Maryland.

1469. Donna J. Robertson, compiler, *Tombstone Inscriptions of Cecil County, Maryland* (Largo, Florida: privately printed, 1995), p. 194.

1470. John Benjamin Tyson Family Group Record provided by Anne T. Gyles, Conowingo, Maryland, from Tyson Vertical File, Cecil County Historical Society Library, Elkton, Maryland.

1471. Donna J. Robertson, compiler, *Tombstone Inscriptions of Cecil County, Maryland* (Largo, Florida: privately printed, 1995), p. 194.

1472. George E. Tyson household, 1900 U.S. census, Cecil County, Maryland, population schedule, enumeration district 24, sheet 18, line 42, p. 218, dwelling 336, family 343; National Archives micropublication T623, roll 620.

1473. Cecil County, Maryland, Land Record JGW8:424–425, Land Office, Elkton, Maryland.

1474. Cecil County, Maryland, Land Record JGW14:391, Land Office, Elkton, Maryland.

1475. George Frist household, 1920 U.S. census, Cecil County, Maryland, population schedule, District Seven, Port Deposit, enumeration district 29, sheet 1, dwelling and family 4; National Archives micropublication T625, roll 670.

1476. Mrs. George E. Tyson obituary, *Cecil Whig*, Elkton, Maryland, 14 October 1938, page 8, column 1, Cecil County Historical Society Library, Elkton, Maryland.

1477. Donna J. Robertson, compiler, *Tombstone Inscriptions of Cecil County, Maryland* (Largo, Florida: privately printed, 1995), p. 194.

1478. Lula M. Churchman estate packet #3573, 1975, Cecil County, Maryland, Register of Wills, Elkton, Maryland.

1479. Herman Mayes Genealogical Collection.

1480. Donna J. Robertson, compiler, *Tombstone Inscriptions of Cecil County, Maryland* (Largo, Florida: privately printed, 1995), p. 450.

1481. Cecil County, Maryland, Marriages 1896–1911:322, Marriage Office, Elkton, Maryland.

1482. Donna J. Robertson, compiler, *Tombstone Inscriptions of Cecil County, Maryland* (Largo, Florida: privately printed, 1995), p. 194.

1483. Donna J. Robertson, compiler, *Tombstone Inscriptions of Cecil County, Maryland* (Largo, Florida: privately printed, 1995), p. 240.

1484. Ibid.

1485. Ibid.

1486. Mrs. George E. Tyson obituary, *Cecil Whig*, Elkton, Maryland, 14 October 1938, page 8, column 1, Cecil County Historical Society Library, Elkton, Maryland.

1487. Donna J. Robertson, compiler, *Tombstone Inscriptions of Cecil County, Maryland* (Largo, Florida: privately printed, 1995), p. 194.

1488. Ibid.

1489. Pearl Astle, 159-50-9604, Social Security Death Index, *Family Search*.

1490. Cecil County, Maryland, Marriages January to June 1918:4, Marriage Office, Elkton, Maryland.

1491. Donna J. Robertson, compiler, *Tombstone Inscriptions of Cecil County, Maryland* (Largo, Florida: privately printed, 1995), p. 194.

1492. Harold Edward Tyson, 218-05-4631, social security application dated 19 April 1937, U.S. Social Security Administration.

1493. Howard Edward Tyson, 218-05-4631, Social Security Death Index, *Family Search*.

1494. Esther Ann Astle Tyson, social security application 212-74-9857 dated 12 April 1972, U.S. Social Security Administration.

1495. Biographical material provided August 2002 by Donald Frist (68 N. Hills Drive, Rising Sun, MD 21911) to compiler. Frist is a cousin.

1496. Cecil County, Maryland, Book January 1, 1928:173, Marriage Office, Elkton, Maryland.

1497. Edward Frist household, 1900 U.S. census, Cecil County, Maryland, population schedule, enumeration district 25, sheet 10, line 2; National Archives micropublication T623, roll 620. Exact date from Herman Mayes Genealogical Collection.

1498. Donna J. Robertson, compiler, *Tombstone Inscriptions of Cecil County, Maryland* (Largo, Florida: privately printed, 1995), p. 203.

1499. Cecil County, Maryland, Marriages 1896–1911:96, Marriage Office, Elkton, Maryland.

1500. Donna J. Robertson, compiler, *Tombstone Inscriptions of Cecil County, Maryland* (Largo, Florida: privately printed, 1995), p. 203.

1501. Edward Frist household, 1900 U.S. census, Cecil County, Maryland, population schedule, enumeration district 25, sheet 10, line 2; National Archives micropublication T623, roll 620.

1502. Oscar Frist household, 1920 U.S. census, Cecil County, Maryland, population schedule, District Seven, Port Deposit, enumeration district 31, sheet 4A, line 32, dwelling and family 92; National Archives micropublication T625, roll 670.

1503. Donna J. Robertson, compiler, *Tombstone Inscriptions of Cecil County, Maryland* (Largo, Florida: privately printed, 1995), p. 203.

1504. Cecil County, Maryland, Will Book T27:149–151, Elkton, Maryland.

1505. Joseph O. Frist obituary, *Cecil Whig*, Elkton, Maryland, 28 November 1979, clipping from Cecil County Historical Society Library, Elkton, Maryland.

1506. Ibid.

1507. Charles E. Frist estate, 11 October 1926, Cecil County, Maryland, Register of Wills, Elkton, Maryland. Also Donna J. Robertson, compiler, *Tombstone Inscriptions of Cecil County, Maryland* (Largo, Florida: privately printed, 1995), p. 203.

1508. Donna J. Robertson, compiler, *Tombstone Inscriptions of Cecil County, Maryland* (Largo, Florida: privately printed, 1995), p. 203.

1509. Ibid.

1510. Herman Mayes Genealogical Collection.

1511. Donna J. Robertson, compiler, *Tombstone Inscriptions of Cecil County, Maryland* (Largo, Florida: privately printed, 1995), p. 235.

1512. Donna J. Robertson, compiler, *Tombstone Inscriptions of Cecil County, Maryland* (Largo, Florida: privately printed, 1995), p. 252.

1513. Herman Mayes Genealogical Collection.

1514. Edward Frist household, 1900 U.S. census, Cecil County, Maryland, population schedule, enumeration district 25, sheet 10, line 2; National Archives micropublication T623, roll 620. Also biographical material provided by Donald Frist (68 N. Hills Drive, Rising Sun, MD 21911) July 2002 to compiler. Frist is a son of John Cresswell Frist.

1515. Biographical material provided by Donald Frist (68 N. Hills Drive, Rising Sun, MD 21911) July 2002 to compiler. Frist is a son of John Cresswell Frist.

1516. Cecil County, Maryland, Marriages 1910–1914:112, Marriage Office, Elkton, Maryland.

1517. Olive Frist, 215-320-8492, Social Security Death Index, *Ancestry.com.* Also copy of original application.

1518. Biographical material provided by Donald Frist (68 N. Hills Drive, Rising Sun, MD 21911) July 2002 to compiler. Frist is a son of Olive Frist.

1519. Edward Frist household, 1900 U.S. census, Cecil County, Maryland, population schedule, enumeration district 25, sheet 10, line 2; National Archives micropublication T623, roll 620.

1520. Cecil County, Maryland, Land Record JGW8:424–425, Land Office, Elkton, Maryland.

1521. Cecil County, Maryland, Land Record JGW14:391, Land Office, Elkton, Maryland.

1522. John Frist household, 1920 U.S. census, Cecil County, Maryland, population schedule, Seventh District, enumeration district 30, sheet 6B, line 61, dwelling 85, family 86; National Archives micropublication T625, roll 670.

1523. Cecil County, Maryland, Will Book V29:96–97, Elkton, Maryland.

1524. Donna J. Robertson, compiler, *Tombstone Inscriptions of Cecil County, Maryland* (Largo, Florida: privately printed, 1995), p. 197.

1525. Biographical material provided by Donald Frist (68 N. Hills Drive, Rising Sun, MD 21911) July 2002 to compiler. Frist is a son of John Cresswell Frist.

1526. John Willard Frist, 216-09-6231, Social Security Death Index, *Family Search.*

1527. Biographical material provided by Charlotte (Frist) Turner (1677 Paradisewood Dr., Paradise, CA 95969) 13 March 2001 to compiler.

1528. Donna J. Robertson, compiler, *Tombstone Inscriptions of Cecil County, Maryland* (Largo, Florida: privately printed, 1995), p. 244.

1529. Edward Frist household, 1900 U.S. census, Cecil County, Maryland, population schedule, enumeration district 25, sheet 10, line 2; National Archives micropublication T623, roll 620. Exact date from Herman Mayes Genealogical Collection.

1530. Oliver Frist obituary, *Cecil County News*, Elkton, Maryland, 11 December 1935, column 3, Cecil County Historical Society Library, Elkton, Maryland.

1531. Baltimore City, Maryland, Marriage Index 1886–1914, original card index, Maryland State Archives, Annapolis, Maryland.

1532. Donna J. Robertson, compiler, *Tombstone Inscriptions of Cecil County, Maryland* (Largo, Florida: privately printed, 1995), p. 215.

1533. Baltimore County, Maryland, Circuit Court, Equity Cases, Docket 18:154 *Elmira Schleigle et al vs. James H. Plummer et al*, 12 August 1908 Packet #10903, Maryland State Archives, Annapolis, Maryland.

1534. Florence Frist obituary, *Oxford Press*, Chester County, Pennsylvania, 29 May 1957, Chester County, Pennsylvania Historical Society Library.

1535. Edward Frist household, 1900 U.S. census, Cecil County, Maryland, population schedule, enumeration district 25, sheet 10, line 2; National Archives micropublication T623, roll 620.

1536. Baltimore City, Maryland, Marriage Index 1886–1914, original card index, Maryland State Archives, Annapolis, Maryland.

1537. Baltimore County, Maryland, Circuit Court, Equity Cases, Docket 18:154 *Elmira Schleigle et al vs. James H. Plummer et al*, 12 August 1908 Packet #10903, Maryland State Archives, Annapolis, Maryland.

1538. Oliver Frist household, 1920 U.S. census, Baltimore County, Maryland, population schedule, City of Baltimore, enumeration district 72, sheet 1, line 63; National Archives micropublication T625, roll 660.

1539. Cecil County, Maryland, Will Book S26:510–511, Elkton, Maryland.

1540. Donna J. Robertson, compiler, *Tombstone Inscriptions of Cecil County, Maryland* (Largo, Florida: privately printed, 1995), p. 215.

1541. Ibid.

1542. Ibid.

1543. Harford County, Maryland, Marriage Book WSF 4:82, Marriage Office, Bel Air, Maryland.

1544. Raymond H. Banks, compiler, *The Banks Compilation of Birth Data of Men with Links to New Castle County, Delaware [including the city of Wilmington] Who Were Born 1873–1900* (No place: privately published, 1996).

1545. Joel Frist household, 1880 U.S. census, New Castle County, Delaware, population schedule, Wilmington Hundred, enumeration district 12, page 23, line 42, stamped p. 283, dwelling 225, family 228, microfilm 1254119, Family History Library, Salt Lake City, Utah.

1546. Catherine A. Frist, probate record, 18905, 1936, New Castle County, Delaware, Delaware Public Archives, Dover, Delaware. Homer was not named in his mother's will, but his wife, Mary, was named.

1547. Herman Mayes Genealogical Collection.

1548. Homer Frist household, 1920 U.S. census, New Castle County, Delaware, population schedule, Wilmington City, enumeration district 78, sheet 1, line 18, dwelling and household 8; National Archives micropublication T625, roll 203.

1549. Catherine A. Frist, probate record, 18905, 1936, New Castle County, Delaware, Delaware Public Archives, Dover, Delaware. Mary Harkins Frist was named in Catherine's 1934 will.

1550. Joel Frist household, 1880 U.S. census, New Castle County, Delaware, population schedule, Wilmington Hundred, enumeration district 12, page 23, line 42, stamped p. 283, dwelling 225, family 228, microfilm 1254119, Family History Library, Salt Lake City, Utah.

1551. George Frist household, 1900 U.S. census, New Castle County, Delaware, population schedule. City of Wilmington, Ward Seven, enumeration district 26, sheet 8, line 37, dwelling 137, household 147; National Archives micropublication T623, roll 155.

1552. Homer Frist, World War I draft registration #A1850, Wilmington, Delaware, microfilm 1570613, Family History Library, Salt Lake City, Utah.

1553. Homer Frist household, 1920 U.S. census, New Castle County, Delaware, population schedule, Wilmington City, enumeration district 78, sheet 1, line 48, dwelling and household 8; National Archives micropublication T625, roll 203.

1554. Francis A. Wallis household, 1920 U.S. census, New Castle County, Delaware, population schedule, Wilmington City, enumeration district 78, sheet 1, line 18, dwelling and household 3; National Archives micropublication T625, roll 203.

1555. Homer Frist household, 1930 U.S. census, New Castle County, Delaware, population schedule, Wilmington City, enumeration district 277, sheet 41A, line 13; National Archives micropublication T626, roll 290.

1556. Catherine A. Frist, probate record, 18905, 1936, New Castle County, Delaware, Delaware Public Archives, Dover, Delaware.

1557. Margaret Wallis, social security application 160-28-7136, U.S. Social Security Administration.

1558. Margaret Frist Wallis, 160-28-7136, Social Security Death Index, *Family Search*.

1559. Wallis–Frist Marriage Certificate Register No. 254, p. 396, Delaware Bureau of Vital Statistics, Delaware Public Archives, Dover, Delaware.

1560. Joan Wallis Hauptle family data, email message from<jhauptle@comcast.net> (55 Grey Wing Pointe, Naples, FL 34113) to compiler 26 May 2003.

1561. Joseph Hendel Wallis (2648 Majestic Drive, Wilmington, DE 19810) telephone conversation with compiler 25 May 2003.

1562. St. James Methodist Episcopal Church Register No. 1 1874–1935 pp. 46, 48, Newport, Delaware.

1563. Ann Eliza Frist Foard probate record, 48521, 1964, New Castle County, Delaware, Delaware Public Archives, Dover, Delaware.

1564. Frist–Foard marriage, card file, Delaware Historical Society, Wilmington, Delaware.

1565. Fowser, Ann, "The Foard Family," copy provided by Ann Fowser (19 Natchez Trail, Medford Lakes, NJ 08055) July 2002 to compiler, hereinafter cited as The Foard Family.

1566. John Hilton Foard probate record, 22677, 1943, New Castle County, Delaware, Delaware Public Archives, Dover, Delaware.

1567. Biographical material provided by Mrs. Franklin Foard (700 Zee Street, Martinsville, VA 24112-3932) to compiler. Mrs. Foard was Ann Eliza (Frist) Foard's daughter-in-law.

1568. Frist–Foard marriage, card file, Delaware Historical Society, Wilmington, Delaware.

1569. Sketch entitled "Foard's Store" undated by unknown author, provided June 2002 by granddaughter Ann Foard Fowser (19 Natchez Trail, Medford Lakes, NJ 08055), copy held 2002 by compiler.

1570. Ibid.

1571. John Foard household, 1920 U.S. census, New Castle County, Delaware, Christiana Hundred enumeration district 149, sheet 11, line 38; National Archives micropublication T625, roll 204.

1572. Biographical material provided by Mrs. Franklin Foard (700 Zee Street, Martinsville, VA 24112-3932) to compiler.

1573. John Hilton Foard probate record, 22677, 1943, New Castle County, Delaware, Delaware Public Archives, Dover, Delaware.

1574. John Hilton Foard probate record, 22777, 1944, New Castle County, Delaware, Delaware Public Archives, Dover, Delaware.

1575. John Hilton Foard obituary, 26 February 1949, card file, Delaware Historical Society, Wilmington, Delaware. No newspaper listed.

1576. Sketch entitled "Foard's Store" undated by unknown author, provided June 2002 by granddaughter Ann Foard Fowser (19 Natchez Trail, Medford Lakes, NJ 08055), copy held 2002 by compiler.

1577. Biographical material provided by Mrs. Franklin Foard (700 Zee Street, Martinsville, VA 24112-3932) to compiler.

1578. Ann Eliza Frist Foard probate record, 48521, 1964, New Castle County, Delaware, Delaware Public Archives, Dover, Delaware.

1579. Nebeker Family Record, copy provided in August 2002 by Ann Fowser (3742 Asbury Avenue, Ocean City, NJ 08226) to compiler.

1580. Ibid.

1581. Ibid.

1582. Ibid.

1583. Ibid.

1584. Ibid.

1585. Ibid.

1586. Ibid.

1587. Ibid.

1588. John Nebeker Frist, death certificate #1122 (1947), Delaware Department of Vital Records, Dover, Delaware.

1589. Ibid.

1590. Frist–Currender marriage, marriage card file, Delaware Public Archives, Dover, Delaware.

1591. Carrie Currender Frist death certificate #2388 (1946), Delaware Department of Vital Records, Dover, Delaware.

1592. Ibid.

1593. Robert Frist household, 1900 U.S. census, New Castle County, Delaware, population schedule, enumeration district 51, sheet 3, line 85; National Archives micropublication T623, roll 156.

1594. John N. Frist household, 1910 U.S. census, New Castle County, Delaware, population schedule, enumeration district 74, sheet 3A, family and dwelling 50, p. 227[?]; National Archives micropublication T624, roll 146.

1595. John Frist, World War I draft registration #A2133, New Castle County, Delaware, microfilm 1570610, Family History Library, Salt Lake City, Utah.

1596. 1920 U.S. census, New Castle County, Delaware, population schedule, Newport, enumeration district 148, sheet 4, line 64, dwelling and family 34; National Archives micropublication T625, roll 204.

1597. Carrie Currender Frist death certificate #2388 (1946), Delaware Department of Vital Records, Dover, Delaware.

1598. John Nebeker Frist death certificate 1122 (1947), Delaware Department of Vital Records, Dover, Delaware.

1599. John Frist probate record, 26846, 1947, New Castle County, Delaware, Delaware Public Archives, Dover, Delaware.

1600. Robert Currender Frist, certificate of delayed birth registration #21314, dated 16 April 1964, Delaware Board of Health, Delaware Public Archives, Dover, Delaware.

1601. Robert C. Frist obituary, *Wilmington Evening Journal*, Wilmington, Delaware, 2 January 1970, p. 36.

1602. Kathryn Casey Frist, social security application 221-03-6472, dated 30 November 1936, U.S. Social Security Administration.

1603. Robert C. Frist, social security application 221-03-2468, U.S. Social Security Administration.

1604. Robert C. Frist obituary, *Wilmington Evening Journal*, Wilmington, Delaware, 2 January 1970, p. 36.

1605. John N. Frist household, 1910 U.S. census, New Castle County, Delaware, population schedule, enumeration district 74, sheet 3A, family and dwelling 50, p. 227[?]; National Archives micropublication T624, roll 146.

1606. James Frist household, 1900 U.S. census, Hamilton County, Tennessee, population schedule, enumeration district 43, sheet 12, line 6; National Archives micropublication T623, roll 1574.

1607. Bertie Hartman obituary, *Chattanooga Daily Times*, Chattanooga, Tennessee, 17 May 1959, p. 29, column 7.

1608. John Hartman obituary, *Chattanooga Daily Times*, Chattanooga, Tennessee, 4 January 1913, p. 3, column 3.

1609. Herman Mayes Genealogical Collection. No confirmation of this date was found in Tennessee records.

1610. James Frist household, 1900 U.S. census, Hamilton County, Tennessee, population schedule, enumeration district 43, sheet 12, line 6; National Archives micropublication T623, roll 1574.

1611. James B. Frist household, 1930 U.S. census, Hamilton County, Tennessee, population schedule, enumeration district 33-82, sheet 5B, dwelling 91, family 93, microfilm 21, Tennessee State Library and Archives, Nashville, Tennessee. Although the census listing is entered as James B. Frist, it is in fact for Mrs. James B. Frist.

1612. Bertie Hartman obituary, *Chattanooga Daily Times*, Chattanooga, Tennessee, 17 May 1959, p. 29, column 7.

1613. Bertie Hartman obituary, *Chattanooga Daily Times*, Chattanooga, Tennessee, 17 May 1959, p. 29, column 7. Precise date is from Herman Mayes Genealogical Collection.

1614. Mary Ann Frist interview, *Chattanooga News*, Chattanooga, Tennessee, 2 February 1917; clipping from William H. Frist, M.D. Genealogical Collection. Mary Baldwin Frist stated in this interview that she had seven great-grandchildren, but that six of them lived in Delaware and the seventh was a one-year-old who was the "apple of her eye" and lived in Lookout Valley. This must have been John's younger brother Roy.

1615. Bertie Hartman obituary, *Chattanooga Daily Times*, Chattanooga, Tennessee, 17 May 1959, p. 29, column 7. Precise date is from Herman Mayes Genealogical Collection.

1616. Herman Mayes Genealogical Collection.

1617. John Vetter death certificate #5130 (1929), Tennessee Department of Vital Records, Nashville, Tennessee.

1618. Ibid.

1619. Marriage date approximated from birth of first child.

1620. Biographical material provided December 2000 from son, John Stanley Vetter, M.D. (FristHealth Richmond Family Medicine, 921 Long Drive, Suite 101, Rockingham, NC 18379), to compiler.

1621. Ibid.

1622. Elizabeth Vetter household, 1920 U.S. census, Walker County, Georgia, population schedule, enumeration district 173, sheet 14B line 94 and 15A, line 1, stamped p. 66 and 67, dwelling 295, family 294; National Archives micropublication T625, roll 281.

1623. Robert and John Vetter obituaries, *Chattanooga Daily News*, Chattanooga, Tennessee, 17 June 1929.

1624. John Vetter death certificate #5130 (1929), Tennessee Department of Vital Records, Nashville, Tennessee.

1625. Biographical material provided December 2000 from son, John Stanley Vetter, M.D. (FristHealth Richmond Family Medicine, 921 Long Drive, Suite 101, Rockingham, NC 18379), to compiler.

1626. Ibid.

1627. Jacob Frist household, 1900 U.S. census, Perry County, Mississippi, population schedule, enumeration district 89, sheet 11, line 35; National Archives micropublication T623, roll 824.

1628. Mrs. Mary Tomlinson obituary, *The Meridian Star*, Meridian, Mississippi, 9 January 1980, p. 11C, column 1.

1629. Lauderdale County, Mississippi, Marriage Book 27:547, Lauderdale County Department of Archives and History, Meridian, Mississippi.

1630. M. F. Parker (roomer), 1920 U.S. census, Lauderdale County, Mississippi, population schedule, City of Meridian, Beat 1, enumeration district 45, artificial p. 148, as indexed by volunteers at Lauderdale County, Department of Archives and History, Meridian, Mississippi.

1631. Mrs. Mary Tomlinson obituary, *The Meridian Star*, Meridian, Mississippi, 9 January 1980, p. 11C, column 1.

1632. Jacob Frist household, 1900 U.S. census, Perry County, Mississippi, population schedule, enumeration district 89, sheet 11, line 35; National Archives micropublication T623, roll 824.

1633. Jacob Frist household, 1910 U.S. census, Lauderdale County, Mississippi, population schedule, enumeration district 42, sheet 18B, dwelling 256, family 282; National Archives micropublication T624, roll 746.

1634. Interview with Mrs. Brooks Lide (2807 Poplar Springs Drive, Meridian, MS, 39305) by Shirley Wilson, 17 April 2002, quotations held in 2003 by compiler. Mrs. Lide was born in 1908 and knew Mary Louise Frist.

1635. "Engagement and Approaching Marriage," *The Meridian Star*, Meridian, Mississippi, 6 September 1925, p. 2, column 1.

1636. Ibid.

1637. Biographical material provided by Charlotte Chesnutt (P.O. Box 412, Montreat, NC 28757) 6 July 2001 to compiler. Charlotte is a niece.

1638. Mrs. Mary Tomlinson obituary, *The Meridian Star*, Meridian, Mississippi, 9 January 1980, p. 11C, column 1.

1639. Karen Dover, abstractor, *Lauderdale County Cemetery Records, Volume IV* (Meridian, Mississippi: Lauderdale County Department of Archives and History, 1992), p. 71. Also viewed and photographed by compiler in 2002.

1640. Jacob Frist household, 1910 U.S. census, Lauderdale County, Mississippi, population schedule, enumeration district 42, sheet 18B, dwelling 256, family 282; National Archives micropublication T624, roll 746.

1641. Helen Cameron death certificate #23337 Volume 1814 (1956), Florida Office of Vital Statistics, Jacksonville.

1642. Thomas Fearn Frist, M.D. "The Frist Story." William H. Frist, M.D. Genealogical Collection (703 Bowling Avenue, Nashville, TN 37215), p. 24.

1643. 1900 U.S. census, Lauderdale County, Mississippi, population schedule, Beat One, enumeration district 18, sheet 1, dwelling 6, family 7; National Archives micropublication T623, roll 815.

1644. Karen Dover, abstractor, *Lauderdale County Cemetery Records, Volume IV* (Meridian, Mississippi: Lauderdale County Department of Archives and History, 1992), p. 71.

1645. Jacob Frist household, 1910 U.S. census, Lauderdale County, Mississippi, population schedule, enumeration district 42, sheet 18B, dwelling 256, family 282; National Archives micropublication T624, roll 746.

1646. "Death of J. C. Frist at Noon Today Follows Stroke of Paralysis," *The Meridian Star*, Meridian, Mississippi, 2 January 1919, p. 3.

1647. Jennie Frist household, 1920 U.S. census, Lauderdale County, Mississippi, population schedule, enumeration district 45, sheet 7B, dwelling 147, family 155; National Archives micropublication T625, roll 882.

1648. Thomas Fearn Frist, M.D. "The Frist Story." William H. Frist, M.D. Genealogical Collection (703 Bowling Avenue, Nashville, TN 37215), p. 24.

1649. Karen Dover, abstractor, *Lauderdale County Cemetery Records, Volume IV* (Meridian, Mississippi: Lauderdale County Department of Archives and History, 1992), p. 71.

1650. "Ex-Resident Dies," *The Meridian Star*, Meridian, Mississippi, 25 March 1943, p. 1.

1651. Karen Dover, abstractor, *Lauderdale County Cemetery Records, Volume IV* (Meridian, Mississippi: Lauderdale County Department of Archives and History, 1992), p. 71.

1652. Alan Garner Cameron, social security application 080-18-0640, U.S. Social Security Administration.

1653. Alan Garner Cameron, social security application 080-18-0640, U. S. Social Security Administration. Also Alan G. Cameron death certificate #74-053171 (1974), Florida Office of Vital Statistics, Jacksonville.

1654. Alan G. Cameron death certificate #74-053171 (1974), Florida Office of Vital Statistics, Jacksonville.

1655. Except where otherwise cited, this sketch is a composite compiled from biographical material provided by Reverend John Chester Frist's two daughters, Jane Frist (P.O. Box 272, 102 Frist Road, Montreat, NC 28757) and Charlotte Chesnutt (P.O. Box 412, Montreat, NC 28575) and his son Thomas Ferran Frist (P.O. Box 1204, 98 Frist Road, Montreat, NC 28757) to the compiler.

1656. Biographical material provided by Reverend John Chester Frist's daughter Jane Frist (P.O. Box 272, 102 Frist Road, Montreat, NC 28757) to compiler.

1657. Biographical material provided by Reverend John Chester Frist's daughter Charlotte Chesnutt (P.O. Box 412, Montreat, NC 28575) to compiler.

1658. Biographical material provided by Reverend John Chester Frist's son John Chester Frist (146 Ensworth Avenue, Nashville, TN 37205) to compiler.

1659. Biographical material provided 12 July 2001 by Thomas Ferran Frist (P.O. Box 1204, 98 Frist Road, Montreat, NC 28757). Frist is a son.

1660. Biographical material provided by Reverend John Chester Frist's daughter Jane Frist (P.O. Box 272, 102 Frist Road, Montreat, NC 28757) to compiler.

1661. Biographical material provided by his son Thomas Ferran Frist (P. O. Box 1204, 98 Frist Road, Montreat, NC 28757) September 2002 to compiler.

1662. Ibid.

1663. Letter dated 8 January 1960 from Donald G. Miller to Charlotte Chesnutt (P.O. Box 412, Montreat, NC 28757), copy provided in January 2002 to compiler.

1664. Except where otherwise cited, this sketch is a composite compiled from biographical material provided by Reverend John Chester Frist's two daughters, Jane Frist (P.O. Box 272, 102 Frist Road, Montreat, NC 28757) and Charlotte Chesnutt (P.O. Box 412, Montreat, NC 28575) and his son Thomas Ferran Frist (P.O. Box 1204, 98 Frist Road, Montreat, NC 28757) to the compiler.

1665. Biographical material provided by Jane Frist (P.O. Box 272, 102 Frist Road, Montreat, NC 28757) to compiler.

1666. Biographical material provided by Charlotte Frist Chesnutt (P.O. Box 412, Montreat, NC 28575) to compiler.

1667. Biographical material provided by John Chester Frist, Jr., M.D. (146 Ensworth Avenue, Nashville, TN 37205) to compiler.

1668. Biographical material provided by Thomas Ferran Frist (P.O. Box 1204, 98 Frist Road, Montreat, NC 28757) to compiler.

1669. Except where otherwise cited, this sketch is a composite compiled from biographical material provided by his children. Also Thomas Fearn Frist's own biographical material on his life cited in this compilation as "The Frist Story."

1670. Thomas Fearn Frist, M.D. "The Frist Story." William H. Frist, M.D. Genealogical Collection (703 Bowling Avenue, Nashville, TN 37215), pp. 33–34.

1671. Ibid.

1672. Thomas Fearn Frist, M.D. "The Frist Story." William H. Frist, M.D. Genealogical Collection (703 Bowling Avenue, Nashville, TN 37215), p. 13.

1673. Winfield Dunn, NCCJ Brotherhood Dinner, 14 April 1983, Introductory Remarks, Thomas F. Frist, Sr., M.D., Honoree, p. 31, William H. Frist, M.D. Genealogical Collection.

1674. Interview with Dorothy Frist Boensch (104 Bellebrook Circle, Nashville, TN 37205), 14 December 2001, by compiler.

1675. Alan Hall, "Thomas F. Frist, Jr., President and CEO, Hospital Corporation of America," *SKY Magazine*, January 1983, p. 27.

1676. "Thomas F. Frist, Sr., M.D. 1910– ," *Modern Health Care*, 10 September 1990, p. 54.

1677. American Retirement Corporation website <www.arclp.com/about.html>.

1678. Ibid.

1679. "Thomas F. Frist, Sr., M.D. 1910– ," *Modern Health Care*, 10 September 1990, p. 54.

1680. Carol Frist (1326 Page Road, Nashville, TN 37205), 13 December 2001 memo to compiler. Carol is a daughter-in-law.

1681. Dorothy Harrison Cate Frist eulogy, 8 January 1998, no pagination, page 8, delivered by nephew George Harrison Cate, Jr., copy held in 2003 by William H. Frist, M.D.

1682. "Mrs. Frist follows husband in death," *The Tennessean*, Nashville, Tennessee, 7 January 1998, copy held in 2003 by compiler.

1683. Interview with Dorothy Frist Boensch (104 Bellebrook Circle, Nashville, TN 37205), 14 December 2001, by compiler.

1684. *Good People Beget Good People: The Life and Legacy of Dr. Thomas F. Frist, Sr.* (Nashville, Tennessee: private published, 1998), p. 7.

1685. Biographical material provided by Mary (Frist) Barfield (1026 Chancery Lane S., Nashville, TN 37215-4552), 13 December 2001 to compiler.

1686. *Good People Beget Good People: The Life and Legacy of Dr. Thomas F. Frist, Sr.* (Nashville, Tennessee: privately published, 1998), p. 4.

1687. Biographical material provided by Thomas Fearn Frist, M.D. and wife Patricia (Champion) Frist (1304 Chickering Road, Nashville, TN 37215), July 2002, to compiler.

1688. Interview with Dorothy Frist Boensch (104 Bellebrook Circle, Nashville, TN 37205) 14 December 2001 by compiler.

1689. Frist Family Group Sheet and biographical material provided by Robert Armistead Frist, M.D. and wife Carol (Knox) Frist (1326 Page Road, Nashville, TN 37205) 12 December 2001 with updates 18 February 2002 and 22 April 2002 to compiler.

1690. Biographical material provided by Mary (Frist) Barfield and her husband, Henry Lee Barfield II (1026 Chancery Lane S., Nashville, TN 37215-4552) December 2001 with July 2002 update to compiler.

1691. Biographical material provided by William Harrison Frist, M.D. and wife Karyn (McLaughlin) Frist (703 Bowling Avenue, Nashville, TN 37215) 5 December 2001 with August 2003 updates to compiler.

1692. Joseph Frist household, 1900 U.S. census, Hamilton County, Tennessee, population schedule, enumeration district 59, sheet 53, line 28; National Archives micropublication T623, roll 1574.

1693. Paul F. Frist obituary, *Chattanooga Daily Times*, Chattanooga, Tennessee, 18 March 1961, p. 9.

1694. Interview with Kate (Groves) Frist, 28 February 2002, in Chattanooga, Tennessee, by compiler.

1695. Katie Irene Groves birth certificate D-313543, State of Tennessee, Division of Vital Records, Ronnie Frist Genealogical Collection.

1696. Interview with Kate (Groves) Frist, 28 February 2002, in Chattanooga, Tennessee, by compiler.

1697. E. L. Groves Family Bible, currently owned by his great grandson, Ronnie Frist (1718 Gray Road, Chattanooga, TN 37421), copy held in 2003 by compiler.

1698. Joseph Frist household, 1900 U.S. census, Hamilton County, Tennessee, population schedule, enumeration district 59, sheet 53, line 28; National Archives micropublication T623, roll 1574.

1699. Original deed, marked as recorded in Deed Book 5, Volume 15, p. 356, Hamilton County, Tennessee, Ronnie Frist Genealogical Collection, copy of deed held in 2003 by compiler.

1700. Paul F. Frist household, 1930 U.S. census, Hamilton County, Tennessee, population schedule, enumeration district 33-82, sheet 5B, dwelling 87, family 89, microfilm 21, Tennessee State Library and Archives, Nashville, Tennessee.

1701. Paul Frist, social security application 415-14-0956, U.S. Social Security Administration.

1702. Paul Frist obituary, *Chattanooga Daily Times*, Chattanooga, Tennessee, 13 March 1961, p. 9.

1703. Mrs. Katie Frist, 1958 membership, National Association Rainbow Division Veterans, Ronnie Frist Genealogical Collection.

1704. Robert Joe Frist, letters to his mother Kate Frist, Chattanooga, Tennessee, from Ronnie Frist Genealogical Collection, copies held in 2003 by compiler. Grammar, spelling, and punctuation are as found in the letters.

1705. "History of the 42nd Infantry Division 'Rainbow,'" <www.grunts.net/army/42ndid.html> (downloaded 6 March 2002).

1706. Letters dated 14 January 1945 and 30 January 1945 from Kate Frist to her son Robert Joe Frist, Ronnie Frist Collection. The letters remained sealed, with the air mail stamps inside, until they came into the possession of Robert Joe Frist's nephew Ronnie Frist in December 2001. The grammar, spelling, and punctuation are as found in the letters.

1707. Letters dated 14 January 1945 and 30 January 1945 from Kate Frist to her son Robert Joe Frist, Ronnie Frist Genealogical Collection.

1708. Ronnie Frist Genealogical Collection.

1709. Ronnie Frist Genealogical Collection.

1710. Ronnie Frist Genealogical Collection.

1711. Paul F. Frist obituary, *Chattanooga Daily Times*, Chattanooga, Tennessee, 18 March 1961, p. 9.

1712. Interview with Ronnie Frist (1718 Gray Road, Chattanooga, TN 37421) 27 February 2002 by compiler.

1713. Interview with Patricia Huguenin (609 Grand Mountain Road Chattanooga, TN 37421-7429) 27 February 2002, by compiler.

1714. Sydney [*sic*] Donald Frist birth certificate 21583 (1930), State of Tennessee, Division of Vital Statistics. Ronnie Frist Genealogical Collection

1715. Sidney Donald Frist obituary, *Chattanooga Daily Times*, Chattanooga, Tennessee, 2 January 1973, p. 2.

1716. Frist Family Group Sheet provided 28 March 2002 by Ronnie Frist (son) (1718 Gray Road, Chattanooga, TN 37421) to compiler.

1717. Biographical material provided by Naomi Willmary (Frist) Rollins (4911 Alabama Avenue, Chattanooga, TN 37409) dated 13 November 2001 to compiler. Mrs. Rollins is the daughter of Sadie Briggs Frist. Jacob Frist Family Bible lists him as Jacob C. Frist, but descendants state that his name was James Charles Frist and he used the nickname "Jake."

1718. James C. Frist death certificate #5468 (1944), Tennessee Division of Vital Statistics, Nashville, Tennessee.

1719. Biographical material provided by Naomi Willmary (Frist) Rollins (4911 Alabama Avenue, Chattanooga, TN 37409) dated 13 November 2001 to compiler. Mrs. Rollins is the daughter of Sadie Briggs Frist.

1720. Naomi Willmary (Frist) Rollins (4911 Alabama Avenue, Chattanooga, TN 37409) letter 13 November 2001 to compiler. Rollins is a daughter.

1721. Richard Forrester household, 1920 U.S. census, Hamilton County, Tennessee, population schedule, enumeration district 197, sheet 3, lines 14 and 15, microfilm 1743, Tennessee State Library and Archives, Nashville, Tennessee.

1722. William C. Briggs household, 1930 U.S. census, Hamilton County, Tennessee, population schedule, Chattanooga, Ward Eighteen, enumeration district 33-60, sheet 20A and 20B, dwelling 410, family 455, microfilm 20, Tennessee State Library and Archives, Nashville, Tennessee.

1723. James C. Frist death certificate #5468 (1944), Tennessee Division of Vital Statistics, Nashville, Tennessee.

1724. James Calvin Frist obituary, 26 October 1952, *Chattanooga Daily Times*, Chattanooga, Tennessee, p. 23, column 6 and 7. Also James Charles Frist obituary (his father), *Chattanooga Daily Times*, Chattanooga, Tennessee, 9 March 1944, p. 11, column 3.

1725. Interview with Patricia Huguenin, (609 Grand Mountain Road Chattanooga, TN 37421-7429) 27 February 2002 by compiler. James Calvin Frist was Pat's oldest brother.

1726. James Calvin Frist obituary, 26 October 1952, *Chattanooga Daily Times*, Chattanooga, Tennessee, p. 23, column 6 and 7.

1727. Evelyn Frist obituary, *Chattanooga News-Free Press*, Chattanooga, Tennessee, 14 December 1983, p. C-14.

1728. Ibid.

1729. Interview with Patricia Huguenin (609 Grand Mountain Road Chattanooga, TN 37421-7429), 27 February 2002 by compiler.

1730. Frist Family Group Sheet provided 27 November 2001 by daughter Susan Frist Dixon (6415 Washington Circle, Chattanooga, TN 37416) to compiler.

1731. Frist Family Group Sheet provided by Naomi Willmary (Frist) Rollins (4911 Alabama Avenue, Chattanooga, TN 37409) 9 July 2001 to compiler.

1732. Frist Family Group Sheet and interview with Patricia Huguenin (609 Grand Mountain Road Chattanooga, TN 37421-7429), 27 February 2002, updated August 2002 by compiler.

1733. Frist Family Group Sheet provided March 2001 by Clarence Harold Frist (419 Turrentine Avenue, Gadsden, AL 35901) to compiler. Harold is a brother. All information is from this source, unless otherwise cited.

1734. Ibid.

1735. Frist Family Group Sheet provided March 2001 by Clarence Harold Frist (419 Turrentine Avenue, Gadsden, AL 35901) to compiler. Harold is an uncle.

1736. Ibid.

1737. Ibid.

1738. Page County, Iowa, Register of Births entry #14, microfilm roll 1,035,208, Family History Library, Salt Lake City, Utah.

1739. Montgomery County Genealogical Society and Bicentennial Committee, *Cemetery Records Montgomery County, Iowa, Townships of Douglass Washington East (Jackson)* (Des Moines, Iowa: Iowa Genealogical Society, 1984), p. 49, citing Section Four; Row 14.

1740. Montgomery County, Iowa, Marriage Record Book 6:93, microfilm 1,481,225, Family History Library, Salt Lake City, Utah.

1741. Montgomery County Genealogical Society and Bicentennial Committee, *Cemetery Records Montgomery County, Iowa, Townships of Douglass Washington East (Jackson)* (Des Moines, Iowa: Iowa Genealogical Society, 1984), p. 49, citing Section Four, Row 14.

1742. Lewis Patton household, 1900 U.S. census, Montgomery County, Iowa, population schedule, Jackson Township, enumeration district 107, sheet 7, line 35; National Archives micropublication T623, roll 450.

1743. Lewis Patton household, 1920 U.S. census, Montgomery County, Iowa, population schedule, Jackson Township, enumeration district 115, sheet 4A, line 9; National Archives micropublication T625, roll 504.

1744. Montgomery County Genealogical Society and Bicentennial Committee, *Cemetery Records Montgomery County, Iowa, Townships of Douglass Washington East (Jackson)* (Des Moines, Iowa: Iowa Genealogical Society, 1984), p. 49, citing Section Four, Row 14.

1745. Frist Family Group Sheet provided by son Manferd H. Findley (4555 Jordan Grove Road, Central City, IA 52214) to compiler.

1746. Montgomery County, Iowa, Marriage Record 12, #5593, microfilm 1,481,228, Family History Library, Salt Lake City, Utah.

1747. Frist Family Group Sheet provided May 2001 by Manferd H. Findley (4555 Jordan Grove Road, Central City, IA 52214) to compiler. Manferd is a nephew.

1748. Ibid.

1749. Family Bible Record, owned by daughter Geraldine Miller (415 S. Eighteenth Street, Clarinda, IA 51632-2515), copy held in 2003 by compiler.

1750. Montgomery County Genealogical Society and Bicentennial Committee, *Cemetery Records Montgomery County, Iowa, Townships of Douglass Washington East (Jackson)* (Des Moines, Iowa: Iowa Genealogical Society, 1984), p. 120.

1751. Herman Mayes Genealogical Collection.

1752. Orpha Frist, social security application 485-38-3895, U.S. Social Security Administration.

1753. Ibid.

1754. Orpha Geesaman Frist, 485-38-3895, Social Security Death Index, *Family Search*.

1755. Nannie Bridgman household, 1920 U.S. census, Plymouth County, Iowa, population schedule, enumeration district 138, sheet 3B, dwelling and family 58; National Archives micropublication T625, roll 506.

1756. Montgomery County Genealogical Society and Bicentennial Committee, *Cemetery Records Montgomery County, Iowa, Townships of Douglass Washington East (Jackson)* (Des Moines, Iowa: Iowa Genealogical Society, 1984), p. 120.

1757. Orpha Geesaman Frist, social security application 485-38-3895, U.S. Social Security Administration.

1758. Geraldine Rosetta Frist Miller, Eickemeyer Funeral Chapel record, provided to compiler June 2002 by husband Dale Miller (415 S. Eighteenth Street, Clarinda, IA 51632-2515).

1759. Frist Family Group Sheet provided by Geraldine (Frist) Miller (415 S. Eighteenth Street, Clarinda, IA 51632-2515), 10 November 2001 to compiler. Mrs. Miller was a sister who has since died.

1760. Ibid.

1761. Mead Person household, 1900 U.S. census, Polk County, Iowa, population schedule, enumeration district 62, sheet 11, stamped p 47, dwelling 218, family 219; National Archives micropublication T623, roll 453.

1762. John S. Frist household, 1880 U.S. census, Marion County, Iowa, population schedule, Swan and Union Townships, enumeration district 118, sheet 10, dwelling 91, family 93, stamped p. 482; National Archives micropublication T9, roll 354.

1763. Pioneer Sons and Daughters Genealogical Society, *Marriages Polk County, Iowa, Book 12 1905–1906* (Des Moines, Iowa: Iowa Genealogical Society, 1986), p. 17.

1764. Blanche Frist, 484-64-9091, Social Security Death Index, *Family Search*.

1765. Ibid.

1766. John S. Frist household, 1880 U.S. census, Marion County, Iowa, population schedule, Swan and Union Townships, enumeration district 118, sheet 10, dwelling 91, family 93, stamped p. 482; National Archives micropublication T9, roll 354.

1767. Mead Person household, 1900 U.S. census, Polk County, Iowa, population schedule, enumeration district 62, sheet 11, stamped p 47, dwelling 218, family 219; National Archives micropublication T623, roll 453.

1768. Joseph Frist household, 1910 U.S. census, Polk County, Iowa, population schedule, Des Moines, enumeration district 65, sheet 7A, dwelling 43, family 45, stamped p. 67; National Archives micropublication T624, roll 418.

1769. Joseph Frist household, 1920 U.S. census, Polk County, Iowa, population schedule, Camp Township, Runnells, enumeration district 69, sheet 1A, line 7, dwelling and family 3, stamped p 58; National Archives micropublication T625, roll 507.

1770. Russell Frist, 482-01-8838, Social Security Death Index, *Ancestry.com*.

1771. Frist Family Group Sheet provided by Steven Frist (601 Maish, Des Moines, IA 50315) to compiler. Steven Frist is a grandson of Russell Edward Frist. Marriage date is approximated from birth of only child and may be much earlier.

1772. Henry Thomas household, 1880 U.S. census, Dallas County, Iowa, population schedule, Boone Township, p. 275, dwelling and family 25; National Archives micropublication T9, roll 335.

1773. Dallas County, Iowa, Marriage Record 1852–1902, p. 149, microfilm 1034112 Item 2, Family History Library, Salt Lake City, Utah.

1774. Elmer Thomas household, 1910 U.S. census, Dallas County, Iowa, population schedule, enumeration district 19, sheet 8, dwelling 172, family 180; National Archives micropublication T624, roll 399.

1775. Ibid.

1776. Ibid.

1777. Ibid.

1778. Henry Thomas household, 1880 U.S. census, Dallas County, Iowa, population schedule, Boone Township, p. 275, dwelling and family 25; National Archives micropublication T9, roll 335.

1779. Ibid.

1780. Dallas County, Iowa, Marriage Record 1852–1902, p. 162, microfilm 1034112 Item 2, Family History Library, Salt Lake City, Utah.

1781. Arthur W. Allen household, 1900 U.S. census, Dallas County, Iowa, population schedule, Boone Township, enumeration district 5, sheet 4, line 56, dwelling and family 81; National Archives micropublication T723, roll 427.

1782. Dallas County, Iowa, Marriage Record 1852–1902, p. 162, microfilm 1034112 Item 2, Family History Library, Salt Lake City, Utah.

1783. Arthur W. Allen household, 1900 U.S. census, Dallas County, Iowa, population schedule, Boone Township, enumeration district 5, sheet 4, line 56, dwelling and family 81; National Archives micropublication T723, roll 427.

1784. Ibid.

1785. Ibid.

1786. Ibid.

1787. Audrey Gilbert, *Preble County, Ohio, the 1900 Federal Census* (Owensboro, Kentucky: Cook & McDowell Publications, 1980), p. 302.

1788. Herman Mayes Genealogical Collection.

1789. Paul H. Frist household, 1920 U.S. census, Wayne County, Indiana, population schedule, City of Richmond, enumeration district 179, sheet 7B, dwelling 174, family 177; National Archives micropublication T625, roll 474.

1790. Violet Genevieve Frist, 308-44-1056, Social Security Death Index, *Family Search*.

1791. Ibid.

1792. Paul H. Frist household, 1920 U.S. census, Wayne County, Indiana, population schedule, City of Richmond, enumeration district 179, sheet 7B, dwelling 174, family 177; National Archives micropublication T625, roll 474.

1793. Ione Sell Hiestand, ed., *Preble County Ohio* (No place: Preble County Historical Society, 1992), p. 171.

1794. Paul H. Frist household, 1920 U.S. census, Wayne County, Indiana, population schedule, City of Richmond, enumeration district 179, sheet 7B, dwelling 174, family 177; National Archives micropublication T625, roll 474.

1795. Marriage approximated based on the birth of the first child.

1796. Family data provided 30 May 2002 by Paul J. Frist (9311 Sandra Drive, New Paris, OH 45347) to compiler.

1797. Russell Frist household, 1900 U.S. census, Madison County, Indiana, population schedule, Green Township, enumeration district 92, sheet 10, dwelling 179, family 184, stamped p. 323; National Archives micropublication T623, roll 386.

1798. Marley Otto Frist obituary, *Anderson Daily Bulletin*, Anderson, Indiana, undated clipping from Patricia Frist Genealogical Collection.

1799. Herman Mayes Genealogical Collection.

1800. Hester Frist, social security application 313-03-2844 dated 25 November 1936, U.S. Social Security Administration.

1801. Ibid.

1802. Hester Frist, 313-03-2844, Social Security Death Index, *Family Search*.

1803. Russell Frist household, 1920 U.S. census, Madison County, Indiana, population schedule, Anderson Township, enumeration district 101, sheet 9A, stamped p. 170, dwelling 191, family 205; National Archives micropublication T625, roll 448.

1804. Hester Frist, social security application 313-03-2844 dated 25 November 1936, U.S. Social Security Administration.

1805. Marley Otto Frist obituary, *Anderson Daily Bulletin*, Anderson, Indiana, undated clipping from Patricia Frist Genealogical Collection.

1806. Russell Frist obituary, *Anderson Herald/Bulletin*, Anderson, Indiana, 1 November 1989, p. A-2, from Patricia Frist Genealogical Collection.

1807. Herman Mayes Genealogical Collection.

1808. John J. Stevens household, 1900 U.S. census, Union County, Indiana, population schedule, Centre Township, enumeration district 130, sheet 5, dwelling and family 92, stamped p. 276; National Archives micropublication T623, roll 406. Exact date from Herman Mayes Genealogical Collection.

1809. Herman Mayes Genealogical Collection.

1810. Lee County, Iowa, Marriage Record 13:418, microfilm 1,903,294, Family History Library, Salt Lake City, Utah.

1811. Ibid.

1812. Herman Mayes Genealogical Collection.

1813. Ibid.

1814. Dane Starbuck, *The Goodriches: An American Family* (Indianapolis: Liberty Fund, Inc., 2001), p. 38.

1815. "Pierre F. Goodrich Dies; Business Executive Had Diversified Career," *The Indianapolis Star*, Indianapolis, Indiana, 26 October 1973, p. 1.

1816. Dane Starbuck, *The Goodriches: An American Family* (Indianapolis: Liberty Fund, Inc., 2001), p. 125. This is presumed to be Decatur, Indiana.

1817. Dane Starbuck, *The Goodriches: An American Family* (Indianapolis: Liberty Fund, Inc., 2001), pp. 123, 124.

1818. Dane Starbuck, *The Goodriches: An American Family* (Indianapolis: Liberty Fund, Inc., 2001), pp. 212, 213.

1819. Dane Starbuck, *The Goodriches: An American Family* (Indianapolis: Liberty Fund, Inc., 2001), p. 285.

1820. Ibid.

1821. Dane Starbuck, *The Goodriches: An American Family* (Indianapolis: Liberty Fund, Inc., 2001), pp. 236, 237.

1822. James P. Goodrich household, 1900 U.S. census, Randolph County, Indiana, population schedule, White River Township, enumeration district 136, sheet 4, line 70, dwelling 87 family 88; National Archives micropublication T623, roll 399.

1823. Dane Starbuck, *The Goodriches: An American Family* (Indianapolis: Liberty Fund, Inc., 2001), pp. 41, 121.

1824. Dane Starbuck, *The Goodriches: An American Family* (Indianapolis: Liberty Fund, Inc., 2001), p. 123.

1825. Dane Starbuck, *The Goodriches: An American Family* (Indianapolis: Liberty Fund, Inc., 2001), p. 125.

1826. Pierre Frist obituary, *The Indianapolis Star*, Indianapolis, Indiana, 26 October 1973, p. 1.

1827. Ibid.

1828. Dane Starbuck, *The Goodriches: An American Family* (Indianapolis: Liberty Fund, Inc., 2001), p. 285.

1829. "Pierre F. Goodrich Dies; Business Executive Had Diversified Career," *The Indianapolis Star*, Indianapolis, Indiana, 26 October 1973, p. 1.

1830. Dane Starbuck, *The Goodriches: An American Family* (Indianapolis: Liberty Fund, Inc., 2001), pp. 212, 213.

1831. "Court: Gifts Tax Exempt," *The Indianapolis Star*, Indianapolis, Indiana, 16 September 1982, p. 47, column 6.

1832. "IRS Reviews Goodrich Tax," *Indianapolis News*, Indianapolis, Indiana, 18 May 1978, p. 40, column 1.

1833. Ibid.

1834. Dane Starbuck, *The Goodriches: An American Family* (Indianapolis: Liberty Fund, Inc., 2001), p. 481.

1835. Dane Starbuck, *The Goodriches: An American Family* (Indianapolis: Liberty Fund, Inc., 2001), pp. 236, 237.

1836. Dane Starbuck, *The Goodriches: An American Family* (Indianapolis: Liberty Fund, Inc., 2001), p. 126.

1837. "Anne [*sic*] D. Goodrich, Polish Prince Wed," *The Indianapolis Star*, Indianapolis, Indiana, 3 May 1952, p. 6, column 1.

1838. Ibid.

1839. Ibid.

1840. Dane Starbuck, *The Goodriches: An American Family* (Indianapolis: Liberty Fund, Inc., 2001), pp. 213, 214.

1841. William C. Tindall household, 1900 U.S. census, New Castle County, Delaware, population schedule, E. Wilmington, enumeration district 28, sheet 23, line 7; National Archives micropublication T623, roll 155.

1842. Ibid.

1843. Marriage date approximated from birth date of first child.

1844. William Cook Tindall, social security application 222-07-0954, U.S. Social Security Administration. Tindall was their son.

1845. William Tindall household, 1920 U.S. census, New Castle County, Delaware, population schedule, Wilmington, enumeration district 73, sheet 3, line 75, dwelling 41, family 50; National Archives micropublication T625, roll 203.

1846. Ibid.

1847. William Cook Tindall, social security application 222-07-0954, U.S. Social Security Administration.

1848. William C. Tindall II probate record, 88815, 1986, New Castle County, Delaware, Delaware Public Archives, Dover, Delaware.

1849. William Cook Tindall, social security application 222-07-0954, U.S. Social Security Administration.

1850. William C. Tindall II probate record, 88815, 1986, New Castle County, Delaware, Delaware Public Archives, Dover, Delaware.

1851. Willard Springer household, 1900 U.S. census, New Castle County, Delaware, population schedule, Wilmington Hundred, enumeration district 16, sheet 1, line 39, p. 201; National Archives micropublication T623, roll 154.

1852. Harold L. Springer probate record, 56073, 1969, New Castle County, Delaware, Delaware Public Archives, Dover, Delaware.

1853. Harold L. Springer household, 1930 U.S. census, New Castle County, Delaware, population schedule, Christiana, enumeration district 90, p. 5B, dwelling 105, family; National Archives micropublication T626, roll 287.

1854. Carolyn L. Springer probate record, 53971, 1968, New Castle County, Delaware, Delaware Public Archives, Dover, Delaware.

1855. Willard Springer household, 1900 U.S. census, New Castle County, Delaware, population schedule, Wilmington Hundred, enumeration district 16, sheet 1, line 39, p. 201; National Archives micropublication T623, roll 154.

1856. Harold L. Springer household, 1930 U.S. census, New Castle County, Delaware, population schedule, Christiana, enumeration district 90, p. 5B, dwelling 105, family; National Archives micropublication T626, roll 287.

1857. Harold L. Springer probate record, 56073, 1969, New Castle County, Delaware, Delaware Public Archives, Dover, Delaware.

1858. Biographical material provided by Harold L. Springer III (1406 N. Harrison Street, Wilmington, DE 19806) 10 July 2002 to compiler.

1859. William L. Springer, probate record, 91552, 1987, New Castle County, Delaware, Wilmington, Delaware. In the event that none of his issue survived, William L. Springer's will named his brother's children.

1860. William L. Springer, probate record, 91552, 1987, New Castle County, Delaware, Wilmington, Delaware. Will written in 1983.

1861. Ibid.

1862. Ibid.

1863. Harold L. Springer household, 1930 U.S. census, New Castle County, Delaware, population schedule, Christiana, enumeration district 90, p. 5B, dwelling 105, family; National Archives micropublication T626, roll 287.

1864. Biographical material provided by Harold L. Springer III (1406 N. Harrison Street, Wilmington, DE 19806) July 2002 to compiler.

1865. Harold L. Springer household, 1930 U.S. census, New Castle County, Delaware, population schedule, Christiana, enumeration district 90, p. 5B, dwelling 105, family; National Archives micropublication T626, roll 287.

1866. Biographical material provided by Harold L. Springer III (1406 N. Harrison Street, Wilmington, DE 19806) July 2002 to compiler.

1867. Edith Springer Baumgartner, probate record, 65875, 1975, New Castle County, Delaware, Delaware Public Archives, Dover, Delaware.

1868. Biographical material provided by Harold L. Springer III (1406 N. Harrison Street, Wilmington, DE 19806) July 2002 to compiler.

1869. Willard Springer household, 1900 U.S. census, New Castle County, Delaware, population schedule, Wilmington Hundred, enumeration district 16, sheet 1, line 39, stamped p. 201; National Archives micropublication T623, roll 154.

1870. Helen S. Stout probate record, 29860, 1948, New Castle County, Delaware, Delaware Public Archives, Dover, Delaware.

1871. Frist Family Group Sheet provided by grandson Paul L. White III (118 Montchan Drive, Wilmington, DE 19807), 9 November 2001, to compiler.

1872. Ibid.

1873. Willard Springer probate record, 20759, 1936, New Castle County, Delaware, Delaware Public Archives, Dover, Delaware.

1874. Willard Springer household, 1900 U.S. census, New Castle County, Delaware, population schedule, Wilmington Hundred, enumeration district 16, sheet 1, line 39, stamped p. 201; National Archives micropublication T623, roll 154.

1875. Charles Masters household, 1900 U.S. census, Kent County, Delaware, population schedule, enumeration district 69, Sheet 6, Line 19; National Archives micropublication T623, roll 153.

1876. Willard Springer probate record, 20759, 1936, New Castle County, Delaware, Delaware Public Archives, Dover, Delaware.

1877. Ibid.

1878. Helen S. Stout probate record, 29860, 1948, New Castle County, Delaware, Delaware Public Archives, Dover, Delaware.

1879. Marjorie S. White probate record, 105594, 1993, New Castle County, Delaware, Wilmington, Delaware.

1880. Marriage approximated from the birth of their first child in 1945.

1881. Willard Springer, Jr. death certificate 518 (1956), Delaware Bureau of Vital Statistics, Dover, Delaware.

1882. Willard Springer probate record, 36508, 1956, New Castle County, Delaware, Delaware Public Archives, Dover Delaware.

1883. Edna L. Springer, social security application 221-30-7022, U.S. Social Security Administration. Date of marriage approximated from birth of first child.

1884. Edna L. Springer, social security application 221-30-7022, U.S. Social Security Administration.

1885. Willard Springer household, 1900 U.S. census, New Castle County, Delaware, population schedule, Wilmington Hundred, enumeration district 16, sheet 1, line 39, p. 201; National Archives micropublication T623, roll 154.

1886. Willard Springer household, 1930 U.S. census, New Castle County, Delaware, population schedule, Brandywine, enumeration district 91, p. 7, dwelling 77, family 78; National Archives micropublication T626, roll 287.

1887. Willard Springer, Jr. probate record, 36508, 1956, New Castle County, Delaware, Delaware Public Archives, Dover Delaware.

1888. Willard Springer, Jr. death certificate 518 (1956), Delaware Bureau of Vital Statistics, Dover, Delaware.

1889. Willard Springer household, 1930 U.S. census, New Castle County, Delaware, population schedule, Brandywine, enumeration district 91, p. 7, dwelling 77, family 78; National Archives micropublication T626, roll 287.

1890. Elizabeth Springer Mahood probate record, 36231, 1956, New Castle County, Delaware, Delaware Public Archives, Dover, Delaware.

1891. Edith Springer Baumgartner, probate record, 65875, 1975, New Castle County, Delaware, Delaware Public Archives, Dover, Delaware. Edith was an aunt.

1892. Ibid.

1893. Ibid.

1894. Willard Springer household, 1930 U.S. census, New Castle County, Delaware, population schedule, Brandywine, enumeration district 91, p. 7, dwelling 77, family 78; National Archives micropublication T626, roll 287.

1895. Edith Springer Baumgartner, probate record, 65875, 1975, New Castle County, Delaware, Delaware Public Archives, Dover, Delaware. Edith was an aunt.

1896. Willard Springer household, 1930 U.S. census, New Castle County, Delaware, population schedule, Brandywine, enumeration district 91, p. 7, dwelling 77, family 78; National Archives micropublication T626, roll 287.

1897. Edith Springer Baumgartner, probate record, 65875, 1975, New Castle County, Delaware, Delaware Public Archives, Dover, Delaware. Edith was an aunt.

1898. Edwin J. Sheppard household, 1900 U.S. census, New Castle County, Delaware, population schedule, Wilmington, enumeration district 45, sheet 24, line 32; National Archives micropublication T623, roll 156.

1899. Esther S. Graves probate record, 66410, 1975, New Castle County, Delaware, Delaware Public Archives, Dover, Delaware. Also Joan Wallis Hauptle (55 Grey Wing Pointe, Naples, FL 34113) telephone conversation 25 May 2003 with compiler.

1900. Herman Mayes Genealogical Collection.

1901. Edward J. Graves probate record, 32533, 1953, New Castle County, Delaware, Delaware Public Archives, Dover, Delaware.

1902. Esther S. Graves probate record, 66410, 1975, New Castle County, Delaware, Delaware Public Archives, Dover, Delaware.

1903. Edward J. Graves probate record, 32533, 1953, New Castle County, Delaware; Delaware Public Archives, Dover, Delaware. His 1952 will named daughters Nancy A. Graves and Carolyn J. Graves, but made no mention of a daughter Eileen.

1904. Kallena Sheppard probate record, 29157, 1950, New Castle County, Delaware, Delaware Public Archives, Dover, Delaware. This record for their maternal grandmother named two granddaughters Carolyn Graves and Eileen Graves, but did not mention Nancy A. Graves.

1905. Edward J. Graves probate record, 32533, 1953, New Castle County, Delaware, Delaware Public Archives, Dover, Delaware. The 1953 petition listing the heirs named Carolyn J. Graves Allen as a daughter.

1906. Kallena Sheppard probate record, 29157, 1950, New Castle County, Delaware, Delaware Public Archives, Dover, Delaware. This record named two granddaughters Carolyn Graves and Eileen Graves. Eileen was not named in the probate record for either of her parents. It is possible that she was Nancy Aileen. If she existed as a separate person she must have died by 1952 as she was not named in her father's will or in the settlement of his estate.

1907. Edward J. Graves probate record, 32533, 1953, New Castle County, Delaware, Delaware Public Archives, Dover, Delaware. All children were presumably named in this estate and Eileen was not mentioned. It is possible that Eileen and Nancy A. Graves are the same person.

1908. Harry Homer Frist Family Record, preserved by his daughter Patricia Jo Frist (Clinton, Indiana, now deceased), copy held in 2003 by compiler.

1909. Ibid.

1910. Ibid.

1911. Ibid.

1912. Ibid.

1913. Patricia Frist Genealogical Collection Item 29.

1914. Harry Frist household, 1920 U.S. census, Vermillion County, Indiana, population schedule, Helt Township, enumeration district 107, sheet 10B, dwelling 248, family 262; National Archives micropublication T624, roll 472.

1915. Patricia Frist Genealogical Collection Item 28

1916. Patricia Frist Genealogical Collection Item 33.

1917. Patricia Frist Genealogical Collection Item 32.

1918. Harry Homer Frist Family Record.

1919. Patricia Frist Genealogical Collection Item 28.

1920. Harry Homer Frist Family Record.

1921. Ibid.

1922. Patricia Frist Genealogical Collection Item 34.

1923. Ibid.

1924. Harry Homer Frist Family Record.

1925. Ibid.

1926. Patricia Frist Genealogical Collection Item 46.

1927. Ibid.

1928. Gary Jones (P. O. Box 142, Montezuma, IN 47862), telephone conversation May 2001 with compiler.

1929. Harlow Peirce Frist death certificate (1975), Vermillion County, Indiana, Board of Health.

1930. Ibid.

1931. Frist–Miller marriage, copy of original marriage license provided June 2001 by daughter Mary Edith Banes (2229 Rainbow Drive, Lafayette, IN 47904-2311) to compiler.

1932. Eliza H. Frist death certificate #034173 (1993), Lafayette, Indiana, Health Department, Lafayette City.

1933. Ibid.

1934. Harlow Peirce Frist, World War I discharge papers, provided June 2001 by Mary Edith Banes (2229 Rainbow Drive, Lafayette, IN 47904-2311) to compiler. Banes is a daughter.

1935. Herman Mayes Genealogical Collection. Also Patricia Frist Genealogical Collection Item 53.

1936. Harlow Frist household, 1920 U.S. census, Vermillion County, Indiana, population schedule, Helt Township, enumeration district 147, sheet 12B, dwelling 285, family 295; National Archives micropublication T625, roll 472.

1937. Biographical material provided June 2001 by daughter Mary Edith Banes (2229 Rainbow Drive, Lafayette, IN 47904-2311) to compiler.

1938. Herman Mayes Genealogical Collection. Also Patricia Frist Genealogical Collection Item 52.

1939. Eliza H. Frist death certificate #034173 (1993), Lafayette, Indiana, Health Department, Lafayette City.

1940. Harlow Peirce Frist death certificate (1975), Vermillion County, Indiana, Board of Health.

1941. Biographical material provided by Mary Edith Banes (2229 Rainbow Drive, Lafayette, IN 47904-2311) February 2001 to compiler.

1942. Frist Family Group Sheet and Robert J. Frist obituary, *Journal and Courier*, Lafayette, Indiana, 26 October 1998, provided by Mrs. Robert Jediah Frist (798 West 1050 South, Brookston, IN 47923-8062) to compiler.

1943. Betty Frist Mayes obituary, *Clintonian*, Clinton, Indiana, 5 May 1990, clipping from Patricia Frist Genealogical Collection.

1944. Herman Mayes Genealogical Collection.

1945. Marshall A. Frist obituary, undated from unknown newspaper, Patricia Frist Genealogical Collection.

1946. Marshall Frist, 303-01-5203, Social Security Death Index, *Family Search*.

1947. Vermillion County Historical Society, *Vermillion County Indiana, History & Families* (Paducah, Kentucky: Turner Publishing Company, 1990), p. 156.

1948. Marjorie Frist, social security application 312-46-0831 dated 23 January 1962, U.S. Social Security Administration.

1949. Marjorie Frist, 312-46-0831, Social Security Death Index, *Family Search*.

1950. Marshall Frist household, 1920 U.S. census, Vermillion County, Indiana, population schedule, Helt Township, enumeration district 107, p. 11A, dwelling 249, family 264; National Archives micropublication T625, roll 472.

1951. Vermillion County Historical Society, *Vermillion County Indiana, History & Families* (Paducah, Kentucky: Turner Publishing Company, 1990), p. 156.

1952. Marshall Frist, 303-01-5203, Social Security Death Index, *Family Search*.

1953. Marjorie Frist, 312-46-0831, Social Security Death Index, *Family Search*.

1954. Vermillion County Historical Society, *Vermillion County Indiana, History & Families* (Paducah, Kentucky: Turner Publishing Company, 1990), p. 156.

1955. "Marjorie Frist of Clinton Dies," undated obituary from unknown newspaper, Patricia Frist Genealogical Collection. Exact date from Herman Mayes Genealogical Collection.

1956. Herman Mayes Genealogical Collection.

1957. "Wayne E. Frist, 38, Dies in Iowa," undated obituary from unknown newspaper, Patricia Frist Genealogical Collection.

1958. Herman Mayes Genealogical Collection.

1959. Abram Frist household, 1900 U.S. census, Baltimore County, Maryland, population schedule, City of Baltimore, enumeration district 289, sheet 17, house number 1112, dwelling 319, family number illegible; National Archives micropublication T623, roll 618.

1960. Interview with Martin Burnett Lyons (30588 Kingston Road, Easton, MD 21601), son of Estella Elizabeth Frist Lyons, September 2002 by Margaret Hepner (600 Falcon Bridge Drive, Joppa, MD 21085). Information conveyed 26 September 2002 to compiler.

1961. Harry H. Lyons household, 1920 U.S. census, Talbot County, Maryland, population schedule, Trappe district, enumeration district 111, sheet 6, dwelling 114, family 114; National Archives micropublication T624, roll 677.

1962. Interview with Martin Burnett Lyons (30588 Kingston Road, Easton, MD 21601), son of Estella Elizabeth Frist Lyons, September 2002 by Margaret Hepner (600 Falcon Bridge Drive, Joppa, MD 21085). Information conveyed 26 September 2002 to compiler.

1963. Ibid.

1964. Ibid.

1965. Ibid.

1966. Frist Family Group Sheet provided June 2002 by Gene and Debbie Fischer III (11615 Joy Lane, Fredericksburg, VA 22407) to compiler. Gene is a grandson of Dolores Mary Frist Klima. All information is from this source.

1967. Frist Family Group Sheet provided June 2002 to compiler by Gene and Debbie Fischer III (11615 Joy Lane, Fredericksburg, VA 22407).

1968. Frist Family Group Sheet provided 2 April 2002 by Margaret Frist Hepner (daughter) (600 Falcon Bridge Avenue, Joppa, MD) to compiler. All information in this biographical sketch came from this source except where otherwise cited.

1969. Bernard Frist household, 1920 U.S. census, Baltimore County, Maryland, population schedule, City of Baltimore, enumeration district 187, sheet 4, line 15 dwelling 69 family 89; National Archives micropublication T625, roll 658.

1970. Daniel Hepner (600 Falcon Bridge Avenue, Joppa, MD), telephone conversation, 21 January 2003 with compiler.

1971. Frist Family Group Sheet provided 2 April 2002 by Margaret Frist Hepner (daughter) (600 Falcon Bridge Avenue, Joppa, MD) to compiler. All information in this biographical sketch and the listing of children came from this source.

1972. Lula Churchman, social security application 212-80-1783, dated 6 May 1974, U.S. Social Security Administration.

1973. Lula M. Churchman estate packet 3573, 1975, Cecil County, Maryland, Register of Wills, Elkton, Maryland.

1974. Herman Mayes Genealogical Collection.

1975. Samuel James Churchman, social security application 221-01-9076, dated 30 November 1936, U.S. Social Security Administration.

1976. Donna J. Robertson, compiler, *Tombstone Inscriptions of Cecil County, Maryland* (Largo, Florida: privately printed, 1995), p. 147.

1977. George E. Tyson household, 1900 U.S. census, Cecil County, Maryland, population schedule, enumeration district 24, sheet 18, line 42, stamped p. 218, dwelling 336, family 343; National Archives micropublication T623, roll 620.

1978. S. J. Churchman household, 1920 U.S. census, Cecil County, Maryland, population schedule, Fourth District Fair Hill, enumeration district 22, sheet 9, dwelling 131, family 133; National Archives micropublication T625, roll 670.

1979. Samuel James Churchman, social security application 221-01-9076 dated 30 November 1936, U.S. Social Security Administration.

1980. Donna J. Robertson, compiler, *Tombstone Inscriptions of Cecil County, Maryland* (Largo, Florida: privately printed, 1995), p. 147.

1981. Lula Churchman, social security application 212-80-1783 dated 6 May 1974, U.S. Social Security Administration.

1982. Lula M. Churchman estate packet #3573, 1975, Cecil County, Maryland, Register of Wills, Elkton, Maryland.

1983. Donna J. Robertson, compiler, *Tombstone Inscriptions of Cecil County, Maryland* (Largo, Florida: privately printed, 1995), p. 147.

1984. Ibid.

1985. Herman Mayes Genealogical Collection.

1986. Ibid.

1987. George E. Tyson household, 1900 U.S. census, Cecil County, Maryland, population schedule, enumeration district 24, sheet 18, line 42, p. 218, dwelling 336, household 343; National Archives micropublication T623, roll 620.

1988. Donna J. Robertson, compiler, *Tombstone Inscriptions of Cecil County, Maryland* (Largo, Florida: privately printed, 1995), p. 450.

1989. Cecil County, Maryland, Marriages 1896–1911:322, Marriage Office, Elkton, Maryland.

1990. Donna J. Robertson, compiler, *Tombstone Inscriptions of Cecil County, Maryland* (Largo, Florida: privately printed, 1995), p. 450.

1991. Ella E. Tyson estate packet #1865, 1966, Cecil County, Maryland, Register of Wills, Elkton, Maryland.

1992. George E. Tyson household, 1900 U.S. census, Cecil County, Maryland, population schedule, enumeration district 24, sheet 18, line 42, p. 218, dwelling 336, household 343; National Archives micropublication T623, roll 620.

1993. John Earl Tyson household, 1920 U.S. census, Cecil County, Maryland, population schedule, District Six Rising Sun, enumeration district 28, sheet 7, dwelling 12, family 8; National Archives micropublication T625, roll 670.

1994. Cecil County, Maryland, Will Book Y32:323–325, Register of Wills, Elkton, Maryland.

1995. Donna J. Robertson, compiler, *Tombstone Inscriptions of Cecil County, Maryland* (Largo, Florida: privately printed, 1995), p. 450.

1996. Ella E. Tyson estate packet #1865, 1966, Cecil County, Maryland, Register of Wills, Elkton, Maryland.

1997. Ella E. Tyson estate packet #1865, 1966, Cecil County, Maryland, Register of Wills, Elkton, Maryland. Exact dates from telephone conversation 28 October 2002 Martha Vianne Absher Gillespie (15225 N. Seventy-Second Dr., Peoria, AZ 85381) with compiler. Mrs. Gillespie is a daughter.

1998. Herman Mayes Genealogical Collection.

1999. Donna J. Robertson, compiler, *Tombstone Inscriptions of Cecil County, Maryland* (Largo, Florida: privately printed, 1995), p. 441.

2000. Biographical material provided July 2002 by Donald Frist (68 N. Hills Drive, Rising Sun, MD 21911) to compiler.

2001. Donna J. Robertson, compiler, *Tombstone Inscriptions of Cecil County, Maryland* (Largo, Florida: privately printed, 1995), p. 441. Date of marriage is from Herman Mayes Genealogical Collection.

2002. Ella E. Tyson estate packet #1865, 1966, Cecil County, Maryland, Register of Wills, Elkton, Maryland. Exact dates from Herman Mayes Genealogical Collection.

2003. Pearl Astle, social security Numident printout dated 10 May 1972 for 159-50-9604, U.S. Social Security Administration.

2004. Pearl Astle, 159-50-9604, Social Security Death Index, *Family Search.*

2005. Cecil County, Maryland, Marriages January to June 1918:4, Marriage Office, Elkton, Maryland.

2006. Charles Ellis Astle, social security form OA-C790 for 179-22-4532 filed 21 August 1956, U.S. Social Security Administration.

2007. Charles Ellis Astle, 179-22-4532, Social Security Death Index, *Family Search.*

2008. George E. Tyson household, 1900 U.S. census, Cecil County, Maryland, population schedule, enumeration district 24, sheet 18, line 42, stamped p. 218, dwelling 336, family 343; National Archives micropublication T623, roll 620.

2009. Pearl Astle, 159-50-9604; Social Security Death Index, *Family Search.*

2010. Donna J. Robertson, compiler, *Tombstone Inscriptions of Cecil County, Maryland* (Largo, Florida: privately printed, 1995), p. 223.

2011. Ibid.

2012. Herman Mayes Genealogical Collection.

2013. Donna J. Robertson, compiler, *Tombstone Inscriptions of Cecil County, Maryland* (Largo, Florida: privately printed, 1995), p. 223.

2014. Harold Edward Tyson, social security application 218-05-4631 dated 19 April 1937, U.S. Social Security Administration.

2015. Howard Edward Tyson, 218-05-4631, Social Security Death Index, *Family Search.*

2016. Esther Ann Astle Tyson, social security application 212-74-9857 dated 12 April 1972, U.S. Social Security Administration.

2017. Esther Ann Tyson estate packet #7872, 25 April 1994, Cecil County, Maryland, Orphans' Court, Elkton, Maryland.

2018. George E. Tyson household, 1920 U.S. census, Cecil County, Maryland, population schedule, District Seven, Port Deposit, enumeration district 29, sheet 1, dwelling and family 4; National Archives micropublication T625, roll 670.

2019. Harold Edward Tyson, 218-05-4631, social security application dated 19 April 1937, U.S. Social Security Administration.

2020. Howard Edward Tyson, 218-05-4631, Social Security Death Index, *Family Search.*

2021. Esther Ann Tyson estate packet #7872, 25 April 1994, Cecil County, Maryland, Orphans' Court, Elkton, Maryland.

2022. Esther Ann Tyson estate packet #7872, 25 April 1994, Cecil County, Maryland, Orphans' Court, Elkton, Maryland. Exact dates are from Herman Mayes Genealogical Collection.

2023. Esther Ann Tyson estate packet #7872, 25 April 1994, Cecil County, Maryland, Orphans' Court, Elkton, Maryland. Exact dates and names of children are from Herman Mayes Genealogical Collection.

2024. George E. Tyson household, 1920 U.S. census, Cecil County, Maryland, population schedule, District 7, Port Deposit, enumeration district 29, sheet 1, dwelling and family 4; National Archives micropublication T625, roll 670.

2025. Ibid.

2026. Cecil County, Maryland, Book January 1, 1928:173, Marriage Office, Elkton, Maryland.

2027. Herman Mayes Genealogical Collection.

2028. Biographical material provided August 2002 by Donald Frist (68 N. Hills Drive, Rising Sun, MD 21911) to compiler. Frist is a cousin.

2029. Herman Mayes Genealogical Collection.

2030. Biographical material provided 18 December 2000 by Dr. Ramsey Hudson Frist (633 Jones Avenue, Morgantown, WV 26505-4722) to compiler. Ramsey is Joseph Osmond Frist's son. All information in this sketch is from this source, unless otherwise cited.

2031. Joseph O. Frist obituary, *Cecil Whig*, Elkton, Maryland, 28 November 1979, clipping from Cecil County Historical Society Library, Elkton, Maryland. Also Joseph Frist, 177-03-4309, Social Security Death Index, *Family Search.*

2032. Joseph O. Frist obituary, *Cecil Whig*, Elkton, Maryland, 28 November 1979, clipping from Cecil County Historical Society Library, Elkton, Maryland.

2033. Blanche Frist, social security application 161-50-0613, U.S. Social Security Administration.

2034. Blanche Frist, 161-50-0613, Social Security Death Index, *Family Search.*

2035. Joseph O. Frist obituary, *Cecil Whig*, Elkton, Maryland, 28 November 1979, clipping from Cecil County Historical Society Library, Elkton, Maryland.

2036. Joseph O. Frist obituary, *Cecil Whig*, Elkton, Maryland, 28 November 1979, clipping from Cecil County Historical Society Library, Elkton, Maryland. Also Joseph Frist, 177-03-4309, Social Security Death Index, *Family Search.*

2037. Joseph O. Frist obituary, *Cecil Whig*, Elkton, Maryland, 28 November 1979, clipping from Cecil County Historical Society Library, Elkton, Maryland.

2038. Blanche Frist, 161-50-0613, Social Security Death Index, *Family Search.*

2039. Frist Family Group Sheet and biographical material provided by Dr. Ramsey Hudson Frist (633 Jones Avenue, Morgantown, WV 26505-4722) 18 December 2000 to compiler.

2040. Ibid.

2041. Frist Family Group Sheet provided by Michael Maria Frist Schell (12402 Broad Road, Conneaut Lake, PA 16316) to compiler.

2042. Donna J. Robertson, compiler, *Tombstone Inscriptions of Cecil County, Maryland* (Largo, Florida: privately printed, 1995), p. 180.

2043. Biographical material provided by Donald Frist (68 N. Hills Drive, Rising Sun, MD 21911), July 2002 to compiler. Frist is a brother. All information in this sketch is from this source, except where otherwise cited.

2044. Donna J. Robertson, compiler, *Tombstone Inscriptions of Cecil County, Maryland* (Largo, Florida: privately printed, 1995), p. 180.

2045. Ibid.

2046. John Frist household, 1920 U.S. census, Cecil County, Maryland, population schedule, Seventh District, enumeration district 30, sheet 6B, line 61, dwelling 85, family 86; National Archives micropublication T625, roll 670.

2047. D. Sterling Frist obituary, *Cecil Whig*, Elkton, Maryland, 30 May 1984, clipping from Cecil County Historical Society Library, Elkton, Maryland.

2048. Donna J. Robertson, compiler, *Tombstone Inscriptions of Cecil County, Maryland* (Largo, Florida: privately printed, 1995), p. 180.

2049. Biographical material provided by Donald Frist (68 N. Hills Drive, Rising Sun, MD 21911), July 2002 to compiler. Frist is a uncle. All information in this sketch is from this source, except where otherwise cited.

2050. Ibid.

2051. John Willard Frist, 216-09-6231, Social Security Death Index, *Family Search*.

2052. Biographical material provided by Charlotte (Frist) Turner (1677 Paradisewood Dr., Paradise, CA 95969) 13 March 2001 to compiler.

2053. John Willard Frist, 216-09-6231, Social Security Death Index, *Family Search*.

2054. Biographical material provided by Charlotte (Frist) Turner (1677 Paradisewood Dr., Paradise, CA 95969) 13 March 2001 to compiler.

2055. Frist Family Group Sheet provided by Charlotte (Frist) Turner (1677 Paradisewood Drive, Paradise, CA 95969) to compiler.

2056. Ibid.

2057. Donald Russell Frist (68 North Hills Drive, Rising Sun, MD 21911-1663), 13 December 2000 letter to compiler. All information in this sketch is from this source, except where otherwise cited.

2058. Donna J. Robertson, compiler, *Tombstone Inscriptions of Cecil County, Maryland* (Largo, Florida: privately printed, 1995), p. 244.

2059. Ibid.

2060. Donald Russell Frist (68 North Hills Drive, Rising Sun, MD 21911-1663) 13 December 2000 letter to compiler.

2061. Doris Frist obituary, *Cecil Whig*, Elkton, Maryland, 18 July 1987, clipping from Cecil County Historical Society Library, Elkton, Maryland.

2062. "1955 Kaiser Manhattan is unusual sight in Cecil County," *Cecil Whig*, Elkton, Maryland, 4 March 1999, Section D, p. 2, columns 2–5.

2063. Donald Russell Frist (68 North Hills Drive, Rising Sun, MD 21911-1663) 13 December 2000 letter to compiler.

2064. Donna J. Robertson, compiler, *Tombstone Inscriptions of Cecil County, Maryland* (Largo, Florida: privately printed, 1995), p. 215.

2065. Ibid.

2066. Harford County, Maryland, Marriage Book WSF 4:82, Marriage Office, Bel Air, Maryland.

2067. Chandler Family Reunion Committee, *A Record of the Descendants of George and Jane Chandler (who emigrated to Pennsylvania from Wiltshire, England, in 1687) with a Pedigree of the Chandlers of Oare, Wiltshire* (No place: Chandler Family Reunion Committee, 1937), p. 645.

2068. Donna J. Robertson, compiler, *Tombstone Inscriptions of Cecil County, Maryland* (Largo, Florida: privately printed, 1995), p. 215.

2069. John Kraus household, 1920 U.S. census, Cecil County, Maryland, population schedule, enumeration district 31, sheet 5B, line 84, dwelling 130, family 131; National Archives micropublication T625, roll 670.

2070. Donna J. Robertson, compiler, *Tombstone Inscriptions of Cecil County, Maryland* (Largo, Florida: privately printed, 1995), p. 215.

2071. Ibid.

2072. Chandler Family Reunion Committee, *A Record of the Descendants of George and Jane Chandler (who emigrated to Pennsylvania from Wiltshire, England, in 1687) with a Pedigree of the Chandlers of Oare, Wiltshire* (No place: Chandler Family Reunion Committee, 1937), p. 645.

2073. Herman Mayes Genealogical Collection.

2074. Chandler Family Reunion Committee, *A Record of the Descendants of George and Jane Chandler (who emigrated to Pennsylvania from Wiltshire, England, in 1687) with a Pedigree of the Chandlers of Oare, Wiltshire* (No place: Chandler Family Reunion Committee, 1937), p. 645. This cites 19 September 1924, Mayes says 16 September 1924.

2075. Herman Mayes Genealogical Collection.

2076. Chandler Family Reunion Committee, *A Record of the Descendants of George and Jane Chandler (who emigrated to Pennsylvania from Wiltshire, England, in 1687) with a Pedigree of the Chandlers of Oare, Wiltshire* (No place: Chandler Family Reunion Committee, 1937), p. 645.

2077. Herman Mayes Genealogical Collection.

2078. The Foard–Smith Family Tree. Also Ann Eliza Frist Foard probate record, 48521, 1964, New Castle County, Delaware, Delaware Public Archives, Dover, Delaware.

2079. The Foard–Smith Family Tree. All information in this sketch is from this source, unless otherwise cited.

2080. Letter from Mrs. Franklin Peach Foard (700 Zee Street, Martinsville, VA 24112-39323) dated 16 August 2001 to compiler, held by compiler in 2002. Mrs. Foard was Anna Roberta's sister-in-law.

2081. The Foard–Smith Family Tree.

2082. Ibid.

2083. Ibid.

2084. Ibid.

2085. Anna Eliza Frist Foard probate record, 48521, 1964, New Castle County, Delaware, Delaware Public Archives, Dover, Delaware. Also biographical material provided by Mrs. Franklin Peach Foard (700 Zee Street, Martinsville, VA 24112-3932) to compiler.

2086. Biographical material provided by Mrs. Franklin Peach Foard (700 Zee Street, Martinsville, VA 24112-3932) to compiler. The information in this sketch was from this source, except where otherwise cited.

2087. Biographical material provided by Mrs. Franklin Peach Foard (700 Zee Street, Martinsville, VA 24112-3932), to compiler.

2088. Frist Family Group Sheet, provided by Ann Fowser (19 Natchez Trail, Medford Lakes New Jersey, 08055) to compiler.

2089. Biographical material provided by Mrs. Franklin Peach Foard (700 Zee Street, Martinsville, VA 24112-3932) to compiler.

2090. Ibid.

2091. Bertie Hartman obituary, *Chattanooga Daily Times*, Chattanooga, Tennessee, 17 May 1959, p. 29, column 7. This proves the relationship. Specific dates and other family information in this sketch are from Herman Mayes Genealogical Collection, except where otherwise cited.

2092. James B. Frist household, 1930 U.S. census, Hamilton County, Tennessee, population schedule, enumeration district 33-82, sheet 5B, dwelling 91, family 93, microfilm 21, Tennessee State Library and Archives, Nashville, Tennessee. Although the entry is listed James B. Frist, it is in fact for Mrs. James B. Frist. The names of Roy Frist Hartman and his uncle Joe Frist are interchanged on this census.

2093. Jacob C. Houts household, 1930 U.S. census, Hamilton County, Tennessee, population schedule, enumeration district 33-82, sheet 5B, dwelling 84, family 86, microfilm 21, Tennessee State Library and Archives, Nashville, Tennessee.

2094. Herman Mayes Genealogical Collection. This marriage was not located in Tennessee.

2095. Jacob C. Houts household, 1930 U. S. census, Hamilton County, Tennessee, population schedule, enumeration district 33-82, sheet 5B, dwelling 84, family 86, microfilm 21, Tennessee State Library and Archives, Nashville, Tennessee. This indicates Miriam was born in Tennessee, not Alabama as stated in Herman Mayes Genealogical Collection.

2096. Joseph Byron Frist probate record, #1115, Chancery Court of Hamilton County, 300 Courthouse, 201 East 7th Street, Chattanooga, Tennessee 37402.

2097. Bertie Hartman obituary, *Chattanooga Daily Times*, Chattanooga, Tennessee, 17 May 1959, p. 29, column 7.

2098. Bertie Hartman obituary, *Chattanooga Daily Times*, Chattanooga, Tennessee, 17 May 1959, p. 29, column 7. This proves the relationship. Specific dates and other family information in this sketch are from Herman Mayes Genealogical Collection, except where otherwise cited.

2099. Ibid.

2100. Biographical material provided by John Stanley Vetter, M.D. (FristHealth Richmond Family Medicine, 921 Long Drive, Suite 101, Rockingham, NC 18379) December 2000 to compiler. All information on this family is from this source.

2101. Ibid.

2102. Frist Family Group Sheet and biographical material provided by Jane Frist (P.O. Box 272, 102 Frist Road, Montreat, NC 28757) 18 December 2000 with multiple updates to compiler.

2103. Ibid.

2104. Frist Family Group Sheet provided by Jane Frist (P.O. Box 272, 102 Frist Road, Montreat, NC 28757) to compiler.

2105. Frist Family Group Sheet and biographical material provided by Jane Frist (P.O. Box 272, 102 Frist Road, Montreat, NC 28757) 18 December 2000 with multiple updates to compiler.

2106. Ibid.

2107. Frist Family Group Sheet and biographical material provided July 2001 by Charlotte Chesnutt (P.O. Box 412, Montreat, NC 28757) to compiler.

2108. Ibid.

2109. Frist Family Group Sheet and biographical material provided by Dr. Robert Chester Faucette (P.O. Box 412, Montreat, NC 28757) 9 January 2002 to compiler.

2110. Frist Family Group Sheet provided December 2001 by Randy and Janie Moore (219 East College Street, Black Mountain, NC 28711) to compiler.

2111. Biographical material provided by Lynda Faucette 11 and 12 July 2001 and Tom Faucette (9486 Capricorn Way, San Diego, CA 92126) 29 December 2001 to compiler.

2112. Biographical material provided 1 March 2002 by John Chester Frist, Jr., M.D. (146 Ensworth Avenue, Nashville, TN 37205) to compiler.

2113. Mary Corrine Frist, obituary notice, *Tennessean*, Nashville, Tennessee, 22 December 2000, p. 7B, column 2.

2114. Biographical material provided 25 February 2002 by Corinne Frist Glover (5477 Eastwind Road, Wilmington, NC 28403) to compiler.

2115. Biographical sketch provided 3 December 2001 by John Chester Frist III (146 Ensworth Avenue, Nashville, TN 37205) to compiler. Updated September 2002.

2116. Frist Family Group Sheet provided by Thomas and Clare Frist (P.O. Box 1204, 98 Frist Road, Montreat, NC 28757) to compiler. Updated 10 January 2002 and September 2002.

2117. Ibid.

2118. Biographical material provided by Thomas Fearn Frist, Jr., M.D. and wife Patricia Champion Frist (1304 Chickering Road, Nashville, TN 37215) July 2002 to compiler.

2119. Ibid.

2120. Frist Family Group Sheet and biographical material provided 28 March 2002 by Trisha and Chuck Elcan (1034 Chancery Lane, Nashville, TN 37215) to compiler.

2121. Frist Family Group Sheet provided 3 December 2001 by Tommy and Julie Frist (4420 Warner Place, Nashville, TN 37205) to compiler.

2122. Frist Family Group Sheet provided 30 November 2001 and updated 1 December 2001 by William and Jennifer Frist (1216 Canterbury Drive, Nashville, TN 37205) to compiler.

2123. Interview with Dorothy Frist Boensch (104 Bellebrook Circle, Nashville, TN 37205) 14 December 2001 by compiler.

2124. Ibid.

2125. Ibid.

2126. Frist Family Group Sheet and biographical material provided by Robert Armistead Frist, M.D. and wife Carol (Knox) Frist (1326 Page Road, Nashville, TN 37205) 12 December 2001 with updates 18 February 2002 and 22 April 2002 to compiler. All information is from this source, unless otherwise cited.

2127. Ibid.

2128. Biographical material provided February 2002 by Robert and Melissa Frist (211 Craighead Avenue, Nashville, TN 37205) to compiler.

2129. Biographical material provided by Scott McClain and Carol Len (Frist) Portis (6205 Hillsboro Road, Nashville, TN 37215) 5 February 2002 to compiler.

2130. Biographical material provided by Carol Frist (1326 Page Road, Nashville, TN 37205) 2 March 2002 and fax update 22 April 2002 by Carol Frist to compiler.

2131. Biographical material provided by Mary (Frist) Barfield and her husband, Henry Lee Barfield II (1026 Chancery Lane S., Nashville, TN 37215-4552) December 2001 with July 2002 update to compiler.

2132. This facility was founded by her father.

2133. Biographical material provided by Mary (Frist) Barfield and her husband Henry Lee Barfield II (1026 Chancery Lane S., Nashville, TN 37215-4552) December 2001 with July 2002 update to compiler.

2134. Frist Family Group Sheet provided by Mary Lauren Allen (108 Westhampton Place, Nashville, TN 37205) March 2001 and biographical sketch provided 13 December 2001 to compiler.

2135. Frist Family Group Sheet provided by Dorothy Sifford (2410 Golf Club Lane, Nashville, TN 37215) January 2001 and biographical sketch provided 14 December 2001 to compiler.

2136. Biographical sketch provided by Corinne Barfield (402 Page Road, Nashville, TN 37205) 13 December 2001 to compiler.

2137. Lee Cole Barfield (A56 Little Hall, Princeton University, Princeton, New Jersey 08544) biographical sketch provided 13 December 2001 to compiler and updated August 2002.

2138. Biographical material provided by William Harrison Frist, M.D. and wife Karyn (McLaughlin) Frist (703 Bowling Avenue, Nashville, TN 37215) 5 December 2001 with December 2002 update to compiler.

2139. Eddie is the surname of an ancestor rather than a nickname as one might suppose, according to daughter Karyn McLaughlin Frist (703 Bowling Avenue, Nashville, TN 37215).

2140. Biographical material provided by William Harrison Frist, M.D. and wife Karyn (McLaughlin) Frist (703 Bowling Avenue, Nashville, TN 37215) 5 December 2001 to compiler.

2141. Sydney [*sic*] Donald Frist birth certificate 21583, State of Tennessee, Division of Vital Statistics. From Ronnie Frist Genealogical Collection. Ronnie is Sidney's son.

2142. Sidney Donald Frist Sixth Grade Report Card, Hamilton County, Tennessee, Ronnie Frist Genealogical Collection.

2143. Sidney Donald Frist Honorable Discharge United States Marine Corps 21 February 1950, Ronnie Frist Genealogical Collection.

2144. Frist Family Group Sheet provided 28 March 2002 by Ronnie Frist (son) (1712 Gray Road, Chattanooga, TN 37421) to compiler.

2145. Sidney Donald Frist death certificate 2 January 1973, Tennessee Division of Vital Statistics, copy in Ronnie Frist Genealogical Collection.

2146. Sidney Donald Frist obituary, 2 January 1973, *Chattanooga Daily Times*, Chattanooga, Tennessee, p. 2.

2147. Frist Family Group Sheet provided 28 March 2002 by Ronnie Frist (son) (1712 Gray Road, Chattanooga, TN 37421) to compiler.

2148. Larry D. Frist death certificate #50-19944 (1950), Tennessee Division of Vital Statistics, Nashville, Tennessee.

2149. Frist Family Group Sheet provided 28 March 2002 by Ronnie Frist (1712 Gray Road, Chattanooga, TN 37421) to compiler.

2150. Ibid.

2151. Frist Family Group Sheet provided 27 November 2001 by daughter Susan Frist Dixon (6415 Washington Circle, Chattanooga, TN 37416) to compiler. All information is from this source, unless otherwise cited.

2152. James C. Frist obituary, *Chattanooga Daily Times*, Chattanooga, Tennessee, 9 March 1944, p. 11, column 3. James was Frank's father and his obituary mentioned Frank's service.

2153. Frist Family Group Sheet provided 27 November 2001 by daughter Susan Frist Dixon (6415 Washington Circle, Chattanooga, TN 37416) to compiler.

2154. Avene Frist obituary, *Chattanooga Daily News*, Chattanooga, Tennessee, 28 September 1962, p. 23.

2155. Ibid.

2156. Frist Family Group Sheet provided 27 November 2001 by daughter Susan Frist Dixon (6415 Washington Circle, Chattanooga, TN 37416) to compiler.

2157. Margaret Frist obituary, *Chattanooga News-Free Press*, Chattanooga, Tennessee, 25 March 1991, p. B-4.

2158. Frist Family Group Sheet provided 27 November 2001 by Susan Frist Dixon (6415 Washington Circle, Chattanooga, TN 37416) to compiler.

2159. Ibid.

2160. Frist Family Group Sheet provided 27 November 2001 by Susan Frist Dixon (6415 Washington Circle, Chattanooga, TN 37416) to compiler. Susan is a sister.

2161. Ibid.

2162. Frist Family Group Sheet and interview with Patricia Huguenin (609 Grand Mountain Road Chattanooga, TN 37421-7429), 27 February 2002 by compiler. All information on this family is from this source, unless otherwise cited.

2163. Ibid.

2164. Frist Family Group Sheet provided by Clarence Harold Frist (419 Turrentine Avenue, Gadsden, AL 35901) to compiler. All information is from this source, unless otherwise cited.

2165. Ibid.

2166. Ibid.

2167. Ibid.

2168. Ibid.

2169. Ibid.

2170. Ibid.

2171. Ibid.

2172. Frist Family Group Sheet provided by Manferd H. Findley (4555 Jordan Grove Road, Central City, IA 52214) to compiler. Manferd is the son of Roy Manford Findley.

2173. Ibid.

2174. Montgomery County, Iowa, Marriage Record 12:31, microfilm 1,481,228, Family History Library, Salt Lake City, Utah.

2175. Frist Family Group Sheet provided by Manferd H. Findley (4555 Jordan Grove Road, Central City, IA 52214) to compiler.

2176. Ibid.

2177. Ibid.

2178. Geraldine Rosetta Frist Miller, Eickemeyer Funeral Chapel record, provided to compiler in June 2002 by husband Dale Miller (415 S. Eighteenth Street, Clarinda, IA 51632-2515). All information is from this source, although Geraldine Miller while she lived provided family group sheets stating the same information.

2179. Ibid.

2180. Frist Family Group Sheet provided by Geraldine (Frist) Miller (415 South Eighteenth Street, Clarinda, IA 51632-2515), 10 November 2001 to compiler. Mrs. Miller has since died.

2181. Ibid.

2182. Ibid.

2183. Ibid.

2184. Frist Family Group Sheet provided by Geraldine (Frist) Miller (415 South Eighteenth Street, Clarinda, IA 51632-2515), 10 November 2001 to compiler. Mrs. Miller was a sister who has since died. All information is from this source.

2185. Ibid.

2186. Frist Family Group Sheet provided by Geraldine (Frist) Miller (415 South Eighteenth Street, Clarinda, IA 51632-2515) 10 November 2001 to compiler. Mrs. Miller was an aunt.

2187. Ibid.

2188. Frist Family Group Sheet provided by Geraldine (Frist) Miller (415 South Eighteenth Street, Clarinda, IA 51632-2515) 10 November 2001 to compiler. Mrs. Miller was a sister who has since died. All information is from this source.

2189. Ibid.

2190. Frist Family Group Sheet provided by Geraldine (Frist) Miller (415 South Eighteenth Street, Clarinda, IA 51632-2515) 10 November 2001 to compiler. Mrs. Miller was an aunt who has since died.

2191. Ibid.

2192. Ibid.

2193. Ibid.

2194. Ibid.

2195. Russell Frist, 482-01-8838, Social Security Death Index, *Ancestry.com*.

2196. Frist Family Group Sheet provided by Steven Frist (601 Maish, Des Moines, IA 50315) to compiler. Steven Frist is a grandson of Russell Edward Frist. All information is from this source, except where otherwise cited.

2197. Joseph Frist household, 1910 U.S. census, Polk County, Iowa, population schedule, Des Moines, enumeration district 65, sheet 7A, dwelling 43, family 45, stamped p. 67; National Archives Micropublication T624, roll 418.

2198. Joseph Frist household, 1920 U.S. census, Polk County, Iowa, population schedule, Camp Township, Runnells, enumeration district 69, sheet 1A, line 7, dwelling and family 3, stamped p. 58; National Archives micropublication T625, roll 507.

2199. Marriage approximated from birth of only child and could have been much earlier.

2200. Frist Family Group Sheet provided by Steven Frist (601 Maish, Des Moines, IA 50315) to compiler. Steven Frist is a grandson of Russell Edward Frist.

2201. Russell Frist, 482-01-8838, Social Security Death Index, *Ancestry.com*.

2202. Frist Family Group Sheet provided by Steven Frist (601 Maish, Des Moines, IA 50315) to compiler. Steven Frist is a son. He was not certain of the year of their marriage.

2203. Family data provided 30 May 2002 by Paul J. Frist (9311 Sandra Drive, New Paris, OH 45347) to compiler.

2204. Marriage approximated based on the birth of the first child.

2205. Helen Louise Frist, social security application 316-20-0021 dated 4 June 1942, U.S. Social Security Administration.

2206. Helen Louise Frist, 316-20-0021, Social Security Death Index, *Family Search*.

2207. Family data provided 30 May 2002 by Paul J. Frist (9311 Sandra Drive, New Paris, OH 45347) to compiler. Paul is the father of the children.

2208. Ibid.

2209. Ibid.

2210. Louise Steele Frist, social security application 312-56-0126, U.S. Social Security Administration.

2211. Family data provided 30 May 2002 by Paul J. Frist (9311 Sandra Drive, New Paris, OH 45347) to compiler. Paul is the father.

2212. Ibid.

2213. Ibid.

2214. Russell Frist, 305-10-6144, Social Security Death Index, *Family Search*.

2215. Biographical material provided by Phillip Stanley Frist (3107 Waterfront Circle, Anderson, IN 46012) 31 May 2002 to compiler.

2216. Russell Frist obituary, *Anderson Herald/Bulletin*, Anderson, Indiana, 1 November 1989, p. A-2; from Patricia Frist Genealogical Collection.

2217. Ibid.

2218. Biographical material provided by Phillip Stanley Frist (3107 Waterfront Circle, Anderson, IN 46012) 31 May 2002 to compiler.

2219. Ibid.

2220. Herman Mayes Genealogical Collection. All information is from this source unless otherwise cited.

2221. Ibid.

2222. Ibid.

2223. Garry Alan Parmer, 241-64-6333, Social Security Death Index, *Family Search*.

2224. Herman Mayes Genealogical Collection.

2225. Ibid.

2226. Ibid.

2227. Marjorie S. White, 221-12-1195, Social Security Death Index, *Family Search*.

2228. Marjorie S. White probate record, #105594, 1993, New Castle County, Delaware, Register of Wills, Wilmington, Delaware.

2229. Marriage approximated from the birth of their first child in 1945.

2230. Frist Family Group Sheet provided by Paul L. White III (118 Montchan Drive, Wilmington, DE 19807) 9 November 2001 to compiler. Paul is a grandson. Paul L. White probate record, 79746, 1982, New Castle County, Delaware, Delaware Public Archives, Dover, Delaware. This record indicates that the mother was Rebecca McCullough.

2231. Paul L. White probate record, 79746, 1982, New Castle County, Delaware, Delaware Public Archives, Dover, Delaware, indicates he died in Sussex County, Delaware.

2232. Ibid.

2233. Marjorie S. White probate record, 105594, 1993, New Castle County, Delaware, Register of Wills, Wilmington, Delaware.

2234. Frist Family Group Sheet of grandson Paul L. White III (118 Montchan Drive, Wilmington, DE 19807) provided 9 November 2001 to compiler.

2235. Ibid.

2236. Harry Homer Frist Family Record.

2237. Ibid.

2238. Patricia Frist Genealogical Collection Items 35 and 38.

2239. Patricia Frist Genealogical Collection Item 36.

2240. Patricia Frist Genealogical Collection Item 37.

2241. Ronald Glen Foltz obituary, undated from unknown newspaper, Patricia Frist Genealogical Collection.

2242. Patricia Frist Genealogical Collection Item 39.

2243. Patricia Frist Genealogical Collection Item 38.

2244. Harry Homer Frist Family Record.

2245. Ibid.

2246. Patricia Frist Genealogical Collection Item 41

2247. Ibid.

2248. Patricia Frist Genealogical Collection Item 42.

2249. Patricia Frist Genealogical Collection Item 43.

2250. Patricia Frist Genealogical Collection Item 44.

2251. Harry Homer Frist Family Record.

2252. Patricia Frist Genealogical Collection Item 46.

2253. Ibid.

2254. Ibid.

2255. Patricia Frist Genealogical Collection Item 47.

2256. Patricia Frist Genealogical Collection Item 48.

2257. Patricia Frist Genealogical Collection Item 49.

2258. Harry Homer Frist Family Record.

2259. Gary Jones (P.O. Box 142, Montezuma, IN 47862) telephone conversation May 2001 with compiler.

2260. Patricia Frist Genealogical Collection Item 51. The compiler of this genealogy was fortunate enough to meet with Pat in Clinton, Indiana, in March of 2001 before her health problems became known and just a month before she died.

2261. Harry Homer Frist Family Record.

2262. Biographical material provided by Mary Edith Banes (2229 Rainbow Drive, Lafayette, IN 47904-2311) February 2001 to compiler.

2263. *Journal and Courier*, Lafayette, Indiana, Sunday, 14 April 1985, from Patricia Frist Genealogical Collection.

2264. Biographical material provided by Mary Edith Banes (2229 Rainbow Drive, Lafayette, IN 47904-2311) February 2001 to compiler.

2265. Ibid.

2266. Biographical update provided by Mary Edith Banes (2229 Rainbow Drive, Lafayette, IN 47904-2311) September 2002 to compiler.

2267. Harry Homer Frist Family Record. Also Robert Jediah Frist, social security application 313-28-8730, dated 22 May 1946, U.S. Social Security Administration.

2268. Robert J. Frist obituary, *Journal and Courier*, Lafayette, Indiana, 26 October 1998, clipping provided 12 March 2001 by Mrs. Robert Frist (798 W. 1050 South, Brookston, IN 47923) to compiler.

2269. Ibid.

2270. Frist Family Group Sheet provided by Mrs. Robert Jediah Frist (798 West 1050 South, Brookston, IN 47923-8062) to compiler.

2271. Robert J. Frist obituary, *Journal and Courier*, Lafayette, Indiana, 26 October 1998, clipping provided 12 March 2001 by Mrs. Robert Frist (798 W. 1050 South, Brookston, IN 47923) to compiler.

2272. Ibid.

2273. "Antiques in Hoosier Homes," *The Sunday Star*, 19 September 1943, clipping provided 12 March 2001 by Mrs. Robert Frist (798 W. 1050 South, Brookston, IN 47923) to compiler.

2274. Robert J. Frist obituary, *Journal and Courier*, Lafayette, Indiana, 26 October 1998, clipping provided 12 March 2001 by Mrs. Robert Frist (798 W. 1050 South, Brookston, IN 47923) to compiler.

2275. Frist Family Group Sheet provided by Mrs. Robert Jediah Frist (798 West 1050 South, Brookston, IN 47923-8062) to compiler.

2276. Ibid.

2277. Ibid.

2278. Ibid.

2279. Ibid.

2280. Harry Homer Frist Family Record.

2281. Betty Frist Mayes obituary, *Clintonian*, Clinton, Indiana, 5 May 1990, clipping from Patricia Frist Genealogical Collection.

2282. Herman Mayes Genealogical Collection. All information in this sketch is from this source, unless otherwise cited.

2283. This compilation consisted of family group sheets with names and vital statistics for descendants. It was provided to William H. Frist, M.D. (703 Bowling Avenue, Nashville, TN 37215) on disk and in hard copy format by Gary Jones (P.O. Box 142, Montezuma, IN 47862), who did the data entry work.

2284. Betty Frist Mayes obituary, *Clintonian*, Clinton, Indiana, 5 May 1990, clipping from Patricia Frist Genealogical Collection.

2285. Harry Homer Frist Family Record.

2286. Vermillion County Historical Society, *Vermillion County Indiana, History & Families* (Paducah, Kentucky: Turner Publishing Company, 1990), p. 156.

2287. Ibid.

2288. Herman Mayes Genealogical Collection.

2289. Vermillion County Historical Society, *Vermillion County, Indiana, History & Families* (Paducah, Kentucky: Turner Publishing Company, 1990), p. 156.

2290. Patricia Frist Genealogical Collection Item 63.

2291. "Wayne E. Frist, 38, Dies in Iowa" undated obituary from unknown newspaper, Patricia Frist Genealogical Collection.

2292. "Wayne E. Frist, 38, Dies in Iowa" undated obituary from unknown newspaper. Also anecdotal Item 64, both from Patricia Frist Genealogical Collection.

2293. Herman Mayes Genealogical Collection.

2294. "Wayne E. Frist, 38, Dies in Iowa" undated obituary from unknown newspaper, Patricia Frist Genealogical Collection.

2295. Ibid.

2296. Patricia Frist Genealogical Collection Item 64.

2297. Ibid.

2298. Ibid.

2299. Frist Family Group Sheet and biographical material provided June 2002 by Gene and Debbie Fischer III (11615 Joy Lane, Fredericksburg, VA 22407) to compiler. Gene is a son.

2300. Ibid.

2301. Ibid.

2302. Frist Family Group Sheet provided by Brian Joseph Fischer (714 Magnolia Road, Joppa, MD 21085) October 2002 to compiler.

2303. Frist Family Group Sheet provided by Dawn Lee Fischer Casey (1212 N. Fountain Green Road, Bel Air, MD 21015) October 2002 to compiler.

2304. Frist Family Group Sheet and biographical material provided 2 April 2002 by Margaret Frist Hepner (600 Falcon Bridge Avenue, Joppa, MD 21085) to compiler.

2305. Ibid.

2306. Ibid.

2307. Ibid.

2308. Ibid.

2309. Ibid.

2310. Ibid.

2311. Frist Family Group Sheet and biographical material provided 2 April 2002 by Margaret Frist Hepner (600 Falcon Bridge Avenue, Joppa, MD 21085) to compiler. Margaret is a sister.

2312. Ibid.

2313. Frist Family Group Sheet and biographical material provided 2 April 2002 by Margaret Frist Hepner (600 Falcon Bridge Avenue, Joppa, MD 21085) to compiler. Margaret is an aunt.

2314. Ibid.

2315. Ibid.

2316. Ella E. Tyson estate #1865, 1966, Cecil County, Maryland, Register of Wills, Elkton, Maryland. Exact dates are from Herman Mayes Genealogical Collection.

2317. Herman Mayes Genealogical Collection.

2318. Telephone conversation 28 October 2002 Martha Vianne Absher Gillespie (15225 N. Seventy-Second Drive, Peoria, AZ 85381) with compiler.

2319. Ibid.

2320. Ella E. Tyson estate #1865, 1966, Cecil County, Maryland, Register of Wills, Elkton, Maryland.

2321. Ella E. Tyson estate #1865, 1966, Cecil County, Maryland, Register of Wills, Elkton, Maryland. Exact birth date from Herman Mayes Genealogical Collection.

2322. Ella E. Tyson estate #1865, 1966, Cecil County, Maryland, Register of Wills, Elkton, Maryland. Exact dates are from Herman Mayes Genealogical Collection.

2323. Herman Mayes Genealogical Collection.

2324. Ibid.

2325. Ella E. Tyson estate #1865, 1966, Cecil County, Maryland, Register of Wills, Elkton, Maryland. Exact dates from Herman Mayes Genealogical Collection.

2326. Herman Mayes Genealogical Collection.

2327. Vernon E. McMullen will, Cecil County, Maryland, Will Book LDR 15:436–438, Register of Wills, Elkton, Maryland.

2328. Vernon E. McMullen will, Cecil County, Maryland, Will Book LDR 15:436-438, Register of Wills, Elkton, Maryland. Exact dates are from Herman Mayes Genealogical Collection.

2329. Ibid.

2330. Herman Mayes Genealogical Collection. All information on Evelyn and her family is from this source, except where otherwise cited.

2331. Donna J. Robertson, compiler, *Tombstone Inscriptions of Cecil County, Maryland* (Largo, Florida: privately printed, 1995), p. 249.

2332. Herman Mayes Genealogical Collection.

2333. Ibid.

2334. Ibid.

2335. Esther Ann Tyson estate packet #7872, 25 April 1994, Cecil County, Maryland, Orphans' Court, Elkton, Maryland. Exact dates from Herman Mayes Genealogical Collection.

2336. George Oliver Gross, social security application 221-05-5641, dated 17 July 1937, U.S. Social Security Administration.

2337. Ibid.

2338. Donna J. Robertson, compiler, *Tombstone Inscriptions of Cecil County, Maryland* (Largo, Florida: privately printed, 1995), p. 217.

2339. Herman Mayes Genealogical Collection.

2340. Ibid.

2341. Ibid.

2342. Ibid.

2343. Frist Family Group Sheet and biographical letter provided by Dr. Ramsey Frist (633 Jones Avenue, Morgantown, WV 26505) 18 December 2000 to compiler.

2344. Ibid.

2345. Frist Family Group Sheet provided by Heidi Frist Derry (213 Ridgeley Road, Morgantown, WV 26505) 26 February 2001, updated 26 October 2001 to compiler.

2346. Frist Family Group Sheet provided by Jonathan Ramsey Frist (1020 Ashton Drive, Morgantown, WV 26505-4722) in 2001 to compiler.

2347. Frist Family Group Sheet provided by Erica Ann Frist Canfield (212 North Emerson Street, Arlington, VA 22203) June 2001 to compiler.

2348. Frist Family Group Sheet and biographical material provided by Michael Maria Frist Schell (12402 Broad Road, Conneaut Lake, PA 16316) in 2001 to compiler.

2349. Ibid.

2350. Biographical material from Herman Mayes Genealogical Collection with update provided by Donald Frist (68 N. Hills Drive, Rising Sun, MD 21911) July 2002 to compiler. Frist is an uncle. All information on this family is from this source.

2351. Biographical material provided by Donald Frist (68 N. Hills Drive, Rising Sun, MD 21911) September 2002 to compiler.

2352. Biographical material from Herman Mayes Genealogical Collection with update provided by Donald Frist (68 N. Hills Drive, Rising Sun, MD 21911) July 2002 to compiler. Frist is an uncle. All information on this family is from this source.

2353. Frist Family Group Sheet provided by Charlotte Frist Turner (1677 Paradisewood Drive, Paradise, CA 95969) to compiler.

2354. Ibid.

2355. Ibid.

2356. Ibid.

2357. Herman Mayes Genealogical Collection. All information on this family is from this source.

2358. Ibid.

2359. Ibid.

2360. Herman Mayes Genealogical Collection. All information on this family is from this source, except where otherwise cited.

2361. Benjamin Franklin Ordog, social security application 264-24-4289, U.S. Social Security Administration.

2362. Benjamin Franklin Ordog, 264-24-4289, Social Security Death Index, *Family Search*.

2363. Herman Mayes Genealogical Collection. All information on this family is from this source, except where otherwise cited.

2364. David Carlton Morris, social security application 211-22-4752, dated 16 March 1946, U.S. Social Security Administration.

2365. David Carlton Morris, 211-22-4752, Social Security Death Index, *Family Search*.

2366. Herman Mayes Genealogical Collection.

2367. Ibid.

2368. Foard–Smith Family Tree.

2369. Foard–Smith Family Tree. Also biographical material provided by Janet Dann (1559 Riff Road, Corning, NY 14830) to compiler.

2370. Foard–Smith Family Tree.

2371. Ibid.

2372. Ibid.

2373. Ibid.

2374. Ibid.

2375. Ibid.

2376. Ibid.

2377. Ibid.

2378. Foard–Smith Family Tree and biographical material provided by Janet Dann (1559 Riff Road, Corning, NY 14830) May 2002 to compiler.

2379. Ibid.

2380. Ibid.

2381. Ibid.

2382. Ibid.

2383. Ibid.

2384. Ibid.

2385. Ibid.

2386. Ibid.

2387. Ibid.

2388. Frist Family Group Sheet provided by Ann Fowser (19 Natchez Trail, Medford Lakes, NJ, 08055) to compiler. All information on this family is from this source, unless otherwise cited.

2389. Ibid.

2390. Ibid.

2391. Ibid.

2392. Ibid.

2393. Frist Family Group Sheet provided by Jane Frist (P.O. Box 272, 102 Frist Road, Montreat, NC 28757) to compiler.

2394. Ibid.

2395. Ibid.

2396. Ibid.

2397. Ibid.

2398. Ibid.

2399. Frist Family Group Sheet and biographical material provided by Dr. Robert Chester Faucette (P.O. Box 412, Montreat, NC 28757) 9 January 2002 to compiler.

2400. Ibid.

2401. Frist Family Group Sheet provided by Randy and Janie Moore (219 East College Street, Black Mountain, NC 28711) December 2001 to compiler.

2402. Ibid.

2403. Biographical material provided by Lynda Faucette 11 and 12 July 2001 and Tom Faucette (9486 Capricorn Way, San Diego, CA 92126) 29 December 2001 to compiler.

2404. Ibid.

2405. Biographical material provided by Corinne Frist Glover (5477 Eastwind Road, Wilmington, NC 28403) 25 February 2002 to compiler.

2406. Ibid.

2407. Biographical sketch provided 3 December 2001 by John Chester Frist, III (146 Ensworth Avenue, Nashville, TN 37205) and updated September 2002 to compiler.

2408. Ibid.

2409. Frist Family Group Sheet provided by Thomas and Clare Frist (P.O. Box 1204, 98 Frist Road, Montreat, NC 28757) to compiler. Updated 10 January 2002 and September 2002.

2410. Ibid.

2411. Ibid.

2412. Ibid.

2413. Frist Family Group Sheet and biographical material provided 28 March 2002 by Trisha and Chuck Elcan (1034 Chancery Lane, Nashville, TN 37215) with September 2002 update to compiler.

2414. Ibid.

2415. Frist Family Group Sheet provided by Tommy and Julie Frist (4420 Warner Place, Nashville, TN 37205) 3 December 2001 to compiler.

2416. Ibid.

2417. Frist Family Group Sheet provided 30 November 2001 and updated 1 December 2001 by William and Jennifer Frist (1216 Canterbury Drive, Nashville, TN 37205) to compiler.

2418. Ibid.

2419. Interview with Dorothy Frist Boensch (104 Bellebrook Circle, Nashville, TN 37205) 14 December 2001 by compiler.

2420. Ibid.

2421. Biographical material provided February 2002 by Robert and Melissa Frist (211 Craighead Avenue, Nashville, TN 37205) to compiler.

2422. Ibid.

2423. Biographical material provided by Scott McClain and Carol Len (Frist) Portis (6205 Hillsboro Road, Nashville, TN 37215) 5 February 2002 to compiler.

2424. Ibid.

2425. Biographical material provided by Carol Frist (1326 Page Road, Nashville, TN 37205) 2 March 2002 and fax update 22 April 2002 by Carol Frist to compiler.

2426. Ibid.

2427. Frist Family Group Sheet provided by Mary Lauren Allen (108 Westhampton Place, Nashville, TN 37205) March 2001 and biographical sketch provided 13 December 2001 to compiler.

2428. Black and Orange Captains are eighth graders selected each year by the students to act as leaders of the school.

2429. Frist Family Group Sheet provided by Mary Lauren Allen (108 Westhampton Place, Nashville, TN 37205) March 2001 and biographical sketch provided 13 December 2001 to compiler.

2430. Frist Family Group Sheet provided by Dorothy Sifford (2410 Golf Club Lane, Nashville, TN 37215) January 2001 and biographical sketch provided 14 December 2001 to compiler.

2431. Black and Orange Captains are eighth graders selected each year by the students to act as leaders of the school.

2432. Frist Family Group Sheet provided by Dorothy Sifford (2410 Golf Club Lane, Nashville, TN 37215) January 2001 and biographical sketch provided 14 December 2001 to compiler.

2433. Biographical sketch provided by Corinne Barfield (402 Page Road, Nashville, TN 37205) 13 December 2001 to compiler.

2434. Ibid.

2435. Lee Cole Barfield (A56 Little Hall, Princeton University, Princeton, New Jersey 08544) biographical sketch provided 13 December 2001 to compiler and updated August 2002.

2436. Black and Orange Captains are eighth graders selected each year by the students to act as leaders of the school.

2437. Lee Cole Barfield (A56 Little Hall, Princeton University, Princeton, New Jersey 08544) biographical sketch provided 13 December 2001 to compiler and updated August 2002.

2438. Biographical material provided by William Harrison Frist, M.D. and wife, Karyn (McLaughlin) Frist (703 Bowling Avenue, Nashville, TN 37215) 5 December 2001 with December 2002 update to compiler.

2439. Ibid.

2440. Ibid.

2441. Ibid.

2442. Ibid.

2443. Ibid.

2444. Frist Family Group Sheet provided by Ronnie Frist (1718 Gray Road, Chattanooga, TN 37421) 28 March 2002 to compiler.

2445. Ibid.

2446. Frist Family Group Sheet provided by Susan Frist Dixon (6415 Washington Circle, Chattanooga, TN 37416) 27 November 2001 to compiler.

2447. Ibid.

2448. Ibid.

2449. Ibid.

2450. Ibid.

2451. Ibid.

2452. Frist Family Group Sheet provided by Manferd H. Findley (4555 Jordan Grove Road, Central City, IA 52214) to compiler.

2453. Ibid.

2454. Ibid.

2455. Ibid.

2456. Ibid.

2457. Frist Family Group Sheet provided by Manferd H. Findley (4555 Jordan Grove Road, Central City, IA 52214) to compiler. Manferd is Stanley Findley's brother.

2458. Ibid.

2459. Biographical material provided by Geraldine Frist Miller (415 South Eighteenth Street, Clarinda, IA 51632-2515) 10 November 2001 to compiler. Mrs. Miller was the final historian for this branch of the family and has since died. Copy held in 2003 by compiler. Also Frist Family Group Sheet provided by Manferd H. Findley (4555 Jordan Grove Road, Central City, IA 52214) to compiler.

2460. Biographical material provided by Geraldine Frist Miller (415 South Eighteenth Street, Clarinda, IA 51632-2515) 10 November 2001 to compiler. Also Frist Family Group Sheet provided by Manferd H. Findley (4555 Jordan Grove Road, Central City, IA 52214) to compiler.

2461. Frist Family Group Sheet provided by Geraldine Frist Miller (415 South Eighteenth Street, Clarinda, IA 51632-2515) 10 November 2001 to compiler. Mrs. Miller was the final historian for this branch of the family and has since died.

2462. Ibid.

2463. Ibid.

2464. Ibid.

2465. Ibid.

2466. Ibid.

2467. Ibid.

2468. Ibid.

2469. Frist Family Group Sheet provided by Steven Frist (601 Maish, Des Moines, IA 50315) to compiler. Steven Frist is a son of Jimmy Dale Frist.

2470. Frist Family Group Sheet provided by Steven Frist (601 Maish, Des Moines, IA 50315) to compiler. Steven Frist is a son of Jimmy Dale Frist. He is not certain of the year of their marriage.

2471. Frist Family Group Sheet provided by Steven Frist (601 Maish, Des Moines, IA 50315) to compiler. Steven Frist is a brother.

2472. Frist Family Group Sheet provided by Steven Frist (601 Maish, Des Moines, IA 50315) to compiler.

2473. Ibid.

2474. Ibid.

2475. Biographical material provided by Phillip Stanley Frist (3107 Waterfront Circle, Anderson, IN 46012) 31 May 2002 to compiler.

2476. Ibid.

2477. Ibid.

2478. Ibid.

2479. Ibid.

2480. Ibid.

2481. Herman Mayes Genealogical Collection.

2482. Garry Alan Parmer, 241-64-6333, Social Security Death Index, *Family Search*.

2483. Patricia Frist Genealogical Collection Item 36. All information is from this source, unless otherwise cited.

2484. Ibid.

2485. Ibid.

2486. Ibid.

2487. Ibid.

2488. Patricia Frist Genealogical Collection Item 37.

2489. Ibid.

2490. Ibid.

2491. Robert Alan Hughes obituary, unknown newspaper, Orlando, Florida, 21 February 1994, Patricia Frist Genealogical Collection.

2492. Patricia Frist Genealogical Collection Item 37.

2493. Patricia Frist Genealogical Collection Item 39.

2494. Ibid.

2495. Ibid.

2496. Ibid.

2497. Patricia Frist Genealogical Collection Item 38.

2498. Ibid.

2499. Herman Mayes Genealogical Collection. Also Patricia Frist Genealogical Collection Item 42.

2500. Ibid.

2501. Frist Family Group Sheet provided by Eric Lynn Jones (P.O. Box 258, Montezuma, IN 47862-0258) to compiler.

2502. Patricia Frist Genealogical Collection Item 42.

2503. Patricia Frist Genealogical Collection Item 43.

2504. Ibid.

2505. Ibid.

2506. Ibid.

2507. Patricia Frist Genealogical Collection Item 44.

2508. Ibid.

2509. Ibid.

2510. Ibid.

2511. Patricia Frist Genealogical Collection Item 48.

2512. Ibid.

2513. Ibid.

2514. Ibid.

2515. Patricia Frist Genealogical Collection Item 49.

2516. Patricia Frist Genealogical Collection Item 49. All information on this couple and their children is from this source.

2517. Biographical material provided by Mary Edith Banes (2229 Rainbow Drive, Lafayette, IN 47904-2311) February 2001 to compiler.

2518. Ibid.

2519. Mary Edith Banes telephone call 3 September 2002 to compiler. Banes temporary address (509 Harvest Run Drive, Las Vegas NV 89145-2980).

2520. Frist Family Group Sheet provided by Eric Brian Skeel (575 David Drive, Ashville, AL 35953) 2001 to compiler.

2521. Frist Family Group Sheet provided by Brittney Varao (9147 W. Desert Inn Road #L204, Las Vegas, NV 89117) 2001 to compiler.

2522. Frist Family Group Sheet provided by Mrs. Robert Jediah Frist (798 West 1050 South, Brookston, IN 47923-8062) to compiler.

2523. Ibid.

2524. Ibid.

2525. Ibid.

2526. Ibid.

2527. Ibid.

2528. Ibid.

2529. Ibid.

2530. Patricia Frist Genealogical Collection Item 63.

2531. Ibid.

2532. "Wayne E. Frist, 38, Dies in Iowa" undated obituary from unknown newspaper, Patricia Frist Genealogical Collection.

2533. Herman Mayes Genealogical Collection. Also Patricia Frist Genealogical Collection Item 64.

2534. Ibid.

2535. Ibid.

2536. "Wayne E. Frist, 38, Dies in Iowa" undated obituary from unknown newspaper, Patricia Frist Genealogical Collection.

2537. Herman Mayes Genealogical Collection. Also Patricia Frist Genealogical Collection Item 64.

2538. "Wayne E. Frist, 38, Dies in Iowa" undated obituary from unknown newspaper, Patricia Frist Genealogical Collection.

2539. Herman Mayes Genealogical Collection. Also Patricia Frist Genealogical Collection Item 64.

2540. Patricia Frist Genealogical Collection Item 64.

2541. Ibid.

2542. Frist Family Group Sheet provided June 2002 to compiler by Gene and Debbie Fischer III (11615 Joy Lane, Fredericksburg, VA 22407). Gene is a son of Dolores Klima.

2543. Ibid.

2544. Ibid.

2545. Ibid.

2546. Ella E. Tyson estate #1865, 1966, Cecil County, Maryland, Register of Wills, Elkton, Maryland. This estate names Ella's children, grandchildren, and great-grandchildren. Also telephone conversation 28 October 2002 Martha Vianne Absher Gillespie (15225 N. Seventy-Second Drive, Peoria, AZ 85381) with compiler.

2547. Ibid.

2548. Telephone conversation 28 October 2002 Martha Vianne Absher Gillespie (15225 N. Seventy-Second Drive, Peoria, AZ 85381) with compiler.

2549. Ibid.

2550. Ella E. Tyson estate #1865, 1966, Cecil County, Maryland, Register of Wills, Elkton, Maryland. This estate names Ella's children, grandchildren, and great-grandchildren.

2551. Ibid.

2552. Telephone conversation 28 October 2002 Martha Vianne Absher Gillespie (15225 N. Seventy-Second Drive, Peoria, AZ 85381) with compiler.

2553. Ibid.

2554. Frist Family Group Sheet and biographical material provided by Heidi Frist Derry (213 Ridgeley Road, Morgantown, WV 26505) 26 February 2001, updated 26 October 2001 to compiler.

2555. Ibid.

2556. Frist Family Group Sheet and biographical material provided by Jonathan Ramsey Frist (1020 Ashton Drive, Morgantown, WV 26505-4722) in 2001 to compiler.

2557. Ibid.

2558. Frist Family Group Sheet and biographical material provided by Erica Ann Frist Canfield (212 North Emerson Street, Arlington, VA 22203) June 2001 with August 2002 update to compiler.

2559. Ibid.

2560. Frist Family Group Sheet provided by Manferd H. Findley (4555 Jordan Grove Road, Central City, IA 52214) to compiler.

2561. Frist Family Group Sheet provided by Steven Frist (601 Maish, Des Moines, IA 50315) to compiler. All information is from this source, unless otherwise cited.

2562. Ibid.

2563. Frist Family Group Sheet provided June 2002 to compiler by Gene and Debbie Fischer III (11615 Joy Lane, Fredericksburg, VA 22407). Gene and Debbie are Marcia's parents.

2564. Ibid.

Part III

1. Frederick H. Hitchcock, *A Calendar of Delaware Will, New Castle County 1682–1800* (reprint; 1911, Baltimore: Genealogical Publishing Company, 1969), p. 25.

2. Henry and Paul Garretson survey, New Castle County, Delaware, warrants and surveys Deed Book C2:15, microfilm 6537, Family History Library, Salt Lake City, Utah.

3. Letter from Mrs. L. J. Lemstra (458 Blackman Street, Clinton, IN) to the York County Historical Society, 21 February 1930, original in file 2243, York County Historical Society, York, Pennsylvania, copy of original held in 2002 by compiler.

4. Joseph Abraham family, Andres Borrell's List of Church Members at Old Swedes Church 8 November 1764, Holy Trinity (Old Swedes) Church Archives, Wilmington, Delaware.

5. Dr. Peter Stebbins Craig, FASG (3406 Macomb Street, N.W., Washington, DC 20016) explored most of the early Garretson families in New Castle County, Delaware, and prepared reports on several men named John and Henry Garretson.

6. This date is estimated and based largely on the land survey in 1676.

7. John Garretson van der Hof will, New Castle County, Delaware, 1694, Delaware Public Archives, Dover, Delaware. This original will lists his sons as Garrett, Casparius, and Cornelius. Will Book B:13–14, microfilm 6539, Family History Library, Salt Lake City, Utah, erroneously listed his sons as Gerhard, Casparius, and Cornelius.

8. John Garretson van der Hof will, New Castle County, Delaware, 1694, Delaware Public Archives, Dover, Delaware.

9. *Delaware History, Volume XX* (Wilmington, Delaware: The Historical Society of Delaware, 1982–1983), p. 138.

10. Peter Stebbins Craig, "The Garretson Families of New Castle County," research report compiled 1994, p. 3. Copy from Craig (3406 Macomb Street, N.W., Washington, DC 20016), held in 2002 by compiler.

11. *Records of the Court of New Castle on Delaware, Volume II 1681–1699 Land and Probate Abstract Only* (Meadville, Pennsylvania: Colonial Society of Pennsylvania, 1935), p. 37.

12. John Garretson survey, New Castle County, Delaware, warrants and surveys Book C2:44–5, microfilm 6537, Family History Library, Salt Lake City, Utah.

13. New Castle County, Delaware, Deed Book A1:135-136, Delaware Public Archives, Dover, Delaware.

14. John Garretson van der Hof will, New Castle County, Delaware, 1694, Delaware Public Archives, Dover, Delaware. This original will lists his sons as Garret, Casparius, and Cornelius. Will Book B:13–14, microfilm 6539, Family History Library, Salt Lake City, Utah, erroneously listed his sons as Gerhard, Casparius, and Cornelius.

15. John Garretson van der Hof will, New Castle County, Delaware, 1694, Delaware Public Archives, Dover, Delaware.

16. Garret Garretson probate record, 1758, New Castle County, Delaware, Delaware Public Archives, Dover, Delaware. His will written 1754. His birth date is approximated.

17. John Hussey will, New Castle County, Delaware, Will Book B:137–139, microfilm 6539, Family History Library, Salt Lake City, Utah.

18. Casparius Garretson will, New Castle County, Delaware, Will Book Misc. 1:90–91, Delaware Public Archives, Dover, Delaware.

19. Cornelius Garretson probate record, 1765, New Castle County, Delaware, Delaware Public Archives, Dover, Delaware. His will dated 26 January 1765.

20. This date is estimated on many factors including that he was known to be married in 1707 and that his wife was born in 1681.

21. John Garretson van der Hof will, New Castle County, Delaware Will Book B:13–14, microfilm 6539, Family History Library, Salt Lake City, Utah.

22. Garret Garretson probate record, 1758, New Castle County, Delaware, Delaware Public Archives, Dover, Delaware.

23. Ibid.

24. John Hussey will, New Castle County, Delaware, Will Book B:137–139, microfilm 6539, Family History Library, Salt Lake City, Utah.

25. Hussey Family Material (undocumented), Friends Historical Library, Swarthmore College, Swarthmore, Pennsylvania.

26. John Hussey will, New Castle County, Delaware, Will Book B:137–139, microfilm 6539, Family History Library, Salt Lake City, Utah.

27. *Delaware History, Volume XX* (Wilmington, Delaware: The Historical Society of Delaware, 1982–1983), p. 138.

28. James E. Hazard (403 Cedar Lane, Swarthmore, PA) letter 23 December 2002, reporting on Garretsons in Quaker Records, copy held in 2003 by compiler.

29. Hussey–Garretson marriage; Kennett Monthly Meeting 1692–1821, Box PH-265, p. 16, Friends Historical Library, Swarthmore College, Swarthmore, Pennsylvania. Nothing is known about their daughter Ann. It is possible that she married first to a Garretson and that this was her second marriage, but conclusive proof is lacking and alternate theories exist.

30. Casparius Garretson will, New Castle County, Delaware, Will Book Misc. 1:90–91, Delaware Public Archives, Dover, Delaware.

31. Garretson–Colender marriage, Kennett Monthly Meeting 1692–1821, Box PH-265, p. 39, Friends Historical Library, Swarthmore College, Swarthmore, Pennsylvania.

32. Kennett Monthly Meeting minutes 1686–1739, Box PH-267 p. 263, Friends Historical Library, Swarthmore College, Swarthmore, Pennsylvania.

33. Garret Garretson probate record, 1758, New Castle County, Delaware, Delaware Public Archives, Dover, Delaware.

34. Ibid.

35. James E. Hazard (403 Cedar Lane, Swarthmore, PA) letter 2 January 2003, report on Garretsons in Quaker Records, copy held in 2003 by compiler.

36. Garretson–Colender marriage, Kennett Monthly Meeting 1692–1821, Box PH-265, p. 39, Friends Historical Library, Swarthmore College, Swarthmore, Pennsylvania.

37. Cornelius Garretson probate record, 1765, New Castle County, Delaware, Delaware Public Archives, Dover, Delaware. His will dated 26 January 1765 named "Cousin Ann Hussey."

38. Garretson–Goodwind marriage, Marriages before 1800, Holy Trinity (Old Swedes) Church Archives, Wilmington, Delaware. It is likely, but not proven, that this is the correct marriage.

39. Frederick H. Hitchcock, *A Calendar of Delaware Wills, New Castle County 1682–1800* (reprint; 1911, Baltimore: Genealogical Publishing Company, 1969), p. 63. The will of her brother Jedediah named her as Hulda Gooding.

40. Cornelius Garretson probate record, 1765, New Castle County, Delaware, Delaware Public Archives, Dover, Delaware. His will dated 26 January 1765 named "Cousin Mary Scot."

41. Sarah Garretson will, New Castle County Orphans' Court Record Group 2545, 1793, Delaware Public Archives, Dover, Delaware.

42. Elizabeth Garretson probate record 1802, New Castle County, Delaware Public Archives, Dover, Delaware. Will dated 2 February 1802 and probated 26 June 1802.

43. New Castle County, Delaware, Deed Book W2:296–298, microfilm 6573, Family History Library, Salt Lake City, Utah.

44. Date of birth estimated from birth date of first son.

45. Cornelius Garretson letters of administration, New Castle County, Delaware, Register of Wills Book G-1:411, Delaware Public Archives, Dover, Delaware.

46. Ibid.

47. Garret Garretson probate record, 1758, New Castle County, Delaware, Delaware Public Archives, Dover, Delaware. Eliakim was named in 1755 as coexecutor of his father's will, so he would have been at least twenty-one at that time, but his birth date was probably closer to 1718–1722.

48. Eliakim Garretson probate record, 1761, New Castle County, Delaware, Delaware Public Archives, Dover, Delaware. Also F. Edward Wright, *Early Church Records of New Castle County* (Westminister, Maryland: Family Line Publications, 1994), p. 109.

49. Garret Garretson probate record, 1758, New Castle County, Delaware, Delaware Public Archives, Dover, Delaware. Jedediah was named in 1755 as coexecutor of his father's will. He would have been at least twenty-one at that time, but his birth date was probably closer to 1725.

50. Frederick H. Hitchcock, *A Calendar of Delaware Wills, New Castle County 1682–1800* (reprint; 1911, Baltimore: Genealogical Publishing Company, 1969), p. 63.

51. Date of birth estimated from birth date of his son.

52. Garret Garretson probate record, 1758, New Castle County, Delaware, Delaware Public Archives, Dover, Delaware.

53. Cornelius Garretson letters of administration, New Castle County, Delaware, Register of Wills Book G-1:411, Delaware Public Archives, Dover, Delaware.

54. Peter Stebbins Craig, "Descendants of Jan Gerritsen Van der Hof," research report, compiled 1994, p. 8. Copy from Craig (3406 Macomb Street, N.W., Washington, DC 20016), held in 2002 by compiler.

55. Peter Stebbins Craig, "Descendants of Jan Gerritsen Van der Hof," research report, 1994. Copy held in 2003 by compiler, p. 8. Also New Castle County, Delaware Deed Book N1:458–460, Delaware Public Archives, Dover, Delaware.

56. Carol J. Garrett, *New Castle County, Delaware, Land Records 1755–1762* (Westminster, Maryland: Willow Bend Books, 1999), p. 30.

57. Letter from Mrs. L. J. Lemstra (458 Blackman Street, Clinton, IN) to the York County Historical Society, 21 February 1930, original in file 2243, York County Historical Society, York, Pennsylvania, copy of original held in 2002 by compiler. The names and birth and death dates of James and Mary Garretson were given in this letter as well as the names and birth dates of their three children. Although the information is not entirely accurate, the dates are used in the absence of contradictory data.

58. Letter, Mrs. L. J. Lemstra (458 Blackman Street, Clinton, IN) to York County Historical Society, 21 February 1930. Also James Garretson probate, 1789, New Castle County, Delaware, Delaware Public Archives, Dover, Delaware. The date of 5 March 1783 was included in the letter and descended in the family, but James Garretson's probate record indicates he was deceased by 28 March 1782. Thus the date of 5 March 1782 is used here.

59. Garretson–Abram marriage, Marriages before 1800 citing p. 881, Holy Trinity (Old Swedes) Church Archives, Wilmington, Delaware, copy of original provided by Archivist Ray Nichols (no book listed) and held in 2002 by compiler.

60. Date of birth estimated from known date of his brother's birth.

61. Letter, Mrs. L. J. Lemstra (458 Blackman Street, Clinton, IN) to York County Historical Society, 21 February 1930, previously discussed.

62. Garret Garretson probate record, 1758, New Castle County, Delaware, Delaware Public Archives, Dover, Delaware.

63. Letter, Mrs. L. J. Lemstra (458 Blackman Street, Clinton, IN) to York County Historical Society, 21 February 1930. Also James Garretson probate, 1789, New Castle County, Delaware, Delaware Public Archives, Dover, Delaware. The date of 5 March 1783 was included in the letter and descended in the family, but James Garretson's probate record indicates he was deceased by 28 March 1782. Thus the date of 5 March 1782 is used here.

64. Garretson–Abram marriage, Marriages before 1800, citing p. 881, Holy Trinity (Old Swedes) Church Archives, Wilmington, Delaware, copy of original provided by Archivist Ray Nichols (no book listed) and held in 2002 by compiler.

65. Mary Abram baptism, Old Swedes Church Archives, Wilmington, Delaware. Her mother's name, Margret, was listed variously in the church records as Margret, Margretha, and Margrete. Original examined in July 2001 and pertinent data copied by compiler.

66. Letter, Mrs. L. J. Lemstra (458 Blackman Street, Clinton, IN) to York County Historical Society, 21 February 1930.

67. Mary Garretson will, New Castle County, Delaware, Will Book M:217–218, microfilm 6540, Family History Library, Salt Lake City, Utah. This date is not compatible with the one (June 1802) given in the Lemstra letter.

68. Cornelius Garretson probate record, 1765, New Castle County, Delaware, Delaware Public Archives, Dover, Delaware.

69. Joseph Abraham probate record, 1772, New Castle County, Delaware, Delaware Public Archives, Dover, Delaware.

70. Joseph Abraham entry, Andres Borrell's List of Church Members, Holy Trinity (Old Swedes) Church Archives, 1 November 1764, Old Swedes Church Archives, Wilmington, Delaware.

71. Carol J. Garrett, *New Castle County, Delaware, Land Records 1755–1762* (Westminster, Maryland, Willow Bend Books, 1999), p. 190.

72. New Castle County, Delaware, Deed Book Z1:383, microfilm 6564, Family History Library, Salt Lake City, Utah.

73. New Castle County, Delaware, Deed Book C2:74–76, microfilm 6565, Family History Library, Salt Lake City, Utah.

74. Letter, Mrs. L. J. Lemstra (458 Blackman Street, Clinton, IN) to York County Historical Society, 21 February 1930.

75. James Garrettson probate record, 1789, New Castle County, Delaware, Delaware Public Archives, Dover, Delaware.

76. Letter, Mrs. L. J. Lemstra (458 Blackman Street, Clinton, IN) to York County Historical Society, 21 February 1930.

77. James Garrettson probate record, 1789, New Castle County, Delaware, Delaware Public Archives, Dover, Delaware. The heirs were listed as Abrams in this probate record, but Abraham is used here to minimize confusion.

78. New Castle County, Delaware, Deed Book F:425–426, microfilm 6539, Family History Library, Salt Lake City, Utah.

79. Mary Garretson will, New Castle County, Delaware, Will Book M:217–218, microfilm 6540, Family History Library, Salt Lake City, Utah.

80. Mary Garretson probate record, 1786–1789, New Castle County, Delaware, Delaware Public Archives, Dover, Delaware.

81. Elizabeth Garretson probate record 1802, New Castle County, Delaware, Delaware Public Archives, Dover, Delaware. Will dated 2 February 1802 and probated 26 June 1802.

82. Letter, Mrs. L. J. Lemstra (458 Blackman Street, Clinton, IN) to York County Historical Society, 21 February 1930. This letter listed the three children as Josiah, Elizabeth, and Gideon. The handwritten versions of the two names Josiah and Jediah are very similar. Since no records were found for anyone named Josiah Garretson and evidence suggests that Jediah was related, the correct name is believed to be Jediah.

83. Jediah Garretson probate record, 1808, New Castle County, Delaware, Delaware Public Archives, Dover, Delaware.

84. Letter, Mrs. L. J. Lemstra (458 Blackman Street, Clinton, IN) to York County Historical Society, 21 February 1930. This birth date is also on her tombstone in St. James Cemetery, Newport, New Castle County, Delaware.

85. Henry and Elizabeth Frist tombstone, St. James Methodist Episcopal Church Cemetery, Newport, Delaware, photo taken July 2001 by compiler.

86. Letter, Mrs. L. J. Lemstra (458 Blackman Street, Clinton, IN) to York County Historical Society, 21 February 1930.

87. Ibid.

88. Audrey Gilbert, *Probate Abstracts Preble County, Ohio, Estates and Guardianships: Cases 2000 through 2999* (West Alexandria, Ohio, privately printed, 1998), p. 152 citing file #2869.

89. *History of Preble County, Ohio, with Illustrations and Biographical Sketches* (1881 reprint, Evansville, Indiana: Unigraphic, 1972), p. 259.

Part IV

1. *Early Church Records of New Castle County, Delaware Volume 2 Old Swedes Church 1713–1799* (Westminster, Maryland: Family Line Publications, 1994), p. 5.

2. Peter Stebbins Craig, *The 1693 Census of the Swedes on the Delaware* (Winter Park, Florida: SAG Publications, 1993), p. 102. Also *Early Church Records of New Castle County, Delaware Volume 2 Old Swedes Church 1713–1799* (Westminster, Maryland: Family Line Publications, 1994), p. 6. In this baptismal record dated 5 September 1714 Conrad Constantine, Mrs. Kerstin Garrison (Kerstin Constantine had married Henric Garrison in April 1714 at Old Swedes Church), and Miss Mary Constantine (who didn't marry Joseph Abraham until December 1714) all served as sponsors.

3. Peter Stebbins Craig, *The 1693 Census of the Swedes on the Delaware* (Winter Park, Florida: SAG Publications, 1993), p. 102.

4. Peter Stebbins Craig, *The 1693 Census of the Swedes on the Delaware* (Winter Park, Florida: SAG Publications, 1993), pp. 101–102.

5. Ibid.

6. Joseph Abraham birth record, Index to Baptisms and Births in the 1700s in Old Swedes Church citing Burr p. 232, original p. 66, Holy Trinity (Old Swedes) Church Archives, Wilmington, Delaware.

7. Ibid.

8. Joseph Abraham probate record 1778–1779, New Castle County, Delaware, Delaware Public Archives, Dover.

9. Abraham–Farrys marriage, Index to Marriages at Old Swedes Church from 1713 to 1799, citing Burr p. 387, original p. 253, Holy Trinity (Old Swedes) Church Archives, Wilmington, Delaware.

10. Joseph Abraham birth record, Index to Baptisms and Births in the 1700s in Old Swedes Church citing Burr p. 232, original p. 66, Holy Trinity (Old Swedes) Church Archives, Wilmington, Delaware.

11. Joseph Abraham probate record 1778–1779, New Castle County, Delaware, Delaware Public Archives, Dover.

12. Abraham–Farrys marriage, Index to Marriages at Old Swedes Church from 1713 to 1799, citing Burr p. 387, original p. 253, Holy Trinity (Old Swedes) Church Archives, Wilmington, Delaware.

13. Carol J. Garrett, *New Castle County, Delaware Land Records 1755–1762* (Westminster, Maryland, Willow Bend Books, 1999), p. 99.

14. New Castle County, Delaware Deed Book F:425–426, microfilm 6566, Family History Library, Salt Lake City, Utah.

15. New Castle County, Delaware Deed Book F:425–426, microfilm 6539, Family History Library, Salt Lake City, Utah.

16. Abraham–Farrys marriage, Index to Marriages at Old Swedes Church from 1713 to 1799, citing Burr p. 387, original p. 253, Holy Trinity (Old Swedes) Church Archives, Wilmington, Delaware.

17. Carol J. Garrett, *New Castle County, Delaware Land Records 1749–1752* (Westminster, Maryland: Family Line Publications, 1998), p. 1.

18. Augustine Constantine probate record, 1752, New Castle County, Delaware, Delaware Public Archives, Dover, Delaware.

19. Carol J. Garrett, *New Castle County, Delaware Land Records 1755–1762* (Westminster, Maryland, Willow Bend Books, 1999), p. 190

20. Carol J. Garrett, *New Castle County, Delaware Land Records 1755–1762* (Westminster, Maryland, Willow Bend Books, 1999), p. 99.

21. Carol J. Garrett, *New Castle County, Delaware Land Records 1755–1762* (Westminster, Maryland, Willow Bend Books, 1999), p. 104.

22. Joseph Abraham family, Andres Borrell's List of Church Members at Old Swedes 8 November 1764, Holy Trinity (Old Swedes) Church Archives, Wilmington, Delaware.

23. New Castle County, Delaware Deed Book Z1:383, microfilm roll 6564, Family History Library, Salt Lake City, Utah.

24. Joseph Abraham probate record 1778–1779, New Castle County, Delaware, Delaware Public Archives, Dover, Delaware.

25. Ibid.

26. New Castle County, Delaware Deed Book F:425–426, microfilm 6539, Family History Library, Salt Lake City, Utah.

27. Mary Abram baptism, Holy Trinity (Old Swedes) Church Archives, Wilmington, Delaware. Original examined in July 2001 and pertinent data copied by compiler.

28. Mary Garretson will, New Castle County, Delaware, Will Book M:217–218, microfilm 6540, Family History Library, Salt Lake City, Utah.

29. Abraham–Garretson marriage, Index to Marriages at Old Swedes Church from 1713 to 1799, citing Burr p. 731, original p. 881, Holy Trinity (Old Swedes) Church Archives, Wilmington, Delaware.

30. Joseph Abraham family, Andres Borrell's List of Church Members, Old Swedes Church, 1 November 1764, Holy Trinity (Old Swedes) Church Archives, Wilmington, Delaware. Agnes not included in the family.

31. Abraham–Garretson marriage, Index to Marriages at Old Swedes Church from 1713 to 1799, citing Burr p. 731, original p. 881, Holy Trinity (Old Swedes) Church Archives, Wilmington, Delaware.

32. Joseph Abraham family, Andres Borrell's List of Church Members, Old Swedes Church, 1 November 1764, Holy Trinity (Old Swedes) Church Archives, Wilmington, Delaware. Margaret not included in the family.

33. Joseph Abraham family, Andres Borrell's List of Church Members, Old Swedes Church, 1 November 1764, Holy Trinity (Old Swedes) Church Archives, Wilmington, Delaware. William was included in the family, but was not on the deed of sales for Joseph's land.

34. New Castle County, Delaware, Deed Book F:425–426, microfilm 6539, Family History Library, Salt Lake City, Utah.

35. Ibid.

36. Joseph Abraham family, Andres Borrell's List of Church Members, Old Swedes Church, 1 November 1764, Holy Trinity (Old Swedes) Church Archives, Wilmington, Delaware. Hannah not included in the family.

37. Joseph Abraham family, Andres Borrell's List of Church Members, Old Swedes Church, 1 November 1764, Holy Trinity (Old Swedes) Church Archives, Wilmington, Delaware. Joseph not included in the family.

38. Isaac Abraham probate record 1790–1808, New Castle County, Delaware, Delaware Public Archives, Dover, Delaware.

39. Abraham–Smith marriage, Index to Marriages at Old Swedes Church from 1713 to 1799, citing Burr p. 219, original p. 49, Holy Trinity (Old Swedes) Church Archives, Wilmington, Delaware.

40. New Castle County, Delaware Deed Book F:425–426, microfilm 6539, Family History Library, Salt Lake City, Utah. Benjamin was not included in this deed of sale for his father's land.

Part V

1. Helen Ramage, *Portraits of an Island Eighteenth Century Anglesey* (Llangefni, Gwynedd, Wales: Anglesey Antiquarian Society and Field Club, 1987), pp. 11–13.

2. Anne Kelly Knowles, *Calvinists Incorporated: Welsh Immigrants on Ohio's Industrial Frontier* (Chicago: University of Chicago Press, 1997), appendix, no pagination.

3. Dafydd Hayes, *Hayes Computerised Indexes Parish Church Marriages Amlwch, Anglesey, Wales 1630–1869* (Buckley, Clwyd, Wales: privately published, no date), pp. 59, 60.

4. Parish Register, Amlwch, Anglesey, Wales #855, British microfilm 104512, Family History Library, Salt Lake City, Utah

5. Anne Kelly Knowles, *Calvinists Incorporated: Welsh Immigrants on Ohio's Industrial Frontier* (Chicago: University of Chicago Press, 1997), appendix, no pagination.

6. Griffith Parry death record (1883), Jackson County, Ohio, Death Records 1879–1900, p. 322, microfilm 301042, Family History Library, Salt Lake City, Utah.

7. Mary J. Hison and Frances Welch, *Cemetery Inscriptions of Jackson County Ohio, Volume II* (Baltimore: Gateway Press, 1982), p. 886.

8. Ecclesiastical Parishes of Anglesey, *Supplied to GENUKI by Joyce Hinde* [*Page generated: 27th November 1999, 22:48 GMT by Brian Pears*] <www.genuki.org.uk/big/wal/AGY/AGY_Pars.html> downloaded 2 October 2002 by compiler.

9. Ann Parry birth record 28 March 1812, Ty Mawr Chapel Church Records 1792–1837, Llanfihangel tre'r Beirdd Parish, Anglesey County, Wales, British microfilm 1482419 Item 8, no pagination, arranged chronologically by date of birth, Family History Library, Salt Lake City, Utah. Mary's maiden name is listed on the birth records for all of their children. The marriage date is approximated from the birth of their first child.

10. Ann Parry birth record 28 March 1812, Ty Mawr Chapel Church Records 1792–1837, Llanfihangel tre'r Beirdd Parish, Anglesey County, Wales, British microfilm 1482419 Item 8, no pagination, arranged chronologically by date of birth, Family History Library, Salt Lake City, Utah.

11. John Parry birth record 3 January 1814, Ty Mawr Chapel Church Records 1792–1837.

12. Griffith Parry birth record 21 August 1816 and Mary Parry birth record 13 March 1819, Ty Mawr Chapel Church Records 1792–1837.

13. Ann Parry birth record 28 March 1812, Ty Mawr Chapel Church Records 1792–1837.

14. John Parry birth record 3 January 1814, Ty Mawr Chapel Church Records 1792–1837.

15. Dafydd Hayes, *Hayes Computerised Indexes Parish Church Marriages Amlwch, Anglesey, Wales 1630–1869* (Buckley, Clwyd, Wales: privately published, no date), p. 60.

16. John Perry household, 1850 U.S. census, Jackson County, Ohio, population schedule, Madison Township, p. 259, household 459; National Archives micropublication M432, roll 698.

17. Ibid.

18. John Pary [*sic*] household, 1860 U.S. census, Gallia County, Ohio, population schedule, Greenfield Township, Gallia Furnace post office, sheet 243, stamped p. 269, line 12; National Archives micropublication M653, roll 966.

19. Ibid.

20. Ibid.

21. Griffith Parry birth record 21 August 1816, Ty Mawr Chapel Church Records 1792–1837.

22. Griffith Parry death record (1883), Jackson County, Ohio, Death Records 1879–1900, p. 322, microfilm 301042, Family History Library, Salt Lake City, Utah. Also Mary J. Hison and Frances Welch, *Cemetery Inscriptions of Jackson County Ohio, Volume II* (Baltimore: Gateway Press, Inc., 1982), p. 886.

23. Dafydd Hayes, *Hayes Computerised Indexes Parish Church Marriages Amlwch, Anglesey, Wales 1630–1869* (Buckley, Clwyd, Wales: privately published, no date), p. 59.

24. Jackson County, Ohio, Marriage Records 1850–1857, p. 133, microfilm 301043, Family History Library, Salt Lake City, Utah.

25. Mary Parry birth record 13 March 1819, Ty Mawr Chapel Church Records 1792–1837.

26. Griffith Parry birth record 21 August 1816, Ty Mawr Chapel Church Records 1792–1837.

27. Griffith Parry death record (1883) Jackson County, Ohio, Death Records 1879–1900, p. 322, microfilm 301042, Family History Library, Salt Lake City, Utah. Also Mary J. Hison and Frances Welch, *Cemetery Inscriptions of Jackson County Ohio, Volume II* (Baltimore: Gateway Press, Inc., 1982), p. 886.

28. Dafydd Hayes, *Hayes Computerised Indexes Parish Church Marriages Amlwch, Anglesey, Wales 1630–1869* (Buckley, Clwyd, Wales: privately published, no date), p. 59.

29. Anne Kelly Knowles, *Calvinists Incorporated: Welsh Immigrants on Ohio's Industrial Frontier* (Chicago: University of Chicago Press, 1997), appendix, no pagination.

30. Mary J. Hison and Frances Welch, *Cemetery Inscriptions of Jackson County Ohio, Volume II* (Baltimore: Gateway Press, 1982), p. 886.

31. Ibid.

32. Jackson County, Ohio, Marriage Records 1850–1857, p. 133, microfilm 301043, Family History Library, Salt Lake City, Utah.

33. Mary J. Hison and Frances Welch, *Cemetery Inscriptions of Jackson County Ohio, Volume II* (Baltimore: Gateway Press, 1982), p. 886.

34. Anne Kelly Knowles, *Calvinists Incorporated: Welsh Immigrants on Ohio's Industrial Frontier* (Chicago: University of Chicago Press, 1997), appendix, no pagination.

35. Dafydd Hayes, *Hayes Computerised Indexes Parish Church Marriages Amlwch, Anglesey, Wales 1630–1869* (Buckley, Clwyd, Wales: privately published, no date), p. 59.

36. Anne Kelly Knowles, *Calvinists Incorporated: Welsh Immigrants on Ohio's Industrial Frontier* (Chicago: University of Chicago Press, 1997), appendix, no pagination.

37. Parish Register, Amlwch, Anglesey, Wales, #855, British microfilm 104512, Family History Library, Salt Lake City, Utah.

38. Compiler's conversation with unidentified Welsh researcher at the Family History Library in Salt Lake City January 2002.

39. Anne Kelly Knowles, *Calvinists Incorporated: Welsh Immigrants on Ohio's Industrial Frontier* (Chicago: University of Chicago Press, 1997), appendix D, Welsh Immigrants to the Jackson/Gallia Settlement, no pagination.

40. 1881 Amlwch, Anglesey, Wales census, addresses of miners, <http://www.parysmountain.fsnet.co.uk/> click on 1881 Amlwch area census, downloaded 27 September 2002 by compiler.

41. Jackson County, Ohio, Deed Book E:519–520, microfilm 301014, Family History Library, Salt Lake City, Utah.

42. Reverend William R. Evans, *History of Welsh Settlements in Jackson and Gallia Counties of Ohio* (Utica, New York: T. J. Griffiths, 1896), p. 26.

43. Mary J. Hison and Frances Welch, *Cemetery Inscriptions of Jackson County Ohio, Volume II* (Baltimore: Gateway Press, 1982), p. 886.

44. Jackson County, Ohio, Deed Book M:253–254, microfilm 301018, Family History Library, Salt Lake City, Utah.

45. Griffith Parry household, 1850 U. S. census, Jackson County, Ohio, population schedule, Madison Township, p. 259, family 458; National Archives micropublication M432, roll 698.

46. Jackson County, Ohio, Deed Book M:317, microfilm 301018, Family History Library, Salt Lake City, Utah.

47. Jackson County, Ohio, Deed Book M:318, microfilm 301018, Family History Library, Salt Lake City, Utah.

48. Jackson County, Ohio, Marriage Records 1850–1857 p. 133, microfilm 301043, Family History Library, Salt Lake City, Utah.

49. Jackson County, Ohio, Deed Book P:366–377, microfilm 301020, Family History Library, Salt Lake City, Utah.

50. Jackson County, Ohio, Deed Book Q:427, microfilm 301021, Family History Library, Salt Lake City, Utah.

51. Jackson County, Ohio, Deed Book R:57–58, microfilm 301021, Family History Library, Salt Lake City, Utah.

52. Griffith Parry household, 1860 U.S. census, Jackson County, Ohio, population schedule, p. 77 dwelling 1114, family 1083; National Archives micropublication M653, roll 992.

53. Griffith Parry household, 1870 U.S. census, Jackson County, Ohio, population schedule, Madison Township, stamped p. 206, dwelling 296, family 300; National Archives micropublication M593, roll 1226.

54. Griffith Parry household, 1880 U.S. census, Jackson County, Ohio, population schedule, enumeration district 195, stamped p. 255, sheet 12, dwelling 98, family 101; microfilm 1255037, Family History Library, Salt Lake City, Utah.

55. Griffith Parry death record (1883) Jackson County, Ohio, Death Records 1879–1900, p. 322, microfilm 301042, Family History Library, Salt Lake City, Utah.

56. Mary J. Hison and Frances Welch, *Cemetery Inscriptions of Jackson County Ohio*, Volume II (Baltimore: Gateway Press, 1982), p. 886.

57. Griffith Parry will, Jackson County, Ohio, Will Book B:464-468, microfilm 301051, Family History Library, Salt Lake City, Utah.

58. Mary J. Hison and Frances Welch, *Cemetery Inscriptions of Jackson County Ohio, Volume II* (Baltimore: Gateway Press, 1982), p. 886.

59. Parish Register, Amlwch, Anglesey, Wales; microfilm 104512, Family History Library, Salt Lake City, Utah.

60. Griffith Parry will, Jackson County, Ohio, Will Book B:464–468, microfilm 301051, Family History Library, Salt Lake City, Utah. William's children were named in Griffith's estate papers, not William.

61. Ibid.

62. Griffith Parry household, 1850 U.S. census, Jackson County, Ohio, population schedule, Madison Township, p. 259, family 458; National Archives micropublication M432, roll 698.

63. Hamilton County, Tennessee Deed Book 324:329, Record L, Volume 13, Register of Deeds, Chattanooga, Tennessee. John F. and Mary Jones both died in New Orleans, Louisiana, by 1 April 1912 according to an affidavit dated 10 November 1915, which was filed in Hamilton County by J. C. Frist.

64. Jackson County, Ohio, Marriage #5420, Court of Common Pleas, Jackson, Ohio.

65. Griffith Parry household, 1860 U.S. census, Jackson County, Ohio, population schedule, p. 77 dwelling 1114, family 1083; National Archives micropublication M653, roll 992.

66. Sarah Ann Parry death record (1888), Jackson County, Ohio, Death Records 1879–1900, p. 326, microfilm 301042, Family History Library, Salt Lake City, Utah.

67. Mary J. Hison and Frances Welch, *Cemetery Inscriptions of Jackson County Ohio, Volume II* (Baltimore: Gateway Press, 1982), p. 886. Hugh is not buried here, but this is presumed to be his wife Sarah.

68. Griffith Parry death record (1883), Jackson County, Ohio, Death Records 1879–1900, p. 322, microfilm 301042, Family History Library, Salt Lake City, Utah.

69. Griffith Parry household, 1860 U.S. census, Jackson County, Ohio, population schedule, p. 77 dwelling 1114, family 1083; National Archives micropublication M653, roll 992.

70. Mary J. Hison and Frances Welch, *Cemetery Inscriptions of Jackson County Ohio, Volume II* (Baltimore: Gateway Press, 1982), p. 885.

71. Griffith Parry household, 1860 U.S. census, Jackson County, Ohio, population schedule, p. 77 dwelling 1114, family 1083; National Archives micropublication M653, roll 992.

72. Mary J. Hison and Frances Welch, *Cemetery Inscriptions of Jackson County Ohio, Volume II* (Baltimore: Gateway Press, 1982), p. 885. This lists David as eleven years old, but he would have only been one year old.

73. Griffith Parry household, 1850 U.S. census, Jackson County, Ohio, population schedule, Madison Township, p. 259, family 458; National Archives micropublication M432, roll 698. Also Jacob Frist household, 1900 U.S. census Perry County, Mississippi, population schedule, enumeration district 89, sheet 11, line 35, dwelling 198, family 203; National Archives micropublication T623, roll 824.

74. Hamilton County, Tennessee Deed Book 324:329, Record L, Volume 13, Register of Deeds, Chattanooga, Tennessee. John F. and Mary Jones both died in New Orleans, Louisiana, by 1 April 1912 according to an affidavit dated 10 November 1915, which was filed in Hamilton County by J. C. Frist.

75. Jackson County, Ohio, Marriage #5420, Court of Common Pleas, Jackson, Ohio.

76. Jacob Frist household, 1900 U.S. census, Perry County, Mississippi, population schedule, enumeration district 89, sheet 11, line 35, dwelling 198, family 203; National Archives micropublication T623, roll 824.

77. Hamilton County, Tennessee, Deed Book 324:329, Record L, Volume 13, Register of Deeds, Chattanooga, Tennessee. John F. and Mary Jones both died in New Orleans, Louisiana, by 1 April 1912 according to an affidavit dated 10 November 1915, which was filed in Hamilton County by J. C. Frist.

78. Griffith Parry household, 1850 U.S. census, Jackson County, Ohio, population schedule, Madison Township, p. 259, family 458; National Archives micropublication M432, roll 698.

79. Griffith Parry household, 1860 U.S. census, Jackson County, Ohio, population schedule, p. 77 dwelling 1114, family 1083; National Archives micropublication M653, roll 992.

80. Mary Jones household, 1870 U.S. census, Jackson County, Ohio, population schedule, Madison Township, stamped p. 207 dwelling 314, family 318; National Archives micropublication M593, roll 1226.

81. Griffith Parry household, 1880 U.S. census, Jackson County, Ohio, population schedule, enumeration district 195, stamped p. 255, sheet 12, dwelling 98, family 101; microfilm 1255037, Family History Library, Salt Lake City, Utah.

82. Hamilton County, Tennessee, Deed Book 64:283–284, microfilm 137, Tennessee State Library and Archives, Nashville, Tennessee.

83. Hamilton County, Tennessee, Deed Book 72:605–606, microfilm 141, Tennessee State Library and Archives, Nashville, Tennessee.

84. Hamilton County, Tennessee, Deed Book 102:639–641, microfilm 156, Tennessee State Library and Archives, Nashville, Tennessee.

85. Jackson County, Ohio, Marriage Book J:399 #4247, Probate Court, Jackson, Ohio.

86. Hamilton County, Tennessee, Deed Book 145:463–466, microfilm 178, Tennessee State Library and Archives, Nashville, Tennessee.

87. Hamilton County, Tennessee, Deed Book 171:232–233, Record O, Volume 7, Register of Deeds, Chattanooga, Tennessee.

88. Hamilton County, Tennessee, Deed Book 152:279–280, microfilm 181, Tennessee State Library and Archives, Nashville, Tennessee.

89. Jacob Frist household, 1900 U.S. census, Perry County, Mississippi, population schedule, enumeration district 89, sheet 11, line 35, dwelling 198, family 203; National Archives micropublication T623, roll 824.

90. *Soard's New Orleans City Directory for 1903* (New Orleans: Soard's Directory County Ltd., 1903), p. 353.

91. Hamilton County, Tennessee, Deed Book 324:329, Record L, Volume 13, Register of Deeds, Chattanooga, Tennessee.

92. Hamilton County, Tennessee, Deed Book 271:458–459, Record K, Volume 11, Register of Deeds, Chattanooga, Tennessee.

93. Magnolia Cemetery, Meridian, Mississippi, photograph taken April 2002 by compiler.

94. Jackson County, Ohio, Marriage Book J:399 #4247, Probate Court, Jackson, Ohio.

SELECTED BIBLIOGRAPHY

This bibliography is not a complete record of all sources consulted in the preparation of this family history. It is primarily a listing of the references cited within the text, although it is not limited to those references.

CITY, COUNTY, STATE, AND FEDERAL RECORDS

California. Los Angeles. Department of Health Services. Death Registrations.

Delaware. Dover. Board of Health. Delaware Public Archives, Dover. Delayed Birth Registrations.

Delaware. Dover. Bureau of Vital Statistics. Delaware Public Archives, Dover. Marriage Certificate Register.

Delaware. Dover. Division of Vital Records. Death Registrations.

Delaware. Kent County. Delaware Public Archives, Dover. Assessments Lists 1759–1798, Deed Books, Guardianships, Marriage Records, Original Probate Records, Orphans' Court Case Files, Will Books.

Delaware. New Castle County. Delaware Public Archives, Dover. Assessment Lists, 1788–1816, 1821, Deed Books, Guardianships, Marriage Records, Original Probate Records, Orphans' Court Case Files, Will Books.

Delaware. New Castle County. Microfilm. Delaware Public Archives, Dover. Tax Lists.

Delaware. New Castle County. Microfilm. Family History Library, Salt Lake City, Utah. Deed Books, Warrants and Surveys, Will Books.

Delaware. New Castle County. Orphans' Court Records. Microfilm. Family History Library, Salt Lake City, Utah.

Delaware. Wilmington. Delaware Public Archives, Dover. Death Registers.

Delaware. Wilmington. Microfilm. Family History Library, Salt Lake City, Utah. Death Registers.

Delaware. Wilmington. Microfilms 1570610, 1570613. Family History Library, Salt Lake City, Utah. World War I Draft Registrations.

Florida. Jacksonville. Department of Vital Records. Death Registrations.

Georgia. Richmond County. Court of Ordinary. Microfilm. Family History Library, Salt Lake City, Utah. Tax Lists.

Indiana. Lafayette. Health Department, Lafayette City. Death Certificates.

Indiana. Randolph County. Health Department, Winchester. Death Record, Book of Lynn.

Indiana. Vermillion County. Board of Health. Death Certificates.

Indiana. Vermillion County. Circuit Court Office, Newport. Jediah Rudolph Frist estate packet #483.

Indiana. Vermillion County. County Clerk, Newport. Birth Records, Deed Books, Marriage Books, Wills.

Indiana. Wayne County. Microfilm 1839242. Family History Library, Salt Lake City, Utah. Court Order Probate Record.

Indiana. Wayne County. Microfilm 413530. Family History Library, Salt Lake City, Utah. Final Accounting.

Indiana. Wayne County. Microfilms 1753568-9. Family History Library, Salt Lake City, Utah. Deed Books.

Iowa. Dallas County. Microfilm 1034112 Item 2. Family History Library, Salt Lake City, Utah. Marriage Records 1852–1902.

Iowa. Lee County. Microfilms 1903294-6. Family History Library, Salt Lake City, Utah. Marriage Volumes.

Iowa. Montgomery County. Microfilm 1022209. Family History Library, Salt Lake City, Utah. 1891 State Census, population schedule.

Iowa. Montgomery County. Microfilms 1,481,225 and 1,481,227-8. Family History Library, Salt Lake City, Utah. Marriage Records.

Iowa. Page County. Microfilm. Family History Library, Salt Lake City, Utah. Death Records.

Iowa. Page County. Microfilm 1020170. Family History Library, Salt Lake City, Utah. 1885 State Census, population schedule.

Iowa. Page County. Microfilm 1429485. Family History Library, Salt Lake City, Utah. 1925 state census, population schedule.

Iowa. Page County. Microfilm. Family History Library, Salt Lake City, Utah. Marriage Records, Register of Births.

Iowa. Polk County. Microfilm 1462725. Family History Library, Salt Lake City, Utah. 1915 state census, population schedule.

Maryland. Baltimore City. Circuit Court. Maryland State Archives, Annapolis. Equity Case File #11793-B, Box 282, *Margaret Ann Frist vs. John Edgar Frist.*

Maryland. Baltimore City. Circuit Court. Maryland State Archives, Annapolis. Equity Index.

Maryland. Baltimore City. Health Department. Microfilms. Maryland State Archives, Annapolis. Burial Permits and Death Certificates.

Maryland. Baltimore City. Microfilms CR 1110, 1122. Maryland State Archives, Annapolis, Maryland. Land Records.

Maryland. Baltimore City. Microfilm. Maryland State Archives, Annapolis. Marriage Books.

Maryland. Baltimore City. Microfilm. Maryland State Archives, Annapolis. Marriage Index 1851–1885, 1886–1914 (original card index).

Maryland. Baltimore City. Microfilm. Maryland State Archives, Annapolis. Will Books.

Maryland. Baltimore City. Orphans' Court. Maryland State Archives, Annapolis. Book RTB:55.

Maryland. Baltimore City. Orphans' Court. Microfilms CR 315 and CR 9616. Maryland State Archives, Annapolis.

Maryland. Baltimore County. Board of Health. Maryland State Archives, Annapolis. John Edgar Frist Death Certificate (1912), F1912, Series C322-19, Acc. No. 50,126-19, location 2/56/9/8.

Maryland. Baltimore County. Circuit Court. Maryland State Archives, Annapolis. Equity Cases, Docket 18:154 *Elmira Schleigle et al vs. James H. Plummer et al*, 12 August 1908 Packet #10903.

Maryland. Baltimore County. Circuit Court. Maryland State Archives, Annapolis. Equity docket packet #9127, *John Edgar Frist vs. Margaret Ann Frist.*

Maryland. Baltimore County. Microfilms CR 1105, 1110, 1119. Maryland State Archives, Annapolis. Land Records.

Maryland. Baltimore County. Microfilm CR 123. Maryland State Archives, Annapolis. Wills.

Maryland. Cecil County. Cecil County Historical Society Library, Elkton. Tax Assessments, 1830–1869.

Maryland. Cecil County. Chancery Court Office, Elkton. *Abraham B. Frist vs. Elizabeth C. Frist* Divorce (1857), metal boxes Ended A–G, loose packet #300.

Maryland. Cecil County. Land Office, Elkton. Land Records, Marriages, Mortgages, Wills and Probate Files.

Maryland. Cecil County. Maryland State Archives, Annapolis. Marriage Book 1840–1851.

Maryland. Harford County. Marriage Office, Bel Air. Marriage Books.

Mississippi. Jackson. State Department of Health. Death Registrations.

Mississippi. Lauderdale County. Chancery Court. Department for Archives and History, Meridian. J. C. Frist Estate #6869, Box 328.

Mississippi. Lauderdale County. Chancery Court, Meridian. Deed Records, Deeds of Trust, Record of Lands Sold to State.

Mississippi. Lauderdale County. Department of Archives and History, Meridian. Marriage Records, White.

Mississippi. Lauderdale County. Probate Court, Meridian. Marriage Books, Wills.

Ohio. Jackson County. Court of Common Pleas, Jackson. Marriages.

Ohio. Jackson County. Microfilm. Family History Library, Salt Lake City, Utah. Death Records 1879–1900, Deeds 1841–1860, Marriage Records 1850–1857, Will Books.

Ohio. Preble County. Probate Court, Eaton. Will Books and Probate Records.

Pennsylvania. Chester County. County Archives, West Chester. Deed Books and Docket, loose estate papers.

Pennsylvania. Philadelphia County. Microfilms 21917, 21932. Family History Library, Salt Lake City, Utah. Deed Books.

Tennessee. Chattanooga. Microfilm M-21. Tennessee State Library and Archives, Nashville. Death Records.

Tennessee. Hamilton County. Chancery Court, Chattanooga. Probate Records.

Tennessee. Hamilton County. County Clerk, Chattanooga. Marriage Books.

Tennessee. Hamilton County. Microfilm 83. Tennessee State Library and Archives, Nashville. Will Books.

Tennessee. Hamilton County. Register of Deeds, Chattanooga. Deed Books.

Tennessee. Hamilton County. Register of Deeds. Microfilms 137, 141, 156, 178, 181. Tennessee State Library and Archives, Nashville. Deeds.

Tennessee. Nashville. Department of Public Health. Tennessee State Library and Archives, Nashville. Death Registrations.

United States. Maryland. Baltimore City. U.S. Social Security Administration. Original Applications.

United States. National Archives, Washington, D.C. Civil War Soldiers and Widows Pension Files.

United States. National Archives, Washington, D.C. Interstate Commerce Commission. Record Group 134. Jacob Chester Frist, Medal of Honor Case File #25.

United States. National Archives, Washington, D.C. Records of the Veterans Administration, Record Group 15. Bounty Land Warrant Application Files, 1812–1855. Unindexed Bounty Land Files. John Frist 1812 File.

United States. National Archives, Washington, D.C. U.S. War Department. Delaware Civil War Military Service Records.

West Virginia. Kanawha County. Microfilm. Family History Library, Salt Lake City, Utah. Death Records and Deed Books.

INTERNET AND ELECTRONIC RECORDS

Germany. Das Telefonbuch. <www.telefonbuch.de/NSAPI/anfrage> [downloaded 17 January 2002 by compiler].

"History of the 42nd Infantry Division 'Rainbow,'" <www.grunts.net/army/42ndid.html> [downloaded 6 March 2002 by compiler].

Social Security Death Index. *Ancestry.com*. Provo, Utah. MyFamily.com, Inc., 1998–2003.

Wales, Anglesey. Ecclesiastical Parishes. Supplied to GENUKI by Joyce Hinde [Page generated: 27th November 1999, 22:48 GMT by Brian Pears] <www.genuki.org.uk/big/wal/AGY/AGY_Pars.html> [downloaded 2 October 2002 by compiler].

Wales, Anglesey, Amlwch. 1881 census, addresses of miners <www.parysmountain.fsnet.co.uk/> [click on 1881 Amlwch area census, downloaded 27 September 2002 by compiler].

NEWSPAPERS

Anderson Daily Bulletin. Anderson, Indiana.

Baltimore Sun. Baltimore City, Maryland.

Cecil County News. Elkton, Maryland.

Cecil Democrat. Elkton, Maryland.

Cecil Whig. Elkton, Maryland.

Chattanooga Daily News. Chattanooga, Tennessee.

Chattanooga Daily Times. Chattanooga, Tennessee.

Chattanooga Free Press. Chattanooga, Tennessee.

Chattanooga News–Free Press. Chattanooga, Tennessee.

Chattanooga Times. Chattanooga, Tennessee.

Clinton Plaindealer. Clinton, Indiana.

Daily Clintonian. Clinton, Indiana.

Indianapolis News. Indianapolis, Indiana.

Indianapolis Star. Indianapolis, Indiana.

Jeffersonian. Baltimore County, Maryland.

Journal and Courier. Lafayette, Indiana.

Liberty Herald. Liberty, Indiana.

Long Beach Press–Telegram. Long Beach, California.

Meridian Star. Meridian, Mississippi.

Richmond Item. Richmond, Indiana.

Tennessean. Nashville, Tennessee.

Villisca Review and Letter. Villisca, Iowa.

Wilmington Evening Journal. Wilmington, Delaware.

PUBLISHED MATERIAL

Ancestral File, version 4.19, Family History Library. Salt Lake City: Family History Library, 2002.

Armstrong, Zella. *Hamilton County and Chattanooga, Tennessee, Volume 1*. 1931. Reprint, Johnson City, Tennessee: Overmountain Press, 1993.

Art Work of Chattanooga, Tennessee. Chicago: Gravure Illustration Company, 1917.

Beaven, Mrs. Arthur (Elsie) Patterson. *Records of Callender and Patterson Family Cemetery*. Perryville, Maryland: Captain Jeremiah Baker Chapter NSDAR, 1942.

Belsterling, Charles Starne. *Paternal Ancestors of Florence Fries Belsterling*. New York: no publisher, 1938.

Cecil County, Maryland, Tombstone Inscriptions, Districts 7, 8, & 9. No place: Genealogical Society of Cecil County, 1992.

Centenary Methodist Church Historical Committee. *Centenary The Story of a Church*. Chattanooga: privately printed, 1962.

Chandler Family Reunion Committee. *A Record of the Descendants of George and Jane Chandler (who emigrated to Pennsylvania from Wiltshire, England, in 1687) with a Pedigree of the Chandlers of Oare, Wiltshire*. No place: Chandler Family Reunion Committee, 1937.

Compiled Service Records of Confederate Soldiers Who Served in Organizations from Tennessee. Micropublication M268. Washington, D.C.: National Archives. Microfilm roll 17. Tennessee State Library and Archives, Nashville.

Craig, Peter Stebbins. *The 1693 Census of the Swedes on the Delaware*. Winter Park, Florida: SAG Publications, 1993.

Darke County Genealogical Society. *Darke County, Ohio, Marriages 1851–1898*. No place: Darke County Genealogical Society, no date.

Delaware History. Volume XX. Wilmington, Delaware: The Historical Society of Delaware, 1982–1983.

Delaware's Industries, An Historical and Industrial Review. Philadelphia: Keighton Printing House, 1891.

Doherty, Thomas P., ed. *Delaware Genealogical Research Guide*. 2d ed. Wilmington, Delaware: Delaware Genealogical Society, 1997.

Dover, Karen, abstractor. *Lauderdale County Cemetery Records, Volume IV*. Meridian, Mississippi: Lauderdale County Department of Archives and History, 1992.

Early Church Records of New Castle County, Delaware. Volume 2. Westminster, Maryland: Family Line Publications, 1994.

Ellis, Ruby Haskins, and Anna Petty Neal. *Lineage Book National Society of the Daughters of American Colonists, Volume II 1001–2000*. Washington, D.C: Judd & Detweiler, 1930.

Evans, William R. *History of Welsh Settlements in Jackson and Gallia Counties of Ohio*. Utica, New York: T. J. Griffiths, 1896.

"Every Evening." *History of Wilmington, the Commercial, Social, and Religious Growth of the City during the Past Century*. Wilmington, Delaware: "Every Evening," 1894.

Garrett, Carol J. *New Castle County, Delaware, Land Records 1749–1752*. Westminster, Maryland: Family Line Publications, 1998.

———. *New Castle County, Delaware, Land Records 1755–1762*. Westminster, Maryland: Willow Bend Books, 1999.

Genealogical Society of Cecil County. *1860 U.S. Census for Cecil County, Maryland*. Charlestown, Maryland: Genealogical Society of Cecil County, 1989.

Gilbert, Audrey. *Abstracts from Preble County, Ohio, Newspaper Obituaries Book VII 1915–1918*. West Alexandria, Ohio: privately published, 1999.

———. *Abstracts from Preble County, Ohio, Newspaper Obituaries Book VIII 1919–1922*. West Carrollton, Ohio: Electronic Print Imagine Corporation, 2000.

———. *Obituary Abstracts 1877–1895 from Preble County Newspapers in Preble County, Ohio, Volume II*. Utica, Kentucky: McDowell Publications, 1983.

———. *Obituary Abstracts 1896–1900 from Preble County Newspapers in Preble County, Ohio, Volume III*. No place: privately printed, 1985.

———. *Preble County, Ohio, Deaths 1867–1907*. Utica, Kentucky: McDowell Publications, no date.

———. *Preble County, Ohio, 1880 Census*. Utica, Kentucky: McDowell Publications, 1983.

———. *Preble County, Ohio, Land Records Volume III 1828–1833 Books 9–13*. West Alexandria, Ohio: privately printed, 1992.

———. *Preble County, Ohio, Marriages 1860–1898*. Owensboro, Kentucky: McDowell Publications, 1981.

———. *Preble County, Ohio, Marriages 1907–1915*. Utica, Kentucky: McDowell Publications, no date.

———. *Preble County, Ohio, Marriages 1916–1926*. West Alexandria, Ohio: privately printed, 1998.

———. *Preble County, Ohio, the 1900 Federal Census.* Owensboro, Kentucky: Cook & McDowell Publications, 1980.

———. *Preble County, Ohio, 1910 Census.* Utica, Kentucky: McDowell Publications, 1984.

———. *Preble County, Ohio, 1920 Census.* No place: no publisher, 1993.

———. *Preble County, Ohio, Personal Property Tax Lists 1827–1834.* West Alexandria, Ohio: privately printed, no date.

———. *Preble County, Ohio, Probate Abstracts Estates and Guardianships Cases 3000 through 3999.* West Alexandria, Ohio: privately printed, 1998.

———. *Probate Abstracts Estates and Guardianships Preble County, Ohio.* West Alexandria, Ohio: privately printed, 2001.

———. *Probate Abstracts Estates and Guardianships Preble County, Ohio, Book 4.* West Alexandria, Ohio: privately printed, 1999.

———. *Probate Abstracts Estates & Guardianships Preble County, Ohio, Cases 5000 to 5999 Book 5.* West Alexandria, Ohio: privately printed, 1999.

———. *Probate Abstracts Preble County, Ohio, Estates and Guardianships Cases 2000 through 2999.* West Alexandria, Ohio: privately printed, 1998.

Good People Beget Good People: The Life and Legacy of Dr. Thomas F. Frist, Sr. Nashville, Tennessee: privately printed, 1998.

Hall, Alan. "Thomas F. Frist, Jr., President and CEO, Hospital Corporation of America." *SKY Magazine*, January 1983.

Harkness' Magazine. September 1872 to August 1874.

Hayes, Dafydd. *Hayes Computerised Indexes Parish Church Marriages Amlwch, Anglesey, Wales 1630–1869.* Buckley, Clwyd, Wales: privately printed, no date.

Hiestand, Ione Sell, ed. *Preble County Ohio.* No place: Preble County Historical Society, 1992.

Hison, Mary J., and Frances Welch. *Cemetery Inscriptions of Jackson County Ohio, Volume II.* Baltimore: Gateway Press, 1982.

The Historical Records Survey. *Hamilton County Tombstone Inscriptions, Volume I.* Nashville, Tennessee: Works Progress Administration, 1939.

———. *Hamilton County Tombstone Inscriptions, Volume II.* Nashville, Tennessee: Works Progress Administration, 1939.

History of Page County, Iowa. Des Moines, Iowa: Iowa Historical Society, 1880.

History of Parke and Vermillion Counties Indiana. Indianapolis, Indiana: B. F. Bowen & Company 1913.

History of Preble County, Ohio, with Illustrations and Biographical Sketches. 1881. Reprint, Evansville, Indiana: Unigraphic, 1972.

Hitchcock, Frederick H. *A Calendar of Delaware Wills, New Castle County 1682–1800.* 1911. Reprint, Baltimore: Genealogical Publishing Company, 1969.

Jones, George J. *German-American Names.* 2d ed. Baltimore: Genealogical Publishing Company, 1995.

Knowles, Anne Kelly. *Calvinists Incorporated: Welsh Immigrants on Ohio's Industrial Frontier.* Chicago: University of Chicago Press, 1997.

Laidley, W. S. *History of Charles and Kanawha County, West Virginia, and Representative Citizen.* 1911. Reprint, Waynesville, North Carolina: Don Mills, 1993.

Meldrum, Charlotte D. *Early Church Records of Salem County, New Jersey.* Westminster, Maryland: Family Line Publications, 1996.

The Mercer County Chapter of the Ohio Genealogical Society. *Probate Court Death Records Mercer County, Ohio, Book 1 1867–1888.* Celina, Ohio: no publisher, no date.

Montgomery County Genealogical Society and Bicentennial Committee. *Cemetery Records Montgomery County, Iowa, Townships of Douglass Washington East (Jackson).* Des Moines, Iowa: Iowa Genealogical Society, 1984.

Morton, Oren F. *A History of Monroe County, West Virginia.* Staunton, Virginia: The McClure Company, 1916.

Nebeker, William G. "Line of Descent of Nebekers." Printed genealogical chart. Salt Lake City, Utah: privately printed, no date. Copy held in 2003 by compiler.

The New Jersey Historical Records Survey Program. *Index of the Official Register of the Officers and Men of New Jersey in the Revolutionary War.* 1941. Reprint, Baltimore: Genealogical Publishing Company, 1965.

Norwood's Directory of Chattanooga 1884–1885. Chattanooga, Tennessee: C. W. Norwood, 1884.

Peat, Wilbur D. *Portraits and Painters of the Governors of Indiana 1800–1978.* Revised and edited by Diane Gail Lazarus. Indianapolis, Indiana: Indiana Historical Society, 1978.

Peden, Henry C., Jr. *Colonial Delaware Soldiers and Sailors 1638–1776.* Westminster, Maryland: Family Line Publications, 1995.

Peterson, Rose W., compiler. *Spring Hill Cemetery, Charleston, West Virginia, Volume III, L–R.* Nitro, West Virginia: Peterson Quality Associates, 1995.

Pioneer Sons and Daughters Genealogical Society. *Marriages Polk County, Iowa, Book 12 1905–1906.* Des Moines, Iowa: Iowa Genealogical Society, 1986.

Powell, Henry Fletcher. *Tercentenary History of Maryland,* 4 vol. Chicago: S. J. Clark Publishing Company, 1925.

Ramage, Helen. *Portraits of an Island Eighteenth Century Anglesey.* Llangefni, Gwynedd, Wales: Anglesey Antiquarian Society and Field Club, 1987.

Record of Pennsylvania Marriages Prior to 1810. Volume I. Baltimore: Genealogical Publishing Company, 1987.

Records of the Court of New Castle County of Delaware Volume II 1681–1699 Land and Probate Abstract Only. Meadville, Pennsylvania: Colonial Society of Pennsylvania, 1935.

Richards, Mary Fallon, and John C. Richards, eds. *Delaware Marriages and Deaths from Newspapers 1729–1853.* Westminster, Maryland: Family Line Publications, 1997.

———. *Marriages from the Delaware Gazette 1854–1859, 1861–1864.* Camden, Maine: Picton Press, no date.

Robertson, Donna J., compiler. *Tombstone Inscriptions of Cecil County, Maryland.* Largo, Florida: privately printed, 1995.

Scharf, J. Thomas. *History of Delaware 1609–1888.* Vol. 1. Philadelphia: L. J. Richards & Company, 1888.

———. *History of Delaware 1609–1888.* 2 vols. 1888. Reprint, Westminster, Maryland: Family Line Publications, 1990.

Shilt, Rose. *Preble County, Ohio, Marriage Records 1841–1859 Volume III.* Union City, Indiana: Gateway to the West Publications, no date.

Short, Don, Mrs., and Mrs. Dale Bowers. *Preble County, Ohio, Marriage Records 1831–1840 From Marriage Book A Volume II.* No place: privately printed, no date.

Silliman, Charles A. *The Episcopal Church in Delaware 1785–1954.* Wilmington, Delaware: The Protestant Episcopal Church in the Diocese of Delaware, 1982.

Smith, Elsdon C. *New Dictionary of American Family Names.* New York: Gramercy Publishing Company, 1988.

Soard's New Orleans City Directory for 1903. New Orleans: Soard's Directory County Ltd., 1903.

Social Security Death Index. *FamilySearch.* Salt Lake City, Utah: Family History Library, 2001.

Starbuck, Dane. *The Goodriches: An American Family.* Indianapolis, Indiana: Liberty Fund, Inc., 2001.

Stidham, Jack. *The Descendants of Timothy Stidham Volume 1.* Morristown, Tennessee: J. Stidham, 1978.

Strassburger, Ralph, and William Hinke. *Pennsylvania German Pioneers, Volume I 1727–1755.* Norristown, Pennsylvania: Pennsylvania German Society, 1934.

Strickland, Jean, and Patricia N. Edwards, compilers. *Perry County, Mississippi, W.P.A. Manuscripts Newspaper Items*. Moss Point, Mississippi: Ben Strickland, 1997.

Swenson, Shirley, ed. *The Nebeker Family Book*. No place: Nebeker Family Association, 1979.

"Thomas F. Frist, Sr., M.D. 1910–." *Modern Health Care*, 10 September 1990, p. 54.

Vermillion County Historical Society. *Vermillion County Indiana, History & Families*. Paducah, Kentucky: Turner Publishing Company, 1990.

Ward, Mary Sam. *Our Spiritual Heritage*. Newport, Delaware: The Women of St. James, no date.

Wilmington City Directory and Business Gazetteer. Wilmington, Delaware: Wilmington Advertising Agency, 1900 and 1902.

Withycombe, E. G. *The Oxford Dictionary of English Christian Names*. 3d ed. New York: Oxford University Press, 1977.

Wright, F. Edward. *Early Church Records of New Castle County*. Westminister, Maryland: Family Line Publications, 1994.

Yount, Beverly. *Tombstone Inscriptions in Wayne County, Indiana, Volume IV*. Fort Wayne, Indiana: Fort Wayne Public Library, 1970.

UNITED STATES CENSUS RECORDS

Alabama. Etowah County. 1920 U.S. Census, Population Schedule. Micropublication T625, roll 15. Washington, D.C.: National Archives.

Alabama. Etowah County. 1930 U.S. Census, Population Schedule. Micropublication T626, roll 16. Washington, D.C.: National Archives.

Alabama. Jefferson County. 1930 U.S. Census, Population Schedule. Micropublication T625, roll 23. Washington, D.C.: National Archives.

California. Los Angeles County. 1900 U.S. Census, Population Schedule. Micropublication T623, roll 91. Washington, D.C.: National Archives.

California. Los Angeles County. 1920 U.S. Census, Population Schedule. Micropublication T625, rolls 104, 118. Washington, D.C.: National Archives.

Delaware. Kent County. 1900 U.S. Census, Population Schedule. Micropublication T623, roll 153. Washington, D.C.: National Archives.

Delaware. New Castle County. 1800 U.S. Census. Micropublication M32, roll 4. Washington, D.C.: National Archives.

Delaware. New Castle County. 1810 U.S. Census. Microfilm 224381. Family History Library, Salt Lake City, Utah.

Delaware. New Castle County. 1820 U.S. Census. Micropublication M33, roll 4. Washington, D.C.: National Archives.

Delaware. New Castle County. 1830 U.S. Census. Micropublication M19, roll 12. Washington, D.C.: National Archives.

Delaware. New Castle County. 1840 U.S. Census. Micropublication M704, roll 33. Washington, D.C.: National Archives.

Delaware. New Castle County. 1850 U.S. Census, Population Schedule. Microfilm 6437. Family History Library, Salt Lake City, Utah.

Delaware. New Castle County. 1860 U.S. Census, Population Schedule. Microfilm 803098. Family History Library, Salt Lake City, Utah.

Delaware. New Castle County. 1870 U.S. Census, Population Schedule. Micropublication M593, roll 121. Washington, D.C.: National Archives.

Delaware. New Castle County. 1880 U.S. Census, Population Schedule. Microfilm 1254119. Family History Library, Salt Lake City, Utah.

Delaware. New Castle County. 1900 U.S. Census, Population Schedule. Micropublication T623, rolls 154–156. Washington, D.C.: National Archives.

Delaware. New Castle County. 1910 U.S. Census, Population Schedule. Micropublication T624, rolls 146–147. Washington, D.C.: National Archives.

Delaware. New Castle County. 1920 U.S. Census, Population Schedule. Micropublication T625, rolls 202–204. Washington, D.C.: National Archives.

Delaware. New Castle County. 1930 U.S. Census, Population Schedule. Micropublication T626, rolls 287, 289, 290. Washington, D.C.: National Archives.

Georgia. Richmond County. 1850 U.S. Census, Population Schedule. Micropublication M432, roll 81. Washington, D.C.: National Archives.

Georgia. Walker County. 1910 U.S. Census, Population Schedule. Micropublication T624, roll 214. Washington, D.C.: National Archives.

Georgia. Walker County. 1920 U.S. Census, Population Schedule. Micropublication T625, roll 281. Washington, D.C.: National Archives.

Indiana. Jay County. 1880 U.S. Census, Population Schedule. Microfilm 1254287. Family History Library, Salt Lake City, Utah.

Indiana. Madison County. 1900 U.S. Census, Population Schedule. Micropublication T623, roll 386. Washington, D.C.: National Archives.

Indiana. Madison County. 1920 U.S. Census, Population Schedule. Micropublication T625, roll 448. Washington, D.C.: National Archives.

Indiana. Marion County. 1920 U.S. Census, Population Schedule. Micropublication T625, roll 452. Washington, D.C.: National Archives.

Indiana. Randolph County. 1880 U.S. Census, Population Schedule. Micropublication T9, roll 307. Washington, D.C.: National Archives.

Indiana. Randolph County. 1900 U.S. Census, Population Schedule. Micropublication T623, roll 399. Washington, D.C.: National Archives.

Indiana. Union County. 1900 U.S. Census, Population Schedule. Micropublication T623, roll 406. Washington, D.C.: National Archives.

Indiana. Union County. 1920 U.S. Census, Population Schedule. Micropublication T625, roll 460. Washington, D.C.: National Archives.

Indiana. Vermillion County. 1870 U.S. Census, Population Schedule. Micropublication M593, roll 365. Washington, D.C.: National Archives.

Indiana. Vermillion County. 1880 U.S. Census, Population Schedule. Micropublication T9, roll 318. Washington: National Archives.

Indiana. Vermillion County. 1900 U.S. Census, Population Schedule. Micropublication T623, roll 408. Washington, D.C.: National Archives.

Indiana. Vermillion County. 1910 U.S. Census, Population Schedule. Micropublication T624, roll 384. Washington, D.C.: National Archives.

Indiana. Vermillion County. 1920 U.S. Census, Population Schedule. Micropublication T625, roll 472. Washington, D.C.: National Archives.

Indiana. Wayne County. 1830 U.S. Census. Micropublication M19, roll 29. Washington, D.C.: National Archives.

Indiana. Wayne County. 1850 U.S. Census, Population Schedule. Micropublication M432, roll 180. Washington, D.C.: National Archives.

Indiana. Wayne County. 1860 U.S. Census, Population Schedule. Micropublication M653, roll 308. Washington, D.C.: National Archives.

Indiana. Wayne County. 1880 U.S. Census, Population Schedule. Micropublication T9, roll 322. Washington, D.C.: National Archives.

Indiana. Wayne County. 1900 U.S. Census, Population Schedule. Micropublication T623, roll 412. Washington, D.C.: National Archives.

Indiana. Wayne County. 1910 U.S. Census, Wayne County, Indiana, Population Schedule. Micropublication T624, roll 388. Washington, D.C.: National Archives.

Indiana. Wayne County. 1920 U.S. Census, Population Schedule. Micropublication T625, roll 474. Washington, D.C.: National Archives.

Indiana. Wayne County. 1920 U.S. Census Soundex Code R-100. Micropublication T560, roll 164. Washington, D.C.: National Archives.

Iowa. Dallas County. 1880 U.S. Census, Population Schedule. Micropublication T9, roll 335. Washington, D.C.: National Archives.

Iowa. Dallas County. 1900 U.S. Census, Population Schedule. Micropublication T623, roll 427. Washington, D.C.: National Archives.

Iowa. Dallas County. 1910 U.S. Census, Population Schedule. Micropublication T624, roll 399. Washington, D.C.: National Archives.

Iowa. Lee County. 1920 U.S. Census, Population Schedule. Micropublication T625, roll 499. Washington, D.C.: National Archives.

Iowa. Marion County. 1880 U.S. Census, Population Schedule. Micropublication T9, roll 354. Washington, D.C.: National Archives.

Iowa. Montgomery County. 1900 U.S. Census, Population Schedule. Micropublication T623, roll 450. Washington, D.C.: National Archives.

Iowa. Montgomery County. 1920 U.S. Census, Population Schedule. Micropublication T625, roll 504. Washington, D.C.: National Archives.

Iowa. Page County. 1920 U.S. Census, Population Schedule. Micropublication T625, roll 506. Washington, D.C.: National Archives.

Iowa. Plymouth County. 1920 U.S. Census, Population Schedule. Micropublication T625, roll 506. Washington, D.C.: National Archives.

Iowa. Polk County. 1900 U.S. Census, Population Schedule. Micropublication T623, roll 453. Washington, D.C.: National Archives.

Iowa. Polk County. 1910 U.S. Census, Population Schedule. Micropublication T624, roll 418. Washington, D.C.: National Archives.

Iowa. Polk County. 1920 U.S. Census, Population Schedule. Micropublication T625, roll 507. Washington, D.C.: National Archives.

Iowa. Warren County. 1870 U.S. Census, Population Schedule. Micropublication M593, roll 423. Washington, D.C.: National Archives.

Louisiana. Ouachita County. 1870 U.S. Census, Population Schedule. Microfilm 552025. Family History Library, Salt Lake City, Utah.

Maryland. Baltimore County. 1860 U.S. Census, Population Schedule. Micropublication M653, roll 465. Washington, D.C.: National Archives.

Maryland. Baltimore County. 1870 U.S. Census, Population Schedule. Micropublication M593, rolls 572, 580. Washington, D.C.: National Archives.

Maryland. Baltimore County. 1880 U.S. Census, Population Schedule. Micropublication T9, rolls 498, 500. Washington, D.C.: National Archives.

Maryland. Baltimore County. 1880 U.S. Census, Population Schedule. Microfilm 1254501. Family History Library, Salt Lake City, Utah.

Maryland. Baltimore County. 1900 U.S. Census, Population Schedule. Micropublication T623, rolls 607, 614, 618, 620. Washington, D.C.: National Archives.

Maryland. Baltimore County. 1920 U.S. Census, Population Schedule. Micropublication T625, rolls 657, 658, 660, 662, 667. Washington, D.C.: National Archives.

Maryland. Cecil County. 1840 U.S. Census. Micropublication M704, roll 164. Washington, D.C.: National Archives.

Maryland. Cecil County. 1850 U.S. Census, Population Schedule. Micropublication M432, roll 290. Washington, D.C.: National Archives.

Maryland. Cecil County. 1860 U.S. Census, Population Schedule. Micropublication M653, roll 472. Washington, D.C.: National Archives.

Maryland. Cecil County. 1870 U.S. Census, Population Schedule. Micropublication M593, roll 583. Washington, D.C.: National Archives.

Maryland. Cecil County. 1880 U.S. Census, Population Schedule. Micropublication T9, roll 507. Washington, D.C.: National Archives.

Maryland. Cecil County. 1900 U.S. Census, Population Schedule. Micropublication T623, roll 620. Washington: National Archives.

Maryland. Cecil County. 1920 U.S. Census, Population Schedule. Micropublication T625, roll 670. Washington: National Archives.

Maryland. Talbot County. 1920 U.S. Census, Population Schedule. Micropublication T624, roll 677. Washington, D.C.: National Archives.

Mississippi. Lauderdale County. 1910 U.S. Census, Population Schedule. Micropublication T624, roll 746. Washington, D.C.: National Archives.

Mississippi. Lauderdale County. 1920 U.S. Census, Population Schedule. Micropublication T625, roll 882. Washington: National Archives.

Mississippi. Lauderdale County. 1930 U.S. Census, Population. Micropublication T626, roll 1153. Washington, D.C.: National Archives.

Mississippi. Perry County. 1900 U.S. Census, Population Schedule. Micropublication T623, roll 824. Washington, D.C.: National Archives.

Ohio. Cuyahoga County. 1900 U.S. Census, Population Schedule. Micropublication T623, roll 1255. Washington, D.C.: National Archives.

Ohio. Cuyahoga County. 1920 U.S. Census, Population Schedule. Micropublication T625, roll 1374. Washington, D.C.: National Archives.

Ohio. Gallia County. 1860 U.S. Census, Population Schedule. Micropublication M653, roll 966. Washington, D.C.: National Archives.

Ohio. Jackson County. 1850 U.S. Census, Population Schedule. Micropublication M432, roll 698. Washington, D.C.: National Archives.

Ohio. Jackson County. 1860 U.S. Census, Population Schedule. Micropublication M653, roll 992. Washington, D.C.: National Archives.

Ohio. Jackson County. 1870 U.S. Census, Population Schedule. Micropublication M593, roll 1226. Washington, D.C.: National Archives.

Ohio. Jackson County. 1880 U.S. Census, Population Schedule. Microfilm 1255037. Family History Library, Salt Lake City, Utah.

Ohio. Preble County. 1850 U.S. Census, Population Schedule. Micropublication M432, roll 723. Washington, D.C.: National Archives.

Ohio. Preble County. 1860 U.S. Census, Population Schedule. Micropublication M653, roll 1026. Washington, D.C.: National Archives.

Ohio. Preble County. 1870 U.S. Census, Population Schedule. Micropublication M593, roll 1259. Washington, D.C.: National Archives.

Ohio. Preble County. 1880 U.S. Census, Population Schedule. Microfilm 1255060. Family History Library, Salt Lake City, Utah.

Pennsylvania. Chester County. 1830 U.S. Census. Micropublication M19, roll 148. Washington, D.C.: National Archives.

Pennsylvania. Delaware County. 1920 U.S. Census, Population Schedule. Micropublication T625, roll 1560. Washington, D.C.: National Archives.

Tennessee. Hamilton County. 1860 U.S. Census, Population Schedule. Micropublication M653, roll 1253. Washington, D.C.: National Archives.

Tennessee. Hamilton County. 1870 U.S. Census, Population Schedule. Micropublication M593, roll 1532. Washington, D.C.: National Archives.

Tennessee. Hamilton County. 1880 U.S. Census, Population Schedule. Micropublication T9, roll 1259. Washington, D.C.: National Archives.

Tennessee. Hamilton County. 1900 U.S. Census, Population Schedule. Micropublication T623, roll 1574. Washington, D.C.: National Archives.

Tennessee. Hamilton County. 1910 U.S. Census, Population Schedule. Micropublication T624, rolls 1501–2. Washington, D.C.: National Archives.

Tennessee. Hamilton County. 1920 U.S. Census, Population Schedule. Micropublication T625, rolls 1742–3. Washington, D.C.: National Archives.

Tennessee. Hamilton County. 1930 U.S. Census, Population Schedule. Microfilms 20–21. Tennessee State Library and Archives, Nashville, Tennessee.

Texas. Denton County. 1880 U.S. Census, Population Schedule. Micropublication T9, roll 1300. Washington, D.C.: National Archives.

Virginia. Monroe County. 1860 U.S. Census, Population Schedule. Micropublication M653, roll 1363. Washington, D.C.: National Archives.

West Virginia. Kanawha County. 1880 U.S. Census, Population Schedule. Micropublication T9, roll 1405. Washington, D.C.: National Archives.

West Virginia. Kanawha County. 1900 U.S. Census, Population Schedule. Micropublication T623, roll 1762. Washington, D.C.: National Archives.

West Virginia. Kanawha County. 1920 U.S. Census, Population Schedule. Micropublication T625, roll 1958. Washington, D.C.: National Archives.

UNPUBLISHED MATERIAL

Abraham, Audrey. Telephone conversation 14 August 2002 regarding Port Deposit Presbyterian Church with compiler.

Alabama. Gadsden. Forrest Cemetery. Tombstone data.

Biographical materials from family members in the form of family group sheets, letters, telephone calls, interviews, faxes, and email are cited within the text and not separately listed in this bibliography.

Brubaker, Clifton Morse. "Copy of the Records from the Church Register of the Port Deposit Presbyterian Church 1938–1943—Book 1 for the 150th Port Deposit Presbyterian Church Celebration 1838–1988." Port Deposit Library, Port Deposit, Maryland.

Carnegie Hero Fund Commission. Pittsburgh, Pennsylvania. Jacob Chester Frist, Award No. 1077.

Craig, Peter Stebbins. "Descendants of Jan Gerritsen Van der Hof." Research report, 1994. Copy held in 2003 by compiler.

———. "The Garretson Families of New Castle County." Research report, 1994. Copy held in 2003 by compiler.

Delaware. Kennett Monthly Meeting. Friends Historical Library, Swarthmore College, Swarthmore, Pennsylvania. 1692–1821 Marriages.

Delaware. Newport. St. James Methodist Episcopal Church Cemetery. Tombstone Data, Church Records.

Delaware. Wilmington. Asbury M. E. Church, card file. Wilmington: Delaware Historical Society.

Delaware. Wilmington. Holy Trinity (Old Swedes) Church. Baptisms and births, marriages, membership lists, tombstone data, and church records.

Delaware. Wilmington. Wilmington and Brandywine Cemetery. Tombstone Data.

Dunn, Winfield. 14 April 1983. NCCJ Brotherhood Dinner. Introductory Remarks. Thomas F. Frist, Sr., M.D., Honoree. William H. Frist, M.D. Genealogical Collection.

du Pont letters. Hagley Museum and Library, Wilmington, Delaware.

"Foard's Store." Undated sketch by unknown author. Provided June 2002 by Ann Foard Fowser, 19 Natchez Trail, Medford Lakes, NJ 08055 and held in 2003 by compiler.

Fowser, Ann. "The Foard Family." Copy provided by Ann Fowser, 19 Natchez Trail, Medford Lakes, NJ 08055 and held in 2003 by compiler.

Frist, David H. Family Bible. Original owned by Geraldine (Frist) Miller's husband Dale Miller, 415 South 18th Street, Clarinda, IA 51632.

Frist, Dorothy Harrison (Cate). Eulogy 8 January 1998, delivered by nephew George Harrison Cate, Jr.

Frist, Frank Peirce. Family Bible. Copy provided by Patricia Jo Frist, Clinton, Indiana and held in 2003 by compiler.

Frist, Harry Homer. Family Record. Original owned by Patricia Jo Frist, Clinton, Indiana and copy held in 2003 by compiler.

Frist, Jacob. Family Bible. Original owned by William H. Frist, M.D., 703 Bowling Avenue, Nashville, TN 37205.

Frist, Jacob. Report card. Original owned by granddaughter Mary Barfield, 1026 Chancery Lane S., Nashville, TN 37215-4552.

Frist, Jane. Genealogical collection. Frist, P.O. Box 272, Montreat, NC 28757, collected the material. Copy held in 2003 by William H. Frist, M.D.

Frist, Jediah. Family Bible. Copy from Patricia Frist Genealogical Collection, held in 2003 by compiler.

Frist, Lizzie. Letter 15 August 1878 from William M. Vetter. Owned by John Stanley Vetter, M.D., FristHealth Richmond Family Medicine, 921 Long Drive, Suite 101, Rockingham, NC 28379. Copy held in 2003 by compiler.

Frist, Mary Ann (Baldwin). Interview. Unpublished manuscript of Wiltse, pp. 9–13. Chattanooga Public Library, Chattanooga, Tennessee. Published copy in *Chattanooga News*, Chattanooga, Tennessee, 2 February 1917. William H. Frist, M.D. Genealogical Collection.

Frist, Patricia. Genealogical Collection. Copy held in 2003 by compiler.

Frist, Ramsey Hudson. Letter 18 December 2000 from 633 Jones Avenue, Morgantown, WV 26505 to compiler.

Frist, Ronnie. Genealogical Collection. Frist, of 1718 Gray Road, Chattanooga, TN 37421, owns collection of his grandmother Kate Frist.

Frist, Thomas Fearn, M.D. "The Frist Story." William H. Frist, M.D. Genealogical Collection, 703 Bowling Avenue, Nashville, TN 37215.

Frist, Thomas Fearn. Narrative labeled "Family History Jacobson Excerpts," owned by William H. Frist, M.D.

Frist, Thomas Fearn. Research report 15 September 1984 from P.O. Box 1204, 98 Frist Road, Montreat, NC 28757. Copy from William H. Frist, M.D. Genealogical Collection.

Frist, William H. Genealogical Collection, 703 Bowling Avenue, Nashville, TN 37215.

Goodrich, Mrs. James P. Letter 14 December 1926 to relative "Mayne," surname not stated. Copy from genealogical collection of William H. Frist, M.D. 701 Bowling Avenue, Nashville, TN 37215.

Groves, E. L. Family Bible. Original owned by Ronnie Frist, 1718 Gray Road, Chattanooga, TN 37421. Copy held in 2003 by compiler.

Hazard, James E. Report 23 December 2002 on Garretsons in Quaker Records. Copy held in 2003 by compiler.

Hepner, Margaret. Genealogical Collection. Hepner, 600 Falcon Bridge Drive, Jappa, Maryland 21085, provided copies held in 2003 by compiler.

Hussey Family Material (undocumented). Friends Historical Library, Swarthmore College, Swarthmore, Pennsylvania.

Index of Obits and Marriages in *Baltimore Sun* 1871–1875, Volume 1 A–J. Baltimore: Enoch Pratt Library.

Indiana. Clinton. Frist Funeral Home Records. Patricia Frist Genealogical Collection.

Indiana. Vermillion County. Helt's Prairie Cemetery. Tombstone Data.

Lemstra, Enid. Letter 26 August 1927 to cousin Anna Alexander, Wilmington, Delaware. Copy held in 2003 by compiler.

Lyons, Martin Burnett. Interview September 2002. Lyons, 30588 Kingston Road, Easton, MD 21601, interviewed by Margaret Hepner, 600 Falcon Bridge Drive, Joppa, MD 21085. Data conveyed 26 September 2002 to compiler.

Maryland. Baltimore. Loudon Park Cemetery. Tombstone Data and Cemetery Burial Records.

Maryland. Baltimore. New Cathedral Cemetery. Tombstone Data.

Maryland. Cecil County. Hopewell United Methodist Church Cemetery. Tombstone Data.

Maryland. Elkton. Cecil County Historical Society Library. Genealogical Data.

Miller, Donald G. Letter 8 January 1960 to Charlotte Chesnutt, P.O. Box 412, Montreat, NC 28757. Copy provided in January 2002 to compiler.

Miller, Geraldine. Family Bible Record. Original owned by Mrs. Miller, now deceased, 415 S. 18th Street, Clarinda, IA 51632-2515. Copy held in 2003 by compiler.

Miller, Geraldine Frist. Eickemeyer Funeral Chapel record. Copy provided to compiler by Dale Miller, 415 S. 18th Street, Clarinda, IA 51632-2515.

Mississippi. Meridian. Magnolia Cemetery. Tombstone Data and Cemetery Records.

Mayes, Herman. Genealogical Collection. Mayes, 11207 South 200 East, Clinton, IN 47842, and Gary Jones, P.O. Box 142, Montezuma, IN 47862, collaborated in producing an unpublished Frist manuscript. Copy held in 2003 by compiler.

Nebeker Family Record. Copy provided in August 2002 by Ann Fowser, 3742 Asbury Avenue, Ocean City, NJ 08226, to compiler.

Pennsylvania. Chester County Historical Society Library. Genealogical Data.

Tennessee. Chattanooga. Citizens Cemetery. Tombstone Data.

Vetter, William M. Family papers. Owned by John Stanley Vetter, M.D., FristHealth Richmond Family Medicine, 921 Long Drive, Suite 101, Rockingham, NC 28379. Copy held in 2003 by compiler.

Wales, Anglesey. Amlwch, parish register. British microfilm. Family History Library, Salt Lake City, Utah.

NAME INDEX

Names are indexed only once on each page. Birth dates for descendants are included in parentheses, when known. This is done twice, once as a child and once as an adult. Thus, an indexed entry with a birth date will lead to the primary information on that individual. Female descendants are similarly indexed under all married names. The abbreviation *ca* for *circa* is used when the birth year is uncertain.

SUBJECT INDEX

Good people beget good people : a genealo

929.2 FRI 00038125

Frist, William H.

Dandridge Memorial Public Library (4-04)

JUL 2 2 2004

NC

DISCARD

DEMCO